THE MAKING OF
ARAB AMERICANS

From Syrian Nationalism to U.S. Citizenship

HANI J. BAWARDI

UNIVERSITY OF TEXAS PRESS
Austin

Copyright © 2014 by the University of Texas Press
All rights reserved
Printed in the United States of America
First paperback edition, 2015

Requests for permission to reproduce material from this work should be sent to:
   Permissions
   University of Texas Press
   P.O. Box 7819
   Austin, TX 78713-7819
   http://utpress.utexas.edu/index.php/rp-form

♾ The paper used in this book meets the minimum requirements of ANSI/NISO Z39.48-1992 (R1997) (Permanence of Paper).

LIBRARY OF CONGRESS CATALOGING-IN-PULICATION DATA

Bawardi, Hani J.
  The making of Arab Americans : from Syrian nationalism to U.S. citizenship / Hani J. Bawardi. — First edition.
    pages   cm
  Includes bibliographical references and index.
  ISBN 978-0-292-75748-6 (cloth : alk. paper)
  ISBN 978-1-4773-0752-6 (paperback)
  1. Arab Americans—Politics and government—20th century.
  2. Arab Americans—Societies, etc.—History—20th century. 3. Arab Americans—History—20th century. 4. Arab Americans—Ethnic identity. 5. Arab nationalism—History—20th century. 6. Syria—Emigration and immigration. I. Title.
  E184.A65B38 2014
  305.892′7073—dc23   2013039741

THE MAKING OF ARAB AMERICANS

Banquet honoring delegations of Arab states to the United Nations, November 1946. Courtesy of the Immigration History Research Project, University of Minnesota.

*For Rushd (Roy) Farah, the son of
Ameen Saleh Yaʿqoub Farah. Rushd was born
December 16, 1922, and died June 21, 2013.*

You say what, then, can the Syrian do if you rob him of his hope of a reformed future in the lands of his birth and childhood?
... The Syrian only has self-reliance and utilizing his talents, intelligence, and excellence to rely on.
... Every word a pupil learns in the American schools is a word learned by all Syrians.... Free your children from the slavery of stagnant traditions and old customs, and they will remain free even in chains and jails.

GIBRAN KHALIL GIBRAN, 1911

CONTENTS

ACKNOWLEDGMENTS	ix
NOTE ON ARABIC NAMES AND TERMS	xiii
INTRODUCTION	1
Chapter 1 ARAB POPULATIONS UNDER OTTOMAN RULE: A BACKGROUND	39
Chapter 2 THE SYRIAN NATIONALISM OF THE *MAHJAR* PRESS	54
Chapter 3 SOLDIERS FOR SYRIA BEFORE WORLD WAR I: THE FREE SYRIA SOCIETY	81
Chapter 4 THE "SYRIA IDEA" AND THE NEW SYRIA PARTY	104
Chapter 5 THE MANDATE YEARS AND THE DIASPORA: THE ARAB NATIONAL LEAGUE AND A HISTORICAL CONTEXT FOR ARAB AMERICAN NARRATIVE	159
Chapter 6 THE ARAB NATIONAL LEAGUE AND THE EMERGENCE OF ARAB AMERICAN IDENTITY	190
Chapter 7 THE INSTITUTE OF ARAB AMERICAN AFFAIRS: ARAB AMERICANS AND THE NEW WORLD ORDER	239
CONCLUSION	296
NOTES	307
BIBLIOGRAPHY	349
INDEX	363

ACKNOWLEDGMENTS

Meaningful research on the Arabic-speaking pioneers in the United States can take place only if their stories are faithfully captured. It is my privilege and honor to be entrusted by Roy (Rushd) Farah with the manuscripts of his father, Ameen Farah (1888–1975). I am deeply indebted to Roy and his wife, Pauline, of Grand Blanc, Michigan, for opening their home and their hearts to my family. They will always have a place in our hearts. Ameen's papers enriched my life beyond measure and provided the tools for advancing the nascent studies on the early Arab immigrants in the United States.

I am deeply grateful to Joy Totah Hilden for giving me unfettered access to the papers of her father, Dr. Khalil Totah, in her home in Berkeley, California. Khalil Totah's work as the director of the Institute of Arab American Affairs from 1945 to 1950 deserves dedicated research beyond the chapter on the institute in this book. I am very grateful to my dear friends and neighbors in Ann Arbor, Michigan, Amal Dalack and her husband, Gregory Dalack, a great-grandson of Orthodox Archpriest Basil M. Kherbawi. Father Kherbawi spent a lifetime in the service of his countrymen. I vow to continue translating to completion "Syrian Immigration to the United States," which he published in 1913.

It has been a privilege to get to know Dr. Fuad Isa Shatara, the founder of the Arab National League, better, thanks to his granddaughter Barbara Tate Cerato; her mother, Gina Shatara; and her aunt, Hope Murphy Shatara. The family provided Dr. Shatara's pictures and an audio disk from the 1930s. Gina Shatara shared her fond memories of this truly remarkable man. The research in this book on Dr. Shatara only begins to explore the staggering importance of this statesman, author, surgeon, and man of peace and vision. Arab Americans suffered a profound loss when Fuad Isa Shatara died on January 8, 1942, at the early age of forty-eight. His vision of coexistence and peace in Palestine lives on through his writings, letters, and commentary in archival repositories from Jerusalem to New York to Flint, Michigan.

Although I had little success in locating the descendants of Ḥabīb Ibrahīm Kātibah, his writings and importance must also be remembered and acknowledged by students of immigration and ethnic studies everywhere. This task is possible thanks to Alixa Naff, who, I discovered after completing this study, preserved Kātibah's papers as part of her collection at the Smithsonian Institution. I am grateful to Joe Hursey and the archivists at the Smithsonian's Museum of American History for accommodating me despite being short-staffed due to the budget sequester. Sadly, Alixa was frail and died before I had a chance to see her during my brief visit to Washington, D.C., to examine her collection. She left a massive wealth of untapped information for future generations of scholars. The Arab American community can ensure her legacy by underwriting proper preservation and cataloging of her collection, including the astoundingly important records of Ḥabīb Kātibah.

I am eternally and deeply grateful to my PhD adviser at Wayne State University, Dr. John J. Bukowczyk, for pushing me to look at the larger picture when others suggested that one file from Ameen Farah's archives would have been sufficient to support my dissertation. He nurtured my intellectual pursuits without compromise for the duration of my doctoral work at Wayne State while also allowing me to tend to my teaching career and care for my family. It is a privilege to be a beneficiary of Dr. Barbara Aswad's kind support, pioneering scholarship, and long experience in Arab American studies. I will always remember with deep appreciation the generous words of encouragement from Dr. Janice Terry when I showed up in her office at Eastern Michigan University clutching several documents from Ameen Farah's archives on Arab American organizations. "That is why we do our work," she said to me, "so you can change it or build on it." My research on the Arabic-language newspapers was greatly enhanced by the kind assistance of Gamil Youssef, the knowledgeable Middle East bibliographer in the Asian and Middle Eastern division of the New York Public Library, now retired. Mr. Youssef accommodated my research needs and made available untapped copies of *Jurāb-ul-Kurdi* and *Al-Funūn* in the summer of 2007. I share his hope that all rare Arabic-language material in the New York Public Library will be preserved on microfilm sooner rather than later.

Two gracious and dear friends lessened the estrangement inherent in pursuing new scholarship that not many people consider valuable: Charles M. Samaha of Saint Petersburg, Florida, a great-nephew of Faris Malouf, one of the founders of the Institute of Arab American Affairs; and Todd Fine, the unstoppable campaigner for preservation of the original Little Syria in Lower Manhattan. Charley's forthcoming biography of his great-uncle will make an invaluable contribution to Arab American studies when it is published. The wealth of information he continues to share with me has enriched my research. I am always happy to translate the treasures we excavate. Words cannot convey the feelings of gratitude and deep affection I have for Todd Fine for helping me across the finish line during a difficult transition for him. Todd deserves the gratitude of all New Yorkers and Arab Americans for his passion and dedication to the cause of saving the last remnant of early immigrant life on New York's Washington Street. His tireless work is also keeping alive the memory and importance of Ameen Rihani and *The Book of Khalid* (1911), the first Arab American novel in English. My sustained conversations with Todd Fine and Charley Samaha on the massive yet untapped body of historical evidence and literature give me hope that studies on Arab Americans will reach the critical mass needed to be a viable field of scholarship.

I am very fortunate to be working with Jim Burr, a senior editor at the University of Texas Press. Jim's interest in this book did not waver as I followed leads across the country before I realized that research can be endless. My sincere thanks go to the editorial board of the University of Texas Press for agreeing to publish this book.

The love, faith, and patience of my wife, Rula Kort Bawardi; my daughter, Salma; and my son, Tarek, keep me going.

NOTE ON ARABIC NAMES AND TERMS

Whenever possible, I have tried to explain variations in the names of organizations depending on differences in translation styles. Sometimes the founders themselves chose names for their organizations not consistent with accurate translation. For example, Jamʿiyat al-Nahḍah al-Filasṭṭīnīyah, the Palestine (or Palestinian) Nationalist Renaissance Society, was named in English the Palestine National League by its founder, Fuad Shatara. Adding to the confusion is the dearth of archival evidence that obscures this society's reemergence as the Arab National League, causing some scholars to assume that each title belonged to a different organization. Some scholars offer their own translations if they come across names in Arabic, not to mention that translations may vary from one scholar to the next depending on his or her language skill.

I follow common practices of transliterating Arabic phonetics in that I minimize the use of symbols to denote Semitic sounds. I generally have not hyphenated names; for example, Abd-ul-Hamid and Abd-el-Hadi are spelled Abdulhamid and Abdelhadi or Abdulhadi unless quoted. Variations in a name's spelling do not change how it is pronounced. The name Husaini is often spelled Husseini or Husayni. I follow the spelling used in relevant citations, for instance, Mikhail Naimy as opposed to the standard Arabic, Nuʿaimah, though my preferences would be Ameen versus Amin and Muhammad versus Muhamed unless citing text. Some Arabic words conveniently connote concepts essential to the discussion. Most Arabic-language text I have used is transliterated in the notes and translated in text.

THE MAKING OF ARAB AMERICANS

INTRODUCTION

A portrait of Ameen Farah (1888–1975), who immigrated from Nazareth to the United States in 1913, is displayed occasionally at the Arab American National Museum (AANM) in Dearborn, Michigan. The attractive displays in this museum, which opened in 2005 across from Dearborn's city hall, introduce students and the general public to facets of Arab immigrant life in the United States during different periods. Museum visitors could see Farah's portrait in a white coat standing in his grocery store; it was displayed just a few feet from the Columbia University graduation gown of an immigrant named Khalil Totah. The motion-activated recording above Farah's portrait explained the centrality of peddling in the immigrant experience and the wide ownership of grocery retail businesses by immigrants to Flint, Michigan. Between the portrait and the gown, a placard on the wall read: "The 1967 [Arab-Israeli] War led to the formation of the first major Arab American national political organization." Referring to the Association of Arab American University Graduates (AAUG), a crucial political organization founded, indeed, in 1967, the inscription stated it was established because "Arabs in America were dismayed at the ways in which U.S. media portrayed the war and at the U.S. government's hostility to the Arabs and Arab American causes."

This narrative presented by the museum—of a quaint, apolitical immigration that parallels the American success teleology yet was followed by a much later political explosion—matches the dominant narrative of political development in Arab American studies and in popular understanding. Nothing in the only national museum dedicated to Arab American history and life or in the aggregate scholarship, for that matter, indicates that Farah and Totah knew each other well or narrates how they respectively operated the first and last major Arab American political organizations spanning four decades, from 1915 to 1950. This episode highlights the central void in Arab American studies and broader historical output, the lack of organizational histories of the mass political groups that established the contours of Arab American identity and of Arab Americans' collective social obligation.

Aside from the practical reality that there has not been significant attention to or archival work on this topic, core conceptual failings have blocked proper investigation into early Arab American political history. The unproblematized acceptance of a narrative of contested identities and sectarian and geographic divisions has obscured the central influence of Syrian nationalism and later pan-Arabism on the political orientations of early intellectuals and journalists and the many avid consumers of their writings. Developing crises—from the Ottoman decline to World War I to postwar colonialism and uprisings to the Palestinian question in the face of Zionist advances—created an environment for urgent and ecumenical collective action. Each organization chronicled in this book helped shape Arab American identity by attempting to embrace a broad nationalism that did not stress identity divisions and that engaged all immigrant cohorts and potential partners. Any reasonable reading of the actual activities of these organizations suggests that historical narratives of rampant sectarianism (alongside Lebanese separatism) in Arab American life have been significantly overstated for the first fifty years of mass immigration and completely misunderstood for the past half century. While it is difficult to assess the beliefs of a majority of the immigrants, analysis of their press output and political activity suggests that contemporary portrayals of the immigrants as apolitical, divided, or apathetic need immediate revision. Many of these notions of ubiquitous sectarianism and Lebanese separatism are based on dated studies or selective translations of particular newspaper articles. Presumptions of incurable sectarianism based on verbal attacks in the Syrian press, especially by particular persistent personalities, create the impression that political awareness and collective action did not exist, and this conclusion has inhibited serious studies on the political activities of the first decades of Arab immigration to the United States.

The project of developing Arab American identity within the framework of organized political advocacy encounters an urgent need for more scholarship and archival collection regarding the generation to which members of these organizations belonged, including their writings, social networks and clubs, and charitable and religious civil-society organizations. Taking advantage of the archives that exist, in this study I build the historical context for four key early political organizations in the United States by connecting the immigrants to Arab cultural and political awareness through their writings and documented attempts at political organization. Doing so establishes that Arab national awareness accompanied the immigrants to the United States from the start of their mass immigration in the 1880s, as evidenced in the Arabic-language press. I present for the first time a description of the impetus and operation of the following national political organizations: the Free Syria Society (FSS), founded in 1915; the New Syria Party (NSP), 1926; the Arab National League (ANL), 1936; and the Institute of Arab American Affairs, 1944.

SYRIAN NATIONALISM

Building the context for this alternative narrative requires an examination of what Philip S. Khoury describes as "the one national independence movement largely ignored by historians of the Arab Middle East": the Syrian nationalist movement.[1] Making the case for the existence of Syrian nationalism and feelings of peoplehood at the outset of mass emigration from the Ottoman Empire is ultimately intertwined with Arab cultural awakening and gathering grievances with the Ottoman Turks before World War I. While the core impactful grievances are still open to debate, for the purposes of this book the articulated grievances justified Arab political demands;[2] they coincided with mass immigration to the United States from the Syrian provinces of the Ottoman Empire, in the Levant and modern Syria, between roughly the 1880s and the start of World War I. Sufficient numbers of immigrants and a scattering of compatriots in the Arab Middle East, Europe, and the Americas acted on these nationalist feelings by demanding independence and developing alternative political visions. The awareness of Syrian identity emerged from within a larger movement of the Arab *nahḍah*, a cultural awakening in the mid-nineteenth century that matured before large-scale immigration from the region to the Americas commenced. The "Syria idea" materialized as the culmination of increased Arab self-awareness and after Western ideas of sovereignty had entered into the discourse of this immigrant cohort before the large-scale emigration.

Syria was not the only name immigrants used to refer to their *bilād* (literally meaning cities or towns but intended to mean country or homeland). References to Syria dating back to the Greco-Roman period gave way to Bilād al-Shām during much of the Arab Islamic rule from the seventh century until administrative and other reforms (*tanzimāt*) by the Ottomans defined Syria's boundaries. Accordingly, Syria encompassed the *wilayet* (provinces), *sanjaq* (literally "flag" but in this context subprovinces), and *mutaṣarrifiyah* (akin to a county) stretching from the modern Turkish border in the north to the Sinai Peninsula and the Arabian Desert in the south and from the western fringes of Iraq in the east to the Mediterranean in the west.[3] The extensive boundaries delimited the coveted country sought by the Free Syria Society, founded by Ameen Farah in 1915, the first of the four organizations. The idea of Syrian sovereignty matured amid suspicions by exiled Syrian nationalists in Cairo and Europe of European territorial ambitions in the rapidly weakening Ottoman Empire. The political plans of achieving independence for Syria accompanied Ameen Farah on his journey to the United States and formed the ideological foundation on which the more successful and increasingly sophisticated New Syria Party was built. The NSP was established in 1926 in direct response to the Syrian Revolt against French colonialism. The revolt was Syrians' response to the dismemberment of Geographic Syria, an area encompassing the modern states of Syria, Lebanon, and Israel and the Palestinian territories in historic Palestine, by the European victors who used the Paris Peace Conferences of 1919 to implement the secret Sykes-Picot Agreement of dividing the region among France, Britain, and Russia. These extremely frustrating events, which coincided with the introduction of political Zionism and Jewish settlement in Palestine, impelled activists to fall on an Arab consciousness to have any hope of responding. The result was an even larger and far more organized political collective, the Arab National League. The ANL prepared the groundwork for continuing organized political advocacy before it disbanded in preparation for World War II. The ANL reconstituted as the Institute of Arab American Affairs after World War II and embarked on a newly professionalized effort of organized Arab American political lobbying and information campaigns seeking increased understanding between the United States and the Arab Middle East.

In this study I argue that the fate of Syria in that period was the core theme that consumed the energies and passion of intellectuals with the support of a large and sophisticated constituency among the first generation of Arab immigrants. As these efforts for achieving national sovereignty on modern footing from U.S. shores yielded the four major formal political organizations studied here, it fostered pragmatic political agendas in the organizations and facilitated among many Syrians a sense of belonging, social participation, and empowerment in their adopted country. As hopes for political unity in Syria were frustrated by the combined French and British policies, practical efforts toward Syrian unity were superseded by the exasperating and politically charged crisis in Palestine. This was the time when Jewish immigration increased with the aid of the British. By the beginning of World War II, the immigrants had been in the United States for twenty-five to fifty years, and many of them and their descendants served in both wars. Observing the problematic trends of political alignment, its members consciously suspended the Arab National League in May 1941, almost seven months before the Japanese attacks on Pearl Harbor, after declaring their loyalty to their adopted country. Their full ascription to Americanism was the culmination of an evolution of strategies of political activism on behalf of beleaguered Syria. In this study I propose a specific event, the Fourth Annual Convention of the Arab National League, in 1939, as coming as close as one can to identifying a birthing moment for Arab American identity.

EXISTING SCHOLARSHIP

The space between Ameen Farah's portrait and Khalil Totah's gown in the Arab American National Museum offers a patchwork of artifacts and images intended to assemble strands of the Arab American experiences into a narrative—a run-of-the-mill tailor's kit, a wedding gown from 1989, and a lifelike plastic replica of a dozen falafel. Nearby, several laminated placards emphasize the centrality of the Arab-Israeli War of 1967; others describe lone Arab adventurers of the mid-nineteenth century and celebrate recent arrivals from Yemen and other parts of the Arab Middle East. The museum's east wing then leaps to commemorate quintessential Arab American success stories on constantly flickering video screens: the educator Christa McAuliffe, who died in the Challenger explosion; Donna Shalala, the first Arab American secretary of Health and Human Services; Diane Rehm, the host and executive producer of *The Diane Rehm Show* on WAMU and National Public Radio; the late Helen Thomas, a longtime White House correspondent for United Press International; the NFL player Jeff George; the consumer advocate Ralph Nader; the U.S.-born Queen Noor of Jordan; and scores of others. The focus on culture, the immigrant experience, the home, and iconic success stories alongside "all-American families" more or less also reflects the dominant strands of scholarship on Arab Americans.

Yet, most of the scholarship has left a glaring gap, a failure to synthesize and document the personal accounts and political activities of the parents and grandparents of these famous Arab Americans, how their activities within sophisticated mass political organizations were shaped by momentous events in the Middle East, and ultimately how political activism aided in their gradual ascription to an Arab American identity. Several reasons explain the gap in the scholarship on early Arab immigrants' political activism. Among the recognizable factors are a general dearth of historiographies, prohibitive immigration restrictions from 1924 until 1965 that halted continuity of understanding of the immigrants' origins and made it much harder to locate research subjects and material once scholarship commenced in the late 1960s, and the absence of systematic efforts to collect material into repositories for Arabic-language books and manuscripts. One of the most debilitating shortcomings in the scholarship has been the negligible scholarly use of the Arab immigrants' own sizable Arabic-language works. Additionally, there is a near absence of transnational perspectives on the immigrants' evolving political strategies and social lives.

Arab American studies and much more recent interpretations of Arab American life from feminist perspectives began to take their present forms as a result of the arrival of a highly educated cadre of immigrants following the repeal of immigration restrictions in 1965. The civil rights movement undoubtedly reinforced the overall disposition held by many pioneering scholars in Arab American studies, among them Michael Suleiman, that a defense of the Arab point of view was compatible with a critique of colonialism and the fight for civil rights. Interactions of these relatively recent Arab immigrants and scholars active in the civil rights movement in the 1960s and 1970s encouraged social studies research on Arab immigration. The early scholarship on Arab Americans was sparked in part by the need to explain an Arab point of view and a narrative of belonging in the aftermath of the Arab defeat by Israel in 1967. This goal fell within the perimeters of the Association of Arab American University Graduates, which came to being as a result of that war. Most of the seminal scholars were connected in varying degrees with the AAUG, including Ibrahim Abu Lughod, Michael Suleiman, Elaine Hagopian, Janice Terry, Edward Said, Barbara Aswad, Abdo Elkholy, and Hisham Sharabi. A few other important scholars were not connected to the founding of AAUG, most notably the crucial Alixa Naff. The main concern of these scholars was contending with an open cultural hostility in the United States toward Arabs and Arab Americans in the aftermath of the 1967 Arab-Israeli conflict. In the process of attempting to explain Arab Americans, they created a basic body of scholarship on the early Arab Americans' immigration experiences, but they largely left out analysis of their political work and aspirations. The studies they produced, however, paved the way for studies on the Arabic-speaking communities through the different perspectives of gender, ethnicity, family life,[4] and, much less so, literature. At present, gathering postmodern interpretations emphasizing feminism, ethnicity, and certain political renditions relies heavily on the work of such scholars for background, if not guidance and mentorship.

The present study is not an attempt to lessen the importance of these pioneering scholars' contributions to Arab American studies. They were responsible for filling a void in social and cultural studies on the Arabic-speaking immigrants, and without their work, material for students of Arab American life would be impoverished, to say the least.[5] However, the bulk of the scholarship they authored seems resigned to an overall assumption that no formal Arab American political activity took place before 1967 due to purported apathy and indifference, inadequate education, and sectarianism. Commonly advanced, as the inscription in the museum illustrates, is that it took the 1967 Arab-Israeli War to galvanize the Arab American community into self-awareness. For example, citing nearly identical statements by a roster of her colleagues who are the pioneers mentioned above, Yvonne Haddad unequivocally declares, "The 1967 Arab Israeli war, with its one-sided press coverage, the general U.S. public support of Israeli aggression, and the apparent deliberate effort by the United States government to prolong the United Nations debate for the ceasefire in the area until Israel had achieved its objectives, shocked the Arab community in the United States and gave birth to the Arab American identity."[6] Janice Terry distinguished post-1967 immigrants who "reflect the national, socioeconomic, religious, and political diversity of the Arab World from earlier arrivals who tended to avoid political or community organizations that operated outside the close confines of specific ethnic, religious or village-based membership."[7]

Even a passing glimpse at the scholarship of the past forty years leaves little doubt that the thousands of initial arrivals up to World War I appeared to care little about political affairs, much less the fate of "a nation." After the 1967 war, palpable hostility arose toward Arabs and Arab Americans because of, Michael Suleiman explicates in his treatment of U.S. press coverage of the conflict in *Arabs in the Mind of America* (1988), the prevailing view that Arabs were the aggressors and Israelis the victims in this and previous wars. Since his study, Suleiman came to realize that what the AAUG failed to do was to conduct a systematic review of sources for a fuller understanding of the failure to build lasting Arab American institutions. Despite this initial lacuna, Suleiman's work remains prominent in the literature on Arab Americans and their descendants partly because he anticipated one of Arab Americans' chief grievances today: "[Arabs] seem to be consistently presented as the 'villains' with the Israelis as the 'heroes' in any conflict or flare-up. Unless this unbalanced presentation is corrected or compensated for, no adequate knowledge of Middle East issues can be rendered to the American public and government, on which to base an impartial and just solution for the many problems of that area."[8]

Suleiman also attempted to "delineate the political identity of Arab Americans from the time of their arrival" through various settings such as "regional, local, national, or international."[9] In exploring political participation by Arab Americans, Suleiman correctly states that knowledge "of the political orientation and activities of the early Arab immigrants to the United States is sketchy at best."[10] At the time, in 1994, Suleiman's claims were a departure from those he made in a 1987 essay in which he relied on some translations from Arabic-language press and accounts of Arab travelers to the United States in the late 1920s and 1930s.[11] Suleiman asserts in the 1987 piece that the immigrants' "attachment to a specific political entity (i.e., country) was to come later after the dismemberment of the Ottoman Provinces,"[12] a reference to World War I or later. He contends that "early immigrants," a label he uses to delineate immigration before 1965, were not concerned with formal political collectives because their affiliations were tribal or clan-based, that national bonds played no part in immigrant affiliations, and that attachment to Syria was nostalgic. They thought of themselves, he writes, "primarily in terms of family and sect and gloried in their former homelands' wonderful *physical* environment."[13] Therefore, the immigrants did not possess a sense of peoplehood or national consciousness. In 2006 Suleiman suggests that Arab pioneers were involved in "community politics" within their groups, but weak "communal solidarity" precluded political participation. World War I, he adds, was a watershed event marked by an "extremely positive" response from immigrants to calls by community leaders to join the U.S. armed forces, while before the war they joined churches, cooperatives, and benefit and social clubs.[14] Suleiman mentions the Arab National League and its founders Fuad Isa Shatara and Ḥabīb Ibrahīm Kātibah based on sporadic sources, but he resolves that in the 1920s editor Salloum Mokarzel of the *Syrian World*, an English-language magazine in New York City, led the first serious effort to establish a broad organization, the Federation of American Syrian Lebanese Clubs.[15]

Absence of historiographies on any of the national organizations—social or otherwise—makes it an arduous task to correct sketchy accounts in the *Syrian World*. Suffice it to say for now that the designation "Lebanese" was debated in the 1930s and 1940s before it was accepted next to the label "Syrian" which was never in question. I will develop this discussion further as part of my treatment of the Syrian press in chapter 2 and again within building the historical context for the league and the institute in chapters 5 and 7, respectively. But the question of why Suleiman and, for that matter, Alixa Naff and their colleagues did not investigate the early political organizations beyond passing reference is an important one, especially because they knew about them well before 1994 and because the records on the Arab National League were secured by Naff some two decades ago.[16] Farhat Ziadeh described the institute to Alixa Naff in an interview she conducted in November 1994,[17] and he named the people involved and indicated that Suleiman had by that time obtained Khalil Totah's memoir from Ziadeh. The memoir, along with the institute's sizable archive and a collection of books, was in the Khalil Totah Library at the University of Washington, where Ziadeh was head of the Near Eastern Languages and Civilizations division.[18]

Lawrence Davidson gives the most complete account of the political activities by the Arab immigrants prior to 1967, mostly in their responses to Zionism after the Balfour Declaration of 1917 promised the granting of "a home for the Jews in Palestine." In the course of his review of U.S. newspapers and government records, Davidson came across the names of Fuad Isa Shatara, the New York City physician who founded the Arab National League (ANL), and the prolific activist Ḥabīb Ibrahīm Kātibah.[19]

After major newspapers were digitized, with the benefit of Davidson's findings it has become easier to locate references to the early immigrants and their political work. But this has left persistent gaps in the historical context and where the newspapers were outside major population centers on the East Coast or have not been digitized. Southeastern Michigan is a case in point. In the years following the Syrian revolt against French colonialism in 1925, Highland Park, Michigan, became home to the New Syria Party; it was mentioned in the New York press and by scholars only when its activities resumed in 1929 under drastically different circumstances. Although Davidson perceptively noted the convergence of activists when their viewpoint was needed, often after a spike in violence in Palestine, no new political organizations on the scale and reach of the NSP would form again until the ANL emerged following a popular uprising in Palestine in 1936.

CONTEMPORARY IMPLICATIONS OF SCHOLARSHIP ON SYRIAN NATIONALISM

The common assumption that Arab Americans have little in common with one another and that their identity is a malleable social construction reveals how Arab American identity is contested without regard for historical context. An introductory statement by Nabeel Abraham and Andrew Shryock in the 2002 collection *Arab Detroit* illustrates how scholarship on Arab Americans in one of the most important centers of Arab American life in the country, southeastern Michigan, ignores an older historical context: "Arab American identity, as expressed in Detroit today, seldom refers to an ancient regional heritage or even a shared culture. It emerged quite recently as part of a complex (and now largely forgotten) reaction to the 1967 Arab Israeli War."[20]

Although Abraham and Shryock purport to complicate the question of what Arab American identity represents, their claims that Shi'a Muslims and Christian Palestinians do not come in contact and that their differing dialects "cause confusion" detract from basic social and historical research into the origins of these communities and their development. However, while I probe Arab immigrant experiences with political action before 1967, this is not to say that the ramifications of the 1967 war for Arab Americans have not been significant and enduring. Young and newly arriving immigrants may not remember 1967, as the editors insist in *Arab Detroit*, but this does not lessen its importance in the lives of Arab Dearborners of any generation. Lessons learned from political upheavals within memory can inform our understanding of Arab immigrants over the breadth of their American experience.

But the process begins by making the early organizations known as a way to engender understandings of historical continuity in Arab American life—a major goal of this study—and by putting political events in perspective before delving into surface identity politics. How the 1967 war indirectly led to the founding of the Arab Community Center for Economic and Social Services (ACCESS) escapes most interested parties, mainly because no full history of ACCESS has been attempted and hardly anything is known about the founders, their communities, or what moved them to act. The implication here, in addition to asserting the need for histories on institutional and civic life, is to draw attention to the connections between political activism on one side and the establishment of charitable and educational campaigns on Arab culture and history on the other.

Renditions of Arab American identity devoid of marking and interpreting happenings in the past become self-perpetuating social constructions, perhaps even replicating hated Orientalisms, devoid of any historical points of reference or documentation and analysis. If the political fallout of the 1967 war yielded the AAUG, the war was only the most recent of many cataclysms that had profound fallout on the lives of Arab immigrants in the United States. The example of how it took earlier and later immigrants working together to create ACCESS underscores the need to document and understand events and fully grasp Arab American life in its continuity and evolution. Gauging nationalist feelings across the span of immigration from Geographic Syria illuminates the ideological and social basis for the construction of Arab American narratives after 1967. Therefore, a utility of this study is to present a formative history for the 1967 reaction, and while I seek to qualify and build on the post-1967 seminal scholarship, I also strive to make sure the impetus and importance behind it is not lost.

A group of nationalist supporters of different factions of the Palestine Liberation Organization (PLO) active in Detroit, most notably the Popular

Front for the Liberation of Palestine, laid the foundation for ACCESS. In their quest to mobilize immigrants behind their goals, the activists discovered that providing needed social services would help them harness a constituency. Accordingly, George Khoury, an engineer from the Palestinian town of Birzeit near Ramallah and a founding member of the AAUG Michigan chapter, approached the AAUG in one of its meetings at a church on Jefferson Avenue in Detroit in 1971 and pitched the idea of founding a social services organization that Khoury named the Arab Community Center for Employment and Social Services. In the meeting Khoury obtained seed funding of $1,000 from the AAUG along with a "friendly amendment." Karen Amin suggested replacing the word "Employment" in Khoury's chosen name with "Economic."[21] Thereby ACCESS, the parent institution of the Arab American National Museum, was born, and its operations would initially be managed by a diverse group including newly arriving Palestinians, second- and third-generation descendents of Shi'a immigrants from the Younis and Amen families, and Yemeni immigrants such as Ali al-Maklani, Muhsin Hubaishi, and Manna' al-Jaberi. Today, ACCESS is the largest social services organization for Arab Americans in the country. When mostly Lebanese Shi'a Muslims settled in Dearborn after the bloody Lebanese civil war in the mid-1970s, many sought ACCESS for various basic services. ACCESS, then, is a by-product of three generations of Arab immigrants working together to create a social safety net for all Arab Americans.

Khoury disclosed that supporters of the Popular Front for the Liberation of Palestine championed the idea of a center for community services. With the AAUG seed money, they helped the Southeast Dearborn community establish an Arab center to aid the larger community. The task of running the center was left for a democratically elected executive committee of residents of Palestinian, Yemeni, and Lebanese descent including Khoury, Alan Aimen, Katherine Younis-Amen, Don Younis, and Helen Atwel. This caused a split with more radical members who were not as keen on assimilative aspects of the center, among them Maoists. Khoury, whose friends also supported the Popular Front for the Liberation of Palestine and Fatah (Fatḥ), the largest PLO faction, founded the diverse Organization of Arab Students at Wayne State University, which became the largest of its kind in the country.[22]

A recent interpretation of the impact of the AAUG underscores the dire need for historiography on political activism and for a sober assessment of the development of Arab American identity from transnationalist and historical perspectives. While *Arab Detroit* treats the meaning of 1967 and earlier political conflicts as distant and forgotten matters, Gary

David interprets the response to the Arab-Israeli War of 1967 as the basis for a narrow and exclusive political category. David argues that formulation of Arab American identity after 1967 contributes to excluding anyone who is not a public activist or does not exhibit observable traits such as Arabic-language skill.[23] Therefore, what Abraham and Shryock consider a largely forgotten war with no bearing on contemporary immigrants' self-perceptions and identity formation, David critiques as a basis for "double marginalization" and a source of disunity. Yet, 1967 led to the creation of the AAUG and helped George Khoury and his politicized new immigrant colleagues to fill a void in social services in collaboration with an older immigrant group they perceived to be more established members of an existing Arab American community.[24] David contends that the war in 1967, according to "virtually all contemporary writers of the Arab American experience, is the pivotal moment in the shaping of what it means to be Arab American,"[25] citing Yvonne Haddad, Michael Suleiman, and Evelyn Shakir. He then adds this quote by an Israeli scholar: "Before that war, Arab American identity was amorphous and dormant."[26] Only with this assumption does it become possible under the prevailing confusion in Arab American studies to debate the meaning of the Arab-Israeli War of 1967 from exclusively anthropological, sociological, or some other theoretical perspective devoid of historiography.

The stories of Palestinians among the 331,958 Arab immigrants who arrived between World War II and 1985 were not all that different from those of many early immigrants who were prevented from returning home by time, distance, or political uncertainty.[27] The Palestinians' stories still tell of their deracination and bitter memories of feeling, for example, "more a foreigner in Jerusalem than in San Francisco."[28] Deracination saturated and also circumscribed the AAUG's work and analysis. Gregory Orfalea affirms the salient belief that Palestinian exiles and refugees in the second wave were unlike the pioneers who made their way to the United States led by "economic concerns and the search for better livelihood."[29] Orfalea argues that the distinction separated the two communities until the war of 1967, the Yom Kippur War of 1973, and the Israeli invasion of Lebanon in 1982. He asserts that 60 percent of the later arrivals were Muslims who were "spiritually alienated" and that the Palestinians, though "drawn by U.S. freedom," were "concomitantly repelled by U.S. policies."[30] Orfalea conforms to the view that early immigrants considered assimilating into the host culture their primary objective: "Whereas early Arab immigrants and their offspring shared in the wholesale adaptation to the mores of America—wanted them, gloried in them—the second wave kept 'their bags packed.'"[31] Orfalea draws on numerous interviews that seem to demonstrate that Arab Americans had "no status, no entity, no consciousness, no existence whatsoever."[32] Such discourse, I argue, is the perspective of the 1967 lens; such is the fog of the loss of Palestine in 1948 after a brief war.

My aim in this study is not to challenge these and similar writings, including a surge of publications treating September 11, 2001, as another formative watershed of sorts. Rather, it is to begin a process of looking at political activism by Arab Americans as a marker of the development of their identity over an extended period that encompassed many violent episodes and political events dating from before World War I. Arab immigrants had a full range of experiences in the United States for seventy-five years by the time the AAUG was founded, and Dearborn did not become home to the largest concentration of Arabic speakers outside the Middle East in a vacuum. Putting the aftermath of 1967 in proper context requires challenging the prevailing discourse in a fundamental way, by looking at Arab American political advocacy as part of a set of complex sociopolitical dynamics on both sides of the Atlantic. By drawing on evidence from immigrants' political and literary writings in their ethnic press, published biographies, and archival evidence, much of it virtually untapped, I seek to answer one aspect of Michael Suleiman's call to redress what "the AAUG failed to do, [which] is the same thing the community and *all* its organizations have neglected to do from the very beginning until now, namely, carry out a proper study of the Arab American community."[33]

HISTORICAL FOUNDATIONS

The work of Alixa Naff and other pioneering scholars presents a starting point. They tell that of the many Syrians, from the estimated 130,000 to 250,000 who made the journey, most were Christians from the Mount Lebanon area and arrived between 1876 and the end of World War I. A breakdown of the numbers is nearly impossible due to unreliable data in immigration records, especially before 1899, when Syrians were lumped together in census records as "Turks in Asia." After 1899 it is generally acknowledged that by the start of World War I about 90,000 had left Syria headed to the United States.[34] A respectable number of the immigrants managed to secure economic footholds in the United States fairly rapidly, Naff affirms: "As a whole [Syrian immigrants] averaged $1,000 annually when the U.S. labor force was averaging about $650 annually."[35] Many used peddling and sedentary trade in housewares and groceries to "operate on their own terms."[36] From supply centers such as Lower Manhattan's Washington Street, Syrians fanned out and eventually covered much of the U.S. heartland, although most settled on the East Coast.[37] Much less is known about smaller contingencies of immigrants in small cities like Flint or Highland Park near Detroit. The available references to individuals from these communities in the papers of the Free Syria Society, the New Syria Party, and the Arab National League offer glimpses at their disproportionate importance in Arab American life. The Flint-based, secret Free Syria Society did not at all have a large membership, but it attracted the seminal literary figures Mikhail Naimy, Nasib Arida, and Muhammad Muhaisen. All the operations of the New Syria Party were run from Highland Park, although its chapters covered dozens of major U.S. cities as well as parts of Mexico. The fourth and last national convention of the ANL held in Flint in 1939 attracted 200 delegates from across the United States in addition to emissaries from Jerusalem.

Economic successes in communities large and small aided immigrants' political activities, but not to the degree that they helped establish churches and parishes beginning in major cities on the East Coast.[38] Also scant is knowledge about Syrian immigrant social clubs and religious societies established by the forebears of the Sunni and Shi'a communities in different U.S. locations, including Dearborn. A dearth of information on the levels of education according to sect adds to the hurdles before this study, mainly because considerable evidence in this book indicates that Orthodox Christians published most of the newspapers and had greater political input; evidently they shared an overall nationalist position with many Maronites and certainly most Muslims, including the Druze derivation of Shi'a Islam. This hurdle becomes distinct when challenging vague claims of uniform sectarian divisions as causes of political apathy and even more so regarding perceptions that Lebanese separatism was based on religious, not political sentiments. The direct role played behind the scenes by French officials and the Maronite clergy remains outside the focus of this study. But the volatility of the ever-shifting political reality before and after World War I added to the bewilderingly fluid social space among immigrants, especially in New York, where most of the immigrant press operated. Research into the operations of the main political organizations reveals that indeed there was general consensus, with the exception of the Maronite newspaper *Al-Hoda*. However, any cursory look at the press without historical context could reveal dissonant tones among editors considered allies in this study during almost any period. This is not due to any fundamental contradictions or ideological differences. It is partly due to expressions of Arab hype—vague oratorical displays that are very difficult to untangle in a purely social-science approach and a lack of specific studies on this phenomenon—and partly from the intense and disparate colonialist pressures by the British and the French, as seen in the example of the visit in 1927 by Prince Shakib Arslan.

The discrepancies can be explained by a cursory look at a master's thesis by Motaz Abdullah Alhourani, a political science student of Michael Suleiman. Alhourani's study relies on a collection of quotes without attention to the historical context and focuses on "the attitudes and orientations of the Arab-American community concerning major issues facing the Arab world at the time of WWI."[39] It is difficult to decipher what these issues were, but Alhourani asserts that *Al-Dalil* newspaper's "support for Ottoman rule was clear and wholehearted in the years 1910 to 1913." He bases his assumption on quotes such as this one dated April 2, 1910: "Turks and Arabs are brothers in nationalism. Their love to their homeland should always lead them to cooperate and unify."[40] Alhourani then contends that *Al-Dalil* advocated Syrian independence by 1913 but only under the guardianship of France.[41] He proceeds to describe how the New York newspaper *Mirāt al-Gharb* (Mirror of the West) "renewed its attacks on Muslim and Druze accusing them of coming to America to make quick profits and then going back to their towns and villages."[42] However, Alhourani gives no specific evidence of attacks by the newspaper. He describes in the same sentence how the Druze editor of *Al-Bayān* newspaper in New York defended it against such attacks. Looking at an aggregate of *Mirāt al-Gharb* editorials from the 1910s by Najīb Diāb, its Orthodox Christian editor, a dialectically different perspective emerges. *Mirāt al-Gharb* invited a series of nationalist sermons by the Muslim heads of the Higher Committee of the Ottoman Administrative Decentralization Party in Egypt, Rafīq al-ʿAẓm and Muhammad Rashīd Rida in Cairo, where many Syrian nationalists sought refuge. Attention to political developments will show that *Mirāt al-Gharb* and *Al-Bayān* were in agreement in their subtle opposition to Ottomanism and carefully navigated a path of decentralization while keeping their attention fixed on independence without provoking the European powers. Between 1925 and 1927 *Al-Bayān* and *Mirāt al-Gharb* dedicated considerable energies and resources to ensure the success of the Syrian revolt. Hence, it is possible, short of a historical context, to draw a desired argumentative outcome based on a flawed premise from sporadic statements in the immigrant press.

Fairly swiftly, economic stability enabled newspaper subscriptions by immigrants who supported a vigorous Arabic-language press across the United States, thereby allowing activists to opine on a variety of topics. The published works produced by early immigrants need to be part of the aggregate knowledge about their lives. Many of the works can mitigate presumptions of political apathy and ignorance and provide an overview of dozens of clubs and societies. One such work is Basil Kherbawi's Arabic-language survey of the Syrian communities in his massive 1913 book, *Tarīkh al-Wilāyāt al-Muttahidah* (History of the United States), which contains a semiscientific survey under the heading "Tarīkh al-hijrah al-Sūrīya" (History of Syrian immigration).[43] Another example is a collection of speeches and poems by Rizk Haddad over his long and distinguished career. Haddad's collection contains vivid and fairly detailed information on the political, social, economic, literary, and psychological affairs of early immigrants.[44] Haddad's eloquent poems capture the essence of immigrants' fears, hopes, and trepidations over horrific conditions in Syria during World War I, their split patriotism between the United States and the homeland, and their dreams of reforms and independence. The range of Rizk Haddad's poems covers the genres of *haju* (diatribe or critique), *madeeh* (compliments and exaltation), *ritha'* (lament), and *qaseed* (nationalist ode). In addition to rivaling the literary prowess of the influential members of the famed al-Rābitah al-Qalamīyah (Pen Bond, known also as Pen League), Haddad's speeches contain critical information for historians and social scientists. He gave the keynote address at the founding ceremony of the United Syrian Society in 1908; he explicated the meaning of the increasingly salient term "New Syria" as the Syria of the diaspora across the globe in an address to the Syrian Ladies Benevolent Society of Brooklyn, New York, in the same year; and he welcomed the Egyptian emissary Prince Muhammad Ali in 1912. Haddad's speeches celebrated Syria's beauty, lamented the temporary slump in the quality of the immigrant press when it hit the lowest point in 1906 amid exchanges of insults, urged Syrians of the diaspora to send aid to beleaguered countrymen during World War I, and welcomed nationalist clergy and reformers when they sought aid as guests of the New Syria Party on behalf of the Syrian cause in 1927. He, like many fellow writers, rallied behind Palestine's plight when the emissaries Jamil Beyhum from Beirut and Emil el-Ghouri from Jerusalem represented the *mufti* of Jerusalem, Hajj Amin al-Husseini, and toured the United States seeking aid from Arab nationalists in 1938 and 1939.[45] Haddad's writings were not unique, as will be discussed later in relation to the *mahjar* (diaspora) press. I also explore the importance of Ameen al-Rihani, who commanded respect as a prolific author and intellectual on both sides of the Atlantic and served as an inspiration for pan-Arabism in the diaspora earlier and longer than any other Syrian-Lebanese writer. The aggregate content of a range of newspapers and writers points to a convergence behind the Syrian and later the Arab nationalist cause commensurate with the political changes in Syria.

A rare overview of the social landscape of southeastern Michigan can be found in Jamil Beyhum's own account of his trip to Michigan as the guest of the Arab National League. Chapter 6 includes a summary of this book, *Filasṭīn: Andalus al-Sharq* (Palestine, the Andalusia of the East), published in 1946, as well as details of the ANL's political activities. Beyhum's account provides information on the Arab Palestinian Renaissance Society under the directorship of Hanna Khalaf, Shiʻa Imam Khalil Bazi's Renaissance Arab Hashemite Club, a Sunni mosque, and a club headed by Sheikh Muhammad Husain Kharoub. Each of these personalities and collectives in the Detroit area deserves examination beyond the present study. There is scant mention of these pioneering immigrants to Dearborn, the heart of what became the largest Shiʻa Lebanese population in the United States from the south of modern Lebanon. Critical knowledge on the social and political inclinations and religious life as well as estimates of the number of Muslim and Druze families in southeastern Michigan are needed to build on the work of Abdo A. Elkholy, who has provided one of the few studies on Muslims in the United States.[46]

Immigrants from Greater Syria (Bilād al-Shām in the vernacular of early Arab rule) began arriving in the United States in discernible numbers in the decade following 1876, the year merchants from Greater Syria participated in the Centennial International Exhibition in Philadelphia and spread the word about economic opportunities in the new industrial giant. Syrian immigration coincided with the massive influx of eastern and southern Europeans until a series of laws were passed to severely restrict immigration from outside northwestern Europe. The laws culminated in the Immigration Act of 1924, also known as the Johnson-Reed Act. This law set quotas restricting entry from any country to 2 percent of the number of people from that country already residing in the United States, based on the Census of 1890, that is, before immigration from eastern and southern Europe peaked.[47]

The early immigrants' homeland is best understood through the network of cultural, social, and economic ties that served to connect towns and major cities across Ottoman administrative districts. Immigrants emphasized Greater Syria's geographical contiguity when they described their political aspirations and defined its boundaries for each other and the West despite the successive adjustments to administrative districts that began in the 1870s. Key activists understood, as later discussion on their political activities will show, that this region was home to predominantly Arab Muslim populations administered by the Turkish Ottoman Empire since the second decade of the sixteenth century. Not all immigrants from Greater Syria identified themselves as Arabs. The population of the region includes significant

FIGURE I.1. *Souvenir of the Philadelphia International Exposition, 1876. Souvenirs were given to merchants who displayed wares. This one belonged to Iskandar Kort, a Palestinian from Jerusalem. Courtesy of Laila Kort family archive, Jerusalem.*

numbers of Armenians, Jews, and Kurds who preserved their distinct identities and sometimes languages despite speaking Arabic fluently.

Over the course of the nineteenth century, economic agreements with the Ottomans gave Russia and Western powers unprecedented leverage over the affairs of the weakening empire despite efforts to modernize the administration and the enacting of the first Ottoman Constitution, in 1876. Modernization and reforms, or *tanzimāt*, by the Turkish Ottomans did little to stop corruption, and hopes of non-Turkish inhabitants of the empire for equality were dashed when Sultan Abdulhamid suspended the Ottoman Constitution the same year it was enacted. Syrians in the United States gradually became worried that European domination of their lands loomed ever closer, as translations from the immigrant press and discussion of what became known as the First Arab Conference in Paris, in 1913, and the political agenda of the Free Syria Society will show. Their anticipation of political change in their homeland turned to alarm when the constitution was suspended again in 1909, one year after it was revived, this time by militant Turks. The events unfolded at a time when Arabs were becoming more aware of both their ancient past and modern Western thought and as significant numbers of immigrants, among them the many who were educated in American and French missionary schools, brought these political ideas and concerns to the New World.

The decades leading up to the mass Syrian emigration were characterized by the region's increasing contacts with Westerners as well as by intellectual activities made possible by improved schools and printing presses brought by foreign missionaries earlier in the nineteenth century.[48] Shared language and dominant Arab cultural memory were major ingredients in the *nahḍah* movement. One of the hallmarks of this awakening was the resurrection of ancient Arabic-language literary and Islamic texts and incorporation into them of social and political developments in the West. Inquiries into ancient texts revealed, for example, the enduring interpretations of Sunni Islam by Saḥīḥ al-Bukhāri, a scholar of Persian ancestry,[49] and Imam Ali's *Nahj al-Balāghah* (Method of eloquence), considered one of the most authoritative sermons in Islam. By the last third of the nineteenth century, printed copies of the Bible, the Qur'an, and Butrus al-Bustāni's *Muḥīṭ al-Muḥīṭ*, the first modern Arabic-to-Arabic dictionary, adorned bookshelves of ordinary people across the Middle East. Thousands of these volumes, along with religious Christian theological works, often written in classical Arabic style characteristic of ancient Islamic texts, accompanied Syrian immigrants. More importantly for the future of Arab American studies and contrary to prevailing impressions, among the immigrants were sufficient numbers of widely read and highly sophisticated scholars who described their experiences and participated in lively debates from the start of the immigration.

The shelves of immigrant libraries teem with classics that reveal what the immigrants read and how *jāhilīyah* (pre-Islamic) and Islamic scholarship reinforced their Arab cultural identity.[50] Arabic-language book collections in the homes of Christian Orthodox Syrians, my research revealed, contain nineteenth-century, first-print editions of *Al-Luzūmīyāt* by Abu al-ʿAlāʾ al-Maʿarri (973–1058) and copies of *Maqāmāt al-Harīri* (The assemblies of Harīri, printed in 1899) on the literary mastery of Muhammad Uthman al-Harīri (1054–1122). Similar classics by al-Jahiz and Abu al-Tayyib al-Mutanabbi as well as *Muqaddimat Ibn Khaldūn* (Ibn Khaldūn's introduction) were reissued by missionary presses in various parts of Syria or Cairo's Bulaq section. More significantly for this study, perhaps, is that the libraries in Syria proper, across the ocean from New York, contained works of pioneering *mahjar* poets, members of al-Rābitah al-Qalamīyah, the Pen Bond, nearly all of whom received at least elementary education in Russian, American, and French missionary schools in Syria. Among writers who made the U.S. East Coast their home are Jubrān Khalil Jubrān (better known as Gibran), Elia Abu-Mādi (better known as Elia D. Madey), Rashid Ayoub, ʿAbdulmassīh Haddād, Nadra Haddad, Muhammad Muhaisen, Mikhail Naʿimah (better known as Naimy), Nasib Arida, and Najīb Diāb. In Detroit were Suleiman Baddūr and ʿAbbas Abu Shaqra, among many from the Bazi, Kharoub, and Saʿdi clans.

The Arab cultural awakening in Syria was a critical ingredient that, combined with the changing political realities in the world, fueled collective action in the United States. Building the context for the formative stage of Syrian immigrant political activism and developing that context through 1951 requires exploring a host of intervening topics such as Ottoman reforms, Turkish nationalism, and nationalist content in *nahḍah* literature in Syria and writings in the Syrian press in the United States as well as challenging pervasive and exaggerated perceptions of intra-Syrian sectarianism mostly pitting Orthodox Christians against Maronites, adherents to a form of Catholicism practiced in what is now Lebanon. Chapter 3 in this study sheds light on how the small Free Syria Society (FSS) was indirectly responsible for the reemergence of *Al-Funūn*, one of the *mahjar*'s most influential literary magazines, which featured early works by such famed members of the Pen Bond as Gibran, Naimy, and Arida. Archival evidence shows Naimy and Arida as members, in addition to Muhammad Muhaisen, who moved to Detroit from New York and co-edited *Al-Difāʿ al-ʿArabi* (The Arab defense, 1921) with Muhammad Husain Kharoub.

The analysis of FSS in this study is presented as the first available evidence that the spark behind political activities in the United States—and, for that matter, in Europe and South America—was ignited by the early anti-Ottoman nationalist societies. The FSS's principles and goals mirrored the political agenda of the larger anti-Ottoman, anti-Turkish Hizb al-Lāmarkizīyah al-idārīyah al-ʿUthmani (Ottoman Administrative Decentralization Party, often called simply the Decentralization Party), at the time headquartered in Cairo. The party's agenda was consistent with the known goals espoused by al-Fatāt, a secret nationalist society in France. The aims of the FSS were in line with a sophisticated political agenda of the leaders of the Syrian national movement who sought to achieve the complete independence of Syria in stages while contending with signs of European expansion and Ottoman decline. Chapter 3 includes a description of how the hopes of the immigrants and the political leadership of the Syrian cause converged in Paris in 1913 at the First Arab Conference. A critical piece of evidence on the genesis of the first political collective is found in letters between Ameen Farah, the immigrant from Nazareth and original owner of the archival records on the organizations under study, and two of his friends. In one of these letters, while Farah was in Cairo contemplating emigration to the United States, the idea of a secret Free Syria Society was hashed out. Equally critical is that Farah joined the Decentralization Party in 1912, the year it was founded in Cairo. It was affiliated with the secret and vehemently anti-Ottoman al-Fatāt party, to which his friend Jubrān Kuzma belonged while in Montpellier, France. Al-Fatāt, a dominant anti-Ottoman nationalist organization, instigated the First Arab Conference in 1913, the year Farah made the journey to the United States and launched his Free Syria Society. Kuzma attended the conference in Paris, where he was joined by a bloc representing the Syrian nationalists in the United States headed by *Mirāt al-Gharb* editor Najīb Diāb. The Paris conference culminated in a subtle agenda that captured the aims of independence that had been espoused by secret and public anti-Ottoman, anti-Turkish societies for years.[51] Although the period immediately after World War I was a time of great anxiety for immigrants, the FSS was too small to make a lasting impact on the goals of political mobilization. However, linkages between the U.S. Syrians and the broader Arab nationalist movement in Syria and Cairo never ceased due to the activity of the press and increased speed of travel aboard steamships.

After World War I the French occupied what became modern Lebanon and Syria in the north, and the British occupied Palestine to the south and extended their control east of the Jordan River through Iraq. This development pushed the coveted goal of a sovereign Syria further beyond reach.

It was, however, France's often violent occupation that ensured the rapid spread of nationalist feelings across Syria as never before and impelled immigrants to launch aid efforts in a bid to rescue their fellow Syrians. Although not every immigrant was behind the cause of Syria's independence and geographical contiguity, opposition to them, my research shows, was kept alive overwhelmingly by the vociferous editor of *Al-Hoda* newspaper, Naʿūm Mokarzel. His brother was Salloum Mokarzel of the *Syrian World*; he took over as *Al-Hoda* editor upon Naʿūm's death in 1932. Naʿūm Mokarzel's relentless opposition to Syrian nationalist goals was aided not by a large immigrant constituency—I found no evidence of that whatsoever—but by, rather, the Maronite clergy's historical position aligned with France and likely by the French government itself. Mokarzel may have relied on a majority of Maronites among the immigrants for wider circulation of his newspaper. However, undue emphasis on Maronite opposition to Syria's independence inclusive of Lebanon, too, can be qualified in two ways. First, Maronites did not participate in any national political organizations proportionate to their superior numbers. This means either that apathy in political matters was largely a Maronite peculiarity or that Lebanese separatism was not as widely shared by Maronites as we are led to believe. Second, a lack of studies on structural assimilation by the 1940s and 1950s makes it easy to ignore the likelihood that many immigrants distanced themselves from the Arab cause in the interwar period by emphasizing Lebanese separatism when it was necessary to profess loyalty to the United States as Arab Americans at the start of World War II. This was a very conflicted time for political activists due to the difficulty of sustaining opposition to the British on the eve of the second global conflict.

I build the context for the Arab National League and explore how immigrant intellectuals maintained a nationalist attachment to Syria in their writings by describing the debates over the implications of using the label "Lebanese" next to or in place of "Syrian." I include conversations from Elia Madey's *As-Sameer* (*Al-Sameer*) magazine debating the frequency of using the terms "Lebanon" and "Lebanese" at the expense of "Syria" and "Syrian" to show that Lebanese identity was not always the salient one, although "the Lebanon" (al-Lubnān), the Mount Lebanon area surrounding Beirut, was part of Syria. The early 1930s were confusing times amid French and British entrenchment but also a time of rising tensions caused by aggressive Jewish settlement in Palestine. The decade began after a Palestinian uprising in 1929 due to worsening conditions among the peasants. Contentions with Zionism and British occupation exploded in another revolt in 1936, gave rise to the Arab National League, and overlapped with signs of an expanding conflict in Europe. The dilemma immigrants faced at the time was twofold: opposition to the British became untenable once war broke out in Europe, and the anticolonialist nature of Arab nationalist sentiments made Lebanese identity more attractive in the American political climate than attachment to Syrian nationalism. Therefore, immigrants had to suspend their political objectives and support the war effort. Identifying as "Lebanese," which until now had been subsumed by identifying oneself as "Syrian," became a convenient alternative to connotations of Arabism or Syrianism that had projected a hostile demeanor toward the colonialist French and British allies in World War II. Naʿūm Mokarzel's advocacy of the French preference for Lebanon's separation from Syria ironically opposed U.S. trusteeship as an alternative to the French Mandate, when nationalists like Ameen Rihani expressed hopes that the United States would play a greater role in securing Syria's independence. The designation "Lebanese" gained popularity after the war just as asserting a Syrian nationalist agenda became politically inopportune and difficult to justify and maintain. Nevertheless, Syrian Americans responded to the new reality of nascent Arab independence by asserting their Arab American identity, as the name of the Institute of Arab Americans Affairs illustrates.

Studies that rely excessively on Naʿūm Mokarzel's writings add to the confusion, as he extracted the support of a subset of immigrants who favored French hegemony over the Lebanon and caused a prolonged spat of unseemly exchanges in the immigrant press. The research I present shows that the Maronite Mokarzel lashed out against others—fellow Maronites, Orthodox Christians, and Druze and other Muslims—for political reasons, thus creating impressions in the pioneering studies on Arab Americans of a permanent sectarian split.

Interpretations of sectarian discord as dominant and impenetrable, combined with a lack of systematic, full translations of entire articles and books, have worked to hinder a sober assessment of immigrants' broad political orientations. Most of the newspaper editors participated in diatribes and insults at different times. However, there are no studies to investigate the causes of their verbal outbursts within a certain time frame or set of events. Any critical assessment should acknowledge the interchangeable nature of hostility on the part of intellectuals who were traditional allies; for example, a Druze and an Orthodox Christian might exchange words but overall remain allies. Also it must be taken into account that basic agreements on a host of issues existed, such as between the Maronite Amin al-Gharib (Ghurayeb) and the Orthodox Najīb Diāb or Nasib Arida, save during the visit of Shakib Arslan in 1927. The political context for the exchanges has been largely missing but is vital to having a realistic understanding of their duration, tone, and causes.

During the political uncertainty and upheavals in the aftermath of the Balkan wars of 1912–1913 and on the eve of World War I, a preponderance of newspapers, intellectuals, and political activists of various persuasions overall opposed Naʿūm Mokarzel. Political rhetoric by Lebanese separatists failed to stifle any of the mass political organizations; one in 1926 was the first large attempt at rallying immigrants in a last-ditch effort to save Syrian territorial integrity. After the largest Syrian revolt against French occupation in the interwar period erupted in 1925, the New Syria Party was formed by diverse immigrants whose sentiments were echoed by the Orthodox and Druze editors of *As-Sameer* and *Al-Bayān*. The consensus held with few exceptions even during the visit by the very controversial Syrian nationalist Prince Shakib Arslan in 1927, despite his known preference for upholding Islam and with it some form of Ottoman existence. As for Shakib Arslan's visit, the reality is far from a simple Christian versus Muslim divide. Gualtieri suggests a severe rift along religious lines and that the "Christian identified papers" *Al-Hoda* and "*as-Sayeh*" (*Al-Saʾeh*) opposed Arslan's visit while the Druze paper *Al-Bayān* endorsed it.[52]

In fact, Naʿūm Mokarzel did not spare *Al-Saʾeh* and its Maronite editor his diatribes for their nationalist posture in the past, as indicated. Support for Arslan, despite bitter memories of hangings of nationalists by the Turks, was ecumenical. Sporadic opposition to Arslan, too, was mixed; among opponents was a small group of traditionally nationalist Orthodox Christians whose views were otherwise indistinguishable from those of the nationalists, Druze or not. The reason had far less to do with sectarianism and more to do with Arslan's largely misunderstood strategy of maneuvering to preserve an Ottoman and therefore Islamic shell to ward off European encroachment.[53] Lack of historical context in recent scholarship accounts for misjudging opposition to Arslan as a sign of sectarianism, although information on the New Syria Party outside the present study is severely wanting. Ameen Farah, himself a Christian, was not only instrumental in preparing for Arslan's visit and the ensuing convention in Detroit's Book-Cadillac and Statler Hotels but also responsible for saving the only semicomplete NSP archive.

Analysis of the First Arab Conference in Paris and its comprehensive political agenda is critical to presenting the FSS and the NSP as steps toward advancing modern Syrian Arab nationalism in the diaspora, and such analysis captures the metamorphosis of the political space and message that came to define the Arab National League.

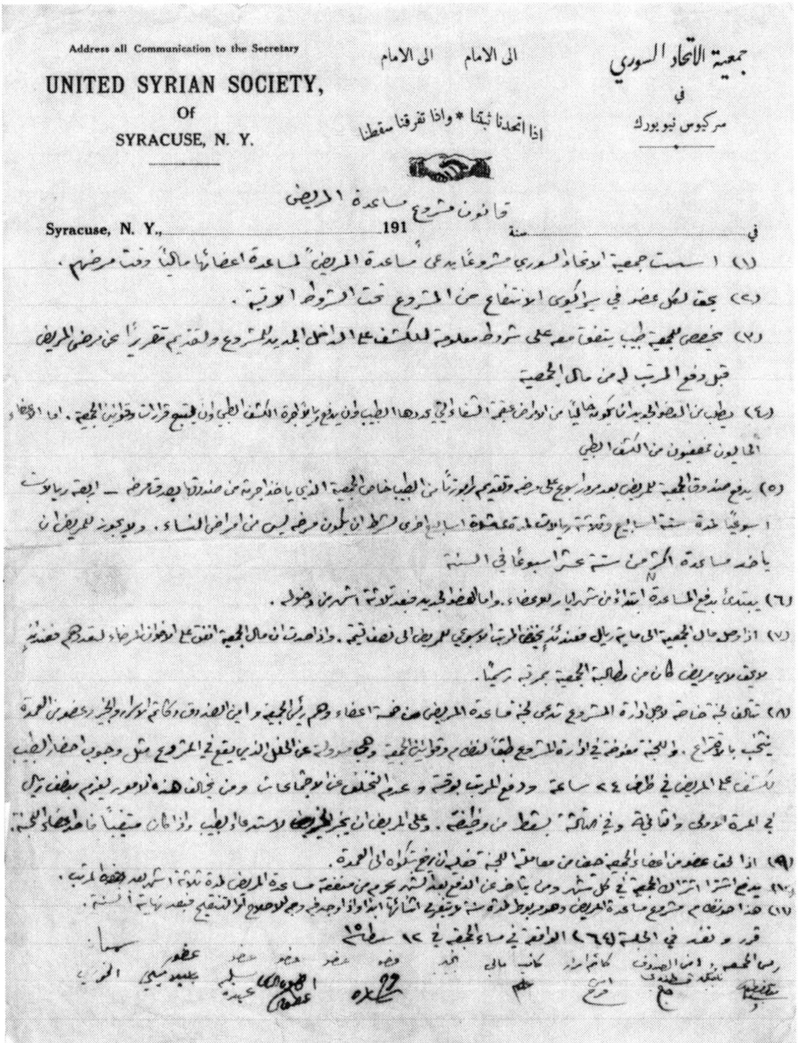

Address all Communication to the Secretary

UNITED SYRIAN SOCIETY,
Of
SYRACUSE, N. Y.

جمعية الاتحاد السوري
في
سركيوس نيويورك

الى الامام الى الامام

اذا اتحدنا ثبتنا * واذا تفرقنا سقطنا

قانون مشروع مساعدة المريض

Syracuse, N. Y., ...191

في ...... سنة

FIGURE I.2. *Insurance document, 1915. One of the few surviving papers of the important United Syrian Society, this document contains the bylaws of the Patient Aid Project, a kind of insurance plan that offered medical care to members by a designated doctor. Ameen Farah is listed as treasurer; his is the third signature from the right at the bottom. Farah Papers, Bawardi Collection.*

Although information on the United Syrian Society is imprecise at best, its nonsectarian status and endorsement of Najīb Diāb, a committed Syrian nationalist, by a large membership inclusive of Maronites suggests that it was possible for consensus behind Syrian nationalism to overcome residual sectarian divisions. My translation of a sophisticated explication of Arab identity by the Arab nationalist and one-time Ottoman parliamentarian ʿAbdulghani al-ʿUraisi during the First Arab Conference problematizes Syrian national identity. Al-ʿUraisi's carefully worded definition of Arab peoplehood left ample room for diverse ethnic, religious, racial, and provincial affiliations in an Arab cultural framework. The motivations for Syrian immigrants' mobilization in the conference centered on hopes of reforming Syria and joining the burgeoning community of modern states; however, the immediate driving force behind articulating a coherent political program had to do with their anxiety over the weakening Ottoman rulers and the imminent British and French occupations.

Inevitably, the discussion contends with competing arguments regarding whether Arab nationalism was viable or even present at the turn of the twentieth century, much less during the second half of the nineteenth century. One such theory is Anthony D. Smith's concept of "ethnie,"[54] which provides the basis of a concept of Arab "peoplehood" relying on common cultural traits. A separate viewpoint is the notion of crediting instead the introduction of institutions by the colonialist powers and the disproportionate role a small elite class played in attaining political awareness.[55] Contributing to the array of competing theories is the doubt cast by Western scholars as to whether Arab cultural identity was capable of ever producing a nationalist project. The archival evidence in Farah's correspondences with his nationalist friends in 1912, presented in chapter 3, provides additional insights on the level of Arab Syrian national coherence. The rationale for bringing into the discussion definitions of Arab Syrian peoplehood is to gain an appreciation of how immigrants perceived themselves at the time. Put succinctly, understanding how they became Arab Americans amid the advent of cultural pluralism in the United States at the outset of World War II requires an assessment of the meaning of their Arabness in relation to standard understandings of nationalism.

Immigrants' identity did not develop based solely on hardened ideas of nationalism. A cultural Arab concept of the nation endured in the idea of *ummah* (the nation), a term first used to describe the early Muslim community. The term permeates the writings of Syrian activists and Arab nationalists in this study regardless of their religious or sectarian affiliations. The term provided the foundation on which Rihani reconciled Voltairian

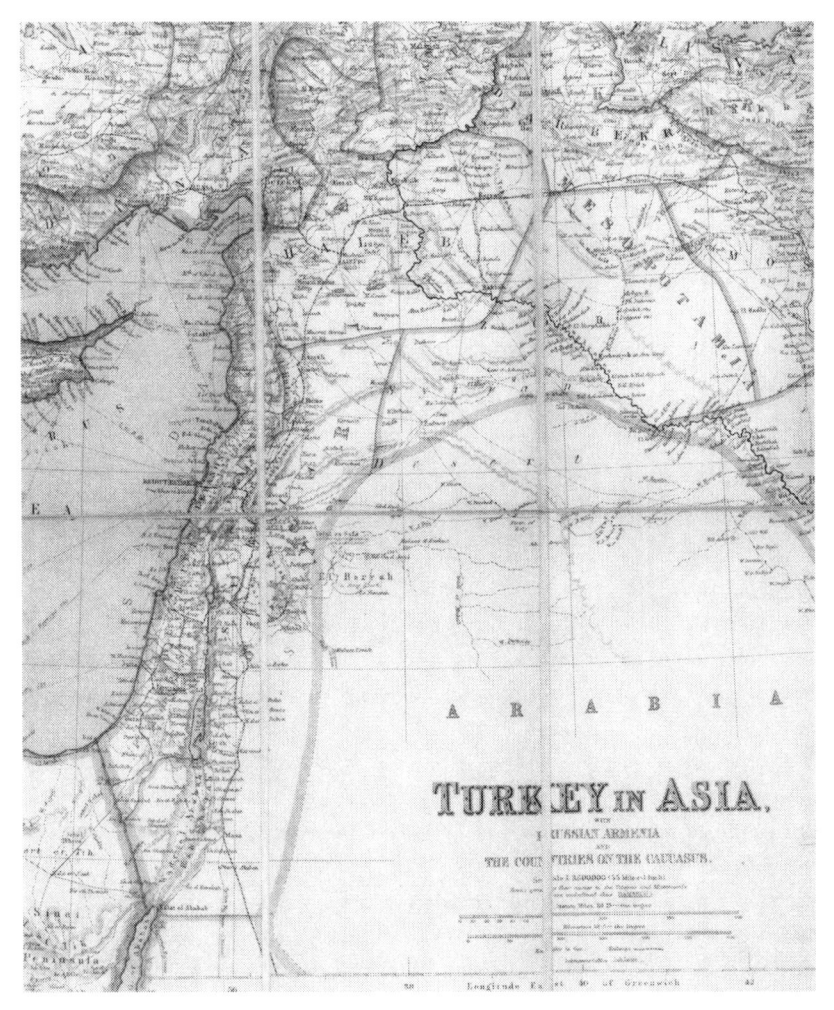

FIGURE I.3. *Ottoman districts in Syria and surrounding areas, circa 1909. The map was produced by Philips and Son. Courtesy of Hatcher Graduate Library, University of Michigan, Ann Arbor.*

thought with that of the philosopher Abu al-ʿAlāʾ al-Maʿarri in his cultural translational project. The concept of *al-ummah* differs from Western discourse regarding nationalism, which is predicated on the dominance of race, ethnicity, or a combination of both despite lofty pluralist interpretations of the French Revolution. The term *ummah* can mean a community, as in the first community in Medina. There the Prophet Muhammad took refuge from persecution in what is known as Hijrah (migration), which also marks the start of the lunar Islamic calendar in 622 CE. It is, therefore, no accident that Rihani and Gibran, both Maronites, modeled their discourse after *ḥadīth* and relied heavily on Islamic classical philosophy. That is, Islamic classical discourses were the source of a flexible identity that can emphasize Arabness or as Gibran and Rihani would have it, skepticism. Gibran's *The Prophet* and Rihani's translations of *Al-Luzūmīyāt* by al-Maʿarri are examples of the influence classical Arabic style had on their writings. They published in Cairo's *Al-Hilāl* in proximity to leading literary figures, perhaps for a vetting by the foremost intellectuals there. They knew and celebrated the works of Jurji Zaydan (1861–1914), Rifaʿa Rāfiʿ al-Tahtāwi (1801–1873), and others in Egypt.

All educated Syrians studied, as do schoolchildren across the Arab world today, classical Arab history. They learned that in Medina (al-Madīna al-Munawara) Muslims formed their first city-state and that within a century multitudes of diverse ethnic, racial, and linguistic groups from the eastern fringes of Persia to Spain joined the new religion. For the most part, Christians and Jews remained separate under Islam and were given sanction as *ahl al-kitāb* (people of the book), meaning fellow monotheists as followers of the Bible or the Torah. These concepts are woven into Arab history and filter into the literature and nationalist message of Syrian American activists, newspaper editors, scholars, and literary figures, among them the leaders of the organizations under study and most of their constituents. Therefore, the colonialist British, French, and Russians projected their influence over the Ottoman Empire by pushing for a system of distinct treatment of the *millet* (religious minority) such as Catholic, Orthodox, Anglican, and other Christians. The *millet* system helped them graft administrative zones of influence under the pretext of protecting minorities. This arrangement did not preclude a universal *ummah*, that is, an Arab and Islamic pluralist conception of an overarching community inclusive of Arabic-speaking *millet*, among them Arab Jews who did not adhere to political Zionism.

Likewise, modernist pan-Islamists like Jamāl al-Dīn al-Afghāni called for unifying all Muslims including Ottoman Turks in a single nation. If this concept was popular among Sunni Muslims in Detroit at the height of Syrian Revolt, such fervor was never an impediment to Christian-Muslim collaboration in the NSP. Including Jews in a vision of a Palestinian society by the founders and activists in the Arab National League and the yet more sophisticated Institute of Arab American Affairs was possible because Islam's treatment of Jews and Christians preserved their communities in all parts of the Middle East and because Jews and Christians in the Arab world overwhelmingly spoke Arabic, often as their first tongue. George Antonius, in his seminal book *The Arab Awakening*, first published in 1938, makes the point that the Arabic language predated Islam, but when Islam outstretched that language, the interplay between Islam and Arab cultural identity became flexible in that Arabs were largely accommodated regardless of their religions.[56] Adding to the flexibility was the position of Christians and Jews as fellow monotheists in the *ummah* that was enshrined in the very classical Arabic and Islamic works the Syrians studied. As indicated, Muslim works could be found alongside Christian ones in missionary schools in Syria and in private libraries. Therefore, I was not surprised in the least when I came across no less than a dozen Qur'ans in the libraries of Orthodox Christian Syrians such as that of the archpriest Basil (Basilius) Kherbawi.

The process of Arabization did not alter the religious practices of Christians and Jews, although Islamization moved further to cover non-Arabs, in keeping with the Qur'an's message that God's revelations through the prophets, Jesus and Moses too, was intended for all mankind.[57] The concept of the *ummah* that immigrants brought with them can be used to specify the attributes of the whole nation or parts thereof. Hence, when they used the term "the Syrian nation" (*al-ummah al-Sūrīya*), as they did often, they referred to the regional, cultural, and political unity that existed within Greater Syria regardless of sectarian divides. When Syria's cause suffered setbacks due to the colonialist policies of the British and the French, the same Arab nationalists responded by invoking the Arab nation (*al-ummah al-ʿArabīyah*), hence pan-Arabism. Not included in the scope of this discussion, it should be noted, is the resurgence of Islamic identity, which began to displace Arab national identity in the lives of immigrants not covered by the time frame of the present study.

The concept of Arab nationalism has had to contest claims of sectarianism that have largely been made out of context. It is true that the overwhelming majority of early immigrants were Christians, but most existing scholarly studies have ignored significant pockets of Muslims and have been hampered by a lack of resources such as translations of Arabic-language writings by the immigrants. Because the concept of *ummah* remains potent in any expression of Arabness, it is vital in building the context for the Arab National League. Hence, from my research, while acknowledging some sectarian discord and even violent incidents, I challenge claims of rampant sectarianism without the specific context of why they occurred and when. In this framework, nationalist content in the writings of Ameen Rihani and to a lesser extent Gibran and such compatriots as ʿAbbas Abu Shaqra, Najīb Diāb, Amin Gharib, ʿAbdulmassīh Haddād, and Elia Madey in the periodicals *Al-Saʾeh*, *Al-Muhājir*, *Al-Bayān*, *Al-Funūn*, and later *As-Sameer*, among other outlets, leaves little doubt that Syria's cause enjoyed ecumenical support by Syrian Christians of different denominations as well as by Muslims. References to the *ummah* in these writings acknowledge commonalities and provide the context for pan-Arabism and Arab nationalism once the Syria idea ran into obstacles after World War I.

The story of immigrants' transition from rallying behind Syrian nationalism into defending Arab nationalism begins with the founding of the New Syria Party in 1926 and continues through the aforementioned confusing times of the European Mandate system over Syria and the founding of the Arab National League. Headquartered in Highland Park, Michigan, with a leadership that was mainly though not exclusively Muslim, the NSP was initially organized to send aid to Syria in response to French atrocities in 1925. In its humanitarian efforts, the party raised significant funds to aid the rebellion against the French that year led by the Druze Sultan al-Atrash. The NSP held national conventions in 1926 and 1927; during the second convention it hosted the Arab nationalist and respected writer Shakib Arslan, Syria's emissary to the League of Nations. As indicated, although Naʿūm Mokarzel's attacks continued against the NSP in the late 1920s and its successor, the ANL, into the 1930s, they did little to hinder the reach and appeal of either organization.[58] The efforts of the NSP alerted Syrian nationalists to the possibility of collecting revenues from the United States and Latin America for a nationalist cause. Most existing scholarship does not account for the party's significance, likely because it was not covered in the English-language press.

A discussion of the structure and operations of the NSP fills a gap in scholarship of the organized Syrian constituency in North America around political causes. The level of organization and the visit by members of the Syrian-Palestinian Executive Council, a body that had its genesis in the push for a Syrian state after World War I, represented the diaspora in international forums. Although each organization deserves dedicated research of its own, I list many of the regional chapters and names of the NSP to show the networking among nationalists across the United States and the leadership in Cairo. But the NSP is significant also in providing evidence of the degree of the Arab American community's integration into the United States during this period. It should be noted that the ages of members in the mid-1920s ranged from late thirties to fifties, which means a great many were pioneer immigrants themselves. This revealed organizational convergence offers a rare opportunity for assessing the political orientations of a representative sample of Syrian immigrants before the records disappear for lack of systematic collection. NSP members were aware of their position of belonging to a diaspora in a powerful country. Although most of their documents and correspondence are in Arabic, they verbalized the need for lobbying Americans and for demonstrating command of the English language. The NSP represents a critical shift in the size, structure, and impetus behind mass efforts by immigrants to aid Syrian Arabs across the waters. Its campaign combined humanitarian aid and political fervor within a transnational network connecting immigrants across the United States with those fighting the French in Syria.

The alternative narrative in this study does not ignore division or discouragement within the ranks of immigrant nationalists. The Druze-led revolt was crushed in 1927, and this was followed by a hiatus in mass-organized political activity from 1928 to 1936, roughly the period of the Great Depression. While the entire subject of the development of Arab American identity is underresearched, that period is a void within a void. It was a transitional period in which political activity took place outside any single organization. The reporting on the Palestinian uprising in 1929 in the immigrant and English-language press reflected a clear competition between Zionists and Arabs regarding who would better represent their respective views in the United States.

Immigrants were aware of what was going on in Palestine, occasionally described as "Southern Syria." But many were also gravely concerned about happenings in what they considered to be northern Syria. The terminology was a natural extension of their political aspirations, especially after a brief Syrian kingdom of roughly "Natural Syria" took hold from 1918 to 1920. The north, that is, Syria and Lebanon, was under complete French control. Palestine, they knew, would be the site of the next battle. Because of the disparate policies of the French in the north and the British in the south, it became more arduous for them to refer to themselves as Syrians or to confine their activities to the Syrian cause. During the confusion wrought by colonialism in the interwar period, activists continued to ask probing questions in *As-Sameer* and other outlets, and they collaborated with Palestinians and Syrian nationalists to explain their point of view at every opportunity. No large organizations existed in this period; however, I present translations from *As-Sameer* and sustained political writings by activists mostly in the New York area as angry responses to news of British policies in Palestine. The loose strands of Arab immigrant life and the increasing need to articulate a political stance in the United States are assembled as background for the reaction to the large Palestinian uprising in 1936 and the founding of the ANL.

After the revolt in Syria abated and before the economic devastation of the Great Depression was halted by the massive mobilization of World War II, Syrian immigrant activists across the United States, aided by known Arab luminaries in American life, united once again to form the Arab National League in 1936. A key figure in its emergence as a continuation of earlier efforts to combat Zionism not connected to the NSP's work was Fuad Shatara, a physician in New York who founded Jamʿīyat al-Nahḍah al-Filasṭīnīyah (translated as the Palestine National League or Palestine Renaissance Society) about 1923. The immigrants' relatively brief experience with the New Syria Party illustrated that it was possible to launch a structured political organization, and Shatara's Palestine National League reemerged as the Arab National League, but only after the urgent need abated in northern Syria. Shatara was aided by the prolific writer and reporter Ḥabīb Ibrahīm Kātibah as well as capable and established Syrian community leaders such as Faris Malouf and George M. Barakat. They succeeded in establishing the ANL as the largest nonsectarian Syrian immigrant political organization in the United States, with a reported membership of 15,000. The ANL held four national conventions, the fourth in Flint the same week in 1939 that war broke out in Europe. The ANL made a point of lobbying the U.S. Congress as well as of explaining Arab culture to American audiences and American culture to Arabs. The ANL captured most of the functions of any current Arab American organization short of exclusive use of English in daily operations.

Decades of acculturation, combined with valuable experience gained by the NSP in political outreach and lobbying, allowed the immigrant activists to experiment with defending Arab causes by speaking of them in terms that the American populace could understand: freedom, liberty, and self-determination. The ANL, on a grander scale, repeated the NSP's strategy of galvanizing Syrian immigrants in the late 1930s by hosting nationalist figures from the old country. This time, the guests of the league were emissaries representing the *mufti* of Jerusalem, Hajj Muhammad Amin al-Husseini. Their visits in 1938 and 1939 helped raise considerable sums of money and support for the victims of British military campaigns and Jewish settlement in Palestine.

The ANL did not survive the mobilization for World War II because Syrian immigrants were aware of U.S. national interests, a cornerstone of which was alliance with Britain against Nazi Germany; thus, continuing their antagonism toward the British put them at odds with U.S. war efforts. However, the ANL represented the last stage in American Syrians' experience before an ascribed identity as Arab Americans was consciously articulated. During the ANL's fourth national convention, amid news that World

War II had commenced in Europe, an articulate pronouncement was made by one of the speakers that the immigrants were no longer "Arabs in America"; rather, they were "Americans of Arab extraction." This is the moment, I argue, that the formation of Arab American identity reached maturity and Syrian immigrants became part of the pluralistic culture in the United States. Research into these events is uncharted territory in terms of existing scholarship and promises to be a major step in the project of writing Arab Americans into American history. Arab Americans consciously decided to maintain their status both as Arab nationalists and American citizens, as evident in this statement in U.S. government records: "The Arab National League [. . .] voluntarily disbanded in May 1941 in order, as its leaders put it, to avoid embarrassing Great Britain's prosecution of the war, and the hope was expressed that Zionists might follow the example and suspend propaganda for the duration."[59]

The metamorphosis into an Arab American identity occurred due to pragmatic thinking during the war but also because immigrants became increasingly aware of their potential as U.S. citizens. Some saw that by working in a fully Americanized environment they could assist a pan-Arab nationalist strategy to combat colonialism and Zionism. This is to say that Syrian immigrants, like Arabs in general, fell on their larger Arab consciousness without losing sight of the agency inherent in being citizens of the United States. Immigrants' reactions to the calamity wrought by colonialism and Zionism after nearly six decades of living in the United States is essential to any understanding of the emergence of Arab American identity in its present form despite a prolonged hiatus of large-scale immigration into the United States. The hiatus was not unique to Arab Americans. It was simply time for Arab Americans to join the millions of Italians, Jews, and Polish immigrants and their descendents in claiming full Americanized identity and declaring their loyalty on the eve of World War II.

When World War II ended, Arab Americans faced a new reality in the Middle East, much like they did after World War I. Having served their country in the war, Arab Americans participated in various stages of high policy on Palestine as contributors to British and U.S. commissions. When the U.S. government tied the fate of displaced European Jews to the work of the commissions on Palestine, Arab American activists accepted entry of a large, though limited, number of Jewish settlers into Palestine. At the same time, they lobbied for entry of newly independent Iraq and Syria to the United Nations to enhance the expanded prestige and global responsibility of the United States. However, by 1946 the British and French scheme of dividing Syria for the duration of the interwar years yielded frontier borders that permanently severed Palestine west of the Jordan River from the rest of Syria, creating Jordan out of a patch of desert east of the river and treating Lebanon as independent. Several countries consequently emerged, each of which also sought legitimacy as a member of the United Nations. Syria and Lebanon became independent in 1946, and Israel was declared a state in 1948 with U.S. and Russian support. The Arab world split into two camps, the Western-supported monarchies on one side and nonaligned countries on the other.

As American military power and influence increased leading up to World War II, the United States slowly assumed British policies and minimized support for anticolonial Arab nationalism. The Arab National League faced an existential dilemma, given its antagonistic stance toward British militarism in Palestine. Predictably, the United States supported the monarchies in Saudi Arabia, Jordan, and Morocco. Lebanese identity as separate from Arab nationalist attachments—a convenient way for nonpolitical segments of the immigrant population to avoid problems—gained currency as an alternative to Syrian national identity, while the larger Arab cause subsumed Syrian nationalism. The result was the pragmatic postwar Institute of Arab American Affairs, which promoted U.S. interests as a way to gain some modest leverage against the increasingly powerful Zionists. The process was begun by Fuad Shatara, Ḥabīb Kātibah, Faris Malouf, and Abdelhamid Shouman, among other individuals, even before the NSP was founded two decades earlier.

Representing Arab nationalisms and Palestinian rights after World War II was considered by members of the institute as a way to forge, potentially, an even-handed policy by the United States. Their approach ideally would serve the interests of the United States and emergent Arab regimes. The institute was a full-fledged Arab American political organization that anticipated the challenges and battles of every Arab American civil rights and lobbying group since. Founded in 1945, its members made a point of representing U.S. interests in the Middle East and produced dozens of publications such as a monthly bulletin that was disseminated to thousands of homes and institutions across the United States. The institute promoted the entry of new Middle Eastern states into the United Nations in 1945 and did what it could to respond to Zionist influence. Working in a complex and contested political atmosphere, members of the institute resisted forceful Zionist lobbying in favor of partitioning Palestine by continuing the ANL's efforts to explain the Arab point of view in congressional hearings. Any talk of Arab nationalism, however, fell on the wrong side of the fence from American foreign policy during this period. The champions of Arab nationalism overseas were for the most part perceived as being on the side of the Soviets, and after news of the Holocaust began to spread across the world in 1945, a broad critique of Zionism became very difficult to maintain.

The institute came up against the U.S. government itself, which was convinced by persuasive lobbying by proponents of Zionism to incorporate support for their political goals into a sweeping policy of containing communism. The result of this support was a series of setbacks for the institute and Arab regimes culminating in a U.S.-recommended partition plan in 1947 that gave the Jewish minority, largely now of new arrivals from Europe, more than half the landmass of Palestine. Arab American activists achieved some success by working with Department of State employees who did not see Arab nationalism as a threat to U.S. interests. Unfortunately for their cause, the institute was no match for the large memberships and funding of the Zionist groups that gave them enormous political clout. Effective boycotts by Zionist groups—for example, of the *New York Times* when its editor questioned Zionist aims or of anyone who lent support to the Institute of Arab American Affairs—raised the stakes for any would-be Arab American organization thereafter. Despite the challenges, Arab Americans recruited many prominent allies, including academics and Jewish luminaries, in the 1930s and 1940s.

Albert Einstein, for a time, opposed political Zionism and the idea of a state for Jews in Palestine, and because of his stance he attracted the attention of Fuad Shatara and his friend the Harvard professor William Earnest Hocking. Several influential personalities in the United States, Jewish and non-Jewish, felt the need to extend economic development to the Palestinian sector in the face of one-sided British policies favoring the Zionists. Among the luminaries were Professor Hocking; the Reform rabbi Judah Magnes; the publisher of the *New York Times*, Arthur Hays Sulzberger; Kermit Roosevelt Jr., grandson of U.S. president Theodore Roosevelt; Virginia Gildersleeve, dean of Barnard College; and the Harvard archeologist Elihu Grant, a Quaker. Individuals who participated in panels, radio broadcasts, and debates with Zionists included Ḥabīb Kātibah, Ameen Rihani, Faris Malouf, Peter George, Philip K. Hitti, and Fuad Shatara. Others contributed to the institute's "Papers on Palestine" series of pamphlets to explain Arab points of view when Zionism was appealing to an expanding share of the older German and Reform Jewish populations.

In working to defend Palestinian national aspirations, the Institute of Arab American Affairs represented a new and distinct stage of political activity in Arab American history sparked by pronouncements made by the Arab National League during its Fourth Convention in Flint in 1939. The situation in Palestine motivated the staff and members of the institute to produce and disseminate the largest body of information in the English language about the political situation in Palestine and about Arab culture, history, and geography until, perhaps, the Association of Arab American University Graduates came on the U.S. stage after 1967. In 1946 the institute published one of the earliest books on Arab Americans' contributions to life in the United States, *Arabic-Speaking Americans* by institute secretary Ḥabīb Ibrahīm Kātibah with the help of Farhat Ziadeh. Early confrontations between the institute and later the league on one side and Zionists on the other foretold battles between Arab Americans and proponents of Zionism in the United States after 1967 that continue unabated today.

Many peripheral topics come into play when looking at Arab immigrants' history of political activism. Despite the animosity between Arab activists and Zionists, Arab-Jewish relations were complex and left room for agreement between the two sides over opposition to political Zionism. The tone of Syrian and later pan-Arab nationalists, though critical of Zionists' territorial ambitions in parts of the immigrants' Syria, remained free of outward or deliberate traces of anti-Semitism until the founding of Israel in 1948. Many activists and political figures in Palestine considered themselves Semites and were familiar with indigenous Jewish communities in the Arab world. Their views allowed them to distinguish between strictly political Zionism and spiritual manifestations of Zionism that left room for the coexistence of Jews and Palestinians. A meeting of the minds allowed for a publication by the institute outlining the pragmatic political aim of binational statehood on equal footing.

In the aftermath of World War II, despite clinging to hopes of pan-Arab unity, immigrants' disposition was largely one of pragmatism; they understood the United States' role as a superpower and considered their proximity to that power as U.S. citizens an asset. Their pragmatism was a lesson they learned from the dejection they experienced following the collapse of the much-touted promises of self-determination by President Wilson after World War I. Even though European colonialism had receded, the U.S. Congress still did not sympathize with Arab nationalism or the ultimate goal of unifying the Arab world. These were the signs of new zero-sum policies of containment at a time when some Arab regimes, including Syria and Egypt, held to a position of nonalignment, fearing renewed foreign domination.

Arab American activists working for the institute recognized the need to serve U.S. strategic interests in the oil-rich Middle East. They hosted Saudi delegates and members of the royal family and facilitated some official contacts with the United States. However, they faced the paradox of balancing their role of fostering relationships with their loyalties to the core Arab cause, the concern over the partitioning of Palestine. At a critical time, the evidence reveals, the Saudis balked on taking a public stand on the issue of Palestine. What followed was a gradual rift between the objectives of the institute and a U.S. pragmatic policy of supporting Arab monarchies as part of an overall strategy of containing communism. Institute leaders' desires of promoting U.S.-styled democracies in Syria and Lebanon gradually became incongruent with their adopted country's hostile position toward any talk of Arab nationalism or political reform. When the United States persisted in supporting partition in Palestine and aligned more closely with Zionism aims, the activists and their constituency found themselves on the wrong side of U.S. strategic interests.

The increased radicalization of the Arab world after Israel was declared a state in 1948 with U.S. support and the bitter battles the institute fought against the Zionist lobby foretold an ominous future for Arab American political activism. The setbacks continued when the Israelis routed the armies of Syria, Egypt, and Jordan in 1967. The fallout of 1967 is beyond the scope of this study, but the retreat from pan-Arabism and the resulting new political reality in the Middle East, unlike standard history purports, did not make a qualitative difference in the way Arab Americans behaved in the United States since the founding of the institute. They faced the same difficulties in influencing hostile U.S. policies toward Arab regimes due to Zionist pressure, and they fought the same uphill battles to raise public awareness about Arabs and their history against a tidal wave of aggressive and frustrating advocacy by their detractors.

Looking into the activities of the Institute of Arab American Affairs after World War II, with the emergence of postcolonial regimes and the founding of Israel, is essential to gaining a realistic grasp of Arab American life in the aftermath of 1967. In general, current scholarship tips overwhelmingly toward postmodern approaches to social constructions of identity and sexuality, while narratives, chronologies of origins, and social history have yet to receive adequate attention. There is a sweeping dearth of narratives on groups of individuals or social history; of historiographies on institutions, civic societies, and political organizations; and of adequate surveys of immigrant literature beyond a general view of the impact of the Pen Bond.

The sources for the narrative of this study come from little-known archives that include the bylaws, minutes of meetings, and correspondences of the four organizations themselves, mostly from the papers of Ameen Farah, ownership of which was transferred to me by his son, Roy (Rushd) Farah of Grand Blanc, Michigan, in 1996. Complementing this resource are published studies and extensive translations from the Arabic-language press, in addition to other collections from the New York Public Library's Middle Eastern Division and Dorot Jewish Division, the Immigration and History Research Center at the University of Minnesota, Hebrew University in Jerusalem, Columbia University, and the Ameen Rihani collection at the Library of Congress. I made some use of the massive materials of each of the following: declassified records of the Office of Strategic Services; the Library of the Antiochian Village in rural Pennsylvania, part of the Antiochian Orthodox Church of North America; the papers of Khalil Totah at the home of his daughter, Joy Hilden Totah, in Berkeley, California; and the library of the late archpriest Basil Kherbawi in the home of Amal and Gregory Dalack, his great-grandson, in my city, Ann Arbor, Michigan. I also benefited from the generous council of the descendants of Fuad Shatara, especially his daughter Gina Shatara of Florida and granddaughter Barbara Tate Cerato of New York.

The present study is an attempt to incorporate Arab-nationalist Syrian thought as a significant marker of Arab American identity development and to urge treating the attendant discussions as an integral part of U.S. social history. It is also a call to pay adequate attention to collecting and preserving surviving material relating to Arab immigrants in various locations so this material may point the way for future research.

ARAB POPULATIONS UNDER OTTOMAN RULE: A BACKGROUND

Chapter 1

The Ottomans succeeded in expanding their rule over Arab populations partially because they understood the role of Islam in the lives of their subjects. The Turks appealed to the predominantly Muslim Arab populations by professing to be the new guardians of Islam and its holy sites and the seat of the caliphate (*khalifah* is the successor to the Prophet Muhammad). While Arabism is acknowledged to have survived Ottoman rule and emerged as the basis of a protonationalism before World War I, some scholars on Arab nationalism question whether nationalist feelings or even feelings of Arabism were present.[1] This is not the view of seminal scholars including George Antonius and Zeine Zeine, whose work is essential in any rendition of Arab nationalism. They mark the mid-nineteenth century and literary innovations as the start of national feelings. Whatever the debate over the origins of Arab nationalist thought, the outcome was an awareness of the importance of national and social coherence despite the often fluid political and social atmosphere, whereby close interaction took place between Arabs from different regions, Turks, Kurds, Armenians, and Jews. This diversity was part of the Ottoman realm within porous boundaries until frontier borders were introduced by colonial powers to serve their aims. When the constitution was reinstated in 1908 after it was suspended by Sultan Abdulhamid in 1877, Ottoman subjects rejoiced because equality under the constitution meant an acknowledgement of their peculiarities. In *The Book of Khalid* Rihani described the scene in 1908 in the "muddy square at the holy stomp of liberty" where the protagonist in his novel exclaimed, "I beheld my old friend the Spouter dispensing to the turbaned, and the tarboushed crowd . . . of the blessing of that triple political abracadabra of the French of more than a century passed. Liberty, Fraternity, Equality!"[2] Rihani's satire notwithstanding, Rashid Khalidi is one of the leading contemporary scholars who has chronicled the transition from Ottomanism to Arabism through the experiences of Syrian political activists, among them ʿAbdulhamīd al-Zahrāwi and Shukri al-ʿAsali, and the role of the press in Syria and Egypt.[3] The story of Arab nationalism is ultimately the story of how Arab-Ottoman association came to an end, on whose terms, and what the colonialist powers did about this process.

Ottoman rule over the Syrian provinces extended from 1517 after the Ottoman Sultan Selim I conquered the Mamluks, the rulers of Egypt, having subdued the shah of Iran in the preceding two years, until World War I.[4] This period in the history of the Middle East was preceded by a string of victories of unbroken succession of "brilliant and great [Ottoman] Sultans" from the fourteenth through the sixteenth centuries.[5] The Ottomans maintained their rule over Arab lands despite attempts by "martial and heroic" Arab figures such as Fakhr al-Dīn and Ḍhāhir al-Umar to challenge their legitimacy.[6] While the efforts at insurrection might serve as early indications that Arabism was not completely lost, they nevertheless failed to unify Arabs or pose enduring political challenges to Ottoman hegemony. Likewise, Aḥmad al-Jazzār, the governor of ʿAkka (Acre), was savage and brutal, and most Arab leaders who challenged the Ottomans were, according to George Antonius, "solitary and self seeking," appearing and disappearing in "tedious succession" without seriously challenging Ottoman rule. An exception would be Muhammad Ali, the Ottoman governor of Egypt, whose rule sparked Syrian nationalist inquiry.[7]

Antonius presents Ali's challenge as the spark behind the idea of an Arab empire during Ottoman rule, but the time was not ripe for Arab national consciousness.[8] Muhammad Ali's long rule in the first half of the nineteenth century, the woes of the Ottoman Empire in navigating European encroachments, and local unrest all contributed to increase Syrians' desires for shedding Ottoman control. Syrians inched closer to developing a modern consciousness of their place within an Arabic-speaking *ummah* during this period. Muhammad Ali, an Albanian by birth and an Ottoman subject, came to Egypt as part of an Ottoman expedition to oversee the evacuation of the Napoleonic campaign of 1798. He allowed Arabs into the army for the first time since the decline of Arab rule and allowed or sent many to be educated in France and elsewhere. Ali reformed the country's cotton production, built the military, and created a large textile industry.

The British dashed Ali's efforts to modernize the Egyptian economy as part of their policy of creating markets for British goods, and they incorporated Egypt into the emerging world economy under European domination.[9] Ali's Egypt, despite his reforms, was never a match for the vast European power driven by a population explosion and backed by a superior navy and a great capacity for industrial output. The imbalance in military might enabled European powers and Russia to dictate their terms to the Ottoman sultan in Istanbul. This European encroachment was accompanied by intense intra-European competition that may have delayed the dismemberment of the Ottoman Empire and consequently prolonged Arab subjects' submission to the progressively decaying Ottomans.[10]

Openness to Europe contributed in no small measure to strengthening Egyptian and Syrian Arabs' conceptions of nationalism, especially after the radical social and political changes brought by the French Revolution in 1789 and Napoleon Bonaparte's invasion of Egypt in 1798. News of the collapse of established rulers in France resonated across Europe and reached the Middle East, prompting a reassessment of the stagnation Arabs and Islam had suffered for five centuries. When Bonaparte was evicted from the region, Muhammad Ali was charged with overseeing the French exit from the area. Ali stayed in Egypt and displaced the remnants of the ineffectual Mamluks who ruled on behalf of the Ottoman sultan in Istanbul.

Soon, innovations in the Arabic language by one of the beneficiaries of this change, Rifāʿa Rāfiʿ al-Tahtāwi, coupled with increased availability of printing presses thanks to Bonaparte's campaign, bridged classical Arabic and Islamic education with the new Western technology and liberal intellectual traditions of the period. As soon as the presses began to operate in the Bulaq section of Cairo, the Arabic lexicon expanded to include such words as *tiyatru* (theater), *jurnāl* (journal), and *al-bosta* (postal service). The developing, dynamic atmosphere attracted many Syrian intellectuals, making Cairo a center for political dissidents seeking refuge from the cruelty of Sultan Abdulhamid and thus exposing them to Tahtāwi's innovative work.[11] Cairo also became a way station to the United States for Syrian nationalists fleeing the Ottoman police and conscription in Beirut, Nazareth, Haifa, Homs, Damascus, and other major cities.

The often exaggerated impact of the West, however, should not obscure the local social context. Arab nationalism in the period can be framed as an overall history that is part of a world history without ignoring local structures and their specific features.[12] Naturally, immigrants' religious lives and clan affiliations mirrored attachments along similar loyalties in Syria. Relations among sects were vulnerable to Ottoman weakness in the face of Europeans who found ways to extend their influence by extending privileged treatment to certain religious groups and in so doing created resentment between some Christians and Muslims. Ali challenged Ottoman rule by launching a successful military campaign across Syria in 1832, led by his son Ibrahim Ali, that reinvigorated Syrian Arabs' hopes of freedom from the Turks. Ibrahim Ali's invasion of Syria and subsequent push for Istanbul were tenuous because Ali was ultimately undercut by the Europeans and because support for Ibrahim among the Syrians was not uniform. Nevertheless, once established in Syria, Ibrahim Ali sought to appeal to the Arabs of Syria by professing: "I came to Egypt as a child and my blood has since been colored completely Arab by the Egyptian sun."[13] Ibrahim's plans, however flimsy because he was not an Arab and was ultimately driven by self-serving concerns, were sensitive to growing sentiments among the local population of distinctness as Arabs based on language, perceived ethnic connections, and a shared past.

An unintended result of Ibrahim Ali's tenure in Syria was the reintroduction of foreign Christian missionaries, who played an important role in the area's cultural and social development. Although European missionaries made previous attempts to proselytize in parts of Syria as early as the sixteenth century, American Presbyterians were the first to assert their presence, in 1820. Their numbers swelled with the arrival of Eli Smith in 1827, followed by French Jesuits in Lebanon in 1831. The ensuing events are pivotal in retrospect: the Americans brought a printing press to Beirut from Malta and, under the directions of Eli Smith, developed in Leipzig, Germany, a new typeface known as "American Arabic." Schools for boys and girls soon opened, and Ibrahim Ali initiated primary school education modeled after the system established in Egypt. With presses now in Syria and Egypt, books were printed in numbers not seen in generations. Equally important is the systematic rehabilitation of ideas and intellectual discourses that had remained dormant throughout Ottoman rule. Formal education extended literacy to the Muslim population as well,[14] but it also allowed a "rehabilitation of the Arabic language as a vehicle of thought" when stagnant classical texts were reexamined and reinvigorated.[15]

Along with schools came uneven development in Muslim and Christian communities due to foreign influence and ultimately, sectarian violence. I contend that Druze-Maronite violence in the mid-nineteenth century had a limited impact on immigrants' nationalist demands and political work. However, the exaggerated role of sectarianism can be put into perspective by a cursory examination of the roots of the intra-Syrian violence in 1860. Sectarian antagonism was urged on by the British and the French, a large Arabic-language study by Muhammad Zu'aitir discloses,[16] as the area was being incorporated into a world economy. Neither the Ottoman Empire nor Arab Syrian communities would be safe from expanding European economies and reach and the resulting intra-European intrigue. One example is that France's Napoleon III instructed his agents to foment conflict in Syria in order to avert internal rebellion while providing locals with the capital necessary to grow and produce silkworms for French industry.[17]

The Europeans saw an opportunity in the worsening economic conditions among farmers. Druze and Maronite peasants rebelled against landlords of both sects, but when the violence reached Druze areas, many of the landlords were killed. France seized the opportunity to spread rumors of impending conflict and dispensed weapons to Maronite peasants, who formed marauding gangs dressed in special uniforms. A German official noted that the gangs of Maronites insisted on humiliating their Druze neighbors. He quoted the Maronite archbishop Abdallah al-Bustāni as saying: "Our blind love for France was the main and direct cause for this disaster which befell us and which left pains and deep wounds that will not heal easily."[18] With France's help the Maronites bought 120,000 rifles and 20,000 handguns in the year preceding the massacre. A British officer recognized that the Maronites were not hapless victims, stating that "it is futile to describe Christians as martyred."[19] However, despite evidence that the Maronites were armed and belligerent, it can be assumed that such a statement was partly motivated by Britain's long-standing policy of guarding routes to India across Syria and Iraq through an alliance with the Druze.

Settlement of the French, British, and Russian strategic arrangements in Syria should be understood as part of the expanding colonial tide across Asia and Africa between 1844 and 1900.[20] The Maronites were willing partners to growing French influence under the ensuing Ottoman capitulations and sought to increase their autonomy in the area of Mount Lebanon. In part to satisfy European demand for reform, an imperial rescript, *Islâhat hatt-ı hümâyûnu*, inscribed the *millet* system into law. Accordingly, Christians increasingly came under French, British, and Russian jurisdiction as religious minorities. Druze victims were seldom mentioned by the Christian-dominated press and were soon forgotten, while the French seized on the one-sided press accounts of sectarian discord and extracted Ottoman acquiescence for sending a large military contingent to Syria ostensibly to protect the Maronite Catholics.

The heavily indebted Ottomans were coerced into granting the Maronite enclave in Mount Lebanon more autonomy, in effect creating a separate administrative entity (*mutaṣarrifīyah*) in the Mount Lebanon area. This administrative change provided the locals with autonomous rule under French protection as a prelude to Lebanese political claims for independence. The decrees promulgated in the 1850s and 1860s on the pretext of mitigating intra-Syrian violence became the justification for the preferred status of foreign Christians living in parts of the Ottoman Empire. The decrees in effect gave Russian, British, and French nationals added leverage in economic and administrative spheres and deepened animosity within sectors of the populous. Therefore, while Jewish and Arab and Armenian Christian *millet* attained some legal protection, European agents moved to control all aspects of Ottoman economic life. Although their efforts were, above all, intended to establish the foreign powers' presence in an atmosphere of intense intra-European competition, they nevertheless strengthened ties between Christian Arabs and Europe.

Syrians who immigrated to the United States under these conditions brought with them memories of the Arab *nahḍah* and sectarian discord. However, the sectarianism was more complex than a Christian versus Muslim rift because not all Christians were Maronites and because burgeoning nationalist feelings cut across religious affiliations. Therefore, intra-Syrian discord had political underpinnings. Although Orthodox Christians largely escaped bouts of violence in the Syrian provinces, they were not, like the Protestants, spared Maronite hostility when they did not acquiesce to French colonialist designs. Furthermore, the sectarian animosity in the United States was confined to a vociferous few, while Maronite Syrians also opposed French domination of Lebanese separatism. The conduct of the Maronite Church in severely punishing dissent, forging alliances with foreign powers, and maintaining Lebanese Maronite purity remains outside the reach of the present study, although I will discuss the signs of Maronite hostility toward Syrian Arab identity as well as the much-publicized sectarian squabbles in the *mahjar* press and the Lebanonization of references to Syria.

Syrians of all sects engaged literary inquiry into Arabic texts, and the knowledge and concepts they gained accompanied them on their journeys to the United States. In particular, more scholarship is needed to gain a better understanding of the reasons behind overrepresentation of Orthodox Christian editors and publishers among the pioneers, especially since most of the early arrivals were Maronites. The missionaries in the Lebanese and other parts of Syria themselves, save very few, were ill equipped to participate in this inquiry because classical Arabic texts remained well beyond their grasp. But they provided the schools and funds for Arab Christian and Muslim scholars who fought off mundane and uninspiring teachings by local priests and turned to manuscripts and ancient Arabic texts. Several, among them Nasīf al-Yāziji, Butrus al-Bustāni, and Ahmad Beyhum, stand out in the annals of the Arab cultural awakening for their translations and explications of Arabic grammar. Even before the close of the nineteenth century, the press on both continents bridged distances and generations of Arab diasporas and their homelands. This is to say, it hardly mattered that al-Yāziji and al-Bustāni were Christians or that al-Bustāni became Presbyterian. They paved the way for Jurji Zaydān, whose books accompanied Syrian immigrants to the United States and whose work on the histories of the Arabic language and Islamic civilization formed one of the pillars of pan-Arab thought in modern times.

Connections to the past often drove Syrians' quests for new knowledge. Al-Yāziji, for example, practiced the medicinal principles of the tenth-century physician and philosopher Ibn Sīna (Avicenna),[21] delved into "the heart of the lost world of classical Arabic literature," and discovered the "desolation wrought by the centuries" before his works helped establish a new standard for the teaching of grammar, logic, and rhetoric, especially for the schools of the American mission.[22] Butrus al-Bustāni, born in 1819, was a Christian who attained the best education possible at the time through the American school in Ain Waraqa. His education in Syriac, Latin, and the "science of his [Arabic] mother tongue" was often delivered by Arab scholars working in the American schools. Al-Bustāni translated the Bible before authoring his two major works, compilations of dictionaries of the Arabic language. In my search for archival material I often find al-Bustāni's *Muḥīṭ al-muḥīṭ* (Circumference of the ocean) and *Quṭr al-muḥīṭ* (Diameter of the ocean) in homes of descendants of early Syrian immigrants to the United States.[23]

The diffusion of books and ideas led to the growth of Arab social and literary clubs across Syria, much as in the American diaspora, Egypt, Iraq, and the Maghrib. The literary clubs eventually nurtured nationalist sentiments. The Society of Arts and Sciences, facilitated by American missionaries in 1847 and with al-Bustāni and al-Yāziji among its members, was transformed into the Syrian Scientific Society (al-Jamʿīyah al-ʿilmīyah al-Sūrīya). Its evolution was one of the first signs of a modern Arab consciousness but not yet a conscious move to break free from the Ottoman Empire. With the press firmly established, this mid-nineteenth-century movement projected its voice to Beirut, Baghdad, Palestine, and Egypt. The society had also among its erudite members the Druze Amir (Prince) Muhammad Arslan and the important Muslim intellectual Husain Baihum. It must be noted here that there was no discernible difference culturally or politically between Damascus, which since antiquity had been a center of culture, and Beirut near Mount Lebanon. Within a generation, descendants of Arslan and Baihum—Prince Shakib Arslan and the Lebanese intellectual Muhammad Jamil Beyhum, respectively—would visit the United States as honored guests of the U.S.-based Syrian political mass organizations under study.

Improved communications and acknowledgment of the Arab and Islamic past in literature motivated immigrants to look toward the Arabian Peninsula for inspiration, thus preparing the way for further political development in the region and Syrian immigrants' wide-reaching political interests. Sharif Husain of Mecca, as guardian of Islam's holiest places in the Hijaz region of western Arabia, challenged Ottoman rule by joining the fight on the side of Britain and the Allies of World War I against the Central Powers. Another source of inspiration to Arab American intellectuals like Ameen Rihani was the success of the Wahhabi movement in eastern Arabia after the war. The Wahhabis gained power and influence in western Arabia in the eighteenth century after an alliance took hold between Muhammad ibn 'Abd al-Wahhab, the inspiration behind a strict interpretation of Islam, and the house of Saud. Shortly before World War I engulfed the region, the Hijaz Arabs represented by Husain Ibn Ali's son Faisal forged an alliance with many among the Syrian nationalists in Damascus. Aside from containing Islam's holiest places, western Arabia was an important symbol for Ottoman religious authority. Therefore, the Ottomans forced the guardians of these holy places, the family of Husain Ibn Ali, to move to Istanbul, the seat of Turkish Ottoman rule.[24] Members of Husain's family are descendants of the Prophet Muhammad's clan, and the Hashemites are therefore highly regarded by most Muslims. Because of Arabia's status as the source of the Arabic language—the dominant cultural marker for Arab collective memory—and because of the Hashemites' "capacity for original and independent thinking,"[25] they also commanded the respect of non-Muslim Arabs.

Syrians in the diaspora and in Syria became increasingly dissatisfied with the Ottoman Turks well before World War I. The frustration of the Syrians, however, did not mean that they were blind to the ambitions of the Great Powers.[26] As I will explain in the discussion on the First Arab Conference in Paris in 1913, this was true on both sides of the Atlantic. Ottomanist sentiments in the last decade of the nineteenth century lingered because of an overwhelming desire for reforms and because of the pan-Islamist sentiments of respected intellectuals such as Muhammad Abduh (1849–1905), 'Abdulrahmān Kawākibi (1848–1902), and Muhammad Rashīd Rida (1865–1935).[27] In addition, Syrian immigrants understood the dangers of colonialism because they read news of European ambitions in the Ottoman Empire—Germany's eastward-driven foreign policy (*Drang nach Osten*) seeking to build railroads connecting Berlin with Baghdad, French and British demands for open markets for their products, coerced contracts with the Ottomans to build railroads, and construction of the Suez Canal with Egyptian Arab chattel laborers. Ottoman industry and trade were suffocated by the excessively high interest Europeans imposed on loans designed to allow lavish living by the Ottoman sultans and their governors in Egypt under the guise of integrating the Ottoman domain into a world economy.[28]

FIGURE 1.1. *Ameen Farah's teaching certificate from the Greek Metropolitan in Nazareth. A translation of this certificate may have helped Farah escape to Cairo through Alexandria, where he taught in a school for Jewish children around 1911 or 1912 before journeying to the United States in 1913. Farah Papers, Bawardi Collection.*

A core of progressive military Turkish reformers along with foreign students and exiles reacted to British, German, and French interventionist policies and Russian land grabs by forming the Young Turks,[29] which gave rise to the Committee of Union and Progress (CUP) and a brief restoration of the Ottoman Constitution in 1908. Syrian public and secret societies formed and began formulating plans for either autonomy within an Ottoman framework or independence in stages. These included al-ʿArabi al-Fatāt (Arab Youth), a Paris-based Arab rendition of the Young Turks; al-ʿAhd (The Promise); al-Muntada al-ʿArabi (Arab Literary Club); and the Decentralization Party (Hizb al-Lāmarkizīyah al-idārīyah al-ʿUthmani).

When the constitution was suspended in 1909, very few Syrian leaders and intellectuals maintained hopes of equality with the Turks, and those who openly opposed Turkish rule, among them Muhammad Rashīd Rida, Muhammad Kurd Ali, and Rafīq al-ʿAẓm, began sharing their cautious plans for independence on the pages of the Syrian press in the United States. Noteworthy is that modern European thought permeated the ideas of reformers across the religious spectrum despite fears of European colonialism. Both ʿAẓm and Kurd Ali understood Western principles of citizenship, as evidenced by their columns in the U.S. Syrian press. ʿAbdulrahmān al-Kawākibi inspired reforms in Islamic thought, while his determined opposition to the domination of Islam by the Turks added to his appeal among nationalists. However, al-Kawākibi's influential book *Umm al-qurā* (Mother of the villages), published posthumously, was itself influenced by the anticolonialist author Wilfred Blunt,[30] who opposed British occupation of Egypt in 1882.

Any division among Syrian nationalists was replaced by a unified anti-Turkish position when Jamāl Pasha, a member of the CUP, executed dozens of Christian and Muslim Syrian nationalists after the Arabs chose to fight on the side of the Allies in World War I. By then the conservative elements in society that struggled with residual loyalty to the Ottoman Muslims transferred their loathing of Ottoman Sultan Abdulhamid to the CUP.

The challenge for Syrian Arab nationalists as World War I drew nearer was to find a way to operate on their own terms given Ottoman repression and Europe's growing appetite for territory, markets, and material. The combination of permanent changes in Arab societies due to the proliferation of Western modes of life and thought,[31] along with lessons learned from foreign control over Ottoman affairs, helped shape the strategies of Arab nationalists in Cairo, across Syria, in Europe, and in the Americas. The Decentralization Party, which had a direct impact on the political message of the Free Syria Society, devised a philosophy of inching toward independence without falling victim to European designs. The Decentralization Party sought to improve the lives of Arab populations within a "constitutional parliamentary Ottoman sultanate based on principles of decentralization."[32] Whatever the approach, catching up to Europe while maintaining political and cultural survival was no easy task. The remainder of this chapter presents examples from archival evidence of the staggering burden shared by Syrian youth and how ideas of political action were transmitted and exchanged outside the press.

The spatial dimension of political involvement by Syrians expanded with the ease of travel in search of education and opportunity. For Ameen Farah and many of his compatriots, the possibilities of reclaiming Syria seemed to be enhanced by the freedoms they gained once out of the reach of Ottoman police. Farah used a temporary leave from Ottoman conscription to escape to Alexandria, Egypt, and from there to Cairo in 1911 before continuing to the United States in 1913. Once in Cairo, he joined the Decentralization Party, which was founded the year Farah departed for the United States. From Cairo, Farah reconnected with childhood friends Jubrān Kuzma, an agricultural student in Montpellier, Nicola Qub'yn, and Muhammad Muhaisen, who also immigrated to the United States. Farah's archives include exchanges between Kuzma and Qub'yn as well.

It is unclear how or when Farah gathered letters not intended for him. It is evident that he made an effort to collect and preserve them. There is room here to discuss only a fragment of the thirty-seven letters mostly dated 1912 and 1913 before sporadic letters were exchanged after the war, in 1919 through 1921. Farah feared that CUP agents might intercept the letters; therefore, he scraped off all names and most references to places on many of the letters with surgical precision. In an atmosphere of persecution and jailings, Syrian nationalists had ample cause for caution. The content of the letters is dense with references to reformers, European ambitions, land acquisition in the Galilee by Zionists, and incidents of acquiescence by wealthy Syrian absentee landowners, as well as diatribes against the CUP, advocacy of interreligious cooperation around the nationalist cause, and talk of reforming the country's agriculture by acquiring and applying scientific methods from the West—in short, most of the main topics of the day. The evidentiary value of these correspondences, however, transcends abstract and intellectual boundaries and offers rare, unassuming, and unfiltered specific evidence of the hopes, fears, political plans, and frustrations Syrians took with them on their journeys in search of ways to build their nation, the idealized Syria. The letters leave no room for doubt that a significant cadre of ordinary Syrians across national borders understood not only the need to wriggle free from Ottoman rule but also the impending dangers of colonialism and the need for a political strategy. The correspondences illustrate that the young Syrians expected a wide conflict over the holdings of the Ottoman Empire and prepared themselves by hatching out plans for achieving independence in stages.

The earliest correspondence is dated February 9, 1912, possibly from Jubrān Kuzma, then a twenty-one-year-old, prolific, anti-Ottoman activist in Montpellier, to Nicola Qubʿyn. On the first page Kuzma describes the prevailing social and political conditions in Syria, including Christian-Muslim relations:

> I love the mere mention of [national] independence and hopes of achieving it, despite the hope-killing clouds of misery over our heads. Policies and politics are changing and glib and we do not know how to settle down. I look at European policies and principles of material gain devoid of all humanity, and I burn over our weakness and inability to resist. . . . When I look at the majority of Christians in our lands, I become filled with fury, and I can't help saying that European policies succeeded to a great extent through schools in dividing and splintering us. Then I look at a large portion of the Muslim youth, and my heart is brought back to life, and my hopes are renewed. Not too long ago, the "Arab Society's Appeal to all Arabs" invited them to unite, Christians and Muslims, in their demands for true Decentralization from the government and explained to them that the government of the Turks [the CUP] is no longer able to protect them from foreign occupation. This invitation, though weak, is like a flash of light shining in our night of total darkness, telling us of the presence of a few free nationalist zealots watching over their country and who won't allow their national identity [jinsīyatahum] to be lost.[33]

Not all notables and people of means were sincere in calling for reforms, Kuzma wrote, but he detected the sincerity of "those who proved themselves to us," referring by name to the reformers Muhammad Kurd Ali; Shukri al-ʿAsali, a parliamentarian who refused a post by the CUP in exchange for his silence; and ʿAbdulhamīd al-Zahrāwī, a member of the Decentralization Party and head of the First Arab Conference in Paris the following year.[34] Kuzma lamented intra-Syrian division: "Some feel that European occupation will, at least, end Ottoman domination and others (among the Muslims) feel it is his duty to hold onto the seat of the caliphate, and yet others have no idea what to ask for."[35] Kuzma, a Christian, predicted a role for Sharif Husain of Mecca in perhaps mobilizing the Bedouin tribes as Syria's "salvation" once they were armed and organized: "What does it matter then if France declares us a protectorate and sends its tanks and armies to our shores? They would not cross too far behind these shores."

Kuzma's understanding of the inner workings of French society, whose opposition to war had a socialist tinge, surpassed the "glib" calls for French intervention: "Many French are angry with their government for sending them to fight for colonialism" after using missionaries to pave the way by "sowing the seeds of division among Syrians," a clear reference to the intra-Syrian massacres in the 1850s and 1860s.

Correspondence dated June 30, 1912, from Jubrān Kuzma to either Qubʿyn or Farah seems to confirm historical accounts of Arabic-speaking subjects being phased out of all meaningful jobs in the Ottoman administration, including the army, by the CUP-led constitutional government in 1909.[36] He confirms the outlawing of all clubs and societies calling for autonomy that year. Kuzma decries in his letter the methods employed by some Zionists of acquiring land through corrupt Ottoman officials, and he curses the Turkish "thieves" who closed down the newspapers *Al-Barq* and *Al-Muqtabas*. Although U.S. immigrants and Syrian nationalists remained preoccupied with the fate of the Ottoman Empire, colonial ambitions, and the practices of the CUP, Kuzma's letter captured signs of the approaching Arab-Zionist conflict, which would worsen between the world wars and emerge as the core political issue on both sides of the Atlantic. This is a translated excerpt of Kuzma's letter:

> [Ottoman Turks] treat Syrian parliamentarians as employees, jail independent writers, and sell our lands to the Jews. Jida, Tel al Shammam, Afoula [towns in northern Palestine] were all sold to the Jews, and soon our beloved Nazareth will become a Jewish-owned town and more people will be evicted and fall victim to a damned band that will increase our misery, steal our trade, and bury our fields with debts. . . . When will Sursuk, Bishara Azzam, Qewar [landowning families including absentee landlords], and the notables understand that the thousands of liras [Ottoman monetary unit] they accept is like a passing rain quick to dry up. As for the land, it is a spring of gold bringing money for eternity. I heard that some shop owners wish that Nazareth would fall into Jewish hands, thinking their spending money would make them rich. They are unaware that the Jew, once settled, is likely to become a merchant or an artisan before he would become a farmer. What blind idiocy! [. . .]
>
> They can see Haifa, Jaffa, and Tiberius filled with Jewish-owned shops. The Jewish farmer buys only from his kin. . . . They can see Shajara, where Jews forced the locals to flee, and now they are going after the

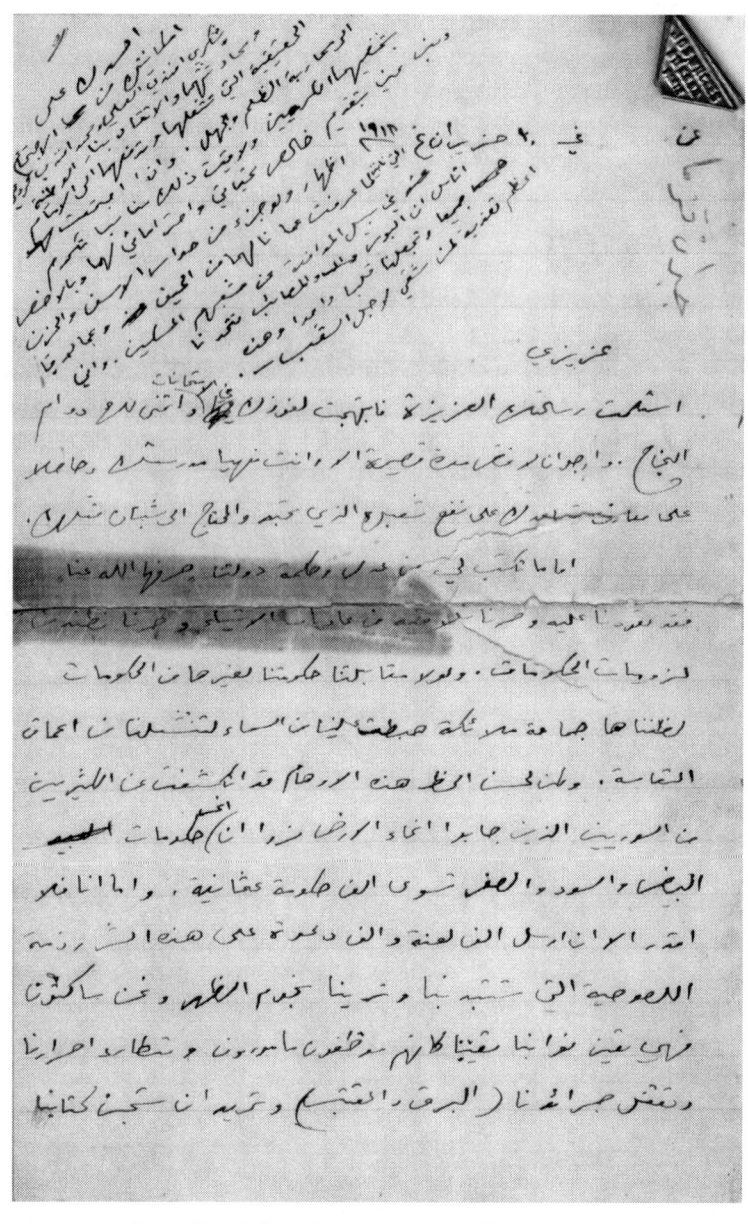

FIGURE 1.2. *Letter from Jubrān Kuzma in Montpellier, France, to either Ameen Farah or Nicola Qub'yn, 1912. Kuzma extolls the virtues of the Syrian nationalist Shukri al-'Asali and lashes out about the Ottoman government. Farah kept thirty-seven such letters. Farah Papers, Bawardi Collection.*

inhabitants of Kafr Kanna, where they accuse them [Palestinian villagers] of killing by placing one of their [Jewish] dead in fields or on the road of Kafr Kanna. The [locals] are then tried by the "fair" Ottoman judges (may God burn their beards and their pockets [because] they never fill). And by bribery and threats they prove the charges and jail the innocents for fifteen or twenty years. . . . Leave the schools aside, as reforming them is not within our means, and take for example the [government-backed] press. . . . I say the press adds corruption atop corruption, and void atop void; for the press knows only to humor the powerful and won't dedicate even a column to educate the commoners [including] the Beirut Lisān al-hāl [Current affairs]. It is filled with lines of killing, stealing, and pillaging and European news of the falling of a pilot or a train wreck—all borrowed from the foreign press. . . . Conditions are ripe for a change. Many youth are motivated and educated [and] filled with a love for the land and ready [to] sacrifice to attain progress and prosperity, but we lack one thing, without which we cannot take one more step forward . . . that is unity, for we are divided. We are scattered intellectually and financially lacking a collective association like those powerful ones that yield great coups. Therefore, I perceive that all we have to work for is to unify behind a society with a scientific and social orientation, more than political, in order to spread the spirit of unity. We do not need youth to throw bombs at processions of the kings and ministers; we need teachers, and apostles preaching unity.[37]

At the heart of the debates on the origins of Arab nationalism is the question of who instigated it and when. Rashid Khalidi's research consistently has expanded the circle of nationalists beyond the notables and landowning elite; he pays attention to the role of professionals and journalists,[38] precisely the kind Kuzma, Farah, Qubʻyn, Muhaisen, and their heroes ʻAsali and Zahrāwi were. An exhaustive discussion of Arab nationalism remains beyond my scope, however. Answers to questions concerning the viability of some of the organizations in this study, will ultimately hinge on whether the case was made for Arab nationalism as a viable force and at what time period. The intent thus far has been to prepare the framework for presenting immigrant political action with a purpose: Syria's independence. The critical examples from the content in the letters above, the fact that Farah was a member of the Decentralization Party, and the fact that he carried these letters across the ocean at great personal risk are part of a process of transplanting Syria's cause wherever Syrians lived before World War I. The rest of the discussion recalls the historical roots of what subsequent chapters describe as an organized political action.

Chapter 2

THE SYRIAN NATIONALISM OF THE *MAHJAR* PRESS

The content of the Arabic-language press is beginning to attract some attention, however disjointed, by a few of scholars of Arab American history. This is no surprise given that the journalistic output is one of the only primary sources outside a scattering of original records and letters of the first arrivals. This chapter presents translations from the early immigrant press in proper historical context to explain the political orientations of immigrants. The Arabic-language press in the United States offers unambiguous and copious evidence of subtle strategies for achieving Syria's complete independence before World War I. Immigrant activists, especially Najīb Diāb of *Mirāt al-Gharb*, agreed with nationalists active in Cairo and Paris on the strategy of using the Ottoman Empire as a shield from European ambitions while working for independence. The conversations in various newspapers advanced differing perspectives such as rejecting participation in an Ottoman coalition, accepting residual Ottomanism, and attaining administrative autonomy. World War I ended talk of coalitions with the Turks, and prospects of European encroachment effected a pragmatic strategy by the Syrians of finessing a transitional period to autonomy, but only as a prelude to independence. The nationalists understood that an abrupt end to Ottoman rule would invite European domination.

The press played a pivotal role in introducing activists to each other in the 1910s, for example, Ameen Farah to the famous authors Mikhail Naimy and Nasib Arida and activists in New York such as Fuad Shatara and Habib Salloum to countrymen across the United States. The press faithfully publicized the activities of the United Syrian Society and other collectives; promoted publications by seminal Syrian literary figures who, like Gibran, lived in the New York area; and kept immigrants apprised on news from Geographic Syria.

Despite the abundant information in the surviving issues of the major newspapers and especially given the dearth of manuscripts and personal papers of Syrian pioneers, translations for research purposes are scant. Effective interlibrary loan services do not seem to alleviate a critical deficiency in language fluency. The lack of specialized studies on the U.S. Arabic-language press, save for Henry Melki's survey for his doctoral dissertation in 1972, obscures the press's centrality to the political aspirations of the immigrants and their literary pursuits. The sample I utilize in this chapter, a fraction of the available issues of Syrian newspapers in the United States, addresses immigrants' awareness of and reaction to specific political developments in Syria.

The immigrant press was an extension of the Arab cultural *nahḍah* and its thrust toward self-awareness. Therefore, my examination begins with viewing the press as stimulating political action and establishing links between U.S. nationalists and their comrades in Syria. The press I have read illustrates long-standing and basic agreement of the Maronite clerical hierarchy with French interventionist policies. Naʿūm Mokarzel, editor and owner of the newspaper *Al-Hoda*, left an enduring impression that he represented a constituency with a defined political agenda. I found no evidence of widespread agreement with his views, only anecdotal commentary in the form of personal diatribes usually by Mokarzel himself.

Distance from Europe and the Middle East and relative inexperience in international affairs shielded the United States from intra-European fighting over Ottoman territories, but many Arabic-speaking immigrants no doubt wondered about the fate of their former homelands and expected the Ottoman Empire to collapse, with unforeseen results. The activists who attempted collective action were extremely committed and sought some role in the impending changes. Arabic-language newspapers and magazines performed double duty by serving the intellectual literary needs of immigrants while also providing news of the old country. The main newspapers often featured writings by Ameen al-Rihani, Khalil Gibran, Mikhail Naimy, Nasib Arida, ʿAbdulmassīh Haddād, Amin al-Gharib, Elia Madey, William Catzeflis, and other well-known authors.

Rihani came to the United States at age twelve, in 1888, before many of the activists in this study were born. He introduced Voltairian critiques of religious zeal in his 1903 book, *Al-Muʾallafah al-thulathīya fi-al-mamlakah al-hayawanīyah* (The trilateral treaty in the animal kingdom), which led to his excommunication by the Maronite Church. Rihani followed this book with dozens of reformist essays and short stories; the first Arab American novel in English, *The Book of Khalid* in 1911; and *Al-Luzūmīyāt*, translations of the poetry of al-Maʿarri. His essays in *Al-Rihānīyāt* (1910) established him as a writer and philosopher of note in Cairo and the diaspora. In the 1920s Rihani turned his attention to exploring Arab dynasties on the Arabian Peninsula in his two-volume *Mulūk al-ʿArab* (Kings of the Arabs, published in English in 1930 as *Around the Coasts of Arabia*). His early writings for *Mirāt al-Gharb, Al-Muhājir, Al-Bayān,* and *Al-Hoda* newspapers and later the English-language *Asia* magazine, among many others in both languages, added to his Americanist views and his skills as a speaker and made him an ideal choice to be a frequent guest of the Foreign Policy Association, founded in 1918 to educate the public on U.S. international affairs, and to deliver a keynote address at the Arab National League gathering in New York in May 1937. Rihani advocated a universal love of country that was free of political prejudices and religious intolerance. With his public stature well established, he made himself available to give speeches and reveled in dealing with the media, but he remained aloof from the mundane organizational affairs of political collectives. Rihani was not the only important writer with nationalist leanings. Literary analysis all too often focuses on Gibran's humanist genius, Naimy's prose, and Arida's poetry and overlooks the Syrian Arab political and nationalist aims they expressed. All of these literary giants received their elementary education in parts of Geographic Syria as the Arab awakening unfolded.

Many eventually prominent Syrians obtained their education in one of the thirty-three schools Americans established by 1860, including the first all-girls school. By 1891 Muslim and Christian students enrolled in American-run missionary schools alone numbered 7,117.[1] In 1865 American missionaries established the Evangelical Syrian College, which eventually became the American University of Beirut (AUB). Dozens of newspapers appeared in Syria beginning in Beirut and Damascus in the mid-1850s. In Jerusalem, a short distance south of Beirut, thirty-six Palestinian newspapers appeared between 1908 and 1928. In Beirut, many newspapers were attached to foreign missions aimed at proselytizing and were run by missionaries who endeavored to use printing and Arabic to reach wider audiences among Syrians. By the late nineteenth century American missionary publications included *Akhbār al-Injīl* (News of the Bible), *Kawkab al-subḥ al-munīr* (Shining morning star), and *Al-Nashrah al-usbūʿīyah* (The weekly bulletin), and Jesuits published *Al-Bashīr* (The good message). This type of educational support by various missionaries, especially Americans, enabled one of the most influential figures in the annals of Arab literature, Butrus al-Bustāni, to publish *Nafīr Sūrīya* (Trumpet of Syria), an Arab anti-Ottoman newspaper.

A small number of Arabic-language newspapers in Syria and Istanbul, the capital of the Ottoman Empire, targeted the Arab subjects of the empire and served as mouthpieces for the central government in Istanbul. Some papers catered to specific readerships; however, most newspapers, including those published by Druze, addressed nationalist affairs of the larger Syrian community, while Southern Syrian (Palestinian) papers, observing the affairs of Syria generally, expressed concern about the rise of Zionism and Jewish immigration. In Palestine, socialist-driven attention to workers' conditions was advocated by *Filasṭīn* (Palestine), published by ʿĪsa al-ʿĪsa, and *Lisān ḥāl al-ʿummāl fi Filasṭīn* (Reporter on the workers in Palestine), published by Ittiḥād al-ʿummāl (Workers Union).[2] The Khalidi family library in Jerusalem houses bound issues of a wide range of publications: *Al-Jawāʾeb*, established in Istanbul in 1860 by Syrian nationalist Ahmad Fāris Shidyāq; *Al-Jinān*, edited by Butrus al-Bustāni in Beirut in 1870; *Al-Muqtataf*, founded in Cairo in 1877 by Faris Nimr; *Al-Manār*, edited by Rashīd Rida in Cairo in 1897; *Al-Muqtabas*, established in 1906 and edited by Muhammad Kurd Ali in Cairo; and *Al-Mufīd*, published in Beirut by ʿAbdulghani al-ʿUraisi.[3]

Palestinian papers that reached Syrian Palestinian immigrants in the United States include *Al-Karmel*, published in Haifa by Najib Nassar; *Al-Quds*, published in Jerusalem beginning in 1906 by Jurji Hananiya; and *Filasṭīn*. Private libraries belonging to the Budairi family published books and other materials despite Jerusalem's relatively small population then. When the political situation shifted after World War I due to British and French occupations, the Budairis issued *Sūrīya al-Janūbīyah* (Southern Syria), its name a sign of impending political changes and a reminder of the historic and cultural contiguity of Syria.[4] Likewise, a passing glance at articles reprinted in *Mirāt al-Gharb* in 1911 through 1913 suggests a common appeal among the major newspapers to all Syrians—Damascenes, Beirutis, and Jerusalemites, many of whom read news of each other's economic developments, social affairs, and most significantly, political responses to Ottoman decay and to Ottoman Turkish propaganda. Economic and social reforms (*islāḥāt*, plural of *islāḥ*) remained a dominant topic in the newspapers, and their potential was reinforced by recounting ancient Arab glories and Western scientific and intellectual feats. Syrian intellectuals, among them Rafīq al-ʿAẓm and Rashīd Rida, recognized the value of appealing to the economically stable Syrian American audiences to hasten the reforms as part of a larger political agenda of seeking autonomy.

The reformers thus contributed regularly in the Arabic press in the United States, especially in 1912 and 1913 over the fate of the Ottoman Empire when it lost almost all of its European territories in the Balkan wars. Dissemination to the United States of newspapers published by Syrian exiles in Cairo was aided by British rule in Egypt beginning in 1882 but did not always escape Sultan Abdulhamid's paranoia during his reign (1876–1909).

When Turkish nationalists restored the constitution in 1908, overlapping the Ottoman sultanate, they too monitored correspondence and publications, forcing closures and deletions of names, as the letters between Ameen Farah and his friends in Nazareth and France will illustrate.

In Part 4 of *Tarīkh al-saḥafah al-ʿarabīyah* (History of the Arab press, the first installment of which appeared in 1913), Viscount Philippe de Tarazi provided a rare tally of all known Arabic-language newspapers and magazines worldwide through 1933, and a good number of them continued to publish for another fifty years.[5] De Tarazi categorized the publications according to sectarian orientation, likely in order to differentiate Ottoman Turkish official newspapers and French-supported publications from nationalist ones. In his accounting, Muslim publishers issued 451 periodicals with either an Arab nationalist or Ottomanist current, compared with 412 publications by Christian nationalists or missionaries. However, one should not read too much into these contrasts based on religion or sect, as many "Christian" and "Muslim" papers expressed nearly identical Arab nationalist and sometimes anti-Ottoman sentiments, while many "Muslim" newspapers rejected Ottoman domination regardless of the Islamic factor.

Classifying newspapers according to their editors' and publishers' sectarian orientations is problematic in discussing the often-recalled divisions in New York. Revisiting this issue from the perspective of professed stances on Syria's nationalist cause by each of the editors will reveal that most major editors and their newspapers agreed on maintaining Syria's territorial integrity, with one exception, *Al-Hoda*. Circulation as a measure of acceptance of a newspaper's orientation, too, is difficult to ascertain due to a lack of empirical information on the Syrian press in the first four decades of emigration from Syria. However, it is possible to piece together a coherent picture of the overall political attitudes of the papers' readers by combining circulation figures during World War II with their political orientations. The figures are listed in declassified surveillance reports by the Foreign Nationalities Branch of the U.S. Office of Strategic Services (OSS).[6] One highly accurate list of publications in the Americas and various parts of Syria and Egypt was supplied to Walter L. Wright Jr. of the OSS by professor Philip Hitti, who at the time was chairman of the Department of Oriental Languages at Princeton University. Hitti was the source of Wright's report dated November 4, 1941, stating that the immigrant press in the United States reached audiences in the Middle East and South America and provided stories and analysis on "items of interest" all over the world. He described both *Mirāt al Gharb* and *Al-Saʾeh* as pan-Arab, *As-Sameer* as Syrian nationalist, and *Al-Hoda* as "opposed to the Pan-Arab Movement."[7]

One year later another brief report accurately described the nationalist tendencies of each of the major publications based on a partial list of newspapers and magazines accompanied by the religious and sectarian affiliations of their editors. These were supplied to the OSS Foreign Nationalities Branch by Defense Service Section employee Habib J. Awad. The initial list includes editors' names, addresses, and orientations. Salloum Mokarzel, who succeeded his brother Naʿūm as *Al-Hoda*'s editor, and J. G. Raphael, editor of *Al-Akhlāq*, are listed as Maronites. The Orthodox editors and their papers in the report are Elia Madey, *As-Sameer*; ʿAbdulmassīh Haddād, *Al-Saʾeh*; Nasib Arida, who succeeded Najīb Diāb, *Mirāt al-Gharb*; and Najib Badran, *Al-Nisr*. The report lists Ameen David, who succeeded Suleiman Baddūr in *Al-Bayān*, as Druze.[8] A subsequent report adds the Detroit *Al-Sabah* without naming an editor and describes it as "nationalist."[9] The incomplete tally of editors alone puts the number of Orthodox and Druze with known nationalist sentiments at six compared to two Maronite newspapers, one of which, *Al-Akhlāq*, regularly published articles by Habib Salloum and Fuad Shatara when they publicly expressed nationalist views and therefore can hardly be considered antagonistic to the nationalist cause of Syria. The circulations according to the OSS reports ranged from 800 to 2,000, while *Al-Hoda*'s circulation may have been much larger, according to its owner. *Al-Hoda* published a variety of views outside of its editor's known preference for Lebanese separation and opposition to Syrian nationalism; nationalist newspapers and editors outnumbered those edited by Maronites, although not all Maronites were antagonistic to Syrian nationalism. A simple deduction dictates, then, that most Syrian immigrants who read newspapers and magazines were accepting of the publications' nationalist tone and information.

Information in the OSS reports does not preclude almost universal loyalty to and love for Lebanon, yet it does challenge the implication that political support for separating Lebanon from Syria was popular or based on religious and sectarian affiliations. Naʿūm Mokarzel may well have championed Lebanese separatism when the idea of a Syrian nation enjoyed considerable support. His divergence is different from disagreements over the visit by the Druze Syrian leader Shakib Arslan, who drew opposition by Maronites and Orthodox alike due to his consistent strategy of propping up Ottomanism as a shield from colonialist agendas longer than any of his compatriots. Aside from that, the picture is far more complex than one of inherent animosity between two camps, one Maronite and one Orthodox, or even divisions over spiritual matters of marriage, communion, and ecumenical worship.

Admittedly, passions were stirred for a long time over ecclesiastics. For example, *Al-Hoda* published a directive by the Maronite patriarch Anton ʿArīdah (aka Anton Butros) in Syria discouraging exogamy and mixing with non-Maronites or offering them communion, and it drew a response in *Al-Nisr* from the Orthodox archpriest and author Basil Kherbawi.[10] However, the issue of national affiliation was not confined to church as was religion and therefore appears to have represented a wider source of immigrant identification. Syria's cause attracted many Maronites alongside activists from other sects. His brother Salloum was more nuanced and open to interaction with others, while the often volatile Naʿūm Mokarzel maintained close associations with French officials, among them George Picot, an author of the Sykes-Picot pact between France and England that ultimately divided Syria into several states,[11] associations that deserve attention beyond the scope of the present study. Here, a background on the immigrant press is intended to explore the extent of agreement on the Syria idea beyond recycled claims of sectarianism.

The official publications that were either Ottoman (later Turkish) or foreign-backed through the start of World War I numbered fifty-one, and twelve of those, de Tarazi discloses, were "Israelite," that is, Zionist and non-Zionist Hebrew newspapers supported by European coreligionists.[12] These semicomplete accounts of Arabic-language periodicals are helpful in tracking some of the immigrants responsible for nationalist rhetoric in the Arabic-language press in the United States. De Tarazi listed Muhammad Muhaisen, a childhood friend of Farah who wrote in *Mirāt al-Gharb* as early as 1914 and 1915, the editor of *Al-Difāʿ al-ʿArabi*, which was distributed in Detroit beginning October 1, 1921.[13] He listed the Druze ʿAbbas Abu Shaqra's newspaper, *Al-Burhān* (The evidence), as starting on October 1, 1920.[14] I have not yet found issues of either newspaper.

A 1913 study of Syrian immigrant communities across the United States at that time suggests that Syrians' literary pursuits matched their proclivity for economic success from the beginnings of U.S. Syrian immigrant life. Basil Kherbawi performed the study for his Arabic-language book *Tarīkh al-Wilāyāt al-Muttaḥidah* (History of the United States).[15] Their economic stability in turn aided newspaper sales early in the Arab immigrant experience. The first Arab immigrant newspaper in the United States was *Kawkab Amreeka* (Star of America), begun in 1892 and published in both Arabic and English by Ibrahim and Najīb ʿArbili, Orthodox Christian brothers from Arbil, Syria. Ibrahim and Najīb were the sons of Yousef ʿArbili, a learned physician and expert in classical Arabic texts and Islamic philosophy, as most educated Arabs often were. The nine ʿArbili siblings and their parents

FIGURE 2.1. Muhammad Muhaisen, circa 1913. On the back of this portrait Muhaisen wrote this dedication to Farah: "Let my picture bear witness to our brotherhood, Ameen." Farah Papers, Bawardi Collection.

are remembered by Arab American scholars as the first Syrians to immigrate as a family, in 1878. Nearly nothing is known of their fate.

Najīb 'Arbili likely took advantage of good relations between the United States and the Ottoman Empire in the late nineteenth century—when American Civil War veterans served as military trainers in Egypt and elsewhere in the empire—to obtain printing presses and Arabic typeset for the newspaper. The 'Arbilis used their connections as former students of an American missionary to overcome Sultan Abdulhamid's prohibition against the export of Arabic type and printing equipment as a means of censorship.

Nonetheless, *Kawkab Amreeka* initially published glowing accounts of Abdulhamid due, I suspect, to the need for printing equipment and safe passage to Syria if needed and in keeping with the good relations between the Ottoman and American governments. *Kawkab Amreeka*'s publishers defined its role as to "develop good relations and understanding between East and West," defend Syrian immigrants facing discrimination and physical attacks, encourage Syrian immigration, foster commerce with the United States, and promote the Chicago World Expo in 1893.[16] Shortly after the founding of *Kawkab Amreeka*, two more Arabic-language newspapers were established in the United States, *Al-Hoda* (Guidance) in 1892, published by Naʿūm Mokarzel in Philadelphia before the paper was moved to New York in 1902, and *Mirāt al-Gharb* in 1896, published in New York by Najīb Diāb, an Orthodox Christian and former apprentice of the ʿArbilis. The uncompromisingly critical tone of both papers regarding Ottoman decay may have been the publishers' response to the conciliatory tone of *Kawkab Amreeka* toward the Ottomans. Nearly all Syrian Arab newspapers in the United States called for reforms; however, in his writings Naʿūm Mokarzel progressively championed separating Beirut and the surrounding area of Mount Lebanon from the rest of Syria, especially after the Ottoman Constitution was restored briefly in 1908. The Orthodox Najīb Diāb joined the Druze, Sunni, and Shiʿa editors and contributors to newspapers in the United States and in Syria who consistently supported the eventual independence of all Syria under one Arab flag.

The immigrant press suffered strange bouts of exchanging insults, often between Naʿūm Mokarzel and other editors of all persuasions. *Al-Hoda*'s editor and publisher baffled his contemporaries by lashing out with venom and vigor against anyone who opposed him. The specific cause and timing behind Naʿūm Mokarzel's belligerent attitude toward his peers, particularly his hostility about any mention of Syria and Syrians, is difficult to determine without dedicated biographical research. Unfortunately, these diatribes became a basis for scholars to ignore otherwise ideologically balanced content in the Syrian press on a host of issues. Challenging the discrepancy is the first line of defense in this study against contemporary constructions of Lebanese exceptionalism based on a romanticized Phoenician past. I surmise, however, that Naʿūm Mokarzel's sectarian prejudices were motivated by a political agenda. His diatribes drew reciprocal rhetoric from Diāb and others, and their exchanges hindered meaningful debates and collective action among the immigrants for a time. They did not go without eloquent and dignified rebuttals. Suffice it to mention for now that Naʿūm Mokarzel's *Al-Hoda* professed to speak for Lebanon, although his provocative remarks were unaccompanied by any perceptible political plan of action for independence, perhaps because he felt assured of French support.

The heated exchanges also invited belligerent responses in *Mirāt al-Gharb*. When news spread that the respected writer Amin al-Gharib, a member of the illustrious Pen Bond, intended to publish the newspaper *Al-Muhājir* (The immigrant) in New York in 1903, Syrian readers welcomed the news warmly because they were fed up with occasional epithets and personal insults on the pages of newspapers large and small. Naʿūm Mokarzel did not share the overall sentiments of welcoming *Al-Muhājir* because of its nationalist tinge. Before establishing his own paper, al-Gharib made a name for himself as a level-headed and prolific writer in the pages of *Al-Hoda* and *Al-Sakhra*. In the first issue of *Al-Muhājir* published on July 25, 1903, its masthead reads, "a Syrian nationalist newspaper" issued every Saturday to "address the immigrants' concerns" and strengthen connections between the homeland and the diaspora "without taking the side of any party or being led by any agenda."[17]

Al-Gharib, a Maronite who did not succumb to Naʿūm Mokarzel's sectarian rants, urged other papers to "promote the Syrian cause and to elevate the nationalist cause by putting an end to sectarian division."[18] *Al-Muhājir* contributed to arresting the slump in literary quality by featuring Gibran's first works, including the celebrated "A Tear and a Smile" (in Arabic, *Damʿah wa ibtisamah*),[19] and it helped exchange innovative prose and poems with the homeland along with other news. Despite *Al-Muhājir*'s appeal among Syrians, Mokarzel cast al-Gharib as one of three enemies of *Al-Hoda*, the other two being *Mirāt al-Gharb* and the nationalist Orthodox archpriest Rafael Hawawini.[20] Hawawini established the Orthodox Archdiocese of North America and published and edited *Al-Kalimah* (The word; still in circulation), the Syrian Orthodox official magazine.[21]

Mokarzel's behavior may not be a simple matter of cantankerous personality. His actions often appear to have been calculated. He lashed out against Syrian nationalists at pivotal times such as during the formation of various aid and later political collectives, which suggests that he actively wished to undermine their agendas. He launched verbal assaults as well when France implemented a policy of devising spheres of influence for itself and cultivating allies to that end.[22] Mokarzel's vehement opposition to expressions of nationalism during this period corresponded with overtures Zionists made to the Maronites of Lebanon as the former sought to purchase land along the Litany River, delineating the borders between modern Lebanon and Palestine. Muhammad Zuʿaitir draws connections between backing Maronite separatism and regional colonial ambitions (for example, British public invitations to carve up the Middle East among European powers as early as 1907),[23] and the French "Cambou declaration" on June 4, 1917, promised the establishment of a Jewish state five months before the British made a similar declaration.[24] These designs, Zuʿaitir argued, cemented Maronite Zionist collaboration on the basis that establishment of a national home for the Jews would help Maronites achieve the same for Christians.[25]

When the disputes on the pages of newspapers peaked in 1906, Syrian intellectuals intervened by urging all to tone down the rhetoric. One example is a poem published that year in *Mirāt al-Gharb* by the widely respected medical doctor and writer Rizk Haddad titled "Tool al-Lisan" (Belligerent language). Between 1901 and 1910 it was Ameen Rihani, "the Voltaire of his time" and one of the diaspora's ablest and most respected scholars,[26] who challenged Naʿūm Mokarzel, his former editor and the husband of his sister.[27] In "Nahnu wa jara'eduna" (Us and our newspapers), a lengthy critique of the state of the Arabic-language press in a letter to a friend, Rihani faults both *Al-Hoda* and *Mirāt al-Gharb* for "useless attacks," "denigrating women and men's honor," "deceitfulness," "incendiary" and "malignant" diatribes, and the uncritical attitudes of their readers.[28]

In the letter to his friend about the state of the press Rihani recounts a report in the New York press on a street brawl among Syrians caused by disagreements over competing Syrian newspapers. He rejects Naʿūm Mokarzel's claim to be a dedicated Maronite Catholic when in fact he had "but a shadow of piety"; Rihani admonishes Mokarzel for being among the "guilty ones, whose guilt is multiplied by his command of the language, which he uses to plant the seeds of ignorance and superstition in the hearts of the simple ones," presumably immigrants from the Lebanon area with modest education.[29] Rihani was at a loss in reconciling Mokarzel's literary prowess with a "filthy vocabulary" and "extreme zeal for Lebanon's independence while denying others [nationalist Syrians] independence."[30]

Rihani's indignation in the face of Mokarzel's threats of "crushing," "pulverizing," "smashing," and "destroying" his opponents may have been caused by the political motivations behind Mokarzel's diatribes; Mokarzel incessantly claimed that he represented Lebanese sovereignty and that Syria's independence was a threat to Lebanese separatism. Of course, hostility toward those who did not subscribe to his opinion may have been his only course of action because nationalist activism in Beirut itself was ecumenical. The secret Beirut Reform Society established in 1876, if that was the inspiration for Naʿūm Mokarzel's Lebanese League of Progress, had a mixed membership of Orthodox, Maronites, and Muslims in that city and may have been the impetus for the anti-Ottoman Beirut Reform Society established in the United States in 1911. Mokarzel, however, expended a great deal of effort to convince readers that he alone represented Lebanese independence and made similar claims during the First Arab Conference in Paris, where he attempted to capitalize on the superior numbers of Maronite immigrants.

Lebanon's separation became a tool for challenging Syria's sovereignty within its natural boundaries. The Beirut Reform Society spearheaded efforts to rid the Lebanon of Turkish rule. It was founded by Faris Nimr, Ibrahim al-Hourani, and Jacoub Sarouf—all Orthodox Christians—and a Catholic, Ibrahim Yāziji, in addition to Shahin Macaris, whose sectarian orientation I have not been able to determine. All of these pioneering nationalists were graduates of the American Evangelical Syrian College.[31] Overall, the religious strife between Druze and Maronites in the 1860s created animosity, but that episode of Syrian history, however painful, cannot be traced to disparate political ideologies, one Syrian and one Lebanese, in the lives of Syrian immigrants until French policies made this division impossible to overlook. That occurred when Lebanon was separated from Syria by the French, who seized on Ottoman collapse and the Syrians' weakness.

Turkish nationalists led by the CUP dashed hopes of autonomy by suspending the 1908 constitution, and a chaotic period ensued through the first phase of Syrian immigration to the United States. The removal of Sultan Abdulhamid in 1909, coupled with news of reportedly countless hangings of Syrians by Turks during World War I, solidified Christian and Muslim resolve to work together for independence. Hence, Naʿūm Mokarzel's preference for statehood for Lebanon separate from the rest of Syria should be understood in the context of foreign intrigue, not domestic developments.

Acknowledging the exaggerated sectarian divisions at this point provides a context for Mokarzel's renewed and intensified attacks in favor of French colonialism during the mandate period. Whether Zionist and French aims converged in Lebanon is beyond my focus, mainly because immigrants would soon turn their attention to the larger Arab cause and Zionist encroachment in Palestine proper. The point here is that Mokarzel's possible collusion with Zionists and certainly with French officialdom should not be mistaken for generic intra-Syrian sectarianism.[32]

Rihani, Gibran, and their circle of formidable friends, thanks to their reputations in the Syrian press in the diaspora and Cairo, rescued the Arabic-language press in the United States from infighting, helped transform it into a model for rehabilitating archaic classical style, and in the process became known as nationalist figures throughout the Arabic-speaking world. Their literati prowess drew responses from Beirut and Cairo to Gibran's series of articles under the title "A Tear and a Smile" in *Al-Muhājir*. The exchanges of insults were not without effect; they caused serious altercations during the first decade of the twentieth century that culminated in the death of a member of the Estefan family in which the Orthodox priest Rafael Hawawini and Naʿūm Mokarzel were implicated.[33] This period marked the height of animosity between the Maronite clergy's mouthpiece *Al-Hoda* and the Orthodox *Mirāt al-Gharb* allied with Hawawini. Amin al-Gharib opposed Mokarzel before distancing himself from the affair. The immigrant press was not stuck in this rut for long and provided a sophisticated medium for news, reports, and analysis of local and important distant events such as when the CUP suspended the constitution. However, more complex political developments caused zealous individuals to continue to weed out mention of Syria and replace those with the term "Lebanese."

Khalil Gibran's book *The Prophet* is available in some forty languages and is one of the best-selling books of all time. Published in 1923, it became synonymous with Gibran's esoteric and spiritual philosophy, which attracts seemingly endless discussion, much of it extolling Gibran's pacifism. But his spiritual writing shows only one side of the Gibran who, according to his cousin and namesake, "could not conceal his nationalistic leanings, and he had committed himself to war long before 1914."[34] Tread "poetically with the Turkish government," Gibran told his confidant Mary Haskell, advocating a "general Allied attack."[35] John Daye's book *Lakom Jubrānakom wa li Jubrāni* (You have your Gibran and I have mine, 2009) provides additional ammunition for assessing a Lebanonization of Gibran.

The point regarding Gibran's nationalist sentiments was made in my dissertation by relying on one of the few studies on the Syrian press in the United States by aforementioned Henry Melki. In 1911, according to Melki's Arabic-language study, Gibran was asked to address a gathering of Boston's Al-Halaqāt al-Dhahabīyah (Golden circles). This is my translation of Gibran's Arabic comments:

> The hopes held by the delirious from the parliamentary government resemble those by the patient's kin when their patient revives before death claims him. The band called "Freemen" [the CUP], though capable of declaring a constitution and removing Abdulhamid and running after reforms, does not want to give up even a single link in the chains with which successive sultans led processions of Ottoman nations. All that the Turk's *ahrār* [Freemen, the CUP] seek is establishing a constitutional government for themselves and absolute rule over the Arabs and all who speak Arabic.

You say what, then, can the Syrian do if you rob him of his hope of a reformed future in the lands of his birth and childhood? Does he become a naturalized citizen of the country to which he immigrated? Or does he seek help from foreign countries throwing his weakness [at the mercy of] European powers—the Druze clinging to England, the Orthodox [Christians] to Russia, and the Maronite to the French—as our fathers did?

He who empties his heart from the illusions and false dreams of the Ottoman state only to fill it with the promises and ambitions of the foreign states resembles one who runs from fire to hell. The Syrian only has self-reliance and his talents, intelligence and excellence to rely on.

The money earned by a solitary peddler is money earned by all Syrians. Every word a pupil learns in the American schools is a word learned by all Syrians. . . . Free your children from the slavery of [abhorrent old] traditions and old customs, and they will remain free even in chains and jails.[36]

A copy of this address can be found in the Jafet Memorial Library at the American University of Beirut. It was republished in *Mirāt al-Gharb* on March 3, 1911, and in *Al-Barq* in Beirut some weeks later as it appears above. Melki published an altered version of the address that can be found in the Jafet Memorial Library in the January 31, 1982, issue of *Al-Anwar* magazine in Beirut.[37] Daye's study lists eleven examples of "Syria," "Syrians," or both being changed to "Lebanon" and "Lebanese" or omitted altogether in the 1982 version published in *Al-Anwar*. The result is that Gibran's commitment to the Syrian cause is turned on its head, suggesting that he was committed to Lebanon's cause of separation from Syria. The alterations, although under a different social climate in Lebanon, create the impression that being a Maronite automatically means favoring Lebanese separation from Syria. An extensive though not exhaustive survey of the Arabic-language press does not suggest intractable animosity between the Maronite Gibran and the Orthodox ʿAbdulmassīh Haddād or that writers or editors were split into two distinct camps along a sectarian divide. Gibran's work appeared in *Al-Saʾeh* magazine and in *Al-Funūn*, which was funded by an Orthodox Christian and co-edited by Naimy. When Naʿūm Mokarzel and Najīb Diāb traveled to Paris for the Arab Conference in 1913, Gibran deeply regretted not attending as well with his friend Najīb Diāb, who represented the "emigrant Lebanese."[38] Any hesitation on Gibran's part to aid countrymen ravaged by World War I due to his pacifist views vanished, and he "actively solicit[ed] funds for his beleaguered country,"[39] encouraged, perhaps, by Rihani.

Post–World War I intra-European territorial compromises forced the

Palestinians to make some references to "Southern Syria" and even to found a newspaper carrying the same name, *Sūriya al-Janūbīyah*. However, political coverage by Syrian newspapers in the diaspora made little distinction in various provinces and districts in Syria. Intellectuals like Mikhail Naimy shared Gibran's attitude, although Naimy was more interested in literature than politics. In 1915, two years before the British issued the Balfour Declaration granting "a national home" in Palestine for Jews, Naimy astutely observed that Palestine was vulnerable to mass Jewish immigration and British colonialism. Considering land acquisition by European Jews in northern Palestine while he was studying at the Muscovite seminary in Nazareth, Naimy wrote:

> In whose brain did this idea [of settling Jews in Palestine] sprout and grow before it traveled like lightning from one end of the globe to the other? I don't know or care. This war filled the land with prophets and dream readers, but the prophet of the Israelites' independence and return to their ancestors' land found millions of followers among the Hebrews who are moved by religious feelings and others who are moved by political and economic benefits.
>
> It is Christianity's misfortune that you can find thousands who deny His [Christ's] teachings . . . [who] told them that he came to pour new wine in a new goblet. Instead they see in the Torah only the dead letter and attributing every event that happened to a prophecy by Ezekiel and his fellow travelers.
>
> Russia makes promises to the Jew of helping him attain this end not because he is liked but to be rid of him. England has a political aim outlined in the press numerous times: to keep Palestine, which is close to its colonies in Asia and Africa, under its control by giving a people independence in name only.
>
> Did the strong in this world agree on how to manage the politics of this world? So have we and our press learned and heard. And thus we and our press remain silent. . . . We are deaf and mute as if this matter does not concern us, as if Palestine is part of Mongol lands or one of the Philippine islands.[40]

Despite scholars' tendency to attribute sectarian affiliations to the various newspapers, their services overlapped to benefit all Syrian readers. *Al-Bayān*, described as a Druze newspaper, was instrumental in publicizing among Syrian immigrants the need for aid relief during World War I when starvation was the primary concern in Syria; *Mirāt al-Gharb* and *Al-Hoda* did so as well. Subtle differences among the newspapers existed, though, such as the uncompromisingly nationalist stance of *Jurāb-ul-Kurdi* editor and publisher Anton Anastasias Zraick in paying no attention to European trepidations toward Arab independence and arbitrarily proclaiming alliances and economic policies. In contrast, *Mirāt al-Gharb* recognized the dangers inherent in political uncertainty and left the door open, however slightly, for using remnants of Ottomanism against the Europeans if need be. *Al-Hoda* led a repudiation of Syrian nationalism and offered instead unwavering support for France's colonialist policies of carving out the Mount Lebanon area.

A survey of newspapers and their leanings provides irrefutable evidence that sectarianism was checked by much larger concerns, such as the approaching war and the future of Syrians' relationship with their homeland. Immigrant activists understood that they were in a position to respond to events in their places of origin and that their responses would inform their standing in their adopted country. These considerations and not being at odds with U.S. interests went into the decision some made to launch formal political collectives with nationalist agendas. The impact of World War I is important to understand but not as the watershed some claim it represented in immigrants' lives. The war itself did not end immigrants' feelings of connectedness to Syria because Syria did not disappear and the national cause gained some steam after Ottomanism and Turkism were no longer factors of consequence. Rather, immigrants saw an opportunity of a peace dividend encouraged, albeit prematurely, in Woodrow Wilson's ideas of self-determination, on the victors' terms, especially since the U.S. role in the war was viewed as benign and noncolonialist.

The positions of Druze and Muslim editors did not differ from those of most non-Muslims on social and political affairs overall. Established in New York City in 1911 by Suleiman Baddūr and ʿAbbas Abu Shaqra—both Syrian Druze—the newspaper *Al-Bayān* counts among the pioneer Arabic-language newspapers. In its very first issue the editors declared that they aimed to "serve the national cause and literature to the best of our ability." By the end of World War I, *Al-Bayān* editors did not consider its nationalist orientation an impediment to professing allegiance to the United States: "No protection is left for us save that which the United States can offer."[41] The nationalist fervor of *Al-Bayān* became apparent during the Syrian Druze revolt against the French in 1925, and it found ample support from all other newspapers save *Al-Hoda*. Another New York newspaper that combined literary works with political analysis was *Al-Saʾeh* (The traveler), first published in 1912 by ʿAbdulmassīh Haddād, a member of the famed Pen Bond, al-Rābitah al-Qalamīyah. During a year at the Russian Orthodox seminary in Nazareth he met two other would-be members of the Pen Bond, Mikhail Naimy and Nasib Arida. ʿAbdulmassīh Haddād's prosperous brother then lured him to the United States in 1907.

Despite resolving to avoid episodes of exchanging insults, the editors and contributors at *Al-Saʾeh* soon found the periodical pulled into unseemly polemical exchanges with *Al-Hoda* simply because they, like most of their counterparts, opposed Mokarzel and favored Syrian independence. Being an Orthodox Christian was sufficient to be on the opposite side of the fence from the mouthpiece of the Maronite clergy, *Al-Hoda*. Covering the First Arab Conference, in Paris in 1913, *Al-Saʾeh* editorials urged Syrians to seek independence under such headlines as these: "The Syrians' National Zeal," "Syria Demands Her Rights," "What Would Syria Need in Order to Achieve Independence?" "Syria and Reforms," "Syria for the Syrians," and "When Will the Muslim and the Christian Become Brothers?" Ameen Rihani, a Maronite, came under attack by *Al-Hoda* during a spike in mass efforts to collect aid for Syrians at the close of the Great War, and the Greek Orthodox ʿAbdulmassīh Haddād of *Al-Saʾeh* defended him.

In addition to newspapers, early immigrants also published magazines, most of which were political in nature. Nasib Arida, whom ʿAbdulmassīh Haddād and Naimy met at the Russian Orthodox seminary in Nazareth, intermittently issued *Al-Funūn* (The arts) in New York between 1913 and 1918. Arida had come to the United States in 1905 and worked in retail while writing for *Al-Hoda* and *Mirāt al-Gharb*. In his writings Arida often expressed his pain over the generally decaying climate in Syria and repression under Turkish rule. In this poem he expresses his frustration over his countrymen's lack of action:

> No, by my God a heartless people receive only death as a gift.
> Let history turn a page of failure and settle its accounts.
> Perhaps rage, perhaps shame, perhaps fire may move the heart of a coward.
> All these are in us, but all they move is the tongue.[42]

Al-Funūn is still considered one of the most influential magazines in Arab literary history despite its constant financial troubles during its short life. The magazine's nationalism accounted for much of its influence. In June 1918 its inside front cover featured an image of a "New Arab Flag" above a line of poetry by fourteenth-century Iraqi poet Safi al-Dīn al-Hilli that immortalized its colors, along with a list of the names of luminaries hanged by the CUP. *Al-Funūn* published writings by most of the period's literary giants before they were identified as members of the Pen Bond in 1920.

The first English-only magazine published by a Syrian immigrant was *The Syrian World*. Founded in New York City by Salloum Mokarzel, Naʿūm's brother, the publication lasted from 1926 to the mid-1930s. Salloum took over publication of *Al-Hoda* when Naʿūm died in 1932. Unlike his brother Naʿūm, Salloum was considered a gentle person. He intended the magazine to help New York's Syrian parents in rearing their U.S.-born children, instilling in them "self-respect, and educating them on [their] honorable lineage and the glories of their nation."[43] Young people's alienation from their parents drew the attention of Khalil Gibran, who wrote this much-quoted message to Syrian American youths on the pages of *The Syrian World*:

> I believe in you.
> I believe in your destiny.
> I believe that you are contributors to this new civilization....
> I believe that you can say to Emerson and Whitman and James,
> "In my veins runs the blood of the poets and wise men of old,
> and it is my desire to come to you and receive, but I shall not come
> with empty hands."[44]

The importance of *The Syrian World* is twofold. First, it is a ready resource for non-Arabic-speaking researchers. Second, it featured writings by the nationalist Ḥabīb Ibrahīm Kātibah, who was born in Yabrud in Syria in 1892, the same year *Kawkab Amreeka* was first published. Kātibah graduated from the American University in Beirut in 1912 and from the Harvard School of Theology in 1918. He championed the Palestinian cause at the early signs of Zionist settlement in 1916 and had a great deal to offer *The Syrian World* because he worked as a correspondent for the *Brooklyn Daily Eagle*, the *Detroit News*, and *Al-Ahram* in Cairo. Kātibah assumed the directorship of the Arab National League in 1936 and worked as the secretary of the Institute of Arab American Affairs from 1945 until his death in 1951; during those years Kātibah's political arguments against Zionism appeared frequently in the *New York Times*, *Chicago Tribune*, and *Los Angeles Times*. It is not clear if his regular contributions to *The Syrian World*, along with those by Philip Hitti, signaled a new pathway in the political lives of Syrian immigrants; this topic demands separate investigation. During the life of *The Syrian World*, compatriots Fuad Shatara and Khalil Totah would join Kātibah on the pages of the magazine. Together they would continue building their constituency among Syrian Americans through the pages of the Syrian press before directing their focus toward the American populace, thus marking a shift in immigrant political activism.

Syrian intellectuals living in Egypt left an important imprint on the Syrian press both in Egypt and the United States. Syrian immigrant nationalist writer Farah Anton was among the first to embody Western modernism and apply it uncompromisingly in his calls for a strictly secular and free Syria and to develop a discourse on the compatibility of Arab culture and secularism. Anton's philosophical beliefs underpinned the modernist national aspirations of many of the early immigrants in this study, especially Ameen Farah, a prominent figure in the organized political activities in southeastern Michigan between 1915 and 1939. One of the many who escaped the reach of Sultan Abdulhamid in Syria to British-occupied Egypt in 1897, Farah Anton advanced his criticism of religious intolerance by both Christians and Muslims from Cairo. He chose the name *Al-Jami'ah al-'Uthmānīyah* (Ottoman college) for his magazine, in which he launched one of the most enduring transnational arguments for unifying and elevating "the Orient" through translating and explicating Ernest Renan's *Life of Jesus*, a book that accompanied many Syrians to the Americas and elsewhere. Anton brought his readers the modernist socialism of Friedrich Nietzsche and Leo Tolstoy as well. Anton was seduced by Enlightenment-laden definitions of the nation and by a humanist interpretation of religion. As a Syrian nationalist in Egypt he was at odds with Egyptians who wanted to preserve a semblance of Ottomanism as a response to British oppression and military occupation. The source of his intellectual disagreement with Egyptian nationalists was his view of the British as the lesser of two evils when compared to the Ottomans. In 1906 he left Cairo for New York, taking with him the skills at political maneuvering he had acquired in the Western-dominated Middle East.

Anton Anastasias Zraick, an Orthodox Christian from Tripoli, published and edited the newspaper *Jurāb-ul-Kurdi* beginning on May 2, 1902. The innocuous description below the title of *Jurāb-ul-Kurdi* categorizes it as a "political, literary, entertaining, critical, independent daily newspaper" with the address of 74 Greenwich, New York City. On its pages, Zraick was one of the most ardent critics of the Ottomans, and his attacks only intensified after the CUP took charge in 1908 and banned his paper from Arab population centers in Syria. Zraick rejected finessing a political path that left the door open for anything but complete independence and an end to Ottoman Turkish rule in any form over Arabs. He did so amid cross-currents of unionism (*ittiḥādīyah*) with the Turks as advocated by the CUP and coalitionism (*i'tilāfīyah*), the main idea behind decentralization, and certainly he rejected Ottomanism in any context. While on a visit to his hometown in 1914 he paid with his life for his nationalist philosophy, which actually encapsulated what Diāb, Baddūr, and other advocates of Syrian independence ultimately wanted. Zraick, his brother, and numerous anti-Turkish Syrians were arrested, tortured, and executed by Turks.[45]

Examining small newspapers and magazines of the time makes it possible to identify many other nationalists, several of whom became closely connected to the political organizations that developed within Syrian immigrant communities in the United States. Among them were editors and publishers Nasif Damous of *Al-Islah* (The reform), New York, 1898; Jouseph (Yusef) Nuʿman Malouf of *Al-Ayyām* (The days), New York, 1897; Salim Sarkis of *Al-Rāwi* (The narrator), New York, 1902, and *Al-Bustān* (The garden), Boston, 1903; Maroun Khalil al-Khouri and Philip Faris of *Al-Jihād* (The struggle), New York, 1904; Shukri Bakhkhash of *Al-Fatāt* (The youth), New York, 1917; Naseem Khouri of *Sūriya al-Jadīdah* (New Syria), Boston, 1910; and Naseeb Amer Wahbeh of *Al-Hurīyah* (Liberty), 1921, and the magazines *Sāhat Ali* (Ali's arena), 1913, and *Al-Hurīyah*, 1920, respectively, all in Detroit.

Neither the chaos of 1909 when the Turkish CUP deposed Sultan Abdulhamid and suspended the constitution nor infighting among editors detracted from the gravity of the Balkan wars. Immigrants began to echo the same fears in their newspapers as expressed by Farah and his friends in their correspondences to and from Cairo, France, and Nazareth that Europeans were poised to pounce on the "sick" Ottoman state. The urgency of events propelled inquiry by activist editors and other U.S. Syrians into democratic precepts and self-rule in an Arab state in Syria. Anti-Ottoman, anti-Turkish secret societies devised a measured strategy of reforming the Ottoman state as a prelude to independence. Their strategy centered on delicately discouraging European domination by using Ottomanism as an umbrella under which plans for complete independence were drawn. Events and newspaper coverage of 1911–1913, examined briefly in the remainder of this chapter, help explain the assertive Arab nationalism of the Free Syria Society and the New Syria Party despite only limited successes.

Events in Europe unfolded in a manner that signaled ominous escalation that seemed increasingly likely to engulf the Ottoman Empire. Like Arabs, the Albanians, Bulgarians, and Greeks sought to wrest free from Turkish control, encouraged by the Young Turk revolution and the restoration of the Ottoman Constitution of 1908. While the dominant European powers maneuvered to extend their control across the Arab Middle East, Italy occupied Libya in 1911, alarming Syrians about territorial dismemberment of Geographic Syria under a similar occupation. When the Balkan nations banded together in an attempt to purge the Turks, France and Austria-Hungary became wary of Russian influence as the guardians of the Orthodox in the Balkans and tried to avert war with Russia. In the Second Balkan War, in 1913, Romania joined the Turks and both lost to Serbia, which became a regional power. The turn of events reaffirmed Austrian fears of Russian expansion, this time through alliance with Serbia. The die was cast, and astute Syrians anticipated the entry of France and Britain into the melee to defend routes to their rich colonies in the Far East. Many Syrians were inspired to heed the Balkans' example of banding together against the Ottomans.

In the December 1912 issue of *Al-'Ālam al-Jadid al-Nisā'i* (The new world for women), an early magazine especially for Syrian women, editor Afifa Karam likened the heroism of Giuseppe Garibaldi, the Italian "hero of freedom," to the anti-Turkish heroism of the people of the Balkans.[46] Karam's account was sandwiched between articles extolling the virtues of U.S. First Lady Ellen Wilson and of the renowned Native American Pocahontas. While tension and military losses piled up, the Turks used all their resourcefulness to muster a fighting force and quell dissent. They employed conscription and spying and invoked their historical status as guardians of Islam's sacred places in Mecca and Medina and the seat of Shaikh al-Islam, the highest authority on Islamic jurisprudence. The Turkish officers' revolt and constitutional reforms over the course of 1908 and 1909 expanded conscription to non-Muslims, who experienced harsh conditions, especially when the Balkan wars escalated. Official Ottoman newspapers spread propaganda, called for *jihād* (struggle), and published one-sided and often inflammatory news of atrocities against hapless Muslims by their Russian-backed Orthodox Serb enemies. The tactics did little to sway the Syrian populations either in Syria or in the United States regardless of religion. They did, however, fuel the anti-Muslim rhetoric in *Al-Hoda*.

A call to arms in the Balkans was issued in the name of Sultan Mehmet V, a Shaikh al-Islam puppet who replaced Abdulhamid. *Jurāb-ul-Kurdi* editor Anastasias Zraick mocked the call to join the "bloodbath" as a ploy by the CUP; a translation of his article title is "The Muslim Caliph Calls for War. Then on to War." Zraick wrote, "If all quarters obeyed [Ottoman authority in the name of Islam], Syria will not obey, nor will all the Arab provinces [that] will not stoop to the level of wild animals. If they [Arabs and Syrians] fight, they will fight in the cause of humanity . . . yes, they will unite with Christians to break the chains of slavery and Turkish oppressive control."[47]

In the same article Zraick criticized attempts at inciting sectarian division among Ottoman subjects as a means of mobilizing the masses against the predominantly Christian Balkans, labeling the provocation as a campaign to avenge Ottoman losses to the "Christian nations" there. The latter, wrote Zraick, "lost their property in battle and regained them with the edge of the sword." The implications of Zraick's response are far-reaching. The rebuke of Turkish posturing in the name of Islam would not have been possible had the traditional loyalty to the Muslim Ottoman Turks among the masses not eroded to reveal an ecumenical Arab ethos. Its appearance here is further indication that immigrant readers in the United States agreed that Arabism, Islam, and Christianity were not mutually exclusive. Zraick's rhetoric supports the Arab nationalist analysis by historians George Antonius and Zeine Zeine that after a period of religious strife due to the erosion of civil laws and effects of the *millet* system, Turkism quickly began to lose hold on the Arab provinces. From the safety of Greenwich, New York, Arab Christian Zraick addressed his remarks to Muslim readers, telling them Turks "slaughter the children, violate the girls, burn the elderly and handicapped by setting their houses on fire. They pillage the churches and destroy them."[48]

On the pages of *Jurāb-ul-Kurdi* Zraick reported accurate translations of the latest agreements signed by the CUP, among them the concession of Salonica to Greece and similar concessions to the Serbs and Bulgarians.[49] Under the calculatedly facetious subtitle "Rejoice! Reforms after These Preludes: Religious Decrees Chain Down Reforms," Zraick mocked any chance of a coalition with the Turks:

> We argued that reform [under Turkish rule] is a mirage, a dream. And we argued that its benefits will not extend beyond the circle of the Turkish race.... Months have passed and now the dreams came crashing down. Did we not say that the victory of the Unionists [the CUP] will finish these hopes? Overnight, telegrams came from the capital warning governors, notables, and newspapers not to say anything that would "scratch the ear." Now the press is caught between two fires, the fury of public opinion if it obeys the orders of silence and the sword of vengeance if it practices its freedom.[50]

Zraick went on to list newspapers closed by the CUP, among them *Al-Mufid* for reporting that dysentery spread in frontier towns and *Al-Thabat* for publishing posthumously an address by anti-CUP officer Nathem Pasha that had previously appeared in another publication, *Lisān al-Hāl*.[51] He published the article in November 1912, and the situation in Syria became even more dangerous when war broke out. Zraick was killed when he visited family in Syria in 1914. His and others' deaths and the need for secrecy, like Farah's carefully removing names from letters, suggest that the CUP monitored Syrians and their press in the United States through spies in New York.

In this volatile political situation, with the Ottoman Turks suffering massive territorial losses and Europe awaiting an opportunity to expand into Turkish territory, Syrian nationalists in the relative safety of Cairo stepped in. In May 1913 *Jurāb-ul-Kurdi* published a series of articles by the head of the Ottoman Administrative Decentralization Party, Rafīq al-ʿAẓm, a Syrian nationalist leader living in Cairo. In the series ʿAẓm explained constitutional government and decentralization. He likened the state to a "compassionate father" and the subject to a "good son: the former is nurturing and the later obedient."[52] ʿAẓm methodically laid out the events behind the Syrian quest for autonomy but appealed to the masses in Syria by presenting an alternative and virtuous rendition of Ottomanism. This strategy, largely misunderstood as Ottomanist loyalty if noted at all, followed the fine line of seeking autonomy within a reformed umbrella state without raising the ire of Europeans.

The cornerstone of this disposition by ʿAẓm and his compatriots across continents was the keen awareness that the Ottoman Empire historically served as a buffer to keep Europe's powers and Russia off each other's throats. ʿAẓm defended decentralization against critics who were bought with titles by the CUP or who succumbed to jealousy. He criticized the CUP's New Provinces Law, which employed "racial origin as a weapon [with which] to kill any semblance of national life."[53] Syrians' astute reading of geopolitical affairs motivated the nationalists to find a delicate balance because of the powder keg Europe had become. But that was not the only ominous sign of conflict. On May 1, 1913, an editorial in *Jurāb-ul-Kurdi* titled "Will the War Take Place?" illustrated Syrians' anxieties over U.S.-Japanese relations surrounding the California Alien Land Law enacted that year that prohibited land ownership by Asians. The interest in Japan was due to the victory scored by the small Japanese state against the Russian giant in 1905, although the article exhibited no sympathy for Japan over the United States. The implication was that if Japan could defeat the Russians, then Syrians, Serbians, and others could repel the Ottomans or, for that matter, the approaching European threat.

In the third part of ʿAẓm's explication of the Syrian nationalist strategy he implied that Ottomanism, a nonbinding federation with the Ottoman state, could be replaced with open confrontation if the CUP—and those who either held hopes of combining forces with the CUP or were bribed by its agents—did not make good on promises of constitutionalism. Noteworthy is that ʿAẓm may have intended his political commentary in the U.S. Syrian press to convey uniform respect for American democratic ideals among the immigrants. He also surely knew that writings in the New York press could bypass Turkish censors so news could reach the Syrian provinces,[54] in part because foreign mail services from the United States were not subject to censorship by the Turks. Similarly, articles in Cairo newspapers *Al-Muqattam* and *Al-Manār* may have been intended for the Syrian diaspora because they were reprinted by the largest immigrant newspapers, *Al-Hoda* and *Mirāt al-Gharb*. ʿAẓm regularly rebuffed his critics, usually cronies of the CUP, who warned against criticizing the Ottoman state during such turbulent times. Still, the gravity of a possible collapse of the Ottoman Empire was an overwhelming concern given the weak position of the Arab provinces. ʿAẓm wrote: "We made clear to all that time is of the essence. Our country was the first to be proposed aloud for partition," a reference to statements by European pundits.[55] The third part of ʿAẓm's analysis in the Syrian press offers a carefully crafted argument of Arab worthiness of sovereignty as a replacement to Ottomanism without overplaying his hand and alienating those with residual loyalty to the seat of the caliph in Istanbul or powerful Europeans, hence the Ottomanist disposition.[56]

Al-Hoda and *Mirāt al-Gharb*, too, covered events of the Balkan wars; expectations of war with Japan, which Japan would surely lose, according to both papers; U.S. policy in the Philippines; and the Ottoman Reparations Treaty, one of the many economic concessions dictated by European powers to the Ottomans. The newspapers' opposition to the Ottoman Turks had a subtle difference from each other: *Mirāt al-Gharb* took a clear stance behind ʿAẓm's strategy and that of the Ottoman Administrative Decentralization Party of achieving independence in stages, while *Al-Hoda* was satisfied with diatribes against the Turks without a clear political agenda beyond Lebanese independence under French guidance. *Mirāt al-Gharb* dedicated more columns to a variety of news than did *Jurāb-ul-Kurdi* with its detailed political analysis.

Before the war *Mirāt al-Gharb* covered news of Iraq, Palestine, and seemingly mundane events from Arab parts of the empire. The newspaper's articles reported that Cairo newspapers circulated in Syria under the noses of the Turks. Under the headline "Palestine: A Description of Current Affairs. Jaffa. Bethlehem. Jerusalem," a correspondent reported that people circumvented the Turkish CUP's ban of *Al-Muqattam* by asking the French postal service, which was not subject to Ottoman scrutiny, to obtain it. Other news items in the same article were the founding of a sports club in Jaffa as a way to skirt a ban on assembly and "jubilation" and support for the Syrian nationalist Shukri al-ʿAsali for refusing the CUP's offer of governorship of the Latakia province in Syria. Such offers of positions were a common tactic the Turks used to silence criticism. Readers could learn about condemnation of the Turks by the people of Jaffa for assaulting an Armenian soldier who was beaten and taken to Jerusalem for trial.[57]

Mirāt al-Gharb kept close watch on papers serving as mouthpieces for the CUP. It published a letter by Rafīq al-ʿAẓm, a Muslim, in which he challenged *Al-Haqq Yaʿlu*, one of the CUP's official Arabic-language newspapers, for calling on the population to slaughter Christians to avenge atrocities attributed to Christians in the Balkans. ʿAẓm noted that official newspapers received protection from Istanbul, while most independent dailies were censored and their owners jailed and even executed.[58] Several newspapers, including *Al-Hoda*, covered the political assassination of Shawkat Pasha, the Arab Ottoman army officer who was instrumental in ousting Abdulhamid on behalf of the CUP, for which he was criticized by Zraick. Only this time, the press reclaimed Shawkat as a brave Arab Iraqi soldier despite his service in the Ottoman army.[59]

The political urgency expressed in most papers was not always shared in *Al-Hoda*, whose owner felt assured of French support for Lebanon's separation and therefore reacted to a different political reality. Nevertheless, *Al-Hoda* was not completely indifferent to the fluid political situation after the wars in the Balkans or to readers' apparent interest in what Cairo Syrians had to say about the future. *Al-Hoda* called for *islāh*, reforms, in Beirut and incessantly reported on the affairs of the Lebanese Renaissance Society. But news of the United Syrian Society, which seemed to enjoy the widest appeal to a diverse segment of the U.S. Syrian population at the time, was far more frequent in *Mirāt al-Gharb* because of the ecumenical society's nationalist leanings. *Mirāt al-Gharb* also sought to emphasize Muslim-Christian reconciliation, reminding its readership that reforms hinged on unity.

As a call to unity, *Mirāt al-Gharb* noted "two important leaps forward" taken by Syrians: "One is closing the ranks among Muslims and Christians after the Muslims realized that the Christians reject foreign [European] rule. The second is that all lost confidence in the rule of the Turks."[60] The article's plea summarized the grievances of the nationalist political leadership in Cairo, which sought to preserve the Ottoman state in name while using the Arabic language in public life and closely watched the ever-looming European encroachment. But the article also appealed to Ottoman Turks to draw lessons from their mistakes before all was lost to European colonialism: "Can you not see the wolf waiting to pounce on this sheep [Syria] in the same manner he kidnapped your previous [Balkan] flock?"[61]

'Aẓm's reformist agenda and masked calls for independence from the Turks by calling for autonomy drew attention to the dire consequences of the Ottoman Reparations Treaty. In the treaty, Germany secured railroad concessions in Anatolia in exchange for surrendering similar contracts in Kuwait to the British, the French touted their interest in Syria, and Russia threatened the Ottoman state over the Armenian problem. All, 'Aẓm explained, are "ominous omens" of expanding conflicts that "foretell of impending calamity" for the weak Syrians.[62]

Given immigrants' anxieties about the future, nationalists among them felt a need to act. Their strategy of extracting independence from the Ottomans in stages was complemented by nuanced efforts to relate their desire for independence to Europe. After all, many Arab nationalists were educated in the West, and articles by leading intellectuals and editors like Muhammad Kurd Ali, editor of *Al-Ra'id* and *Al-Muqtabas*, were laden with news of science and technological inventions. But the Arab nationalists across the Americas, Europe, Egypt, Syria, and elsewhere understood that their keen desires for progress alone would not lessen European appetite for expansion, given Europe's colonialist track record of gaining coerced capitulatory agreements like ownership of the Suez Canal in Egypt by British and French investors. The added worry of rising tensions in the Balkans among Europe's big players convinced Arab nationalists that it was time to pitch their case for independence forcefully. This is the background for their plans for making their aspirations clear in what became known as the First Arab Conference in Paris, in 1913.

The invitation to American Syrians to attend the planned conference in Paris was extended by Najīb Diāb, editor of *Mirāt al-Gharb*. He worked closely with 'Aẓm, who in turn coordinated with Syrian nationalists in France. Diāb's relationship with 'Aẓm was a natural outgrowth of several factors, not the least of which was the high value 'Aẓm and the Decentralization Party placed on the "science of organized efforts."[63] Another factor was the rigorous practice of reprinting 'Aẓm's literary and political commentary in the Cairo, Beirut, and U.S. Syrian press. He announced the conference in *Mirāt al-Gharb* on May 5, 1913, appealing to the widest audience possible under the title "Da'wa ila abna' al-ummah al-arabiya" (An invitation to the children of the Arab nation). Diāb's invitation on the pages of his newspaper explained the reasons for the conference. Among the reasons he listed "three problems in Turkey": "The Ottomans' debt to Europe, which can be solved only by an infusion of money in exchange for contracts to build railroads and irrigation projects; the 'Arabic problem,' and the 'Armenian problem.'" The convergence on Paris of Syrian nationalists from several continents for the conference would mark a defining moment for Syrian nationalism and for immigrants' potential as lobbyists. The call itself is indicative of immigrants' grasp of impending changes and awareness of their value in an attempt to influence the course of events. Conference attendees may have perceived themselves as emissaries of progress on a mission to bring the promise of sovereignty and long-sought reforms to Syria.

SOLDIERS FOR SYRIA
BEFORE WORLD WAR I: *Chapter 3*
THE FREE SYRIA SOCIETY

Najīb Diāb, publisher and editor of *Mirāt al-Gharb* newspaper in New York City, reported in May 1913 about a formal request by student activists in France to hold a conference for Arab nationalists. The request was sent to the Higher Committee of the Ottoman Administrative Decentralization Party at its headquarters in Cairo. Diāb told his Syrian readers in the Americas that the students were alarmed by the "insinuations in the European press and winks in clubs by gentlemen [the polity]" concerning the fate of Syria. The insinuations were seen by the students as hints at adding Syria to European colonies extending from Egypt to the Far East. European ambitions were due "to the mismanagement of the Turks."[1] Diāb expressly sought the participation of the diaspora communities in America and Europe and set these agenda points: "nationalist life and resisting occupation," the rights of Arabs in the "Ottoman Kingdom," the necessity of reforms based on decentralization, and immigration to and emigration from Syria.[2]

Academic studies on the Paris conference have revealed that the signatories of the invitation were all members of either the Decentralization Party in Cairo or al-ʿArabi al-Fatāt (Arab Youth, often called al-Fatāt) in Paris. Two of them, ʿAbdulghani al-ʿUraisi and Shukri al-ʿAsali, served as Arab representatives in the Ottoman Parliament.[3] Al-Fatāt's involvement indicates that, in addition to the Decentralization Party's known preference for superior organization, the call for the conference was ultimately a move toward independence from Ottoman rule.

Because al-Fatāt remained a secret organization to the end, it is difficult to confirm that Jubrān Kuzma, Ameen Farah's childhood friend from Nazareth, and others were actually members who may have borrowed the idea of the secret Free Syria Society from al-Fatāt. Members of al-Fatāt often chose death at the hands of the CUP before revealing the names of their comrades, and its very existence was not confirmed until after the collapse of Ottoman rule.[4] However, by Antonius's description, stipulations in al-Fatāt's bylaws seem to match those implemented by the Free Syria Society in Flint. Savvy strategies began to take shape on the eve of World War I utilizing the Decentralized Party's highly developed organizational skills, the considerable experience of ʿAẓm, Zahrāwi, and ʿUraisi in international affairs and Ottoman administration, and the vigor of al-Fatāt's youthful nationalists.

The nationalists gathered in Paris from June 18 to June 23, 1913, for the First Arab Conference. The endorsement of Najīb Diāb by the United Syrian Society is a sign that many Syrian immigrants chose him as their representative to the conference in Paris. Naʿūm Mokarzel attended and represented Lebanese separatism against demands for Syrian national and territorial integrity by nationalists from Lebanon, Palestine, Egypt, Istanbul, Iraq, Damascus, Mexico, and the United States.[5] The convergence prompted the Syrian Druze nationalist Shakib Arslan to dub the event "the Syrian Conference." Participants appear to have understood that they needed to define themselves on their terms at a critical moment in the region's and their own history and to demonstrate a level of sophistication that would pave the way for statehood and future dealings with Turks and Europeans alike. A comprehensive definition of Arab nationalism by ʿAbdulghani al-ʿUraisi opened the conference:

> Groups, in the opinion of political scientists, do not meet this right [nationalism], unless they, according to the German scientists, share one language and ethnicity [ʿunsur]; and according to the Italians, unless they share one history and one set of customs; and according to the French, a unified political goal. Hence, as we observe the Arabs from all political angles, we will know that Arabs share a unified language and a unified ethnicity and a unified history and unified traditions and unified political ambitions. . . . Based on this, I say the first right of groups of nations is the right of (national) citizenship [jinsīyah], whereby we are Arabs above political colors, and we preserved our shared attributes and distinctiveness for numerous centuries despite all we suffered at the hands of the Istanbul administration, such as political absorption or colonial subservience or racial intermingling.[6]

The eclectic attributes proposed by ʿUraisi as the basis for national Arab identity were meant to reestablish Arabism on a modern footing. In making the case for Arab national coherence, ʿUraisi proposed an Arab distinctness unconfined by racial, ethnic, historical, and cultural attributes alone but a combination of all these. Most of all, as a leader among Syrian nationalists, he understood the value of having a platform from which to irrevocably declare that the time had passed when Arabs were subjugated under the Turkish yoke. ʿUraisi and other nationalists with property and families in Syria understood the risk of grave harm to themselves and family members at the hands of Turkish nationalists for their position. Their fears were justified, as the CUP killed many of the Syrian participants, including ʿUraisi and ʿAbdulhamīd al-Zahrāwi.

The Decentralization Party issued the only known comprehensive account of the conference, to counter misinformation campaigns by the CUP to discredit the gathering. The result of the Decentralization Party's report was a meticulous outline of each session and transcripts of all of the speeches as well as an interview for a French newspaper with al-Zahrāwi, the head of the conference. The report also contained a list of telegrams and letters of support from five continents. These records are especially helpful in illustrating the prominent role of U.S. Syrians, particularly United Syrian Society emissary Najīb Diāb, on behalf of the Syrian diaspora.

In his interview with the French press, ʿAbdulhamīd al-Zahrāwi did not overplay his hand, in keeping with ʿAẓm's stated goals on behalf of the Decentralization Party in Egypt. He maintained that Arabic-speaking people are part of the Ottoman family and are entitled to their rights of "preserving the national life generally [and] . . . implementing reforms, in particular on the basis of decentralization." Mindful of wealthy Syrians in the diaspora and the possibility of their repatriation, he demanded that the Turkish government independently "examine carefully the issue of immigration and migration."[7] In emphasizing the participation of the Syrian diaspora from Europe and the Americas, he attempted to signal to the reporter and French readers that the coveted reforms did not diverge from Western sensibilities and lifestyles. After all, these Syrian nationalists had hung their hats in the West.

Zahrāwi, no doubt, was aware of the antagonism between the CUP and the French and British due to increasing German investments in and weapons exports to the Ottoman Empire. Nevertheless, Zahrāwi hinted in the interview that all options remained open to the Arabs if they were prevented from achieving their coveted autonomy. Although the Decentralization Party advocated autonomy under an Ottoman umbrella, Zahrāwi subtly reminded the reporter that defending a country within a defined boundary, that is, sovereignty, had been an accepted Western concept since the French Revolution. Zahrāwi likely was encouraged in making his remarks by agreement among the nationalists in al-Fatāt and the Decentralization Party on averting the replacement of Ottoman control with European colonialism and on addressing the young nationalists' strong preference for declaring their desire for independence outright.

The reporter raised the specter of pan-Islamism under the pretext of the Ottoman state by asking, "Do you back Ottoman unity for the sake of religious bond?" Zahrāwi reminded the reporter of intra-Muslim wars between the Ottomans and the Persians and emphasized the need for unhampered reforms in the Arab provinces. An Ottoman collective, he indicated, would not stand in the way of reforms and progress. But Zahrāwi's defiance was unmistakable when he hinted that warfare was an option should the Ottomans resist Arab autonomy: "I repeat my statements in Cairo; our plans will change dramatically."[8]

In his address at the conference, "The Wishes of the Syrian Immigrants," the publisher and editor Najīb Diāb, who traveled to Paris to represent U.S. Syrian immigrants, stated that compatriots in Syria were asking for their rights, not seeking mercy. The immigrants were forced to leave their homes, he explained, because of "repression, high poll taxes, and backward governors . . . [and] dispersed seeking freedom in the land of freedom." He proposed that "you in Shām [meaning Syria] and we in the country of Uncle Sam [bilād al-'amm Sām]" engage in transnational unity: "We raise our voices with you in asking for our rights, but not for mercy, and demand reforms under the crescent [symbol on the Ottoman flag]."[9] Having delivered a political message of preserving continuity under an Ottoman shell to keep Europe at bay, Diāb exposed the nationalists' aims behind addressing immigration and migration to and from Syria. He declared that immigrants' familiarity with the West would be useful in efforts to Westernize the homeland; reforms would convince many in the diaspora to return and bring back "the knowledge of Europe and America, their literature, politics, arts, and social sciences, therefore restoring to the Orient its past glory. These are the wishes of the immigrants [al-muhājirūn]."[10]

Elaborating on his rebuke of the hardened nationalism of the Ottoman Turks, Diāb reminded the participants, and no doubt the Ottoman police and European observers, that during the previous twenty-five years in the diaspora, Syrians had tried to reason with the government of Abdulhamid but were "rebuffed and suffered spies who tried to silence our presses in the land of freedom and often sowed divisions among us and splintered us into warring sectarian camps and made reports and sent many, one after the other, to Yeldiz Qushwa [an Ottoman prison], while the capital issued ugly charges against us and sentences of expulsion and death [until] . . . we were forced to part our ties with the homeland."[11]

In the Paris conference, where Arab-nationalist demands were declared in the presence of a thoroughly mixed convergence of Muslims and Christians, Diāb delivered the United Syrian Society's message of preserving Syria's unity. His remarks unmistakably rebuked Lebanese parochialism but were not hostile to the Maronite Syrians from Beirut and the Mount Lebanon area: "We still long for Syria and never forgot her promise, for she is our loving mother and Lebanon is her heart. How can you separate the heart from the mother?"[12]

Naʿūm Mokarzel's speech, in contrast, was a short and boisterous ridicule of the Turks in a tone characteristic of his rhetoric against his enemies in *Al-Hoda*. He told a parable likening the Ottoman Empire to "an old hag" and warned against replacing it with "multiple hags," a reference to Turkish officers of the CUP. He boasted that the Lebanese made up the majority of immigrants in the United States, giving the false impression that he represented either all who came from the Lebanon region or the majority of the immigrants. His intention apparently was to reinforce an attitude that to be Lebanese is different from being Syrian. Mokarzel remained silent on any framework or vision for the future of Lebanon, much less Syria. For him, French sponsorship of Lebanese separatism, part of Ottoman capitulation to France's demands, was all that mattered.

The dense publication on the conference proceedings offers many lessons about Syrian immigrant networks of political activists across the globe. The Syrian transnational coalition combined the demands of Syrians in New York, Cairo, Damascus, Beirut, Europe, and elsewhere by issuing resolutions on questions raised by the participants. Diāb and others called for speed in implementing reforms such as giving Arabs a political role in the Istanbul central government and establishing decentralized administrative branches in Arab population centers.

Maronites from Beirut demanded including foreign advisers, meaning French officials, in a future government to widen the authority of local administration. A heated debate erupted, ending with approval of an expanded role for the local administration in Beirut and dismissal of the proposed representation for French agents. Resolutions called for Arabic to be included as an official language in the parliament. Jubrān Kuzma demanded that Arabic be used in school curricula at all levels. A resolution passed that military service be confined to soldiers' areas of residence to keep Syrians out of Ottoman battles with Europe, a lesson learned from the wars in the Balkans. But the conferees kept the door open for Syrians' military service in extreme emergencies, perhaps a sign that if it came down to it, a fight against European colonialism was not altogether out of the question. A paramount demand was made for financial accountability by the Turkish authorities to preclude further encroachment by European creditors.[13] The inception and proceedings of the conference place immigrants at the heart of Arab nationalist demands. Their positioning took place at a pivotal time before World War I effected fundamental changes in the political history of the Middle East and the lives of Syrian Americans.

The participants adopted a call by Diāb to hold a follow-up conference in New York,[14] and an invitation was promptly telegraphed to *Mirāt al-Gharb* but with no dates indicated. The invitation was printed in *Mirāt al-Gharb*,[15] as were regular telegrams of progress sent by Diāb, along with letters of support for the conference from diverse parts of the United States and Mexico.[16] *Mirāt al-Gharb* reported on a June 18 article in the Cincinnati *Commercial Tribune* about the Paris conference and local Syrian immigrants' interest in being represented there by Najīb Diāb.[17] The *Commercial Tribune* quoted a Cincinnati businessman as saying Syrians expected certain issues to be discussed: "Syria is a province in the Ottoman Sultanate with a population that exceeds that of Anatolia itself, yet it has no voice in the government. A Syrian cannot utter his thoughts publicly. This is the reason behind the [Paris] Conference."[18]

The Paris conference pulled together the hopes and fears of Syrian nationalists across the globe despite their divisions over strategy such as the extent to which opposition to Ottomanism was to be made clear. If Arab grievances against the Ottomans added nationalism to the "cauldron of effective political ideologies in the Arab provinces,"[19] the Paris conference was the place where this nationalism found coherence and expression within a Syrian framework. Although it would take the mandate years before nationalism reached all of Syria, the importance and strength of U.S. Syrians became evident. Not only were they shielded by distance from harm at the hands of Turkish nationalists, they also resided in an emerging power that had no claims on Ottoman territories. That was a good thing given the aggressively colonialist track record of the French, Germans, and British. The mostly Muslim officers of the Decentralization Party skillfully invoked Syrian Americans as evidence of the secular nature of the desired reforms, thereby reassuring France of their plans. Their strategy was balanced with warnings during the conference and in the press in the United States and Cairo that if reform did not come to fruition, a fight would ensue. ʿAẓm and Zahrāwi insinuated that the fight would not be against Ottomanism but rather against the CUP's ultranationalist ideology and against Europe if need be. In this way they made clear to France that Syrians were serious about an autonomy free of European meddling. In just twelve years, history proved that Syrians nationalists' intuition was on the mark; war would sweep across the globe, the French would ignore their message and occupy Syria, and Syrians would make good on their promises to fight back. The diaspora in the United States would then band together behind the first large national Syrian organization, the New Syria Party.

Nationalist sentiments expressed in the Arabic-language press provide the background for chronicling and discussing the inception and short life of the secret Free Syria Society. As described earlier, immigrants endeavored to establish newspapers to inform readers about their homelands, to learn of each other's opinions and concerns, and to advertise their products and import-export businesses. Newcomers to the United States from Syria in 1913, just before World War I ignited, read or heard about immigrants' successes and failures, learned that nationalist sentiments existed wherever Syrians lived, and shared a keen grasp of impending changes signaled by events in the Balkans and elsewhere. Ameen Farah's two years in the relative freedom of Cairo before making the journey to the United States enabled him to ponder new possibilities of harnessing scattered Syrian talents. His close proximity to the Decentralization Party in Cairo, where ʿAẓm wrote his sermons to immigrants in the United States, and Farah's conversations in letters with his peers Jubrān Kuzma and Nicola Qubʿyn must have encouraged him to embark on a plan of organizing Syrians behind political demands. The plan materialized in the form of the Free Syria Society.

This small and short-lived collective was not the only one of its kind. But it is one that can be documented thanks to Farah's papers, and it illustrates how nationalist feelings resulted in political work on U.S. soil before the United States considered taking part in World War I. The FSS is unique in other respects as well; it is the last society to have navigated Ottomanism, Western secularism, and the minefield of seeking independence prior to World War I given clear signs of Western ambitions. The precolonial, pre–World War I period in which the society's political conceptual framework came into being preceded political activism by Syrian immigrants in the United States. The immigrants transitioned from unwilling Ottoman subjects into U.S. citizens with a plan of action for Syria, creating more sophisticated organizations.

The bylaws for the FSS may have traveled to the United States from Egypt with Ameen Farah, but the small organization came to life in Flint, likely in 1914. As a strictly political organization, the FSS transplanted to the United States long-term secular goals, including the Decentralized Party's explicit aims of achieving complete independence in stages. Meticulous recordkeeping by Ameen Farah is supported by George Antonius's documentation of the political aspirations of the Decentralization Party and al-Fatāt.

Ameen Farah's role in the FSS was no accident. He did not come from the landowning or intellectual elite; his father, Saleh, and his grandfather

Ya'qoub were nationalists, learned Orthodox clergy, and historians in their own right.[20] Ameen's mother, Amina, was literate and a well-respected figure within the Farah clan and among Nazarenes. Farah's archives abound with letters from his father, some of which chronicle Arab and Islamic histories and past glories and setbacks. Upon the death of her husband, Amina took on the role of matriarch and became the center of social activities and gatherings for the family. Her letters to Ameen, much like those from his father, exude an awareness of their status as an educated family closely connected to their social environment in the Galilee area of Palestine.

Ameen was typical of graduates of the Russian *maskubīyah* (Arabic corruption of "Muscovite") or Greek-run seminaries among the six other Nazarenes who accompanied him to the United States in 1913. Although not considered elite, they possessed language skills in English and French and spoke Turkish and Greek fluently, as did most educated youth. Unlike many Syrian immigrants who were from Lebanon (a short distance to the north of Nazareth) and reportedly traveled below deck, the Nazarenes traveled above deck, often kept detailed records of their journeys, and took with them enough funds to survive the first months in the new country.[21] Often they were encouraged to immigrate by kin and townspeople already in the United States. In Ameen Farah's case, encouragement came from two sources, his cousin Nazir, who had settled in Flint about a decade earlier, and ongoing, danger-fraught conscription in the Turkish Ottoman army.

In his youth Ameen Farah served as a de facto teacher during a stint as a conscript, possibly in 1910 and part of 1911. During the Balkan wars, army service often ended in death from exposure or unsanitary conditions if not from the war itself. A friendly Turkish *uzbashi* (sergeant) granted Ameen a temporary leave, which he used to escape to Alexandria and from there to Cairo. While in Egypt he joined the Ottoman Administrative Decentralization Party and may have started writing an autobiographical novel, *Rushd wa Suha*.[22] Although not of particularly high literary quality (he was probably around twenty-one years old when he started writing it), the novel is an early example of writing about and aspirations for equality in accessible language, a departure from the severity and grandeur of difficult-to-understand Arabic classical rhymed prose. Farah echoed sentiments by his friends Kuzma and Qub'yn by drawing lessons from the humanist philosophy of Renan, Voltaire, and Tolstoy. These sentiments the Syrian youth unknowingly shared with Ameen al-Rihani, Khalil Gibran, and Elia Madey. Indeed, the sentiments continued to inform Farah's thinking in the United States when he contacted Gibran's friends Mikhail Naimy and Nasib Arida for the purpose of launching the Free Syria Society.

FIGURE 3.1. *Ameen Farah's Ottoman identity document. The Arabic script is Ottoman Turkish, no longer in use. The Islamic Hijri year 1330 at the bottom left corresponds to about 1911, during Farah's conscription and the year he escaped to the relative safety of Cairo. Farah Papers, Bawardi Collection.*

Under "Dedication" in his novel, Ameen is unequivocal about his aims, as if to foretell his life's journey of working for Syria's salvation:

> I dedicate this, my novel, to the contemporary youth of Syria in their birthplace and all the locations of their diaspora on the five continents. This youth that endeavors to elevate the homeland, restore his dignity, and expends the utmost efforts to destroy old structures of darkness, such as the structures of sectarianism, ignorance, and repression. In their places he builds, under the eastern sun, the luxurious and solid composite of justice, science, and tolerance. To these noble souls with whom I share the association of the same homeland, origin, language, and life's journey, I present the novel *Rushd wa Suha*. Ameen Farah.[23]

As indicated previously, the United Syrian Society (USS) espoused a nationalist agenda even though the society itself was not a political organization. However, the political leanings of the USS seem to correspond to those of the Free Syria Society because Syrian nationalists' political agenda was at least partly forged outside Syria's borders by 1913, and most if not all orientations of the Syrian immigrant population appear to have been represented in the USS.[24] Other societies in the New York–New Jersey area and elsewhere existed, but few commanded wide appeal based on shared goals. Some served specific functions such as offering a kind of health insurance, while others were small and ephemeral. Bits and pieces of translations from the Syrian press will continue to complicate the picture because it remains difficult to ascertain which societies can be considered regional or national and which are small and fleeting if the archival evidence and transnational context are not considered. Such uncertainty is one of the dilemmas facing this study moving forward.

Basil Kherbawi's 1913 Arabic text on U.S. history and that of Syrian immigrants provides the earliest significant hints of structural political acculturation and primary-group affiliations of church and village. Nothing in Kherbawi's study precludes political awareness, although it is obvious from his introduction that he navigated his book away from politics and sectarianism and relied on respondents' accounts and figures of their organizations and societies. Kherbawi amassed information for his book by sending out hundreds of questionnaires to Syrians in all parts of the United States for the purpose of documenting their social, political, economic, artistic, and religious lives. Kherbawi's conclusions based on his semiscientific study suggest that organizations of various orientations existed at the outset of immigration and that for many Syrians, thriving businesses in fixed locations, rather than peddling door to door, existed earlier than previously be-

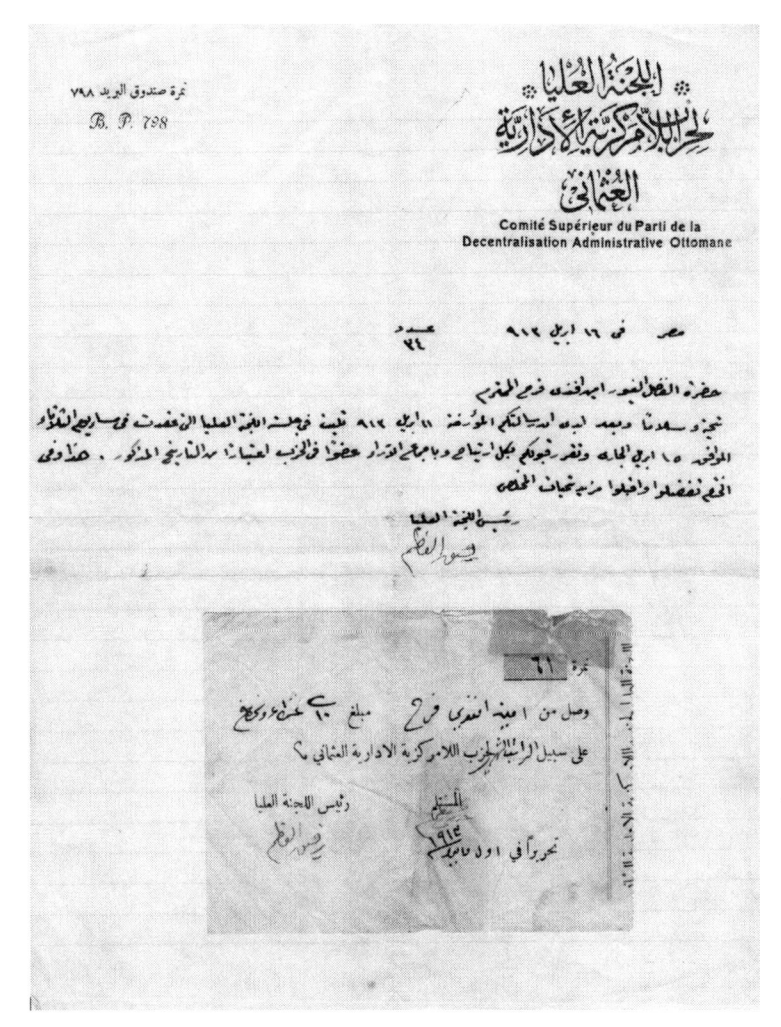

FIGURE 3.2. *Certificate informing Farah of his acceptance into the Ottoman Administrative Decentralization Party, April 16, 1913 (top), and receipt of Farah's membership dues, May 1, 1913. Both documents were signed by Rafīq al-ʿAẓm. Farah Papers, Bawardi Collection.*

lieved. In terms of structural assimilation, Kherbawi chronicles inroads several immigrants made into political life by securing high positions in the Republican Party and winning elections.[25]

Kherbawi provides a long list of prominent Syrian figures in literature, politics, and commerce, including the earliest Syrian associations and clubs, starting with the Orthodox Benevolent Society, founded in 1895,[26] and al-

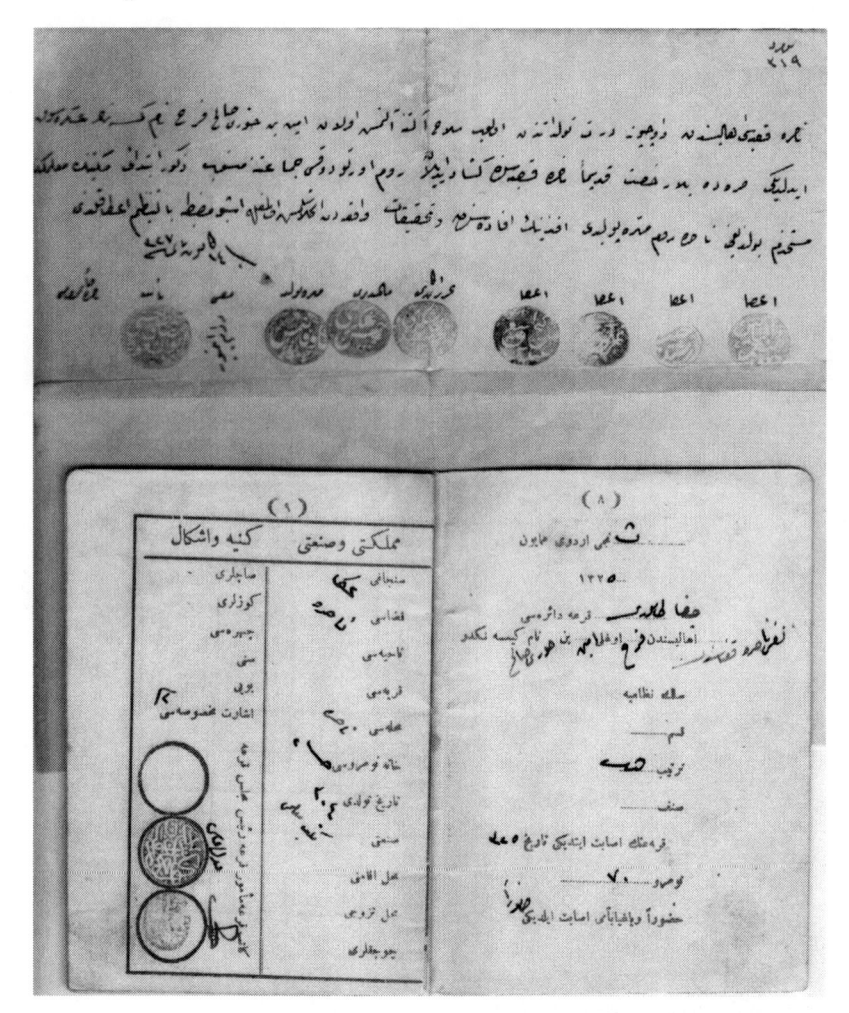

FIGURE 3.3. *Farah's teaching credentials in Ottoman Turkish (top) and his Ottoman army ID (bottom). Farah used the teaching credentials to escape Ottoman conscription, traveling first to Alexandria and then to Cairo. Farah Papers, Bawardi Collection.*

Muntada al-Sūri al-Amrīki (Syrian-American Literary Club), founded in 1908. Kherbawi reports that the Lebanese Renaissance Society had nearly 5,000 members spread across fifteen chapters, but he was keen to disclose that the information was supplied by the society itself, an indication that he took the figure with a grain of salt. Kherbawi presents information on women's benevolent societies and their work in tenement houses and an excerpt from the bylaws of the Jam'īyat ittiḥād al-'ummāl al-Sūrīya (Syrian Workers Union Society).[27] He notes Nasif Malouf as a leading figure in the American Red Crescent;[28] the book has an extensive list of churches and their respective societies among other social and literary clubs and organizations.

The examples of abundant organizational life did not lessen the challenges before the FSS. To Ameen Farah, fragments of their disagreements in the Syrian press were familiar, but in his novel, *Rushd wa Suha*, he was concerned with one root cause of sectarianism, the wars in the Balkans. A newcomer, however, he missed the brunt of intra-Syrian sectarian disputes in the press and may have been filled with hope upon reading commentary by Diāb, ʿAẓm, and Rashīd Rida. He set as a goal enlisting a small, educated, and motivated constituency to imbue the masses with ideas of sound reforms still fresh in his treasured letters with Kuzma, Qubʿyn, and Muhammad Muhaisen, his childhood friends. Farah somehow brought to the United States Jubrān Kuzma's letter to Nicola Qubʿyn dated December 1, 1912, that was intended as the seed for a secret political party on the "five continents." Ameen's motives for making good plans to build the political party were fresh memories of dreadful life under the Turks, ultimately the reason behind his journey to the United States in 1913. He brought with him his intellectual baggage, documents, ideas, and small though respectable capital. Once in New York he was finally able to read in the Arabic-language press echoes of his discontent against the Turks, among them Mikhail Naimy's call for a "Palestinian friend" to answer "Southern Syria's" call in the face of Jewish immigration. Farah did just that while simultaneously embarking on organizing a cadre of Syrians. Between the time Ameen arrived in the United States and the time he read Naimy's "Palestine, a Jewish Kingdom" in *Al-Hoda*, World War I had commenced and Arabs of the Hijaz region in western Saudi Arabia had joined the Allies against the Ottomans and Germans.

The fight between the "new imperialists," like the Syrians' plans for independence, was in the making. The emergent colonialist Germans' competition with France over North Africa and restive Slavic groups in the Austro-Hungarian dynasty brought Europe closer to the brink of war. The assassination of Austrian Archduke Franz Ferdinand by a Serbian rebel set in motion events that led to World War I and ultimately the settlement of the "Eastern question," a term at the time for the Ottoman Empire's fate and eventual dismantling. Arab provinces were caught in the middle precisely as Syrian leaders feared would happen. Although it took time for the dust to settle, the collapse of the empire and the defeat of the Turks heightened the Arabs' hopes of change. During these momentous changes, appealing to as many Syrians as possible was paramount for Farah and his FSS if the aims of the Arab Conference in Paris were to be implemented. The only difference was the lessened likelihood of maintaining an Ottoman shell because the CUP began executing Arab nationalists, including moderates like ʿAbdulhamīd al-Zahrāwi, head of the Arab Conference in Paris, and his colleague ʿAbdulghani al-ʿUraisi, as well as expatriate Zraick, editor of *Jurāb-ul-Kurdi*.

Mikhail Naimy, whose writings attracted the attention of Farah as a newcomer, was a renowned author and future member of the influential Pen Bond. However, literature, not politics, was Naimy's passion. He joined the FSS along with Nasib Arida and an undetermined number of Syrians in New York, Detroit, and elsewhere. Naimy's membership in the FSS can be confirmed in two ways. He published his account of it without mentioning Ameen Farah by name in his autobiography, *Saboun*.[29] Naimy's account gives clues as to the challenges facing organizing attempts and the subtleties of sociopolitical changes contributing to the relative success of future organizations. In his autobiography Naimy discloses a letter from Nasib Arida dated November 19, 1915, expressing his willingness to "exert great efforts in Free Syria [Society]" as an endeavor that "resembles a flash of hope in the dark nights."[30] Arida's letter was a follow-up to a previous conversation in which Naimy suggested bringing Arida's magazine, *Al-Funūn*, "back to life with the help of comrades in Free Syria [Society]." Naimy continued: "A correspondence ensued with the group [in Flint] until it became clear that the members not only lacked funds but also the qualifications to spread an ideology and to free countries."[31] Naimy, among the literati, demonstrated a strong preference for translations of Western works and for poetry as opposed to political action. In his autobiography he expresses his lack of confidence in "A. F.," clearly a reference to Ameen Farah, and the need for "a free Syria . . . that would unify our literary strengths and guide them with wisdom to enlighten Syria, lighten its load, and expose the meaning of life . . . because our contact with the West must move in us living powers that lie under the ashes of ignorance and the spell of the past."[32]

An eight-page letter Naimy wrote to Farah on March 7, 1915, offers a more realistic explanation of the story of his short-lived engagement with and pessimistic view of the FSS. Naimy's involvement in the FSS began with the letter in the same year the FSS was founded; he wrote it apparently in response to Farah's inquiry upon having read Naimy's article on Palestine's fate and Jewish settlement. The Naimy letter is a rare and uncharacteristic example of his otherwise humanist ideas. It is baffling because it illustrates Naimy's adamant negation of any chance of building camaraderie among all Syrians, as he deemed Muslims racially different from Christians. Naimy's bizarre reasoning must have been a shock to Farah in his hopes of building the secret society. Most of all, the letter was laden with apathetic hyperbole that Naimy used to absolve himself from doing what he could as a member of the FSS. Instead, he charged that Syrians were inherently ill equipped to join the modern world. Naimy's letter exposed his animosity toward Muhammad Muhaisen, a progressive social thinker, perhaps due to Naimy's professed ideas about Muslims:

> You ask me about the Syrian movement, and I wish you explained what you meant by the Syrian movement. Do you mean our writers' cracklings in the newspapers, and I am one of those who crackle, or what money was raised by some societies to aid the distressed in the homeland? This is all I saw from this "Syrian movement." . . . No sooner the war ends, you'll see our authors returning to congratulating a friend with a newborn or consoling another for loss of a kin. You'll see the money melt away without calming pains or satisfying a thirst.
>
> Our disease is that time passes at the rate of 60 minutes per hour, whereas we progress by twenty. . . . Our movement to rally Christians, Muslims, and Druze is half a century too late.
>
> Tell me how can you hope to see the Muslim who was in the past absolute master of this country and the one who had the final word, greet the Christian, the infidel pig, as a brother or at least as an equal in political and civil rights? . . . The thousands who ascend the steps of mosques in Syria did not reach this level of mental and social evolution.
>
> I wrote my piece "To the Sons and Daughters of Lebanon" thinking that the size of the calamity may move them to unite. . . . I called on the men to join the fight knowing that they could not win but to show the world and our own that we value our freedom. . . . I roamed among the Syrians urging them to fight for Syria. Here is what a passerby told me after reading my piece: "I see you came up with a new one. You want us to go to war? By God, if Syria is ruined a thousand times, I won't throw myself in front of the cannon for its sake." . . . And when I told him that I would go once I see enough of my comrades do the same, he looked at me with disappointment.
>
> No, my brother, there is a great gap between Christians and Muslims. Aside from religious difference, we are different nationalities [*jinsi*], which I discussed in "The Caravans of Nations" [in *Mirāt al-Gharb*], which was not to the liking of Muhammad Muhaisen, who answered that Syrians are Arabs not 'ajam [Persian or non-Arab]. The truth as I see it that some Muslims in Syria may be Arabs but not Christians.[33]

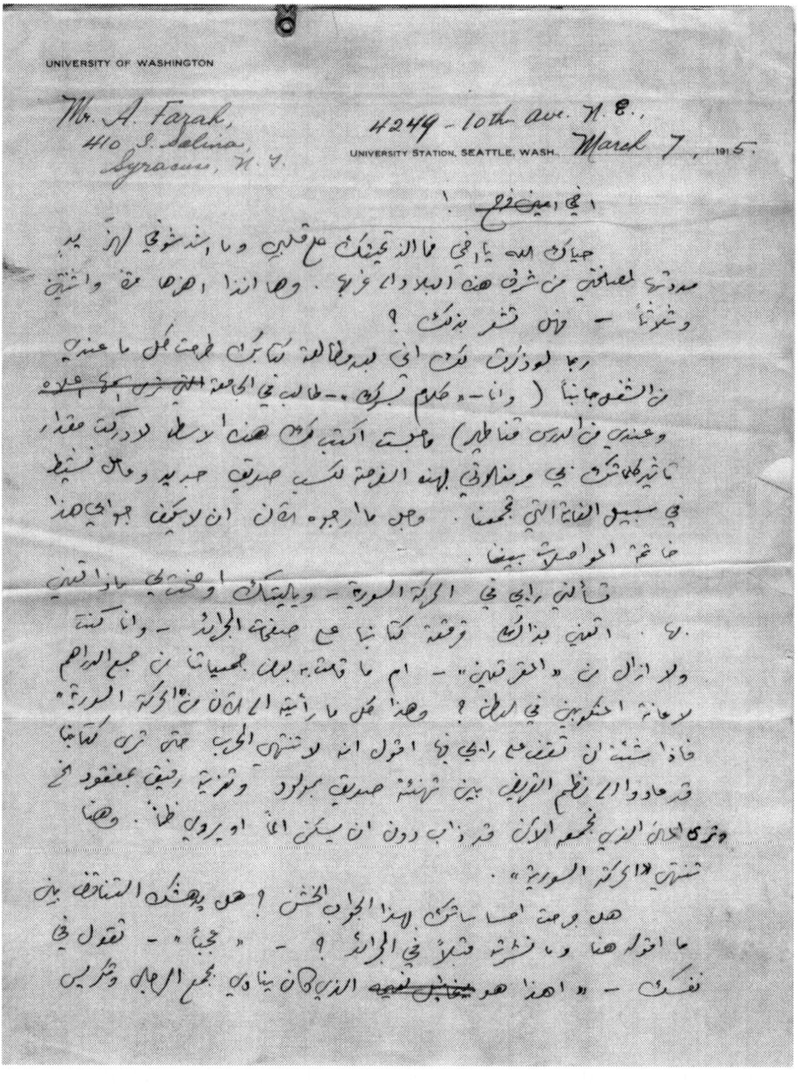
UNIVERSITY OF WASHINGTON

Mr. A. Farah,
410 S. Salina,
Syracuse, N. Y.

4249 - 10th ave. N. E.,
UNIVERSITY STATION, SEATTLE, WASH. March 7, 1915.

FIGURE 3.4. *Letter from Mikhail Naimy to Ameen Farah, March 7, 1915. Farah drew red lines across all references to names, probably as a sign of disapproval of disclosing names while a member in the secret Free Syria Society. Farah Papers, Bawardi Collection.*

The curious letter, albeit characteristic of the author's legendary command of the Arabic language, concluded that there was no possible way for Muslims and Christians to unite given their inherent racial ('*irqi*) differences. For two reasons it remains difficult to determine what caused Naimy's extreme views: he was Orthodox, not Maronite, for whom such views were more accepted; and his autobiography was carefully sterilized and offered no explanations, including the likely reply by Farah. It is important to mention that a native Arabic speaker can recognize hyperbole as a familiar feature in an unassuming correspondence among acquaintances. The hyperbole in Naimy's letter, however, was a far cry from his characteristically vivid descriptions of life in Russia or of trees and plants in Walla Walla, Washington, or his deeply insightful interpretations of human experiences.

It is possible that Naimy's ultimate goal may have been to dissuade Farah from squandering resources at the disposal of the FSS on anything other than such literary pursuits as saving *Al-Funūn*. Farah drew lines in red across all references to names and dates in Naimy's letter, likely because he had asked the indifferent author to avoid mentioning names. These markings mean that Naimy's membership in the FSS was secured prior to March 1915, when he wrote the letter. Another clue to Naimy's disposition was that Muhaisen, a Muslim, was the head of the New York chapter of the FSS. A letter by Muhaisen dated May 13, 1915, on official stationery of the FSS confirmed that Muhaisen was the head of the chapter in New York, the home of Naimy when he was not in college in Washington State and of Arida. It is safe to assume that Naimy's professed interest in the society was disingenuous because of his admitted suspicion of Muslims. His attitude toward Muslims and his public disagreement with Muhaisen account for his criticism of Farah for admitting members—perhaps Muhaisen—without "checking their background."[34]

Funding by Ragheb Mitrage for *Al-Funūn* may have been the sole reason behind Naimy's joining the Free Syria Society after Farah secured the membership of the wealthy Mitrage, his friend and neighbor in Flint. It may have worked as Naimy hoped, given that Ragheb Mitrage eventually provided the funds necessary to reissue *Al-Funūn*. On April 4, 1917, Arida wrote Naimy indicating that he had asked Mitrage to "give him the good news of issuing *Al-Funūn* once again."[35] Arida indicated that Mitrage had invested $2,000 (the equivalent of almost $45,000 now) and promised to raise $5,000 more. Arida, Naimy, Gibran, and other prominent early figures in *mahjar* literature were able to publish what became some of the most prized jewels in modern Arabic literature in *Al-Funūn*. Hence, despite its small member-

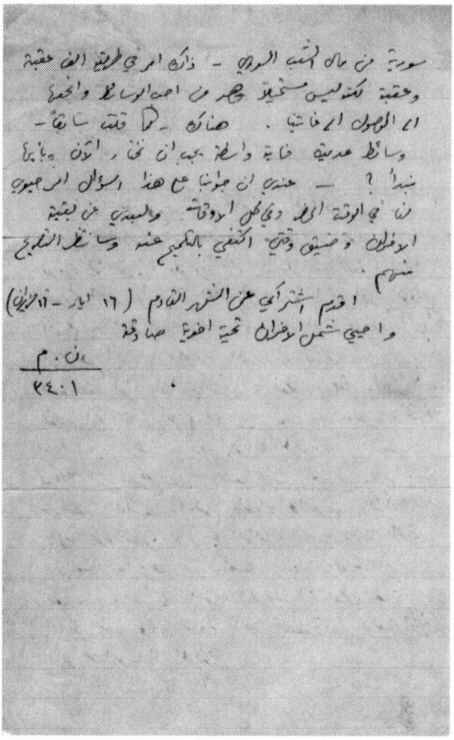

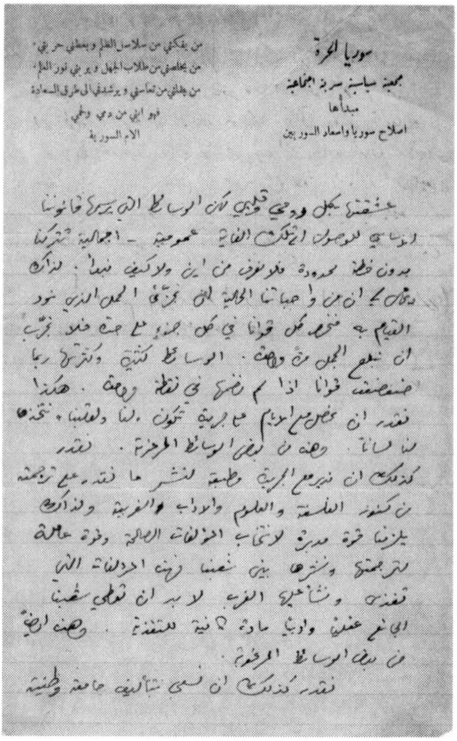

FIGURE 3.5. *Pages of a letter to Ameen Farah, 1915. The letter is signed N. M./3401, but the handwriting appears to be Mikhail Naimy's. Its author wrote on both sides of a sheet of the special stationery Farah provided to members of the secret Free Syria Society. The letterhead reads, "Free Syria. A secret political social society. Its principal goal is reforming Syria and the happiness of Syrians." The letter casts doubt on the society's ability to achieve its goals and criticizes the bylaws as "general" and lacking a "specific plan of action." The proposed solutions were a magazine and publishing house to translate "treasures from Western sciences and philosophy." Farah Papers, Bawardi Collection.*

ship, the FSS facilitated the survival of *Al-Funūn* for several years, while the FSS sharpened its experience in political activism from the United States.

Other members of the FSS did not share Naimy's views on Islam. In one of his letters on the society's stationery, Muhaisen listed five members by their initials and Arida, whom he mentions by name, therefore inadvertently breaking the code of secrecy. Muhaisen described the Christian Arida as "an upstanding and polite man with proud spirit." The letter, which Muhaisen signed with his secret name and number, "M.M./3301," indicated that he and Arida exchanged vows of "everlasting fraternity." Muhammad Muhaisen became known as the most vocal advocate of Syrian national unity through his writings in *Mirāt al-Gharb*, *Al-Bayān*, and his own publications in Detroit. He would move to Detroit and publish *Al-Difāʿ al-ʿArabi* with ʿAbbas Abu Shaqra, the future head of the Detroit branch of the New Syria Party. Another official letter among Ameen Farah's papers was signed with the initials of Mikhail Naimy in reverse, N.M./3401, in Naimy's distinctive handwriting. Accompanying it were dues for May and June 1915. Its writer focused on the idea of securing a magazine and a publishing house to speak for the society and to publish translations of "treasures of Western philosophy, science, and literature."[36]

The society's political aims were established before the political outcome of the war became known. The Free Syria Society's bylaws were unequivocal when it came to the society's goals and objectives. After an empty space for the name of the society were Articles 2 and 3:

> 2. The utmost goal of the society is the complete independence of Syria in stages, from decentralized administration to administrative autonomy, then complete independence ending with republican rule. During each of these stages, the Executive Committee and its branches issue bulletins and instructions as to the society's plans for that time in dealing with the government and the country.
>
> 3. The society is secret and political, as are its members, meetings, decisions, and administrative affairs. All of the society's affairs are to be conducted in secret. Since this is a secret society, it can achieve objectives that are otherwise impossible to achieve; its hand would be free and its members safe from the traps that are erected by the enemies of the homeland and humanity [the CUP].[37]

The society's bylaws stipulated that a general central office was to be established on each continent, with branches operating independently. The leadership was to emanate from either the branches or the central location. Only Syrian men and women twenty years of age or older qualified for membership so long as they would be willing to struggle until death, if necessary, in Syria's cause. Extending equal membership to women during this period of Arab history was consistent with postwar feminist thinking. By 1919 Huda Shaʿrawi, an Egyptian feminist, had led nationalist demonstrations, established the Egyptian Feminist Union, and denounced the veil.[38]

All members of the society, according to the bylaws, were equal and obligated to consider each other as family. Candidates for membership were obliged to swear allegiance and have existing members vouch for them. Section 4 further described the value and aim of working together:

> The most important means of achieving the stated goal [Syria's independence] is to unify the members of all faiths to create one nation [*ummah wāḥidah*], the Syrian motherland, [and] the return of all its children among the immigrant diasporas and the dispersed.... [Other goals include] working on elevating [Syria] economically and intellectually by promoting her products and building colleges and universities ... and severe and total boycott of its enemies and occupying foreigners.[39]

When the United States entered the war in April 1917, 15,000 Syrian immigrants or their descendants joined the U.S. military. Their reasons varied. Though saving Syria and taking revenge on the Turks were dominant reasons for enlisting, spikes in nativist anti-immigrant attitudes across the United States and tightened immigration and citizenship controls may have influenced their decisions too, as service allowed the Syrians to gain citizenship. Uncle Sam's Syrian doughboys included Ashad Hawie of the army's 42nd Rainbow Infantry Division. Hawie distinguished himself when he captured a German officer and led a grenade attack against the elite Prussian Guard.[40] Joining the army and buying war bonds became widely practiced patriotic duties for Syrian Americans and especially attractive as Syrian and American patriotisms converged behind unified ideals of freedom. Syrian intellectuals and the immigrant press urged Syrian Americans to volunteer for military service. One of the most prolific recruiters was Ameen Rihani, who wrote to his friend ʿAbdulmassīh Haddād upon witnessing the devastation of the population while on a visit to Syria: "Syria's salvation is possible only at the hands of a strong Syrian American Army that fights for its freedom on its soil. My pen, tongue, heart, fortune, and offspring are at the service of my homeland."[41]

Farah, Naimy, and many other Syrians served in the U.S. Army. Farah's service, he would write in his diary, was an extension of his patriotic duty as a Syrian nationalist. When his sergeant encouraged him to apply for U.S. citizenship—granted to all servicemen—Farah was not yet ready to discount chances of returning to Syria. It must have been painful for Farah to ponder spending the rest of his life in the United States without a chance of seeing Syria again. He recalled that he "gratefully and politely declined."[42] Nevertheless, Farah eagerly shipped out to join the 85th Infantry Division at Camp Custer in Battle Creek, Michigan, lured by the possibility of fighting

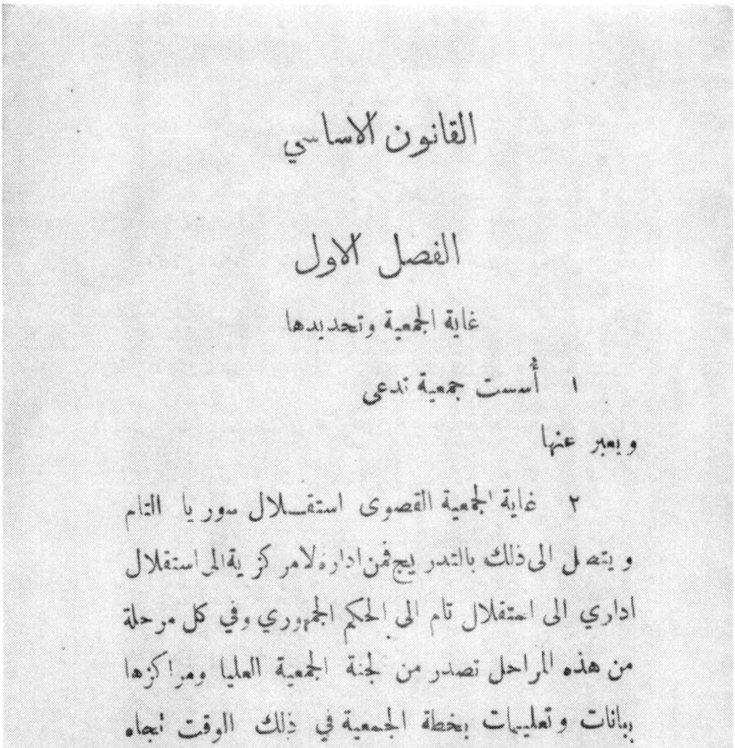

القانون الاساسي

الفصل الاول

غاية الجمعية وتحديدها

١. أُسست جمعية تدعى

ويعبر عنها

٢. غاية الجمعية القصوى استقلال سوريا التام ويتوصل الى ذلك بالتدرج يجب فمن ادارة لامركزية الى استقلال اداري الى استقلال تام الى الحكم الجمهوري وفي كل مرحلة من هذه المراحل تصدر من لجنة الجمعية العليا ومراكزها ببانات وتعليمات بخطة الجمعية في ذلك الوقت انجاه الحكومة والبلاد

٣. الجمعية سياسية سرية واعضاؤها ومجتمعاتها وقراراتها وادارتها تجري تحت ستر الخفاء . ومعلوم ان الجمعية في حال كونها سرية تعمل في سبيل غايتها ما لا تستطيعه لو كانت علنية فتكون مطلقة اليدين ويبقى اعضاؤها في مأمن من الوقوع في الاشراك التي ينصبها لهم اعداء الوطن والانسانية

FIGURE 3.6. *A page of bylaws of the Free Syria Society. The eight-page document provides for structure, operations, methods, financial planning, communications, and conventions for delegates of this small political society founded by Ameen Farah in 1915. Farah Papers, Bawardi Collection.*

FIGURE 3.7. *Ameen Farah (center) in Uncle Sam's army with two American friends, 1919. The photograph was taken at Camp Custer, Michigan. Farah Papers, Bawardi Collection.*

the Ottoman army in which he served as a conscript. The war ended before he reached battle.

The FSS may not have been the resounding success Farah hoped it would be, but the importance of the experiment became evident after the dust of international intrigue settled in the Paris Peace Conference in 1919 and a stark new reality of impending French and British occupations emerged. Arab Syrians' hopes of achieving statehood suffered a blow in 1917, before the war ended, when a letter from Lord Arthur Balfour, the British foreign secretary, to Walter Rothschild, a powerful Jewish banker in Britain, promised to create a "a national home for the Jews in Palestine," thus signaling British support for mass immigration by European Jews. The dire consequences of the Balfour Declaration for Palestinians planted the seeds of anti-Zionist political activism. But in the short term the symbolic importance of coveted Syria as the object of immigrants' patriotism invigorated collective action on a new footing. I devote attention to the last effort in the cause of territorial contiguity of natural Syria before colonialism set in. After Europeans settled the loose ends of the war and put down the Syrian revolt, Palestine became the core issue attracting political mobilization around the larger Arab nationalist cause.

Farah and many of his peers in the FSS may not have noticed Louis Brandeis or Rabbi Silver and their work on behalf of the World Zionist Organization, but several Syrians who began their education at the American University of Beirut before enrolling in America's finest universities did notice and began to formulate a response to Zionism. While Farah was writing for *Al-Bayān*, *Al-Hoda*, and *Mirāt al-Gharb*, Syrian graduates of the finest U.S. universities like Fuad Shatara, Ḥabīb Kātibah, and Philip Hitti began to educate the readers of the *New York Times*, *Detroit Free Press*, and other English-language newspapers on the worsening conditions for Palestinians and the perils of Zionism.[43]

Chapter 4

THE "SYRIA IDEA" AND THE NEW SYRIA PARTY

Amid the uncertainty surrounding the fate of Syria during World War I, most Syrians supported U.S. entry into the war hoping it would mitigate European ambitions and bring Syria closer to self-determination. They hoped rising American prestige, backed by a foreign policy committed to national sovereignty, would be Syria's salvation and lead to its independence. By the time the reluctant U.S. military joined the fighting in 1917, many Syrians had already enlisted, extending a fairly common phenomenon of Syrians serving in the U.S. military since the Spanish-American War.[1] Communication was halted during World War I between activists and the nationalist champions of the First Arab Conference in Paris, who now were scattered in France and Egypt. The initial U.S. reluctance to enter the war created feelings of uncertainty and anxiety as intense famines unlike any in generations ravaged Syria's population. Although Damascenes and Jerusalemites alike feared the militarily superior Europeans might thwart their desires for national sovereignty, many nationalists—among them Jubrān Kuzma, Ameen al-Rihani, and exiles in Cairo—hoped that the inevitable end of Ottoman rule with European victory would bring them closer to their goals. Others, like Fuad Isa Shatara and the Druze nationalist Shakib Arslan, preferred to prevent bringing the conflict to Syria, fearing the aftermath of a direct European military presence. The political program of asserting Arab demands beyond Ottoman rule was already under way prior to the war, but limited choices due to the generally weak position of Arabs affected pragmatic Anglophile and Francophile dispositions on the part of many reformers. For the nationalists in the Middle East, South America, the United States, Europe, and Cairo, apparitions of colonialism remained strong. A contingency of American Syrians joined nationalists in 1919 for the postwar Paris Peace Conference. In the three years that followed they watched as their fears of colonialism became reality. When anti-French discontent exploded in open revolt in Syria by 1925, the New Syria Party was U.S. immigrants' response. The NSP began as a campaign for humanitarian aid following the Druze-led

Syrian revolt and quickly transformed into a last-ditch effort to keep alive the Syria idea and Syrian statehood.

Nationalists' maneuverings and stated hopes of independence comprised the political framework for al-Fatāt, the Decentralization Party, and the Free Syria Society; they also formed the context for the New Syria Party after the war, with one difference: autonomy from the Turks was no longer a prerequisite for independence, as the Ottoman Empire no longer ruled. The NSP still sought sovereignty in Syria based on historical and inalienable rights of self-determination under persistently severe political pressures and under the familiar banner "Syria for Syrians." The political changes arising from European occupation of much of the Middle East after the war began to transform Syrian nationalist demands, including those in Palestine, into an Arab nationalist goal of ending foreign occupation. In response to the complexities of shifting political borders to meet Europeans' expanding ambitions, Syrian immigrants split their efforts to meet challenges on two fronts: French occupation of modern Syria and Lebanon and British supremacy over Palestine and with it, Zionist encroachment. Although Shatara and Kātibah responded to Zionism even before the Balfour Declaration, Southern Syria (Palestine) had to wait during more pressing aid efforts on behalf of the Druze revolt to the north.

The political impetus for the NSP, the idea of Syria's independence within its natural geographic borders, antedates World War I. Making a case in this study for the NSP as a national organization of consequence in Arab American history depends on presenting a transnational historical context for two connected developments: sending aid and mobilizing political action following each calamitous event. Describing the available documents on this organization from Farah's collection in this chapter, due to scant archival evidence, will alleviate understandably cursory mention of NSP in Arab American studies. In addition, general public perceptions of Arab Syrians in the United States, especially in view of the emergent global power status of the United States after the Spanish-American War in 1898 and World War I, began to matter to immigrant activists. Although a coherent U.S. foreign policy in the Middle East would emerge only after World War II, the battle for public opinion in the United States over the fate of geographic Syria was already at hand. The New Syria Party was the first front in which Arab Americans fought through mass organization.

Inevitably, the historical context for the NSP is informed by analysis of the Free Syria Society before it and by the obvious need for a new strategy of pan-Arab nationalism once the Syria idea ran into the obstacle of arbitrary

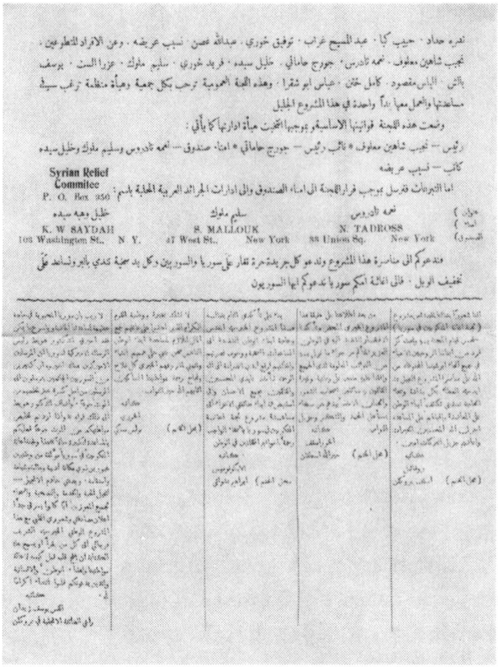

FIGURE 4.1. *This document announces the establishment of the Syrian Relief Committee in response to the famines during World War I. The committee comprised members of the Syrian Ladies Benevolent Society, the United Syrian Society, and the Homs Fraternal Society. Nadra Haddad, Nasib Arida, and ʿAbdulmassīh Haddād, all nationalist members of Al-Rābitah al-Qalamīyah, were among its members. ʿAbbas Abu Shaqra is listed as a volunteer. On the bottom of the second page (left) are endorsements by the ranking clergy of each of the main churches without mention of their sectarian affiliations. The aid was sent through a consortium of American foreign missionaries (Mujammaʾ al-Irsaliyat al-Ajnabiya al-Amrikiya). Courtesy of Dr. Norman Bishara, Ann Arbor, Michigan.*

borders imposed by Europeans in agreement with the Russians before the Bolshevik Revolution. These changes forced immigrants to shift their priorities in accordance with where the urgency was greater, north or south, although their core Arab-nationalist demands remained constant. Moreover, both organizations sprang out of urgent aid efforts in response to disastrous conditions befalling Syrians before structures were established or political agendas were shaped around conditions in the United States.

Carving Syria into spheres of influence for the French in the north and the British in the south was stipulated in 1916 in the secret Sykes-Picot

Agreement that also took into account the concerns of czarist Russia. The Bolsheviks made Sykes-Picot public in 1917 after they deposed the Russian monarchy. That same year the Balfour Declaration by the British built on these arrangements by seeking a permanent presence close to the strategic Suez Canal. Immigrant activists and their supporters responded to each of these overlapping developments as they arose. In the early 1920s, motivated by Jewish settlement in Palestine as stated in the Balfour Declaration in 1917, Fuad Shatara established Jamʿīyat al-Nahḍah al-Filasṭīnīyah and named it the Palestine National League in English. The organization would resurface in 1936 as the Arab National League.

Researching the transcontinental nature of immigrants' responses to unfolding events overseas is complicated by the scatterings of information on political collectives, most of which were either local or short-lived. This sketchiness is even more debilitating when it comes to examining political activism and organizational work in Arab American studies—or lack thereof. This and the subsequent chapters present translations from the largest collection of documents describing operations of these largely unknown organizations in order to mitigate the growing confusion arising from attention to scattered archives and selective translations. Disclosing as many names as possible from archival records in context accomplishes two objectives: first, to provide adequate and necessary translation from mostly Arabic-language archives with records of the organizations; and second, to delineate the prominence of the organizations under study in relation to a growing list of names and groups from Arabic- and English-language newspaper snippets and various other sources. Newspaper accounts often create an impression that ad hoc activism around Fuad Shatara's work in New York—for example, by William Catzeflis, a member of the famed Pen Bond, and Amin Zeidān—was a major part of the ANL's work. It was not. Likewise, relying on snippets of news without context assigns undue importance to Salloum Mokarzel, who was not dedicated to Syria's cause. More to the point, individuals with established reputations in Syrian communities across the United States were more likely than not to support collective action after calamity made political action unavoidable. The same activists could not possibly favor Lebanese separatism and champion Syria's cause. Therefore, to belong to the NSP or the ANL was a result of years of active anticipation of political changes and resulting political awareness. The founding and leading of the NSP was dictated by the proximity of activists to events in Syria and a track record of literary ability and political engagement. Individuals with capabilities and proximity to the Druze revolt made their presence known on the pages of the press on both sides of the Atlantic, and they played leading roles in aid efforts during the famine. In *Al-Akhlāq*, in addition to the unwavering nationalist disposition of Orthodox clergymen Rafael Hawawini and Antony Bashir, the works of ʿAbbas Abu Shaqra, Ḥabīb Kātibah, and Fuad Shatara appeared alongside articles honoring Afifa Karam and Suleiman al-Bustāni, both deceased by then.[2] An absence of historiographies on political action and the main activists allowed Michael Suleiman to note political activism by immigrants while overlooking the NSP as a major organization. This statement is a case in point: "It was not until the late 1920's, however, that serious effort in this direction [establishing a national organization] was made, especially by Salloum Mokarzel."[3] Salloum, although he did not share his brother Naʿūm Mokarzel's penchant for harsh behavior, was not a major figure in any of the national political organizations. Salloum published the first English-language periodical, *The Syrian World*, and participated, as Suleiman noted accurately, in the Federation of Syrian and Lebanese Clubs, which had a "mild" interest in Arab issues.[4]

Examining the New Syria Party requires assembling incidents of how Syrian immigrants acted on their existing political awareness before the formal organization created chapters across the Americas by 1926. Two pieces of evidence before me as I write serve as examples. One is accessible to any researcher with sufficient Arabic-language skills on the thousands of pages of *Mirāt al-Gharb* newspaper recorded on microfilm. The other is from an original page of *As-Sameer* newspaper. *Mirāt al-Gharb* of October 2, 1917, contains an article titled "Lajnat tahrīr Sūriyah wa Lubnān" (Committee for the Liberation of Syria and Lebanon) about a letter of thanks to former U.S. president Theodore Roosevelt (1901–1909) for representing "real Americanism" in speeches when he called for freedom for Armenians and Arabs once the war ended. The letter from the committee answers Roosevelt's endorsement of "Mr. Mitchell," presumably John P. Mitchell, saying its members would be "employing all means at the committee's disposal" to promote Mitchell's election in New York City's mayoral race. An article in *As-Sameer* titled "Al-Ṣuhyūnīyah tanhazim" (Zionism retreats in defeat) and dated December 3, 1936, reports on a debate between Fuad Shatara and David de Sola Pool, an important Jewish scholar and rabbi of the Spanish and Portuguese Synagogue, the oldest congregation in the United States.

The evidentiary value of the 1936 *As-Sameer* article is straightforward, given Shatara's leadership role in the ANL later that year, as supported in numerous accounts from newspapers and other sources. The 1917 *Mirāt al-Gharb* article is laden with hints that Syrian immigrants were adopting more American customs, as evident in their eagerness to participate in local elections and their endorsement of Mitchell for his agreement with Roosevelt on issuing war bonds, something the immigrants also keenly supported. Each of these topics would require a historiography. Until that takes place, the *Mirāt al-Gharb* article is merely a tantalizingly interesting snippet of newspaper. The implication here is that as more scholars pay attention to Arabic-language material, more names will be tossed around but need historical context from events in Syria and early immigrants' collective life to tie them together. In the same manner, the New Syria Party is mentioned in Suleiman's 2006 study as having met with Secretary Henry L. Stimson in 1929 in conjunction with the Arab National League, the same as the Palestine National League, or Jamʿīyat al-nahḍah al-filasṭīnīyah, as founder Fuad Shatara named it. But the ANL did not exist as such until 1936 under different, albeit related, circumstances in Palestine. In fact, two years before 1929, the NSP held two national conventions, and it declined only with the demise of the Great Syrian Revolt in 1927 and the devastation of the Great Depression in the 1930s.

It is unclear whether the Palestinian Wailing Wall uprising in 1929 led to the meeting Suleiman mentions or whether the meeting resulted from a sharp spike of rhetoric in the press by proponents of Vladimir Jabotinsky's extreme branch of the Zionist movement in the United States. The shifting political reality of severing northern Syria from its southern part, Palestine, accounts for the immigrants' rallying behind Palestinian inhabitants of what was still considered Syria, at least among U.S. Syrians. The same reality accounts for a change in the very concept of the Syria idea in the United States and the rise of Arab nationalism and hence the Arab National League. All these changes affected immigrants' political strategies of action and self-awareness as they forged ahead with structurally integrating into their larger communities. Many organizations and societies are barely discussed in a national or international framework, and the impetus behind them and dates of their inception are vague. Equally ill defined are the organizations' agendas, accomplishments, and shortcomings. The question of whether some of these collectives like the NSP carved distinct places in Arab American history is muddled as well by lumping formal mass political organizations with marginal social collectives. Here I intend to add perspectives on the effects of the revolt on Syrian Americans, such as galvanizing a large number of immigrants across the country behind the NSP.

Finally, recurring mention of federations of American Syrian Lebanese clubs without a cogent history of such umbrella organizations adds to the confusion. There were many federations of local societies in the first decades of the twentieth century. The most prominent was the Syrian American

Federation of New England, founded in 1932. I agree with Suleiman that they had mildly Arab orientations but only because the federations were social clubs with wide appeal. Salloum Mokarzel's role in them was marginal because his preference for Lebanese parochialism was rebuffed in favor of keeping alive their Syrian identity. In fact, Charles Samaha, a great-nephew of Faris Malouf, provided that in September 1934, just before the Third Annual Convention of the Syrian American Federation of New England, a debate ensued over whether to add the word "Lebanese" to the name. Most of the members were from the Lebanon area of Syria, and Lebanon had functioned with French support as a separate country. Faris Malouf, as chairman of the constitution committee, mailed his report and a copy of the proposed constitution with an organizational name change to federation president Michael Abodeely, who in turn mailed copies of the amendment to all member clubs. In Malouf's report, to assist the member clubs in their interpretation of the proposed constitution, he defined the word "Syria" in these terms: "strip of land extending from the Taurus range and the Euphrates in the north to the Sinaitic peninsula in the south, and hemmed in between the Mediterranean Sea on the west and the desert on the east, measuring approximately four hundred miles long by about one hundred and fifty miles wide."[5] Only then was the federation's constitution amended and the name changed to the Syrian and Lebanese American Federation of the Eastern States.[6] Syrian ascription never disappears from the names of various federations, and it took a while before "Lebanese" was added to the names of federations in other parts of the country.[7]

Another example of the attachment to Syria, the idea and the place, was the passage of many resolutions championed by Faris Malouf upholding Palestinian rights in the face of British policies. Eventually, Malouf achieved his goal of establishing the Federation of Syrian and Lebanese Clubs in 1950 without abandoning the Arab cause.[8] Faris Malouf's leading role in Arab American history and the importance of the federations await dedicated research. He continued the pioneering contributions by members of the Malouf family to the *nahḍah* movement and political activism in the organizations in this study.

The writings of Ameen Rihani capture the relationship between concerns over Syria's fate and the larger Arab-nationalist demands before and after World War I. Through his experiences one can see that the Syrian cause was at once foundational in Arab-nationalist history and inseparable from subsequent ideas of pan-Arab nationhood. At the outset of the twentieth century Rihani was respected by non-Arab Americans as well as Arabs, including leading intellectuals in Egypt, after his *Al-Riḥāniyāt* appeared in Cairo

FIGURE 4.2. *Faris Malouf, 1938. Malouf organized the Syrian Educational Society in New York in 1916, advocated U.S. citizenship for Syrian immigrant veterans, and served early Arab American federations in leadership roles. Courtesy of Charles M. Samaha, Saint Petersburg, Florida.*

in 1910. His quest to graft the "strenuosity" and materialism of the West upon the East and the spirituality of the East on the West borrowed from the works of Arab and Muslim philosophers and the humanism and political commentary of Thomas Carlyle, Ernest Renan, François Voltaire, and Ralph Waldo Emerson.[9] Western education, missionary work, and aid efforts following famines after World War I, and Syrians' early attempts to build schools in Syria were inextricably intertwined. Educational institutions contributed to the successes of charitable work based in the United States as much as did the political upheavals that created charities. Correspondence by Naimy, Farah, and Farah's Nazarene friends indicates that Syrians viewed an emphasis on education as a tool with which coveted social and political reforms could be attained. Schools and education inevitably facilitated organized political involvement by immigrants on behalf of Syria. In this respect Syrian political aspirations, although soon to be at odds with French and British plans, were still considered by Syrians to be compatible with progress in the Western sense of the word.

Several schools of higher education in science, literature, and agricultural technology existed in major cities in Bilād al-Shām (Syria) by the late nineteenth century, some established with the help of missionaries. The U.S.-based Society of Friends (Quakers) established a boys school in Ramallah, Palestine, and the British, Germans, and French founded schools such as the Collège des Frères in Jerusalem and the Patriarchal School in Beirut. These schools did not dominate Syria's educational system and competed for students with the Arab-run national schools that were established at a local level (*madāris waṭanīyah*). The local schools' political orientations were toward uniform nationalism or an independent Syria in some form. Apart from the dire need for aid during World War I, Arab schools like the Arab Men's Teacher Training College in Jerusalem (later known as the Government Arab College), al-Amiriyyeh school in Jaffa, and al-Rashidiya school in Jerusalem educated a class of sophisticated statesmen, some of whom completed their educations in al-Azhar, the Sorbonne, the American University in Cairo, or the American University of Beirut. These became alternatives to such Turkish schools as Sultaniyeh College and Istanbul University, where fewer notables attained educations. Ameen Farah's involvement in collecting aid to support alternative educational institutions was unhampered by the Great War despite his emigration and contributed to his key role in the NSP. But Farah was not alone. Transnational aid efforts continued after Syrians sent considerable amounts of aid during World War I and continued until one of these efforts evolved in 1925 into the NSP. For example, in July 1920 Hanna Khabbaz, an important author and affiliate of the Protestant church in Homs, Syria,[10] visited the United States to raise funds for the Homs National College.

Khabbaz had visited Flint the previous year and met Ragheb Mitrage and members of the Druze Hamady clan.[11] On his return to the United States, Khabbaz gave a speech in Pittsburgh in Arabic on the first Sunday of July 1920 titled "Life, Freedom, and Righteousness."[12] A committee took up Khabbaz's cause of collecting funds for the college in Syria with links to Flint. Committee members who came together in New York included William Catzeflis, Hanna Nahhas, Abdallah Daʿās, Kāmil ʿArīdah, and others.[13] Following the Paris Peace Conference in 1919, societies and small collectives led by Syrians from the Lebanon and Palestine formed in different parts of the United States to draw attention to Zionism. One of these, the Syrian National Society, published the *Syrian National Bulletin* in Boston. Nationalist Syrian immigrant Ḥabīb Ibrahīm Kātibah, who wrote frequently in the Syrian and U.S. press and would play a pivotal role in the affairs of the Arab National League and the Institute of Arab American Affairs, dedicated the February 1919 issue to "Syria for the Syrians under the guardianship of the United States."[14] In bulletin articles Kātibah discussed the origins of the word *esh-Shām* (or *al-Shām*) and anticipated British and French designs in the region following the Balfour Declaration. He wrote that the borders of Syria "do not exclude Palestine, as is commonly and mistakenly held by a great many of the people of this country [the United States] and Europe." He attributed this error to the "exclusive interest the Christian people of these countries have in the 'Bible Land.'"[15] Hence, Syrians' fears of European colonialism in 1913 continued to color their political commentary after the war.

Ḥabīb Kātibah was born in Yabrud, fifty miles northeast of Damascus, in 1892. He graduated from the Syrian Protestant College (later American University of Beirut) in 1912 and enrolled at Harvard Divinity School in the United States the following year. He completed his academic work specializing in Islam and philosophy at Harvard in 1918 and began to write for newspapers and magazines. In 1924 he was hired as a staff writer for the *Brooklyn Daily Eagle* to cover the Middle East. In 1929 he traveled extensively throughout Syria, Egypt, and Iraq as a foreign correspondent for the *Boston Globe* and the *Detroit News*. In 1933 Kātibah began two years of editing *Syrian World*. He authored several books in Arabic and English, among them *Other Arabian Nights* (1928), *Romances and Folktales* (1929), and *New Spirit in Arab Lands* (1940), in addition to unpublished manuscripts and a translation of the *Orthodox Prayer Book* from Arabic. During World War II he served as senior script editor for the Arabic desk in the Office of War Information. After the war he worked as the New York correspondent for the Cairo-based *Al-Ahram*. Hence, Kātibah's importance in this study draws on the breadth of his experiences as they relate to the contours of Syria's history from his perspective as an immigrant activist.[16] Kātibah knew Fuad Isa Shatara through their work in opposing Jewish immigration. Kātibah began his official work of running the Arab National League at Shatara's invitation in September 1936.

Fuad Isa Shatara was born in Palestine in 1894, attended the British College in Jerusalem, taught for one year, and spent another in Cairo before completing two years of studying medicine at the American University of Beirut. He was conscripted into the Ottoman army in 1914 and managed to escape to the United States, reaching New York in mid-November 1914. He graduated with honors from Columbia University's medical school and practiced medicine in New Jersey and New York until his untimely death in 1942. He founded the Palestine National League about 1923 and relaunched it as the Arab National League in 1936 in response to the general strike in Palestine that year. Numbering anywhere between 10,000 and 15,000 members, the ANL remains the largest Arab American organization per capita to date.[17]

Kātibah was not alone in his activism. Graduates of the Syrian Protestant College, which became the American University of Beirut after 1920, unceasingly put their education and knowledge of Western societies at the service of the Syrian cause once in the United States. Kātibah endeavored to engage the West, including the United States, in support of the Syrian cause following World War I. His arguments in 1919 when Jewish settlement in Palestine with British support became cause for alarm were not very different from demands the NSP would make six years later. However, Kātibah presented the relations of Syria with the West as cooperative and quoted statements by Congressman Julius Kahn, an anti-Zionist Jew, to call attention to Jewish division over "political Zionism." Kātibah argued, that Zionism was "an effort to settle a country already settled and develop a country already developed or being developed by the people themselves."[18] Kātibah invoked scientific surveys published by Encyclopaedia Britannica and biblical studies to paint Natural Syria as surrounded by "the sea on the west, Mount Taurus on the north, and the desert to the east and south."[19] These were the same claims of the First Arab Conference in Paris in 1913, and it made no difference in 1919 what part of Syria was threatened by which colonialist power. The Syria idea was the core issue of the impending British entrenchment in Palestine.

A distinction between political Zionism seeking statehood and the Jewish faith were emphasized in the wake of the Paris Peace Conference, which was attended by a group of Syrian immigrants. An endorsement of Judaism was articulated by Kātibah based on this distinction that would be repeated by Syrian immigrant activists through the creation of Israel in 1948 and beyond. News from Palestine relayed to Syrians a realistic picture of the strides made by the Palestine Bureau that was put in place by the World Zionist Organization and subsequent efforts for agriculture, settlement, and finance. Because Palestine was considered part of Syria, as Kātibah emphasized, Zionism became a cause for alarm among Syrian nationalists. Kātibah welcomed Jewish immigration to Palestine as part of "natural" economic growth in Syria. "We object strongly," he wrote, "to a Jew backed up by a corporation that has a permanent fund [the Jewish National Fund, an English corporation] which will buy and improve the land for him and then sell it to him on the condition that he will not sell it again [to non-Jews]."[20] Before the NSP and later the ANL dominated immigrants' organized political activities, societies on the U.S. East Coast, where Kātibah and Shatara lived and worked, stood behind a unified resolution reaffirming Arab national demands. The Syrian National Society, the New Syria League of New York, the Syrian American Club of Boston, and their branches listed their demands on the last page of the single issue of the *Syrian National Bulletin*:

OUR PLATFORM

Now Therefore, Be it Resolved

I. That Turkish authority—actual or nominal—should not be re-established.

II. That the New Syria shall be a federated union of provinces, each province autonomous within its own borders, yet bonded through one central government into one great nation from the Taurus Mountains to the Sinai Peninsula, free from the difficulties and dangers which beset the severance of one nation into varied spheres of influence, which are bound to hinder the full and freest development of one common people.

III. That the United States assume guardianship and administration of Syria until such time as the Syrians are able to perform the functions of full self–government.[21]

The political framework of inviting the involvement of the noncolonialist United States was intended to moderate French and British hegemony, emphasize Syria's geocultural integrity, and respond to colonialism and Zionism; it was part of a transnational strategy of creating unity among Syrian nationalists in the chaos that followed the fall of Turkey and the Paris Peace Conference in 1919. In the year that followed, violent resistance to British policies erupted among Palestinians, and the British suspected that Palestinian leader Amin al-Husseini was one of the organizers behind the protest.[22] His brother was *mufti* of Jerusalem, the highest religious authority in Palestine, at the time; in 1921 Amin himself would occupy that role. While taking refuge in Damascus, Amin al-Husseini was sentenced to a ten-year imprisonment, but he was pardoned due to his wide appeal and willingness to mediate between Palestinians and the British.

The events brought Amin al-Husseini to the attention of immigrant activists from all parts of Syria. Aside from expulsions, which would become a permanent feature of British dealings with Palestinian leaders, deracination seemed to characterize the experiences of Syrians already abroad. When Ameen Farah resumed contact with his childhood friends after the war, it was under a new set of challenges, as the Turks were no longer an impediment to Syrians' coveted independence. In the chaos of the war's aftermath, at times, impediments to Syrians' goals were not easily recognized. The French and British proclaimed their intentions to smaller, weaker nations and used the League of Nations to obtain legitimacy for control over strategic territories, among which Syria certainly was.

A process of acculturation to Western modes of conduct in economic and social affairs, already in place since Ottoman capitulations, made for an even more complicated social space. The early Jewish settlements in Palestine became in many cases part of the local social mosaic. The fiery nationalist Nicola Qubʿyn now worked for the British in Asyut, the largest town in Upper Egypt, and had other priorities—a recent newborn "Christmas present" he named Albert—that prevented him from visiting Ameen Farah in the United States; Qubʿyn's sister was soon to wed a British national working for his government in Egypt.

Qubʿyn informed Farah in a letter after the war that Jubrān Kuzma had established an Arab-run school (*madrasah waṭanīyah*) in Nazareth that lasted a while despite "repression by the Greek Basilica until it was forced to close its doors."[23] Kuzma contacted Qubʿyn concerning a planned project of sugar production in Galilee, he wrote. Qubʿyn concluded by telling Farah that he was waiting for things to settle down in Syria so he could return because he was fed up with being treated as an outsider in Egypt. The same year, Farah acted on a promise he made to himself during his stint in Uncle Sam's army of publishing *Rushd wa Suha*.[24] Though the message in his novel remained pertinent, the political reality was changing very rapidly, and the friends' plans for an international secret society fighting for Syria's independence were complicated by a new reality in which European influence took precedence.

On June 30, 1922, Syrian immigrants from Flint to Boston and elsewhere received ominous news from the homeland and local newspapers that the U.S. Congress endorsed the Balfour Declaration in reluctantly ratifying the League of Nations charter. The mandate legalized by the League of Nations on July 24 went into effect per the San Remo Agreement on September 19, 1923, with the language of the Balfour Declaration. Immigrant activists, most notably Kātibah, Shatara, Malouf, and Hitti, explained the Syrian side in the U.S. press largely through the *New York Times*. They spoke to audiences whenever they could to inform them that Palestine was part of Syria and the conflict was not religious in nature.[25] The general public in the United States interpreted the conflict as a religious one because of ignorance of Islam and because the Turks who fought against the Allies were predominantly Muslims, not to mention the widespread news, thanks to the tireless efforts of Henry Morgenthau, of atrocities Turks committed against Christian Armenians. Hence, the contours and personalities took shape in the uphill battle of educating the U.S. public on Arab history and religions.

Few Americans outside those doing missionary work understood that Christian Arab populations had lived throughout the Middle East since ancient times, and it mattered little that a great number of activists were

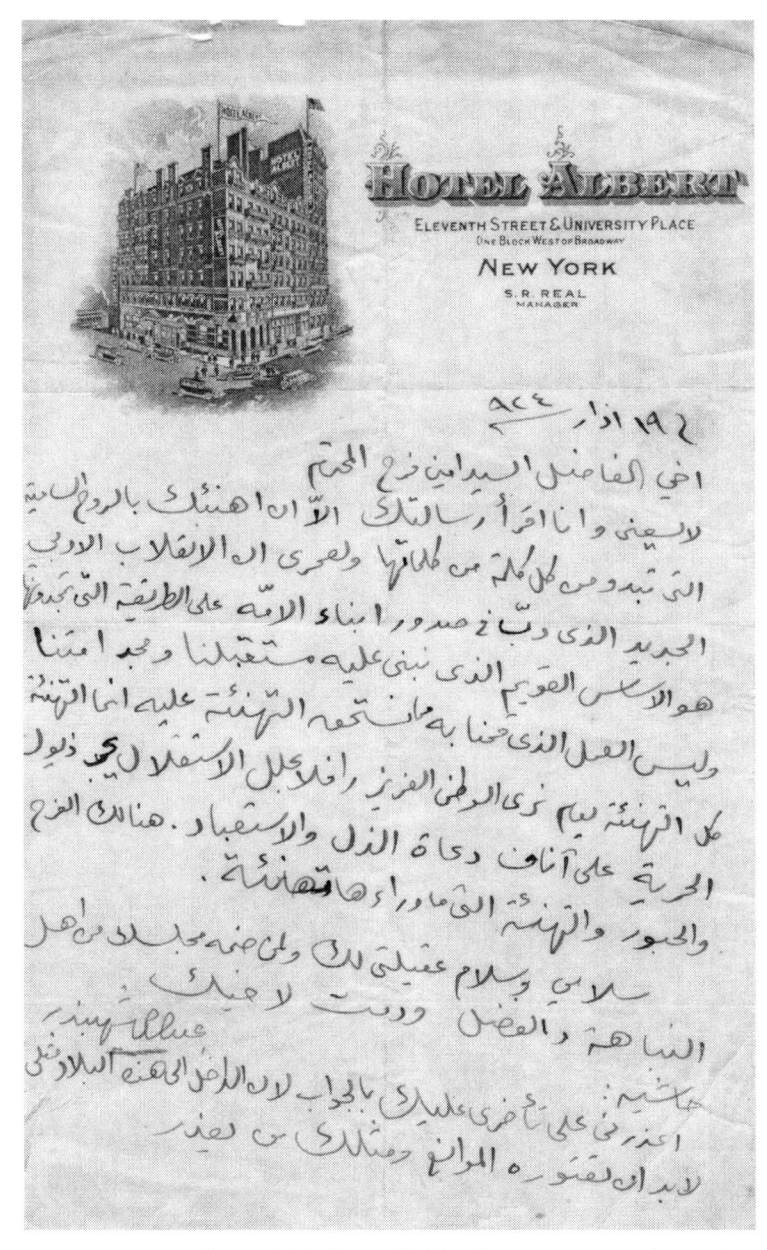

HOTEL ALBERT
ELEVENTH STREET & UNIVERSITY PLACE
ONE BLOCK WEST OF BROADWAY
NEW YORK
S. R. REAL
MANAGER

١٩ اذار ٩٢٤

اخي الفاضل السيد امين فرح المحترم

وصلتني واناأقرأ رسالتك الآ ان اهنئك بالروح السامية
التي تبدو من كل كلمة من كلماتها ولعمري ان الانقلاب الأدبي
الجديد الذي دبّ في صدور ابناء الامة على الطريقة التي يجدها
هو الأساس القويم الذي نبني عليه مستقبلنا ومجد امتنا
وليس العمل الذي حنا به مانتعبه الرنة عليه انما الرنة
كل الرنة بما في الوطن العزيز واقبل جلل الاستقلال يحيي ذوو
الحرية على أنات دعاة الذل والاستعباد. هنالك الفخ
والخلود والرنة الحقا ورائ ها متهانئة.

سلامي وسلام عشيرتي لك ولمن حوله محبك من أهل
النباهة والفضل وديت لا عدمت

جاثم:
اعتذر من علي أفندي عليك بالجواب لان الراحل الى قطر البلاد رشي
لابد ان تقصر به الموانئ ومثلك من يعذر

FIGURE 4.3. *Letter from Abdelrahman Shahbandar to Ameen Farah, March 19, 1924. Shahbandar was replying to Farah's letter of thanks for visiting Flint as part of a delegation to raise awareness about the Syrian issue and seek support from the diaspora. Farah Papers, Bawardi Collection.*

Christians. When the situation reached a boiling point in Syria in 1925, this ignorance of the Middle East was an opportunity for Naʿūm Mokarzel to fuel suspicion against Islam and Muslims in the English-language press on behalf of the French government's policies in Syria. On November 29, 1925, an article signed by Mokarzel was published in the *New York Times* under the title "Syria a Religious Problem: A Western Power's Protection Is Declared Essential until Islam Learns to Be Tolerant—Situation Unchanged Since the Crusades." The article painted Islam as the eternal enemy of civilization and of the West, and it tied the conflict to the Crusades from Europe's medieval era. The article left no doubts that Christians did not belong in the Arab Middle East and that French intervention was their only salvation.

H. I. Kātibah answered Mokarzel's attack on Islam and advocacy of French occupation, also in the *New York Times*, under the title "Islam and Christians in Syria." Kātibah explained that the occupation would take "a French soldier with bayonet in hand over the head of every Mohammedan there" and wondered if the French were willing to go to that extent "in their infatuation with the Syrian Christians." Another reply came from Emile Morhig, the director of the Independence Party of Syria in New York, in the same issue of the *New York Times*. In a clear reference to the work of the Syrian Relief Committee, Morhig wrote that Druze and other Muslims came to the aid of Maronite Christians among others when the siege of the Turks by the Allies caused devastating famines during World War I.

There is no evidence that meaningful numbers of Syrians from the Lebanon or elsewhere advocated French occupation and the separation of Lebanon from the rest of Syria once the mandate became entrenched. This is to say that two developments occurred: growing opposition to French policies muffled progressive Francophile sentiments, and past experience gained by mobilizing the immigrants behind aid efforts made the transition to political mobilization easier. After all, Nadra Haddad, ʿAbbas Abu Shaqra, and Nasib Arida were among the nationalists who served on the board of the Syrian Relief Committee as encouraged by U.S. neutrality. By 1917 the inertia of aid efforts contributed to Rihani's idea of creating the Syrian Liberation Committee (Lajnat tahrīr Sūrīya). Gibran answered his friend's call and proudly served as its secretary: "Great tragedies enlarge the heart. I have never been given the chance to serve my people in a work of this sort."[26]

Incongruent French and British policies meant that Syrians' challenges in Jerusalem and the Galilee differed from those in Damascus, Beirut, and Homs, where the French attempted to imprint their stamp in a colonial competition of cultural brutality with the British. Yet Syrian nationalists' problems were compounded by internal divisions, tribalism, self-serving notables, and poverty in rural areas. Meanwhile, the violence in Palestine continued to escalate due to the British policy of allowing Jewish settlement even when Jewish arrivals "rarely filled the [British-imposed] quotas."[27] The French faced mounting opposition from the Syrian population and responded with increased militarism. Opposition in the French Parliament, coupled with increased awareness of recurring atrocities by French troops, resulted in uniform opposition in France and Syria to the French Mandate but not in an official capacity by Western governments. In the United States, press reports ranged from characteristically more accurate coverage by the *New York Times*, for the time being, to less so in the *Los Angeles Times* to verging on anti-Arab racism in the *Chicago Daily Tribune*.[28]

Despite divisions among Syrians, the uncertain status of Syria and their persistent aspirations for independence turned the country into a tinderbox. Discontent with French policies began to spread to rural areas commensurate with French mistreatment of Syria's Druze population. The situation reached a critical point in terms of media coverage in the United States in October 1925 after the French killed 1,200 Syrian prisoners of war and destroyed parts of Damascus under orders from Maurice Sarrail, the French high commissioner general. The killings were covered in the Arabic- and English-language press,[29] drew condemnation from France's allies, and caused considerable embarrassment to the French government. Even the British were provoked to intervene, drawing the French government's attention to the atrocities Sarrail had ordered.[30] Syrians on both sides of the waters found themselves unified behind a popular revolt. News coverage helped introduce immigrants to leaders of the revolt in Syria including Michele Lotfallah, a Palestinian Christian; Abdelrahman Shahbandar, a progressive Sunni clergyman; and the Druze Sultan Zeid al-Atrash.[31]

Amid foreign occupation and the spread of nearly unrestricted violence, pressures quickly taxed Syrian immigrants' limited means and influence. Pressures came from the two competing colonialist powers, Zionists searching for a solution to past repression in Russia and anti-Semitism in Europe, and a growing need for aid in all parts of Syria due to the worsening economic conditions and wars. The NSP led efforts to connect immigrants with their former homelands during a critical period in the region's history.

Ameen Farah, like many Syrians, resolved to participate in an organized effort to counter French and British occupation in Syria on the heels of the reported brutality by French troops. He had renewed old contacts with Jamal al-Husseini, secretary of the Palestine Arab Action Committee and brother of Hajj Amin al-Husseini. Farah contacted Jamal Husseini and

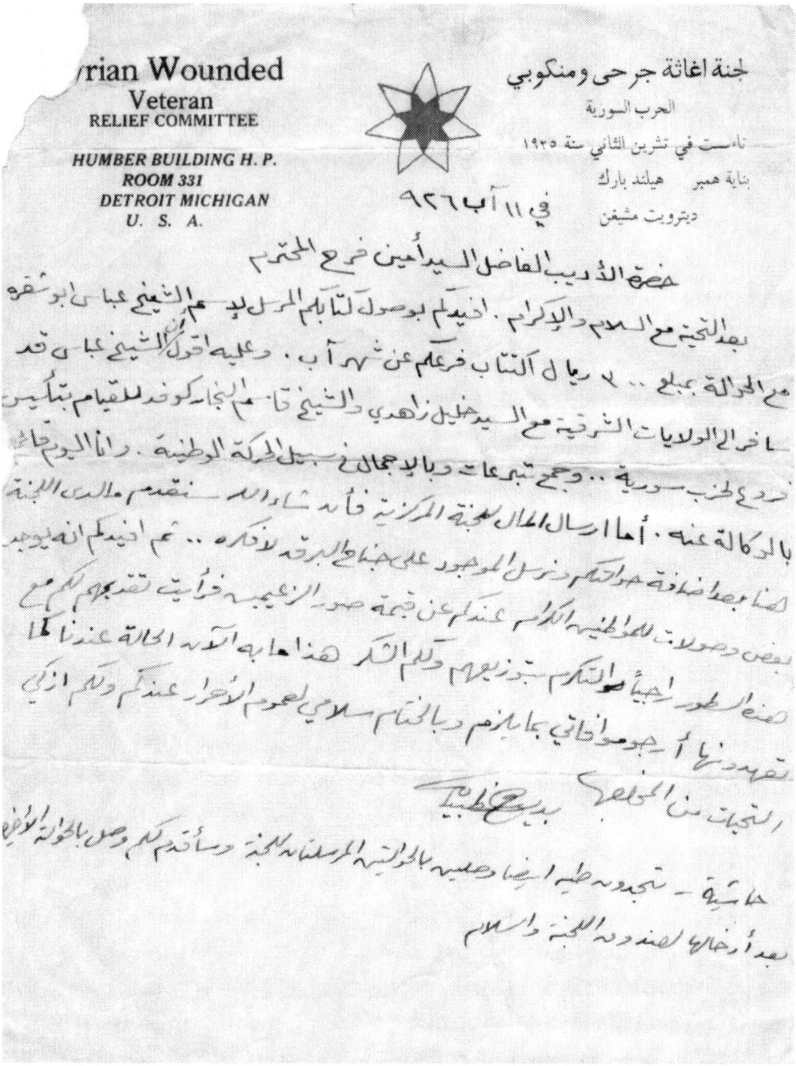
...rian Wounded
Veteran
RELIEF COMMITTEE

HUMBER BUILDING H. P.
ROOM 331
DETROIT MICHIGAN
U. S. A.

لجنة اغاثة جرحى ومنكوبي
الحرب السورية
تأسست في تشرين الثاني سنة ١٩٢٥
بناية همبر هيلند بارك
ديترويت مشيغن

في ١١ آب ٩٢٦

حضرة الأديب الفاضل السيد أمين فرح المحترم

المخلص
بديع ظبيان

FIGURE 4.4. *Letter from Badiʿ Thibiyan to Ameen Farah, August 11, 1926. Thibiyan sent the letter from the headquarters of the Syrian Wounded Veteran Relief Committee. He acknowledges receipt of $300 from the Flint branch and writes that ʿAbbas Abu Shaqra, Khalil Zahdi, and Sheikh Qasem al-Najjar were touring the eastern United States to establish NSP chapters. Farah Papers, Bawardi Collection.*

reminded him of the previous "project of Reverend Benjamin Haddad" in Lebanon to the north of Nazareth with the brothers Kamal and Hilmi Husseini prior to Farah's departure from Nazareth.[32] In his letter Farah asked for a copy of the bylaws of the Palestine Higher Executive either to weigh a decision of whether to send funds through the committee to the Druze fighting the French or to use the document as a blueprint for the bylaws of a planned collective in Michigan. Ragheb Mitrage, who financed Arida and Naimy's *Al-Funūn*, and a Druze friend, Fuad Abu ʿAjram, joined Farah in figuring out the best channel for their patriotic sentiments as the revolt spread. By this time, January 1925, Syrian nationalists in Flint maintained membership in their city's Pan-Syrian Party, which would later add "Affiliated with the New Syria Party" to its letterhead. Not enough material is available on the Pan-Syrian Party in Flint, but existing documents suggest that it was active in contacting members of the U.S. Congress to lobby for a proactive role by the United States in the face of French violence even before the prison massacre.

Volunteers initially assembled information for periodic reports about the NSP's activities, bookkeeping, and preparation for public events. The party grew very rapidly due to the euphoria caused by Syrian rebels' speedy military victories in 1925 and early 1926. With more chapters and presumably donations and inquiries, an executive committee was assembled and set about hiring someone with a command of the English language to oversee administrative operations. The level of organization and financial stability attained by the New Syria Party is evident in its offering $3,000 (equivalent to $39,000 in 2013) to Nathmi Anabtawi, who appeared to be the most suitable candidate for the job. Anabtawi pounced on the offer and ignored hints that the party needed to use some of its budget for office expenses and the like. He responded: "I received your telegram offering me the secretariat job for a salary between $2,500 and $3,000. I accepted the offer immediately asking you to make the salary $3,000, the reason being that family affairs demand that I send some money to the homeland."[33] In this short letter of acceptance Anabtawi left the matters of office necessities to Ameen Farah and indicated without further explanation that his plan, presumably for how he would manage the NSP's affairs, was "known and needed no elaboration" due to "time constraints." He concluded by adding a side note characteristic of Arab hyperbole, emphasizing that money was secondary to the more important task of "doing what's necessary to serve the *ummah*."

Unfortunately for the party, Anabtawi proved self-serving, incompetent, and mostly concerned about pursuing his own education and financial gain. Along with his salary, the NSP faced problems associated with transitioning into using the English language and fashioning a fitting agenda for an American audience—a new undertaking indeed for this generation of newcomers—let alone establishing a national presence. The challenges did not stop its members from projecting Syrians' national demands onto the international stage, especially at the League of Nations in Geneva, where the Druze exile Shakib Arslan unofficially represented Syria and Palestine. An overarching problem, clearly, was the brutally effective campaign by the French against the rebels in Syria, and immigrants did not abandon their support for the NSP until the revolt was put down completely in 1927. A more immediate dilemma may have been related to getting aid into the right hands and maintaining unity. Farah inquired about the fate of funds in a letter to his old friend Najib Nassar, editor of *Al-Karmel* newspaper in Palestine, after a long introduction and side conversation. After requesting a subscription to be sent to NSP headquarters in Detroit, Farah informed the journalist about the party and its aims and accomplishments in responding to propaganda by the French. He alluded in his letter to the Flint affiliates' confidence in U.S. Senator William E. Borah, chairman of the Senate Foreign Relations Committee.[34]

Getting to his point in carefully crafted language, Farah confided to Nassar that "a great deal of funds" had been sent to the rebels through what he called the Jerusalem Committee, headed by Muhammad Amin al-Husseini: "As a member of the party's executive committee (the only Christian member in it) I want, confidentially, to know from you for certain if the money is safe in the hands of the Jerusalem Committee and whether the committee is capable of accomplishing the task or not . . . whether it is spent on salaries, rent and equipment, and so on. . . . We do not think ill of any members of the committee, nor do we know any of them personally, but public money is easily squandered."

Farah disclosed to Nassar that the longer the revolt lasted, the more people would be attracted to the ranks of the nationalists and would send aid to the homeland. He added that Syrians were astonished by the success of the rebels and were filled with pride as a result.[35] Besides the immediate concerns of logistics and administrative pains, long-term and recurring obstacles appeared on the horizon during the NSP's experiment with mass political organizing. Farah's observation that the party drew strength from the revolt implied that the party would grow weaker without it.

Feelings of unity among Syrians before and immediately after World War I were born of shared memories of the past and a common language, the elements of *nahḍah*. But the reasons that Christians, Shi'a, and Sunnis in Highland Park, Michigan, would rally behind a Druze-led revolt and that

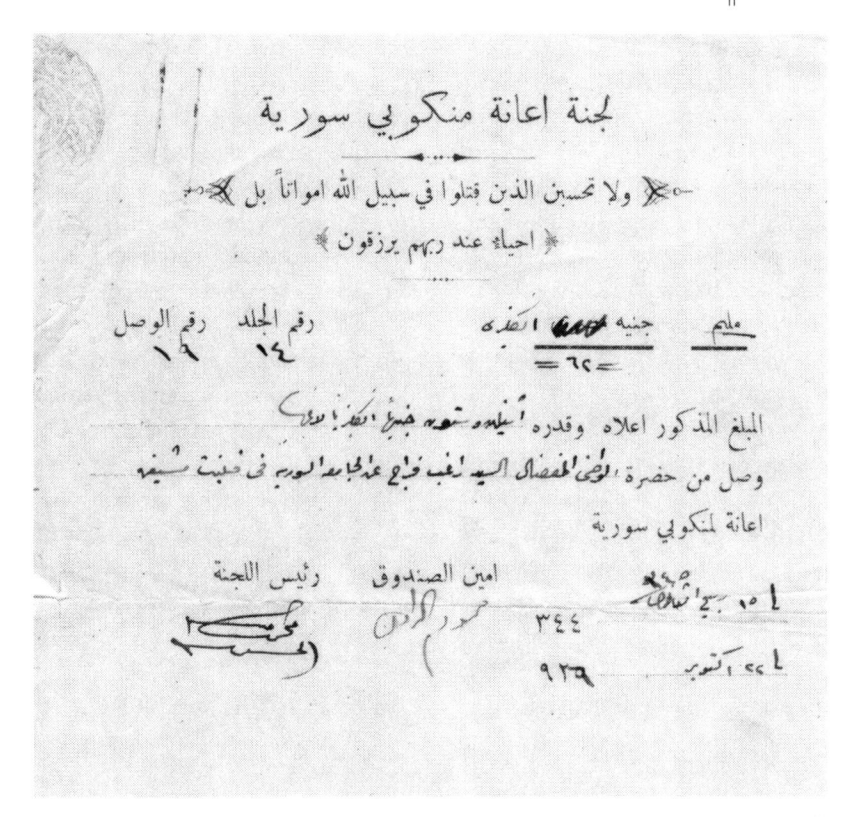

FIGURE 4.5. *Receipt for sixty-two pounds made out to Ameen Farah on stationery of the Committee for the Aid of Syrian War Victims, October 22, 1926. It is signed by the head of the committee, Hajj Amin al-Husseini, who transferred the funds from his Jerusalem office to the Syrian rebellion. Farah Papers, Bawardi Collection.*

most strata of Syrian society, save notables—whose economic interests often intertwined with French policies—would join the rebellion have to do with the realization that Syrian resistance posed a serious challenge to colonialism in general.

Recent scholarship acknowledging the significance of the Syrian revolt helps put immigrants' experiment with the NSP in perspective as an important undertaking on both sides of the Atlantic. Michael Provence, in *The Great Syrian Revolt and the Rise of Arab Nationalism*, examines the alliances and military training under Ottoman rule attained by the leaders of the revolt, and he qualifies salient perceptions that the revolt was the work of primordial networks of feudal lords seeking to preserve their landholdings and positions.[36] Provence concludes that the Syrian revolt was the most significant challenge to colonialism in the interwar period and as such was the reason Sarrail clamped down on news reports from Syria.[37] Immigrants, thanks to the U.S. press, were not hostage to the news blackout by the French on incidents of brutality and the gains attained by the rebels. Members of the NSP responded to the needs of the Druze in the Shouf Mountains and Suwaida and later in Houran near the border with Trans-Jordan. Provence provides a framework for NSP's inevitable demise when he describes in detail how the French razed villages and exiled or executed the rebels they captured.

The first report on the operation of the NSP establishes that the collective was founded in February 1926 and describes its operations for the three months prior to the date of the report, May 3, 1926. My translations of the reports capture traces of immigrants' awareness and interpretations of their activities in the NSP based on the only known records. For example, addressing the report to Farah, a Christian, is implicit acknowledgement of nonsectarianism by the collective. The report does not make extensive references to spirituality or outward expressions of piety, nor does the Druze author and important intellectual 'Abbas Abu Shaqra claim a distinct role in the NSP.

These are the highlights of the report addressed to "the venerable Ameen Farah, member of the executive committee of the New Syria Party," during a general time of euphoria after rebel gains in Syria:

> In the name of the true and sacred national duty, I present to you the three-month account since the establishment of the New Syria Party, which is the first general body ['umūmīyah] in the history of Syrian immigration, established by a resolution of the First General Syrian Convention to achieve the noblest aims and stipulated for its founding in its charter.
>
> The first three months ... were a period of building the foundation of the party, during which an office was opened and branches were established after arduous and lengthy correspondences and negotiations. The places where branches were formed are St. Paul, Minnesota; Grand Rapids, Michigan; Flint, Michigan; Norphlet, Arkansas; Saginaw, Michigan; Princeton, West Virginia; and Greater New York. Al-Bakūra al-Durziya [a Druze society] in Detroit joined the party, and there are letters in the office promising new branches in Newark, New Jersey; Danbury, Connecticut; Messina, New York; and Norfolk, Virginia, and we received a letter from Naseeb Rashid, a committee member in Norwalk, Connecticut, informing us of the establishment of a branch in Georgetown, North Carolina.

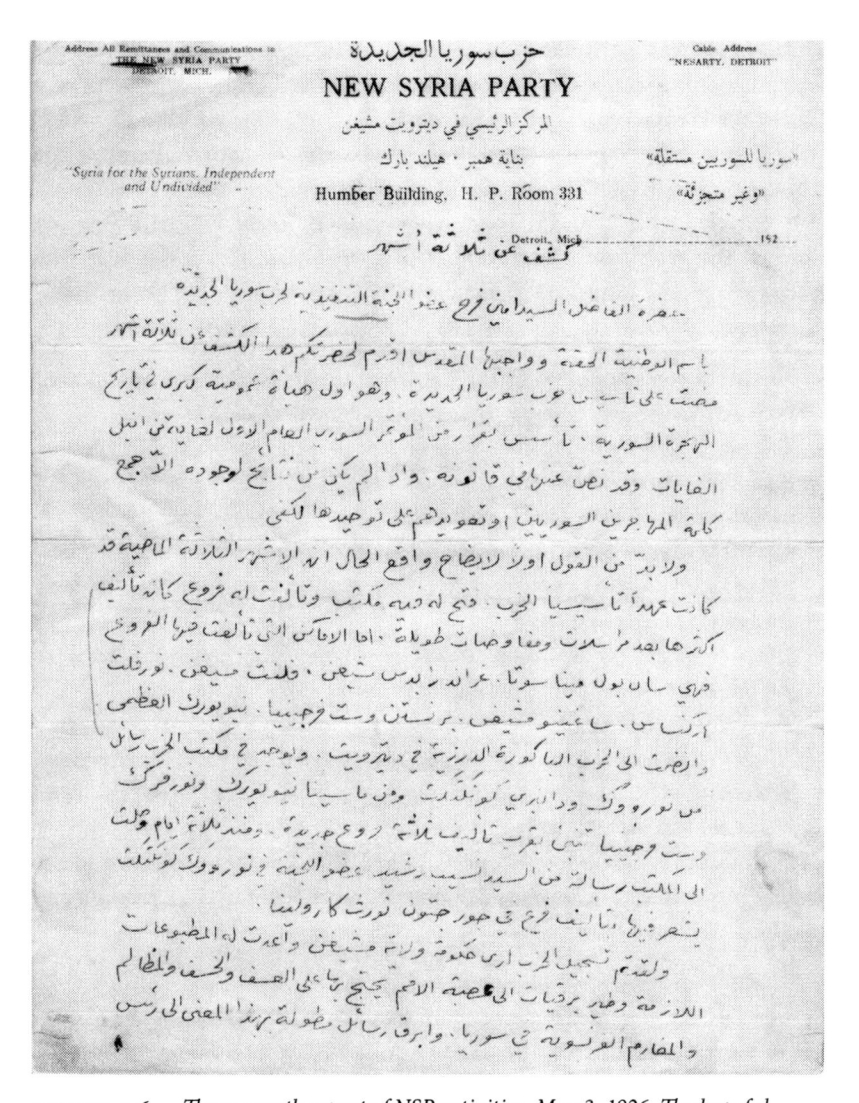

FIGURE 4.6. *Three-month report of NSP activities, May 3, 1926. The hopeful three-page report describes the NSP as "the first great body in the history of Syrian immigration"; it lists several new chapters and outlines plans to aid Syria, "a single coherent region of the Arab regions." Farah Papers, Bawardi Collection.*

The party was registered with the state of Michigan, stationery for its use was prepared, and telegrams were whisked to the League of Nations protesting the French repression and atrocities in Syria. Telegrams to this effect were also sent to the president of the United States, Senator William Borah, Charles Crane (coauthor of the ill-fated King-Crane Report to Woodrow Wilson in 1919), and numerous newspapers in the United States and Europe. The report said important events were disclosed to the "[*Detroit*] *News*, one of the leading newspapers in this country."[38] The report listed other highlights:

- The party communicated to the leaders of the revolution the immigrants' preparedness to lend support financially and intellectually.
- The party telegraphed Prince Shakib Arslan and Ihsan al-Jabiri alerting them that they could officially represent the membership in councils and European conventions.
- The party offered its backing to the executive committee of the Syrian Palestinian Delegation in Egypt and asked King Abdulazīz Āl-Saud to turn his attention to the Syrian issue.
- The party raised funds through public events, increased awareness throughout the country, and published details of Syrian events in the press.
- The party disseminated reports from the headquarters of the national revolution through the Committee to Aid the Afflicted and disseminated these letters and received acknowledgment of donations sent to Jerusalem, from which aid was distributed to the intended destinations.
- The executive secretary of the party visited branches for the purpose of enhancing cooperation between its Central Committee and the Committee to Aid the Afflicted.[39]

Along with the list of chapters, the report identified forty-nine members in Detroit, seventeen members of al-Bakūra al-Durziya, and an average of fourteen members in each of the branches established to that date. It closes with optimistic predictions for more successes in the future.[40] Two aspects of the report help answer impending attacks by the French mouthpiece Na'ūm Mokarzel: first, there is no evidence that the Druze members of the NSP constituted a majority; second, they founded the party as a kind of immigrant equivalent to Druze prominence in Syria. Al-Bakūra al-Durziya, one of the oldest Arab Druze American societies in the country, transferred its seventeen members to the NSP after the latter was founded by a cross-section of immigrants concerned about French imperialism.

The strain of sporadic news that some Syrian leaders were forced to surrender to the French added to a general air of chaos and uncertainty. The

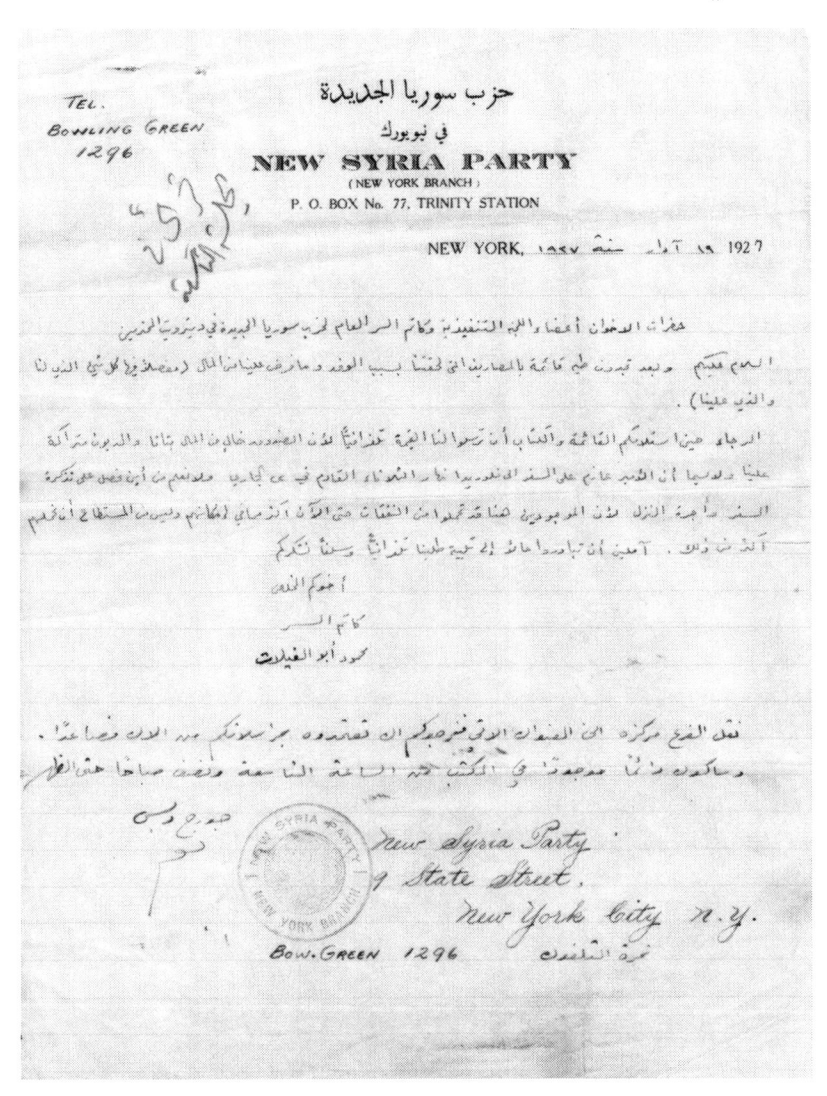

FIGURE 4.7. *Letter from Mahmoud Abulfilat of the New York chapter of NSP, March 19, 1927. He urgently asks for funds to cover expenses of the visiting delegation. Farah Papers, Bawardi Collection.*

relatively few Syrian immigrants in general faced a monumental public relations task, and most members were still building their own economic lives while also carrying the burden of financing the NSP. Farah, who had just established his prosperous A. Farah and Khouri grocery retail business in Flint, followed the report with an undated correspondence to the NSP's office in Highland Park. In it he expressed concerns over differences between Detroit's two competing chapters of the party that were exacerbated by the precarious military position of the rebels and disparate levels of education among the members. Farah suggested a solution to problems on the local scene—to form a separate committee not affiliated with the NSP but sharing its political aims. This, Farah wrote, would lead to "disinfecting the [NSP] body of the whims and germs of Detroit's clannish societies [ahlīyah]."

Farah suggested a strategy of insulating the proposed committee from anticipated political posturing in preparation for a second NSP convention.[41] In a subsequent correspondence he urged John (Hanna) Nasr of Detroit to meet his obligations to the tripartite collectives of the Masonic Society, the Orthodox Fraternity, and the Syrian Club, "all of which demand that you serve the cause of the homeland."[42] Farah absolved Nasr of the criticism by others that he was a "leftist socialist" and requested that Nasr leave the Masons alone for a time and dedicate a year of service to the homeland through the NSP: "If nothing comes of it, we can both withdraw knowing that we did our part."

Details of the party's day-to-day operations in Farah's papers and correspondences paint a realistic picture of any political collective under stressful conditions. Seeking ways to have an impact in the homeland despite monumental difficulties illustrates a consciousness of the members' collective duty. But the feeling of obligation collided with the limits of immigrants' capabilities as they pondered making their presence known. Their aim was to weigh in on the decisions made by the League of Nations by publicly lending their support to the rebels. In response to Farah's letter to the NSP headquarters, Lutfi al-Saʿdi informed Farah that he had met Nasr, who seemed to have listened to Farah and answered Saʿdi's call to join a meeting for like-minded individuals. Saʿdi and Hanna Nasr were joined by Nicola Khouri, Ahmad Diāb, George Nasr, Salahaddin al-Ayoubi, and Hasan Jabiri in Saʿdi's office, and they decided to form a chapter of patriots. However, in a planned follow-up meeting, Saʿdi regretted that only he, Hanna Nasr, Khouri, and Diāb showed up; they decided instead to attend the party's general meeting in room 303 of the Humber Building at the party's headquarters in Highland Park.

In the general meeting it became evident, Saʿdi reported to Farah, that the conflicting backgrounds in "social class, environment, and education" made for a bitter exchange. This convinced Hanna Nasr and Nicola Khouri that the idea of an alternative party would not attract a sufficient number of like-minded individuals.[43] Although it is not explicitly mentioned in the correspondence, I estimate that intra-Muslim division exacerbated by disparate

FIGURE 4.8. *NSP delegates from the United States, Canada, and Mexico attending the banquet in honor of Shakib Arslan at the Book-Cadillac Hotel, Detroit, January 15, 1927. Farah Papers, Bawardi Collection.*

educational backgrounds accounted at least in part for problems within the party. Farah's plans to channel aid through the Husseinis in Jerusalem due to the French blockade of the rebels most likely did not meet the approval of all Shi'a members. Farah attempted to assess the gravity of the situation in a correspondence he sent to Suleiman Baddūr, himself a Druze and the co-publisher and editor of the widely regarded *Al-Bayān* newspaper. In the letter Farah confessed his worries: "Lately, lack of confidence in the Jerusalem Aid Committee has spread among the immigrants. Is there any merit to this?" He asked for clear and honest answers from the editor because the party put its full trust in the committee during the first convention due to the danger that financial aid from immigrants would stop if the "rumor spreads."[44] I have found no reply from Baddūr among Farah's papers.

Despite sporadic internal discord and what must have been their oppressively demanding business lives, members remained committed. Correspondence from the chapters sometimes used the business letterhead of members' retail and manufacturing businesses. For example, a letter from Ali Muhyiddīn listed the return address as "Mahadeen Bros. Manufacturers of Lace Embroideries, 469 Summit Avenue, West Hoboken, N.J.," reflecting

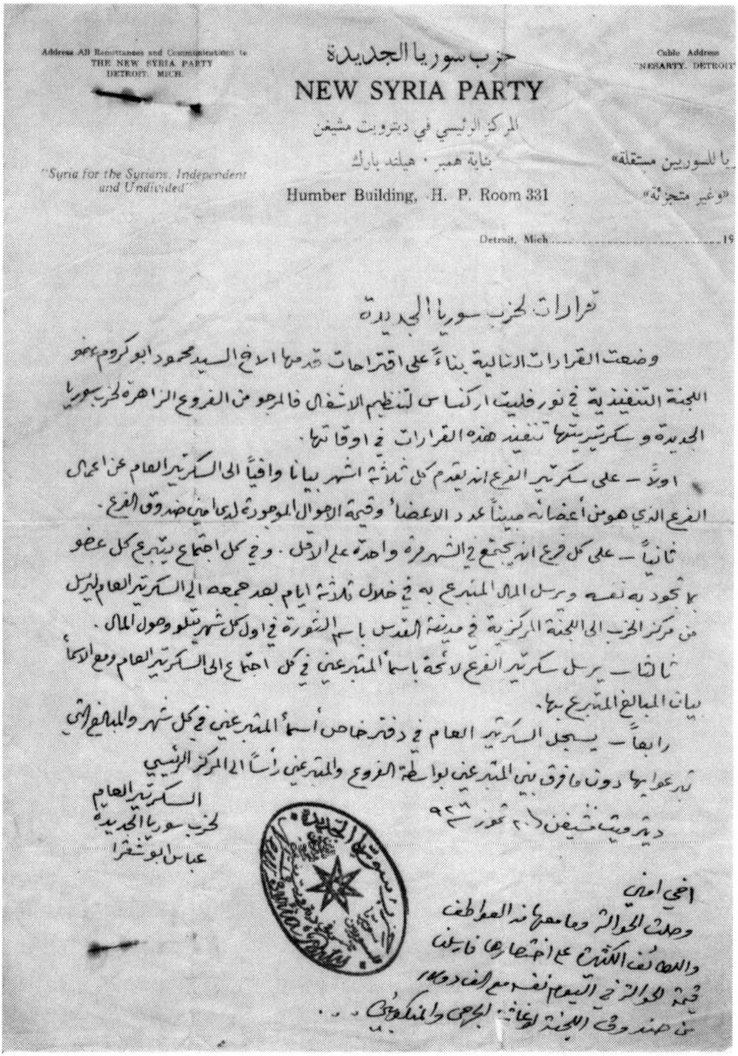

FIGURE 4.9. *Amendments to the NSP bylaws, July 20, 1926. These were requested by Mahmud Abu Kuroum of Arkansas and signed by ʿAbbas Abu Shaqra. The letterhead indicates the party's headquarters in Highland Park. Farah Papers, Bawardi Collection.*

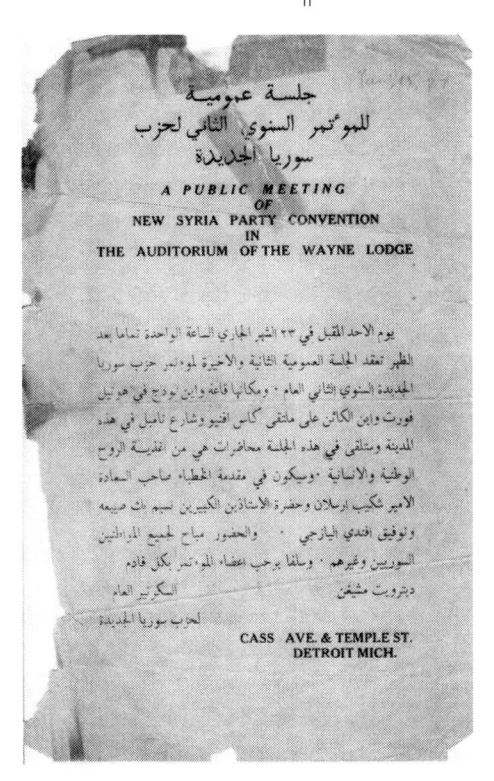

FIGURE 4.10. *Public invitation to a meeting on January 23, 1927. The invitation announces that Shakib Arslan, Nasīm Saybaʿa, and Tawfīq al-Yāziji would speak at the meeting as part of the NSP's Second Annual Convention. Farah Papers, Bawardi Collection.*

the name spelling he adopted. The letter expressed Muhyiddīn's opinion on an issue already under discussion in Michigan, that of establishing an English-language Syrian information center in the diaspora. He wrote that this was an old and sound idea supported by many. The idea of an information office was a critical line of thinking and an indication that immigrants began to see the need for enhancing their effectiveness in their communities. Influencing public opinion would be the very essence of subsequent efforts by many NSP members who transferred their membership to the Arab National League and later the far more sophisticated Institute of Arab American Affairs.

It may have been too soon for the relatively small Syrian immigrant population to influence the polity or imprint its stamp on the American cultural and social composite, but that did not stop the members from trying or mean the NSP was not a representative body of Syrian immigrants. A full information office may have been beyond their level of resources and sophistication. However, Muhyiddīn anticipated the emergence of a new generation of Syrian Americans when he expressed his hopes that the problem would be solved with time. NSP member Muhyiddīn, who would later join the ANL, did not stop there; he expressed his compatriots' frustrations at the entrenched indifference of the U.S. government to what emergent Syrian American citizens viewed as the United States' global obligation. He pointed out the need to rally even more immigrants behind political work. His letter continues:

> But most importantly, our lack of confidence that even minimum tangible results can be achieved from propaganda in America because all our efforts in the past and experiences of knocking on doors taught us that there is no use. Even if we owned a newspaper like the [New York] Times we have little hope of convincing America of intervening in Syria, and the French understand only force. . . . We are in need of propaganda within our ranks in order to unify our stance and assemble a legion that contributes money and alleviates harsh financial conditions in the homeland. After we are unified and confident, we can knock on America's doors, but the condition of the party in its present shape does not escape you; if you launch another party, this may cause confusion with dire consequences . . . especially if you hand the affairs of running the office to Mr. Nathmi [Anabtawi]. I say this frankly because Nathmi is incapable of such work, as we tested him and found him to be hasty, and he has personal aims of mostly financial gain; you'd best keep the current secretary. If you had to change the administration, why not call for an extraordinary meeting of the executive committee to discuss the best ways of unifying efforts and shaking off this stoicism? . . . If peace reigns tomorrow, it will take years for this wretched ummah's wounds to heal. Let us concern ourselves only with collecting money, for this is how we can benefit the homeland. Every year we spend on propaganda in America and elsewhere is a loss, and I believe that the surest way to collect funds is to increase members and branches.[45]

Farah wrote Muhyiddīn on the same day that the latter wrote him, that is, before Farah had a chance to read its contents. In his letter Farah deemed it necessary to establish a Syrian information office in the *mahjar*, a matter that was approved by the Pan-Syrian Party in Flint, now affiliated with the NSP in Detroit. The information office would have two functions, to increase membership and to disseminate information to newspapers, books, and magazines and in other printed material in the United States and beyond. Despite the difficulties in finding a qualified person to manage the information office, Ameen Farah wrote that the manager had to be fluent in English. Abu Shaqra, although a well-respected and capable author in his native language, fell short of this requirement. "We need a person who can compose political reports, translate, and author propaganda . . . and roam the country and inject the spirit of nationalism in the nationalists and inspect the branches," Farah wrote. He suggested Nathmi Anabtawi before he learned of Muhyiddīn's qualms about his choice. Armed with a commission by NSP officers Salman Yousef Azzam and Najm Haidar, Farah budgeted $3,000 for the task divided as follows.[46]

Salary for the director of the office: $2,100
Stationery and stamps: $150
Pamphlets and books: $250
Travel expenses: $200
Miscellaneous expenses: $300

Anabtawi became an obstacle and may have hindered the party's efforts in some respects. His posturing is worthy of note because it illustrates the party's earnest albeit unfulfilled desire for an educated operator as it targeted public opinion in the adopted country and in the League of Nations. A communication from the unscrupulous Anabtawi underscored Arab immigrants' awareness of the need to expand their reach beyond the confines of their own community despite the trouble of overcoming the hype and large egos of unspecified individuals in Detroit. Anabtawi's scant though pretentious communications, carrying a return address in New Haven, Connecticut, indicated that Muhyiddīn's fears were well founded. Anabtawi said he deeply regretted writing that a report sent to the branches by ʿAbbas Abu Shaqra was incomplete, and he explained in his letters how busy he had been with his annual exams and made several trivial observations. Anabtawi likely dampened spirits by condemning sending the considerable amount of $5,000 in aid to the rebels as embarrassingly trivial, saying that it would not "replace 10 destroyed homes."[47]

Anabtawi's response to Farah's question about the best ways to organize the office was a classic show of lip service, the very trait *nahḍah* intellectuals discouraged: "You are like one asking to run a factory by writing letters only," he replied, then preached that capable management "requires predicting events before they occur."[48] Anabtawi, probably mindful of the party's need for someone with fluency in English, ended the response with yet another unsubstantiated claim that he wrote an article for *The Nation* "amounting to four printed pages (single spaced)" and would send a copy to Farah once it was published. He also wrote that he provided information to "a lady" writing for *Asia* magazine that would "appear shortly."[49]

In July 1926 Abu Shaqra sent a list of resolutions by the executive committee of the NSP to all branches in an apparent effort to engender organization and accountability. He disclosed that several decisions were adopted based on recommendations by Mahmud Abu Kuroum, a member of the executive committee in the Norphlet, Arkansas, branch, and that secretaries of branches were required to present comprehensive reports every three months of membership, available funds, and accomplishments. Other recommendations included the following.

1. Each branch was required to meet once a month, collect donations, and send the money within three days to the general secretary, who in turn would send the money, the month it was collected, from the party's headquarters to the Central Committee in Jerusalem in the name of the revolution.
2. The secretary of each branch was to send to the general secretary a list of the donors and the respective amounts they donated.
3. The general secretary was to document in a dedicated register the names of the donors each month and the amounts they donated regardless of whether the donations were sent to the branch or directly to the headquarters.[50]

The report ended by informing Farah that the money transfer he sent was received and forwarded along with $1,000 to the Committee to Aid the Afflicted in Jerusalem.

Some letters to Farah explained the humanitarian aid component of the party's function. I could not discern from the available documents if all aid sent by way of Jerusalem and other venues was intended for the rebels or if different channels were used for different destinations. Either way, the intense suspicion toward any insurgents in the United States—still in the shadows of the Bolshevik Revolution and the Red Scare just six years prior—must have made it necessary to maintain the humanitarian aspect of sending aid.

In August Farah received a letter from Badi' Thibiyan under the dual English and Arabic letterhead of the Syrian Wounded Veteran Relief Committee Lajnat I'anat al-Mankūbīn fi Sūriya. The Arabic text indicated that the committee was founded in November 1925 and its address was the Humber Building in Highland Park, the same building as the party's headquarters. This lone letter from the relief organization confirms that the NSP was preceded by a massive effort to collect funds by the same group that assumed the NSP name in the first convention. The letter was sent from Highland Park to Farah in Flint:

> Venerable Mr. Ameen Farah,
> Greetings. This is to confirm your letter to Sheikh ʿAbbas Abu Shaqra with the amount of $300.00 for August. Sheikh ʿAbbas departed to the eastern states with Khalil Zahdi and Sheikh Qasem al-Najjar as a delegation to establish branches for Syria's party and collecting aid for the national cause. I am serving today in his place. As for sending the funds to the Central Committee, we, God willing, will add your receipts to what we have and send the total speedily.[51]

A letter from Muhammad Musa al-Tawil to "the nationalist zealot [and] the head of the Syrian Arab Committee," Farah, indicated that reports about the NSP in *Al-Bayān* and likely press outlets in the Middle East attracted requests for aid from Islamic humanitarian organizations in Syria, although their links to rebel leaders remained unclear. Significantly, the reach of the Syrian Arab Committee appeared to breach the northern frontier of British control in Palestine into French-claimed Lebanon and Syrian territories:

> Greetings. Our [Syrian Arab] committee decided to write your committee [NSP] seeking to invoke your sympathy and asking your aid and help and backing us in our humanitarian endeavors in Galilee. We are distributing essential sustenance to more than 12,000 in Shām lying in Ghoutah and the surrounding villages [from the Baqaʿ Valley in northern Palestine to Damascus], among them the elderly, widows, and orphans. They came to us exhausted by hunger [and] seeking refuge, and we sheltered them and consoled them and did not spare any effort in bandaging their wounds and calming their severe pains. The Arab Syrian immigrant community [*jaliah*] met its obligations toward the afflicted in Lebanon. As for those who suffered in Damascus, do they not deserve some of the sympathy of the generous [ones] who race to serve the needs of others with their wealth?[52]

The short letter continues seeking to evoke generosity with embellished language and reiterating the dire need in Syria.

Nearing the convention planned for January 1927, Farah explained his reluctance concerning several issues to the executive committee of the NSP in a letter to Abu Shaqra.[53] He called for careful evaluation of the pros and cons of inviting Shakib Arslan, Michele Lotfallah, and Nasīm Saybaʿa to attend the second annual convention of the party. He expressed his reluctance to advocate for or support the idea, but he added a warning to his compatriots not to hold a convention without an explicit agenda, definite objectives, and careful planning "from beginning to end." Farah strongly urged Abu Shaqra to decide on a venue for the convention so preparations could begin. He drew Abu Shaqra's attention to the necessity of spelling out the party's charter, arguing that providing such clarity of purpose by the NSP would help to avoid chaos. Farah ended the correspondence by expressing deep reservations on two counts: "The presence of luminaries among us is premature, not to mention expenses that would reach no less than $5,000. Some may make promises born of zeal for the cause [forgetting that] the biggest immigrant communities [New York] made promises to [Abdelrahman] Shahbandar when he was among us, none of which came to fruition." Finally, Farah politely confessed to his friend, "We as a party are not sophisticated to a degree that enables us to play an international role without falling into pitfalls due to lack of experience."[54]

Bearing smudges of smoke, likely as a result of the fire that consumed his business in 1929, Farah's papers contain a large number of carbon copies of drafts of correspondence he authored in his role in the NSP. One of those is an announcement Farah sent to *Al-Bayān* and *Al-ʿĀṣimah* under the title "Memorial Services."[55] In it he announced plans to honor men of the revolution martyred at the hands of the French. The memorial service was conducted at the Young Men's Christian Association in Flint and drew a crowd from Saginaw, Bay City, and other cities. Farah's letter to the press states that he and Abu Shaqra gave speeches followed by those of Badiʿ Thibiyan, secretary of the Committee to Aid the Victims of the Syrian War; Hanna Nasr of Detroit; Ragheb Mitrage, secretary of the party's affiliate in Flint; and Muhammad Abi ʿAjram the committee's treasurer, also in Flint, who spoke in English. The event concluded with speeches by Said Zahrah of the Detroit NSP and Amin Saab of Flint. Farah continued: "You could see the drenching tears fall on the faces of the men and women in silence. The memory of [martyrs] Rashid, Adel, Fadl, and Fuad moved all into deep sighs and choked moans."[56]

Sporadic notices celebrating initial victories by Syrians against the French were usually sent on official NSP stationery from the central headquarters in Highland Park, and Abu Shaqra and Farah continued their debate about the approaching convention. Abu Shaqra in an apparent response to a letter from Farah acknowledged the gift to the party of a subscription to the Palestinian *Al-Karmel* newspaper and donations sent by Flint affiliates that were sent to Syria along with $100 from the central office. In response to Farah's concerns about inviting the luminary Shakib Arslan, Abu

Shaqra defended the suggestion as a way of introducing Syrian leaders to the immigrant community.[57] Abu Shaqra contended that the financial benefits of Arslan's visit would outweigh the expense and said he perceived an advantage in learning firsthand the state of high policy in Europe and the revolution and therefore the best ways to proceed. He said responses to the proposed visit indicated the chapters' willingness to cover the expenses and offered another incentive: "The mere announcements in the newspapers of the visit by the three [Syrian delegates] would enhance [the NSP's] stature in every respect." Abu Shaqra agreed with Farah about the benefit of the visits and assured him that more than three months would give ample time to prepare. Abu Shaqra closed by apologizing to Farah for not being in the office when Farah visited Highland Park and explained that he took "leave to visit the public library to collect the names of members of the American Congress [House of Representatives] to distribute articles as I did to members of the Senate."[58]

The financial contributions through al-Husseini in Jerusalem did reach their intended recipients in the Shouf Mountains of Syria and later in Houran. Letters from Sultan al-Atrash acknowledging donations from Farah, Abi ʿAjram, Mitrage, and others in the party are further confirmed by Hasan Amin al-Buʿaini's extensive Arabic-language study of the Druze in Syria.[59] Al-Buʿaini credits the New Syria Party as a source of funds without indicating that it was an immigrant organization in Detroit.[60] Buʿaini's discourse and Michael Provence's account backed by extensive research stand in contrast to testimony in 1926 to the League of Nations from the commission investigating the revolt. The committee described Syrians unfavorably: "Ignorant or unmindful of any better fate, they are deeply rooted in their serfdom and are as conservative as their masters [Druze leaders]. They have no aspirations for a system of greater social justice nor for a better communal life."[61]

The idea that Syrians were fit only to be wards of France and Britain until they were ready for self-rule was the essence of the mandate idea at the close of the war and hardly a new mode of thinking by colonialist powers. As for the NSP in the United States and its affiliates in South America, they were not dissuaded by French propaganda and claims of civilizing indigenous peoples by colonizing them. American Syrians had the advantage of being insulated from the multitude of unscrupulous notables in Damascus vying for influence by working for the French. Immigrants maintained their support for the Syrian revolt for its duration because they faced fewer pressures than did the population in Syria.

Letters of acknowledgment from Sultan al-Atrash of the immigrants' efforts were an incentive to send more aid. The carbon copy of a handwritten form letter signed by Druze leader al-Atrash shows that he promised to continue the fight until death in the face of "reckless rage, repression, and daily destruction by the French" and confirmed that aid from American Syrians "alleviated great pains" and was of great help. Al-Atrash urged the immigrants to send more, saying "maximum financial aid is needed." The rebel leader said aid should be "sent through the Committee for the Syrian War Afflicted in Jerusalem, headed by Hajj Amin al-Husseini, the president of the Supreme Islamic Council" as the best route for sending funds.[62]

In December 1926 carbon copies of the handwritten official report on the activities of the New Syria Party for the previous year were mailed to all branches of the NSP by its executive secretary, ʻAbbas Abu Shaqra.[63] The documents contain the only available account of the operations of the NSP in 1926. The immigrants' enthusiasm for establishing branches of the NSP can be explained in terms of the momentum created by U.S. news coverage of French atrocities and political bravado by Shakib Arslan, representing Syrians at the League of Nations. The NSP, now in its second year, invited Arslan to visit the party's office in Detroit despite Farah's doubts. Recognizing the political benefit of tapping into immigrants' access to the U.S. polity in the United States in making a case against the French in the international arena, the Druze Prince Shakib Arslan and his colleague Ihsan al-Jabiri accepted the invitation from the NSP to the Syrian and Palestinian delegation's headquarters in Geneva. Confirmations were received by the Detroit NSP, according to Abu Shaqra's report, from the executive committee of the delegation in Cairo, which agreed to send secretary Nasīm Saybaʻa and committee member Tawfiq al-Yāziji. The report indicates that Prince Michele Lotfallah in London declined the invitation due to poor health, and it declares the establishment of several chapters across the United States and South America.

Although the party expressed a keen interest in lobbying and public relations campaigns, some in the rank and file of the NSP took delight in behaving quixotically. For example, each chapter chose a rebel leader as its namesake. Abu Shaqra reported that five new chapters had been established by the roaming delegation: in Hopewell, Virginia, the chapter was named after Tawfiq Holoheider; the Quincy, Massachusetts, chapter was named after Ahmad Zaki Pasha; a chapter in Washington, D.C., was named after Faris al-Khouri; a Yucatan, Mexico, chapter was named for Hasan al-Atrash; in Parker, Texas, a second chapter was named after Hamad al-Barbour. The immigrants were aware of, although not prepared to accept, French advances against the nationalists after the latter had gained swift victories.

When the French launched a counteroffensive with fresh troops and massive armaments, news of the devastation of dozens of villages by the French added to the Syrian Americans' resolve.

Nevertheless, the immigrants' enthusiasm hinged on the survival of the rebellion and its leaders. Naming chapters after favored rebel heroes and intellectuals suggests hints of Old World affiliations, perhaps even some variations in sensibilities and approach. Again, these divisions, like possible intra-Muslim disputes within the NSP, must be understood in perspective as insufficient to undermine the organization. The subtle differences and even nondescript discord in Detroit did not alter the main thrust behind the NSP or smother the core idea of Syria's independence, however unlikely under the mandate. The idea of supporting the revolt against a common enemy remained intact. Moreover, this nationalist goal by the NSP seems to have absorbed all other peripheral and minor collectives and superseded Fuad Shatara's existing Palestine National League. Contentions that immigrants—and by definition the NSP—were split over supporting the rebellion along sectarian lines are fed by Mokarzel's diatribes and opposition to Shakib Arslan and by disregard for the historical context of rapidly evolving political realities. Arslan was a controversial personality irrespective of Mokarzel's indiscriminate opposition to him and to any agenda outside Lebanese separatism. Although the Islamist Arslan was educated by Ibrahim al-Bustāni, a major Christian *nahḍah* figure, and in French by Augustus Adib in missionary schools, his political ideology was shaped by the disappearance of political freedom in Syria commensurate with spotty prosperity brought by rising foreign influence amid Ottoman policies of capitulation. The discrepancy, from his perspective, allowed for his association with the dean of pan-Islamist thought Jamāl al-Dīn al-Afghāni.[64] The conservative pan-Islamist Prince Arslan, who represented the Houran district of Syria in Istanbul through World War I, maintained his unwavering opposition to Europeans even when the main Arab fighting force in Arabia joined the Allies in 1916, going as far as criticizing the First Arab Conference in 1913 while the Ottoman state was fighting in the Balkans. Although he consistently distinguished himself from the Turks by emphasizing that he was an Arab, he alienated some Syrian nationalists, among them typically nationalist Orthodox Syrians. In Mokarzel's charges that the NSP was a Druze organization, he ignored support for Arslan among Christians, the small number of Druze across the United States and South America to support NSP chapters, and the considerable aid from several sources that was sent by the party. Ultimately, the NSP was possible only as an ecumenical effort.

In 1926 the French imported thousands of troops from France and colonies in Africa and began a massive assault against the rebels, who possessed outdated weapons and meager supplies. Pressure against the rebels did not sap the morale of the chapters but did signal that their collapse, as Farah feared, could spell disaster for the NSP because supporting them was its primary goal. The members continued to find ways to react to unfolding events and setbacks. In what can be interpreted as part hyperbole and part sincere nationalist zeal, the news of the surrender of Abdel-Ghaffar al-Atrash to the French, Abu Shaqra reported, "upset the nationalists of the chapter named after him in Norphlet, Arkansas. Accordingly, the members resolved to rename the chapter after Sayyah Hammoud al-Atrash [another Druze rebel]."[65]

The French attacks hastened the immigrants' resolve to hold the conference. Majīd Arslan in Buenos Aires and George Haddad, editor of *Al-Qalam al-Hadidi* (The iron pen) in São Paulo, Brazil, acknowledged receipt of an invitation from the NSP.[66] The party sent invitations to the Hasan al-Atrash chapter in Yucatan, Mexico, and to dignitaries and wealthy immigrants, among them Jaber Shuqair, Amin al-As'ad, Abdullah Omar, and Abdelhamid Shouman, founder of al-Bank al-'Arabi (Arab Bank). The party signaled the leadership in Palestine in an apparent effort to funnel aid to the Syrian fighters through the relief committee in Jerusalem headed by Hajj al-Husseini and expressed its wishes that Abdelrahman Shahbandar attend the convention in Detroit. In response, al-Husseini telegraphed an urgent appeal for immigrants to send "generous aid." The content of al-Husseini's letter and the plans for a national convention in January 1927 were published in *Al-Bayān*, Abu Shaqra reported to the chapters.[67]

The last of Farah's manuscripts of 1926, collectively titled "Receipts and Disbursements," are in the handwriting of Kamel Hamady, a prosperous merchant in Flint, and on the letterhead of the successful Hamady supermarket chain. Hamady's report indicates totals of $482 received and $401 spent. The accounting does not indicate the amounts sent to Jerusalem apparently separately by the Pan-Syrian Party in Flint.[68]

By December 7, 1926, the Second Annual Convention of the New Syria Party was set and a program disseminated to the branches by 'Abbas Abu Shaqra. He announced that the program was based on recommendations made by Ameen Farah after being ratified by the executive committee and the branches. Stipulations in the program included some penciled-in corrections in Farah's handwriting:

1. The Convention is to begin on the 15th of January 1927 at 2:00 p.m. in Detroit.

2. The Convention will consist of the Executive Committee of the current year, the general secretary, and chapter delegates.
3. Delegates are to meet with the Executive Committee and present the minutes of their elections that must be ratified by the secretaries.
4. A preparations committee and a committee to keep the order are to be elected from the ranks of the delegates.
5. The Executive and delegates are required to attend the first general session to welcome the visitors and hear speeches. Admission will be open to the public. Those prepared to give a speech must submit their names to the preparations committee, which will assemble a list of all speakers.

The program for the secondary sessions gave further details:

1. A summary of the sessions of the Central office will be read to all in attendance and reports of all accomplishments and projects in the [branches'] first year [1927] will be printed and distributed to the attendees.
2. Thorough accounting and ratification of the budget.
3. Voting on any necessary amendments and changes in the Party's bylaws as needed.
4. Elections of the Executive Committee for a new term after the Convention and clarifying their functions, numbers, and authority.
5. Election of the General Secretary and Treasurer in a formal session of the presumptive [new] Executive Committee.
6. A new agenda is aimed at increased aid to Syria financially, intellectually, and politically.
7. A separate agenda is aimed at expanding the Party and increasing communications among its chapters.
8. Determining a budget for the coming year.

Farah added that the Flint branch would hold working sessions in nearby Flint and instructed chapters regarding procedures:

Chapter Delegates
Each chapter can send one representative or more.
1. Each chapter has one vote regardless of the number of delegates; however, a single delegate can have as many votes as the chapters represented by that delegate.
2. No delegate is allowed to represent more than three chapters.
3. Individual members can attend and share suggestions without voting. However, if 10 members attend from a branch, they are granted one vote.
4. Voting will be denied to any chapters that are not current on their dues.

5. The Executive Committee is elected for one year or until the following Convention is held.
6. The common interest of the Party and the homeland must be served by taking into account the intellectual capabilities, honesty, and managerial experience of the Executive Committee without paying any attention to sectarianism and [village or clan] affiliation (al-jam'īyah).
7. The sessions of the Committee are private unless it is deemed appropriate inviting other members.[69]

The convention took place as planned and was attended by Shakib Arslan accompanied by Nasīm Sayba'a. The two men served as the delegates representing Syria and Palestine, respectively, in Cairo and the League of Nations in Geneva. The *Detroit Free Press* of January 15, 1927, covered the convention's opening day under the headline "Syrian Prince Pledges Fight. Nationalists Will Carry on War for Liberty, Say[s] Prince. Here for Convention." The article reported that "one hundred delegates from all parts of the United States" were present. Capturing the fighting mood of the Syrian rebels against the French after the atrocities of the previous years, the reporter wrote, "There will be no handshaking with the French and no cessation of fighting by the Syrians until Syria wins, by arms or diplomacy, her independence." The article continued: "The prince was accompanied to Detroit by Naceem bey Saybya [Nasīm Sayba'a, the Palestinian delegate residing in Cairo], who represents the nationalistic movement of the Syrians in Egypt." The newspaper quoted Sayba'a regarding his education at the American University of Beirut: "'It was there we learned the principles of democracy.'"

A January 17 article in the *Free Press* reported on the convention proceedings in more detail and covered the activities of Na'ūm Mokarzel and others who opposed the Syrian nationalists and Arslan. The newspaper reported that the prince addressed the opening session in the Fort Wayne Hotel in a "one-week convention of the New Syria Party, which was formed here a year ago and of which Detroit is the national headquarters. The organization had about forty locals scattered throughout the United States, mostly east of the Mississippi river."[70] The *Free Press* article cited specifics from speeches by Shakib Arslan and others about the French Mandate's trail of "wanton destruction of more than 500 villages and the slaughter of 30,000 young men" and Syria's trade deficit of 600,000 francs due to the worsening economic conditions.[71]

Sayba'a made a plea for charity to the *Free Press* as the "treasurer of the relief committee for Syrian refugees" on behalf of "100,000 in dire need." The January 17 article mentioned speeches by Fred Massey, Hanna Nasr,

FIGURE 4.11. *NSP conference, Statler Hotel in Detroit, January 27, 1927. The NSP's guests had returned to Michigan after visiting the U.S. South and the East Coast. Ameen Farah (second row, third from right) stands next to Muhammad Abi 'Ajram (fourth from right). Prince Shakib Arslan is seated in the center, left of 'Abbas Abu Shaqra. Farah Papers, Bawardi Collection.*

and S. Joseph of Hannibal, Missouri, among others. It said participants reacted indignantly to reports that a faction from Mount Olivet, North Carolina, had sent a letter to Senator Simmons of that state charging that Emir Arslan "was the right-hand man of Djemal [Jamāl] Pasha, murderer of Syrians during the war." They "hotly branded the charge as 'enemy propaganda inspired by France'" and declared that France itself recognized Arslan as a hero of his people.[72]

Intra-Syrian division over Arslan's visit was a matter of divergent political approaches. Aside from Ameen Farah, one of the most dynamic activists in Flint was a Syrian Orthodox Christian from the Lebanon named Najib Abu Samra (later just Samra). His stance on Syria's independence and the mandate was no different than Farah's, but Samra, like others regardless of denomination, never forgave Shakib Arslan for what many felt were visions of pan-Islamism through Turkish executions of nationalists during World War I. In fact, Samra's absence from the NSP conference, given his prolific activities on behalf of Syria's cause, was conspicuous. This intranationalist—and intra-Orthodox, for that matter—difference of opinion was not the same as Mokarzel's long-standing opposition to a wide range of dispositions around him regardless of the source.

Tacit advocacy in favor of French intervention by *Al-Hoda* picked up steam during World War I just as *Mirāt al-Gharb* expressed fears of carving Lebanon out of Syria. Because Syria's cause encompassed Palestine within it before the mandate changed that reality, Palestine was also in Mokarzel's crosshairs. Najīb Diāb responded to a request by Ameen Rihani to comment on Rihani's article on Palestine in *Al-Fatāt*; in his editorial Diāb captured the immigrants' postwar bewilderment over the impending role of the British and the French.[73] Diāb gingerly approached the sensitive subject of the future of Syria in a series of articles titled "The approaching Syria" ("Sūriya al-Muqbilah"). Many Syrians felt indebted to the French and the British for purging the Turks, Diāb suggested, while also expressing his preference for a united Syria and presenting a four-point platform:

> First, Syria should have complete administrative independence under French protection with the backing of the other allies.
>
> Second, a representative parliament of the population should be established without regard to sectarian and ideological beliefs.
>
> Third, no privileges should be granted that favor any part of Syria in representation or otherwise.
>
> Fourth, the minority should not attempt to gain overrepresentation or privileges by any means, as this would negate the spirit of democratic representation and unity; the rights of the Muslim majority should be guaranteed according to the declarations of the aims and programs of the protecting powers.[74]

A survey of *Al-Hoda* articles, ads, and editorials surrounding the main events in Syria throughout the early 1920s reveals spikes of claims by Naʿūm Mokarzel that only the Lebanese League of Progress of New York represented the demands of the Lebanese people.[75] Mokarzel's postwar attacks against his detractors increased as Arslan's publicized visit neared, but his attacks against Syrian nationalists began several years earlier when he continually criticized Prince Faisal's government and supporters in his daily editorial column "Khawāṭer" (Whims) under titles such as "Who Are the Faisalites?" and "Why Are They?" These were mixed with a strange sort of jingoism targeting other Syrians in articles such as "It [Lebanon] Is a Paradise Except for the Lazy and the Traitor," which extols the virtues of the

French.⁷⁶ By January 1926 Mokarzel was seeking to trivialize the Syrian rebellion under numerous headings: "The French Finish off Remnants of the Rebels"; "The Rebels Gather in Eastern Jordan"; "No Traces Are Left of the Revolution"; and "50 Rebels Are Taken Prisoners."⁷⁷

Days before the Detroit NSP convention, *Al-Hoda* claimed that "Syria's Affairs Are Returning to Normal," citing an article in the *Herald Tribune*. Mokarzel published selective news about the resumption of the publication of *Al-Muqtabas* and *Al-Ra'i al-ʿām* (Public opinion) without mentioning that the French suspended both or that fresh French troops had landed in Tripoli.⁷⁸ On January 12, 1927, Mokarzel took aim at Shakib Arslan. In his "Al-Khawāṭer" column Mokarzel cited a long list of pejorative names directed against him that he attributed to the January 10 issue of *Al-Bayān*. In typical form Mokarzel resorted to sectarian incitement; he charged that the prince was in Detroit to "incite against the Christians in a Christian country" and wrote, "If we were in Druze lands, our blood would be spilled," without explaining who "we" meant. He attacked Arslan as "flippant," a "backstabber," and "poor in money and principles." The next day an *Al-Hoda* headline announced that "Druze Chiefs Depart Syria," based on an article in the *Evening Sun*. On January 13 Mokarzel pulled out all the stops in an article titled "He Killed Your Loved Ones; Won't You Kill His Incitements?" He accused Arslan of being instrumental in killing 60,000 Lebanese young men and women and directed his attacks against charities and aid to Sultan al-Atrash. He said Arslan was "living on crumbs of Lotfallah's party" and all who welcomed Arslan acquiesced to his crimes. Mokarzel urged resistance to the convention's visitors:

> Fight the Palestinian-Syrian delegation in this manner:
> —Do not attend any meetings attended by a Druze.
> —Consider the Christians in the delegation only to be Druze-in-the-making, for their sectarianism is worse than that of the worst enemies of your religion.
> —Do not host any of these unwelcome guests.
> —Do not participate in feasts attended by any members of the delegation.
> —Do not donate any money to the delegation, for these donations will only contribute to bloodshed, burning of homes, and destruction of churches after looting them.

In the weeks leading up to and following the convention while the prince was in the United States, Mokarzel repeatedly called on his readers to circulate a question he posed in Arabic in his newspaper and in English to members of the U.S. Congress: "What will you be doing [about Arslan's visit]?" The January 18, 1927, issue of *Al-Hoda* listed the names of people who supported its stance and opposed Arslan, nearly all of whom were residents of Mount Olivet, North Carolina, likely the group behind the protest reported in the *Detroit Free Press* two days prior. On January 18 the *Free Press* ran an article about the hundreds of protesters to Arslan's presence in Detroit. George N. Asmar, a spokesman for the exclusively Maronite Syrian Christian Association, told the reporter that Arslan was a "fugitive from Syria under sentence of death." Asmar was referring to a death sentence by the French against Arslan and many opposition leaders in absentia. Asmar elaborated: "The French government and its policies are favored in Syria and in the great Mt. Lebanon."[79]

The Maronite spokesman labeled Nasīm Saybaʿa a fugitive and said the Druze "delight in the killing of women and children." He warned against raising funds for them from "our humble people."[80] Asmar contended that "of 250,000 Syrians in the United States, not more than 25,000 are members of the new Syrian Party," and that among the approximately 18,000 Syrians in Detroit, 15,500 were Christians.[81] These exaggerated numbers by the self-styled spokesman of the Syrian Christian Association likely had the unintended effect of inflating the ranks of the NSP well beyond its actual numbers; 15,000 members would have amounted to a significant 6 percent of the entire Syrian population in the United States. Asmar's claims could mean only that the overwhelming majority of NSP members were Christians—precisely the opposite of what the Maronites, Mokarzel, and the French government wanted people to believe. Hence, the NSP did not seem in danger of any coherent internal opposition outside Mokarzel's characteristically personal attacks.

Dodging any mention that Muslims in Syria vastly outnumbered Christians or that many among the rebels were Christians strained the argument that Druze Muslims killed Christians at will, not to mention that the fight involved the French, not fellow Syrians. There is no evidence that Mokarzel mobilized a sustained following from the majority Maronites or that he convinced them to throw their lot in with the French. Many natives of Mount Lebanon acted on their own accord due to social conditioning. Although their numbers were superior, they did not represent an organized group. He certainly stood out when he conjured a strategy relying on religious incitement in the United States, where Christians constituted a commanding majority. But this position was easily dismissed when other Christians including Melkites, Orthodox, and Catholics also opposed the French as bitterly as the Muslims in the Shouf Mountains and across Syria. Apparently the extreme rhetoric by Maronites at the behest and in coordination with Mokarzel and the French government indicates that Arslan's visit may have rattled the French.

The tenuousness of the arguments against Arslan no doubt provided an avenue for NSP members to reinforce nonsectarian nationalist bonds. Mokarzel simply renewed the kind of pejorative attacks against an entire class of people who differed with him on the French Mandate that he had made when European intervention after World War I was the issue. Mokarzel's vociferousness, masked by the specter of religious intolerance, was a smokescreen for political aims. Although Saybaʿa steered as far away as he could from politics in his remarks to the *Detroit Free Press*, Mokarzel did not spare him. Despite the need for aid in a devastated Syria, Mokarzel labeled Saybaʿa a liar, a thief, and despicably intolerant. Even Saybaʿa's Christian faith meant nothing to Mokarzel based on his version of history: "The Druze used to be Christians, and now they are the enemies of Christian civilized life, traces of which should have been found in Arslan himself."[82] Regardless of these comments by Mokarzel and his narrow circle, vehement disapproval of Arslan occurred because of his long-standing strategy of using Ottomanism as a cover for Arab autonomy and beyond, although he never abandoned the Syrian Arab cause. The hundreds of protesters reported in the *Detroit Free Press* had completely different reasons to oppose Arslan. Theirs was a peculiar disposition of considering Lebanon a bastion for France based on suspicions about Muslims and Islam. However, the violent nature of the European occupations that replaced the Ottomans served to vindicate Arslan's agenda and made him a fit candidate to represent Syrians internationally.

Successful nevertheless, the convention ended with a second general session on Sunday, January 23, after the prince and his entourage returned from touring the southern states. Invitations by the party announced a public meeting.[83] The invitation announced that Arslan, Saybaʿa, and Tawfīq al-Yāzijī would give speeches that would be "food for the nationalist and human spirits."[84] An accompaniment to the invitation reads like a personal appeal from Nasīm Saybaʿa for his "brothers the Syrian and Lebanese immigrants of all religions, orientations, and views" to hear him "explain the true condition in the [home] country [*al-bilād*]." Intended perhaps as a response to French propaganda, the invitation asserted Saybaʿa's "firm belief that his brothers being away from their original homeland [and receiving] distorted news and their many businesses do not permit them to form a clear idea about what took place, and goes on still, five thousand miles away." Sayba'a would support his words "with proof and answer any question he is asked."[85]

The New Syria Party may have reached its organizational limits with Arslan's visit, not to mention the members' financial reach. Although I found only Farah's papers to describe the party's financial dealings, the documents reveal that the New York chapter and the Flint affiliate, the Pan-Syrian Party, carried more than their share of the expenses for the delegation's travels. The first correspondence after the convention from Abu Shaqra to the Flint chapter warned that only a meager $113.50 remained in the party's bank account, likely because most of the funds were sent to Jerusalem. Abu Shaqra sent Anabtawi to Chicago at the party's expense and asked him to go to Wisconsin, where "some nationalists might lend support."[86] No records indicate whether he did make the trip. Signs of fatigue in the chapters appeared once the euphoria of Arslan's visit subsided and reality set in. A correspondence from one of the convention speakers, S. Joseph, on the stationery of his Hannibal Mercantile Company sheds some light on the convention's financial shortcomings. On March 17, 1927, Joseph wrote that he paid $85 in dues from the members of his chapter and expressed his "displeasure toward the secretary," a reference to Nathmi Anabtawi, because no account was given on the activities of the party in the previous two months. Joseph asked for a copy of the budget in English.[87] This request suggests that immigrants may have been on the cusp of using English in their daily interactions or shedding their knowledge of the Arabic language, or they simply developed a preference for English to force a qualitative change in intra-Syrian immigrant interactions.

Abu Shaqra's prediction that the visit by Arslan might attract the attention of the press was on the mark. *Al-'Āṣimah* (The Capitol), a budding publication in Washington, D.C., contacted Ameen Farah and sent him several issues of the magazine through the managing editor, Elias Joseph. The issues accompanied a letter that declared the publication "a nationalist magazine . . . which you can consider your own in every sense of the word . . . [S]end to me all you wish to publish, and it will be published at no expense."[88] Hence, another considerable voice of a Christian editor upholding nonsectarian support for the nationalist cause was added to *Al-Bayān*, *Mirāt al-Gharb*, *As-Sameer*, and other publications.

The prolonged stay of the prince and his desire to visit Florida took its financial toll on the chapters. By March 19, the New York chapter reported a zero balance. This translation of the New York chapter's budget serves as a rare record of Arslan's itinerary while in the United States for the convention:

Expenses:
$512.39   Reception for the prince and the delegation before departing to Detroit
$117.65   Hotel February 9–15 [upon returning from Detroit]
$43.00   Prince travels to Boston
$84.85   Hotel February 17–23
$211.33   Hotel February 24–March 10
$8.00   Nurse for the prince
$248.65   Prince travels to Washington

Aside from the money the NSP sent for the rebels, the $1,225.98 in expenses was partially covered by the receipt of membership dues and donations totaling $921.00, leaving $304.98 owed by the Detroit office. The statement provided that the hotel expenses of March 13–22, the date of the prince's departure to Florida and the southern states, would probably cost another $300, "not to mention additional expenses when he and Mr. Sayba'a return until their departure."[89]

The convention and visitors no doubt uplifted the spirits of many immigrants, but it was difficult to ignore the worsening reality in Syria. The rebels would keep fighting into the spring of 1927, but their fate looked inevitable. The French had been waging a massive counteroffensive for nearly a year.[90] By the time the NSP convention took place in January 1927, the rebels were in a state of retreat toward Houran, and many were already in the desert near the borders of modern Jordan. Given the relative ease of sending aid from Jerusalem through Trans-Jordan to the desert in the east, a rebel refuge there could explain the increasingly prominent role of al-Husseini in channeling aid and Sultan al-Atrash's request that aid be sent through Jerusalem. Despite their best intentions, the immigrants' resources were limited.

Besides the troubled financial picture, the military devastation of the rebellion by the far superior French army left in its wake other threats to the welfare of the party from within. In frank language Ameen Farah complained about the problematic Martyrs (Fir' al-shuhadā') Chapter of the NSP in Detroit for making more demands on the party than its members were willing to contribute. Farah's predictions concerning financial burdens were realized when losses in Syria precipitated the NSP's collapse. The party's internal fissures may have been a reaction to the defeat of the rebels. Farah complained that financial constraints were due to ineffectual branches that compounded the Flint chapter's problems of assuming the command of a party that was bankrupt and owed large amounts of money. He complained that not all branches sent in their $10 monthly dues on time, which "caused all efforts to be spent on collecting money" to repay the expenses of the guests of the convention in January. He added that the Flint chapter paid $538 to the aid committee and $226 to the party, and on behalf of the Flint chapter he asked that a call for funds be sent to the branches. It remains unclear what distinguished the Martyrs Chapter, one of two in Detroit, but Farah expressed the executive committee's displeasure with that chapter, saying its proximity to the headquarters was harmful and had caused many altercations. He suggested that the Central Committee revoke the chapter's affiliation.[91]

The first report in 1927 from Abu Shaqra, dated April 23, contained a resolution to name the Detroit chapter after the rebel leader ʿUqlah al-Qattami; the resolution came from a formal session in Flint on April 19 and 20 of the executive committee comprised of Farah, Ahmad Diāb, and ʿAjram. The resolution was presented to the Detroit Central Committee in response to a suggestion by the Saint Paul, Minnesota, chapter, which was named after the Syrian luminary Zeid al-Atrash. After urging the branches to adhere to the bylaws in a somewhat convoluted summary of the rules set forth during the second convention, the resolution stated that nothing was accomplished in the three months after the convention, it bitterly complained about hiring Anabtawi without identifying him by name, and it asked to increase the executive committee from three to seven people.

The four proposed additions from the Shiʿa community were Ahmad Hamzi, Khalil Bazi, and Hassan Hammoud from Detroit and Abdallah Ghannoum from Toledo. The Saint Paul members, Asʿad Ghaith, Saleh Hammoud, Hassan Abu Abbas, Ali al-Qaderi, Kamel Heider, and the president of the branch, Abdelrazeq al-Qaderi, signed the suggestion.[92] A member of the Mullen, West Virginia, chapter, Ali Salman Tabi Abi al-Hisn, urgently called on Farah to dismiss "misunderstandings" and implement actions: "The Arab world awaits the decisions of the convention."[93] As if to draw a connection between the effects of the conference and France's policies in Syria, he wrote, "Even France itself, I tell you, is contemplating striking Syria to weaken the cause." He urged the headquarters to instruct the chapters and to organize its financial affairs. His letter is another example of a member's demands for a more sophisticated way of running the organization's affairs: "Take heed of the American public, commercial, and political projects; the central office always needs delegates."[94] On April 29 the expected demand for funds to cover the prince's return trip to Europe on

May 7 came from the New York chapter in a short letter typed in Arabic.[95] The letter was preceded by receipts from Abu Shaqra acknowledging a payment of $150.20 by the Flint chapter to Nasīm Saybaʿa in addition to two previous payments of $300 and $76.[96]

The party continued to function for the remainder of 1927, perhaps until news of the defeat of the revolt reached all branches by summer. The convention, as evidenced by the eleven remaining NSP official documents, exemplified the kinds of problems confronting all new organizations, not the least of which was raising funds. Syrians, like any immigrant group, still contended with the demands of building their own financial lives. Regardless, the pressure of the mandate was too much to bear without strategic partners for the Arab Syrian cause, the isolationist stance of the U.S. government, and the American public's lack of basic knowledge about the immigrants' backgrounds. Given that France had a free hand in Syria as supported by the preeminent global powers, there was little prospect for military success at any time. Nevertheless, despite dampened spirits, letters from the branches suggested that the NSP leadership could do things better, and members appeared to maintain a level of expectation for a more sophisticated leadership.

The records of the NSP point to an impending metamorphosis in Syrians' mode of operations in expecting a level of efficiency that was not quite there yet. Religious and sectarian differences played absolutely no role in the rise, operations, and decline of the NSP, notwithstanding diatribes of a personal nature in *Al-Hoda* and elsewhere orchestrated by Mokarzel that still targeted Christians as often as they did Muslims. Opposition to Arslan, too, was mixed and left the Syria idea as a core issue intact until the mandate changed immigrants' focus and with it their perceived role as citizens in their adopted country.

While still a guest of the party, Saybaʿa wrote a note to Farah on the stationery of the Seville Apartment Hotel in Detroit. In his note Saybaʿa expressed doubts concerning an unrealistic plan concocted by Anabtawi for Saybaʿa to collect aid across the United States. He complained that there was no one to help with such a plan and no committee to ensure its implementation: "Am I expected to go to cities, invite people I don't know, give speeches, and collect aid? And who would help me with all of this?"[97] Encouraged by Fuad Shatara's work, Saybaʿa indicated his desire to travel to New York: "I have a chance of succeeding [there], or else I will return to Egypt asking God to crown your efforts with success where mine fell short of the desired results."[98] The distinguished guest reluctantly asked for the remainder of the funds to defray the cost of his return to Cairo.

Ameen Farah's cautious letter of response three weeks later was a regretful recap of the party's shortcomings during Sayba'a's stay in Michigan and puzzlement at the tendencies by "those who boycotted us financially for personal reasons."[99] When the party received Sayba'a's request for aid, Farah wrote that he "was perplexed as to the best ways to help when the party resembles a body wracked with disease." Farah was mindful in his letter of the changes in 1927. The 1925 revolt was being gradually and brutally put down, but not before French prestige was badly bruised, to which the NSP contributed in no small measure, if only by hosting France's archenemy Shakib Arslan. The NSP did more than that when it managed to send considerable amounts of money to the rebel leader al-Atrash in Houran.

In 1927 negotiated arrangements between the French and the relatively wealthy class of Syrians gave rise to a "politics of notables," which took precedence over open military confrontations.[100] In Farah's view, expressed to Sayba'a, suppressing any division within the NSP was crucial "so the enemies won't know that weakness struck roots in the party.... We were faced with two choices, either we split the party and discard the rotten branch, or we declare its end and sign the death warrant."[101] I am uncertain as to who or what was behind the NSP's troubles in Detroit. However, severe external pressures by the mandate should not be discounted, nor should the Syrians' relatively small numbers in the face of the combined might of the preeminent military powers on the planet.

Farah's letter of response to Nasīm Sayba'a ended with news of a gathering in Detroit to raise funds that would be shared equally by the party in Detroit and the aid committee in Jerusalem. Farah expressed hope that the New York chapter would be better qualified to face the tasks ahead.[102] His intuition would prove correct, as the same course of events in Geographic Syria had already sparked the nationalist zeal of more sophisticated and highly educated Syrians among New York's much larger and older immigrant population. New York Syrians took up Syria's cause fresh from the best U.S. colleges. While the NSP rallied behind the revolt in the Shouf Mountains to the north, activists in New York kept a close eye on developments to the south in Palestine and did what they could for the NSP. Meanwhile in Detroit, a report on the party's activities came in April from the executive committee that only twenty-two of a total of thirty-four chapters, with fifty-one possible votes, actually voted for adding the four proposed new members to the executive committee. Next to the subhead "Telegram from Egypt" was news that the party received a telegram from Najib Shuqair, secretary of the Syrian-Palestinian delegation in Egypt. The telegram was approved in the general meeting of the delegation in Egypt, which "resolved to send gratitude to the NSP for its national and humanitarian role."[103]

Another telegram reached the party from Muhammad Amin al-Husseini, the head of the Islamic Council and president of the Central Relief Committee in Jerusalem. The letter was translated from Arabic to English, distributed on the branch's letterhead, and published in *Al-Bayān* along with Husseini's article "Al-Jihād wa al-jumūd" (Struggle and stoicism). The letter apparently was published with the hope that it would stir up emotions and hasten aid to the thousands of distressed Syrians gathered in Azraq, an ancient oasis in the southern Syrian desert, now in eastern Jordan, where many Syrian rebels took refuge. Under the subhead "Banquet" in the report was an item about a fundraiser held on April 22 at the request of the Dr. Shahbandar Chapter of the NSP. The event produced $300. Elsewhere in the report Abu Shaqra advertised 1,050 one-dollar raffle tickets for a chance to win prizes such as two diamond rings and two gold bracelets donated by the NSP women members of Tampa, Florida. Other subheads in the report, including "New Chapters," "Aid," "Resignation," "Party's Program," and "Two Telegrams," inform members about plans to establish new chapters in Mexico, an inquiry by Elias Sabbagh to do the same at Michigan State College, and the overdue resignation of Nathmi Anabtawi.

In an indication of the remarkable effect of the party's work and his own political strategy, Prince Shakib Arslan asked on behalf of the Syrian delegation in Europe that the NSP send a telegram to the French foreign secretary informing him that Arslan represented the party's wishes and that no agreements regarding Syria should pass without the NSP's approval. At the time, French public opposition to the war in Syria offered a ray of hope for Syrian nationalists. Arslan, Ihsan al-Jabiri, and Riad al-Sulḥ, the Syrian delegates to Geneva, were encouraged by the receptiveness of French officials toward restoring the Mount Lebanon area to Syria—which would have ended Lebanese separation—and creating a representative assembly, a constitution, and a reduction of French troops in Syria to 15,000. Arslan's request corresponded with French attempts to pacify unrest with promises of independence in stages. This opened the way for a representative assembly that in 1929 would draft a constitution. The French high commissioner rejected the proposed constitution, thereby ushering a prolonged period of posturing by the French that splintered Syrian resistance and delayed constitutional representation for two decades.

Despite Farah's pessimism, the NSP still filled a gap in immigrants' desires for a political role in the fate of their old homeland. The question the NSP experiment revealed with regard to influencing high policy was whether immigrants could withstand failures by the political leadership in Syria.

In June 1927 Farah informed Abu Shaqra of his successful effort to dissuade Ahmad Diāb from resigning from membership in the NSP. Farah asked executive secretary Abu Shaqra to send a declaration of Diāb's decision to mitigate the effects of his resignation in a previous report; Abu Shaqra did so on June 16.[104] A final request in Farah's papers from the Detroit office pleaded with its members to send much-needed aid to the Jerusalem Aid Committee and urged them to use their extensive connections as merchants to "wealthy American clients and agents."[105]

Once back in Egypt, Nasīm Saybaʿa sent a final correspondence marked "private" to "my dear and kind friends, Ameen Farah and Ragheb Mitrage." This tender letter expressed the statesman's regrets for falling short of helping Syria's cause and lamented the "dark days" wasted on trying to mend fences among "those who claim leadership," a reference to the Syrian-Palestinian delegation in Egypt.[106] The problem, Saybaʿa explained, was the untimely disagreement among the delegates just when a report by French High Commissioner Auguste Henry Ponsot was submitted to the League of Nations.[107] Ponsot appeared to relent to dozens of complaints by Syrian nationalists to the Mandatory Commission of the League of Nations that the French were not living up to their responsibilities in helping Syrian development as stipulated in the mandate charter.

Saybaʿa informed Farah and Mitrage that he had resorted to writing in *Al-Muqattam* and *Kawkab al-Sharq* to impel the parties into agreement. He enclosed copies of those writings with his letter. He recounted his efforts to again seek consensus while in New York when disagreement within the delegation in Egypt became apparent. Saybaʿa bitterly complained that his pleas for the delegation to speak to the French with one voice went unanswered. As a result, when the French "sensed division in Paris and in Cairo, they sent the delegation on their way." He wrote that "Ponsot came to Syria intent on creating new statelets, killing Lebanon's constitution, and preparing one for Syria without consulting the Syrians as if they did not exist." Ponsot thus caused the dissolution of the Jerusalem Aid Committee, Saybaʿa wrote. The pressures of the mandate represented an indirect threat to immigrants' attempts to close rank because they undermined consensus among the political leaders, most of whom were reeling in exile.

Discord reached a critical level, pitting nationalists against each other on the pages of newspapers in Syria, Palestine, and Egypt. "It came to pass," Saybaʿa wrote, "that the Syrians destroyed their own good name with their own wrongful hands. I do not deny that the failure of the revolt caused fear and confusion," but disunity among the leaders played into the hands of the French, who remained fearful that the revolt might return. Sayba'a mentioned rumors that "some wrote to the New Syria Party in America asking them to withhold aid from Amin al-Husseini and by default from Sultan al-Atrash." Sayba'a considered their request "an unforgivable crime." He urged the Syrian diaspora in Egypt to send aid instead of forming useless parties or relying on Syrian workers in America of modest means.[108]

Sayba'a's letter led Farah and his close friends to reconsider their representation as officers of the NSP in the delegation to Egypt. A short memo from Farah and Muhammad Abi 'Ajram to the NSP's executive committee, dated December 30, 1927, on the letterhead of the Pan-Syrian Party in Flint explained the decision:

> Greetings. During the Second Convention of the New Syria Party, the executive committee empowered Tawfīq al-Yāzijī to represent the party in the Palestinian-Syrian conference in Egypt. Due to fissures in the ranks of the above delegation, the executive committee decided to refrain from being represented and informed Mr. Yāzijī of this decision until agreement is restored. Our party will continue to support the *mujahideen* and their children and has not changed its stance from the national delegation in Europe.
>
> The Executive Committee of the New Syria Party in America
> Ameen Farah   Muhammad Abi 'Ajram

Despite setbacks caused by French policies, ineffectual members, and the demands of life in a new country, the NSP experiment illustrated that collective action was not only possible but in fact inevitable. The obstacles ranged from logistical challenges to recruitment of the talents to oversee administrative work to the insurmountable pressures of contending with two international powers on the scene. Facilitating the delivery of aid proved as difficult as navigating the French and British imperialist hegemony over Natural Syria. The great distance did not sever the diaspora from the unfolding events any more than it did their strong ties to their homeland; rather, it caused a delayed reaction to unrelenting political changes and shifting frontiers as the Syria idea survived in the Americas longer than it had in Egypt or perhaps Syria itself.

The changing geopolitical reality did not dissuade Syrians but only changed the way they referred to themselves. In 1927 the Jerusalem Committee for the Refugees was renamed the Committee for Palestine's Victims

(Jamʿīyat Mankūbī Filasṭīn, as in afflicted by disaster), but its members still looked to immigrants for sympathy and support. Thanks to the NSP, the door was wide open for another round of collecting aid from the diaspora. In 1930 Adel Arslan and Issa Bandak, who would become the education minister in Syria and the mayor of Bethlehem, respectively, toured the United States as guests of the Syrian Palestinian Society for seven months on behalf of the reinvigorated committee, which was still headed by Hajj Amin al-Husseini.[109] The door opened by the NSP would remain open for the duration of another phase in Arab American activism: pan-Arab concerns and the work of the next national political organization, the ANL. Transferring NSP memberships to the ANL went hand in hand with drawing lessons from the ill-fated yet important experiment of the NSP.

The end of the Druze-led revolt, tendencies of self-preservation by the regime in Jordan under King Abdullah, the British-installed son of the sharif of Mecca, and the separation of Palestine from the "Syrian mother" brought on the fulfillment of Kazim al-Husseini's prediction that Southern Syria would no longer exist. The Syrian cause became part of the larger struggle for Arab independence that continued despite the new political borders. Hence, simultaneous national struggles allowed for an eclectic group of nationalists under the rubric of overarching pan-Arabism. In the U.S. arena it was a matter of Syrian activists turning to Palestine, where the need was greatest. Talented and determined American Zionists, like their counterparts in Palestine, forced responses from Syrian Americans. Some of those Zionists were born and reared in Southern Syria, or Palestine, by advancing their own political program with British help. Syrians' responses to events in Palestine were in line with the trajectory of Palestinian national identity and the emphasis on Zionist activities.

Anti-Zionist activism articulated by Fuad Isa Shatara and Ḥabīb Ibrahīm Kātibah stand in contrast to the NSP's attempts to forge a national organization to tackle international policy. Businessmen, already strained, largely ran the NSP with limited help from students and a few administrators experienced in organizing grassroots efforts. The NSP was the product of a generation anchored in a Syrian nationalism that predated the mandate, Zionism, and the emergent realpolitik of World War I. Arab cultural history remains the fuel behind nationalist demands even in the present. However, operating within the terms of the West in Syria became the prudent choice for Syrian notables increasingly concerned with local conditions. French military might and, less so, its own lack of experience and economic resources, not provincialism—sectarian or otherwise—ended the NSP experiment.

The mere fact that the New Syria Party had sizable membership with chapters across the United States and Central and South America confirms an awareness of Syrian political identity across the waters and a desire to fight for Syria's territorial integrity. The translations of archival documents from the Farah papers and other sources mitigate the persistently debilitating unreliability surrounding Arab immigrants' early history and, I hope, open the debate on the extent of politics as a marker in Arab American life. Additional evidence surely waits to be excavated and examined. It is possible to produce a narrative based on mass political work by immigrants once the material is assembled. The NSP's political lobbying at the time was still concentrated on events in Syria and on political support to Syrian leaders in exile. But in two short years the party's efforts evolved from sending aid and reacting to political events in Greater Syria to becoming an active political player.

Despite the evasively one-sided history of the French Mandate, which a few works like that by Michael Provence and the Arabic-language scholarship have challenged, the present examination of the NSP illustrates how French militarism and a perception of U.S. impartiality emboldened immigrants' political agenda beyond sending aid. The NSP hosted the official Syrian-Palestinian delegates to the League of Nations, mustered meaningful amounts of aid, and as the French devastated the Syrian rebels militarily, became an asset to the leaders of the Syrian revolt in their fight on the stage of world public opinion in the League of Nations. This chapter prepares the way for investigating the Arab National League and the Institute of Arab American Affairs by documenting plans to establish an information office, among other measures, in the United States. The combined archival evidence on the Free Syria Society and the NSP qualifies the frequently quoted statement by the intellectual Philip Hitti in 1924 that Syrians were "by no means of one accord as to things political."[110] Moreover, in this chapter I have addressed a gap in Arab American political activity in the 1920s and, perhaps more importantly, proposed that it was possible to coagulate sporadic activism under a single, national, formal, political organization. The ANL was established nine years after the second and last NSP convention was held. Even then, in 1936, Abu Shaqra attended the organizational meeting for the ANL in the name of the New Syria Party, bringing with him Farah and a contingent of the Detroit activists.

More research is needed to confirm the amounts of aid the NSP sent to the rebellion in Syria and to chronicle the emissaries' itinerary. Arslan's appeal and contacts were extensive, and he may have tried to bridge the immigrant communities in New York with the NSP's members in Michigan. In folders bulging with documents that await any attention I found a letter

Shakib Arslan wrote to Ḥabīb Kātibah two years after the end of the revolt that confirms many arguments put forth in this study on the importance of the NSP beyond U.S. borders, the futility of claims of sectarianism, and the practicability of Syrian nationalism despite the military defeat. In this reply to Kātibah, Arslan, who likely spent time with Kātibah while in New York, addressed the activist affectionately: "My Ḥabīb, light of my eyes, may God benefit the homeland with his dedication."[111] The prince defiantly declares that the road to Syrian statehood and independence is moving forward despite all obstacles—the British-French alliance; the weakness of the League of Nations before these two powers; the economic, political, and military weakness of the homelands; and the rampant corruption by many seeking positions under the French system of rule in the name of patriotism. Arslan concludes, "Undeniably, the nationalist community in the diasporas has a great effect in supporting the Syrian national cause."[112]

THE MANDATE YEARS AND THE DIASPORA: THE ARAB NATIONAL LEAGUE AND A HISTORICAL CONTEXT FOR ARAB AMERICAN NARRATIVE

Chapter 5

On August 6, 1936, three months after the largest Palestinian revolt until that time culminated in a prolonged general strike, the founding of the Arab National League was reported in a communiqué in the Arabic-language publication *Al-Saʾeh*.[1] The ANL was replacing the Arab Renaissance Society (Jamʿīyat al-Nahḍah al-ʿArabīyah). A letter from Fuad Isa Shatara to Ameen Farah clears up confusion about several variations of the names of the organization that was the precursor to the league. Occasional interchangeable references to the ANL and the Palestine Renaissance Society, as well as the appearance of other social groups with some Arab orientation, suggest that a single national political organization was not present during the nine years following the Syrian revolt in 1925 save for the New Syria Party. This, however, does not mean a cessation of individual and coordinated support for Arab causes. This was a period of adjustment to the political realities of the mandate and the practical pressures of the Great Depression. In this chapter I chart immigrants' lives during that confusing period through their writings, and I trace the genesis of the Arab National League to events and personalities on the U.S. East Coast before the NSP was founded.

In the years that followed the Syrian revolt against the French, Syria's cause was kept alive by persistent albeit sporadic gatherings of activists from New York, Michigan, and elsewhere. Arabic-language magazines and newspapers, especially *As-Sameer* in New York, continued to provide a forum for conversations among immigrants in which they maintained their connection to their Arab past and Syrian identity. The rebels' defeat by the French and severe economic hardship in the United States account for the lack of a single national political organization from 1927 until the founding of the ANL in 1936. Here I attempt to fill this uncharted period within the scantily researched history of the Syrian immigrants and conditions leading to the founding of the ANL.

Proposing a context for the transition from a Syrian national cause to an Arab one is congruent with Rashid Khalidi's discourse on Palestinian identity. Khalidi has found that the years 1908 to 1921 influenced the trajectory of Palestinian national identity. Ḥabīb Kātibah would work alongside Ismail Khalidi, Rashid Khalidi's father, in the office of the Institute of Arab American Affairs after World War II before Rashid's birth. Kātibah predicted Rashid Khalidi's assessment of the importance of that period in his unpublished manuscript draft titled "The Arab Challenge." Although the Ottoman Constitution, not responses to Zionism, took precedence in Kātibah's analysis, the forces of colonialism in all parts of Syria were connected and corresponded more or less to the same period. Kātibah opened chapter 5, titled "Fateful Years: 1908–1915," in his manuscript with these words:

> The period between 1908 and the outbreak of the first world war was one of the greatest, most bizarre, emotion-charged periods in the history of the Arab lands. It was as if suppressed feelings and impounded forces of all sorts had been suddenly released and, driven by the pressure of outside conditions and events, the Arabs were forced to improvise a *modus operand* without delay. Like a vast mural, the significance of this period dawns upon the observer only after he discovers the central theme in the mind of the artist.[2]

He viewed the ill-fated "Ottoman Revolution," a term meant to signify reviving the Ottoman Constitution in 1908, as equally important to any in world history and "an indication that strength and ubiquity" of yearnings for democracy and equality are more powerful than Sultan Abdulhamid's "elaborate system of espionage."[3] The euphoria and fraternizing that ensued among Turks, Arabs, and Armenians, Kātibah wrote, was looked upon "askance by the political vultures who had been hourly awaiting the demise of the sick man of the Bosphorus." The political vultures, he explains, are the "European imperialists."[4]

During the same period Syrian immigrants in the United States began to pay special attention to Palestine, even as they coalesced around the Syrian cause, because of the Zionists' aggressive land acquisition, especially in light of the Balfour Declaration in 1917. Zionist pressure in Palestine would be viewed as part of colonialist expansion once activists from all over Syria turned their attention to the Syrian Revolt against the French in 1925–1927, when the situation was dire. The New Syria Party lingered after 1927, but the mandate and the dismemberment of Greater Syria made it harder for nationalists to refer to themselves as Syrians or Southern Syrians. By 1929 and a new uprising, this time in Palestine against the British and the gathering Zionist influence, immigrant activists were forced to defend their points of view in the United States in opposition to the Zionists more than to the French. Indeed, the public-opinion battle over Palestine in the English-language press became an essential front in defending the larger Arab defiance to the mandate as a whole. The violence and ensuing Palestinian uprising of 1929 offer examples of how both the Zionists and the Palestinians formulated defenses of their respective views. A balanced approach to exploring the conflict can be found in *Palestine, a Decade of Development*, a special publication in 1932 of the American Academy of Political and Social Science; it covers both viewpoints and illustrates the stark differences that came to characterize the Zionist and Arab (Syrian and Palestinian) positions.[5]

One of the reasons behind the decade-long absence of national political organizations was the Great Depression, beginning with the stock market crash in October 1929. The years of the Depression undoubtedly took a heavy toll on Syrians in Highland Park. Although many of them had just become established economically, Michigan's economy suffered a drastic slump in sales of automobiles, the state's principal industry. The center of political activity shifted to New York at the same time Palestinian and Zionist activities emerged as the core rallying issue for the immigrants. It took a while for immigrants to grasp the political reality arising from the British and French occupations of Syria. Divided into spheres of European influence, Syria faced a profoundly uncertain future. As the Europeans dug in under the pretext of the League of Nations mandates, they also fed the colonized Arab populations a steady diet of promises of freedom and independence.

Further complicating the new political arrangements was the British sanction of Jewish immigration into Palestine. This contradictory British policy promised the Zionists a homeland in lands inhabited by the Palestinians, whose welfare was declared a British responsibility under the charter of mandate. The incoherent and provocative British policy was ill equipped to deal with increased militancy by newly arriving Jews and the indigenous Arab population. The New York–based ANL had to face the reality of rapid Zionist gains in Palestine that were matched by a deterioration of the quality of life for Palestinians. The dream of an independent Syria became untenable as firm Arab leadership and coherence gave way to infighting and posturing by Syrian notables who found themselves forced to deal with the British and the French on colonial terms. Indeed, the verbal collapse of terminology about Syria when trying to distinguish modern Syria, Lebanon, and historic Palestine or Southern Syria reveals the impact of colonialism. The mandate required these distinctions before the emergent Arab nation-states made them inevitable.

Rashid Khalidi finds that critical developments in Palestinian cultural and political identity occurred from the Balfour Declaration in 1917 to the ratification of the San Remo Agreement by the League of Nations in 1922;[6] those developments were largely the impetus behind the ANL. The British and French Mandates widened the gaps separating the Arab nationalists in Damascus, Beirut, Baghdad, and Jerusalem, which made the realization of any part of their political aims at the time all but impossible. This is not to say that the idea for the ANL in the early 1920s emerged from distinct historical circumstance any more than did the idea for the New Syria Party, but neither was the emergence of the ANL disconnected from the NSP or the early responses to Zionism after the Balfour Declaration in 1917 as described by Lawrence Davidson.[7] This is to say the activities connected to the Syria idea transformed into responses to Zionism by largely the same activists who reacted to French and later British militarism during the mandates.

Immigrants felt the effects of these events even before they perceived Zionism as a threat. What brought Britain and France to the region was Syria's location and the Europeans' expanding strategic concerns. After all, Europeans were concerned about oil concessions in Iran, a short distance to the east, and pursued a policy aimed at securing additional concessions for extracting oil in Mosul, Iraq, deemed by the secret Sykes-Picot Agreement in 1916 to lie within the French area of influence. The colonialist powers came to an agreement whereby the British gained control over what became northern Iraq in exchange for cash payment to the French. Access was assured by both colonialist powers to the Far East through the Persian Gulf. But this foothold sank into the quicksand of uprisings in 1920 and 1921 by the Palestinians in response to the equally determined and far less restricted Zionists and to the Great Syrian Revolt.[8] British reliance on oil after converting from coal began to drive its policy in the Middle East and led to an Anglo-Iraqi agreement in 1932 supposedly ending the mandate. Shatara and his compatriots in New York, among them Faris Malouf, George Barakat, and Ḥabīb Kātibah, spoke out in defense of Syria in the same breath they voiced concerns over the future of Palestine.

The literature on the interwar period in the Middle East is voluminous. However, due to the influence of Zionism, Palestinian identity itself is anything but the straightforward story it ought to have been.[9] An inherent limitation in the present study, which approaches events in the Middle East from the vantage of the Palestinian and Arab side, is the lack of an assessment of the repression exacted on Jews in Germany in the 1930s. Suffice it to say that the Zionists' successes did not always come automatically or easily, and there is no intention herein to overstate their power, especially when occupation and internal divisions left the Palestinian and Arab sides perpetually weak. Immigrant activists and their Palestinian counterparts faced similar pressures, ranging from Zionist plans to create a Jewish majority in Palestine to British failure to reconcile contradictory promises to both Arabs and Jews.

The Syrians' first battle in their quest to influence public policy was to simply maintain visibility as U.S. citizens. In the 1937 edited volume *One America*, an inquiry into "the national minorities," Kātibah, who freelanced as a reporter for the *Brooklyn Daily News* and the *Detroit News*, began his contribution titled "Syrian Americans" with a rebuke: "It is a strange moment, and hard to explain, that the Syrians, one of the most ubiquitous of peoples, have been among the least known."[10] Seeking common ground with readers, Kātibah put a human face on the mysterious Arabs from the ancient Middle East, describing a periodization of Syrian immigration and social integration in the United States in three stages. He considered the late nineteenth century the first stage, a romantic time of discovery that he called the "peddling" stage. The second stage was one of "orientation," from the turn of the twentieth century to the close of World War I; in this stage businesses were established on a modern footing—clothing and linen manufacturing in New York and grocery stores and restaurants in the Midwest. In the third stage, from the mid-1920s to the mid- to late 1930s, Syrians gave up their forebears' nomadic ways and "diversified," or entered "completely into American heritage" and became U.S. citizens active in all areas of American life.[11]

The Syrian experience in the Detroit area serves as a microcosm of Arab Syrian acculturation and adjustment to life in the United States that conforms to Kātibah's assessment. The same is true in Flint. As early as 1932, Ameen Farah was invited to serve on the McKeighan for Governor Committee in support of the former Republican mayor of Flint. His involvement probably resulted from the connections Farah gained among his countrymen during his political activism for the New Syria Party. A survey of surviving issues of the Arabic-language *As-Sameer* magazine edited by Elia D. Madey completes—and perhaps complicates—the picture of immigrant self-awareness in the 1930s. During the brutal Depression, immigrants had one eye on their homelands while developing a sense of belonging as U.S. citizens. In the April 15, 1932, issue of *As-Sameer*, Philip Hitti celebrated the fifty-second anniversary of the American Oriental Society, Naʿūm Mokarzel was eulogized, Arab history in late antiquity was celebrated, and unjust taxes imposed on the Muslim majority in Lebanon outside Beirut were criticized by mostly Christian activists.

In characteristically academic style, Hitti informed the readers that they might be astonished to learn that the American Oriental Society had existed since 1842 and its 730 researchers and scientists were dedicated to the study of the religions, languages, and philosophies of the East.[12] Hitti conceded that the United States did not have a trading partner in Arab lands, impelling "folks here to learn Arabic." Nor did the "Stars and Stripes shade Muslim and Arab heads." The other 120 million Americans, he added, were unaware of the presence among them of 60,000 Arabic-speaking immigrants. The immigrant figures cannot now be determined accurately, but an editor's footnote in the *As-Sameer* article explains them this way: "Dr. Hitti relied on official statistics, although some ignore the census and rely on their imagination saying that Arabic-speakers number 300,000."[13]

Madey's sharp and witty eulogy of Naʿūm Mokarzel, the former editor of *Al-Hoda*, refined the man down to his essence. Mokarzel died while on a political crusade in Paris to support the Lebanese presidency of the Maronite candidate Émile Eddé against his progressive opponent Bishara al-Khouri. Mokarzel's death ended thirty years, Madey wrote, of "personal leanings and sectarianism; for journalism ascends with its people's civility and plummets with their decline."[14] Madey credited the man with turning a small weekly newspaper into a large daily newspaper and with financial prowess, among other characteristics:

> And he was able to amass from nothing a large fortune of no less than a quarter of a million dollars. We would have liked to publish the details of his life, but we saw that *Al-Hoda* [Mokarzel's newspaper] ignored the matter as did the other newspapers.... Suffice it to say that he left a void in the journalistic world that can be filled by someone like him.... Therefore, his death is an intense loss to those who admire him. God's mercy. Our sympathy to his widow and family.[15]

It was the impending political reality of propping up a Lebanese state that endured, not Mokarzel's antics. Lebanese separatism was reinforced by isolated antagonism to Arab nationalism expressed by Maronites from the Mount Lebanon area. Sporadic accounts of the antagonism combined with the evidence of insults being exchanged in the Syrian press largely due to Mokarzel's brazen assaults. The political sectarian system of government in Lebanon explains the lengths to which French policies, and perhaps also Mokarzel, went to achieve their aims. In response to French policies supported by Émile Eddé, an article in the same issue of *As-Sameer* criticized the French-dominated Lebanese republic's repressive taxes in the mostly Muslim South Lebanon, as if predicting the economic undercurrents behind the costly civil war some forty years later.[16] The French allowed the first census in Lebanon's history to be carried out in that year, 1932, to justify the confessional system of government whereby the presidency was reserved for a Maronite, the prime minister post for a Sunni Muslim, and the speaker of the Chamber of Deputies for a Shi'a Muslim. However, the French held sway in all matters, and the executive branch prepared all legislation, which was then approved by the deputies. To keep this unbalanced arrangement afloat, the Maronites were guaranteed a majority irrespective of numerical proportionality.[17]

The immigrants' rebuke of French-backed policies based on sectarian affiliation seemed to be widespread. Editorials in subsequent issues of *As-Sameer* admonished advocates of the painful divisions seeking to separate Syrians from Lebanese when the immigrants' numbers were relatively small:

> We spent fifty years trying to make the American population understand which is the country we came from. We were destined to say to them that we are from Syria and never gave Lebanon a thought until the recent while. So, they came to understand that there is a country called Syria, though for the most part they do not understand where it is located. Or have we forgotten that when they asked, we answered Suryya. "Do you mean Siberia?" We would say no. Do you mean Serbia? We would respond negatively, repeating, Syria.[18]

The unsigned author of the piece questioned the wisdom of adding the title "Lebanese" to the names of the Syrian American Clubs in some cities and lamented the lack of good sense in these "useless" antics.[19] The article drew a rebuttal from a countryman who felt that listing the Lebanon was necessary to educate the U.S. population on the specific districts from which Syrians came—"Houran, Alawite [Islamic sect in northern Syria] mountains, Beirutis, Damascene, Biqa'is [from the Baqa' Valley], Alepans, Tripolians, Homsis."[20] Other issues of *As-Sameer* carried translations of field hollers,[21] likely as a way to uplift spirits during the Depression or as a sign of appreciation for black countrymen. Elaborate eulogies commemorated the deaths of the "admired Palestinian leader" Musa Kazim al-Husseini and King Husain of the Hijaz (Sharif Husain of Mecca).[22]

The Syrian Revolt against French occupation led to the formation of the New Syria Party and was rooted in the same set of events that led to the founding of the Arab National League and its predecessor the Palestine Renaissance Society. World War I and its aftermath set in motion a sequence of events that led to an uprising and general strike, only this time in Southern Syria, or Palestine. Syrian American activists from the Lebanon region shared the devotion to Palestine's plight. When the Palestinian journalist ʿĀref al-ʿĀref decried the impending separation in Versailles of Palestine by dismembering Syria,[23] he echoed sentiments by the nationalist Ameen Rihani, the journalist Najīb Diāb, and scores of others from Detroit to New York. The transnational framework of Syrian nationalism transcended locations by drawing on the common denominator of Arabism. The importance of Syria to the Palestinians, hence, was "an indication of devotion to Arabism."[24] The importance of Palestine to the Syrians is part of the same formula.

The reciprocity was evident in the wake of World War I. In 1918 the victorious Arab army and the British entered Damascus, where Prince Faisal, son of Husain Ibn Ali, the sharif of Mecca, established a Syrian government. In 1919 representatives in the Syrian National Congress, the temporary government, came from all parts of Syria including Palestine.

The congress emphasized Syria's unity by rejecting British and French designs of carving out a separate Lebanon and Palestine and prepared the way for the inquiry by the King-Crane Commission into the fate of Syria at the behest of Woodrow Wilson ahead of the Paris Peace Conference. In March 1920 participants in the Syrian Convention sought Syrian "natural unity" and proclaimed Faisal king of Syria. In April the League of Nations gave France power over Syria's fate; in July France destroyed the Syrian fighting force at the Battle of Maysalun.[25] After the fall of Faisal, the gravity of the situation set in among the Palestinian leadership. Musa Kazim Pasha al-Husseini, the preeminent political leader in Palestine, declared his intentions: "Now after the recent events in Damascus, we have to effect a complete change in our plans here. Southern Syria no longer exists. We have to defend Palestine."[26] Palestinians within the Faisal government in the north and those living in other parts of the region as well as Beirutis, Aleppans, and Damascenes living in Jerusalem, Jaffa, or Haifa found themselves unable to move freely through the main cities of Syria. In the United States the reaction to these events was delayed until the Druze-led revolt against the French subsided in 1927. However, in Palestine, people continued to build organizations for religious, civil, and political leadership with nominal financial contributions from U.S. nationalists.

It was no accident that Hajj Amin al-Husseini gained prominence through efforts to collect aid for the Syrian rebellion in 1926 and beyond. Al-Husseini, who commanded the respect and loyalty of members of the ANL, assumed leadership in Palestine following a revolt in April 1920; he already had credentials as a nationalist. He belonged to the Husseini family that is acknowledged to be descended from the Prophet Muhammad's

Hashemite clan, he participated in the fight against the Turks in the Arab Revolt in 1916, and he traveled to Damascus to support Faisal in the Pan-Syrian Congress in 1919. His tenure was initially aided by a strategy of the newly appointed high commissioner Herbert Samuel of utilizing local leadership to implement the mandate pending its ratification by the League of Nations. Although the ultimate goal of the British was to secure the mandate through military occupation, they fueled passions by appointing Samuel, a committed Zionist, as high commissioner over Palestine despite grandiose speeches and photo opportunities with local clergy and notables.

By that time the King-Crane Report, which concluded that the 90 percent Arab population objected to their country being divided and settled by European Jews, had come to nothing and was suppressed in the United States. The World Zionist Organization was not deterred by Syrian popular sentiment from insisting that "inarticulate" nomads sparsely inhabited Palestine, even when Jewish voices acknowledged the contrary: "It was now coming to be realized that Palestine was not empty."[27] In 1921 the Third Palestine Congress met in Jerusalem, and Kazim al-Husseini was appointed president, primarily to express the population's discontent with the British and the practices by the Jewish National Fund of excluding Arab labor from Jewish-owned land and the fund's vast investments.[28] The British sanctioned these policies in breach of the language of the mandate, which was delivered to the Palestinians "from the British Crown directly."[29] Upon his arrival Samuel spoke to a gathering of Palestinian notables in the name of the "victorious allied powers" who "entrusted to [Britain] a Mandate to watch over the interests of Palestine and to ensure to your country that peaceful and prosperous development which has so long been denied to you."[30]

A second Palestinian official delegation journeyed to London to emphasize the Palestinians' grievances of unequal development and Jewish settlements. Churchill dismissed them with the words "talk to Weizmann," a response that left intact the prospect of European Jews becoming a majority in Palestine,[31] as Chaim Weizmann was president of the World Zionist Organization. Skillful posturing by the British at the behest of powerful pro-Zionist lobbyists in London delayed the delegation, but the British government relented somewhat in the face of renewed demonstrations in Palestine on the anniversary of the 1920 uprising in Jaffa. Samuel drafted a statement for Churchill that allowed for a Palestinian legislative council, but he withheld granting it legislative power.[32] Because of its conciliatory tone, the statement became known as the first white paper. Subsequent Palestinian delegations to London during 1922–1923 were aided presumably by Arab immigrants like Salim Farah, son of former mayor of Nazareth Raji Farah, and certainly by Palestinian politicians like Jamal Bey al-Husseini with ties to immigrants in the United States. Such expertise enabled the delegation to quote the May 20, 1921, issue of the *Jewish Chronicle*, where a call appeared for the creation of a "Palestine that was as Jewish as England is English or Canada is Canadian." The delegation rejected, to no avail, Samuel's decision to make Hebrew an official language without their consent when Jews comprised about one-tenth of the population in Palestine. In February 1922 the delegation from Palestine stated its grievances in a booklet outlining the historical roots of the conflict and recent events.

The delegation reminded the British of their promises to "recognize and support the independence of the Arabs within the territories included in the limits and boundaries proposed by the Sharif [Husain of Mecca]."[33] The statements mirrored Arab Palestinian reaction to the Balfour Declaration: "This Declaration ... fell as a thunderbolt from the blue on the Arab population of Palestine."[34] Significantly, in a reference to U.S. Arabs' objections to the Balfour Declaration, without naming a source, the delegation's statement listed the United States among venues where protests against it took place.[35] The Arab delegation noted that prominent Zionists on the Political Committee of the International Zionist Congress promoted the appointments of Balfour and Samuel to their posts and influenced the issuance of the Balfour Declaration.[36] The delegation pointed to popular discontent that led to the formation of "Moslem and Christian leagues ... in large towns and villages." The authors drew inspiration from the establishment of the ecumenical Palestinian Congress in 1919 and subsequent gatherings to combat Britain's policies. Although the delegation did not consent to open Jewish immigration and prospects of a national home for Europeans in their land, they did not overplay their hand, choosing instead to appeal to a sense of fair play by writing that "the word of an Englishman ... would ever stand for righteousness and Justice."[37]

Syrian immigrants may have influenced the language of the delegation concerning possibilities of coexistence in, for example, a reference to the "incontrovertible evidence of the toleration of Arabs towards their Jewish guests who live in peace and harmony with their Arab neighbors."[38] In one decade this statement would serve as the prototype for Fuad Shatara's preferred binational democratic state comprised of Arabs and Jews. Nevertheless, Palestinians were told by Britain's Parliamentary Commission of Inquiry investigating the disturbances of May 1921 that "there can only be one national home in Palestine, and that a Jewish one, and no equality in the partnership between Jews and Arabs, but a Jewish prominence as soon as the numbers of that race are sufficiently increased."[39]

British High Commissioner Herbert Samuel had the power to abolish the council at will, cast a decisive vote in the case of an impasse, and stop any appeals from reaching the League of Nations; he finally appointed an Arab council in Palestine. The delegation members in London—the nationalists Kazim al-Husseini and Amin al-Tamimi and the Maronite Wadiʿ al-Bustāni—rejected the Palestinian leadership's proposal to visit the United States in 1921 to build support among Arab immigrant communities and then spend the fall in London.[40] This debate within the leadership over Palestinians' demands in London was telling of the ongoing connections between the immigrants and the leadership in Palestine. The recommendation to visit the United States was probably made at the behest of Jamal Bey al-Husseini. As did many of his educated peers, he understood the value of reaching out to U.S. immigrants, with Ameen Farah among the many he knew, not to mention Salim Farah, who offered advice to the delegation in London. The British continued to profess at critical junctures that they did not contemplate the "disappearance or subordination of the Arab population, language, or culture."[41] Yet Churchill assured the uncompromising Polish Zionist Vladimir Jabotinsky that Jewish settlement in Palestine was a "right and not sufferance."[42]

In many respects immigrants shared in their compatriots' powerlessness. Until the dust and chaos of World War I settled, the Balfour Declaration in 1917 was mitigated by Wilsonian promises of self-determination for the former subjects of the Ottoman Empire. The discourse in Rihani's *Letters to Uncle Sam* was echoed in earnest hopes of achieving fairness once the United States became involved in the Paris Peace Conference. It was not very easy for most of the immigrant community amid the confusion of mandate policies and the Great Depression to understand the impact of British practices in Palestine. But news of the worsening conditions of the Palestinian people continued to reach the pages of *As-Sameer* and other publications. Adding to the confusion was that British policy differed from French rule because the British had to navigate the demands of both Zionists and the Arab Palestinian inhabitants, and they did so by making contradictory statements while imposing military administration. The Arab activists in the United States understood they had some leverage because they were in contact with the Palestine delegation in London. It was not possible for the Palestinians on either side of the Atlantic to stop the British from buying time until the ratification of the mandate by the League of Nations in 1922, but they did react by planting the seeds for the Arab National League.

Churchill hinted that Palestine could not absorb open Jewish immigration and that there was a possibility of granting Palestinian citizenship to both Arabs and Jews. From this statement came the white paper. However, his and other such statements were subsequently reversed when permanent claims by Zionists in Palestine were allowed. In the lead-up to the creation of the ANL in 1936, another British commission investigated the largest Palestinian uprising until that time and found nothing in the first white paper to prevent "the ultimate establishment of a Jewish State."[43] Meanwhile, Palestinians' attempts to gain a semblance of representation and power over their destiny achieved little, despite their willingness to listen and desire to be heard.[44] Palestinians sent their grievances annually to the League of Nations despite not having official or direct links to it. For their part, Zionists, aided by "severe pressure" from their British counterparts in the British government,[45] forged ahead with their development despite scant Jewish immigration.

The mandate, Balfour's fateful declaration, and yet another popular uprising in Palestine in 1929 kept the bleak situation in Palestine on immigrants' minds throughout the 1930s and eventually added to galvanizing support behind a single organization, the ANL. The intellectual Elia Madey condemned Balfour's declaration for planting a "dreaded seed" that thrived by "drawing the blood of the Arabs and the Jews."[46] Balfour's crime, the seminal *mahjar* author declared, was "not the crime of a day or a year, rather, the crime of an age." Madey's Arabic-language article "The Revolt of 1929" in the next issue of *As-Sameer* ended with a poem titled "Do Not Steal Our Home!"[47] The poem became required reading for successive generations of pupils in the Middle East and was suggested by newspapers as a suitable anthem of the national cause. His recollection of the night he delivered his poem at a pivotal moment provides a clue to immigrants' efforts to pull together. During a gathering on August 15, 1929, at the Hotel McAlpin in New York, "a nationalist body [*hay'ah waṭanīyah*] was created . . . to protest against British policy in Palestine."[48]

The uprising by the Palestinians in 1929 aided the Zionists in the United States in their appeal for support among American Jews. Like previous resistance, this convulsion in Palestine following disputes over access to the holy sites highlighted the need for even-handed policy by the British. Among New York's sizable Jewish population and in Zionist circles in Britain, the causes of this latest uprising were blamed for the most part on intrinsic Arab anti-Semitism, while "no word of censure touched the Jews . . . [who] exacerbated the Christian and Muslim population."[49] The direct cause of the incident was the unprecedented act, mostly by Polish Jewish settlers, of placing tables and chairs in a public pathway leading to the Burāq

(Wailing Wall) section of al-Haram al-Sharif complex, which holds al-Aqsa mosque and the Dome of the Rock, Islam's holiest places in Palestine.

The British had prevented the Jewish worshipers the previous year from blocking the passageway, in keeping with time-honored custom and Ottoman laws forbidding exclusive control of the area by any single religious party. The settlers did not relent, and British troops removed their tables and dividers by force. Demonstrations by Jewish worshipers through Arab neighborhoods were followed by massive demonstrations by Muslims until, as a British observer at the time put it, Palestinians were "inspired by a sort of desperate desire to achieve by blows what protest failed to do."[50] As a result, dozens were killed on both sides, including an *imam* (Muslim clergyman) and three Palestinian women.

An exhaustive report on the events was written by Sir John Hope Simpson in consultation with the high commissioner and a collection of Jewish and "Arab," that is, Palestinian, organizations. The detailed Simpson report was obtained by many immigrants and used extensively in debates.[51] It confirmed most of the grievances by the Palestinians at the time. High unemployment, the major cause of their unrest, was linked to the "desperate position" of the *fellāh* (farmer).[52] The report computed the numbers of cultivable *dunums* (a *dunum* is 1,000 square meters) available to Palestinians and disclosed that in the small village of Beir Zeit (Birzeit) near Ramallah, for example, 115 Palestinian families, a significant number, lost access to land and relied on remittances from family members who "emigrated to America from the village."[53]

The report revealed the vast difference in financial support received by the Palestinian or Arab and Jewish or Zionist sides. Regarding the formidable funds from abroad, Simpson found that the Palestine Foundation Fund, the financial source for the Colonization Department of the Zionist Organization, was "so over-capitalized" that the amount spent on the settlement of each family exceeded its needs,[54] while the same organization demanded "very little from the settler himself."[55] In this respect, Simpson drew a sharp distinction between the early Jewish cooperative farmers—whom the Palestinian Arab report called "neighbors" and who lived in harmony with the indigenous inhabitants—and those who adhered to the practices of the Jewish National Fund.

The events of 1929 played a role in redressing divisions among American Jews over Zionism when the events were interpreted to bolster the Zionist agenda of creating a state in Palestine.[56] U.S. newspapers (with the notable exception of the *New York Times*, which for the time being was not sympathetic to the idea of Zionism) regarded the events with a uniform perspective, thus handing proponents of Zionism a major public relations victory. The *Chicago Tribune* and most of the Jewish presses reduced the events to "Arab riots." It became clear to Syrian activists, especially in New York's Lower Manhattan, where most Arab Syrians settled not far from Jewish immigrants, that influencing public opinion about the conflict depended on how the U.S. press presented this and other events in "the Holy Land."

As a result of the sharp differences in perceiving the events in Palestine, vigorous debates ensued among the parties. Most major newspapers in Chicago, Washington, and Los Angeles indignantly blamed the Arabs in dozens of articles for massacring the ancient Jews in a religious or racial war.[57] Some portrayed the British and Zionists as heroes struggling to defend the "Jewish National Fund colony of Chulda,"[58] as the Jewish Telegraphic Agency described a settlement. The semi-active Syrian organizations banded together in response to the unprecedented news coverage of the events in Palestine, while the Zionist Organization of America tried to "succor Jews stricken in the Wailing Wall riots."[59] Coverage of the events of 1929 was intense and, save that of the *New York Times*,[60] depicted the Palestinians as outlaws and enemies of Jews and Christians.

Arab immigrants were compelled to respond to the way the press covered the news from Palestine and to explain the grievances of Palestinians to the U.S. population at large. After the Palestinian uprising started in August 1929, the *New York Times* reported that "Arabian citizens" met in the Woolworth Building office of New York attorney Selim Totah and issued a statement explaining that the source of the troubles was not religion. They decried the "unfairness of the Jewish press in dealing with the present Palestine rioting."[61] The signatories were listed as Fuad Shatara, president of what the reporter called the Palestine National League; 'Abbas Abu Shaqra, the general secretary of the by-then largely defunct New Syria Party; and Abd M. Khateeb, secretary of the Young Men's Moslem Society of America.

The group, composed of immigrants and other activists from all parts of Syria, agreed that economics and politics were the cause of the troubles in Palestine, where "a minority race was given a permanent home at the expense of the Majority." They said the "deplorable events are the outcome of the Balfour Declaration." The activists declared, "The Wailing Wall is merely an incident" that was symptomatic of a larger social and economic reality. The *New York Times* reported that the group sent a statement "seeking an American sense of freedom and justice to uphold Arabs in their struggle for national independence" to President Herbert Hoover, Senator William Borah, and Secretary of State Henry Stimson. It sent similar cablegrams to

Pope Pius XI, Cardinal Hayes, British Prime Minister Ramsay MacDonald, and the League of Nations headquarters.[62]

The immigrants, apparently alarmed at the hostile tone of news coverage and prospects of even more Jewish and Western support for the Zionists, fell on their larger Arab and Muslim consciousness. Hence, the Palestine question and immigrant strategy became subsumed in a larger Arab context. Accordingly, they sent telegrams to Saudi King Abdulaziz Ibn Saud; Imam Yahya of Yemen; King Riza of Persia; and King Faisal of Iraq, whom the British installed in Baghdad after the French deposed him in Syria. The telegram to the Arab and Muslim dignitaries stated, "Situation dangerous and calling for help. British policy responsible for present conditions. Sacred rights of Arabs as a nation deserving independence and principles you are promulgating in Arabia are menaced by Jewish aggression."[63] U.S. Zionists capitalized on general ignorance of Middle Eastern history and religion in the United States by painting all Arabs as Muslims bent on the destruction of "the Jewish state."

The Lebanese-Syrian intellectual Ameen Rihani weighed in on the events, arguing to the press that Palestinians did not object to Zionism "as a cultural and spiritual movement" but rather to newcomers with "funds in one hand and the Balfour Declaration in the other . . . the vanguard of a dream of conquest, a dream of empire, which the Arabs must resist . . . to the end."[64] Salim Farah, son of Nazareth mayor Raji Farah and brother of Flint resident Neman Farah, helped the Palestinian Council contribute to the Simpson Report when it was consulted. Salim Farah graduated from Cornell and the agricultural school of the University of Illinois before traveling to London to testify before the British Parliamentary Commission of Inquiry; he provided information on the numbers of dispossessed families and lost agricultural surplus in the face of Jewish settlement.[65] His father, as mayor at the close of the Ottoman era, had access to numerous land registry documents.[66]

By this time other Syrians were vocal on the pages of newspapers in many parts of the United States. Some would become key to the success of the ANL. One of those was Najīb N. Samra, a neighbor of Ameen Farah in Flint. He ran a display of "oriental rugs, Damascene brassware and inlaid wood at the Rosenbury and Son store" while living in Bay City, Michigan. As cited in the local paper, Samra said he felt disturbed by a motion picture he saw showing a tag over a mosque declaring "Death to the Christian who sets foot in this temple."[67]

This experience, along with the heightened interest in "the Holy Land" after the 1929 Wailing Wall incident, helped spark Samra's eloquent contributions in the *Bay City Times* in the early 1930s and later in the *Flint Journal* after he moved to Flint. But the implications of Samra's rebuke of stereotypes of Islam are far-reaching in that he, as did many Syrian activists in small cities, anticipated future challenges for Arab Americans that persist to this day. The perceptions that all Arabs are Muslims and that all Muslims are hostile to the West became a continual obstacle for generations of immigrant activists in advancing an Arab political perspective to the U.S. population. Moreover, the stereotype Samra described would be the direct motivation for descendants of the Syrian immigrants, among them U.S. Senator James Abourezk and Arab Americans from four generations, to establish an Arab American civil rights organization five decades later, in 1980: the American Arab Anti-Discrimination Committee.

Samra's articulation of what was called the Arab side of the conflict with Zionism from the depth of the Great Depression foretold the difficulties the ANL would face getting its message across a few years later. True to the spirit of the Arab *nahḍah*, Samra's opinion columns in local newspapers summoned ancient Arab glories but also posited racial and cultural compatibility of Arabs and Jews. In March 1930 Samra educated his readers on the history of the Arabs while making the case that the 1929 disturbances were a symptom and not the cause of the troubles. He blamed political Zionism and reaffirmed that Jews and Arabs had lived in harmony for centuries: "The Jews and Arabs spring from the same Semitic stock. Racially they are congenial."[68] In the article Samra indignantly refuted rampant claims that Arabs were an inferior race and recounted Arab contributions to mathematics, astronomy, chemistry, and physics. He reminded the newspaper readers that Dante, Galileo, and Columbus were all influenced by Arab thinkers.

Samra appealed to some readers' presumed penchant for the exotic to get his point across, perhaps banking on the popularity of film star Rudolph Valentino's rendition of "the sheik" at the time. He came to know Rihani, with whom he shared membership in an association dedicated to the Syrian Arab cause. The association and the Orientalist tinge in Samra's writing style, conjuring exotic imagery of the East to connect to U.S. readers, suggest a strategy by Samra and Rihani of looking to ancient renditions of Arabism. Farah's archives confirm that Samra obtained a copy of Rihani's book *Kings of Arabia* in 1930.[69] Like Rihani, Samra defended "the terrible Bedouin" as a prototype Arab who was "not the wild fellow he is imagined to be ... not treacherous [but] loyal."[70] Samra repeated his sermon on the Arabs' glories in the *Bay City Times*. Despite this, he could not avoid being seen as an outsider. The *Midland Republican* in Michigan repeatedly referred to

Samra as "this Arab" despite acknowledging his service in the U.S. Army Medical Corps in World War I.

Many of the personalities who would soon join the executive board and advisory committee of the ANL and the Institute of Arab American Affairs contributed to newspaper articles and participated in debates across the United States. One attempt to foster understanding of the conflict from both vantage points was that of the American Academy of Political and Social Science in *Palestine, a Decade of Development*. This major critique captures Arab Palestinians' core grievances, reveals collaborative work of immigrants and their compatriots overseas, and illustrates the liberal nature of Palestinian and Arab aspirations and their willingness to share the land with Jewish constituencies on an equal basis. Syrians, regardless of their geographical locations, were referred to generically as Arabs, and given the vast disparity in numbers and access to press in favor of the Zionist side, they found it nearly impossible to get their point across, which makes this series published by the academy worth investigating.

The contributors were scholars, politicians, and activists from both sides of the Atlantic: Aouni Abdelhadi, a native of Nablus, graduate of the Sorbonne, co-founder of the anti-Ottoman al-Fatāt society in Paris, and legal counsel to the Supreme Islamic Council in Jerusalem; Jamal Bey al-Husseini and Omar Saleh al-Barghuthi, members of the Arab Council; the U.S.-educated lawyer Mughannam E. Mughannam; Fuad Shatara; Ameen Rihani; and Columbia graduate Khalil Totah. The American Academy of Political and Social Science invited Totah to co-edit and secure Arab contributors for the series of articles alongside Harry Viteles.[71] These contributors were balanced by Viteles and other capable proponents of Zionism, among them Isaac Ben-Zwi, Bernard Joseph, Frank Adams, J. Elazari-Volcani, A. P. S. Clark, W. Preuss, Alfred Bonné, I. J. Kigler, and W. F. Albright.

Fuad Shatara's contribution in the academy's even-handed approach made the case for a binational state in Palestine with majority rule. His commitment to sharing the rule and the land with a Jewish population was intended to head off a politically dominant role for Zionism and was in keeping with a general consensus among Syrians that Jews already were an integral part of most population centers in the region anyway. Although Shatara began speaking from a distinctly Palestinian perspective, he and his colleagues forged a flexible strategy with regard to Palestine, the new center of conflict. The strategy would gain predominance in view of Kazim al-Husseini's ominous observation that Southern Syria no longer existed. Shatara elaborated on the possibilities of the binational state by addressing two questions: "Is Arab-Jewish unity in Palestine possible?" and "What are the motives behind Arab opposition?" He framed his answers in the reality of Zionist leader Chaim Weizmann's *imperium in imperio*, a Palestine as "Jewish as England is English or America is American," forcing Palestinians, in the British writer Israel Zanwill's satirical words, to "trek along" or be "hewers of wood and drawers of water." Shatara wrote that "in this *Judenstat*, a Jewish majority is a *sine qua non*."[72]

Shatara's answer to competing claims to Palestine by Arabs and Jews was to create a binational state that could be home to both populations, based on the distant and modern history of the Middle East. Not seeking to exalt the ancient Ghassanite Arabs, who were Christianized at the hands of the apostles, Shatara acknowledged the Arab Jews of the long, illustrious Umayyad rule in Spain.[73] These are joined in the article by a partial roster of Jews opposed to Zionism, among them Henry Morgenthau, Professor Jacob Israel DeHaan, Judah Magnes, and Rabbi Landman, editor of the *American Hebrew*. The "most convincing" Jewish anti-Zionist for Shatara was Judah Jastrow of the University of Pennsylvania, who in the appendix of his own book published a petition opposing Zionism signed by 300 Jewish leaders.[74]

Rihani took issue with the title of his piece chosen by the editor, "Palestine and the Proposed Arab Federation," because it implied a sense of "detachment and conjecture." Ever the pan-Arabist, Rihani explained that Palestine was "neither inside nor outside any general Arab movement, but a part of a territory that was wrested from the Turks by the Allies."[75] Driven by his observations and travels in Iraq and the Arabian Peninsula, Rihani blamed colonialism for creating a federation of "separate sovereignties." Such a federation did not exist where all shared the same degree of independence, Rihani wrote; rather, it was a federation plagued by significant disparity of rank and need.[76] He restated the national aspirations of the Syrian nationalists prior to the Turkish Constitution of 1908 and the secret societies' efforts to bring the "northern territories" in Iraq, Syria, and Palestine together with Arabia.[77] Rihani recollected British promises to the Arabs of independence.[78]

In his essay "The Balfour Declaration," Aouni Abdelhadi analyzed the contradictions in British promises to Arabs and Jews and the selective application of the postwar agreements reified by the League of Nations. For example, he recalled that Palestine was placed in "Area A," according to paragraph 4 in Article 22 of the Covenant of the League of Nations, based on Wilson's speech at Mount Vernon in 1918, promising self-determination to all former Ottoman subjects. Article 22 contradicted crafty and convoluted language in Article 95 that singled out Palestine to be administered by a mandatory "power to be determined" and left intact promises to establish a Jewish national home.[79]

Jamal Bey Husseini tackled the mandate's responsibilities for the "development of self-governing institutions" in his piece, "The Proposed Palestine Constitution."[80] He outlined structures of a self-sustaining government under the subtitles "Executive," "The Judiciary System," and "Legislation" and contrasted a coveted constitution for the Palestinians with "The Constitution—Made in England" and "The Constitution versus the Mandate." Husseini noted that the Palestinians were never in need of repeated calls for constitutional and legislative councils to nudge them toward self-governing institutions and democracy by the mandate and that their Iraqi and Syrian brethren, who were "not higher in the grade of civilization nor have they had more experience in democracy than the inhabitants of Palestine, are now enjoying much wider measures of self government than this Constitution gives to the Palestinians."[81]

Arguing for the Zionist side, contributors often employed an effective strategy of equating the Zionist program in Palestine with the "white man's burden," intending, perhaps, to make Zionist aims palatable to British and American audiences. Bernard Joseph drew a wedge between the Zionists on the side of the civilized world and the indigenous inhabitants of Palestine. He deemed the "simplest" of Ottoman Muslim religious codes to be "founded on elementary principles of justice . . . and suited only to the needs of a simple peasantry ignorant of the ways of twentieth-century organization."[82] A. P. S. Clark painted a picture of Jewish progress in which the "primitive agricultural country" inherited by the presumably advanced Zionists leaped to progress when "Germans made their way to the Holy Land."[83] Rather than refute the mandate, Clark presented it as a British phase while referring to Jews as the descendants of the "German Templar Colonies."[84] J. Elazari-Volcani wrote that they brought millions in capital investment with them.[85]

Alfred Bonné proposed a congruence of European strategic concerns with establishment of a Jewish state. Having laid claim to the port city of Haifa as part of biblical "Samaria," the Zionists were partners in "the struggle of the powers for control of the oil-bearing regions."[86] The pipeline extending from Mosul in "Mesopotamia" to Haifa in Palestine was to be administered by a port authority under the British high commissioner and built with the help of Jewish capital. What remained, he wrote, was providing for security for the pipeline through British domination and the help of Zionists as their only reliable allies. Bonné, however, would enlist Palestinian and other farmers in his vision of a Jewish-colonialist enterprise by compensating them adequately. As if to suggest Zionism would facilitate an outpost for the West, he predicted that a war between Britain and its enemies in the East would make the pipeline a "theatre of war."[87]

The immigrant activists and their organizations faced an uphill battle on many fronts. Reports by British commissions following uprisings, the Simpson Report among them, made for arduous and sad reading for them, especially as they knew the U.S. public remained largely unaware of and unconcerned with events in Palestine. Under these conditions it was far more digestible for Americans in general when the Zionist side sounded upbeat by showcasing improvements in all spheres of industry and agriculture in Palestine. Zionist settlers were heralded by their advocates as emissaries of the civilized world in a backward place. The immigrant activists and their compatriots had to keep Palestinian communities from disappearing from the Western lexicon because of the appeal of biblical mythology and ignorance about Arabs and Islam. Thus, simply being referred to as an Arab slowly transformed into an indictment as a Muslim and an alien in a Westernized Zion. Arab nationalists were not in a strong position to challenge British policy, particularly the Balfour Declaration. Yet their worsening reality became increasingly tied to the ebb and flow of European imperialist policies over the places they claimed as their homelands. Therefore, Arab nationalist demands for control over their affairs and resources, however eloquent, simply did not make for good business for Britain and France or for expanding U.S. interests in the Middle East.

The Arab National League came to fruition when the British proved incapable of implementing an even-handed policy based on their experts' recommendations, and their mishandling of policies led to a general revolt and a prolonged strike in 1935 and 1936. The Passfield White Paper of October 1930 called for limits on Jewish land acquisition and settlement but was dismissed a year later due to opposition from British Jewish constituents. In a letter to Chaim Weizmann on March 13, 1931, Ramsay MacDonald, the British prime minister, committed to opening Palestine to Jewish immigration. In doing so he effectively reversed British policy in what became known as "the black paper" from a Palestinian point of view. In 1934 Jewish immigration reached 60,000, and in 1935 it grew to 62,000.[88] The sudden rise in immigration was coupled by a rapid increase of land acquisition by the Jewish Agency and a proliferation of armed Zionist groups, beginning with the Haganah and later its right-wing offshoot known as the Stern Zvai Leumi.[89]

Massive immigration further alienated the Palestinians, who could not muster an effective strategy to overcome British intransigence. Once again, an uprising erupted in Palestine in 1933 amid desperate calls from Palestinian leaders to attack the British and the Zionists.[90] The Palestinian leadership's failure to improve living conditions was exacerbated by a global recession and high unemployment among both Palestinians and Jews. Young, militant Palestinians formed the Istiqlal, or Independence Party, and began to challenge Amin al-Husseini's leadership in a show of general discontent. A Muslim cleric, Izz al-Din al-Qassam, employed guerilla warfare against the British and the Zionists. The British killed Qassam and hundreds of his comrades in 1935. The heavy-handed clamp-down exacerbated widespread feelings among Palestinian peasants who were convinced that playing under Britain's rules was futile.

When Qassam was killed, the Irgun and Zvai Leumi headed by Jabotinsky split from the largest Zionist fighting force, the Haganah. Qassam's death and worsening conditions triggered the largest uprising to that time across Palestine; it was centered in Jaffa. In 1936 the Palestinian popular committees with few ties to large feudal families or political parties declared a general strike. By April 25, 1936, the Palestinian leadership, responding to popular demands for action, formed the Arab Higher Committee (al-Lajnah al-ʿArabīyah al-ʿUlyā) under the leadership of the *mufti* Amin al-Husseini. A massive popular demonstration during the Palestinian general strike forced unity among Husseini's Arab Party, the National Defense Party dominated by the Nashashibi family, Abdelhadi's Independence Party, and the Reform Party headed by Hussein al-Khalidi, all working with Christian leaders of various sects.[91] The strike had little political value, although it lasted eleven months, and resulted in even worse living conditions for the Palestinians. During that time, the Zionists prepared themselves for future conflict, illegally importing machinery for weapons manufacturing from Poland and elsewhere and building weapons factories, sometimes under the watchful eyes of the British.[92]

When the British moved to control the violence in 1936, one thousand Palestinians and eighty Jewish settlers already had been killed.[93] The British arrested Palestinian leaders and escalated measures to include house demolitions, curfews, exiles, and imprisonment of thousands of Palestinians. According to the Ministry of the Colonies, between December 20, 1935, and March 30, 1936, there were 348 killings, 140 incidents of sabotage, 190 kidnappings, and 9 mine explosions. This bout of killings of Jews and Palestinians on a wider scale than before revealed the vast disparity in military hardware and training between the Palestinian side and the well-equipped Zionist gangs working outside British control. By the time the rebellion was crushed, a staggering 19,792 Palestinians had been killed and wounded at the hands of the British and the Zionists in 1936 alone, while the Jewish side suffered 415 casualties from 1936 to 1939.[94] More immediate to immigrants was the difficulty they faced in relating the events as they occurred to citizens of their adopted country. The escalating destruction, mostly on the Palestinian side, moved supporters on both sides within the United States further apart, but hopes of dialogue remained alive due mostly to some Jewish opposition to Zionism. The rhetorical battles in the United States tailored events in Palestine from Zionists' vantage point for the purpose of gaining sympathy and support.

Hajj Amin al-Husseini called off the strike in response to fresh promises from the British, but hunger and dire conditions among Palestinians and mediation by Arab leaders also influenced his decision. Immigrants' political efforts were once again reinforced by their desire to address the humane needs in the homeland. They found a venue for these sympathies by contributing to future British and American inquiries. In 1936 and part of 1937 an all-British panel authored the Peel Commission, named after Lord Earl Peel but known also as the Palestine Royal Commission. This commission was charged with investigating the cause of the uprising and strike in Palestine. Palestinians officially boycotted the investigation, citing a hostile British posture amid mixed British assurances that this was an impartial body not answerable to the British government.

The British assured Palestinians that the commission aimed to implement the provisions in the Mandate Charter equitably, but they also signaled that Jewish immigration to Palestine would not stop. Nudged by the dominant Europeans, Arab kings and governments, most notably the monarchs of Trans-Jordan and Morocco, pressed reluctant Palestinians to testify before the Peel Commission and await its recommendations.[95] By that time a pattern of empty promises by the British convinced the Palestinian leadership to hold back when faced by commissions, especially since there was no sign that the British intended to slow Jewish immigration. However, some of the Palestinians themselves interpreted al-Husseini's reluctance and the resulting delay in presenting Palestinians' grievances to the Peel Commission as proof of his failure as a leader. Hussein al-Khalidi, for instance, lamented that the "lost months" could have been used to prepare answers "with precision and care"; he declared that the *mufti* Amin al-Husseini's testimony "was not on the same level as the head of the Jewish Agency."[96]

The *mufti*'s answers, it was suggested, may have caused "some of the Commission's members to change their minds concerning the country's independence."[97] The *mufti*'s status as the preeminent leader due to his opposition to British policies and unrestrained Jewish immigration, however, was secure among Palestinians and the diaspora because there were no indications that anything the *mufti* could have done or said would have caused the British to rein in the Zionists or repair the systematic obstruction of Palestinian civil society and institutions during the mandate. Palestinians' demands remained the same: abandoning the failed Jewish commonwealth without rejecting Jews or Judaism, slowing or limiting Jewish immigration, preventing the transfer of large plots of Arab-owned land to Jews, ending the mandate, and reaching an Anglo-Palestinian agreement allowing for an elected national government like those drafted by the British in Egypt and Iraq or between France and Syria.[98] The recommendations of the Peel Commission were Britain's answer, yet they proved devastating for Palestinians because they presented the idea of giving the Jewish settlers most of the water resources and fertile land in Palestine under the guise of solving the problem through partition. At the time the British were facing an increasingly belligerent Germany and feared a wider conflict in Europe, and they became once again interested in securing the support of the Arab countries they occupied. In 1938 the British Woodhead Commission rescinded the partition as unworkable without making any fundamental change in overall policies toward the Palestinians. Although the Twentieth Zionist Congress also rejected the commission's plan, talk of partition emboldened Zionists as the world inched closer to a second global war.

The specter of partitioning Palestine fueled the energy of the immigrant activists, but their ability to effect political changes depended on reaching the general U.S. population and polity. Although they were capable and articulate, the Syrian immigrants' small numbers presented a serious problem. This handicap was alleviated somewhat by some Jewish opposition to Zionism as a political philosophy. Intra-Jewish debates in the 1930s through the end of World War II grew more complex. Overall, non-Zionist and anti-Zionist Jews felt compelled to defend Jewish cultural identity against two powerful forces: political Zionism and German anti-Semitism beginning in 1933 with the reign of the German Reich. In some respects the outcome of the debate had significant implications for the future of Arab American activism. While influential Jews in Britain successfully harnessed official British sympathy, European Jews were still subjected to increasing repression in Germany.

In 1933 most American Jews adhered to an effective boycott of German products to protest treatment of Jews by Hitler's Third Reich. The boycott was proclaimed by an umbrella organization, the American League for the Defense of Jewish Rights, which represented 288 organizations and sought to reach beyond the 4 million Jews in the United States to enlist "all Americans."[99] Zionist leaders pounced on this idea with specific demands. When the boycott began in 1933, Weizmann, for example, envisioned the settlement of 250,000 Jews in Palestine at the cost of $25 million to be paid by the League of Nations and "interested governments."[100] Weizmann made his remarks at a reception given in his honor by the American Palestine Campaign, the Zionist Organization of America, and the Jewish Agency for Palestine. In the same event, Louis Lipsky, Morris Rothenberg, Samuel Schulman, and Samuel Untermyer urgently advocated that Jews around the world turn "all eyes to Palestine."[101]

Untermyer warned of "impending doom" hanging over the heads of Jews "who have not already been destroyed." Assimilation into German life was attacked by some Zionists as a "bitter irony of history" and an attempt to "put blinkers on our eyes" by speakers at the Zionist Congress in Prague on August 21, 1933.[102] Two years later, Rabbi Barnett Brickner of Cleveland urged a delegation of the 45,000-member women's Zionist organization Hadassah to help avoid "extermination of 9,000,000 Jews" by making Palestine the homeland for German Jews.[103] The boycott against Germany was effective enough to force a plea from the Germans to end it, but it also provided an opportunity for Zionists to incentivize the Hitler regime toward the "transfer" of Jews to Palestine. During the Zionist Congress in Prague, revisionist Zionists were angered by the 265 votes in favor of a mild resolution "invoking unspecified League help for German Jews" presumably to keep lines of communication open with the Nazis.[104] The congress, nevertheless, issued statements decrying crimes against Jews in Germany and a "plea to Jewish people to accept the view that Zionism is the only solution of the Jewish question."[105] Proponents of Zionism therefore linked their political agenda in Palestine with German anti-Semitism.

Zionist organizations thrived in the United States and were further invigorated by intermittent violence in Palestine, most of all the Palestinian uprising in 1929. The disparity in organizational skills and resources in favor of the Zionist side in the United States was matched by British influence behind Zionist aims in mandate Palestine. This influence allowed the Zionist project to "graft modern political Zionism onto Jewish history."[106] Palestinian self-awareness and fears of Jewish settlement were rooted in the social and economic developments affecting farmers and peasants during Ottoman rule, as Rashid Khalidi has explicated in *Palestinian Identity*. However, the Palestinians' political responses and identity in the early twentieth century became intertwined with "one of the most potent narratives in existence, that of Israel and the Jewish people."[107] As Palestinian identity in the Middle East continued to develop in relation to Zionism, the picture in the United States did not change despite the New Syria Party experiment. Arab immigrants, many now in the United States for a full generation, reacted to political events in all parts of Syria. But when Zionism became an imminent threat, Palestine occupied a prominent role in their agendas. The difference was that U.S. Arabs by that time had experienced structural integration as parents of U.S.-born children and through work, marriage, and service in the U.S. military. That is to say, Arab activists drew closer to Arab Americanism at the same time they endeavored to defend Palestine, the part of their homeland that was under threat. Therefore, six years before the French occupation galvanized a sizable proportion of immigrants behind the "Syria for the Syrians" slogan, the Palestine National League issued Kātibah's booklet *The Case against Zionism* in response to the attempts at appropriating Palestine for Zionist political aims. In the forty-four-page booklet Kātibah methodically refuted Zionism on religious, political, moral, and historical grounds: "Zionism is an anachronism, it is a superimposition of a distorted modern tendency on an irrational ancient doctrine."[108]

The progressively intractable Arab-Israeli conflict obscured occasional agreements between idealistic American Zionists—that is, those who did not necessarily espouse a political agenda or a Jewish state—and their Arab counterparts who did not object to Zionism as a Jewish spiritual restorative movement. Zionist ideology ranged from individuals actively working toward a political community, a Jewish commonwealth, to those who perceived Palestine as a place for a spiritual restoration of the Jews of the Bible. There were also Jews who did not subscribe to either interpretation and rejected Zionism in any form, political or spiritual. Aside from direct responses to events in Palestine, public debates with political Zionists became one of the Arab immigrants' primary functions. This is where opposition to Zionism by American Jews and non-Jews bolstered the Arab Americans' positions in the 1930s. The varied viewpoints provided fertile ground for debates in which Arabs and Jews found themselves on the same side of the divide from American Zionists.

Global developments, however, continued to inform debates among the parties in the United States. Zionists used anti-Semitism to strengthen their position. As a result, the Palestinian side in the United States had to fend against repeated charges of anti-Semitism and often relied on anti-Zionist Jews for a successful defense. Rabbi Elmer Berger, who lived in Flint and forged enduring friendships with the activists and especially with Najīb Samra, criticized some of the tactics employed by the Zionists in the late 1930s and early 1940s. This is how Berger explained the tactics in his memoirs: "Zionist exploitation of the genuine tragedy" in Europe began as "'secret' fund raising efforts" and "glamorized Zionist fundraisers barnstorming local Jews with cloak-and-dagger tales of spiriting Jews out of Europe and of purchasing arms for the Zionists in Palestine."[109] It was difficult for Berger and certainly others later on to "resist the Zionist propaganda" of associating Zionist interests with defeating Hitler. But even at the height of Zionist pressure after World War II, Rabbi Berger came to the realization that "the Zionist plan of handling the problem of Jews in Europe who could escape—or might survive Hitler—was a trap."[110]

At the heart of opposition to Zionism was preserving Judaism as a spiritual and religious identity wherever Jews lived. Berger, for example, defended his American identity against being "expatriated" to the Jewish state, and he objected to being "endlessly reminded of the undemonstrated [Louis] Brandeis dogma that to be a good American it was necessary to be a good Zionist."[111] Part of the untold story of the debate between U.S. Arab immigrants and their Jewish counterparts is limited access to information and general disregard of intra-Jewish debates. By the time Hitler's crimes became known, Elmer Berger would emphatically state in his memoir that no Arab viewpoint was circulating in the United States.

An early and potent critic of political Zionism was Albert Einstein. His opposition became the basis of his acquaintance, if not friendship, with Fuad Shatara, the founder of the Arab National League. The word "communities" as opposed to "nation" was key to Einstein's rejection of Zionist aims in Palestine in his address "Our Debt to Zionism" in April 1938.[112] Einstein credited Zionists with reviving "a sense of community" among Jews, and he decried anti-Semitism, then declared "Now the fateful disease of our time—exaggerated nationalism, borne up by blind hatred—has brought our work in Palestine to a most difficult stage."[113] He still advocated immigration to Palestine but not as a way of achieving a majority by all means nor at any cost: "I should much rather see reasonable agreement with the Arabs on the basis of living together in peace than the creation of a Jewish state. . . . A return to a nation in the political sense of the word would be equivalent to turning away from the spiritualization of our [Jewish] community."[114]

It was Einstein's pacifist views and ideas on dialogue and coexistence that attracted the attention of New York surgeon Fuad Shatara several years before the uprising and general strike in Palestine in 1936.[115] Apparently Shatara wrote the scientist as early as 1930, encouraged by Einstein's views on coexistence in Palestine. On December 16, 1930, Einstein replied to Shatara: "Your letter . . . is an Excellent prove [sic] to me that I am following the right path."[116] Einstein mentioned in his reply that he proposed a conference between "Arabian and Jewish trustworthy representatives" on the pages of the newspaper *Filasṭīn* and asked Shatara to suggest participants from the Palestinian side. But the scientist was not in the New York area at the time, which limited his interaction with Shatara. Einstein listed his return address "for the next two months at California Institute of Technology, Pasadena, California."[117]

In a follow-up letter on February 7, 1931, Shatara informed Einstein that he and other Arab Americans were asked by Rabbi Louis I. Newman to comment on a piece by the rabbi in the December 12, 1930, issue of the *Jewish Tribune* titled "The Fundamentals of an Arab-Jewish Condorat." Shatara did just that. In his letter to Einstein he enclosed a copy of his response to the rabbi's piece under the title "A Proposed Solution for the Arab Jewish Controversy in Palestine."[118] Einstein responded in a letter in German in February 1931 indicating that Shatara's idea of "laying down weapons is reasonable [or desirable]." He suggested involving Judge Brandeis and Morris Cohen before going public and circulating the issue in bigger circles.[119] Available correspondences between the two men continued well beyond Einstein's 1937 address in which he rejected political Zionism. Two years after the violence in Palestine, in April 1938, Shatara contacted Einstein on the official stationery of the ANL to congratulate the scientist on his courage and clear-headed leadership upon delivering his address "Our Debt to Zionism" at a Seder service in New York's Hotel Astor. Shatara signaled that he did not reject Zionism out of hand: "It is my humble opinion that if Zionists will follow your advice, the historic friendship between the Jews and Arabs will be restored, peace will reign in Palestine, and the two cousin races can then collaborate toward upbuilding of a Semitic civilization."[120]

The implications of Shatara's comments would have allowed for coexistence with Zionism in Palestine as perceived by Einstein. Given the reality of uneven development of Jewish and Arab sectors in Palestine, the prolonged conflict would ultimately result in the opposite. The league's stationery may have given Einstein pause, as he investigated the organization in a confidential inquiry he made to Haim Greenberg, an editor at the *Jewish Frontier*.[121] Greenberg's answer was mixed. He conceded that Shatara was a practicing physician with "the reputation of an honest man in medical circles, as well as the community as a whole."[122] However, Shatara's loyalty to the now exiled *mufti* Amin al-Husseini was sufficient to cast doubt on his objectives. Greenberg advised granting Shatara "an informal meeting" and asked to be present because, he wrote, Shatara's personal integrity was contradicted by his political affiliations and support of the policy of the "exiled Grand Mufti of Jerusalem," Amin al-Husseini.[123]

The Einstein exchanges serve as one example of how immigrants had to overcome British policies before forging ahead with their case in their communities in the United States. The British deposed the *mufti* of Jerusalem in 1937 in preparation for arresting him because of his role in the revolt the previous year and after it became clear he would not consent to partitioning Palestine under the prevailing conditions. Other factors behind their decision were the *mufti*'s rejection of annexing the Palestinians' land to Jordan under Abdallah's rule and his active rallying of Palestinians against the British when the partition plan was made public in July.[124] The British arrested other members of the higher committee, forcing many into exile.

Shards of information shed light on how the Syria idea transitioned to circumspection over the fate of Palestine. During Jewish immigration to Palestine in 1935, none other than Mahmoud Abulfilat, the Palestinian former president of the New York chapter of the NSP, chronicled his encounter with Jewish would-be settlers on the ocean liner *Rex*.[125] After avoiding his fellow New Yorkers who were seeking a new life in Palestine, Abulfilat acquiesced when the traveler insisted on "getting to know and understand a Palestinian" and suggested forming an Arab-Jewish society to ensure equality. Fed up with British intransigence and unrestricted Jewish immigration into Palestine, the activist responded that dialogue was pointless when the Palestinians were becoming the "Red Indians [*hunūd humr*] fleeced of funds, land, and country."[126] The two Jewish New Yorkers did their best to convince their Palestinian co-traveler of their good intentions, Abulfilat reported.

When the ship sailed the Mediterranean and became packed with Jews from Germany, Russia, and Eastern Europe, one Jewish traveler reassuringly expressed his desire to help "the region thrive economically."[127] His encounters with a multitude of Jewish immigrants shocked the Syrian Palestinian activist, and he recalled their effects on him when the ship dropped anchor on Palestine's coast: "I formed a different opinion on my destiny and that of my country's current plight, and I will write to *As-Sameer* on this matter soon."[128] He did so the same year in the August 15 issue under the subhead "Mushāhadati fi Bilādi" (My Observations in My Country). Ever mindful of intra-European affairs, *As-Sameer*'s subsequent issues in 1935 likened the arms buildup in Europe to a "labor that will give birth to a creature" that might destroy the "civilization of the twentieth century."[129] Sporadic articles celebrated Anton Saʿadeh's Syrian National Party as the best hope for natural Syria's unity,[130] yet numerous others tried to interpret unfolding developments in Palestine by revisiting the aftermath of the 1929 rebellion and the Balfour Declaration.

The communiqué published in the August 6, 1936, *Al-Sa'eh* announcing the formation of the Arab National League was actually an endorsement by authors William Catzeflis, Amin Zeidan, and Philip Khouri of plans by Shatara to reinvigorate his organization, the Palestine Renaissance Society. The authors were not among the founders of the league, nor did they play a major role in its operations. Urging readers to "unite in the new organization to defend the old homeland, especially Palestine,"[131] this communiqué confirmed the shift from defending Syria against the French occupation to the plight of Palestine to the south. Shatara referred to the nascent Arab National League under two distinct names: Jam'īyat al-Nahḍah al-Filasṭīnīyah (Palestine Nationalist Renaissance Society) and, in English, the Palestine National League. Fuad Shatara sent this letter to Farah on March 26, 1925:[132]

> Greetings. I received your letter on the 19th this month. In response I can tell you that in New York there exists Jam'īyat al-Nahḍah al-Filasṭīnīyah, which was founded several years ago to combat the Zionist movement and which achieved worthwhile deeds in the cause of the homeland. The society collected some $25,000 [more than $300,000 now] to support the national movement for the delegation in London and for propaganda here. The address of the Society is: Palestine National League. 16 W. 27 St. New York City. The annual membership is $5.00. There are other ways of helping the homeland, among them subscription to *Filasṭīn* [newspaper], which struggled for the homeland and is in need of the support of patriots. Its annual subscription is $6.00 annually. The editor will send me several issues for new subscribers. This is what came to mind that I wanted to share with you [plural] with my thanks for your national zeal.
>
> Yours,
> Fuad Shatara

Despite these variations in the name of the society that became the nucleus of the Arab National League, Ḥabīb Kātibah confirmed that they were one and the same. In the Arabic translation of Kātibah's *Arab Speakers in Americans*, a 1946 publication by the Institute of Arab American Affairs of *Al-Nāṭiqūn bi al-Ḍād fi Amrīkā*, a more detailed account than the original English version, Kātibah mentions that Abdelhamid Shouman, who later founded the Arab Bank in Palestine, was among the co-founders of the Palestine National League. Thus, the PNL by any name apparently waited until the New Syria Party and the Druze revolt had run their courses before re-emerging as the Arab National League. Perhaps the most accurate account of the founding of the ANL as well as other organizations under study here

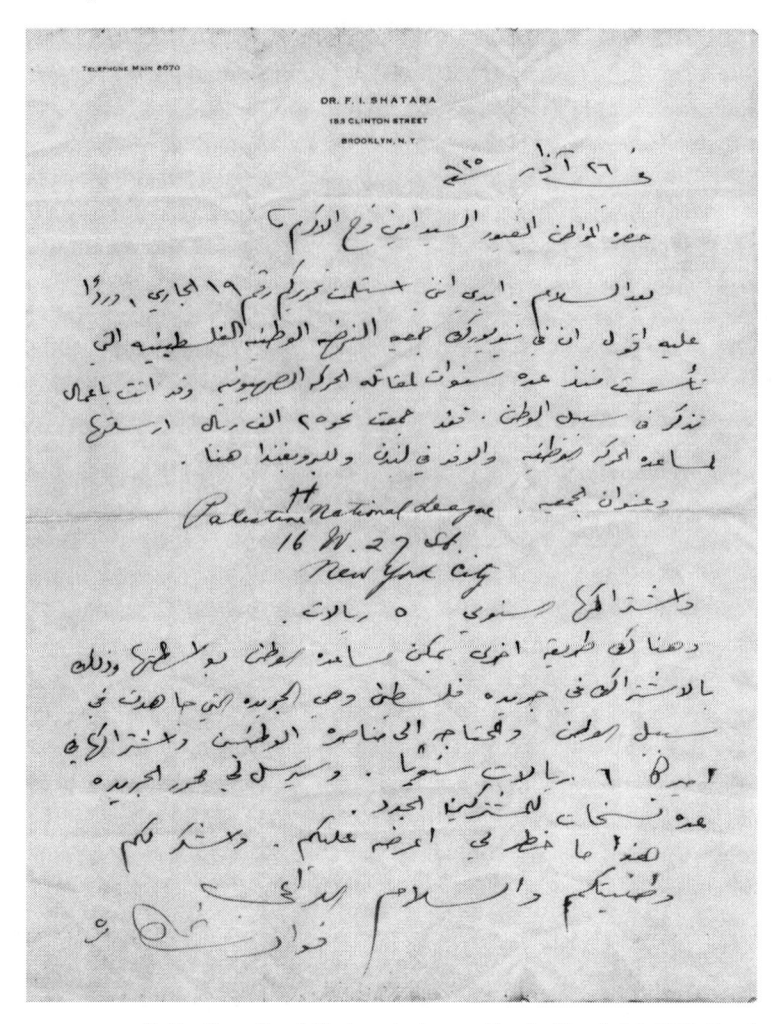

FIGURE 5.1. *Letter from Fuad Shatara to Ameen Farah, March 26, 1925. Farah Papers, Bawardi Collection.*

can be found in Kātibah's *Al-Nāṭiqūn bi al-Ḍād fī Amrīkā*. Kātibah provides a brief historical genesis of the ANL and the institute after listing the NSP in 1926 in this manner:

> In 1923, Dr. Fuad Isa Shatara founded the Palestine National League, considered the first society whose aim was defending the cause of Arab Palestinians. In fact, these intermittent nationalist movements were a prelude to the Arab National League, which was founded in 1936 in New

York by Fuad Isa Shatara, who served as its president as long as he lived until its dissipation at the end of 1939. The big success of this *formal organization* [emphasis added] is attributed to Dr. Shatara, who worked tirelessly and sacrificed a great deal.[133]

As yet, little else is known about the Palestine National League outside the few clues provided in the institute's 1946 publication. More is known about what that collective would become, the Arab National League, thanks to Lawrence Davidson's investigation of newspaper articles and government records.[134] Farah's archive completes the picture in the next chapter.

Chapter 6

THE ARAB NATIONAL LEAGUE AND THE EMERGENCE OF ARAB AMERICAN IDENTITY

The Arab National League disseminated hundreds of copies of an Arabic-language pamphlet titled "Bayān al-Jāmi'ah al-'Arabīyah" (Statement [or pronouncement] of the Arab [National] League) in 1937. The short reader explained the organization's principles and sought members in Michigan, home of an active constituency and the New Syria Party a decade earlier. Partial translations of the statement and other documents in this chapter present in their own voices a sense of Syrian immigrants' developing loyalty as citizens of the United States and the external forces that shaped their choices and views. The pamphlet included an application for membership on the back page. The pamphlet suggested a coming of age for the immigrant activists regarding their aims and their recognition of the grim political reality as budding Arab Americans of Syrian, including Lebanese, ancestry. The activists posited a fresh perspective on how best to achieve political independence in Syria by forging a new emphasis on belonging to their adopted country. Proposing a role for the ANL within a framework of forging ahead as Americans, the statement presented a varied agenda that addressed social and economic concerns:

> Whereas the Arab National League is a free society established in New York specifically for the service of the Syrian country (al-Bilād al-Sūriyah) by drawing on its American atmosphere—the most advanced democratic atmosphere in the world—the League considers its duty to disseminate its principles and hopes so that the Arab world is aware of its true political, economic, and social aims. Thereby, all who support the goals of the League among the Arabic-speaking population in the United States, Canada, Mexico, and all Latin America can lend their support.[1]

Within this declaration several subheads followed the heading "Basic Principles of the Arab League." The activists expressed their wishes of maintaining Syria's natural boundaries and declared Palestine their new core issue. The organization called for "complete independence of the Syrian nation as a united, coherent political unit within the natural geographic borders of Natural Syria." The borders as spelled out correspond to previous geographic boundaries by the Faisal government and the First Arab Conference in Paris in 1913, articulated often by Rihani, Shatara, Malouf, and Kātibah, and adopted by the American Syrian Lebanese Clubs (AMSYRLUB) in 1934. The league's principles considered the prevailing political situation of colonial encroachment as a temporary phase requiring first, "effective resistance to Zionism, the biggest threat to Syrian unity." The remainder of the principles echoed now age-old reformist goals of compulsory education, social reforms, separation of religion and governance, and "promoting the same in all Arab countries through education, representative governments, and a coalition of Arab nations in the spirit of cooperation in intellectual and political fields . . . on the basis of justice and comprehensive peace."[2]

Toward achieving the stated ends, the document suggested social reforms, beginning with forbidding political appointments and—in a clear reference to French-concocted confessional politics in Lebanon four years prior—ending elections based on sectarian affiliations, as well as allocating time for religious education outside formal class sessions. Points 3 to 7 emphasized education, including sports, in uniform and collective programs supported by Arab governments. Under "Economic Reforms," the league called for unified tariffs; improved transportation; health codes; agricultural cooperatives technically supported free of charge as in the Egyptian model; workers unions and protection of women and child laborers; encouragement of national industries; technical and sanitary improvements in food production; large irrigation projects with the participation of the concerned Arab governments to pump water from the Euphrates River in Iraq and the ʿĀsī (Orontes) River running through Turkey, Syria, and Lebanon; a conservation policy; low-interest agricultural and industrial lending institutions; and cancellation of all exclusive and preferential economic contracts to foreigners. The document concluded the basic principles with an unmistakable signal that the "temporary reality" was a prelude to pan-Arab unity:

> In putting forth this "Announcement," which is inspired by its democratic surroundings, the Arab League (al-Jāmiʿah al-ʿArabīyah) does not presume to be merely one that dictates conditions, rather one that expresses hopes motivated by selfless advice and sincere zeal devoid of all personal gains so that the Arab world in its budding life of independence may have ultimate success and prosperity. The Arab League is keenly interested in the first place in the welfare of the overwhelming majority of the peaceful population that withstood the lion's share of sacrifices,

repression, and hardship. May God lead our path, to the benefit of the greater Arab world.[3]

On page 6 of the declaration, the "League's Plea" encapsulates the philosophy of its founding in the form of a letter to the Arab immigrant constituency. Here again is an indication of a genuine realization by the ANL's growing following as the third and largest Arab American organization to date that living in the United States and considering themselves beneficiaries of a democratic system gave them an edge. Several points addressed in the pamphlet end with a plea for readers to become members:

> If you believe with a pure heart in these principles put out by the Arab League as the basis for its working agenda and hopes for the future of the Arab countries, the league calls on you especially to join hands in achieving these goals.
>
> You may think to yourself: even with great numbers, what good can a group do thousands of miles away from Arab countries? It is distance that places loyal nationalists in an excellent position to render true service to the homeland free from personal and financial gains.[4]

The plea declares that the ANL's founding in the United States and elsewhere in the Americas was necessary during the transitional period experienced by Arab countries; that is, it would monitor the development of political life and promote the ascendance of democratic life over forces of "reactionary and selfish" thinking. Another benefit of founding the league lay in "establishing a link between the Arab countries and the greatest democratic republic in the world." The ANL argued in favor of one of its core duties undertaken by Shatara, Kātibah, and their friends—that of educating "American public opinion concerning the Arab orient, which is beginning to bear fruit [and] is one of the most important accomplishments of the organization."[5]

Two months after the general strike in Palestine began in April 1936, Shatara began assembling an advisory board to advocate for the Palestinians in letters bearing his address, 153 Clinton Street in Brooklyn. He contacted Philip Hitti to ask for his support and listed a dozen names of academics and luminaries he contacted.[6] Among the recipients of the letter were William Hocking, Edward Bliss, Reverend Abraham Rihbani, archeologist Elihu Grant, and John Finley. In his letter Shatara pointed out to Hitti that the American public "has been given only one side of the story" and that the "channels of publicity have been practically closed to all attempts to present the Arab side." In September 1936 Shatara contacted Kātibah to ask him to consider running the league, and he reluctantly inquired what salary

FIGURE 6.1. *Fuad Isa Shatara, circa 1936. Born in Palestine, Shatara escaped the Ottoman army and eventually practiced medicine in New Jersey and New York. He founded the Palestine National League in about 1923 and relaunched it as the Arab National League in 1936. Courtesy of Shatara's daughter Hope Murphy Shatara.*

Kātibah would expect.[7] The source of his reluctance was the members' preference for sending money overseas. "All they [ANL members] are interested in is to send money to Palestine," Shatara complained in his letter. He made the case for concentrating some of the league's resources for the U.S. front. Although Kātibah's reply—or any of Shatara's papers—is yet to be found, he apparently accepted the offer. However, the limited resources of the league

[Arabic text - right column:]

– ۱ –

بيـــان الجـــامعة العربيـــة

توطئة

لما كانت الجامعة العربيـــة في نيويورك جمعية حرة أنشئت لخدمة القضايا العربية عموما وقضية البلاد السورية خصوصا مستمدة النور والهداية من محيطها الامير كي الذي هو ارقى محيط ديموقراطي في العالم فانها ترى ان من واجبها اذاعة مبادئها وامانيها كي يقف العالم العربي على حقيقة اغراضها السياسية والاقتصادية والاجتماعية فيوازرها كل من يوافق على هذه المبادئ. من ابناء اللغة العربية في الولايات المتحدة الامير كية وكندا والمكسيك وسائر جمهوريات اميركا اللاتينية.

مبادئ الجامعة العربية الاساسية

۱ – ان تقوم بكل ما في وسعها من الاعمال بكل الطرق المشروعة في سبيل استقلال البلاد السورية التام وحدتها السياسية مع السعي الدائم للتفاهم والتعاون مع سائر الامم العربية في الامور السياسية والاقتصادية والتهذيبية.

۲ – البلاد السورية هي وحدة سياسية تامة لا تتجزأ.. تجمعها جبـال طوروس فالحـابور فنهر الفرات شمالا فبادية الشام شرقـا فخط رفح والعريش جنوبـا فالبحر المتوسط غربـا.

[Arabic text - left column:]

– ۸ –

ولا نرى وسيلة لذلك افضل من الانضمام الى عضويتنا وخير البر عاجله

طلب الانضمام

لقد قرأت بيان الجامعة العربية في نيويورك وانا اوافق على مبادئها المثبتة فيه واحبذ مشاريعها وبناء عليه اريد الانضمام الى عضويتها.

الاسم – بالانكليزية والعربية واضحا –

عنوان الشارع – بالانكليزية –

عنوان المدينة والولاية –

وها انا مرسل لكم حوالة بستة دولارات اميركية قيمة اشتراكي.   الامضاء.

ARAB NATIONAL LEAGUE
303 FIFTH AVENUE
NEW YORK, N. Y.

FIGURE 6.2. *The declaration of the ANL. Page 8 (left) includes a membership form asking for the applicant's "Name in English and Arabic, Street Name in English, City and State," a fee of $6, and a signature. Farah Papers, Bawardi Collection.*

would remain split between influencing public opinion at home and sending much-needed aid to the thousands who were killed by the British and the Zionist gangs throughout the life of the ANL.

The statement continued that in addition to the many debates, speeches, and newspaper articles, the league published books and pamphlets in the English language such as its special publications, thousands of which were distributed, and a "book by Mss. Mattel Mugannam, a book by Taufiq Kanʿan, a book by Wadie Bustani—*all in English* [italics mine] and sought to form the Friends of the Arabs Society comprised of thinkers, authors and professors."[8] Although the membership application was in Arabic, on the back it asked the would-be members to give the information in English.[9] Asking for information in English was inevitable since the targets of membership included the offspring of Arab Syrian pioneers, now in the United States for an average of twenty to thirty years, although Kātibah and Khalidi began to transition to English in most of their communications as these were increasingly directed at the general public and polity. Transitioning to using the English language was one of the recommendations made by the activists in the New Syria Party, as the translations of NSP correspondences have shown. The officers and members of the ANL understood the need to appeal to a wider constituency within the general population. The proceedings of the ANL's Fourth National Convention, in 1939, illustrate that the goal became targeting assimilated Syrians or their U.S.-born children. Overall, it is safe to say that the increase in the numbers of the U.S.-born Arab Americans began to stretch the limits of using Arabic in everyday interactions, although the Arabic-language press still served first-generation immigrants.

Section 2 of "The Constitution and By-Laws of the Arab National League" was published separately in both languages in an attractive booklet format in about 1937. The document succinctly and officially reestablished the objectives of the organization and elaborated rules for members and officers in matters big and small. Although the league was conceived to help Syria and the Arab world by influencing the United States from within, the activists perceived as one of their functions to illuminate the way for Arab countries toward prosperity and independence. Its bylaws outlined in English, among the ANL's objectives, "to render political, cultural, educational, and economic service to the Arab countries; to use its best endeavors, by all legitimate means, to secure the independence of those countries among those that have not yet secured their independence with all their natural territories and boundaries intact."[10] The bylaws provided that membership was open to "any person of whatever race or creed who subscribes to the principles of the League," and they delineated the rights and obligation of members, the rules, and procedures concerning meetings, elections, and quorums. The Arabic-language side of the bylaws more or less reflected the same rules, albeit with one stark difference—an added section 15 with an oath of allegiance (translated to English): "Each member is to recite this oath of allegiance before joining: I swear before God, the homeland, my honor, and all I hold dear to be faithful and loyal to the Arab countries and their causes, to serve them with all my strength, to never say or do anything that might harm them, and to preserve and honor the principles of the Arab League."[11]

The letterhead on the ANL's official stationery listed the officers: F. I. Shatara, M.D., president; David Ramadan, vice-president; Joudy Esmail, treasurer; Ameen Zeidan, secretary; and Ḥabīb I. Kātibah, director. The

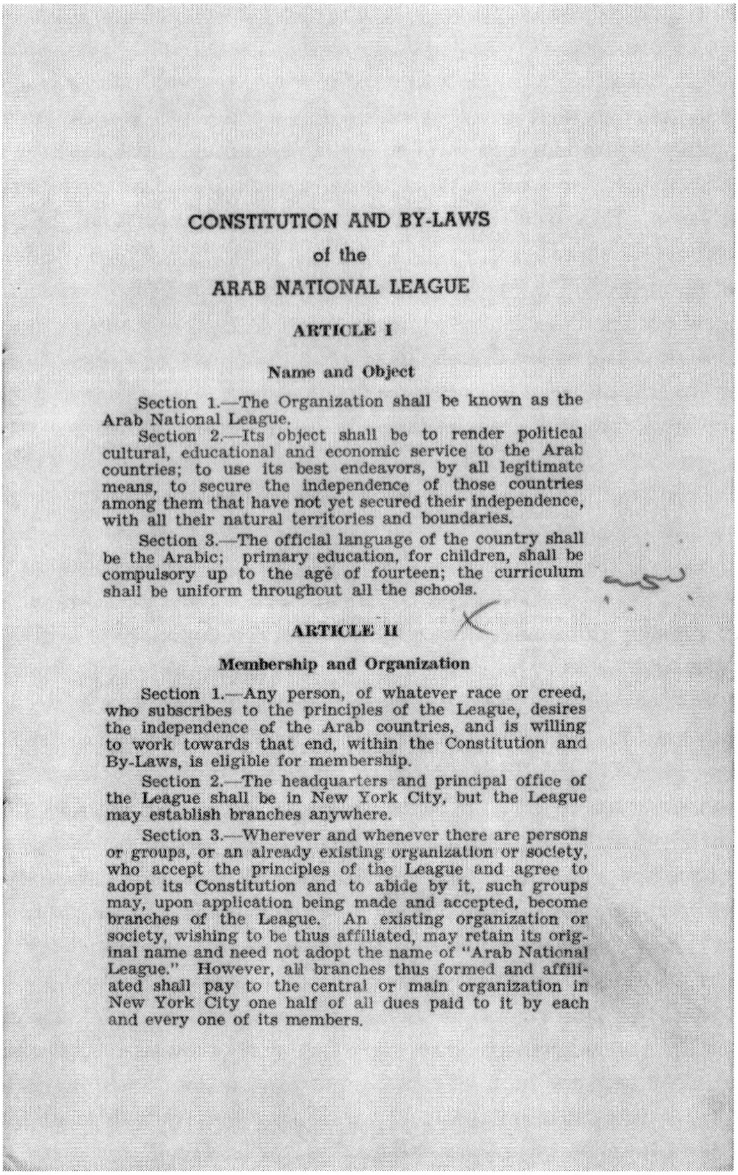

CONSTITUTION AND BY-LAWS
of the
ARAB NATIONAL LEAGUE

ARTICLE I

Name and Object

Section 1.—The Organization shall be known as the Arab National League.

Section 2.—Its object shall be to render political cultural, educational and economic service to the Arab countries; to use its best endeavors, by all legitimate means, to secure the independence of those countries among them that have not yet secured their independence, with all their natural territories and boundaries.

Section 3.—The official language of the country shall be the Arabic; primary education, for children, shall be compulsory up to the age of fourteen; the curriculum shall be uniform throughout all the schools.

ARTICLE II

Membership and Organization

Section 1.—Any person, of whatever race or creed, who subscribes to the principles of the League, desires the independence of the Arab countries, and is willing to work towards that end, within the Constitution and By-Laws, is eligible for membership.

Section 2.—The headquarters and principal office of the League shall be in New York City, but the League may establish branches anywhere.

Section 3.—Wherever and whenever there are persons or groups, or an already existing organization or society, who accept the principles of the League and agree to adopt its Constitution and to abide by it, such groups may, upon application being made and accepted, become branches of the League. An existing organization or society, wishing to be thus affiliated, may retain its original name and need not adopt the name of "Arab National League." However, all branches thus formed and affiliated shall pay to the central or main organization in New York City one half of all dues paid to it by each and every one of its members.

FIGURE 6.3. *English-language side of ANL constitution and bylaws, 1936. Farah Papers, Bawardi Collection.*

executive committee members were E. J. Audi; Joseph Bateh; Joudy Esmail; George Kheiralla, M.D.; Ali Muhyiddīn (Mahadeen); Hassan Mahmoud; David Ramadan; and Ameen Zeidan.

Acting on its goal of educating the American public, the ANL produced the booklet *Whither Palestine? A Statement of Facts and of Causes of the Arab-Jewish Conflict in the Holy Land* among its first publications.[12] The forty-eight-page book, which can still be found in various libraries, is divided evenly between explaining Palestine's ancient and more recent history and refuting Zionist biblical claims and the Balfour Declaration. A dense read, the document drew on the findings of various commissions and inquiries and includes tables explicating census data and trade balances and an elaborate bibliography of previous works by both sides in the conflict. One striking analysis presented in *Whither Palestine*? is a critique of the total dependence of what became idealized Jewish industries and farming communities in Palestine, such as the touted agricultural cooperatives Rishon Le Zion and Rishon Jacob, on outside subsidies from Baron Edmond de Rothschild, the original recipient of the 1917 Balfour Declaration. As a result of those enterprises' dependence on Rothschild, the booklet states, "the rest of the population is taxed in order that the proprietors of these industrial concerns may be in a position to pay the wages of their laborers and to make a profit for themselves."[13]

Insofar as reiterating Syrian immigrants' attachment to American democracy, the philosophical underpinnings of the league's positions on economics were in line with capitalist precepts. The relative economic success of the activist immigrants and their followers informed their political views and nudged them into an alignment with conservative strands of U.S. politics. Increased U.S. investment in the oil-rich region encouraged the league's message of promoting democracy while bringing the activists closer to the Arabists within the State Department.

Throughout 1936–1937, *Mirāt al-Gharb* mirrored many of the ANL's sentiments. The consistently nationalist newspaper decried the rise of Jewish immigration and land acquisition amid worsening conditions for the locals, and it defended Anton Saʿadeh, the longest holdout for pan-Syrian unity, when Lebanese authorities arrested him. Having provided a forum for literary luminaries during much of its history, editorials in the newspaper lamented prospects of losing the cherished classical Arabic-language style to neglect. It faithfully published announcements on ANL activities and protested plans to partition Palestine,[14] all amid a seemingly unstoppable flood of anti-Arab attacks in the U.S. press. On May 10, 1937, a public invitation was issued in the pages of *Mirāt al-Gharb* for a town meeting to be convened in New York City by the Arab National League on June 5, 1937.[15] It was a major gathering by the ANL to honor Ameen Rihani, who delivered the keynote speech and at the time was touring under the sponsorship of the Foreign Policy Association. The meeting was broadcast on WNYC radio, and an audio recording to the meeting can be heard at a website honoring Rihani by members of his family in the United States.[16]

Shatara began his introduction of Rihani by reading two telegrams from Hajj Amin al-Husseini and Prince Adel Arslan congratulating the honoree and extending support to the league. The *New York Times* report on the evening to honor Rihani, with 300 gathered to discuss the "so-called 'Arab side' of Zionism," disclosed that when a lone voice interrupted the speaker with "'Down with the Jews,' he was booed."[17] W. E. Hocking was also invited by the league to address the audience. The Harvard professor emphasized the Palestinians' rights in Palestine on legal grounds and reminded the audience that the Balfour Declaration was not intended to create a Jewish state. Regardless, he explained, "the difficulty is that the more zealous Zionists have never been content with the Balfour Declaration."[18]

Opposition from New York's Eastern European Jewish community to the airing of this event on the radio was swift and fierce. Two days after the ANL banquet a telegram was received by New York City mayor Fiorello La Guardia's office from Jacob Dabronsky, president of the National Council of Young Israel: "Resent deeply the aid and comfort given by a newtorkcity [sic] institution to the defenders of the Arab looters rapers and murderers of Jewish old men women and children in the Holy Land."[19] Within two days of the broadcast the commissioner of plant and structures for New York City in charge of municipal radio broadcasting, Frederick J. H. Kracke, and program director Seymour Siegel found themselves responding to a request by the mayor to submit a report on the broadcast.[20] The two officials appeared before the New York Board of Aldermen in city hall and desperately defended freedom of speech and WNYC for airing the ANL program. Alderman Samson Inselbuch of Brooklyn introduced a resolution charging that the program was anti-Jewish and therefore anti-Semitic, even after the radio station aired a Jewish side of the issues in a program on June 11 that featured Louis Lipsky and Zionist leaders Rabbi Stephen S. Wise, Abba Hillel Silver, and Pierre Paasen.[21]

The *New York Times* reported that the "aldermanic wrath" following Rihani's tour, sponsored by the Institute of International Education and attended by the street commissioner of Boston, Faris Malouf, was alleviated by letters from Jewish leaders in support of Kracke's decision. Rabbi Wise commented to the *New York Times* that charges of anti-Semitism were "absurd ... as if Arabs and Jews alike were not Semites."[22] After being peppered with questions from city aldermen, Kracke enunciated WNYC's policy of not engaging in topics involving religious conflict.

Rihani still served as the most visible representative of pan-Arab nationalism. His work as a frequent guest of the Foreign Policy Association and his command of the English language only added to his already considerable stature. His political views, transnational persona, and pragmatic approach of educating fellow citizens on the basic history and events in Syria made a perfect fit for the league. No complete record of Rihani's speaking tour has been assembled, but his compatriots on three continents were familiar with his publications. He did describe a speaking tour in a letter to his brother Albert on February 14, 1937. The unassuming letter is a valuable window onto the itinerary of a prolific activist and intellectual who was respected by his peers and whose importance in Arab American life is yet to be excavated:

> If you have a map, open it and walk with me from Wheeling W. Va., 480 miles to Chicago then from Chicago, the next day, 420 miles to Minneapolis, Minn. We arrived Friday morning the 12th and had lunch with some members of the Foreign Policy Association who heard my presentation on the political situation in the Arab countries except for Palestine, then back to the hotel for rest.[23] At 7 o'clock we put on formal attire and joined a banquet attended by 300 well-informed people.... On a long rectangular table I sat to the right of the president and one of the Jews, Rabbi Abramowitz to his left ... [In the allotted half hour] I summed up the Arab-Zionist problem ... and sat down. Abramowitz commenced his defense of Zionism weeping and wailing: "We haven't a home in the whole world. How can you deny us Palestine our only home for three thousand years" etc. [During questions and answers] I said ... what would you say to seven million Jews living and thriving in the United States? He was perplexed and his answer was incoherent babbling.

After Rihani won the debate for the Arab side, in his view at least, he and the rabbi each received a check for $175.

> We returned to the hotel at 10 o'clock, changed clothes and resumed travels to Minneapolis at 11 o'clock, spending the night on the train. We arrived in Chicago Saturday morning, changed trains, and resumed the journey to beautiful Cincinnati, arriving last night. Today we awakened to write you this letter one hour before riding another train to West Vir-

ginia 400 miles away from here. So, we traveled one thousand miles in three days to defend the rights of Arabs. This is the kind of work I do. Do you think it is tiring?[24]

Rihani's travels also took him to Flint, where he knew many people including Ameen Farah. The *Flint Journal* reported on the activities of the "noted Arab leader" who was "looked upon as the 'Voltaire' of the Arab emancipation movement."[25] Rihani met with Arab leaders of Flint in the home of Najīb Samra while touring universities at the invitation of the Foreign Policy Association. The newspaper reported that the context of Rihani's lectures on the controversy between Arabs and Jews in Palestine was the widespread rejection by "Arab kings" of Britain's partition plan.

On his way back to Syria from his speaking tour, Rihani sent several letters from the American *S.S. Exeter* Export Line on July 31, 1937. One was an affectionate letter to the young Laila al-Sa'di,[26] daughter of the ANL member Lutfi al-Sa'di, formerly a member of the NSP. In a separate letter to Hajj Amin al-Husseini, Rihani sent three invitations—to Husseini, Aouni Abdelhadi, and Ragheb, presumably Ragheb Mitrage, his old Pen Bond colleague and a supporter of *Al-Funūn*—to visit him on the ship when it docked in either Haifa or Jaffa on August 8, 1937.[27] He explained the invitation with a single statement: "There are fundamental issues on which I want to be apprised of your opinion,"[28] and he asked the dignitaries to respond to the ship's return address in Alexandria, Egypt, where a stop was scheduled. It is not clear if Rihani officially represented the ANL in Jerusalem, the hotspot of Arab nationalist activities at the time. What was becoming evident by 1937 was that the center of attention shifted to Palestine in the south from Syria and the Lebanon proper to the north. The physical location of the opposition to British colonialism was accompanied by increasing emphasis on Palestine as generally an Arab, not Syrian, concern.

Rihani's connection to the ANL was long-standing, given his consistent advocacy for political rights for the Arab population and intellectual stature, as was his association with al-Husseini, whom he addressed as "my dear friend." Rihani influenced al-Husseini's already moderate disposition toward the United States' growing importance due to Arab immigration, Zionism, and an expanding economy. These compelling reasons explain why, in August 1937, the *mufti* expressed to the American consul in Jerusalem, George Wadsworth, his hopes that the United States would not become an imperialist country and could appreciate the Palestinians' dilemma with regard to Jewish settlement.[29] In the same conversation al-Husseini voiced his frustration over the Zionists' levels of political and financial power and his awareness of the likelihood that the United States would back Zionism due to effective lobbying by its advocates.

In the months leading up to al-Husseini's encounter with the U.S. consul, *Mirāt al-Gharb* reported details on Zionists' opposition to precluding a Jewish majority in Palestine and any concessions to Arabs by the Peel Commission.[30] Charitable work and fund-raising for humanitarian aid made up much of that work and coincided with a function of the *mufti*'s office in Jerusalem. As the work of the ANL continued to reach members through regular bulletins, collaboration between the League and Husseini's office was a matter of course.

A letter published in July 1937 in *Mirāt al-Gharb* from the *mufti*'s emissary 'Izzat Tannous, a medical doctor turned diplomat, confirms the link between the ANL and the Arab Higher Committee, still led by al-Husseini from his exile in French-occupied Lebanon before he fled to Baghdad. Tannous announced that the purpose of his official visit to the United States on behalf of the Arab Higher Committee was "to meet the patriots here; to thank them for all their services to Palestine, and to strengthen the spirit of cooperation and mutual support between the homeland and her children abroad."[31] The letter indicated that Tannous had been in the country long enough to enjoy a "hospitable reception" in New York and all the cities he visited. He emphasized the "flood of emotions" the immigrants expressed at the news of hardships experienced by those in Palestine, and he remarked on the ANL's response to the tragic conditions:

> The [Arab] National League in this country took care to collect funds from all citizens in the United States to aid the orphans who lost both parents and the widows. Arabs answered the call and gave generously . . . The Arab League is an ardent nationalist lot [*kutla*] spread across the entire United States working tirelessly day and night to uphold Arab stature, doing what it can to expose the truth to the people, and to raise funds to send to those in the most dire need.[32]

Notwithstanding the Arab Americans' earnest efforts, social and political changes in Syria continued. The pressures of colonialism and age-old exchange of ideas with the West contributed to the infusion of socialist views into Arab-nationalist thought. The political emissaries who visited the ANL brought with them traces of these changes. The word *ba'th*, Arabic for "rebirth" or "resurgence," could be found on President Roosevelt's desk in a letter from an emissary of Amin al-Husseini named Muhammad Jamil Beyhum. A renowned man of letters, Beyhum sent his message days after his delegation arrived in New York on November 11, 1938.[33] Beyhum and Emil

FIGURE 6.4. Detroit News item on Jamil Beyhum (left) and Emil el-Ghouri, November 21, 1938. Representing the mufti of Jerusalem as guests of the Arab National League in Detroit, they attended the league's Third Arab Convention after a stop in New York City. Courtesy of the Detroit News Archives.

el-Ghouri, at the time the Arab Higher Committee's delegate to Cairo and London, were honored guests of the ANL. The urgency of their visit was underscored by the immigrant activists' participation in the most recent British inquiry, when the Arab Higher Committee issued its belated decision on February 6, 1937, to present its case before the Peel Commission. The Arab Higher Committee was represented by Issa Bandak, who toured the United States accompanied by Adel Arslan in 1930; Jamal Bey al-Husseini, who previously served as emissary to the *mufti* in the United States; and Khalil Totah, the Columbia graduate, principal of the Friends Boys School in Ramallah, and former director of the Arab College in Jerusalem. Other contributors to the Peel Commission were intimately familiar with the immigrants through newspaper coverage and visits; among them were author George Antonius, Muhammad ʿIzzat Darwaza, Fuad Saba, Yaʿqoub Farraj, George Mansour, and Archbishop Gregorios Haddad.[34] Sectarianism was not a factor of consequence in the work for nationalist causes, and hopes of pan-Syrian unity began to yield to an overall Arab nationalism and pan-Arab unity. However, increasing difficulty of travel and communication in Geographic Syria more frequently necessitated that most of the emissaries and political actors in Palestine come from the vicinity of Jerusalem.

By the time the ANL became organized and its leaders began to set a course of action, intra-European intrigue stepped in once again. Future combatants in the approaching global conflict, the Allied and Axis powers, began tightening their grips on pathways to the East. The Syrian lands and Egypt once again were staging areas for military operations due to their strategic locations. Beyhum's visit was met by a mixture of general ignorance of Arab history and suspicions that a convergence of Arab nationalist and Islamic zeal in defense of Palestine might not be in the best interest of the soon-to-be-allies against Germany. Adding to this perception was the formal rejection of the partition plan for Palestine by an assembly of 450 Arab and non-Arab Muslim representatives in the Arab National Congress in Bloudan, Syria, in September 1937.[35] These were not official government emissaries, as very few of their countries were independent; rather, the rejection of the partition plan was a show of spontaneous and widespread protest against British and French imperialism.

Momentum in defense of Palestine slowly mounted between December 1931, when the World Islamic Conference took place in Jerusalem, and November 1936, when a similar conference was held in New Delhi, where Beyhum estimated that 35,000 Muslims called for an end to Jewish immigration.[36] Among those responding to the Arab popular voice and taking up Palestine's cause were Egyptian official Mustapha al-Nahhasin in London, Abdulazīz Āl Saud of Saudi Arabia, Nuri al-Saʿīd of Iraq, and Imam Yahya of Yemen. Although the growing support strengthened hopes of pan-Arab unity, it also raised the stakes for the Arab governments. Independence for these burgeoning nations was illusive at best, but defying the vastly more powerful British could halt any talk of independence. To complicate matters further for the Arab countries, their independence was a minor concern for Britain and its allies compared to the rising specter of Nazism.

In this politically charged atmosphere, Beyhum and Ghouri labored to convince their audiences across the United States that they were not anti-Semitic but anti-Zionists, that Muslims, Christians, and Jews had lived in Palestine as Palestinians for hundreds of years and still could without political Zionism.[37] The dignitaries brought with them the hollow ultimatum that "if the British and the Americans continue[d] their present policy in Palestine," they risked a boycott by all Arabs and Muslims, "including the 80,000,000 in India, who are all in sympathy with our people in the troubled Near East [because of] the Zionist invasion."[38] The delegation embarked on a busy schedule of meetings with immigrant leaders in New York at Hotel McAlpin before a large gathering was assembled. Beyhum, who gained a reputation as a staunch anti-Zionist in Lebanon, visited *Al-Hoda*'s presses, encouraged by a long-distance encounter with Naʿūm Mokarzel in 1913.[39] He met with Naʿūm's brother, Salloum Mokarzel, who visited the notable scholar with a contingent of proponents of Lebanese independence.

Beyhum was told that "[Salloum] Mokarzel's views on Palestine are different from ours, and he cannot be convinced to change them,"[40] which did not surprise the scholar from Beirut. Beyhum critically noted the naïve assumption among some notables in Palestine that the Balfour Declaration would not lead to the Palestinians' deracination.[41] He noted a more dangerous arrangement in which Lebanon would become a "Phoenician" Maronite state and would be bolstered by a Jewish Zionist state to the south, referring to the planned Israel.[42] Salloum Mokarzel interrupted Beyhum's presentation to ask questions, while Fauzi al-Barudi, publisher of *Al-Islāh* newspaper, maintained a more distant approach. After the meeting, *Al-Hoda* joined *Al-Bayān*, *Al-Nisr*, *Mirāt al-Gharb*, and *As-Sameer* in publicizing the delegation's activities and preparing for the visitors' appearances across the United States. When it was time for the dignitaries to depart the United States, Salloum Mokarzel enthusiastically addressed a farewell gathering on January 7, 1939.[43]

Beyhum was not dissuaded by rampant hostile propaganda by the league's detractors from believing in American pragmatism with regard to U.S. interests in the Middle East.[44] He reminded newspaper readers and audiences that 500,000 Jews had found refuge in Palestine. He noted the U.S. State Department's position declared in 1938 that its interests did not extend beyond the welfare of U.S. nationals in Palestine. Beyhum expressed what he considered realistic Arab demands in his letter to President Roosevelt. In doing so, he officially reflected the wishes of Hajj Amin al-Husseini. After explaining Arabs' cultural ties with the Jewish people and Arabs' peaceful intentions toward all concerned, he concluded his letter by extending a hand of friendship while also reminding the U.S. president of his obligations to nascent nations:

We Arabs hope that you preserve the principles nurturing small nations that seek independence and self-government. We hope that you support the overwhelming majority in Palestine against an unjust minority working tirelessly against it. As an emissary of the Arab Higher Committee, I ask of you that you grant us the policy of good neighbor, which you employ in your dealings with other nations—whether you consider us loyal friends or foes that differ with you.[45]

Beyhum received a stock response from Undersecretary Wallace Murray informing him that the government will "give utmost attention and consider all factors."[46]

Beyhum's fears that the Zionists held sway over U.S. public opinion dissipated with each encounter with people from all walks of life. He addressed the subject of reaching out to the U.S. public in a section of his book under the heading "The Americans Are Closer to Our Views than Their Official Statements Suggest."[47] He renewed contacts with Arabists from his travels in Arab cities, among them professor Robert Carson of the American University in Cairo, who arranged for a media specialist to aid the delegation in its mission.[48] Genuine attention from reporters and non-Zionists immediately upon arriving in New York alleviated Beyhum and Ghouri's earlier fears. Beyhum described their concerns while in Paris en route to the United States that Zionist propaganda might result in their being denied entry: "I whispered to Dr. Tawfiq Wahbe [a French Syrian], 'I prefer not to talk to reporters so as to avoid giving the Zionists ammunition with which they can deny us entry to the United States.'"[49]

Although Beyhum was soon heartened by enthusiasm from numerous encounters with American supporters, he also met with many Jewish personalities, including advocates of political Zionism. While he was in New York, a meeting with a rabbi was arranged by Ibrahim al-Zain, a Maronite clergyman from Damascus. Beyhum considered lobbying a viable option in the United States because of the general receptiveness he witnessed by Americans to the grievances of the Palestinian Arab side. He dedicated a chapter to "The Arab Fronts Overseas" and another chapter to "The Front in the United States," in which he explained that "Palestine itself is not the battleground between Arabs and Zionists; it is only the object of these battles. The battleground is Europe and the American continent, especially England and the United States."[50]

Beyhum recalled many instances of prominent people adopting Palestine's cause once they became more aware of the situation there. One of those people was Judge William B. Brown of Grand Rapids, Michigan. The judge attended a speech Beyhum delivered in the People's Church and later a reception in honor of the delegation organized by A. S. Yared, president of the ANL's chapter in Grand Rapids.[51] During the reception the judge stood up and declared that he "ruled among people for thirty years in justice and fairness" and heard "the Zionist side and called for addressing their grievances." The judge continued, "Now that I heard the Arab side and absorbed the elements of their position, I can see the facts clearly and decided that they absolutely have a right."[52] Ahmad Yousef Najm, a local activist formerly of the New Syria Party, took the liberty to send a note to Judge Brown and the *Grand Rapids News* on behalf of Beyhum in which he thanked the newspaper for covering Beyhum's speech in the People's Church and expressed gratitude to the judge for his "fair stance."[53]

The delegation reached the Detroit area, and the *Detroit News* covered it on November 23, 1938. The newspaper gave the "Syrian nobleman" and the "exiled secretary of the Palestine Arab Party" the opportunity they sought to attempt influencing public opinion in the United States. It reported their efforts to "correct what [Beyhum] charges are misinterpretations of the present conflict 'put in the minds of people through paid propaganda.'"[54] Beyhum reiterated the nationalists' stance toward Jews, that a million of them lived in peace in Arab nations and that arid Palestine could not absorb more than the 400,000 Jewish arrivals the British government permitted.

Beyhum advocated coexistence under a democratic government. He took care to differentiate between Jews and Zionists and refuted claims of a religious war while affirming Arab demands for freedom in the face of oppression caused by the Zionist movement. Beyhum explained Palestinians' grievance to the *Detroit News*: "In other words, our very existence in the land we hold dear is threatened . . . we are becoming foreigners in our own land." He drew on the strength of nascent Arab countries in making his points: "Among us in Egypt and Syria and Irak [sic] are many Jews. We merely want a democratic government like that enjoyed in America, where all will be proportionately represented."[55] The dignitaries objected to Zionist claims that "Fascist money and propaganda of the totalitarian powers were behind the Arab revolt." Acting on strict instructions from Hajj al-Husseini, Beyhum responded that the archaic weapons in Arab hands were "the same used to fight the Turks. Were we to accept help we probably would be better off. But we do not choose between masters; we do not care to make ourselves subservient to Italy or Germany in a fight against England."

His remarks to the *Detroit News* are reflected in Beyhum's book in describing his travels and activities. He explained in the book that his visit corresponded with concerted efforts by a "consortium of fascists and Nazis" to rally the Arab street against the would-be Allied powers in 1938 and 1939. Beyhum admitted that he was fooled by media outlets belonging to such interest groups into thinking that they could be used to fight Zionism.[56] He approached al-Husseini in exile in the village of Karnail, Lebanon, to consult with him on whether it would be a good idea to stop by Rome and Berlin in order to harness the American affiliates of European anti-Zionists. Beyhum recalled the encounter in his book and may have intended his recollection of events as a response to charges that the *mufti* had turned Nazi: "He advised me not to do so and strenuously insisted that I not contact any of these parties and said to me letter for letter [*bi al-ḥarf al-waḥid*]: 'If we protest against Great Britain because it issued the Balfour Declaration and helped implement it by force and violence, this is a matter between us and the British and we have no use for a third party's interference.'"[57]

Beyhum and Ghouri resurrected long-forgotten cultural links with the "English-speaking people [who] have founded our schools, universities, and missions" and urged them to "help the Jews by all means. But why at the expense of the Arab nation?" Ghouri, like many of his colleagues and predecessors, had attained higher education in the United States; he capitalized on the Arab constituency's links to the extended community in Detroit by telling the *Detroit News* that there were 250,000 Americans of Arab descent in the United States, among them 30,000 mostly American citizens living in Detroit.[58]

Beyhum's authoritative treatises on the history of the Middle East and Arab women attracted the attention of newspaper editors and Arab immigrants from all parts of the Middle East. Those who read his works included Muhammad Bin Thani and 'Abdelsalam Bin Tahamah al-Sa'idi of the Moroccan immigrant community; Yemeni immigrants; the Sudanese delegation to the Islamic conference in Bloudan, which made an unsolicited official endorsement; and prosperous merchants of Greater New York.[59] The Muslim Student Association of New York, headed by Hassan Hammoud, honored the delegation at a large banquet when Beyhum returned to the city in July 1939.[60] Beyhum attended a church service officiated by Metropolitan Antonios (Antony) Bashir of the Orthodox Archdiocese of North America, who gave a "fiery sermon against colonialists."[61] A separate, "spectacular" banquet honoring the delegation was held in the Opera House of the Academy of Music on January 7, 1939, and presided over by Rizk Haddad.

In Beyhum's account of his visit to Flint, he gave special tribute to the ANL's chapter there and its president, Ameen Farah, whom Beyhum described as "consumed by loyalty fused with industriousness and courage."[62] Farah began preparations for the delegation's visit on November 4, 1938, by contacting Fuad Mufarrij, a visiting activist concerned with reviving agriculture in Syria's rural villages with support from donations in the United States. Mufarrij volunteered his time to help Kātibah in the day-to-day operations in the league's headquarters in New York. In his reply to Farah's letter about coordinating activities for the delegation's visit Mufarrij acknowledged Farah's "true nationalist spirit, which the Flint chapter expressed at every occasion," and he confirmed sending regular reports outlining the "benefit of organized work and the necessity of widespread information campaigns."[63]

Fuad Shatara sent a letter about the Detroit convention to ANL chapters and affiliate clubs and societies across the United States. Shatara informed the affiliates in typed Arabic text that the "Third Arab Conference" would be held in Detroit November 24–26, 1938. Shatara asked supporters to hold special meetings if necessary to designate two delegates to represent each chapter and respond to the league's address at 303 Fifth Avenue, New York. The place of the convention was given in English as "The Progressive Arabian Hashemite Society. 10401 Dix Ave, Dearborn Michigan." The contact at the Hashemite Society was listed as its president, Ali Rustum.[64]

On November 21, 1938, Farah sent out carbon copies of a leaflet announcing "a grand reception in honor of the Arab delegation" in fiery language presumably intended to move the recipients' passions. The reception would be held at Dearborn's Arab Hashemite Club, a center for early Shi'a immigrants, and would feature inspiring speeches by Muhammad Beyhum and Emil el-Ghouri for the benefit of "bludgeoned Palestine." He invited all Arabic speakers in Detroit, Dearborn, Highland Park, Hamtramck, Flint, Saginaw, Bay City, Michigan City, Grand Rapids, Grand Haven, and Toledo to attend.[65] Farah's follow-up activities with Mufarrij are logged in a letter from Farah to Kātibah in which he reported on the Flint chapter's activities during a formal session held on November 25, 1938. The chapter's activities included sending five telegrams to President Roosevelt to counter Zionist lobbying, electing a new board member, and sending $180 to Jerusalem, $100 to Damascus, and $200 to ANL headquarters toward the chapter's dues.

Emil el-Ghouri sent a request for another gathering to the Flint Nazarenes from his hotel in Detroit.[66] It was answered by a second banquet celebrating the delegation in Flint's Community Hall. At the banquet Mahmoud Hamady and Tawfiq Mansour competed in bidding for a gold bracelet offered by Adele Samra, the wife of the master of ceremony, Najīb Samra. Beyhum later fondly recalled the event.[67] On December 12, 1938, Farah sent a telegram to the Arabic-language dailies and magazines asking them to report on the successful event, declaring that the benefit had collected $2,000 for Palestine. A rare issue of the Arabic-language *Al-Bayān* newspaper in Farah's collection has front-page coverage of the banquet and the amount raised under the headline "The Arab Delegation Is Welcomed by the Flint, Michigan, Immigrant Community in a Fine Reception."[68]

Beyhum's chronicle and analysis in his book *Filasṭīn: Andalus al-Sharq* complement Farah's and other archives with a wealth of information on names and locations of activists in the Detroit area. The ANL's strategy of defending Syria by taking up the cause of Palestine linked the immigrant communities of Shiʿa and Sunni Muslims and Christians to the events in Syria and to each other. Documentation of the social lives and habits of Detroit Arabs at this time and for the preceding fifty years is nearly nonexistent despite useful Arabic-language material in the Burton Historical Collections of the Detroit Public Library and doubtlessly the homes of old families across southeastern Michigan.[69] All strands of Arab Syrians in southeast Michigan in addition to Grand Rapids and Michigan City to the west answered the call to meetings and rallies by the league. Aside from vague reference to what appears to have been intra-Muslim name-calling by Beyhum, no specific Christian-Muslim animosity was mentioned in his account outside the well-known position of Naʿūm Mokarzel. Among the groups that answered the call by the league were the Arab Palestinian Renaissance Society headed by Hanna Khalaf; the Muslim diaspora in Dearborn represented by the Renaissance Arab Hashemite Club (Jamʿiyat al-Nahḍah al-Hashimiyah) headed by Imam Khalil Bazi; and the nearby Sunni mosque and club headed by Sheikh Muhammad Husain Kharoub.

However—and here is the vague reference to intra-Muslim problems—Beyhum indicated that he "criticized sectarian name-calling although [all] united behind the common nationalist goals."[70] Officers of the Hashemite Club, an important venue for early Shiʿa Muslims in Detroit, included its president Hamid Musharraf, executive director Abdallah Berri, and treasurer Fayez Hasan, all from Jabal ʿĀmil, Lebanon. The activities of the league suggest that Lutfi al-Saʿdi and Muhammad Musa secured the participation of many in the community.[71] The rallies for Palestine apparently coincided with Ramadan festivities of Eid al-Fitr that mark the end of a month of fasting. The November 26, 1938, issue of the Beirut newspaper *Al-Nahar* described Eid al-Fitr as well as the flood of emotions from participants in rallies following speeches by Beyhum, the Shiʿa Khalil Bazi, and the Sunni Husain Kharoub.[72] The league, for the time being, enjoyed larger membership than any other Arab American organization because of its appeal across diverse orientations. The reason for that appeal perhaps was that

Arab nationalist sentiments toward colonialism and Zionism trumped sectarian allegiances.

Over the course of 1938 and 1939 the delegation visited Grand Haven, Michigan, and cities in Florida, as well as Cincinnati, Los Angeles, and Houston, where a banquet was held at the YWCA and headed by Suleiman Dawoud. They also visited a host of small cities where wealthy immigrants gave generously.[73] Beyhum's account does not provide a precise itinerary of the delegation's tours during 1939. However, it can be gleaned from his accounts that a much larger amount of money was raised when the delegation visited more established and presumably wealthier immigrants such as those in Mexico City, Chihuahua, Monterrey, Tampico, and Torreon, Mexico.[74] In his recollection of the delegation's visit to Tampico, Beyhum explained how funds were managed. After a lavish banquet, Tampico league member Mahdi Ahmad Ibrahim suggested giving the proceeds to the delegation to deliver to the *mufti* in Jerusalem. The delegate publicly declined accepting funds, explaining that "according to the custom during the official visit, the delegation does not directly accept donations; rather, they are sent to a separate committee, which would then send the funds to Palestine's war victims [*mankūbīn Filasṭīn*]."[75] This is a reference to Lajnat Mankubī Filasṭīn (Committee for War Victims in Palestine) under the care of the *mufti* al-Husseini directly. Beyhum surmised that the incident in Tampico, reported in the ANL's monthly bulletin on July 17, 1939, would augment confidence in the delegation's mission. In a footnote on the same page he explained the strategy for handling funds: "This was the plan that earned us complete confidence; we instructed the committee that collected the funds to send the funds by means it saw fit to three intermediaries: Omar Daouq in Beirut, Talʿat Pasha Harb in Cairo, and Hajj Yaseen Diab in Damascus. They in turn deliver the money to [the Committee for War Afflicted in Palestine]."

Besides their travels in Mexico, the ANL's guests also briefly left the United States to answer an invitation from established Nazarenes in Cuba led by the nationalist Emile Farah. They were welcomed to the island by the Arab Palestinian Society, the Lebanese Society, government officials, and Cuban dignitaries. The success of the visit to Cuba alarmed the delegation's detractors, likely Maronites working with the French, who sent an emissary of their own to the island.[76]

Beyhum's account of his time in the United States helps piece together a story that otherwise is as scattered as the surviving archives on the Arab National League. When the emissaries came to Detroit in 1938, a group of Syrian Arab women led a crowd of 400 that gathered in the magnificent train station near Michigan Avenue to welcome the visitors of the ANL before a long procession accompanied the delegation to the Leland Hotel. Ghouri's address to supporters that evening was followed by a tribute to Beyhum by Sheikh Husain Kharoub, the leader of the Sunni immigrant community in Michigan.[77] One week before receiving the delegation in Detroit, Fuad Shatara, as president of the ANL, participated in "one of the most important panels on the Arabic cause," hosted by the Foreign Policy Association. A forum in Boston's Kelly Plaza was attended by 500 men and women "representing the educated class in this distinguished town." During the panel discussion Shatara responded to his opponent's claims that the population in Palestine welcomed the Zionists save for a small band of terrorists, and he answered questions from the audience.[78] On November 26, 1938, another lecture and debate took place between the visiting dignitary Fuad Mufarrij and Morris Bookstein. It was hosted by the Connecticut Valley branch of the Foreign Policy Association and held in Kimball Hall in Springfield, Massachusetts.

Activities like these and the unwavering nationalist position of the bishop of the Orthodox Syrian community scored some successes for the Arab cause in the public relations arena. A retraction by the Council of Churches of Christ in America of its support for Zionism was one tangible result achieved by the league and the Syrian Orthodox Archdiocese. Apparently, the council had sent a memo to President Roosevelt urging him to use his office to press the British to keep immigration to Palestine unrestricted. The ANL joined protests against the policy that were led by Archbishop Antony Bashir, Arab leaders, and the Greek Orthodox hierarchy across Syria. The protest leaders delivered the objections to the general secretary of the Council of Churches of Christ. The council responded with a letter to Archbishop Bashir informing him that "at no time has the [council] endorsed any proposal for the creation of a Jewish State in Palestine or any program of political Zionism."[79]

Farah's papers indicate that the momentum created by the delegation's visit kept organized political activities going through 1939. After Beyhum and Ghouri's return tour of the southern states, Cuba, and Mexico in 1939, Syrians in Flint evidently felt confident enough to host that year's national ANL convention. In the process, they created a record of the league's operations, other documents and correspondences, and the most complete list of ANL organizational and individual affiliates across the Americas. Although incomplete, these records allow a far more sober assessment of the political maturity of the Syrian Arab immigrants in the United States. Letters from Beyhum and Ghouri upon their return to New York expressed genuine gratitude to Ameen Farah and sought his council on various issues. Once back in New York, Beyhum sent a Christmas greeting to Farah, while Ghouri, in Lexington by the end of January 1939, told Farah he would like very much for Fred (Farīd) Farah and Subhi Farah, both of the Flint Farah clan, to accompany the delegation to Cuba around February 15 or 18, 1939. In the same letter, Ghouri indicated a delay in the Cuba trip so he and Beyhum could "wander among traveling salesmen in the small cities of southern states."[80]

The flurry of activities around the delegation's visits was part of an overall strategy of influencing public opinion in the United States and London. Ghouri had in 1936 authored a semi-comprehensive position from the Arab point of view published by the Royal Institute of International Affairs.[81] The emissaries' arguments during their visits remained within the confines of the key points Ghouri outlined in his report. Amid these efforts, widespread Arab and Muslim protest against British policies in Palestine was exacerbated by the expulsion of members of the most likely Palestinian legislative body and coincided with unprecedented military mobilization by the United States and the European allies. German support of fascist Spain was one of many ominous signs of the Germans' growing belligerence, yet the ill-prepared British chose neutrality. As Arabs endeavored to convey their grievances to the English-speaking world, news of discontent among India's vast numbers of Muslims enhanced the possibility that U.S. Arab immigrants might have access to their adopted country's government and perhaps hoped that U.S. policies would differ from those of the British that had caused that discontent.

In September 1939 Hitler's army stormed into Poland, ushering in the start of World War II. British mobilization in response meant using the United Kingdom's considerable leverage to enlist its colonies in the fight, just as it had done in the previous world war. Arab populations whom the British considered part of its dominion would not be exempt from this mobilization. The British resorted to calming the fears of friendly Arab regimes at early signs of tension in Europe, having created monarchies in Arabia and Trans-Jordan, precisely to secure strategic depth when needed. The carrot part of an alternating carrot-and-stick strategy by the British entailed nominal success for the Arab office in London in the form of British promises of restricting Jewish immigration and slowing plans to divide Palestine.

The looming war with Germany, not Arab pleas, accounted for Britain's temporary flexibility. The Woodhead Commission in August 1938 declared "impracticable" the plans to divide Palestine as recommended by the Peel Commission the previous year. The Woodhead Commission finding was a ray of hope that reinvigorated immigrants and bolstered their connections to Arab political initiatives. Farah telegraphed the national office of the league rejoicing in the news of the Woodhead report and received a typed letter in Arabic from Kātibah sharing the sentiments. Kātibah informed Farah that he had cabled the delegates in the Arab office in London to congratulate them and press for a "united front for common goals."[82] However, the hardships facing European Jews made it exceedingly difficult to ignore the desire of many of them to leave Europe. The dreadful conditions for European Jews presented an opportunity for Zionists to promote Palestine as a viable destination. American Jewish groups pressed their case to the American public and polity with a predictable outcome, given their relatively large numbers.

The March 4, 1939, issue of the *New York Times* offered Shatara—indeed, Arab nationalists everywhere—both vindication and ominous news. Syrians' long-held historical claim to Palestine as part of Syria was confirmed with the British "official release of the 1916 McMahon correspondence to Hussein, the Sherif of Mecca, promising the establishment of an Arab state that will include Palestine after defeating the Turks and Germans in the war [World War I]."[83] It is not clear if all related records were released, but the article reported on stalled talks between the British and Zionists over the idea of an independent Palestine with majority rule. Agreement between Syrians in the diasporas and the Palestinian delegation in London over extending full rights to the Jewish population in Palestine was verbalized numerous times. However, British hints at a Palestinian state caused Rabbi Wise to break off talks with the British and return to the United States.[84]

The implications of the 1916 correspondence and the British-Zionist stalemate following Wise's return from London can be understood only as part of the big picture. A sweeping new strategy was beginning to emerge whereby the Zionists understood their considerable voting power in the United States and resolved to use it to pressure the British. Oswald Villard and other editors of *The Nation*, on behalf of a "large section of independent liberal and labor opinion," sent a telegram urging British colonial secretary Malcolm MacDonald to "'desist' from any plans to create an independent [binational] State in Palestine."[85] They warned that "such action would arouse indignation among Christians and Jews alike" just when Britain faced the Nazis: "The effect upon American attitude toward Great Britain would be literally disastrous."[86] Adding more weight to the threat of political reprisals, U.S. Representative Charles Buckley of the Bronx telegraphed Secretary of State Cordell Hull demanding that he "remind Great Britain that the Palestine mandate is not to be tossed aside."[87] The *New York Times* article carried reports from Palestine of the discovery of twelve dead Palestinians in a cave who were killed by Jewish terrorists and of the subsequent retaliation by a youth who wounded a Jewish settler before escaping to the "old city" of Jerusalem.[88]

Shatara, a committed binationalist, that is, favoring one state for both Palestinians and Jews with majority rule, sent a letter to Villard at *The Nation* asking him to "reconcile [his] reputation as a liberal with such meddlesome interference to prevent the people of Palestine from attaining their independence" and invited the editor to a debate after suggesting that Villard read George Antonius's newly published *Arab Awakening*.[89] Villard's unsigned and terse reply argued for "one place of refuge for the Jews" and ended with subtly injecting the specter of Nazism: "I have never been accused of 'meddlesome interference,' except by Germans."[90] In his rebuttal to Villard's remarks Shatara attempted to isolate political Zionism as the cause of the conflict and reiterated that Jews could find refuge in Palestine without "trampling" on the "most elementary principles of democracy." The surgeon closed by again calling on Villard to "discuss the facts and debate this issue in true American fashion."[91]

It is important to keep in perspective the disparity of power between the ANL and the collection of Jewish organizations with direct links to the World Zionist Organization and its even wider reach. Arabs as well as the mostly Eastern Europeans on the Jewish side knew that British policy was subject to change depending on Britain's needs. But the ANL and the Arab diaspora generally represented countries that had yet to gain their bearings after centuries of neglect at the hands of foreign conquerors including the Ottoman Turks. Among the Zionists on the Jewish side were scores of intellectuals, labor leaders, union members, and generally a population that experienced and participated in European industrialization. Not only were activists and leaders on the Arab side prevented from communicating across British and French spheres of influence, but they were hindered in their efforts by European perceptions that agrarian life and lack of industrialization in the Middle East were signs of inferiority.

The British were familiar with Chaim Weizmann, who settled in Britain at age thirty and worked as a professor of chemistry. Weizmann's sensibilities and perceptions toward the underdeveloped Palestinian peasant, whom he described as "primitive," ignorant, and prone to believe whatever he was told, were compatible with those of self-styled British gentry.[92] Even when the British government of Neville Chamberlain issued the infamous white paper through colonial secretary MacDonald, it proposed not halting Jewish immigration but rather reducing it to 75,000 for the years 1940–

1945. The stipulation in the white paper of a binational state was something Shatara, Kātibah, and their guests like Beyhum advocated at every opportunity. It seemed that the British were finally heeding their own diplomats' recommendations by issuing the white paper, therefore making possible the realization of all Arab Palestinian goals, albeit motivated by the specter of military conflict in Europe on a massive scale. MacDonald's plans unraveled in the face of pressure brought to bear by U.S. Zionists,[93] who were backed by the steamroller of British politics, Winston Churchill, and other colonialists in the League of Nations.[94] Just before the war engulfed the world and consumed all talk of an independent Palestine, and amid the changing British whims, the Arab National League proceeded with plans to convene in Flint at the behest of Farah and the Flint chapter. Under these circumstances and given their length of time in the United States, service in World War I, and increasing cultural integration, the immigrants began to think of themselves as equal citizens.

In the somewhat optimistic though volatile atmosphere, an end to the mandate seemed a distinct possibility. The Arab diaspora forged ahead, emboldened by British gestures, albeit from a position of weakness, and by a rising awareness among nations under British control. Most of all the immigrants had their achievements and experiences in the United States to draw on, the last of which was a successful fund-raising tour by Beyhum and Ghouri. The central office pressed ahead with plans for a national convention to be held in Flint in September 1939. Farah did not hesitate, as he had with the 1927 convention of the NSP. He and his compatriots were ready to work.

On April 17, 1939, the same day the latest British white paper was issued, Fuad Shatara wrote to Farah, Henry Igram, and George Samra at the Flint chapter of the league: "It may be a long ways yet to September and the forthcoming Arab convention, but we thought it might be a good idea to put out feelers to the various organizations and influential individuals throughout the United States, Mexico, Canada, and Central America."[95] Apparently, the success of the Beyhum-Ghouri visit encouraged Farah and his compatriots to consider Flint a destination for immigrant nationalists in the Americas and a venue for a convention and a *mahrajān* (festive rally). Shatara offered "all the assistance and cooperation" needed from the league's headquarters in New York and confided the organizations' urgent need of funds to the "most loyal and understanding group [in Flint] affiliated" with the league.

Upon Fuad Shatara's offer of support from the headquarters in New York for a convention in Flint, Ameen Farah replied to Kātibah confirming that the motion was seconded and carried in the Flint chapter's official meeting to hold a convention for the Arab National League in Flint "under the auspices of the chapter" and that the board voted to "work earnestly on a worthwhile convention with sufficient political and financial gains for the cause abroad and to sustain the New York office financially for the next year."[96] Accordingly, Farah requested from ANL headquarters the names of the league's chapters, informal affiliates, and "individuals who do not hesitate in the service of the homeland. After receiving your reply, we will decide the next steps speedily. I assure you of our unshakable support." In his gleeful response Kātibah assured Farah of unwavering support from the national office, backed by Shatara and members of the executive board. Farah received the list he requested of groups and individuals across the United States, Canada, and South America. It is not clear if the list was complete; however, the surviving English-language pages show thirty-six affiliates or chapters in addition to fifty-seven individuals.

Each of their addresses, notwithstanding some overlaps when the chapter and the contact person had the same address, was an outpost for the league. The list had been edited and corrected by the national office. Typed notes explained the functions of some individuals, and most names next to the affiliates appeared in Arabic only. For example, next to A. Badr of Dearborn on the first page, the Arabic text specifies his role: "Ahmad Badr Conference Secretary." The Arab National League of Chicago was accompanied with its contact, Mahdi Ahmad Ibrahim, and so forth. The list of ANL affiliates was attached along with a list of members of Congress complete with party affiliations and respective states. The addresses of affiliates supplied by the ANL national office were spread across the country, and the individual contacts were as diverse as the Arab immigrants themselves. It must be stressed that the diversity of religion, region or town, and clan did not preclude political uniformity by virtue of being included as affiliates of the ANL. The Maronites did not have a prominent presence that I can discern from the roster, and many had Muslim names. The lists and supporting letters and documents suggest that when the immigrants approached this stage of collective political activism they were more articulate and more organized than at any time in their history. Notwithstanding the overlap of addresses, the number of chapters and contacts for a community the size of an average city indicates that in its fourth year the ANL had emerged as a representative body of Arab immigrants in the United States.

Coherence of political outlook, immigrants' expectations, and camaraderie among the league's associates engendered social and communal cooperation overall. In this atmosphere Syrians as a community appeared to be positioned to share in the ensuing social changes of World War II, which remolded U.S. society in almost every conceivable way. The war diminished age-old sectarian divisions among U.S. immigrants of older, mostly northwestern European Protestant, Eastern European Catholic, and Jewish descent. It expanded the role of the federal government in ways that later would contribute to redressing Jim Crow laws. War mobilization forced all segments of U.S. society to fall behind the goal of defeating the Axis powers. For Italian, Polish, Jewish, Arab, and indeed all the immigrant groups of the turn of the twentieth century, the latter part of 1939 was a time to declare unwavering loyalty to their adopted country. The dominant Anglo-Protestant population was compelled to acknowledge and accept the cultural characteristics of the "new immigrants," a term used to describe the mostly Eastern European arrivals between 1870 and World War I. For Syrian Arab immigrants, the urgency of aiding fellow Syrians and the rising expectations as loyal U.S. citizens during the impending global conflict prompted them to garner whatever currency their commitment to the war effort could bring. The ANL convention served as the stage on which an emergent Arab American identity was declared, exactly on the day when World War II with all its uncertainty was declared in Europe.

Ameen Farah's manuscripts contain a small stack of copies of letters he sent inviting collectives and individuals to the conference and asking the Arabic-language periodicals and dailies to announce the event to their readers. Careful to address specific interests and attributes of his recipients, he apparently made sure no two invitations were alike. In his invitation to his old pal Madey, editor of *As-Sameer*, Farah recalled the magazine's nationalist history. After the niceties and the necessary information about the event, Farah wrote to Madey: "As-Sameer took a distinguished and serious stance in defense of the homeland. Considering the critical situation—excessive repression by the colonialists, the continuation of the revolution in Palestine, and rumbling of volcanoes in Syria—your presence in the conference adds to its relevance and intended benefit."[97]

In a flurry of letters and preparations, the stage was set for the convention. Plans entailed securing an automobile to be raffled, a block of rooms in Flint's fine Hotel Durant, menus for the banquet, a meeting hall, and a festive finale at the farm of Tawfiq Mansour, where the *mahrajān* with games, music, and food would await the guests. Farah's papers contain several snippets of long newspaper articles extending to readers an invitation to the convention. The announcements in *As-Sameer* described the preparations and promoted the conference by recalling a July 1939 article by Ahmad Yousef Najm in which he extolled the benefits of public engagement, political activism, and mobilization:

[Najm] explicated with clear evidence and examples the importance of [political] advocacy in the advancement of nations.... Of course this advocacy cannot exist without strong organization, efficient action, and a unified path. Achieving common goals depends on attainable and commonly held principles addressing the situation at hand. Official invitations are on the way to committees, societies, and chapters.... If you receive this invitation—or if you did not for some reason—make yourself a "committee of one" so that you can help the conference come to fruition. If you have a suggestion or a critical observation, send it to the league's office or to the Flint chapter in Michigan and lend a hand.[98]

In addition to the local concern of lobbying and mobilizing, the preparations coincided with the return of Beyhum and Ghouri to Jerusalem, where they reported to the *mufti* on their experiences and on Farah's tireless work.

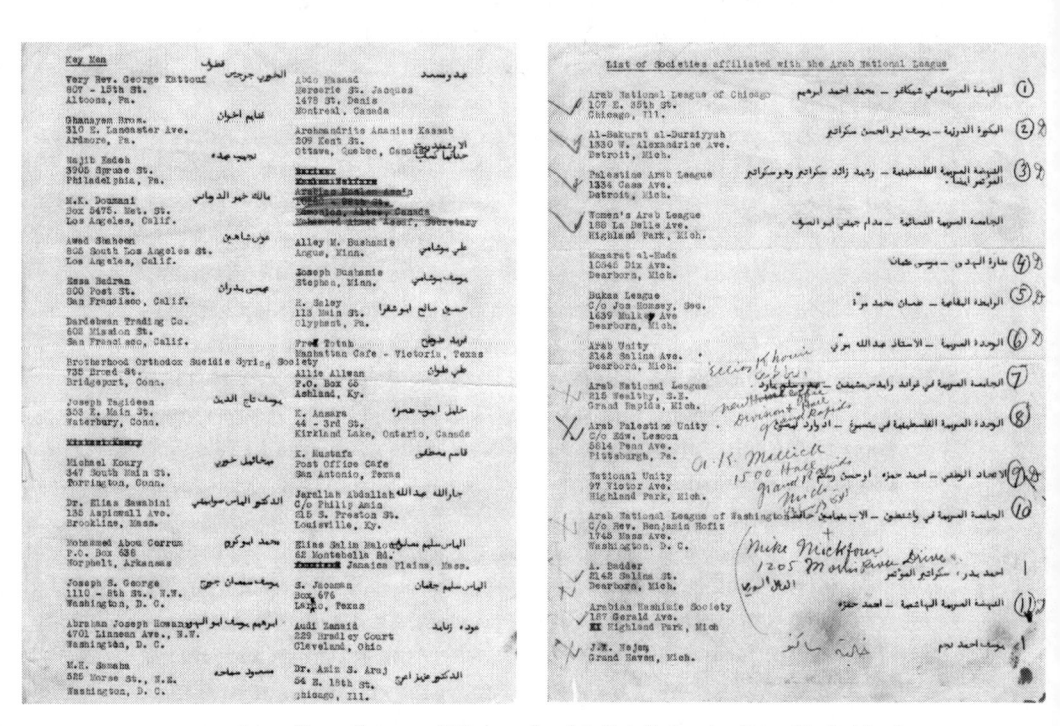

FIGURES 6.5. *Pages from an ANL membership list. Extensive lists of individuals and socialites affiliated with the ANL suggest a membership in the thousands, not hundreds. The scattered nature of ANL documents makes it difficult to piece together a complete picture of the league's structure and operations. Farah Papers, Bawardi Collection.*

HOTEL DURANT
FLINT, MICHIGAN

OFFICE OF THE MANAGER

July 25, 1939

Mr. Emmett M. Sobe
1409 North Saginaw Street
Flint, Michigan

Dear Mr. Sobe:

In accordance with your request we are submitting herewith rates in effect at the Durant during the Convention of the Arab National League.

Single room with private bath $2.50, $3.00, $3.50 and $4.00
Double room with private bath $4.00, $4.50 and $5.00
Room with twin beds and private bath $5.00, $5.50 and $6.00

We are enclosing three sample menus for a banquet you contemplate having in connection with your Convention.

We are putting at your disposal a large reception room on the mezzanine floor at no cost to you. In addition, there is to be a registration desk on the mezzanine floor to register your delegates.

We thank you for this opportunity to be of service to your organization and look forward with pleasure to receiving definite reservations from you.

EWW/eh
Encl.

Cordially yours,

Earl W. Wahl
Manager

FIGURE 6.6. *Hotel Durant room rates for the ANL convention. The elegant hotel in Flint offered the conventioneers sample menus as well. The hotel was built in 1920 and named after the founder of General Motors, William C. Durant. Farah Papers, Bawardi Collection.*

Their testimonies and Farah's long-standing acquaintance with the *mufti* through fund-raising for the New Syria Party fourteen years prior netted Farah a letter that he doubtlessly cherished proudly as part of his impeccably preserved archives. It is addressed to him by name from Hajj Amin al-Husseini on the stationery of the Central Committee to Aid the War Victims (al-Lajnah al-Markazīyah li Iʿānat al-Mankūbīn), the same committee to which all funds were sent. Immigrants generally shortened its name to Lajnat al-Mankūbīn. The short letter from Husseini, dated July 17, 1939, underscores the importance of the immigrants' humanitarian work, especially after the exile of the *mufti* and most of the Palestinian leadership by the British for opposing unrestricted Jewish immigration:

> The kind and gentle Ameen Effendi Farah,
>
> Greetings. The delegation comprised of the two dear brothers Jamil Baik Beyhum and Emil Effendi al-Ghouri is back in the homeland. They both speak highly of you and greatly appreciate all the financial and moral support you extended to them during their humanitarian mission for the benefit of your afflicted brethren among the Arabs of Palestine. Your kindness is deeply felt. May God bless you and reward you accordingly.
>
> We have no doubt that these suffering victims [*al-mankūbīn*] will always be the destination of your proven compassion and aid given your loyalty and faithful nationalist zeal. We urge you to remind the brothers to always expedite their humanitarian deeds nonstop.
>
> In conclusion, accept my sincere gratitude. Please give our greetings and abundant gratitude to each of our brothers, members of the Flint diaspora, who shared in this good deed. May God keep you.
>
> Chairman of the Central Aid Committee of Palestine's War Victims.
> [Signed] Muhammad Amin al-Husseini

The ANL's bulletin for August 1939 announced that Professor Elihu Grant would be the keynote speaker in the convention slated for September 2–4 and that a Pontiac automobile would be raffled.[99] According to the bulletin, Grant, a member of the American Friends Mission, an archeologist, and a retired Harvard professor, not only offered to cover his own expenses but also "launched a campaign to raise $10,000 from American donors to be sent to the Arab revolution in Palestinian through the Friends school in the city of Ramallah, Palestine." The bulletin announced that a group from the league's New York office would attend as well. A member of the New York contingent, Professor Farhat Ziadeh later recalled that he was invited to attend the convention along with Fakhri al-Shaykh, an Iraqi

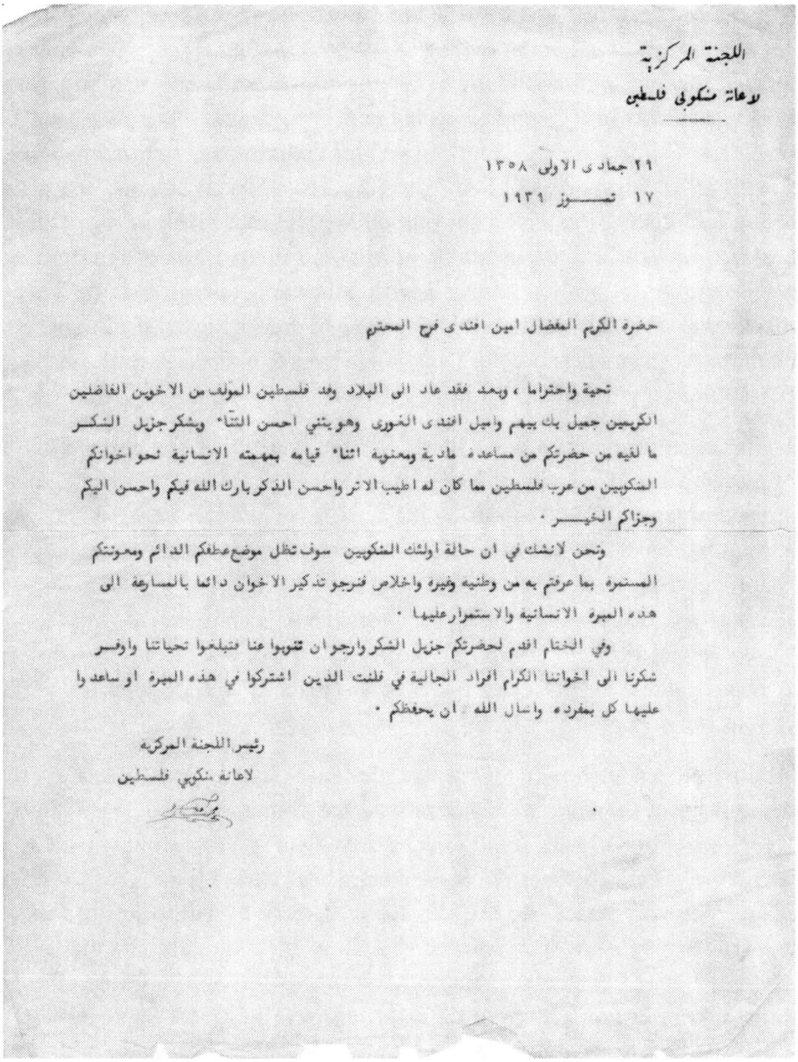

اللجنة المركزية
لإعانة منكوبي فلسطين

٢٩ جمادى الاولى ١٣٥٨
١٧ تمـــوز ١٩٣٩

حضرة الكريم المفضال امين افندى فرح المحترم

تحية واحتراما ، وبعد فقد عاد الى البلاد وفد فلسطين المؤلف من الاخوين الفاضلين الكريمين جميل بك بيهم واميل افندى الخورى وهو يثني احسن الثنا ويشكر جزيل الشكر ما لقيه من حضرتكم من مساعدة مادية ومعنوية اثنا قيامه بمهمته الانسانية نحو اخوانكم المنكوبين من عرب فلسطين مما كان له اطيب الاثر واحسن الذكر بارك الله فيكم واحسن اليكم وجزاكم الخيـــر .

ونحن لانشك في ان حالة اولئك المنكوبين سوف تظل موضع عطفكم الدائم ومعونتكم المستمرة بما عرفتم به من وطنية وغيرة واخلاص فنرجو تذكير الاخوان دائما بالمسارعة الى هذه المبرة الانسانية والاستمرار عليها .

وفي الختام اقدم لحضرتكم جزيل الشكر وارجو ان تنوبوا عنا فتبلغوا تحياتنا ووافر شكرنا الى اخواننا الكرام افراد الجالية في فلنت الذين اشتركوا في هذه المبرة او ساعدوا عليها كل بمفرده واسال الله ان يحفظكم .

رئيس اللجنة المركزية
لاعانة منكوبي فلسطين

FIGURE 6.7. *Letter from Hajj Muhammad Amin al-Husseini to Ameen Farah, July 17, 1939. Farah Papers, Bawardi Collection.*

graduate student at Columbia University, and another Iraqi scholar, ʿAbd al-Majid ʿAbbas, who received his doctorate from the University of Chicago.[100] The group set out from New York in al-Shaykh's automobile of "ancient vintage," setting the stage for an accident in which activists Mufarrij and Shaykh would die soon after the convention.[101]

Fuad Mufarrij had just returned to New York after a four-month journey across the United States during which he refused to accept gifts but addressed the media often and promoted the league. Mufarrij's humanitarian work was widely known and respected in part because of his passionate engagement with improving education and his dedication to improving living conditions in rural areas of Syria and Iraq. His observations and speeches before and during the ANL's convention suggest that many in the Middle East had far-reaching expectations of immigrants in terms of remittances and donations but also as lobbyists with political potential. Mufarrij's perspectives as a visiting dignitary during the conference are telling. But his remarks to league members before it began convey equally important political expectations upon the immigrants by their fellow Syrians:

> The upcoming conference will reflect the strength of the nationalist movement in this country. I hope that the participants will strengthen their organizing abilities during the conference and put them on solid foundations . . . You [Syrian Arab immigrants] gained wide experience through your work in the past. I hope, indeed I trust that you will continue with that which is worthy and avoid previous mistakes. . . . Just as you uphold the homeland in her struggle, so, too, you can be sure the homeland and the patriots are with you—appreciative and supportive of your work.[102]

The ANL leadership, in an attempt to arouse passions and rally support, requested that the *mufti* al-Husseini send his fountain pen to be auctioned at the convention to raise funds. The initiative was indicative of the wide appeal the *mufti* attained even in exile, mostly because of his consistent stance against British policies and the massive settlement by Europeans in Palestine. The Syrian Americans learned that the *mufti*'s fountain pen was to be auctioned in the conference. Ḥabīb Kātibah explained: "the leader of Palestine's Arab Legion answered the request from the Arab League by sending his personal pen to be auctioned . . . to help with the expenses of the office in New York."[103] Kātibah disclosed the full content of the letter from the *mufti*, who confirmed sending his pen by "special delivery."[104] Among the delegates listed in the bulletin, Madame Jenny Abu al-Souf was chosen to represent the Women's Arab League in Detroit, while the Baqaʿ League of Dearborn chose Sheikh Abu Ali Huroub and Taʿan Muhammad Murrah to be the official representatives. The ANL particularly commanded the involvement of the Shiʿas and Sunnis of Detroit. A postscript at the bottom of the last page of the bulletin under "Conference Updates" reported on a letter from Fayez Hasan of the Hashemite Club in Dearborn indicating that

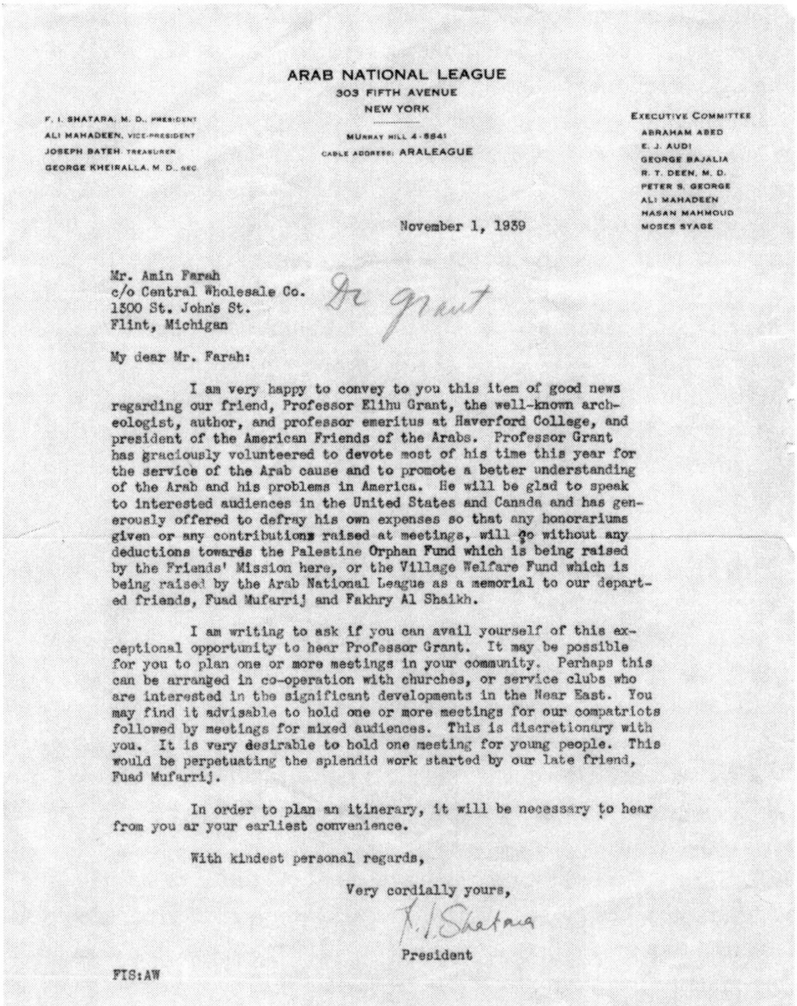

ARAB NATIONAL LEAGUE
303 FIFTH AVENUE
NEW YORK

F. I. SHATARA, M. D., PRESIDENT
ALI MAHADEEN, VICE-PRESIDENT
JOSEPH BATEH, TREASURER
GEORGE KHEIRALLA, M. D., SEC

MURRAY HILL 4-5841
CABLE ADDRESS: ARALEAGUE

EXECUTIVE COMMITTEE
ABRAHAM ABED
E. J. AUDI
GEORGE BAJALIA
R. T. DEEN, M. D.
PETER S. GEORGE
ALI MAHADEEN
HASAN MAHMOUD
MOSES SYAGE

November 1, 1939

Mr. Amin Farah
c/o Central Wholesale Co.
1500 St. John's St.
Flint, Michigan

Dr Grant

My dear Mr. Farah:

   I am very happy to convey to you this item of good news regarding our friend, Professor Elihu Grant, the well-known archeologist, author, and professor emeritus at Haverford College, and president of the American Friends of the Arabs. Professor Grant has graciously volunteered to devote most of his time this year for the service of the Arab cause and to promote a better understanding of the Arab and his problems in America. He will be glad to speak to interested audiences in the United States and Canada and has generously offered to defray his own expenses so that any honorariums given or any contributions raised at meetings, will go without any deductions towards the Palestine Orphan Fund which is being raised by the Friends' Mission here, or the Village Welfare Fund which is being raised by the Arab National League as a memorial to our departed friends, Fuad Mufarrij and Fakhry Al Shaikh.

   I am writing to ask if you can avail yourself of this exceptional opportunity to hear Professor Grant. It may be possible for you to plan one or more meetings in your community. Perhaps this can be arranged in co-operation with churches, or service clubs who are interested in the significant developments in the Near East. You may find it advisable to hold one or more meetings for our compatriots followed by meetings for mixed audiences. This is discretionary with you. It is very desirable to hold one meeting for young people. This would be perpetuating the splendid work started by our late friend, Fuad Mufarrij.

   In order to plan an itinerary, it will be necessary to hear from you ar your earliest convenience.

   With kindest personal regards,

         Very cordially yours,

         F. I. Shatara
         President

FIS:AW

FIGURE 6.8. *Letter from Fuad Shatara to Ameen Farah, November 1, 1939. Shatara emphasizes educating Arab American youth and asks Farah to set up speaking engagements for Professor Elihu Grant, who offered to cover his own expenses. Farah Papers, Bawardi Collection.*

he, Ahmad Hamza, Abdallah Berri, and the president, Ali Samhat, would represent the club. Days before the conference, the overwhelmed Kātibah informed Farah that he would send "hundreds of copies of the books and pamphlets in our possession to be distributed to the delegates" in Flint, and he indicated that he could not help in selling raffle tickets door to door; instead, he delegated the task to the ANL's youth club in New York.[105]

By all reports, the gathering was characterized by feelings of pan-Arab unity and an aura of anti-British sentiments on the Indian continent and in other colonies. The sentiments constituted the backdrop for the observations of Ameen Rihani, one of the league's luminary supporters, in *Asia* magazine on "Spanish Morocco." Rihani did not advocate responding in kind to domination and conquest and was keen on the unity of Arabs wherever they lived, including "this Arab region under Spanish colonial rule."[106] The bulletin of August 18, 1939, reported on Rihani's article in *Asia* magazine defending pan-Arab unity against a proponent of the Zionist point of view who claimed that such unity was a myth.

It is unclear how many immigrants returned to parts of Syria based on political convictions, but such occurrences were not uncommon. One example of the commitment of the U.S. immigrants to their cause was Mahmoud Abulfilat's volunteering fourteen months of service to the Arab revolution. Abulfilat was the former treasurer of the Arab National League who reported in *As-Sameer* on his encounter with Jewish would-be settlers from New York on their way to Palestine. It is safe to assume that foreign occupation made travel arduous, as did the abysmal economic conditions in all parts of Syria due to the occupations and unrest.

The organizers in Flint, who were by now established members of their community and had inherited other concerns and day-to-day responsibilities that also required their attention, and the national office made good on their professed philosophy of appealing to Americans' sense of fair play. Announcements of the upcoming convention in the *Flint Journal* on August 3, one month before it began, exude confidence. The *Flint Journal* was told that as part of the preparations more than 200 delegates from all parts of the Americas were slated to meet in the city's premier hotel and that renowned authority Elihu Grant, a "collateral descendant of General Ulysses Grant" and author of the newly published book *Palestine Today*, would be the keynote speaker.[107] The *Flint Journal* also indicated the possibility that "His Highness Muhamad Ben Essau [ibin Isa], crown of Albahrayn [Bahrain]," who at the time was touring the United States, might be present. Ameen Farah was reported as chairman of the convention committee. The article listed local contributors, among them retail grocery business owner Thomas

FIGURE 6.9. *ANL convention program. With Germany's invasion of Poland, World War II started in Europe just before the convention began. Convention participants professed loyalty to their adopted country as Arab Americans, not Arabs in America. Farah Papers, Bawardi Collection.*

Mansour, Edward Romley, Samuel Igram, and respected marksman and butcher Fred Farah. The reception committee included Emett Sobe, Harry Tali, and Salahaddin al-Ayoubi.

The activists used the planned convention to declare their unwavering loyalty to the United States on the pages of the *Flint Journal*, which had reported on the Arab immigrants for years. As members of the Flint extended community, Farah and Samra provided a source of steady information on the Middle East whenever called upon by the *Journal*. Their familiarity and prominent economic standing presents a microcosmic picture of the Syrian immigrants' impact in similar cities across the United States. The convention would not have a national impact as such or influence national policy—the Syrians were too few to achieve that—but the gathering galvanized pockets of Syrian activists in cities big and small across the United States where they represented constituencies behind an emergent core issue of the Arab Middle East, the fate of Palestine.

Apart from anticipating global conflict, the immigrants built a political agenda for the ANL by advancing savvy positions on current affairs. Six months before the convention, on March 1, 1939, Najīb Samra, the head of the ANL's defense committee, lobbied against Ambassador Joseph P. Kennedy's attempt to influence British policy on behalf of the Zionists. The ambassador had said in London that "drastic restriction of Jewish immigration into Palestine and the abolition of the British mandate over the Holy Land would have a disastrous effect on public opinion in the United States."[108] Samra wired a telegram to Secretary of State Cordell Hull informing him, with his somewhat embellished sense of history, that the ambassador's assertions were "not consistent with the noblest American traditions." Samra alerted the secretary that among the Arabs many were Christians, while also contrasting Syrian culture with the socialist traditions brought to the United States by Polish Jews. He again appealed to higher ideals: "Christian American Arabs in Michigan believe that American sentiment will never condone the eviction from their homes of those whose forefathers literally followed the Master to the place named Golgotha 1,900 years ago, by introducing to the Holy land a strange combination of atheism and political Zionism. We appeal to your proverbial sense of justice."[109]

A week before the convention the *Flint Journal* reported last-minute details regarding the league's gathering, including the backgrounds of the main personalities. Fuad Mufarrij was introduced as one of the attending dignitaries and "general secretary of the Arab National bureau at Damascus," who would be the "toastmaster at a banquet at 7 p.m., September 4."[110] Mufarrij had come to the United States in the spring to represent

Syria in the New York World's Fair, likely encouraged by prospects of independence promised by the Franco-Syrian treaty negotiated that year. But then the French government cancelled the Syrians' plans and "withdrew the privileges of self-government from Syria," the *Flint Journal* reported, referring to the French government's refusal to ratify the treaty dictated to the Syrians by France's own politicians. The *Flint Journal* introduced Elihu Grant, professor of biblical literature at Haverford College in Pennsylvania and an authority on the Near East. Grant, who led archeological expeditions in the area in 1927, had been the superintendent of the American Friends school in Ramallah near Jerusalem from 1901 to 1904. The organizers also expected Flint's mayor, Harry Comings, to give welcoming remarks at the banquet. The names of the other speakers were announced a week before the event; among them were Fuad Shatara, Boston attorney Faris Malouf, Judge Arthur J. Lacey, Lutfi al-Saʻdi of Detroit, the Reverend Herbert Gans, and Mrs. John E. Sickles.

The convention took place as planned on September 2, 1939, just one day after the German invasion of Poland and ended on September 4, one day after the entry of France and Britain into history's largest global conflict. Ziadeh recalled, however, that the "enthusiasm generated by the speeches of the young scholars and the hospitality of the hosts in Flint and Dearborn seemed at the time to dull the news of the outbreak of World War II."[111] The proceedings opened with business sessions and adjourned on a Sunday for the picnic at the home of Tawfiq Mansour on Corunna Road as planned. Nazir Farah, Ameen Farah's cousin, captured glimpses of the open-air festivities on film. The fund-raiser was attended by several hundred people who, despite the uncertainty due to the developments in Europe, enjoyed barbecued meat and games.

In the filmed recording, Subhi Farah, Ameen's brother-in-law, could be seen auctioning the Palestinian flag on a stage flanked by the guests of honor, including Fuad Shatara. The proceeds went to aid the Palestinians who were affected by British reprisals after their revolt was put down and their eleven-month general strike left people worse off than before. After recounting ancient Arab heritage and glories of the past, something he did at every occasion, Najīb Samra explained the objectives of the convention to the *Flint Journal*. He said the Arab National League was "primarily interested in creating a great democracy in the Arab World, patterned after the United States. . . . We also hope to create better understanding between America and the Arab lands."[112] On September 1 the *Flint Journal* announced that Emily Mutter Adams from the Detroit Symphony Orchestra would perform in the league's Labor Day banquet.[113]

League members exercised good judgment in inviting a reporter to the various events. When the conference concluded, the *Flint Journal* reflected the league's intended message: Arab Americans were seeking American justice and American-style democracy for their beleaguered kin in their former lands. American immigrants' demands for Syria's independence were professed throughout the convention along with the immigrants' unwavering loyalty to the government and Constitution of the United States.[114] Grant, a professor and biblical studies expert as well as president of the Friends of the Arabs Society, observed that Britain's treatment of Arabs was a "piece of political chicanery unmatched in history."[115] He told the audience that Palestine was more open to pilgrims of all faiths during Turkish rule than it had been over the previous twenty years. Grant addressed widespread perceptions that Arabs were exotic nomads incapable of civilized life: "Arab countries in the Near East have power, the genius, and the honor to save themselves from within; they only need sympathy and help from the outside." The archeologist attacked the Balfour Declaration as the root cause of the problems in Palestine because "it was drafted in consultation with American Jewish leaders but was opposed by Jews of idealism and insight." He declared that none had the right to "change the fundamental economics of another people."[116]

Mindful of receding isolationism in the United States and increased German danger, the convention issued a resolution on record before the banquet. It asserted "unmitigated allegiance and undivided loyalty to the United States in view of the turbulent conditions in the world."[117] The resolution continued: "Our unconditional support is hereby pledged to our government in whatever course it is deemed necessary to pursue for the safety and happiness of the people of the United States, of whom we are proud to have become an integral part." The league forwarded copies of the resolution to President Roosevelt and Secretary Hull. Samra reiterated the sentiments of unwavering loyalty to the United States: "We love our fatherland [Syria] but we owe allegiance to no other country than the United States."[118]

Grant's nuanced remarks were matched by an equally eloquent speech by Mufarrij, the Syrian diplomat and political science professor at the American University of Beirut. Expressing hopes for a democratic homeland, Mufarrij, "the reformer" (*al-musliḥ*), wished for independence of Arab countries as the means of awakening the "Arab mind, spirit, and soul" and achieving a "cultural renaissance, social justice and modern civilization."[119] Inspired by the sight of such a highly organized group of established immigrants in the United States, the visiting dignitary Mufarrij remarked, "I am impressed by your affirmation that you are American citizens of Arab extraction—not

Arabs in America. This world has been upset by all kinds of minority groups whose hearts belong to the country in which they lived. Arabs know this minority problem from experience in Palestine."[120]

There are sporadic examples of references to Arab immigrants as "Syrian Americans" and less frequently "Arab Americans." These are meant to generally describe the immigrants rather than consciously ascribe to them an American identity while maintaining their ancestral character. But considering the timing and historical moment, the term "Syrian Americans" had a profoundly more significant meaning. This pronouncement marks a birthing moment for Arab American identity. Defending Syria hinged on reaping the fruits of U.S. citizenship; lobbying, as was acknowledged by members of the New Syria Party, became a critical part of the immigrants' strategy. Prospects of likely military service in the approaching war left no doubt about the immigrants' ultimate loyalty.

The conference ushered in signs of social development and maturity beyond political aims. Members of the first U.S.-born generation of Syrians were present at the convention and had something to contribute. Attorney Joseph Joseph, a descendant of the first Syrian settlers in Flint,[121] sounded a great deal like Ameen Rihani when he offered a pluralist vision for the Syrian Arab Americans; Joseph acknowledged his forebears' attachment to their Arab culture while inviting his generation to celebrate being U.S. citizens. Flint's residents could read in the *Journal* how the young Joseph "urged that all Arab Americans teach their children pride in their ancestry—a people which gave birth to many sciences."[122] Shatara drew attention to the next step in the history of the Middle East: "Arabs do not believe in selective democracy—we believe it is just as valuable in Arab lands as in the United States."[123] The convention attracted delegates from across the United States, including the Harvard law student Hikmet Oseiran, and several dignitaries—among them a representative of the First Congregational Unitarian Church in Flint—and Mayor Pro-Tem George V. Gundry. Shatara as president and the league's other officers were reelected during the business segment of the convention.

Before month's end, however, the ANL suffered the first of several crippling blows. Both Fuad Mufarrij and Fakhri al-Shaykh met untimely deaths in an automobile accident in route to either Detroit or Chicago immediately after the festivities at the Mansours' farm. Ziadeh was spared a similar fate because he passed up the ill-fated trip and returned with ʿAbbas to New York. The calamity "severely shook the morale" in the New York office, Ḥabīb Kātibah told Ameen Farah.[124] The energies of the league immediately turned to remembrances and eulogies for the departed activists.

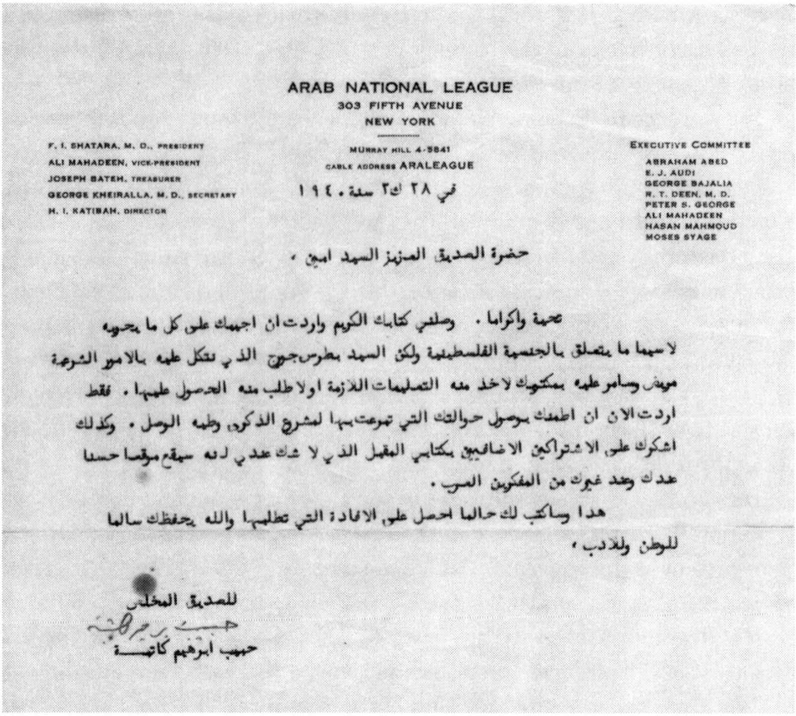

ARAB NATIONAL LEAGUE
303 FIFTH AVENUE
NEW YORK

F. I. SHATARA, M. D., PRESIDENT
ALI MAHADEEN, VICE-PRESIDENT
JOSEPH BATEH, TREASURER
GEORGE KHEIRALLA, M. D., SECRETARY
H. I. KATIBAH, DIRECTOR

MURRAY HILL 4-5841
CABLE ADDRESS ARALEAGUE

EXECUTIVE COMMITTEE
ABRAHAM ABED
E. J. AUDI
GEORGE BAJALIA
R. T. DEEN, M. D.
PETER S. GEORGE
ALI MAHADEEN
HASAN MAHMOUD
MOSES SYAGE

في ٢٨ ك٢ سنة ١٩٤٠

حضرة الصديق العزيز السيد امين ،

تحية واكراما . وصلني كتابك الكريم واردت ان اجيبك على كل ما يحويه
لاسيما ما يتعلق بالجنسية الفلسطينية ولكن السيد بطرس جورج الذي نتكل عليه بالامور الشرعية
مريض وسامر عليه بمكتبه لاخذ منه التعليمات اللازمة او لاطلب منه الحصول عليها . فقط
اردت الان ان اطمنك بوصول حوالتك التي تبرعت بها لمشروع الذكرى وطيه الوصل . وكذلك
اشكرك على الاشتراكين الاضافيين بكتابي المقبل الذي لا شك عندي انه سيقع موقعا حسنا
عندك وعند غيرك من المفكرين العرب .

هذا وساكتب لك حالما احصل على الافادة التي تطلبها والله يحفظك سالما
للوطن وللادب ،

للصديق المخلص
حبيب ابرهيم كاتبة

FIGURE 6.10. *Letter from Ḥabīb Kātibah to Ameen Farah, January 28, 1940. Kātibah promises to check with ANL legal expert Peter George on Farah's Palestinian citizenship. Farah Papers, Bawardi Collection.*

The next correspondence came in November, in Shatara's usual typed English-language style, informing Farah that Grant was volunteering his time to lecture on behalf of Palestinian charities for a year at his own expense.[125] The archeologist further offered to donate any honoraria to the Palestine Orphans Fund, "which is set up by the Friends' Mission, or to the Village Welfare Fund which is raised by the Arab National League as a memorial to our departed friends, Fuad Mufarrij and Fakhri al-Shaykh."[126] Shatara went on to ask Farah to arrange speaking engagements for Grant within the diaspora and to arrange speaking opportunities for "mixed audiences," that is, of immigrants, second-generation Syrian Americans, and general American audiences of diverse backgrounds, because, Shatara explained, it was very advisable to hold one meeting for young people. Doing so "would be perpetuating the splendid work started by our late friend, Fuad

Mufarrij." The future of Arab American political activism, therefore, seems to have been assured.

The activists would soon decide what shape their activism would take amid the postwar political reality. But seasoned activists understood that much would be at stake after the war and expressed the need to resume their political work even during the war. It is important to point out that the experience of World War I was not far from the older immigrants' minds. Farah, for one, never lost hope of returning to what remained of his beloved Syria. When Palestine was once again part of the global theater of war, his anxieties, perhaps mixed with a hint of opportunity, impelled him to ask Kātibah about the prospects of regaining the right to return to Palestine. His hopes would remain just that because Zionists would reemerge even more powerful after the war as the weakened British lost leverage over them. The last ANL letterhead correspondence in Farah's collection during the war was from Kātibah to Farah answering an inquiry concerning Palestinian citizenship. Kātibah apologized for not offering new information because, he explained in his letter, the legal expert, Peter George, was taken ill and could not address Farah's question. Kātibah thanked Farah for a contribution he had sent to New York in memory of the departed Mufarrij and Shaykh.

The league faced a strategic decision of whether to continue operations in the face of the reality the war presented. Opposition to America's ally Great Britain, in terms of pressing for an end to the mandate and for Palestinian statehood, potentially contradicted pronouncements of loyalty and willingness to unite behind U.S. war efforts. Loyalty to the United States meant not opposing or weakening the British. The situation risked putting Arab American activists at odds with U.S. national interests just when many of them and their U.S.-born offspring began to enlist in the U.S. armed forces. A period of anticipation and uncertainty ended, and the ANL decided to suspend its operations for six months before the United States openly declared war on the Axis powers of Germany, Italy, and Japan after the attack on Pearl Harbor in December 1941. Young men from the Khouri and Farah clans filled the footage in Nazir Farah's film in their military uniforms marching in formation and rehearsing rifle drills. For the Arab National League, indeed for the entire Middle East, all bets were off once again. One of the implications of suspending the league's operations at this critical juncture in U.S. history is that the word "Arab" would never be used in the titles of Arab immigrant organizations again without the word American attached to it.

In his book *Filasṭīn: Andalus al-Sharq*, published one year after the end of World War II, Jamil Beyhum succinctly summed up the fate of the league and similar political setbacks of the Arab office in London. Under the subhead "The Cracking (*tasaddu'*) of Arab Fronts in Europe and America," the scholar wrote of the fissures: "How sorry, indeed sad, I am because the Arab fronts collapsed in England and those in the Americas nearly followed suit, while the Zionists replenished the battlefield with their inexhaustible reserves."[127]

Among the important reasons for the collapse, Beyhum wrote, were divisions over a unified course of action even after the establishment of the Arab League, also called the League of Arab States, founded in Egypt (not to be confused with the immigrants' Arab National League) despite overwhelming sympathy for Palestine. He attributed the failure to a "void of higher leadership in Jerusalem during and after the war" due to the absence of al-Husseini, who remained in exile by the British government. The direct reason, Beyhum wrote, was the war—the Arab Office in London was closed, the Arab National League disbanded, and the "voices of Arab societies across Canada and the United States faded into whispers."[128] Additionally, a series of deaths among those who championed Palestine's cause abroad plagued the nationalists: Rihani in Lebanon, George Antonius in Palestine, Prince Majīd Arslan in Argentina, Rizk Haddad, *Al-Bayān* editor Suleiman Baddūr, Fuad Mufarrij—"for whom we all expected a glorious future in serving the nationalist cause"—Nasib Arida, and Suleiman al-Qanawati in Mexico.[129]

Zionists completed the transfer of the center of their operations from England and Geneva to New York. Their strategy was to forge an "alliance with the U.S. government with all the implied influence and power this would bring their cause."[130] Far from a monolith, Zionism encompassed different views. The moderate Louis Lipsky, for example, differed from the hawkish Rabbi Wise over the issue of partitioning Palestine. Lipsky was willing to discuss partition, while Wise, assured of congressional support, remained committed to Zionist control over all of historical Palestine.[131] By August 1937 Wise's Zionist Organization of America extracted Senate Resolution 174 to "request" that the State Department submit any information it might have on the Palestine issue to the Senate and to relate to the British "with a forthright indication of our unwillingness to accept any modification of the mandate without the knowledge and consent of the Government of the United States."[132] The strategy of bypassing the State Department and securing congressional backing was complemented by seemingly unrelenting choices Zionists made in Palestine that would bear fruit once the factions closed ranks at their convention at the Biltmore Hotel in May 1942 in New York as the British weakened and the United States emerged a global superpower.

While never abandoning plans for a Jewish state to include all of Palestine, many Zionist settlers there understood the value of British might in defeating the Nazis despite deep disagreement over Britain's desire to create a country for both peoples with representative government. Therefore, Jewish militants took a stance to oppose any agreement with their Arab neighbors,[133] coupled with a decision by Zionist leader David Ben-Gurion: "We shall fight with Great Britain in this war as if there were no White Paper, and we shall fight the White Paper as if there was no war."[134] The coherent strategies and internal realignments set the Zionist movement apart from the immigrants' organizing efforts, especially in view of the persistently dire conditions in the Arab world. Intra-Arab intrigue and incongruent priorities in Jordan, Lebanon, Syria, Palestine, and Iraq, not to mention the severe pressures of the mandate and the war, made it very difficult for immigrants to forge ahead with a straightforward strategy because its aim was complicated by instability of Arab leadership. Intra-Palestinian divisions, due largely to alternating British policies of divide and conquer, made for uneven development of the Jewish and Palestinian sectors in all spheres and therefore hindered sound footings for dialogue.

British and French efforts to suppress Arab independence for the duration of World War II devastated the Arab National League's core message, and a period of uncertainty set in like that experienced after World War I. But Arab Americans had to contend with the reality of postwar international relations. When news of the Holocaust spread, "the public conscience of the West came to embrace the notion that the settlement of surviving Jews in Palestine could atone for the horrors that Western civilization had inflicted upon them."[135] U.S. reluctance to recognize partition plans subsequent to the Peel Commission was "colored by the fact that six million Jewish lives were lost in the Nazi Holocaust."[136] Meanwhile, British policy in Palestine sought to prevent any chance of revolt by exiling and outlawing the leadership and preventing its regrouping for the duration of the war. This was the absence of leadership noted by Beyhum, and it is a source of confusion in terms of immigrants crafting a coherent strategy.

In the U.S. arena, this was the time, as professed during the ANL's Flint convention, to rally behind the United States during the country's steady move to shed remnants of isolationism and forge an alliance against the Axis. A vehement and increasingly unified Zionist and Jewish mobilization began to take shape in 1939 and followed the Biltmore Program in 1942 of setting as a priority the establishment of a Jewish commonwealth,[137] as well as Ben-Gurion's strategy of utilizing the Jewish lobby in mustering U.S. political and military capabilities.[138] The Biltmore Program unequivocally declared the "Zionist aims with regard to establishment of a Jewish state in Palestine." Zionists envisioned that the "new world order that will follow victory cannot be established on foundations of peace, justice, and equality, unless the problem of Jewish homelessness is finally resolved."[139] As with the aftermath of World War I when the Balfour Declaration set in motion mass Jewish settlement in Palestine, the approaching conflict, Zionists decided, was an opening for establishing a state in Palestine.

A major factor in the Arab National League's nominal successes in the international arena, however modest, can be attributed to maintaining links to the homeland by sufficient numbers of immigrants who possessed a firm nationalist agenda and acted on it by sending remittances or charitable contributions to family members and national leaders. Frequent visits by dignitaries from Palestine reinforced the links and solidified immigrants' resolve to do what they could for the Arab Syrian-Palestinian cause. Regardless of the increasing violence in Palestine, Fuad Shatara's ascendance to the leadership of the ANL and his commitment to the coexistence of Palestinians and Jews indicated a moderate direction for an Arab American stance on the conflict. The ANL refined immigrants' experiments with advocating for democratic rule and debates with detractors, and it facilitated pragmatic links to Arabists in official and informal circles—what immigrants viewed as their rights as American citizens. The ANL experiments represented the final political signpost to becoming Arab American.

Despite the overlap of Syrian nationalist thought and the Palestinian national experience in the approach of World War I due to geographical and cultural contiguity, I find agreement between Rashid Khalidi's assertion of a distinct "Palestinian identity" in response to external political and cultural pressures and my own arguments that an Arab American identity was further shaped by formal political activities during the same period. Palestinians did possess the sense of self and place at the same time these feelings began to form elsewhere in Syria, but these experiences were influenced by the various agendas of the Turks, the British, and the French. Syrian nationalists adapted to the changing reality after World War I and the San Remo Agreement in accordance with nationalists in Syria. I add the argument that navigating a pragmatic approach to subsume the Palestinian narrative within the larger Arab nation was a strategic course of action by the ANL because Palestine emerged as a core issue for all Arabs. Arab American political life would be affected by the fate of Palestine and the path Arab regimes took after World War II. However, the ANL continued a process of validating Arab American identity by vindicating Arab culture and nationalist goals. The political borders imposed by European imperialist powers did not hamper the ANL's efforts to defend the Arab cause as much as did members' domestic concerns in the United States once its entering the war was certain. Pragmatism demanded utilizing a façade of overarching Arab nationalism. This strategy achieved mixed results and could be considered a major reason for the ANL's attempts to explain the seemingly mysterious and exotic Arab and Muslim East to largely unaware Americans. Making sure they were accepted as loyal Americans once the United States mobilized to aid the British and the French when the war began in Europe just before the ANL Fourth Annual Convention started took precedence over fighting British imperialism in Palestine and elsewhere.

For the Palestinian leadership in Jerusalem, developing a successful strategy proved a more complicated matter. The Balfour Declaration became irreversible British and U.S. policy, thus creating a widening demographic and political imbalance in favor of the Jewish population. More significantly, the Balfour Declaration resonated in Europe and the United States as the primary means of redressing European anti-Semitism, which intensified with the rise of Nazism in the 1930s and culminated in its historic crimes against the Jews. Against this background, one of the setbacks to the Arab National League came when the *mufti* ended up in Germany. Al-Husseini escaped arrest by the British in July 1937 for opposing their support of the Zionists and spent two years in Lebanon under French surveillance before he was forced to flee to Iraq. Husseini established contacts with the Nazis, who welcomed him as a leader of anti-British Arab nationalism in 1941. His visit immediately invited condemnation of the *mufti* as a Nazi collaborator and exposed the limits of the support he could count on from immigrants. Zionists continue to associate the *mufti* and his cause with Nazism into present times.

Adherents to Zionism were not the only ones who attacked the league because of its connection to the *mufti*. On April 27, 1942, the editor of *Al-Hoda* attacked *Al-Sa'eh, As-Sameer*, and the Arab National League as treasonous because of the *mufti*'s stay in Germany, where he evidently felt safe from the British. On May 2 Ḥabīb Kātibah responded to an article in *Al-Hoda*, citing the danger that if its charges went unaddressed they would "expose several individuals to punishment [and] might bring innocent men before the law."[140] Kātibah wrote, the report in the OSS archives provides, that the ANL was dissolved before the United States entered the war and before the *mufti*'s flight to Berlin: "How can you say, then, that the Arab National League supports the *mufti* in his present policies?" Kātibah did not back away from the fundamental reasons the ANL was founded—for "the defense of the Arab cause in general and the Palestinian cause in particular." He likened the goals of the ANL to those of the American patriots who fought Britain and distanced the league from the *mufti*'s decision to go to Germany:

> The overwhelming majority of the members of the Arab National League, like myself, do not approve either of the Mufti's present policies or his flight to Berlin. We regret that he did not seek political refuge in Egypt or in Saudi Arabia . . . it was the British imperialists who have driven the Mufti to the lap of Hitler; the Mufti and others beside him, who were so driven, have ceased to distinguish between British imperialism and Nazism, especially because Nazism was being presented to them in other than its real color, seeking their friendship while the imperialists who professed democracy were driving them out of their homes. . . . Times are grave and critical; adherence to facts is best under such circumstances. Otherwise your false charges are more disloyal to the ideals of Americanism than the acts of its outspoken enemies.[141]

The defensive posture by the eloquent Kātibah exposed deep vulnerabilities under a new reality where Arab causes often lacked sustained support in the West. Future Arab American activism would have to labor to put a human face on Arab history, traditions, and persona before political gains could be contemplated. But the immediate danger for Kātibah and his supporters was that his name would be linked to Nazism by unscrupulous detractors. Merciless attacks on Kātibah and Shatara would continue for years after the Arab National League was suspended. Charges of belonging to the Nazi Party once the Zionists made good on capitalizing on anti-Nazi sentiments contributed to the early death of Shatara and drained the activists financially and mentally. On at least two occasions Kātibah was forced to fend off charges that he was a Nazi sympathizer, in 1946 by an associate editor of *In Fact* magazine and in 1947 in the *Daily Mirror*. The ANL's association with Jerusalem's Hajj al-Husseini also worked against it despite Kātibah's rebuke of the *mufti*'s visit to Germany and despite suspending the ANL well before the United States entered the fight. *In Fact* apparently labeled the two activists Nazi members of the Bund, a U.S.-based consortium of German sympathizers who opposed a Jewish boycott of German businesses in Yorkville, Manhattan, relying on a congressman's statements in the *Congressional Record*.

A draft of a rebuttal by Kātibah in response to a letter from associate editor Victor Weingarten of *In Fact* on November 12, 1946, illustrates the extent of Kātibah's distress over the implication that he was a traitor.[142] Kātibah revealed "inside information" to Weingarten to help explain that the league was comprised of affiliate organizations and chapters all over the country and that the affiliates "were completely independent in their internal policies" and hence expressed diverse opinions, not all of them sophisticated. Kātibah acknowledged that some "immature" members' "violent emotions against the British carried them to the extent of favoring the Nazis and Fascists, out of sheer spite to the British." But "none of them," he added, "had full realization of what Nazism really implied or connoted."[143] Of these individuals, Kātibah explained, most changed their views when the war began. Kātibah reminded Weingarten that the league was dormant long before the war started and confessed his preference for keeping it alive to combat "intensified propaganda by the Zionists."[144]

Kātibah conceded that he and Shatara attended one Bund meeting in 1938 but refused an invitation to speak or sit on the platform, although he learned much later that Shatara spoke at a subsequent meeting of the Bund. Kātibah never believed that Shatara might have expressed any sympathy with Nazism; he considered his friend "one of the staunchest champions of democracy among the Arabic-speaking Americans" who enjoyed the respect and support of most of his colleagues at work. However, in his very honest letter Kātibah implied that Shatara's "dictatorial" style alienated some members in the ANL and "indirectly" contributed to dissolution of the ANL. Kātibah reported his attendance at the Bund meeting in his deposition to the Civil Service Commission when he was appointed senior editor in the Arabic section of the Office of War Information (OWI) in 1942, a position he held until the end of the war.

The ANL was not tied to any political organization; according to Kātibah, the FBI scrutinized the minutes of the organization's meetings, given Kātibah's service in the OWI.[145] Kātibah seemed to understand that sharing inside information in a bid to defend his character in his letter to Weingarten did not matter when the underpinnings behind these attacks were political: "I could go on and on but unless you are inclined to open your ears to the 'facts' what use is it?"[146]

Antagonism against Shatara spilled into his work at the Long Island College Hospital and Post Graduate Hospital, where certain colleagues harassed him because of his views. When Shatara was forced to take an indefinite leave from work by a hostile colleague, the pressure may have been too much. Shatara, according to the New York Police report, killed himself. Shatara's daughter said being denied practicing his profession was a factor contributing to his apparent suicide. Shatara's association with the

Bund, although limited, became occasion for maligning his and Kātibah's reputations as "Arabianazis," "Arabastards," "men hostile to the Allies," and "Asiatic Knights of the Ku Klux Klan" from the "burrow in Asia."[147] These incendiary labels were emboldened through a smear campaign in Congress by mostly Jewish congressmen sympathetic to Zionism whose real targets were the Arab point of view.[148] The Institute of Arab American Affairs was attacked as an agent for the Arab Office representing the League of Arab States established after the war. Implementing the Biltmore Program of establishing a Jewish state with a majority Jewish population during the war meant subordinating Jewish identity and religion to Zionist ideology, whereby the latter would become the "logical and inevitable outcome" of the former.[149] Hence the ANL offered, the OSS papers indicate, to suspend its work if the Zionists did the same.

Nevertheless, the Arab National League's objectives as spelled out in its English-language bylaws were unique for a political Arab American organization. Its objectives opened new avenues for the next phase in Arab American activism. Printed in English and Arabic in an attractive and durable cover and widely disseminated, the well-worded ANL bylaws reflected the understanding and sophistication attained by immigrants at this stage of their American journey. Their efforts came together in Flint in a convergence of intensified British repression, a rise in Zionist influence in the United States, anti-Semitism in Germany, and World War II, all just before the extent of Nazi crimes against Jews, Poles, and others became fully known in the United States. These factors did not, alone or combined, dampen Syrians' newfound empowerment as Arab Americans. Feelings of belonging changed the rules for Arab Americans. Arab Americans had found their voice in a long process of explaining and defending their history, culture, and political views. Their collective activism, an extension of previous battles for citizenship and inclusion, helped them find their voice. Continued disasters in their ancestral lands, especially in Palestine, would put their collective voice to the test in arduous debates with organized and capable American Zionists. Much would change in the Middle East and Arab American life after World War II, much that would require immigrants to fall on their emergent Arab American consciousness as a means of influencing the course of events in their own lives and in the Middle East. The experiments of the New Syria Party and the Arab National League prepared the activists and their constituents for the new challenges of rallying Arab Americans behind Palestine's cause while also serving their adopted country.

THE INSTITUTE OF ARAB AMERICAN AFFAIRS: ARAB AMERICANS AND THE NEW WORLD ORDER

Chapter 7

Prolonged and severe immigration restrictions from 1924 to 1965 were a factor preventing meaningful contacts between the two major waves of Arab immigrants. As a result, a chronic detachment rendered illusive any coherent Arab American narrative. Fifteen years separate the Institute of Arab American Affairs (1944–1950) from the Association of Arab American University Graduates, founded in 1967. Although many of the early activists and their constituents either died or grew frail during those years, a basic question remains: What accounts for the void in political activity in these lost years? Answering this question requires tackling the reasons and prevailing conditions surrounding the rise and decline of the Institute of Arab American Affairs.

In this final chapter I establish the institute as the culmination of decades of political activism and social adjustment by the Syrian immigrants who became Arab Americans. The institute is a link to Arab American political work on behalf of the homeland, the very cause that in previous chapters I traced to the dawn of Arab *nahḍah* and the ensuing ideas of Syrian nationhood and later Arab nationalism. The institute experiment was a prelude to the battles and obstacles Arab Americans still face in a hostile environment in their adopted country and an extension of their increasingly sophisticated attempts at raising Americans' awareness of Arab political views, culture, and history. Institute members started the pragmatic strategy of representing U.S. interests in the oil-rich Middle East, defended Arab Americans' right to participate in domestic and foreign policy discussions, and ultimately paved the way for future attempts at guarding against politically motivated discrimination and disparaging stereotypes. Combating effective propaganda campaigns by American Zionists and raising funds for the Palestinian refugees after 1948 in a politically hostile environment drained the institute's resources and led to its demise after a productive five years.

The institute began its work in the middle of a pragmatic strategy by the Zionists of emphasizing the plight of displaced Jewish persons in Europe af-

FIGURE 7.1. *Institute of Arab American Affairs banquet, November 29, 1946. The event at the Waldorf-Astoria Hotel in New York City honored the delegations to the UN General Assembly from Egypt, Iraq, Lebanon, Saudi Arabia, and Syria. Courtesy of the Immigration History Research Project, University of Minnesota.*

ter World War II as a justification for Jewish immigration to Palestine. The strategy facilitated the creation of a Jewish majority in Palestine and compounded the challenges of making a case for Palestinian statehood in the United States. Despite the poor prospects for Palestinian statehood due in part to repressive British Mandate policies and Zionism, Palestine's cause emerged as a core issue for Arabs and Arab Americans alike even before 1948. The present examination of the institute helps explain the space in which the AAUG and every Arab American secular and Muslim organization has operated, as the institute experienced an environment in which balancing politically motivated anti-Arab sentiments in the media and academia became a difficult task. Members of the AAUG recognized the need for social services and understood that building effective and sustainable safety nets for immigrant communities required a rebuke of one-sided if not damaging perceptions of Arabs and Muslims. An apparently broad societal preference for Israel and the need to tell their own story—and in the process bring balance to information on the Middle East—motivated studies by AAUG members. Long before Suleiman posited, in *Arabs in the Mind of America*, that sympathy for Israel transforms into intense hostility against Israel's enemies,[1] commensurate with almost uniform media bias in favor of Israel's positions, the institute fought the same battles. It is possible that the immense burden of responding to hostility by the media, polity, and even academia made it difficult for AAUG members to conceive that the institute fought those battles on a comparable scale. Certainly, severely limited contacts between the two groups of activists were a factor in limiting mutual awareness and comprehension. The Arabs' defeat by Israel in June 1967, known as the Naksah, meaning dejection or glumness across the Arab world and the diaspora, played a role in obscuring battles fought by the Free Syria Society, the New Syria Party, and the Arab National League. However, the Institute of Arab American Affairs remained linked to the previous struggles of Arab awakening and national development. Its leaders were the Syrians from the Beirut area, Aleppo, and Ramallah who now identified themselves as Arab Americans. By the 1940s, as the experiences of the ANL showed, the immigrants could rely on a sizable community of intellectuals with connections to the American University of Beirut.

Members of the Bliss family are a case in point. Daniel Bliss founded the Syrian Protestant College, and its name was changed in 1920 to the American University of Beirut. His son, Howard Bliss, convinced Woodrow Wilson to send the King-Crane Commission to investigate the wishes of Syria's inhabitants prior to the Paris Peace Conference in 1919. Howard Bliss's son, also named Daniel, became a minister and a third-generation advocate for Arab culture and political rights. He kept his father's and grandfather's aspirations alive by seeking even-handed U.S. policies in the Middle East.

Between the turn of the twentieth century and the suspension of the institute's operations in 1950, the quest for statehood by Iraq, Syria, and Lebanon caused institute members to assume the position of facilitators among these emergent states and the United Nations Organization during its for-

FIGURE 7.2. *Daniel Bliss, 1948. Reverend Bliss is boarding a Pan American flight to attend the inauguration of the new AUB president, Stephen B. L. Benrose, on October 1. Arab delegates to the UN displayed images like this one to emphasize cultural links between the United States and the Arab world. Totah Archives, courtesy of Joy Totah Hilden.*

mation in 1945 and beyond. In projecting their vision, Arab American activists relied on their Arab heritage and the relationships they cultivated with a few professional diplomats in the State Department. Thus, aiding burgeoning Arab nations became a vehicle for Arab Americans to implement long-held hopes of reforms in their ancestral lands and to do so from their acquired positions of influence as U.S. citizens, however limited that influence may have been.[2] Records of the institute's activities are voluminous, and an exhaustive discussion of its short life is better left for a separate study. However, establishing the institute as a major political organization representing an aggregate of Arab Americans helps pull together new strands for an Arab American narrative.

Most of the surviving 3,000 to 4,000 pages of institute records can be found in the archives of Khalil Totah, although there are original announcements and pamphlets among Ameen Farah's papers and a scattering of bulletins, letters, and publications in the libraries of Columbia University, Harvard, Haverford College, and the New York Public Library. The records include some previously classified UN documents; transcripts of speeches and rebuttals by Totah, members of the Arab Office established by Arab states in Washington, D.C., and delegates of Arab states in various settings; testimonies before congressional committees and the Anglo-American Committee of Inquiry; pamphlets and propaganda posters from the vantage points of the institute, the Arab Office, and Zionists; and numerous snippets from U.S. and Arabic-language periodicals in Egypt, Iraq, Syria, and Lebanon. The rising Arab-nationalist tide, prospects of independence for Arab countries, and growing U.S. prestige and strategic interests in the oil-rich Middle East created momentum behind political participation by Arab Americans and contributed to unprecedented attention in the United States to events in the Middle East. The institute was well positioned to serve as a bridge between its members' ancestral lands and their adopted country, a new superpower. Persuading the American public of their points of view, hence, became the basis for critical, although uneven, battles between Arab Americans and the friends and proponents of Zionism.

The ominous future of Palestine also provided the motivation for renewed political work as the institute became a new tool for continuing the work of the Arab National League. But representing Arab nations made the institute a target for spying and attacks by U.S. Zionist groups, as the papers of Khalil Totah and other evidence in this study illustrate. In addition, the emerging geopolitical reality of East-West antagonism ultimately harmed the institute because the British and the French handed the United

States a legacy of regional alliances that split the Arab world into two camps along the divide of the Cold War: oil-rich monarchies including Iraq, Jordan, and Morocco that allied with the West versus nationalist strongholds attempting to stay on a path of nonalignment, among them Syria, Libya, and Egypt.[3] Although Arab Americans operated from a newfound sense of pride, having participated in the war like other ethnic groups, once these arrangements began to solidify, the institute's political work became complicated by a general complacency on the Palestine question.

Arab Americans' need for an organization like the institute became overwhelming even before World War II came to an end in 1945. The necessity to respond to proponents of Zionism, as the activists in the Arab National League came to realize, became even more pressing after the Biltmore Zionist Conference in 1942 threw its considerable weight behind the idea of a "Jewish commonwealth" in Palestine. Accordingly, Zionist militants stepped up their sabotage operations to achieve that goal and assassinated potential proponents of even-handed British and later UN policies on the issue of Palestine. The Stern Zvai Leumi gang killed Lord Moyne, a British official residing in Egypt in 1944,[4] therefore inviting in 1945 the British Defense Regulations authorizing military rule. The regulations and other measures by the British failed to curb the weapons buildup by Zionist groups. The next year Zionists blew up the King David Hotel even after the Anglo-American Committee of Inquiry recommended entry of 150,000 Jews into Palestine. Despite worsening odds, given the growing power of the Jewish lobby in the United States and the weakening of the British military in the international arena by the end of the war, institute members participated in the Committee of Inquiry. In 1947 the institute did its best to avert partitioning Palestine after yet another commission, this time the UN Special Committee on Palestine (UNSCOP), took up the issue after the British abdicated their responsibilities as the mandate power over Palestine. When the UN appointed another special envoy, Count Folke Bernadotte, a decorated war hero who saved Jews from Nazi death camps, he too was killed by the Irgun and Stern gangs;[5] he fell victim to a campaign to empty the major Palestinian cities of non-Jewish residents in the lead-up to declaring Israel a state in 1948.[6] The institute continued to do what it could to influence the course of events as the situation in Palestine worsened, but ultimately all its financial support dried up. The regional arrangements of the Cold War rendered Arab nationalist regimes unfriendly toward U.S. interests and therefore undeserving of U.S. economic, much less military, assistance. When the United States ensured support to friendly monarchies that avoided the risks inherent in acting on the Palestine question during the Cold War, Arab Americans operated on the assumption that U.S. support might yield some benefit for their larger Arab national cause.

Geographic Syria was no longer the battlefield for Arab Americans by the time the ANL disbanded in 1939. When Arab Americans resumed their organized political activities after the war by founding the institute, they set their aims at salvaging an even-handed U.S. foreign policy in the Middle East without abandoning hope that Arab unity would materialize once the British and French occupations faded away. Mobilization for World War II had resulted in the suspension of the ANL but not an end to the activists' political aspirations. The shock of Fuad Shatara's death in 1942 apparently by suicide likely prolonged the hiatus in political work. Arab Americans and their supporters restarted their political work from the perspective that they elected to suspend their activities in the Arab National League as a patriotic duty. Once Allied victory was at hand, institute members felt justified in resuming their defense of the Arab viewpoint as U.S. citizens. Pluralist attitudes after the war allowed institute members to express their views before often receptive audiences in meeting halls, on university campuses, on radio airwaves, on the pages of major English-language newspapers, and in congressional hearings. Based on archival and supporting evidence, it is clear that the institute espoused a sophisticated agenda that systematically and ably worked toward achieving political objectives through information campaigns, membership drives, and appeals to a sizable segment of the population, including American notables and Jewish luminaries. Building on the 1939 convention of the ANL in Flint, where the potential for gaining members from the ranks of U.S.-born activists became evident, they debated a new direction for the new organization. I estimate that the vanguard of the ANL and Arab-nationalist movement held sway over the direction the institute took because they supplied the critical funds but also because activists initially thought of reviving the work of the Arab National League as a way to bolster pan-Arab unity.

During the war, Arab Americans drew the attention of the Foreign Nationalities Branch of the Office of Strategic Services, as discussed earlier. The OSS began amassing information on the activities of various groups in what its operatives interchangeably identified as an "Arabic-language community" and "Arab-Americans" in the United States. The secret reports noted undisputed opposition by the majority of Arab immigrants to Zionism and the creation of a "Jewish Army," a reference to a British agreement in 1940 to allow recruitment of a Zionist fighting force from within the British military. Reports in the considerable collection of OSS documents also confirm that the ANL willingly and voluntarily disbanded in May 1941 as a show of solidarity behind the Allies six months before the Japanese attack on Pearl Harbor.[7] The reports accurately captured the disillusionment felt by Arab Americans at the rise of Zionist power in Palestine with British help and the increased support Zionists received from the United States. Aside from Western support for Zionism, Arab Americans, who began promoting mutual understanding between the United States and Saudi Arabia, began to feel somewhat let down by the Saudis' neutral tone when their support on Palestine was needed. As part of their advocacy for the Arab leaders, *Al-Bayān* and *Al-Sa'eh* editorials complained about the overall lack of media coverage on the visit of Prince Faisal, as the Saudi minister for foreign affairs, and his brother Prince Khalid as well as the scant notice by Congress when the brothers represented their father, King Āl Saud.[8] However, when asked about Palestine, Faisal refused to take a stance in support of the Palestinians and other Arab states.[9] This was one of the first signals that not all Arab regimes would be keen on democratic reforms. The Saudi royal clan relied on the United States and the West for survival and control of the country's vast national wealth in exchange for granting them access to oil. The United States preferred that its Saudi ally avoid volatile topics and antagonizing the British, especially during the war, and it certainly demanded the same once the Cold War commenced. The arrangement expanded to demanding similar timid behavior from Arab governments to constitute a new status quo designed to serve U.S. national interests. The institute's prophecy of representing U.S. interests in the Middle East, therefore, went unfulfilled because its core issue, the question of Palestine, remained a liability that was—and remains—contradictory to the larger strategic goals of the United States.

Although accurate analysis sometimes escaped OSS operatives, Nabih Fares and later Farhat Ziadeh, who knew many of the personalities of the Arab National League and the institute very well, were knowledgeable and possessed a command of the written Arabic language. Therefore, the OSS records contain a fair amount of reliable information on the players and some activities of the ANL and the institute. Reports provide good information on the orientation and circulation of each of the major Arabic-language newspapers and some translations of various articles, and some challenge the self-importance of *Al-Hoda* and Mokarzel and even contain voluntary interviews with "nationalist leaders" Faris Malouf and George M. Barakat. Ziadeh gave some idea in his OSS reports about the transition from the ANL to the institute.

"Combating Zionism," that is, pursuing the Palestinian question, was the primary impetus for the institute, according to a July 1944 OSS report, although such an undertaking was not without hazards because Jewish merchants "have not hesitated in the past to boycott any Arab-American merchant who gave active support to the Arab cause."[10] In New York, where Jews constituted a significant part of the city's population, such a boycott would have crippled any business. The founders of the institute apparently agreed on several issues: that an organization should be established, that it should be in New York, that it needed to include a Muslim and a Christian as secretaries—as confirmed by the positions of Ḥabīb Kātibah and Ismail Khalidi—and that a general meeting should be held soliciting the participation of the widest possible number of "Arab American communities in the country." The veracity of the OSS report is substantiated by the funding of the organization at the second organizational meeting, although the amount in the OSS records was set at "$8000 out of a quota of $25000 set for the first year."[11] The roster of institute founders suggests that only capable individuals with considerable experience were involved, those who had keen knowledge of U.S. society and geopolitical affairs.

The papers of Ameen Farah and Khalil Totah provide the most accurate accounts of when and how the institute was founded. A Western Union telegram from Ahmad Badder in Dearborn on November 14, 1944, one of eight telegrams announcing the arrival of participants in the institute's first organizational meetings, informed the institute's headquarters in New York that representatives from Dearborn would be attending the conference. Two telegrams followed, the first listing Imam Khalil Bazi, Muhammad Faraj, and Ibrahim Alawane and indicating they would arrive by plane to attend the conference and the second telegram providing that John (Hanna) Nasr would represent the Arabian Society of Detroit.[12] The "remaining men of the first Arab movement and their supporters," Kātibah indicated in his book *Al-Nāṭiqūn bi al-Ḍād fi Amrīkā*, laid the idea for the Institute of Arab American Affairs the previous month in New York City.[13] This can be interpreted to mean that the same nationalists involved in the ANL and NSP constituted the backbone for the institute. Confirmation of the prominent role by the same immigrant Syrian nationalists also raises questions about any role or contribution by the U.S.-born generation, although it does suggest the older generation's focus on the fate of Palestine. Before the year was over, the institute acted to head off plans for creating a Jewish commonwealth, fearing that it would lead to a state with a Jewish majority. Archbishop Antony Bashir, head of the Syrian Orthodox Archdiocese, wrote to Tom Connally, chairman of the U.S. Senate Foreign Relations Committee, on behalf of what Bashir perceived to be Connally's Arab American constituency. The

معهد الشوءون العربية الاميركية
نشأته ـ مبادئه ـ مآتيه ـ اَمانيه

لقد مضى على تأسيس معهد الشوءون العربية الاميركية عامان اصاب فيهما نصيبا وافرا من النجاح. وهو ما زال يطمح الى توسيع نطاق عمله ويجد في سبيل الوصول الى اهدافه العليا حتى يصبح معهدا يعتز به الاميركيون المتحدرون من اصل عربي والعالم العربي اجمع. هذه غايته القصوى. وتحقيق هذه الغاية منوط في المقام الاول بكل مواطن ينطق بالضاد في الديار الاميركية.

فمعهد الشوءون العربية الاميركية هو منظمة اميركية اعضاءه وموظفوه اميركيو الجنسية وكثيرون منهم من مواليد هذه البلاد

ولا نستطيع ان نعرب عن اغراض المعهد واهدافه بافضل مما اعرب عنه دستوره الاساس بالذي ورد فيه «ان غرض المعهد هو ان يعمل كاداة خير وتفاهم متبادل بين الولايات المتحدة والاقطار العربية وشعوبها اني كانوا».

وتحقيقا لهذا الغرض قام المعهد باعمال لم يتسن لموءسسة مثلها ان تقوم بها في وقت قصير منذ نشأته في ٢٥ تشرين الثاني (نوفمبر) سنة ١٩٤٤ نقتصر على ذكر بعض منها الماما ـ

١ ـ إتخذ المعهد مكتبا له تحت رقم ١٦٠ برودواي ـ نيويورك ـ فاصبح هذا المكتب موردا لكثير من الصحف والمجلات والجمعيات ترتاده لتقصي اخبار الشرق العربي وقضاياه واماله

٢ ـ يصدر المعهد نشرة اخبارية شهرية بثماني صفحات طافحة بالاخبار والتعليقات وانباء التقدم العربي الحديث مما يندر العثور عليه في الصحف او المجلات الاميركية عادة.

٣ ـ ينشر المعهد مطبوعات قيمة في شتى المواضيع المتعلقة بالشرق العربي نذكر منها مقالات ووثائق في القضية الفلسطينية ـ الاميركيون الناطقون بالضاد ـ التقدم العربي في فلسطين ـ مذكرة جوابا على اقتراحات اللجنة الانكليزية الاميركية ـ الازمة في سوريا ولبنان ـ قائمة باحدث المصادر العلمية والادبية عن مختلف نواحي الشرق العربي

FIGURE 7.3. *Page from the Institute of Arab American Affairs' biannual report, 1947. Farah Papers, Bawardi Collection.*

archbishop urged the chairman to "defer consideration of the Palestine resolution now pending before your committee until representatives of Americans of Arab descent are given the democratic opportunity to present the side of the native Arab majority of the Holy Land."[14]

The first available working notes of a general meeting by the institute—for the first time, mostly in English—provided that the organization was founded in fall 1944 "with the purpose of promoting friendly relations and understanding between the Arab World and the United States of America" and convened a meeting on February 17, 1945. That meeting was attended by Faris Malouf, Iliyas Sawabini on behalf of Husni Mahfouz, Simon Rihbany, Joseph Sado, Ramiz Haddad, Mahmoud Sadaka, Abbas Nasrallah, John Hazam, Peter George, Hamdan Ghannam, E. J. Audi, and Isa Bateh. Arif Jabara was represented by Fayyad Barakat of Oklahoma City, and Khalil Bazi from Detroit was delegated to represent John Nasr. The notes list telegrams of support from Ahmad Najm of Grand Haven, Michigan, and a similar message from Adel Haleem asking that Ismail Khalidi represent him. The notes indicated that Ḥabīb Kātibah, Farhat Ziadeh, Ibraheem Kheel, and Jack Kaibani were present to offer their advice. After approving the minutes of the November 1944 meeting read by the secretary Ismail Khalidi, those present agreed to hold an annual meeting on May 26, 1945, charge a committee of legal experts with finalizing the language of the bylaws, and form an interim executive committee composed of Faris Malouf as its president and Joseph Sado, Hamdan Ghannam, Fayyad Jabara, E. J. Audi, Peter George, and Ismail Khalidi as members. The executive committee then met separately to discuss establishing an office for the institute. The next day, Philip Hitti was asked to attend a special meeting and was elected unanimously as temporary president. Accordingly, Hitti appointed a staff with $5,000 ($63,000 in 2012 money) "laid at his disposal for that purpose." Apparently, Hitti's function was to oversee a new election by the executive committee, which chose Ali Mahadeen as the institute's president and Ismail Khalidi its secretary. The first order of business of the new executive board was to send a telegram to the House Foreign Affairs Committee and Senate Foreign Relations Committee asking them to confirm the "aspiration for independence" of Syria, Lebanon, and Palestine.[15]

With this organized cadre of activists, the institute's work commenced. In March, Kātibah and Farhat Ziadeh were engaged full time and Ismail Khalidi part time, and Miss Kareema Khouri was hired to do stenographic work in Arabic and English.[16] Kareema Khouri appears to have stayed very busy, as the March report lists translation and dissemination of several speeches by Hitti. Among these were transcripts of telegrams sent to Chairman Thomas Connally of the Senate Foreign Relations Committee and to the Department of State in support of the admission of Syria, Lebanon, and Palestine into the world body being formed. According to the same report, the request also was "released to English press." The institute sent a "night letter" to American representatives at the UN meetings in San Francisco urging support for those countries. It reprinted articles concerning the conditions in Palestine based on reports by British official Hope Simpson and a booklet it published on "dealing with Arab history and problems" and sent them to participants at the UN.[17] At that time, the institute's temporary location was at 666 West 188th Street in New York City.

Once the institute's administrative structure was in place, seventy established and seasoned activists met and elected Faris Malouf as its new president, Shukri Khouri as vice president, Ismail Khalidi as secretary, and Isa Bateh as treasurer. An executive committee subsequently was formed, headed by Ali Muhyiddīn, the seasoned activist now known better as Ali Mahadeen, and including Faris Saʿd, Yousef Saʿd, Abbas Nasr-Allah, Fuad Jabara, Ilias Odeh, Hanna Hazam, and attorney Butrus (Peter S.) George. Philip Hitti was invited to serve as executive director in March 1945 after the institute took residence at 160 Broadway in New York. Shortly thereafter, Ḥabīb Kātibah was employed to run the office, and Khalidi became treasurer and head of Arab affairs, while Farhat Ziadeh handled English correspondence and literature. In the same year, Khalil Totah replaced Hitti as executive director.[18]

The progress report for the period beginning June 1, 1945, lists the accomplishments of the organization. By that time the institute had issued and mailed out its bulletin to "a list of 5,000 Americans and 4,000 of our people." In addition to *Arabic-Speaking Americas*, *Arab Progress in Palestine*, and *The League of Arab States*, the activists finalized the organization's constitution, sent a number of letters to editors, organized branches in Canada and Mexico, as well as in the United States, and set up a speakers bureau. The institute began organizing an "American advisory council" and a women's auxiliary, and it cooperated with the Arab Bureau of Information,[19] which will be discussed later. By the end of October, the office staff held regular meetings and reported to the board of directors. The organization sent 2,000 copies of its monthly bulletin to public and university libraries, to "leading men of our country," and to new chapters in Lansing and Detroit in Michigan, in Indianapolis, and in Wilkes-Barre, Pennsylvania. The institute also began monitoring the media. Perhaps responding to a perceived incident of Arab-baiting, the institute's new executive director, Khalil Totah, protested remarks made by Congressman John M. Coffee of

Washington, who was quoted as saying, "I say to Hell with these secret private arrangements with the Arab maggots, I smell oil." The congressman wrote back to Totah explaining that he said, "Arab magnets [sic] not Arab maggots."[20]

Before Totah joined the institute on October 1, 1945, as the executive director, Kātibah and Ismail Khalidi compiled lists of 118 prominent Arab American activists across the United States and brief descriptions of their orientations and strengths. These would have been representative affiliates, speakers, and sources of support. They listed libraries in major universities in the United States and Canada as well as "Orientalist" scholars in the Americas. Among the papers in Totah's archives are lists of "Americans of Arab Origins" compiled by the institute's members. The institute prepared its constituency for political action by supplying the chapters with names and party affiliations of all U.S. senators and congressmen and their mailing addresses in Washington, D.C., and dedicated the last page of the monthly bulletin to the monthly activities.[21]

The institute officers worked to earn the confidence of Arab nationalists through its publications, speaking tours, and the like.[22] This confidence helped the organization keep its agenda grounded in the pressing need of aiding emergent Arab governments in the Middle East from an Arab American perspective. That is, its agenda and philosophy navigated a balance between Arab and U.S. interests. This is also to say that the Arab Americans struck the balance they sought when the ANL experiment came to an end; defending Palestine after the war, they realized, no longer contradicted their loyalty to the United States. In fact, they considered advocacy for an even-handed policy in the strategic Middle East to be in the best interest of the United States. Armed with this new sense of purpose, the institute harnessed the collective power of Arab Americans. Publications in Farah's manuscript collection and other material confirm the list of accomplishments in the institute's booklet and its leaders' intention to increase membership. As I have with the previous organizations, I have translated and reproduced some of the institute's Arabic-language documents that cannot be found outside private archival collections. For example, the institute, according to this Arabic-language booklet among Farah's papers, organized the following:

- Sent a delegation to the conference on future international organization in San Francisco that would become the UN.
- Testified before the Anglo-American Committee of Inquiry in 1946 and followed that inquiry with a wide-ranging critique of the committee's recommendations.

- Published and dissemminated several research papers on Palestine, among them *Papers on Palestine I* (1945, fifty-four pages), *Papers on Palestine II* (1947, ninety-three pages), and *Papers on Palestine III* (1947, sixty-seven pages); *The Palestine Reality* and *Arabic Language, Arabic Literature, Arabic Philosophy* (1945); *Arabic-Speaking Americans* and the Arabic version, *Al-Nāṭiqūn bi al-Ḍād fī Amrīkā*, as well as *Arab Progress in Palestine* and *Introducing the Arabs to Americans* (1948); and *Arab Refugees in the Holy Land: A Man Made Catastrophe* (1949).[23]
- Published and disseminated 4,000 copies of a monthly bulletin.
- Systematically disseminated printed material to 250 journalists, 250 radio commentators, members of Congress and main offices in the Capitol, and universities across the United States.
- Participated in lectures, forums, and radio broadcasts on the Palestinian issue and all other Arab countries.
- Published a study defending Syria and Lebanon against French atrocities in 1945.
- Sponsored ads in newspapers explaining the Palestinian issue.[24]

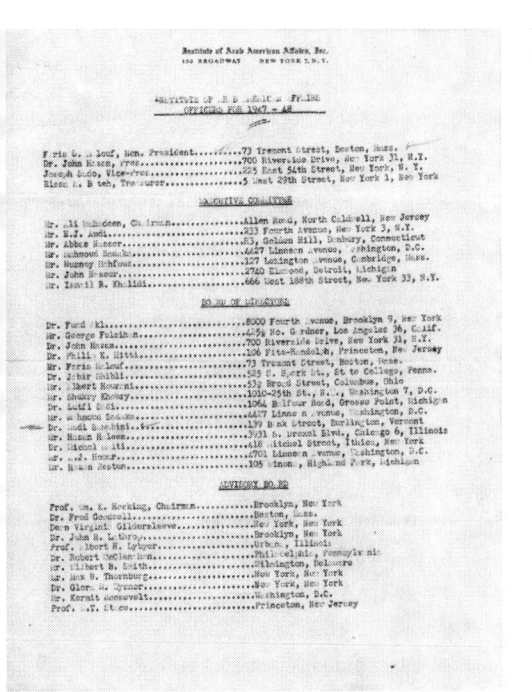

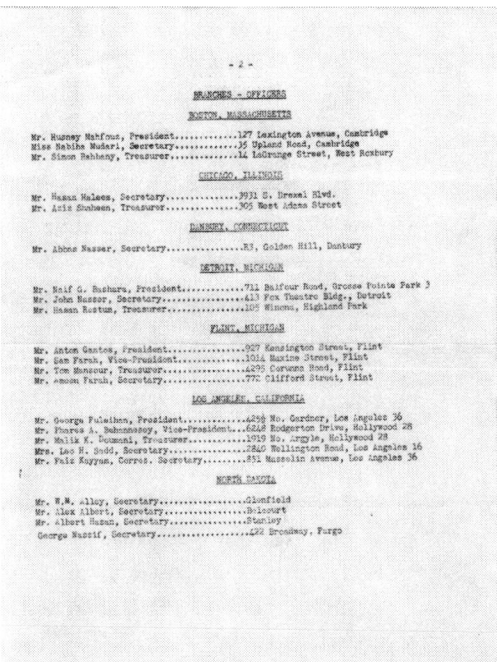

FIGURE 7.4. List of the Institute of Arab American Affairs' chapter officers, 1947–1948. Shown here are two of the three pages of officers of chapters across the United States. Totah Archives, courtesy of Joy Totah Hilden.

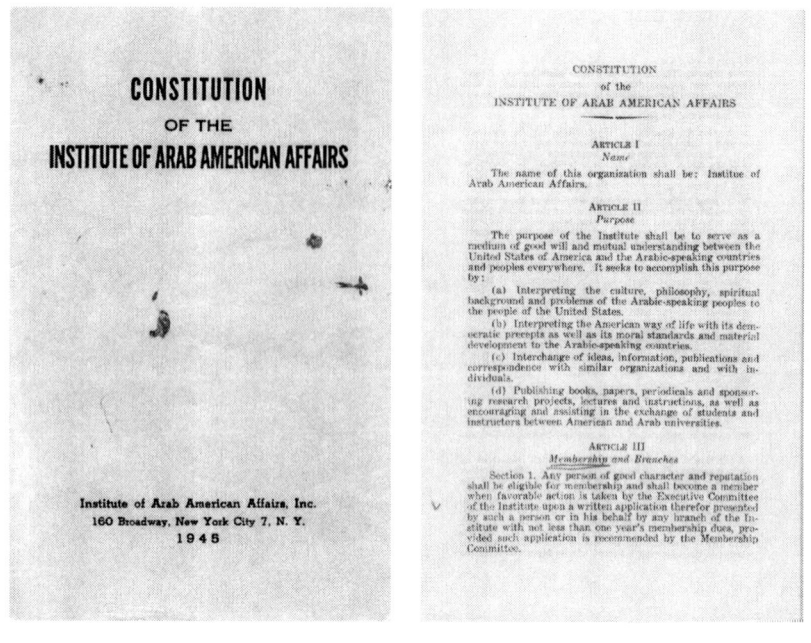

FIGURE 7.5. *Cover and first page of the Institute of Arab American Affairs' constitution, 1945. It was authored and signed by Philip K. Hitti as acting executive director before Khalil Totah became the director. Farah Papers, Bawardi Collection.*

The pamphlet spelled out the institute's message, affirming its aim of "nurturing feelings of mutual understanding between the United States and the Arabic-speaking peoples." Emphasizing the contiguity between the institute's core messaging and previous efforts of political mobilization and cultural work, the pamphlet sums up the institute's founding as "a logical outcome of the preceding formidable efforts that added thirty-three years of experience to its operations."[25] This statement acknowledged that the institute was a conscious extension of existing political work under still unfolding political developments. In other words, the activists resumed work on at least some of the core issues that concerned the ANL before the war.

The institute's English-language constitution outlined the organization's purpose as "to serve as a medium of goodwill and mutual understanding" between the United States and Arabic-speaking populations and governments by "interpreting" the culture of the Middle East to the U.S. population and by "interpreting the American way of life with its democratic precepts as well as its moral standards and material development to the Arabic-speaking countries." Finally, it refers to an "exchange of ideas and information" and mutually beneficial intellectual pursuits such as cultural exchanges, publications, and research.[26] The constitution sets forth rules for executive authority, elections, membership, procedures, and financial operations.

Another pressing concern for the institute, as was the case for each of the organizations previously discussed, was its charitable work. In the case of the institute, this took the form of the Village Welfare Movement (In'ash al-qura), a charity organization, in memory of Fuad Mufarrij—the Syrian honored guest of the ANL in that organization's Fourth Convention, and Khalil al-Shaykh, his companion from Iraq, who both died in an automobile accident on the day the convention ended in September 1939.

Besides performing charitable work, the institute sent Faris Malouf to the San Francisco conference where the United States and Britain led talks on establishing the UN. The "Manifesto of the Institute of Arab American Affairs on Palestine" was expressly intended to address the hundreds of delegates representing about fifty countries at the conference.[27] The manifesto described the institute's objectives as including contributing to the proceedings of the embryonic United Nations. Submitted to the "honorable delegates of the United Nations Conference on International Organization" in San Francisco in April 1945, it most saliently advanced a political message by the Arab Americans within the context of their newfound objectives as Americans. The name of the institute appears in the center column of the three-column, double-sided, one-page publication. On the right foldable side is a quote from Woodrow Wilson's Fourteen Points to "assure sovereignty" to the former Ottoman provinces after World War I and a similar quote on the left side from the Atlantic Charter in 1941 precluding territorial gains by the great powers and promising self-determination once World War II was won. The manifesto mentioned the unsettled situation in Palestine, announced the institute's message of promoting understanding between the United States and Arabic-speaking peoples, and submitted seven considerations "in the name of thousands of loyal American citizens of Arabic-speaking stock."[28]

Point 1 in the succinct statement recalled the offer of Palestine by the British official Lord Balfour, "which was not his to offer," to the wealthy Jewish personality Baron Rothschild as an "unhappy experiment which brought in its wake revolts, bloodshed, and deep resentment." The harshest words in the manifesto—now that the war was over—were directed against the British for their "shameful breach of faith with millions of Arabs" in violation of the letter in the covenant of the League of Nations that development of a mandated Palestine was a "form of sacred trust of civilization."

The Jewish home became a fact, the paragraph continues, to which Jews "look upon with pride" after the Palestinians accommodated in ten years the equivalent of the United States allowing 80,920,000 immigrants in the same proportion.[29]

Points 2 and 3 in the manifesto outlined British investigations and the empty words that followed them in successive white papers regarding the harm of open Jewish immigration and land acquisition. Starting with "demands of a national home in Palestine," the Zionists became emboldened by the "success of their propaganda in the United States and have been demanding the whole of Palestine as their national state." Although the White Paper of 1939 providing for a binational state for all was rejected by "both sides," the manifesto indicated that "Arabs have since tacitly accepted it." The manifesto proclaimed this British-brokered idea of coexistence as a tacit recognition of the Arabs' right to decide their fate and an implicit recognition of their geographic, economic, and historic contiguity with the neighboring Arab states that were about to "take their place among the democratic and progressive nations of the world."[30]

Point 4 recalled the continued Arab association with Palestine, "the land of Canaan" before the advent of "Joshua or even Abraham." This association continued through the arrival of Islam to the geographic and cultural span of Syria. Accordingly, Point 5 stated, "security demands that Palestine be kept in the Arab fold" because a Jewish nation would be impracticable. Point 6 invoked a remark by Prime Minister Churchill after the Yalta Conference in 1945:[31] "The Arabs rendered good and meritorious service to democracy in the present war. All the national resources of Egypt, Iraq, Syria, and Lebanon have been at the disposition of the United Nations. Arab fighters are today with our forces that have penetrated the citadel of Nazism." Finally, Point 7 concluded that having borne more than their share of granting refuge to Jews, "it is our earnest belief and hope" that the solution would create an atmosphere of true democracy and security everywhere, "not in the artificial creation of a Jewish state in Palestine."[32]

Thus, the institute's leaders hoped Arab nation-states might capitalize on rising U.S. prestige. Expressions like "our earnest belief" seem to express the hope that U.S. interests would be compatible with those of the budding Arab states and Arab Americans alike. It should be noted here that implying a broad pan-Arab nationalism by the Arab Americans in their agenda—an outcome of the shifting political reality away from Syrian nationalism and closer to the core Arab issue of Palestine—was by this time secondary to their goals of participating in high politics as Arab Americans serving U.S. interests. That goal was behind their involvement in the process of attaining statehood for the newly formed Arab states in the United Nations. They conceived of their unique position as an opportunity to represent the interests of the United States in all of these would-be Arab states in light of the massive oil deposits and dominant American commercial interests in Saudi Arabia. Conversely, the members' generation-long journey in the United States allowed them to deconstruct the persistent aura of Oriental mystique around the Middle East through their contributions in books, in the press, and in social, religious, and political circles.[33] Belonging to and remembering an extended Arab heritage enabled the institute to project its intermediary position. In fact, upon his employment as executive director, Khalil Totah proceeded to implement the institute's message by sending a personal note addressed to "Fellow Countrymen in Arab Lands."

The institute's activities attracted the attention of foreign and local Zionist groups. In addition to spending lavishly on propaganda in the United States, the New York proponents of Zionism collaborated with their counterparts in Britain on monitoring the institute's activists and tracking its friends and supporters. When Ismail Khalidi served as Arabic-language secretary of the institute before becoming its treasurer in 1945, the Jewish Agency for Palestine infiltrated the institute and began collecting information on its members. J. L. Teller sent a telegram to that effect to Eliahu Epstein, head of the Jewish Agency's Washington office: "My reporter learned Institute for Arab American Affairs headed by son of late Mayor [of Jerusalem] Khalidi. Investigating further. May have full picture their setup countrywide time your return New York."[34] An undated and anonymous report in the Central Zionist Archives in Jerusalem by an informant divulged mostly fanciful talk devoid of any specifics about the institute's hallway being "full of Arabians" and how "the Doctor" (Totah) greeted him and mentioned plans about asking him to translate nondescript material from Italian.[35] By the time the institute began to function in April 1945, the Jewish Agency for Palestine signaled to the World Zionist Organization in London that it endorsed the work of a consortium of several U.S. Zionist organizations named the American Zionist Emergency Council and headed by Rabbi Stephen S. Wise.[36] A memorandum dated July 10, 1945, by Gotlieb Hammer of the Jewish Agency confirmed that the council had spent $300,877.61 on implementing the agency's agenda. The funds were allocated under "Disbursement" to pay for expenses related to "Administrative," "Political," "Press," "Publications," "Community Contact Department," "Research," "American Palestine Committee," and committees overseeing "Intellectual Mobilization," "Allied P.O.W. Groups," "Labor Relations," and "Speaker Bureau." Despite the threat these activities posed to the Arab causes and Palestinians' welfare, Totah and Khalidi maintained reciprocally cordial correspondences with Epstein of the Jewish Agency. In their correspondences, an amicable agreement was reached for exchanging printed material and publications between the institute and Epstein, including the institute's bulletins.[37]

Less cordial was the response by A. S. Yahuda to the manifesto on Palestine the institute sent to the UN conference. His fourteen-page refutation of the institute's grievances against British colonial policies began by distinguishing between Arabs and Christians, that is, as being mutually exclusive categories. He asserted that the institute activists were mostly self-styled "Americans of Arabic-speaking origin" but implied that they were Christian and hence not Arabs because they emphasized the "linguistic, not the racial solidarity with the Arabs." Based on this, Yahuda concluded that they were a fringe group in defiance of the majority of the Lebanese Christian immigrants who did not support the "Pan-Arab movement which is based on racial and nationalistic grounds."[38] Yahuda cast doubt on the desire of the Arab inhabitants of Palestine to join an Arab state and claimed that "King Husain of the Hedjaz" (sharif of Mecca) and his son Faisal went further than giving their "full consent" to the Balfour Declaration: "They expressed most enthusiastically their support of the British policy which was upheld by them all the time, since the liberation of Palestine until the ratification of the Mandate through the League of Nations in 1922 [in San Remo]."[39] Further, Yahuda told the delegates to the UN in his rebuttal that Hussein and Faisal consented to the creation of a Jewish national home in Palestine and "Transjordan." Yahuda stated in his pamphlet that Jewish investment brought the Arab population in Palestine to "a much higher civilized level" and that "all the Arabs of Syria, Lebanon, and Iraq were fighting against Great Britain and her allies on the side of Turks and the Germans."[40] Complete and sharp differences on the future of Palestine characterized Arab-Zionist debates. The commitment to Zionism in the name of Jews weakened anti-Zionist Jews and gnarled the distinction between Zionism and Judaism. Eventually, the debate became increasingly described simply in terms of Arab versus Jew.

The institute's widely disseminated materials were usually written in English, although appeals for aid and some announcements were bilingual in order to appeal to former members of previous organizations and first-generation immigrants as well as their U.S.-born offspring. All the materials were printed or typed. Ongoing charitable campaigns that predated mass immigration by Jews to Palestine in the interwar period continued and became concerned with the plight of dispossessed Palestinians. For example, the Village Welfare Movement to aid the "farmers of the Arab world" was adopted by the ANL at the behest of Fuad Shatara before his untimely death in November 1942; the fund connected the Arab National League and the institute as much as did pronouncements of loyalty to the United States during the ANL Flint convention.[41] Fund-raising for the Village Welfare Movement overlapped with drives for a hospital in Al-Hosn, Jordan, and the Arab Orphanage Committee of Haifa, founded in January 1940 and headed by Judge Muhammad Barad'i Abbasi in the beleaguered Arab section of that port city west of Nazareth. Abbasi visited the U.S. branch of the Orphanage Committee in New York during November 1947 and traveled to Flint, where Ameen Farah was instrumental in helping make his visit fruitful on behalf of the institute. In recognition of his efforts, Farah received an official letter of thanks signed by Sa'id Dajani, the deputy president of the orphanage in Haifa, dated December 11, 1947. The letter indicates that the executive board had decided to acknowledge Farah's efforts in its general meeting held on December 10, 1947.

The need to address the problems of the Palestinians sent other charitable organizations searching for support from Arab Americans. The Jerusalem-based General Arab Orphans Committee in Palestine, founded December 3, 1939, also received financial help from the Arab Americans who were members of the ANL before joining the institute. Donations from Arab Americans helped house hundreds of children who had lost their parents to Jewish and British violence that sometimes followed comparatively subdued Palestinian attacks, and immigrants sent dozens of orphans to be educated in engineering and agricultural colleges in Egypt, Jerusalem, and Beirut. The schools had elaborate stone structures, workshops, farms, wine cellars, sports facilities, and dorms.

Although some operated independently, many charitable organizations were affiliate clubs, committees, and societies that maintained ties to the institute. Farah's archives contain numerous snippets of newspaper articles, invitations to events, and reports that suggest widespread charitable work during different periods. As when banquets benefiting the Syrian Red Crescent were held before World War I, a fund-raiser was held by the institute's Flint affiliate, the American-Arab Committee for Democracy, managed by Najīb Samra, to raise money for refugees. Some charities now affiliated with the institute can be traced to much older immigrant social clubs such as al-'Usbah (The Bond) and the oldest Flint-based social club, the apolitical al-Watan (The Homeland) club, which long continued to draw older members of the Mansour, Farah, Joseph, and other pioneer families around card games in homes of members including that of Ameen's son Roy Farah.[42]

Charitable works were a major part of immigrants' nonsectarian public services, which they sometimes provided in conjunction with worldwide organizations. However, the political undercurrents of loyalty to Syria and its afflicted cannot be ignored. Such were the precepts that attracted formidable non-Arab allies in Palestine's cause, among them the Society of Friends and luminaries like Virginia Gildersleeve, dean of Barnard College, in whose name an international fund was established to provide training and services to women globally.[43]

A challenge facing a successful public relations campaign by the Arab Americans was the perception that the independence-driven Arab nationalists espoused radical ideology and could have threatened the Allies at the outset of World War II. In retrospect, this perception was the beginning of a new global order in which choosing a path outside the alliances of the war became unsustainable until these pressures yielded the Cold War. I will not delve into the modern manifestations of state nationalisms, but for the purposes of this discussion, subtle though critical tendencies of resorting to an ascribed Lebaneseness in the late 1930s became an increasingly viable respite from seeming too Syrian, that is, too nationalistic, when yielding to the will of the Allies was the measure of one's loyalty. These considerations, however, did not dissuade members of the institute, or for that matter members of the Arab National League, from upholding the cause of the Palestinians; it simply made their work even more arduous.

A *New York Times* article from 1938 helps to put this analysis in perspective. The article, "Pan Arabism Adds to Unrest," displays a map of the Middle East with the Arabic-speaking regions blackened, including the east coast of the Persian (Arabian) Gulf and a caricature-like sketch of the *mufti* Amin al-Husseini, although his photo was widely available at the time, atop the caption "The Grand Mufti of Jerusalem is head of the greater-Arabia drive." The subtitle captures the essence of the article: "Movement for Union of Near East States Complicates the Problems of the Powers."[44] The article ties the Peel Commission's suggested partition plan for Palestine to "nationalist agitation" and provides an explanation: "the problem of Palestine . . . is the problem of insurgent nationalism."[45] The writer adopted the views ably disseminated by the ANL that "the political division between Syria and Palestine is quite artificial, with little basis in either geography or history. The same applies to Trans-Jordan." However, the reporter added that "it is less true as regards the Lebanon republic, for there the majority of the people are Christian. They are also more commercial and Europeanized than the Syrians and their outlook is towards the sea rather than the desert."[46]

Contrasting desert-bound Arab nationalists to civilized, pro-Western

Lebanese indicates the image problem Arab Americans have long had to endure, not to mention the creeping dichotomy between Arab and Lebanese based on the same formula. That perception would continue to hamper their attempts at appealing to a wider American constituency. While the institute's membership drive was stridently Arab American, even during the institute's fourth year Khalil Totah was still fighting anti-Arab propaganda and Lebanese separatist campaigns. He protested one such attack on the Arab cause by *Al-Hoda*, the *Chicago Tribune*, and the *New York Times*. The newspapers claimed that entire Druze tribes joined the Zionists against Arab countries.[47] The continuation of the battle with *Al-Hoda* even after Lebanon became fully independent and chose a path of Arab cultural identity—thereby opposing Zionist encroachment in Palestine and Zionist efforts in Lebanon in the 1940s—gives credence to Muhammad Zuʿaitir's analysis of longstanding complicity of some Maronites with the Zionists' aims.[48] The institute had to work especially hard to make the point that it was a loyal U.S. organization concerned with the Arab region of the Middle East and interested in simple fairness.

Its membership solicitations extolled the institute's message of mutual understanding between East and West and its dedication to becoming a "source of pride to Americans of Arab extraction and the Arab world generally." Before listing recent publications and accomplishments of the institute, the membership flyer reads, "Hence, the Institute is an American organization, its members and employees possess American citizenship, and many among them were born in this country."[49]

Totah's personal philosophy of loyalty to the United States and the Allies leaves no doubt that he, as did other institute activists, navigated serving U.S. interests with a balanced approach to the political turmoil in Palestine. As it did for many of his generation, the victory over Nazism fed his sense of enthusiasm and his hopeful outlook. A draft of Khalil Totah's unpublished autobiography describes the Allies' victory over Nazism and the resulting atmosphere in 1945: "The year 1945, it will be recalled, was a year of triumph of forces of democracy over the forces of totalitarianism. Men's hearts, enthused by victory, were full of hope and faith in a future of world peace and prosperity."[50] The atmosphere prompted the institute's "bold Manifesto" delivered by a delegation to San Francisco headed by Faris Malouf and Philip Hitti.

While the United Nations charter was debated in 1944, the Syrians suffered one final thrust of French brutality aimed at staving off their hard-earned independence. The French destroyed a quarter of the Syrian capital city, Damascus, including thousand-year-old landmarks, before the United

States and Britain intervened. American advocates of Syrian independence were doubtlessly heartened when they read the news of U.S.-led efforts to rein in the French, thus allowing Syria's complete independence. In what can be considered a historic stance by the United States against the victimization of Arab populations by a European power (the second being Eisenhower's ultimatum to France, Britain, and Israel to clear out of Egypt after their "tripartite aggression" in 1956), Harry Truman sent a message to the French on May 28, 1944, urging them to "renounce the use of force . . . and to put an end to this mode of settling international disputes."[51] These were some of the earliest attempts by the United States to assert its presence in the Middle East and evidence of the country's newfound economic and military might. It was within the context of expanding U.S. prestige that the institute urged Joseph C. Grew, acting secretary of state, to "present an appeal for support of the independence of Syria and Lebanon"; it invoked the sacrifices of the Syrian Americans, "American citizens of Arab origin," who lost their lives in the fight by U.S. forces to liberate France.[52]

Having consistently called on President Roosevelt to grant Lebanon and Syria a place at the planned conference in San Francisco,[53] the institute found its position enhanced when in June 1945 President Truman endorsed the newly founded League of Arab States, a bloc of mostly semi-independent and a few independent Arab states seeking recognition in the emergent world body.[54] Totah's archives indicate considerable lobbying by the institute toward this and other political ends:

> Mass meetings were arranged under the auspices of the Institute and some of its branches in major cities, particularly in Boston, Mass. Radio talks were broadcast, especially one by a member of the Board, Dr. Michael Malti of Cornell University. Notes of protest were cabled to the powers concerned, and in general, public opinion was repeatedly informed of the basic issues of self-determination involved. Soon afterwards these Arab states were recognized by the United Nations as completely sovereign and independent. The Syrian mandate was at an end and the frontiers of freedom were further extended.[55]

By the time the institute settled into its permanent office at 160 Broadway in New York, a coordinated effort between the institute and Archbishop Bashir had targeted Connally as chairman of the Senate Foreign Relations Committee to delay a resolution for partition and Jewish immigration until Arab Americans could present their arguments to members of the Senate committee.[56] The institute and Bashir aimed to counter the strategy deployed by Zionists to resolve the problems of displaced Jews after the war.

Ironically, Arab Americans who urged U.S. intervention following World War I based on the Wilson administration's Fourteen Points that called for self-determination now found themselves fighting off Zionists driving the interventionist tidal wave after World War II.

The isolationist approach of William Borah, Louis McFadden, and others in Congress gave way to American global prestige after the war. If Zionist aims "smacked suspiciously of serving a superficially Jewish, rather than the broader, national interest" in the eyes of older German immigrants,[57] it became exceedingly difficult to articulate opposition to interventionism after the United States won the war against the Nazis, fascists, and Japanese. Arab Americans, however, maintained their distance from conspiracy theories that, for example, "Jews, the British, and Roosevelt were conspiring to bring the nation into war."[58] Archbishop Bashir suggested that Hitti, Malouf, and Lutfi al-Sa'di of Detroit represent Arab Americans' views on Palestine. It is worth noting that all, including Bashir, were until recently considered Syrian immigrants or descendents thereof. As for the plight of the displaced persons, in a reference to Europeans, including Jews, the archbishop wrote to Senator Connally that "far from resolving the problem of persecuted and homeless refugees whose unfortunate lot is before us, it would endanger the pillars of stability in the Near East and would alienate the Arab and Muslim world from the affection of our beloved America."[59]

The progress reports that were disseminated to the institute's chapters for the first few months of 1945 abound with entries of daily activities. The March 6, 1945, report announced that Hitti had sent a telegram to Egyptian Prime Minister Mahmud Fahmi al-Nukrashy and the Cairo conference, where the League of Arab States was being formed, and that the telegram and Nukrashy's reply had been "translated, mimeographed, and sent to Arabic press."[60]

In the beginning of its operations in February and early March, the institute had opportunities to implement its stated goals of facilitating better understanding between Arabs and the United States on multiple levels. The institute operated on the premise that being close to decision makers in the United States would ultimately allow it to facilitate the membership of Arab states in the new world body. Membership would then serve U.S. interests in the region but would also enable Arabs to address their core issue, Palestine. That was the reasoning behind telegrams to President Roosevelt and Secretary Edward Stettinius urging Syrian and Lebanese representation in San Francisco. A more direct approach was hosting the Arab delegates, many of whom were nationalist graduates of the Syrian American College (American University of Beirut) or universities in the West. Pragmatism dictated that the institute play along in terms of regional political arrangements by supporting monarchies served by the U.S. policy of containment. On March 22, 1945, Philip Hitti informed the State Department that his institution, Princeton, would receive the Iraqi regent on April 2, and he invited an undersecretary of the State Department to attend the reception. The State Department understood the value of the institute's strategy. The response came from Paul H. Alling announcing the State Department's approval for the institute to host the Iraqi regent.[61] The fact that the Iraqi monarch was a descendent of Faisal, the nationalist king of the coveted Syria for a brief while, must have made the institute's decision to host him appear even more agreeable, although Britain still retained control over Iraqi affairs and natural resources.

The July bulletin to the members, the organization's first monthly publication, explained that the regent was actually the young "H. R. H. Prince Abdullah Regent and Heir Apparent of Iraq,"[62] the son of Faisal and grandson of Sharif Husain of Mecca. The bulletin declared the emergence of the "Arab nations as the important factor in the world of tomorrow . . . [because] natural resources [and] strategic position make them either a cockpit of contending powers or a secure link between peaceful nations."[63] The bulletin reminded the institute's constituency of the discovery of "almost unlimited quantities of petroleum . . . [in] level lands and constant climatic conditions"; it reintroduced the Arab Middle East as an "interminable air base, a bridge between continents more so than in the days of caravans . . . [and] a focal point of interest" that at once justified U.S. attention and the institute's advocacy of improvements there. In a thinly veiled swipe at either the Soviet Union or Europeans, the bulletin described the interest of the United States in the Middle East as being "free from the sordid greed and political machinations which have marred the relations of some other powers." Instead, U.S. interest was tied to the dawn of Arab *nahḍah* and the older "institutions of learning founded by [American missionaries] . . . long before there was even conjecture of petroleum under the sandy dunes of Arabia."[64]

As if showcasing its successes, the institute reported to its members on a banquet honoring Prince William Phillips, a special assistant to the secretary of state who spoke of the "great importance upon the strengthening of our cultural relations with the Near Eastern people."[65] Present at that banquet was Nuri al-Saʿīd of Iraq. It is worth noting here that the tumultuous nature of the Middle East still hampered prospects of a coherent strategy combining the institute's energies and whatever leverage Arab states may have had over U.S. policy. The Palestinian leadership experienced mayhem due to expulsions and internal competition, but Nuri al-Saʿid would meet his demise when the monarchy was violently overthrown in 1958. However, for the duration of its existence, organizers of the Institute of Arab American Affairs did what they could to live up to its objectives of presenting the Arabs of the Middle East in a favorable light while also projecting U.S. prestige.

The institute's bulletin served as its medium of reports and analysis. One issue discussed the performance of Arab countries at the UN, where Saudi Arabia, Lebanon, and Syria were represented in an international conference for the first time. Another item reported on a reception at the residence of the Syrian delegate that previously was the home of William Howard Taft, U.S. president and later chief justice of the Supreme Court.[66]

The institute obtained a steady source of operating funds by building its membership through thousands of letters and "contribution blanks" asking recipients to join.[67] As a result the organization could, at least in its messaging if not in broadcasting, compete with Zionist communications. The funds helped in publishing pamphlets, of which it sent hundreds of copies to institutions on the organization's lists. The bulletin reported that institute leaders asked for an audience with Roosevelt "similar to the one granted Rabbi Wise."[68] The last internal report of 1945 described considerable efforts spent in the office to prepare "facts and figures on the Palestine problem" to be put at the disposal of the institute's delegation appearing before the Anglo-American Committee of Inquiry in Washington on January 11, 1945.[69] The invitation by the Anglo-American Committee of Inquiry to the institute was a vindication of its political work and credibility with the U.S. government. The inquiry was begun purportedly to investigate the feasibility of settling more European Jews in Palestine after the war by consulting with Arabs and Jews. In an "emergency meeting" to discuss the invitation by the joint American and British committee, the institute's executive committee voted in December 1945 to contribute to the inquiry. The decision was an extension of previous testimony by Philip Hitti before the House of Representatives Foreign Affairs Committee in mid-February. At the time, Hitti faced a hostile Congress backed by an organized Jewish-Zionist constituency expecting congressional support not only for unrestricted Jewish settlement or vague language for a homeland in Palestine but also to "reconstitute Palestine as a free and democratic Jewish commonwealth."[70]

Hitti's full testimony was published in a series of essays and documents issued by the institute under the title *Papers on Palestine*. The institute expanded its capable roster with notables from academia and public life, and in a meeting the executive committee selected six people to give testimony in Congress regarding Jewish immigration to Palestine: Faris Malouf, Khalil

Totah, Philip Hitti, John Hazam, William Hocking, and Wilbert Smith. Reform Rabbi Judah Magnes, an anti-Zionist Jew, also testified at the congressional hearings. At the same meeting of the executive committee, Smith was asked to serve on the advisory board of the institute along with Hocking and Virginia Gildersleeve of Barnard College for Women. Regular appearances by the institute's officers and chapter delegates across the United States were intended to bolster its position on a host of issues beyond Palestine. The board and members of the institute provided interviews and information on the Arab world to *Time* magazine, *Fortune*, and General Motors of New York. Khalil Totah and John Nasr appeared at a session in Detroit of the Foreign Policy Association and addressed a crowd of 300 at Temple Isaiah in Long Island. Totah visited Flint on December 9 and collected $500 in donations. Ismail Khalidi addressed students at Barnard College.

A resolution proposed by lawmakers Robert F. Wagner of New York and Robert Taft of Ohio called for a Jewish state in Palestine. The congressmen justified their position by reminding their colleagues of the plight of displaced Jews in Europe after the war. As a result of this political pressure, when the Anglo-American Committee's report came out, it was little more than skillful maneuvering reminiscent of the Balfour Declaration despite belated language by the British attempting to limit Jewish immigration. The committee recommended allowing 100,000 people to enter Palestine immediately and leaving the door open for more despite declarations by the British foreign secretary, who reminded the committee that there were millions of displaced persons in Europe, among whom Jews were only a part. Because of supporters like Wagner and Taft, American Zionists simply opposed any quotas in order to leave the door wide open for unlimited Jewish settlement in Palestine. Vague language in the committee's report would guarantee the rights of all of Palestine's inhabitants and a democratic state where the rights of all religions were respected.[71]

The debate over Palestine focused the institute's energies. Although the printing and distribution of educational propaganda by the institute rivaled any in Arab American history, quantitatively speaking, the institute could not compete with even one promotional campaign by the American Zionist Emergency Council. The latter ensured the circulation of 16,000 copies of *Palestine: Land of Promise* to "congressmen, government officials, educational and religious leaders, journalists, diplomats, and state and local officials."[72] However, a unique feature set the institute's efforts apart from subsequent debates with Zionists and the uncompromising stance of American Zionists: the institute kept alive Shatara's ideas on binationalism, calling for the coexistence of Palestinians and Jews within a democratic state in Palestine. Shatara, like Judah Magnes, understood the risk to Palestinians posed by the Zionists' ability to bring about the transfer of large numbers of Jews to Palestine. Added to the more than half-million Jews already in Palestine, it became clear that additional arrivals from Europe would turn the Palestinians into a minority. Accordingly, Magnes's testimony to the committee calling for a binational democratic state was transcribed and published by the institute as part of the *Papers on Palestine* collection.[73]

Reprints of articles by Totah, Hitti, Kātibah, and other commentators likewise were sent to groups on the institute's mailing lists. An internal report provided the numbers of copies of the organization's publications sent at large as follows: American Friends, 1,000; Radio Commentators, 250; Educators, 100; Judiciary, 50; Congressmen, 1,000; High Schools, Colleges, and Public Libraries, 250; Press and Radio Periodicals (including columnists), 250; Clergy, 500; American Organizations, 50; Governors, 48. Records indicate that the same literature was also sent overseas, as follows: Arabic Papers and Periodicals, 50; Near East Colleges, 15; Kings, Heads of Arab Governments, Legislatures, Department of Foreign Affairs, Chambers of Commerce, and Organizations, 150; prospective members of Arabic-speaking origin, 1,000.[74]

The institute had plans for a membership drive in Detroit and appealed to its chapters across the United States to reach second- and third-generation Arab Americans. It provided lists of "Literature Obtainable on Request," "Bibliography on the Arab Near East," monthly bulletins 1 to 7, *Arabic-Speaking Americans*, "Conflict in the Middle East" by Philip Hitti, and "Christians and Zionists" by A. L. Warnshuis,[75] secretary emeritus of the International Missionary Council. The last, a reprint of an article in the *Christian Century* from November 21, 1945, is an example of the range of support generated by the institute. The article by Warnshuis begins with this statement:

> Hypocrisy seems to characterize the support that many Americas give to Zionism. Consciously or unconsciously, their underlying idea is that it will be so much easier and pleasanter if the Jews would go to Palestine, or any other part of the world, rather than to have more of them come to America.... Our political parties put Zionist planks into their platforms—to get votes. Resolutions are introduced into Congress—to get votes. Proposals are made to Britain, the mandatory, to get votes. Not a fair statement [assessing] problems in Palestine but our own selfish interests determine our attitudes. Plain speaking is needed so that our irresponsible actions may be reconsidered.[76]

Zionists, too, were hard at work opposing any strides made by Arab nations and challenging the institute at every turn. Although one must consider the effects of the Holocaust, the institute's binationalist philosophy, as part of its "greater effort expended and centered upon the long-standing problem of Palestine,"[77] met a constant drive for a Jews-only dominion in Palestine that began long before the anti-Semitic wave in Germany. Anti-Zionist Americans of various persuasions and backgrounds looked at subsequent events and found Zionist opposition to binationalism perplexing not only because it predated the Holocaust but also because a binational state would have given relief to thousands of Jews. Totah, in his unpublished autobiographical draft, summed up the institute's challenges:

> The Zionists, highly organized, well financed, and deeply entrenched in the political and economic framework of these key countries [the United States and Britain], proceeded to use their advantageous position to control public opinion, to put pressure on the government, and to influence, if not dominate, their foreign policies in this area of the East. . . . It is on this sorry one-sided and seemingly hopeless scene that the Institute of Arab American Affairs appeared as the champion of truth, justice, and freedom [aided by] thousands of intelligent and serious-minded citizens whose knowledge of Palestine was frequently limited to the biblical period and [who] were hungry for the facts in the present-day controversy. These facts were presented to them by the Institute.[78]

Compared with the mind-boggling loss of life and destruction of World War II globally, the Palestine problem was an obscure human tragedy, much like demands for self-determination seemed to the great powers after World War I. But Palestine's plight attracted bitterness and sharp exchanges among the witnesses and committee members of the Anglo-American Committee of Inquiry,[79] making the United States as much a battlefield as Palestine. Einstein, who previously condemned Jewish terrorism, faulted the colonial British for instigating friction between Arabs and Jews, and he still opposed a Jewish state in the lead-up to the commission's recommendations.[80] Although he was conciliatory when it came to a Jewish-dominated state in Palestine, Einstein's constant advocacy for allowing the flow of Jewish immigration into a volatile situation exposed the contradictions inherent in resolving a European problem in Palestine. Earl Harrison, Truman's envoy to the displaced persons in Germany, was compelled to agree that Jews must be sent to Palestine, "where they want to go," as if in a vacuum. For his part, the embattled British chairman of the committee, Sir John Singleton, was attacked by an economist, Robert Nathan, over Britain's neutral attitude toward land acquisition by the Zionists. However, what Zionists faulted as a neutral attitude came on the heels of decades of uneven developments in favor of the Jewish population in Palestine under British watch during the mandate before the British washed their hands of all responsibilities.

The horrific Holocaust became a factor in the equation after the war. Joseph Schwartz, director of the American Jewish Distribution Committee, declared that 6,000,000 of a population of 7,500,000 Jews perished, and of those "600,000 want to go to Palestine."[81] Zionists were joined by growing numbers of anti-Zionists in opposing the white paper's recommendation to limit the entry of Jews to Palestine in the lead-up to the war; now, after German atrocities, the ardent Zionist Stephen Wise, would contend that "the Christian World owes the Jews some reparation."[82] Perhaps due to the institute's flexibility, divisions within the U.S. Jewish community persisted. Judge Joseph Proskauer of the American Jewish Committee opposed the creation of a Jewish state, calling instead for an all-inclusive, democratic one. However, he insisted on Jewish immigration "as of right not on sufferance,"[83] parroting Churchill's words to his British Jewish constituency in the early days of the mandate.

Another Jewish voice opposed to Zionism and the Biltmore Program, Lessing Rosenwald of the American Council for Judaism, "advocated integration of refugees into a number of countries."[84] On behalf of the Arab side, some in the institute opposed opening Palestine for further Jewish immigration because, Hitti explained, Palestinians viewed a settler as a warrior. Hazam challenged Hitti on that point, arguing that Arabs would "probably not oppose the Jewish refugees if they could be convinced that the Zionists would renounce plans for political and economic domination." The hearings before the Anglo-American Committee of Inquiry and news of suffering in Europe motivated the Arab side to show flexibility and compromise. As a result, many on the Arab American side became open to the idea of permitting 200,000 Jews in exchange for forgoing the establishment of a Jewish commonwealth.[85] For his part, Ernest Bevin, the British foreign secretary who was present at the hearings on Britain's behalf, reminded the committee that Jews were among the displaced masses in Europe numbering in the millions; Bevin created confusion by urging the commission to refer the issue of displacement to the UN but neglecting to explain whether he was referring to only the Jewish displaced or asking that the UN take up the matter of the trusteeship on Palestine.

The findings of the Anglo-American Committee of Inquiry were predictable, given the rationale and expectations in Washington and London for alleviating Jewish refugee problems in Europe. Upon taking office, Truman informed the newly elected British prime minister, Clement Atlee, of the American people's firm belief that Jewish immigration should not be restricted to Palestine.[86] The British began to fathom the Arabs' need for unity after Nuri al-Saʿīd committed to fight the Nazis after crushing his rival Rashid Ali in Iraq. This development was a crucial turn away from Ali's short-lived flirtation with Germany as a possible ally for Iraq's independence from the British. When the more measured militarism of the Haganah and other groups in Palestine targeted Palestinians and British alike, the increasing appetite in the United States for global economic expansion poised them to replace the war-fatigued British. The British were trying to get the United States behind their own plans for the region, but because they had emerged weak from the war and relied on U.S. military muscle, they were not in the best bargaining position. If the British were trying to mitigate their previous mistake by now setting and enforcing limits for Jewish immigration, their reliance on the United States made them vulnerable to pressure by American Zionists. This new formula caused talk of binationalism to recede. Thus, Walid Khalidi argues, the Anglo-American Committee of Inquiry transformed the British Mandate "into a condominium with the United States as a senior partner."[87]

The institute's leaders did their best to refute calls for partitioning Palestine in a memorandum addressed to Undersecretary of State Dean Acheson in August 1946. There was a debate within the institute regarding the number of Jews who should be allowed into Palestine. However, they began to fear that a Jewish majority was within reach that would lead to the expulsion of the Palestinians.[88] An excerpt captures the gist of their twenty-four-page response to the Anglo-American Committee of Inquiry's findings: "We firmly believe that the Arab World will spurn any solution of the problem of Jewish homelessness or so-called statelessness at its expense alone, or on the basis of privileges and prerogatives given those displaced Jews in Palestine that are not countenanced anywhere else."[89] Nevertheless, the institute recommended admitting 100,000 Jews "who were victimized by Nazi and fascist persecution" and recommended that neither side dominate the other in Palestine but rather that "the fullest measure of self-government" be promoted to end the violence.[90]

The testimonies by Hitti, Malouf, and K. S. Mitchell before the House Foreign Affairs Committee, along with articles and letters to newspapers by Arab Americans and supportive luminaries, were published in *Papers on Palestine: A Collection of Statements, Articles, and Letters Dealing with the Palestine Problem*. The preface to the publication declares that the institute "deems it a public duty to publish the following papers dealing with the problem of Palestine, with the hope that the reader might be able to formulate a more intelligent opinion about it."[91] In the thirty-five-page bound volume, Hitti, a professor of Semitic studies at Princeton, refuted exclusive Jewish biblical claims regarding settlement in Palestine under the title "Palestinian Arabs Descended from Natives before Abraham." Other contributions were professor William Ernest Hocking's "Arab Nationalism and Political Zionism," professor Jabir Shibli's "The Voice of the Arabs," and from Sir John Hope Simpson (of the Simpson Report of 1930), "The Palestine Reality." Letters were reproduced from J. W. Bailey to the Greensboro Committee for the Abrogation of the White Paper, from professor H. Soltau in response to a *New York Times* letter, from Philip Marshal Brown to the *New York Herald Tribune*, and from Stuart C. Dodd, also to the *New York Herald Tribune*.

The institute's work also was intended to strengthen ties between the U.S. polity and visiting Arab dignitaries in banquets and forums, including participating in the Foreign Policy Association's gathering titled "The Arab League in World Politics" in November 1946.[92] The annual meetings still attracted delegates from all parts of the United States, including Ameen Farah, who represented Flint in June 1946 and earned a special commendation from the board for his dedication.[93] The activities overlapped with raising funds for Palestinian orphanages, which eventually taxed the immigrants' limited resources. In what amounted to a distraction, given the institute's multiple priorities, hosting Arab delegates to the UN became a regular activity. Arab hospitality and ancestral links dictated the social aspects of the encounters. Faris al-Khouri, the Syrian prime minister, had led the Syrian delegation to the United Nations conference in San Francisco. Aside from being the first high-level Syrian official to visit the United States, Khouri was an acknowledged major *nahḍah* intellectual with links to the American University of Beirut.

Its pragmatism brought the institute closer to approaching the West in terms Westerners could understand. This strategy coincided with a similar approach by emissaries from the immigrants' ancestral homelands who accompanied the delegates. One example that exposed the vulnerability inherent in being associated with the Arab side as well as the prospects for success was that of Ahmad Shuqeiri, head of the Washington Arab Office, an official information center for Arab states. Shuqeiri was registered with the U.S. Department of Justice as a foreign agent in fall 1945. The blatantly and increasingly racist *Washington Daily News* described Shuqeiri as a "smoothie" unlike "those Saudi Arabian princes at San Francisco—all ready to hop on a camel and hump it across the desert."[94] The institute's core mission to represent the United States in its relationship with the Arab world set it apart from the Arab Office. However, several members of the institute offered advice to the newly formed Arab states during meetings of the UN Assembly in 1945 and 1946. In addition, intellectuals and statesmen involved with the Arab Office were no strangers to Arab Americans and the United States; among them were Charles Īsawi, the celebrated Princeton academic; Albert Hourani, a seminal historian and participant in the Jerusalem hearings of the Anglo-American Committee of Inquiry; and the well-known, Western-educated Anwar Nashashibi, Cecil Hourani, and Musa al-'Alami.

The Arab Office came under intense attack by the Anti-Nazi League on the right wing of the American Zionist movement. Likewise, neither the institute nor the Arab League, representing Arab states, was spared the onslaught of Zionists simply because they opposed the creation of a Jewish state with a Jewish majority in Palestine when Jews comprised only 35 percent of the population. The Arab side's vulnerability was worsened by being scrutinized constantly. The credibility of the institute was great enough to prompt President Truman to recommend the institute to British Prime Minister Clement Atlee as a viable consultant body.[95] Arab League Secretary General Abdelrahman Azzam considered the institute independent of the Arab Office, which was a lobbying body.[96] A single misstep by Anwar Nashashibi, a Palestinian attached to the Arab Office, of addressing a gathering of the Blue Star Mothers ultimately led to the closure of the Arab Office because Jewish groups considered the women's organization anti-Semitic. The mistake perhaps could have been avoided had the leadership had the awareness not to accept the group's invitation.

The Arab Office, Arab League, and Institute of Arab American Affairs shared basic agreement on larger questions concerning Arab statehood and the fate of Palestine before the founding of Israel in 1948. However, there may have been underlying reasons for a general lack of coordination on all issues. These reasons might have to do with the suspicion the organizations faced due to general ignorance of the U.S. population about the Arab world, Zionists' ongoing aggressive efforts to safeguard their agenda against all detractors, and the intrinsic racism toward foreigners that extended to U.S. foreign policy. All these factors made it easy for the Anti-Nazi League to attack the Arab Office by instigating a raid by the Federal Bureau of Investigation with the help of Illinois Congressman Adolph J. Sabath. The raid frustrated the Arab intelligentsia's pro-Western agenda of seeking to improve Arab-American relations at a crucial juncture in the history of the Middle East,[97] that is, when young nations seeking democratic reforms were assessing their relationship with the West. The institute did not escape alarmist accusations of anti-Semitism by Zionist pundits such as William Safire despite extracting recognition from personnel in the State Department as the representative of a U.S. constituency with legitimate demands.

The tone with which institute activists were attacked became increasingly linked to the activities of the Arab states. Oil wealth and natural sympathies with Palestinians heightened opposition by Zionists, who also sought to undermine any collaboration between Arab Americans and Arab governments. Safire's attacks are a case in point. Implying a collusion between the institute and foreign agents, Safire charged that "where, formerly, Arab propaganda activities were limited and sporadic, within the past 12 months, well-coordinated Arab-American organizations, apparently well-financed, have sprung up with branches in the major cities."[98] Of course, the Arab states were not always keen on defending the larger Arab cause in favor of preserving powerful positions for themselves, as OSS reports accurately noted. None of the Arab governments save Saudi Arabia, where the monarchy enjoyed unwavering U.S. support for strategic national security reasons, was stable, and most would give way to authoritarian military dictatorships by the 1950s. While Zionist organizations received ample funds from their supporters, no record indicates that the institute benefited from Arab governments. Compared to Zionist resources, the institute's remained miniscule, with a maximum budget of $36,636.96 in 1946–1947 and $11,773.28 cash on hand.[99]

Paying for lavish full-page newspaper ads and, according to institute and newspaper reports, stacking debates with Christian Zionists and heckling opponents became commonplace Zionist tactics. Voting power and boycotts initially enabled pro-Zionists to silence most of their detractors despite some internal differences over priorities. The revisionist Hillel Kook's "loud clamor" of support for the War Refugee Board's U.S. efforts to rescue European Jews, for instance, was contested by the Zionist establishment's first priority of establishing the state as agreed in the Biltmore Program.[100] The extent to which the institute withstood attacks in the public sphere illustrates why ongoing Arab American political organizations would be difficult to maintain, notwithstanding periods of heightened alarm or calamity in their ancestral homelands. But more than anything it was persistent individual writing and lobbying by many proponents of Zionist aims on multiple levels and in various settings that yielded results. These efforts were often intended to inflame public sentiments and began to gather steam at the close of the war, when loose ends awaited solution.

On June 7, 1945, the *New York Times* published a set of letters to the editor, "The Levant Crisis Debated," from varying perspectives, including

```
                Institute of Arab American Affairs, Inc.
                  160 BROADWAY    NEW YORK 7, N.Y.


                         FINANCIAL STATEMENT
                                  of
                     THE INSTITUTE OF ARAB AMERICAN AFFAIRS, INC.
                                 from
                         June 1st, 1946 to June 1st, 1947

        Bank Balance 6/1/46                                      $ 8562.01
                                 RECEIPTS

        Contributions..................................$25189.37
        Membership.....................................  1730.00
        Speeches.......................................   913.86
        Pamphlets......................................   202.03
        Entertainment..................................    18.70
        Due Former employees on S/S....................    20.99
                                      TOTAL RECEIPTS            28074.95
                                      TOTAL CASH               $36636.96

                              DISBURSEMENTS

        Printing and Publication...........................$ 2242.50
        Salaries - Officers    $11951.70
                   Office        3566.50 ...................  15518.20
        Traveling Expenses.................................   1166.45
        Part Time Help.....................................    572.61
        General Expense....................................    226.46
        Postage............................................   1054.95
        Furniture and Fixtures.............................    184.69
        Telephone and Telegraph............................    457.52
        Rent...............................................   1443.75
        Advertising and Subscriptions......................    470.00
        Office Expense.....................................   1517.80
        Towel Service......................................      8.75
                                      TOTAL DISBURSEMENTS         $24863.68

        Cash on Deposit........$11705.64-6/1/47
             Petty Cash Balance...   67.64      TOTAL CASH ON HAND   11773.28
```

FIGURE 7.6. *Statement of revenues and expenses for the Institute of Arab American Affairs, 1946–1947. The institute received donations equivalent to more than $258,000 in 2012 dollars, exceeding those of its contemporary Arab American organizations, but it faced a Zionist machine capable of raising millions. Farah Papers, Bawardi Collection.*

Kātibah's.[101] One letter's author, Frederick Eisner, opposed pressuring the French to stop the carnage in Syria and justified the bombing of Damascus as a necessary measure against "disorder." Eisner raised the specter of Nazism and the usual Maronite invocation of Islamic sectarian violence: "Have we indeed reached, only a few weeks after the defeat of Nazis, already a state of affairs where mobs boldly displaying the swastika banner are permitted to attack convents and to stone the very symbol of Christianity?"[102] It mattered little that such an incident was not likely to have taken place in Syria, as the writer's objective was to play on public ignorance. Nazism never took root in Syria, which served, as did Egypt, Jordan, North Africa, and Lebanon, as launching pads for U.S., British, and, once liberated from Nazi occupation, French military operations.

The institute, for its part, mindful of continued massive Jewish immigration to Palestine, periodically petitioned the White House to stop unlimited immigration. As cited in the *New York Times*, the institute made the fateful prediction that after forming a majority in Palestine, "the Jewish state will be automatic" and added, "It is then and only then that Zionists will concede to let the principle of free election and majority rule operate in that country."[103] In another message to President Truman by way of a letter published in the *New York Times*, Khalil Totah charged that Jewish settlement in Palestine was "purely imperialistic" and that Zionist propaganda was a "subterfuge for its [Zionism's] political aims" that predated the postwar Jewish displacement problem.[104] These rebuttals by institute leaders must have seemed meek in the face of emboldened Zionists backed by powerful politicians like Herbert Hoover, who suggested transferring Palestinians to Iraq as a solution.[105]

Totah, the institute's executive director, and his friend Rabbi Elmer Berger of the Council for Judaism said hecklers made debates an unpleasant ordeal for all opponents of Zionism. Berger and Khloussi Khairy of the League of Arab States (Arab League) were "howled down" by a disapproving audience in a debate with Louis Lipsky and other Zionists.[106] Police officers patrolled the debate halls to keep order such as during a radio broadcast by WJZ. Both Berger and Totah recalled the unfair tactics employed against them in their memoirs. Berger empathized with the Palestinian Totah's frustration in the face of intimidation and maltreatment by hosts and audiences alike. He cited Totah's recollection of an event arranged by the B'nai B'rith in which two Zionists, who spoke well beyond their allotted time, and Professor Harlow, an ardent Christian Zionist, outnumbered him.[107] During the debate, Totah's stock argument that Jews and Arabs lived in peace until the advent of Zionism must have seemed immaterial to reinvigorated supporters of Zionism, as did his arguments that controlled Jewish immigration to Palestine should not override the majority's hopes of equality, let alone drive Palestinians into exile in two years.

The institute bore the brunt of well-financed programs by the Zionist side. As early as June 1945, a campaign to raise $4 million to combat anti-

Semitism by reaching every man, woman, and child in the United States was launched by the Joint Defense Appeal of the American Jewish Committee and the Anti-Defamation League of B'nai B'rith.[108] While news media reported on the effort, a confidential memorandum from Philip Chasin to its chairman, Nathan M. Ohrback, described it as a "gigantic undertaking that requires facilities, strongly constructed . . . built up over a period of ten years of special techniques and experience in defense work."[109] Chasin helped organize fund-raising for the Anti-Defamation League of B'nai B'rith. In 1941 he became the executive director of fund-raising for the Joint Defense Appeal sponsored by the American Jewish Committee and the Anti-Defamation League.[110] To opponents of Zionism, the professed reach of Chasin's program had a chilling effect. In the ostensibly confidential memo he did not mince words in using anti-Nazism as the pretext for such a huge undertaking while anti-Nazi sentiments were still fresh: "Every dollar spent today has greater fighting value in terms of tomorrow. There is no better time to capitalize on the momentum of the nation's anti-Nazi feeling than today."[111] The "militant effort to expose and destroy anti-democratic forces in America" was presented by Chasin as a

> high-powered educational program, geared to reach every man, woman, and child every day of the year, . . . a program through the press, . . . over radio, . . . through advertising . . . comic books . . . schools . . . speakers . . . community services . . . movies . . . churches . . . labor . . . and special groups, . . . a program that expands in accordance with expanded needs. This is a coordinated defense program . . . involving professional techniques and mass media geared to reach all the 136,000,000 American men, women and children.[112]

The memorandum goes on to list accomplishments under the project to that point in 1945:

> We have averaged more than 56,000 individual stations broadcasts this year [as of June 1945] as against 60,000 last year, averaging more than 216 individual station broadcasts a day . . . every day in the year! Our series of 26 full-page ads are now running in 397 newspapers, as contrasted with 234 in the preceding year, with a current total of 2,000 insertions as against 1,000 last year, and now reaching a total dollar value of advertising space estimated at $691,520. This campaign is now appearing as a series of twelve posters on 1,000 billboards being displayed in 130 cities and valued at $250,000. It has been readapted on 16,000 car cards, being displayed in the transportation system of 24 cities, through space on payroll envelopes, blotters, and millions of matchbook covers.

Chasin reported that "all newspapers and magazines are covered including 1,900 dailies with 43,000,000 in circulation—the rural press, the foreign language press, the Negro press, the labor press—with 10,000,000 readers receiving and using some material from the division."[113] In addition, 330,000 books and 9 million pamphlets were distributed to "libraries and institutions where they are accessible to the public," and the organizers arranged for speakers through nonprofit lecture bureaus to address 7,200 audiences for a total listening audience of 30 million. Through the cooperation of comic-book publishers and writers in adapting their material, the committee produced and distributed 6 million comic books. The memo listed the activities of the Legal Investigation Division, apparently the spying arm of the Anti-Defamation League, to collect information on detractors of the Joint Defense Appeal's views. Chasin explained the investigation as part of the "defense program, whereas, all such detractions are deemed to be 'manifestations of anti-Semitism'"; that is, all criticisms of Zionists were deemed anti-Semitic and used to "guide over-all operations of the defense program." Chasin disclosed in his memo that the Research Division of the Anti-Defamation League (ADL) project stored 20,000 volumes and more than 2 million "individual items of pertinent information to the defense program, catalogued in the clipping file over a period of ten years—rare official documents sought after by government agencies, analysts, and writers."[114]

Aware of this massive undertaking,[115] which now enjoyed cover by the ADL, a large Jewish American civil rights institution, Totah lamented in his memoir that the institute "could only manage to insert an advertisement of one-half page in the *New York Times* in its five-year history. Even that half-page was paid for by a Jew."[116] The League for Peace with Justice in Palestine obtained full-page ads pleading in large bold letters: "ZIONISTS MISLEADING WORLD WITH UNTRUTHS FOR PALESTINE CONQUEST. Urgent that Americans be informed at once of facts concealed by Zionists vital to solution of problem of displaced persons."[117] The institute managed to run some ads after 1948, one of which appeared in the *Waterbury Republican*. The bold letters in this ad read: "Who Are the Aggressors Now?" The rest of the ad blames the incursion of Zionist forces well beyond the partition plan of 1947 after a short, uneven war against ill-equipped Arab forces on the "naiveté" of Americans that "led them to believe that Zionists would sit perfectly content with a partitioned Palestine as recommended by the United Nations General Assembly on November 29, 1947."[118] The apparently sporadic ads pale when compared with hundreds of pro-Zionist ads. For example, a group called the Nonsectarian Anti-Nazi League ran an ad with the title "Arab Fascist Propaganda in America Exposed."[119] In a shot across the bow of established German Jews, one ad declared: "Letter to the Terrorist of Palestine," telling Menachem Begin's Haganah that "the Jews of America are for you [except] the rich Jews."[120] To keep pressure on the British in Palestine, other ads by Zionists targeted British attempts to secure a desperately needed loan from the United States to address the war's devastation in England. One read, "Kill that Loan, Lest You Forsake Your Conscience," inducing House Majority Leader John William McCormack to oppose the loan in Congress to financially strapped Britain.[121]

Ads became celebratory once Israel was declared a state in Palestine in May 1948. An advertisement titled "Gained Glory for Israel. Chief On Good Will Mission to U.S." from the Reception Committee for Menachem Begin was signed by hundreds in welcoming a man who was on Britain's wanted list for terrorist acts. The ad termed Begin's actions a "revolutionary war . . . as long as Israel had not gained its complete independence in Palestine's historic boundaries."[122] Zionists who maintained extreme views left no doubt that their objectives had not been met since some parts of historic Palestine were still inhabited by Palestinians. Establishing a Jewish state in Palestine as a solution to historic persecution or anti-Semitism in Europe became palatable enough to either justify or ignore the expulsion of Palestinians from Palestine's major cities and the flattening of hundreds of villages in 1948.[123]

Amid heated and chronically uneven debates in the United States over the partition issue and Jewish immigration to Palestine, two groups figured prominently on the Arab Americans' side, calling on all to heed the Palestinians' voices. For this, they did not escape the dubious attention of the ADL. The first was the Committee for Peace and Justice in the Holy Land, chaired by Virginia Gildersleeve, with Kermit Roosevelt Jr., grandson of Teddy Roosevelt, on its board. The second was the League for Peace with Justice in Palestine, headed by Benjamin Freedman, an anti-Zionist Jewish American from New York.

True to Chasin's plans of employing various methods of dealing with critics of Israel, the B'nai B'rith, albeit espousing a civil rights agenda that effectively kept in check racists and anti-Semitic extremists, made spying and confronting critics of Israel a major objective. The background for this posture dates to a decision by the Jewish Agency between 1945 and 1947—in agreement with the Biltmore Program—that the "Jewish state would have to be seized by force."[124] This strategic decision, though, amounted to a very effective low-intensity war on the weakened British and the poorly armed Palestinians and employed the considerable resources of American Zionists for public relations campaigns. Hence, methods used by the ADL to combat anti-Semitism came to include lumping critics of Zionism within the category of anti-Semites. The organization's official monthly reports for May and June 1948 were titled "Anti-Semitism and the Palestine Issue," parts 1 and 2.[125] The dense twenty- and twenty-nine-page reports followed the activities of the Committee for Peace and Justice in the Holy Land, specifically Virginia Gildersleeve, Kermit Roosevelt, Bayard Dodge (former president of the American University of Beirut), and Max Thornburg. Further, the May report identified Pentagon employees and civil servants who opposed the partitioning of Palestine, among them Captain Michael Fielding, Colonel Charles Wellington Furlong, and Colonel Ronald V. C. Bodley. The list in the June report is even longer. It named Merwin Hart, Upton Close, Gerald Smith, Gerald Winrod, Lawrence H. Smith, Ed Gossett, and John Rankin, in addition to the Institute of Arab American Affairs, the Arab Office, and Freedman's League for Peace, along with Ḥabīb I. Kātibah, identified as a member of the ANL and now the institute.

The last item in the May report was dedicated to opposition to Zionism in the *Bergen Evening Record*, the *Arizona Star*, and the *Chicago Tribune*: "While anti-Zionism and sympathy for the Arab cause are not necessarily indicative of anti-Semitic prejudice, there are many whose pro-Arab utterances and activities have contained sufficient expressed or implied anti-Semitism to give cause for concern."[126] Similarly vague language implicated Gildersleeve and Roosevelt: "In several instances, anti-Semitism has been read into some anti-Zionist attitudes which stem from ostensibly sincere opposition to the establishment of the Jewish State."[127] The report goes on to postulate that Gildersleeve and Kermit Roosevelt "may be contributing to the increase of anti-Jewish sentiment in the United States."[128]

The seemingly nuanced language of the ADL reports—for example, that sympathy for the Arab cause was not necessarily indicative of anti-Semitic prejudice—did not preclude spying on these Arab sympathizers. The rationale for spying was that their opinions opposing Zionism could contribute to anti-Semitism. The two-part report, taken in its entirety, implicitly called for reprisals against Israel's critics while acknowledging the "caliber of those who have indicated their approval of [Gildersleeve's] Committee's stand on Palestine." An example of anti-Jewish sentiment in the report was that of Congressman Ed Gossett (D-Texas), who drew "unsolicited support of bigoted groups" and was deemed an anti-Semite from the Zionist point of view because of a speech he delivered in the U.S. House of Representatives on April 8, 1948. Gossett made reference to a recent "historic statement" on the Arab position issued by Hajj Amin al-Husseini, whom the ADL report described as the "notorious anti-Semite and Nazi collaborator, the Grand

Mufti of Jerusalem." More egregiously, the ADL report continues, "Gossett urged a reading of the Grand Mufti's statement and inserted the full text into the Congressional Record."[129] There is no evidence that the report explored the content of Husseini's statement. Although the ADL report distinguished between Gildersleeve's and Freedman's groups, it deemed their statements to be "sufficiently complementary for joint dissemination" without providing evidence that they in fact were issued jointly.[130] The convoluted reports of B'nai B'rith were even less equivocal in their condemnation of the Institute of Arab American Affairs, described as a successor to the ANL; ADL monitoring of the institute was summarized in its "Facts" report of June 1946.

In the aftermath of the proclamation of the state of Israel, the June ADL report listed the institute at the top of suspect organizations without mention of the Arab American organization's advocacy of coexistence with Jews in a binational state: "The bitter struggle [for] Israel . . . has proved a bonanza to anti-Semites. . . . They have unleashed a fresh attack against Jewry in recent months, compounded of distortions and malice."[131] Although no specific examples were provided of anti-Jewish bigotry by the institute in the report, the most virulent condemnation was leveled against the institute for adding "the pro-Arab fanatic" Benjamin Freedman, a Jew from New York, to the board. The report noted the addition of "notable Americans" to the institute's advisory board as well.

The tone and large volume of pro-Israel commentary can be quantified when incidents of intimidation as a result of this pressure are documented. The tone and content of *New York Times* coverage of the Arab-Israeli conflict, for example, tilted sharply in favor of Zionism after an effective boycott nearly bankrupted the newspaper. The publisher of the *New York Times*, Arthur Hays Sulzberger, refused to support the creation of Israel because he believed it would create problems for Jewish Americans who were woven into the fabric of U.S. society.[132] When Sulzberger made good on his beliefs by canceling an advertisement submitted by the American League for a Free Palestine, a U.S. front for the militant Irgun Zvai Leumi led by Menachem Begin, the newspaper suffered a massive and effective boycott by mostly Eastern European department store advertisers. The correspondence and records from this "frightening experience," as executives of the newspaper referred to the boycott, were "locked away . . . in a safe in the *Times*' offices."[133] Hence, unlike the Arab American activists who found it increasingly difficult to juxtapose their political work with a coherent strategy by leaders in Palestine or the emergent Arab states, Zionists' large following in the United States and coherent political plans of focusing on creating a state became a jointly engaged front of participants with largely similar goals. The United States was one front in this battle. Palestine was another.

While Arab Americans confronted opposition at home, the Irgun under the command of Menachem Begin, a recent Polish settler in Palestine, was joined by the Lehi (Stern) gang to target Palestinian civilians and British personnel for violence after the war.[134] That was the backdrop for assassination campaigns that included the aforementioned killing of Lord Moyne, the British minister of state for the Middle East, and the bombing of the King David Hotel in Jerusalem that killed scores of Palestinians, Jewish civilians, and British nationals.[135] These actions in part pressed the war-fatigued British to instruct Foreign Secretary Ernest Bevin to refer the matter of Palestine to the United Nations. The British seemed to recognize their mistake in having aided the Zionists and now intended, it seemed, to rectify the situation by advocating for a democratic state with majority rule, as attempted with the Peel Commission and the prewar white paper. Arab Americans reacted by attempting to throw in their lot as proud citizens with America's rising prestige on the eve of another redrawing of the political map in Palestine. However, the British were weakened by the war to an extent that rendered them secondary to the emerging superpower status of the United States and Russia.

Even Jewish communists in Palestine who in the 1920s condemned Zionism as an imperialist tool did not defy mobilization behind the Jewish state. They changed their position after World War II. Misguided ideals by these communists of raising the status of Palestinian *fellāhin* under the banner of socialism facilitated Jewish communists' support for an early brand of idealistic Zionism.[136] Jewish nationalism won over international proletarianism, in the later view of Natan Sharansky, a right-wing Russian immigrant who became an Israeli politician.[137] The once pro-worker Jewish idealists conveniently rejected the ideal of a democratic binational state. Thus, nuanced and varied interpretations of Zionism consolidated further behind an exclusively Jewish state.

Overall, the relatively small number of Arab immigrants and the weakness of the Arab states rendered dissemination of the institute's position on the core issue of Palestine untenable. As indicated in the introduction, unlocking the orientations and interests of the U.S.-born generation requires separate research. Arab Americans observed how Truman followed the Roosevelt administration's policy of cultivating friendships with Arab regimes for the ends of containment and securing access to Saudi oil. Truman maintained Roosevelt's tacit assurance to the Saudis that the United States would not make any fundamental changes to its policy in the Middle East. Support to Zionism was the exception, as was the case when the United States endorsed the San Remo Agreement, which legalized the League of Nations and the Balfour Declaration. High policies of the Cold War contributed to the rise of corrupt military regimes in the Arab countries. While Arab Americans envisioned a unified and reformed Arab world, the wealthy Saudi ruling family did not share these visions at a time when the region's economy relied increasingly on oil revenues. U.S. interest, too, would not have been served by assertive and transparent democracies as much as by ensuring the survival of friendly regimes. Maintaining friendly regimes meant that insurgents were targeted by a hostile U.S. foreign policy in what became known as the Truman Doctrine. It did not matter to the U.S. government if insurgents were not communists or that they enjoyed popular support at home. The emergent political status, suffice it to say, was contrasted by well-informed Jewish voters in New York and the motivation to match.

Jewish Americans gained access to Roosevelt and later Truman and ensured the same to Theodore Herzl, Rabbi Wise, and the radical Rabbi Hillel Silver. The outcome of their access was the rejection on behalf of the Zionist movement of any white paper on Palestine and attainment of "justice" for the Jews seeking "a Jewish national home."[138] Persistent lobbying of Congress by a large constituent of mostly Eastern European Jewish immigrants affected a final turn in American policy during Truman's term after the president was "hounded," as the Israeli ambassador in Washington, Michael Oren, put it, by Zionists and their allies to give in to their demands on Palestine.[139] The Truman administration's hesitation before sending the fact-finding Anglo-American Committee of Inquiry to Palestine was met with alarm and accusations by Silver and others that Truman was balking on supporting a Jewish commonwealth.[140] Voting power made this alarm tangible.

For their part, key lawmakers responded to the domestic reality of a large constituency seeking a Jewish commonwealth by working to ensure the success of the Zionist program, often by sponsoring preemptive initiatives. The Wagner-Taft bipartisan resolution favoring a Jewish state in Palestine was an attempt to preempt the British, the UN, the White House, and professional diplomats in the U.S. government. The senators accompanied their move with a speaking tour, further restricting the State Department's options,[141] while acting on their own preference of supporting Zionist aims. Seeking to forge a U.S. political path, Undersecretary of State Dean Acheson welcomed any comments and suggestions from a host of Jewish and Arab Americans to the Anglo-American Committee of Inquiry, including any from the institute, after inviting the same from representatives of friendly

Arab governments and Zionist organizations.[142] However, an even-handed approach or the mere admission of a large number of Jews into Palestine did little to satisfy Zionists who "accused the Committee of sacrificing their political aspirations to charity."[143] The result was a statement in Truman's Yom Kippur address on October 4, 1947, calling for a "viable Jewish state in an adequate area of Palestine."[144] Hence, Truman signaled his acquiescence to the Jewish state and left the size of the adequate area to be decided on the ground with little interference from outside.

The hearings before the Anglo-American Committee of Inquiry were an occasion for Palestinian representatives like Jamal Bey al-Husseini to work with Khalil Totah and Judah Magnes on refuting demands by David Ben-Gurion, Golda Meyerson (later Meir), and others for exclusive statehood over a to-be-determined part of Palestine. After the Anglo-American Committee concluded its work, conditions worsened, from the Palestinian and Arab American standpoint, with dizzying speed. The short-lived Morrison-Grady Plan to settle 100,000 Jews and partition Palestine into three autonomous enclaves was refuted by Rabbi Abba Hillel Silver. He effectively killed the plan by demanding access to all parts of Palestine and open-ended immigration, adding this ultimatum: "For the Jews of Europe it is now Palestine or death."[145]

From a nationalist Arab perspective, the events after World War II that led up to the establishment of Israel amounted to another bout of further dismemberment of the former Natural Syria by colonialists. This time around, the UN Special Committee on Palestine replaced the League of Nations in deciding the political map of Palestine. The special committee recommended partition, but before the UN Security Council voted on the question, Britain announced its withdrawal date from Palestine,[146] thus giving Zionists a timetable to declare statehood and removing any incentive for flexibility or further talk of binational statehood. The institute targeted one of two U.S. officials, Secretary of State George C. Marshall, who foresaw a protracted conflict and the possibility of U.S. military entanglement to keep the peace if a Jewish state was declared over the objection of Palestine's majority inhabitants. Two months before the UN issued its partition plan, Resolution 181, Totah wrote to the secretary of state urging a strategic perspective on the region's stability. He used the example of Zionist militarism of the Stern operative Rabbi Baruch Korff, who plotted to bomb London in July 1947 in retaliation for the British refusing entry to the *Exodus*, a ship loaded with Jewish refugees.[147] Totah criticized what he termed "recruiting volunteers," that is, the *Exodus*, to defy Britain, a U.S. ally, and he made the case that risking alienation of the Middle East by giving in to Zionist plans

> **Institute of Arab American Affairs, Inc.**
> 160 BROADWAY NEW YORK 7, N.Y.
>
> ANNUAL REPORT
> INSTITUTE OF ARAB AMERICAN AFFAIRS
> JUNE, 1948
>
> This organization has entered upon its fifth year of existence. Its last four years have been critical and exciting, but the year which we have just completed is, perhaps, the most disturbing and discouraging to us who are working for Arab American friendship. This is so because we have seen our United States government dealing this friendship an almost deadly blow on November 29, 1947, when it went out of its way to press the U.N. into favoring the partition of Palestine. A few months later Arab-American friendship gained a new lease on life, only to be staggered by President Truman's recognition of the Jewish State. As things stand at present, mutual understanding between our old homes and our new country is being subjected to a great strain. Therefore, it is here that we come in to accomplish our mission of serving "as a medium of good will between the U.S.A. and the Arabic-speaking countries."
>
> We are often faced with the query "what are you doing at the Institute?" Though sometimes asked in a critical and disparaging tone, it is a fair question and here is the answer:
>
> 1. PUBLICATIONS
>
>   It is said that the pen is mightier than the sword. Proceeding on this theory, it might be said that our major effort is expended in pen work as is shown by the following publications:
>
>   PAPERS ON PALESTINE III 67pp. which is a collection of articles by distinguished Jews who oppose political Zionism.
>
>   Kermit Roosevelt's article "Partition of Palestine" 16pp.
>
>   Dean Gildersleeve's letter to the Times, January 22, 1948.
>
>   Dr. C.R. Watson's article "The Partition of Palestine".
>
>   Rev. C.T. Bridgeman "When Solomon Nodded".
>
>   Peace for the Holy Land; 3000 reprints of this advertisement by Gildersleeve-Roosevelt Committee.
>
>   America and the United Jewish Appeal: a most significant editorial by the Arizona Daily Star condemning the Zionist program. Sent to all subscribers as well as editors of every newspaper in the United States.
>
>   Eleven Christian Groups in Zion Hit Partition - 2 column story in the New York Post.
>
>   Speech in Congress by Lawrence Smith (distributed)

FIGURE 7.7. *Page 1 of the Institute of Arab American Affairs' annual report, June 1948. The page bears Khalil Totah's opening remarks about the deepening dilemma for Arab Americans in general and the institute in particular. In the four-page report Totah reports some gains but concludes on the last page that "a sense of defeatism is encountered.... The voice of the Institute is practically the only one in this country which is boldly crying for much needed Arab American friendship." Farah Papers, Bawardi Collection.*

would nullify the Truman Doctrine's aim to contain communism: "for if we are right in guarding the door in Greece and Turkey against interference . . . we would be right in defending the other door . . . in Arab lands and defending the rights of Arab majority against the Zionist minority."[148]

If the institute made an impact in the United States, neither UNSCOP nor its principal secretary, the "influential" Ralph Bunche, who experienced an "emotional identity" with the Zionists,[149] ever had to consider the Palestinian side. In fact, much of the Palestinian leadership was still reeling in exile. Moreover, those who expelled them, the British, now decided to remain aloof from all the proceedings of the UN Security Council and the eleven U.S.-picked UNSCOP members. UNSCOP resolved to grant more than half of Palestine's landmass as a giveaway to the Jewish minority, which at the time owned 6 percent of the land. Truman, in defiance of State Department and Pentagon officials who opposed the drastic UNSCOP land grant to the Zionists, launched an extensive lobbying effort in support of partition.[150] At the same time, the Zionists successfully secured the support of friendly members of Congress, who "pressured UN delegates with threats of the withdrawal of US economic assistance from their countries if they did not vote for the UNSCOP proposal."[151] Small countries that relied on the United States for voting rights in the UN—Cuba, Haiti, and Ethiopia among them—"were threatened with the loss of American financial and political backing if they failed to approve the partition."[152] Ten senators acted in unison to pressure the Philippines, and "thirty-one leaned on Greece" for the same purpose.[153] The Arab League assumed responsibility for filling the political gap left by Britain's destruction of the Palestinian leadership.

Britain declared the termination of the mandate on May 15, 1948, before the UN General Assembly voted on the UNSCOP partition plan. Completely unchecked due to British weariness after World War II and attacks by the Zionist fighters, the Haganah launched a series of raids on Arab population centers, inviting whatever resistance the Palestinians could muster. The Haganah and Zvai Leumi, now working in concert, filled the vacuum created by the British failure with frightening efficiency. In one documented massacre of 250 mostly elderly residents and women and children in the village of Deir Yaseen, they created fear in major Palestinian population centers.[154] The post-boycott *New York Times* was typical of the insensitive U.S. news coverage of the incident, reporting the massacre as "house-to-house fighting" under a headline in what became characteristically antiseptic language: "200 Arabs Killed, Stronghold Taken."[155] Over the past two decades, more Israeli historians have come to terms with this and other atrocities as a larger campaign of terror to evict Palestinians from their lands.

During the Zionist movement's intense lobbying effort to secure a state, President Truman, who is largely remembered as a friend of Israel for extending U.S. recognition upon its founding, occasionally lashed out against the relentless pressure by refusing to speak to the Zionist leaders and suspending all arms sales to the Middle East, which had a much larger impact on Israel as the largest beneficiary of these arms shipments.[156] The president relented to his old partner in haberdashery, Eddy Jacobson, by agreeing to receive Jacobson's friend Rabbi Silver only to watch Silver storm into the Oval Office and pound on the president's desk with his fist. This incident in 1947 led the president to complain that "terror and Rabbi Silver are the contributing causes of some, if not all, of our troubles."[157] Severely lagging in popularity, Truman knew to keep similar sentiments to himself for the 1948 election. In his diary, only recently unearthed, he complained about the intensity of lobbying by American Zionists: "The Jews, I find are very, very selfish. They care not how many Estonians, Latvians, Finns, Poles, Yugoslavs or Greeks get murdered or mistreated as D[isplaced] P[ersons] as long as the Jews get special treatment. Yet when they have power, physical, financial or political, neither Hitler nor Stalin has anything on them for cruelty or mistreatment to the underdog."[158]

On May 12, when declaration of Jewish statehood loomed, Truman called in Secretary of State Marshall and Undersecretary Robert Lovett, as well as two staunch proponents of Zionism, Clark Clifford and David Niles. Marshall made his best case against recognition of Israel as a state, alerting the president that this would be seen as a "very transparent attempt to win the Jewish vote."[159]

In the lead-up to the war of 1948 in Palestine, the Haganah's far superior numbers and advanced weaponry routed the 21,500 bedraggled Arab soldiers, roughly a third the number of the Zionist forces, who came from neighboring Arab states.[160] In 1948 anywhere from 78 to 83 percent (800,000 to 1,200,000) of all Palestinians living in Palestine either fled as a result of Deir Yaseen and other massacres or were expelled.[161] Despite the violence, the newly homeless Palestinians did not expect that their ordeal would last very long. They had no reason to suspect they would spend the rest of their lives as refugees. Accounts of these events in the discourse belonged mainly to Palestinian historians until recently. The large body of literature favoring Zionism, with explicit backing from the ADL and other Jewish groups friendly to Zionism in the United States, made it very difficult to disseminate accurate information on the 1948 Palestinian Nakbah. Other historians strained to communicate the stories of the Palestinians who led productive lives, went to universities, practiced all kinds of trades and industries, owned homes in which they lived for generations, and possessed distinctive culture with their own foods, folk arts, stories, dance, and literature.[162] Hence, remembrances of Palestine became a contested terrain from the outset and added a new dimension to the divide between Arab Americans and a growing number of Jewish Americans who felt that supporting Israel at all costs was a fitting response to representations of the Holocaust.

The institute survived through 1948 and the end of 1949, likely due to the desperate need for aid by newly orphaned and homeless Palestinians. On the U.S. public scene, the institute spent far more time defending itself and the Arab side than expanding its reach, as Faris Malouf had hoped to do. Friends of the Arab side did not fare any better. An incident that was casually reported by the *New York Times* offers a perspective on their hardships. Feeling harassed by fellow New Yorkers for his views on Palestine, Benjamin Freedman brought suit against his detractors, the Nonsectarian Anti-Nazi League, just when tensions were running high in 1948. Because of the general revulsion toward Nazism, opponents of the Zionists became fair game for intense criticism, as happened to Freedman during his litigation. During the court proceedings, a note he wrote to himself on the edge of a newspaper article brought ridicule and humiliation: "It was worth all the effort." The newspaper article was titled "U.S. Reassures Arabs on Any Palestine Shift." Somehow, this note and the article found their way to the court and served as damning evidence against Freedman. The note helped paint Freedman as an agent for the Arabs by the defense attorney of the Anti-Nazi League, and that label was thereafter used systematically to draw attention away from Palestinians. His association with Kātibah and the institute, which the B'nai B'rith monitored closely, was just as damning. In court, Freedman, who was born Jewish but received Catholic training, was pressed to answer what his religion was. When he labored to explain his background, the magistrate, Hyman Bushel, derisively stated to him, "Oh, I see, the Jews put you out, but the Catholics won't have you."[163] The alarmist title of the article about the incident in the *New York Times* is another example: "Witness Admits to Aiding Arab Cause."

An unqualified setback in Palestine that resonated among the immigrants was the murder of Count Bernadotte, the UN mediator. He had built his reputation by rescuing thousands of Jews and soldiers from Nazi prisons. In his June 28 proposal for UN partition plans, Bernadotte included "the suggestion that Jerusalem be placed under Jordanian rule, since all of the area around the city was designated for the Arab state."[164] For his efforts, he was killed by members of the militant Lehi (Stern) gang;[165] the assassination caused shock and added to the frustration of the Arab Americans.[166]

Khalil Totah's reactions in the *New York Times* to the Zionists' triumph in Palestine ranged from introspective laments and recollections of the dismal roles played by the superpowers.[167] He warned of future war if the Palestinians' mounting grievances were not addressed, but his warnings were based on Arab political resolve and military capabilities that were mere illusions until the 1948 reality and the weakness of the Arab forces hit home.[168]

As aid efforts preceded the creation of the New Syria Party and the Arab National League, they now became a major running concern for the institute throughout its existence. Aid activity deepened in 1947 when Zionist militants increased their attacks, taxing the organization's meager resources. In February 1948 Flint's branch of the institute received Judge Abbasi and Isa Nakhleh, a representative of the Arab Higher Committee to the United Nations. Arab Americans in Flint helped the visitors raise money for Palestinian children orphaned by British militarism or attacks by Zionist militants.[169] Their visit was followed by Shafiq Mansour's visit to the Detroit YMCA seeking funds for the General Arab Orphans Committee in Palestine. Like the Arab Americans in Flint and the population in Palestine, the institute in New York was ill prepared for the events of May 1948, when Israel was declared a state. The organization's membership rosters still reflected a healthy count for 1947–1948, and the financial statement for the fiscal year ending in May 1948 showed an income of $27,583.27, expenses of $24,733.28, and a net savings of $14,506.82,[170] a slight decrease from the previous year's receipts and cash flow but still enough to run the office. Money was only one side of the story, though. The future turned bleak by May 14, 1948, the day that marked Israel's statehood covering 70 percent of historic Palestine. The shock of displacing most of the Palestinian population and the prospects of losing entire cities to Jewish settlers must have seemed unfathomable.[171]

Deep feelings of humiliation and a sense of loss set in wherever Arabs resided after the quick defeat of the Arab armies. Most Palestinians from the Galilee, Haifa, Jaffa, and 'Akka became refugees almost overnight. In the minutes of the annual meeting of the institute's board of directors on June 5, 1948, institute president Faris Malouf responded to questions as to whether the Institute of Arab American Affairs should continue with its work. He pleaded that in the next ten years there would be a far greater need for the institute than ever before, and he suggested a long-range plan.[172] By June 11, minutes of the executive board meeting emitted an aura of gloom and dismay. For unknown reasons, Kermit Roosevelt resigned from the advisory board of the institute, and it was resolved by the board to request that Benjamin Freedman withdraw his membership. The committee discussed the

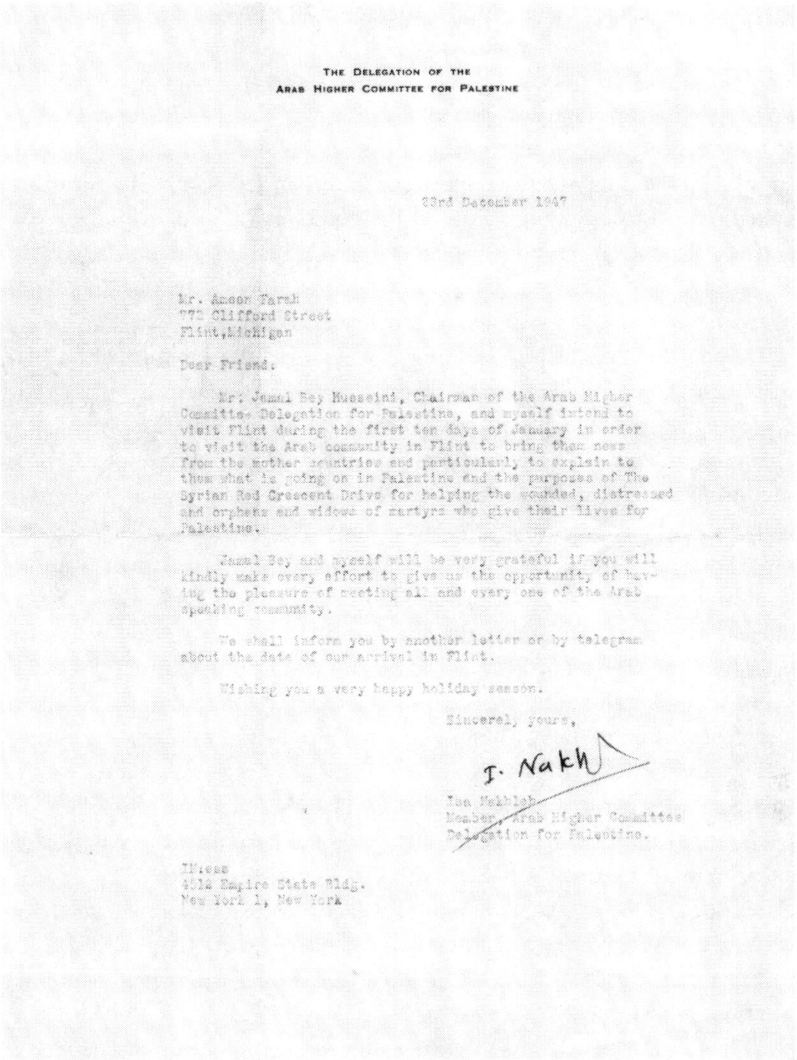

THE DELEGATION OF THE
ARAB HIGHER COMMITTEE FOR PALESTINE

23rd December 1947

Mr. Ameen Farah
772 Clifford Street
Flint, Michigan

Dear Friend:

Mr: Jamal Bey Husseini, Chairman of the Arab Higher Committee Delegation for Palestine, and myself intend to visit Flint during the first ten days of January in order to visit the Arab community in Flint to bring them news from the mother countries and particularly to explain to them what is going on in Palestine and the purposes of The Syrian Red Crescent Drive for helping the wounded, distressed and orphans and widows of martyrs who give their lives for Palestine.

Jamal Bey and myself will be very grateful if you will kindly make every effort to give us the opportunity of having the pleasure of meeting all and every one of the Arab speaking community.

We shall inform you by another letter or by telegram about the date of our arrival in Flint.

Wishing you a very happy holiday season.

Sincerely yours,

I. Nakhleh

Isa Nakhleh
Member, Arab Higher Committee
Delegation for Palestine.

IN:ema
4512 Empire State Bldg.
New York 1, New York

FIGURE 7.8. *Letter from Isa Nakhleh to Ameen Farah, 1947. Ameen Farah was known to the Arab Higher Committee in Palestine not just from his old association with Jamal Bey al-Husseini but also through his work for the NSP and ANL. Nakhleh emphasizes the importance of Flint's "Arab speaking community," a label that now covered residents of Syrian, Lebanese, and Palestinian origins. Farah Papers, Bawardi Collection.*

future of the institute at length, and by a vote of 5 to 4 defeated a motion to continue with work as before. However, the board decided to keep Khalil Totah as executive director until September to dedicate $2,000 for ads outside the New York metropolitan area and to work on coordinating aid collection campaigns in order to avoid competition and conflicts among societies seeking aid from Arab Americans and their friends.[173] The institute's annual report listed publications on the events in Palestine including "Papers of Palestine III" and the critical editorial "America and the United Jewish Appeal" in the *Arizona Daily Star* (hence the interest by the B'nai B'rith in this newspaper), as well as many accomplishments.

Despite the "critical and exciting" five years of the institute's life, 1948 was, according to the institute's report, "perhaps the most disturbing and discouraging to [those] who are working for Arab American friendship. This is so because we have seen our United States government dealing this friendship an almost deadly blow on November 29, 1947, when it went out of its way to press the UN into favoring the partition of Palestine."[174] In the same year, the Flint chapter of the American Middle East Relief Organization, headquartered at 777 United Nations Plaza, New York, was incorporated and began raising funds along with other chapters for relief and works projects.[175] By the end of 1949, William E. Hocking and Virginia C. Gildersleeve sent a letter urging renewed support, despite the calamity, to maintain the function of the institute.

The year 1949 was also a dismal one as hopes of regaining even a part of Palestine through diplomacy were lost and with that loss, any hope that the Arab armies would amount to anything when confronting the superior Zionists. Arab Americans watched as the Israelis annexed Jerusalem and declared the city Israel's capital. Henceforth the Zionists claimed ownership of the city. "It is to be hoped," Ben-Gurion warned, "the General Assembly will correct the mistake which its majority made and will make no attempt whatsoever to impose a regime on Jerusalem against the will of its people."[176] Thus the city that had defied a single religious dominance throughout its documented history became Jewish.

The institute's December 1949 bulletin boldly posted the headline "Israel Is Aligned against the Whole World," with this statement under it: "We are not surprised at Israel's flagrant defiance of the United Nations' resolution to internationalize Jerusalem." The bulletin proceeded to recall the largely forgotten murder of Count Bernadotte, Israel's "flouting" of UN resolutions on returning territories it occupied illegally, and "the vital matter of looted Arab homes, confiscated property, and money in banks, which Israel refused to release. Now comes Jerusalem!"[177] The bulletin reported on

TELEPHONE BARCLAY 7-6456

Institute of Arab American Affairs, Inc.

160 BROADWAY   NEW YORK 7, N. Y.

HONORARY PRESIDENT
FARIS S. MALOUF

PRESIDENT
JOHN HAZAM

VICE PRESIDENT
JOSEPH SADO

TREASURER
EISSA A. BATEH

ADVISORY BOARD

CHAIRMAN
WILLIAM E. HOCKING
MADISON, N. H.

VIRGINIA GILDERSLEEVE
NEW YORK CITY

FRED GOODSELL
BOSTON, MASS.

JOHN H. LATHROP
BROOKLYN, N. Y.

ROBERT McCLENAHAN
PHILADELPHIA, PA.

KERMIT ROOSEVELT
WASHINGTON, D.C.

WILBERT SMITH
WILMINGTON, DEL.

WALTER T. STACE
PRINCETON, N. J.

MAX THORNBURG
NEW YORK CITY

GLORA WYSNER
NEW YORK CITY

EXECUTIVE DIRECTOR
KHALIL TOTAH

December 1st, 1949

Dear Friend:

    Now as never before American public opinion needs to be informed, needs to know the real issues in the Middle East, to be based on fact rather than emotion or fancy. If it is not so informed, our government may be misled into policies which are inimical to our genuine interests. This danger is real.

    The Institute of Arab American Affairs of 160 Broadway, New York City, is an American organization devoted to placing the truth before the American people. It has done so with distinction and success for five years. It has appeared on the radio, on the platform, in churches and clubs. It has a monthly Bulletin and has put out nine publications. It watches the press and has had many letters to the editor published. It is a valuable information center which is the only one of its kind in the United States. Its work is needed now more than ever. It must go on. The enclosed "ad" is an indication of how American public opinion is changing.

    But today the Institute is in desperate need of funds to carry on. If it cannot get them, the result may be grave harm to our people. We are, therefore, appealing to our fellow Americans to come to the aid of this work quickly and generously.

    Enclosed is an envelope in which you can send your contributions. We earnestly ask you not to delay. Every day counts. This needed work must continue.

Sincerely yours,

William Earnest Hocking
Chairman
Board of Advisers

Virginia C. Gildersleeve
Member
Board of Advisers

FIGURE 7.9. *Letter from William Hocking and Virginia Gildersleeve to members of the Institute of Arab American Affairs, 1949. The well-regarded academicians ask for support in the abysmal time following the creation of Israel. They promoted the institute as an American organization serving the country with accurate information on the Middle East. Farah Papers, Bawardi Collection.*

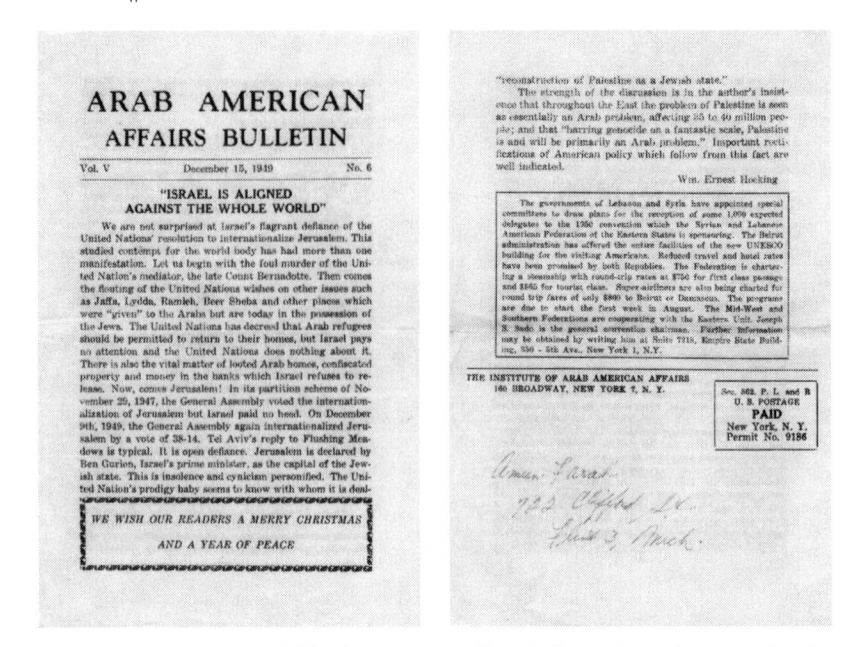

FIGURE 7.10. *Institute of Arab American Affairs Bulletin, December 1949. Farah Papers, Bawardi Collection.*

the General Assembly granting Libyan independence "as soon as possible"; elections in Syria, Egypt, and Iraq; and a Fulbright agreement between the United States and Egypt.[178] Even if the world was aligned against Israel, as Khalil Totah hoped, what mattered was that any help from the Saudi Arabs—Palestine's best hope for actual support—was not part of the U.S. strategy. A letter from Totah to Hocking on December 19, 1949, confirms that the institute approached the Arabian American Oil Company (ARAMCO) for support to no avail. In his letter Totah conceded that ARAMCO did "not propose to help us in our work. It is fear which seems to prevent them from coming to our assistance."[179] It is also possible that the Israelis may have intimidated the Saudis into sidestepping the Palestinians through their superior military capabilities.

Adding insult to injury, in a subsequent letter, on January 16, 1950, Totah explained to Hocking that the Legation of Lebanon in Washington complained about not receiving a receipt for a contribution of $20 it made to the institute. Totah closed with this news: "It is with great regret that I have to inform you about the decision of our Executive Committee on January 13th, 1950 to suspend the operations of the Institute as of January 31st, 1950. . . . It is a pity and a shame as there is room for the Institute but we cannot go on without funds."[180]

In his reply to Totah's January letter, Hocking expressed his regrets and insisted that there was "a need of considerable urgency [for the institute]. What other agency speaks for the Arab world to Americans, and for the American friends of the Arab world to the Arab? There is the politically-pointed material put out by the various [Arab] embassies. . . . But where is the Near East adequately voiced?"[181]

The institute held on until January 26, 1950. A headline in its January 15, 1950, bulletin confirmed the organization's demise: "The Institute of Arab American Affairs Temporarily Suspends Operation." The reasons for the "deplorable" situation were that the institute did not receive the support it deserved and that it lacked funds. Though there was plenty of blame to go around, it is clear that pressure tactics by American Zionists were successful. The bulletin assigned the "major share" of the blame upon

> the whole American community for its apathy and especially for its timidity in the face of Zionist provocation. Neither the American stakeholders with their extensive investments in the Middle East nor the Arabic-speaking businessmen, particularly those in the Greater New York area, evinced anything but a mild and wary interest in the institute; among the relatively few who made donations, many gave only grudgingly and sometimes in mortal fear of economic consequences on their businesses. Such was and is the strange state of mind engendered by the vociferous Zionists and their well meaning but ignorant fellow-travelers.[182]

The institute experiment offers a perspective on the Arab American saga through the prism of continued nationalist feelings and action. The importance of the institute's records is that they provide clues on the interplay between the social and the political spheres in the lives of Arab Americans. This is to say that political action within the institute's core message of engendering goodwill between the United States and the Arab world deepened Arab immigrants' American experience, albeit under grueling circumstances. I hope future studies will follow strands of this research for a perspective on contemporary Arab Americans' experiences with political work in the 1950s. Certainly, the institute and the other organizations discussed in this volume did not exist in a vacuum. An adequate narrative on Arab American life must expand the present study to encompass other contemporary organizations with challenges and aims that are overlapping, and perhaps identical, with those of the institute. These organizations include the former National Association of Arab Americans (NAAA), the American

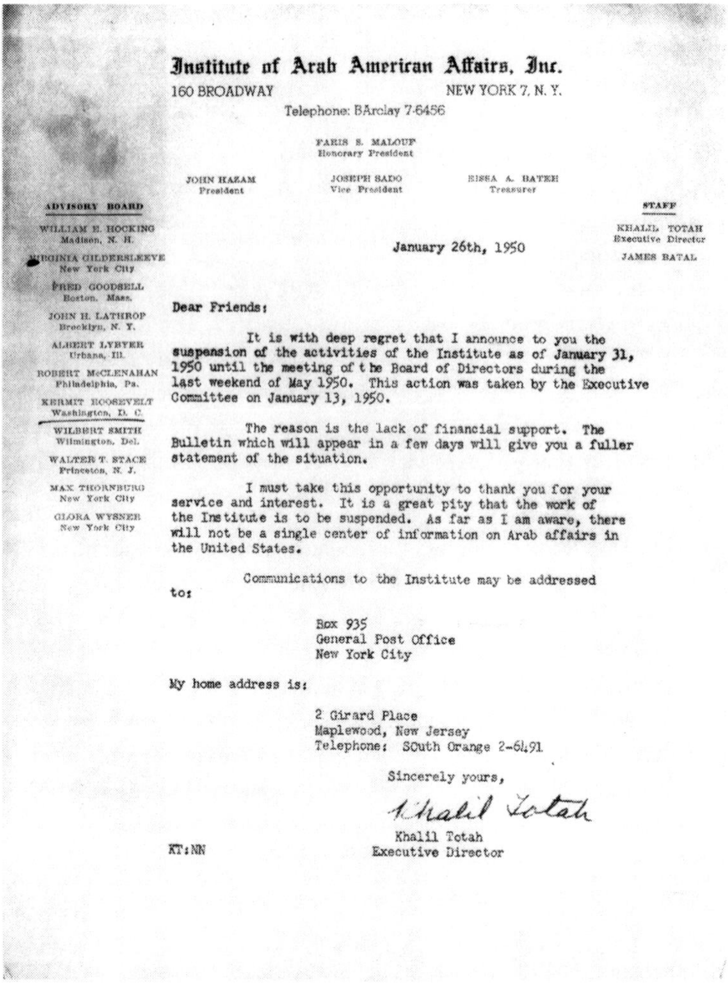

Institute of Arab American Affairs, Inc.

160 BROADWAY   NEW YORK 7, N. Y.

Telephone: BArclay 7-6456

FARIS S. MALOUF
Honorary President

JOHN HAZAM   JOSEPH SADO   EISSA A. HATEM
President   Vice President   Treasurer

ADVISORY BOARD

WILLIAM E. HOCKING
Madison, N. H.

VIRGINIA GILDERSLEEVE
New York City

FRED GOODSELL
Boston, Mass.

JOHN H. LATHROP
Brooklyn, N. Y.

ALBERT LYBYER
Urbana, Ill.

ROBERT McCLENAHAN
Philadelphia, Pa.

KERMIT ROOSEVELT
Washington, D. C.

WILBERT SMITH
Wilmington, Del.

WALTER T. STACE
Princeton, N. J.

MAX THORNBURG
New York City

GLORA WYSNER
New York City

STAFF

KHALIL TOTAH
Executive Director

JAMES BATAL

January 26th, 1950

Dear Friends:

        It is with deep regret that I announce to you the **suspension of the activities of the Institute as of January 31, 1950** until the meeting of the Board of Directors during the last weekend of May 1950. This action was taken by the Executive Committee on January 13, 1950.

        The reason is the lack of financial support. The Bulletin which will appear in a few days will give you a fuller statement of the situation.

        I must take this opportunity to thank you for your service and interest. It is a great pity that the work of the Institute is to be suspended. As far as I am aware, there will not be a single center of information on Arab affairs in the United States.

Communications to the Institute may be addressed to:

        Box 935
        General Post Office
        New York City

My home address is:

        2 Girard Place
        Maplewood, New Jersey
        Telephone: SOuth Orange 2-6491

Sincerely yours,

Khalil Totah

KT:NN   Khalil Totah
                                             Executive Director

FIGURE 7.11. *Letter from Totah to institute members, 1950. This final official communication to members laments suspension of the only U.S. center of information on Arab affairs. Any voice for Arab Americans in political affairs would await the founding of the AAUG seventeen years later when that organization's founders unknowingly picked up where the institute left off. Totah Archives, courtesy of Joy Totah Hilden.*

Arab Anti-Discrimination Committee (ADC), the Arab American Institute (AAI), the Council on American Islamic Relations (CAIR), and the largest service institution, the Arab Community Center for Economic and Social Services (ACCESS).

An examination of Arab immigrant political mobilization can improve understanding of the present because the figures involved were tied to the creation of modern groups like ACCESS, and Middle Eastern political concerns still dominate the work of each of the current organizations. Put differently, establishing the institute as a sophisticated national political organization is a means to gauge any contiguity in Arab American organizational life, or lack thereof, by drawing attention to the effects of homeland politics on the founding and operations of Arab immigrant collectives over time. Such an investigation would be useful in preparing the groundwork for possible links in the political battles fought by the institute and the AAUG and inevitably also for assessing the full impact AAUG had on subsequent efforts to sustain Arab American institutions.

The institute's message of building goodwill and mutual understanding between the United States and the Arab world became the basic principle of most, if not all, Arab—and increasingly Muslim—American organizations. The dilemma for these organizations is identical to that experienced by the institute: their proximity to volatile domestic and foreign political affairs simply because they belong to Arab or Muslim heritage. The question, albeit one that has not been addressed previously, is not so much whether proximities to political events have had a bearing on the formation and sustainability of Arab American organizations. They do. Rather, we should ask how our understanding of Arab American identity is affected if political mobilization continues to be overlooked. This is also a way to put ongoing constructions of a distinct Lebaneseness, as this research inevitably proposes, in proper perspective.

Palestine, the institute's core issue, did not benefit from the institute playing host to Arab delegations to the United States. Matters worsened when demands of settling European Jews in Palestine gave rise to actually partitioning Palestine by the new world body in favor of the Jewish minority. But it was the overall imbalance in the strategic picture whereby the vanguard of Arab nationalism, Syria and Egypt, were deemed to be on the wrong side of U.S. national interest that doomed the institute by placing it too on that opposite side. Therefore, it was not possible for the institute to act on its members' newfound sense of belonging or render service to the United States in the Arab Middle East as its leaders envisioned it could do. While American Zionists ensured a persistently skewed picture of Arabs

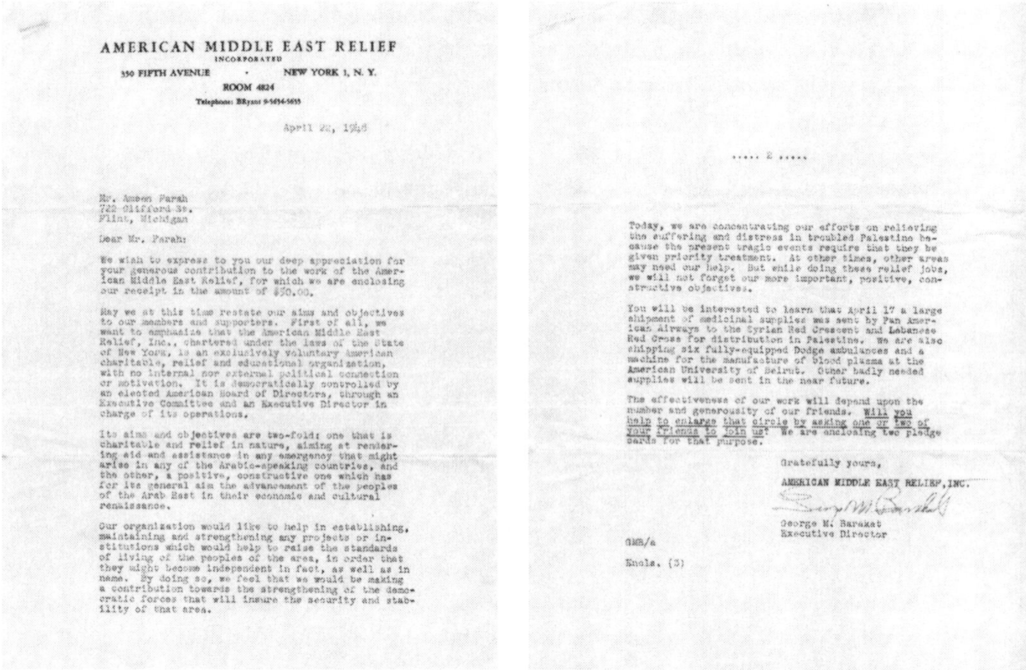

AMERICAN MIDDLE EAST RELIEF
INCORPORATED
350 FIFTH AVENUE · NEW YORK 1, N. Y.
ROOM 4824
Telephone: BRyant 9-5654-5655

April 22, 1948

Mr. Ameen Farah
722 Clifford St.
Flint, Michigan

Dear Mr. Farah:

We wish to express to you our deep appreciation for your generous contribution to the work of the American Middle East Relief, for which we are enclosing our receipt in the amount of $50.00.

May we at this time restate our aims and objectives to our members and supporters. First of all, we want to emphasize that the American Middle East Relief, Inc., chartered under the laws of the State of New York, is an exclusively voluntary American charitable, relief and educational organization, with no internal nor external political connection or motivation. It is democratically controlled by an elected American Board of Directors, through an Executive Committee and an Executive Director in charge of its operations.

Its aims and objectives are two-fold: one that is charitable and relief in nature, aiming at rendering aid and assistance in any emergency that might arise in any of the Arabic-speaking countries, and the other, a positive, constructive one which has for its general aim the advancement of the peoples of the Arab East in their economic and cultural renaissance.

Our organization would like to help in establishing, maintaining and strengthening any projects or institutions which would help to raise the standards of living of the peoples of the area, in order that they might become independent in fact, as well as in name. By doing so, we feel that we would be making a contribution towards the strengthening of the democratic forces that will insure the security and stability of that area.

..... 2 .....

Today, we are concentrating our efforts on relieving the suffering and distress in troubled Palestine because the present tragic events require that they be given priority treatment. At other times, other areas may need our help. But while doing these relief jobs, we will not forget our more important, positive, constructive objectives.

You will be interested to learn that April 17 a large shipment of medicinal supplies was sent by Pan American Airways to the Syrian Red Crescent and Lebanese Red Cross for distribution in Palestine. We are also shipping six fully-equipped Dodge ambulances and a machine for the manufacture of blood plasma at the American University of Beirut. Other badly needed supplies will be sent in the near future.

The effectiveness of our work will depend upon the number and generousity of our friends. Will you help to enlarge that circle by asking one or two of your friends to join us? We are enclosing two pledge cards for that purpose.

Gratefully yours,

AMERICAN MIDDLE EAST RELIEF, INC.

George M. Barakat
Executive Director

GMB/a

Encls. (3)

FIGURE 7.12. *George Barakat's appeal to Farah for aid, April 1948. Barakat, a key figure in the United Syrian Society, the ANL, and the Institute of Arab American Affairs, now headed the American Middle East Relief Organization to aid refugees displaced by Israel. Farah Papers, Bawardi Collection.*

and drowned out Arab American messaging with their own until support for the institute dried up, the Cold War was the overarching strategic factor that prevented Arab Americans from continuing political work the institute had begun. Advocacy of nationalist agendas or charting a nonaligned path as Egypt and Syria attempted to do became nearly impossible to defend during the Cold War. Palestinians became known as refugees and used up what was left of the institute's resources. Between the demise of the institute in 1950 and the emergence of the AAUG in 1967, the Cold War rendered subversive any advocacy of the Palestinians' national demands because, among other reasons, Egypt and Syria, which maintained a nationalist Arab posture, obtained weapons from Eastern Bloc countries to counter what they viewed as an Israeli military threat after losing the Golan Heights and Sinai Peninsula to Israel in 1967.

Intra-Arab conflict and complex political developments beyond the scope of the present study led to the general radicalization of parts of the

Middle East in the face of a U.S. foreign policy of containment.[183] Suffice it to say here that pressures on the part of the West, under the pretext of containing the spread of communism, generally rewarded friendly conservative regimes and alienated those that attempted to chart their own path separate from East-West relations and Cold War politics. These policies contributed to splitting the Arab world along ideological lines of pro-West monarchies in Saudi Arabia, Jordan, and Morocco against the nonaligned Syria and the regime of Jamal Nasser (Abd-al-Naser) in Egypt.[184] Ironically, these nonaligned countries were deemed "revolutionary regimes" by the United States,[185] meaning they were believed to have Soviet leanings, just when some members of the institute wished perhaps that anticommunist sentiments in the United States would aid them against Eastern European Zionists who espoused socialist ideas.[186] Compliance in supplying oil or access by these monarchies became the basis of a new status quo. Calls for pan-Arab nationalism, however, disturbed the equilibrium in U.S. foreign policy.[187] This policy, based on U.S. fears about Arab nationalism, would have major implications for the development of Arab American identity inasmuch as Arab Americans' efforts to build bridges between the United States and their homelands and to advance a counternarrative to Zionism were stymied. Fears of nationalist sentiments and the potential for flirting with Eastern Bloc countries undermined coherence in the ranks of Arab Americans because the chances of bridging their adopted home with the Arab Middle East would be reduced if they maintained a nationalist stance. Participating in the political process, as the institute sought to do, clashed with U.S. antagonism toward Arab nationalist regimes, while Zionist groups painted the institute as an agent of Arab countries. Every Arab American organization since the institute has faced similar dilemmas because of the Palestinian problem while also feeling the need to fight against unrelenting negative stereotypes of Arabs and Arab Americans.

CONCLUSION

Much has changed since the demise of the Institute of Arab American Affairs, yet two generations removed, every contemporary secular and Islamic organization with Arab American membership still espouses the institute's goals and objectives. The American Arab Anti-Discrimination Committee proposes to serve "as a public voice for the Arab American community in the United States on domestic and foreign policy issues and [to educate] the American public in order to promote greater understanding of Arab history and culture."[1] Nor has the cultural essence of Arab identity changed. The works of Elia Madey, Mikhail Naimy, Nasib Arida, Gibran Khalil Gibran, 'Abdulmassīh Haddād, and their colleagues in the Pen Bond adorn textbooks across the Arab world, and it is still possible to assess the Arab Spring from the vantage point of Ameen al-Rihani's pan-Arab thought. Each of these generations was shaped by the same cultural awakening—*nahḍah*—that formed and accelerated national awareness on the part of "Geographic" Syrian Arabs before thousands of them found their way to Manhattan, Highland Park, and Norphlet, Arkansas. Once on U.S. soil, their experiences were profoundly shaped by political changes in their homelands, and as a result, substantial numbers among them joined, between 1915 and 1950, the political organizations presented in this book.

Narrow sectarian parochialism and distance did not stop the Arab immigrants from answering humanitarian pleas in their homelands in times of crisis, and World War I did not erase the salience of their Syrian identity. They rallied to Syria's aid when famine and other disasters struck, and they continued organizing political collectives even when the future of their coveted Syrian state became ominously uncertain. Calls for aid were not interrogated, whether they came from the Shouf Mountains, Beirut, or Nablus; their call was for a free Syria for the Syrians, not for Syrian Muslims, Orthodox Christians, or Maronites.

Before the onslaught of World War I and the mandate era, the Free Syria Society echoed the agenda of the tactful Ottoman Administrative Decentralization Party of Cairo and the nationalist al-Fatāt of France. The FSS echoed calls to the First Arab Conference in Paris in 1913 from nationalists on four continents for achieving complete independence. The discussion on the political sermons by Rafīq al-ʿAẓm and the proceedings of the 1913 Arab conference leave little doubt about Syrians' intentions and strategy. These ideas were the foundation of the Free Syria Society founded by Ameen Farah from Nazareth and the reason his modest effort attracted the membership of the diverse cadre of Ragheb Mitrage, Nasib Arida, Muhammad Muhaisen, and the enigmatic Mikhail Naimy. When the European powers imposed new borders to suit their imperialist plans, the Syrians of Jerusalem, the Baqaʿ, Ramallah, Beirut, Nablus, the Shouf Mountains, and all parts of Greater Syria fell on a larger Arab consciousness.

The New Syria Party's rallying cry, "Syria for the Syrians, Independent and Undivided," printed on the letterhead of all its correspondence from its headquarters in Highland Park, Michigan, captured the urgency felt during the Great Syrian Revolt by Arab immigrants from New York to Minnesota and from Michigan to Mexico. Even before immigrants came together for the NSP in 1925, educated Syrians from the Lebanon, among them Ḥabīb Ibrahīm Kātibah and Faris Malouf, had joined Fuad Shatara from Ramallah and a number of graduates of the former Protestant Syrian College in founding the Arab National League (formerly the Palestine National League) in the early 1920s. When discontent against British Mandate policies exploded in mass protest and spawned the yearlong general strike in 1936 in Palestine (formerly Southern Syria), the Arab National League found it necessary to begin a systematic effort of raising public awareness about the Middle East. Zionist plans and illegal Jewish settlement in Palestine emerged as the next battle for an even greater number of Arab immigrants. When World War II started in Europe during the league's Fourth Annual Convention in Flint, Michigan, it was time for "Americans of Arab extraction," as Fuad Mufarrij observed in the convention, to join their countrymen in the war.

The basic historical outline of these organizations, although the documents are scattered, has been available for years. So what kept information on the activities of Fuad Shatara, Ḥabīb Kātibah, Faris Malouf, Peter S. George, Ismail Khalidi, and the organizations they worked so hard to found and maintain from coming to light sooner? More importantly, what, if anything, would the information in this book change in terms of Arab Americans' experience with political organizing and social development? Manuscript collections are certainly rare finds, and language has been an impediment for many scholars over the past forty years. However, an excavation of the past begins with investigating the reasons scholars with access to the necessary documents and the requisite linguistic knowledge failed to ask the right questions. Lawrence Davidson has shown it is possible to trace electronic newspaper reports to government records and explore new leads on the early Arab immigrants' political activities. Was it that difficult in the aftermath of the humiliation of the 1967 Arab defeat and the magnitude of hostility toward Arabs in public and private settings in the United States to consider the possibility of previous years of tireless work by organizations like the Arab National League and the Institute of Arab American Affairs? Perhaps it was. Many of the seminal scholars in the field of Arab American studies who commenced their scholarship after 1967 and founded the AAUG were convinced that they were operating in a more hostile political space than anyone before them had faced.

Part of the answer, in fact, hinges on limited contacts the scholars might have had with the pioneering generation. As an example, when the young Joseph Joseph professed his dual Arab American loyalty at the ANL's convention in Flint in 1939, Michael Suleiman was a five-year-old boy living in Palestine. By the time Suleiman came to the United States in 1956, Palestine, on whose behalf the ANL was founded, was no longer even recognizable, and the meaning of the term "Southern Syria" had been tenuous since 1923; the Institute of Arab American Affairs had ceased to exist six years earlier; and Shatara, Totah, Malouf, and Kātibah had passed away.

The AAUG was primarily concerned with finding a way for its members to publish and present the Arab point of view when these views were unpopular, to say the least. Under these conditions, inquiring into the political activism of members of the older immigrant community perhaps should have been a priority. Whether this is a fair expectation, as I suggested earlier, is in question. However, one utility of the present study is finding out what it would take for Arab American political organizations to survive. My final correspondence with Michael Suleiman before his death suggests that, indeed, some connections among the activists existed across immigration restrictions and the cataclysmic political events in the Middle East. He disclosed to me that both second-generation Lebanese American Abdeen Jabara and Hisham Sharabi, a newcomer, were involved in the ADC and had links to the AAUG before that. This is significant because they belonged to different generations that span the length and stringency of immigration restrictions. More to the point, he indicated that the AAUG "was formed by both recent arrivals and third generation [Arab Americans] (Abdeen in particular). Zogby [James Zogby, AAI founder and a third-generation Arab American] became very active in late 1970s, especially with work on Palestinian Human Rights Campaign. But the NAAA [National Association of Arab Americans] attracted a lot more second- and third-generation [Arab

Americans]."[2] Could they have learned from each other? Did Zionist pressure and hostility toward Arabs in the United States block that possibility? Or was this disconnect caused by the alienation of the second generation from their Arab heritage? Perhaps that is why the space in the Arab American National Museum leaps from the post-1965 displays to celebrate Danny Thomas and his generation's Americanness.

A contributing factor for the wide gap between the AAUG and the preceding generation of Arab Americans is that careful surveys of existing material never took place. Built on the prolonged immigration restrictions lasting from 1924 to 1965, by the time Alixa Naff and a few others began recording oral histories from the Syrian pioneers, most of the members of the institute and the league, and certainly the NSP and FSS, had died, were frail, or were scattered across the United States. Loss of the Arabic language and acceleration of structural assimilation, too, played a role. The large body of work by Alixa Naff, herself a second-generation Arab American, contained 450 interviews over thirty years yet could not solely have addressed the need for comprehensive study of the community. However, the lack of systematic collections accounts for the absence of qualitative questions into early Arab Americans' political activities. The reason this discrepancy persists, in the view of Janice Terry, a pioneering scholar in Arab American studies, has to do with a lack of mentorship, encouragement, and guidance from the Arab American community at large.

The available scholarly material often does not include Arabic-language manuscripts and adequate translations. Had collection efforts been undertaken, the archives used in this study, which I located in 1995–1996, and many like them would have changed the discourse on Arab American history of political mobilization and indeed changed our understanding of the contours of their identity formation.

Part of realistically assessing the impact of the scholarship of AAUG members on the cultivation of an Arab American narrative is considering how inquiry into the immigrants' past would have to include a critical, honest, and penetrating look into the fog of both disasters, in 1948 and 1967. Such an inquiry would have had to pierce through two distinct political and social stages: pan-Arabism as a movement to unify the Arab world based on nationalist feelings and the decline this movement suffered after the defeat of 1967. It is not helpful to continue to ignore the persistence of rallying by the Arab Americans behind the homeland following calamitous events in the Arab Middle East. Arab Americans, however scholars conceive of their identities based on malleable theories of social construction, still rally on the steps of city halls and sidewalks in times of political crisis or triumph much as those before them did when motivated by pan-Syrian and later pan-Arab feelings. These common threads in their lives across generations hold clues as to how they forged pragmatic agendas from their position as U.S. citizens, that is, the same activities of their contemporary Arab and Muslim American organizations. The Arab American past is laden with lessons on strategies for the future of Arab American institutions. It is time to consider the lessons as part of a more complete narrative of Arab immigrant experiences.

By looking at the prominence of political involvement by early immigrants in this study, I attempt to understand the reasons behind the failure to maintain a sustained political presence in the United States, given the intelligibility, sophistication, and coherence of the ANL and the institute. We need to address why the Institute of Arab American Affairs ultimately unraveled and why Arab Americans still lack a political voice in national politics. What happened—is happening—to Arab American constituents? Indeed, why would ACCESS, a social services organization, fare better than the political body that provided the seed money for it?

The work of the AAUG and the scholars associated with it has certainly been significant, but it needs to be put into the context of the larger Arab American experience. When the institute declined partly due to lack of financial support in the wake of the Nakbah, but mostly due to tremendous internal and external pressures arising from Zionism and the Cold War, there seems to have been a void for many years—at least in my understanding, as I remain mindful of my own stances concerning more considered investigation of the past—not only in political activism and mobilization but also in social studies on the immigrants. A steady stream from thousands of publications antagonistic to the Arab point of view found its way to most U.S. citizens. This stream continues to intensify, though the targets are increasingly Muslims and the perpetrators are a new brand of American nativists and an extreme brand of self-described Christian conservatives. Given the AAUG's preoccupation with self-preservation after the 1967 war and the spike of hostility toward all enemies of Israel, as Suleiman, Khalidi, Said, Sharabi, and others have ably explicated, one has to wonder if the handful of AAUG scholars alone would have been able to write Arab Americans into the discourse on immigration and ethnicity in this country. Arab Americans alone cannot be responsible for securing the dissemination of reasonably reliable information on Arabs, Islam, and Arab Americans and making such information available through elementary schools, colleges, pamphlets, movies, news broadcasts, television productions, and so forth!

Combating stereotypes is as much a problem for Arab Americans today as it ever was. But for Arab Americans a historical perspective is needed on how they became a prime target for relentlessly demeaning stereotypes if the future of existing civil rights and service organizations is to be more secure. The Arab American Anti-Discrimination Committee, perhaps the largest of all Arab American grassroots organizations, was founded in 1980 by U.S. Senator James Abourezk, who represented South Dakota in Congress from 1971 to 1979. Its purpose was to "encourage a balanced U.S. foreign policy in the Middle East" and to "support freedom and development in the Arab world."[3] Achieving these goals was complicated by the more immediate and pressing need to defend Arab Americans and Arab heritage against discrimination and stereotypes. The ADC was Abourezk's response to a covert operation by the FBI that used ugly stereotypes of Arabs as part of an elaborate sting. In that operation, known as Abscam (for Arab scam), FBI agents disguised as wealthy Arab sheiks offered congressmen cash for favors. At the time, young activist Helen Samhan, later the executive director of AAI, illustrated the loaded political implications of the Abscam scandal by questioning whether anyone would get away with an operation called "Jewscam" or "Blackscam."[4]

Where Arab Americans go from here may depend on understanding their collective experience based on historical assessment of the past. In some respects, the founders of the ADC picked up where the institute left off. The ADC has had the same goals and faces the same challenges the institute and Arab American University Graduates faced, but it parallels the institute more than the AAUG. The ADC has expanded its appeal to include all Arab Americans and newcomers, not just university graduates. By the early 1990s the ADC attracted the attention of the media, political actors, and academia as the voice of the emergent Arab American community. The difficulty of connecting the institute, which faded by 1950, to an ADC founded in 1980—given their identical goals and the pressures of the 1967 war—also offers clues as to the difficulty inherent in writing a coherent Arab American narrative.

Adding to these complications are the fundamental political changes in the Arab Middle East. When mass immigration resumed in the United States after 1965, newer Arab immigrants belonged to a multitude of nation-states, many of which did not exist until well after World War II. Yet, the work by the institute to ease the entry of these countries into the United Nations is not part of the Arab American story. Even more obscure is the context behind Fuad Shatara being designated the first envoy representing the Saudi Arabian monarch in the United States in 1924, one year after he seeded the Arab National League. Three decades later, Faris al-Khouri, a major figure in the Arab *nahḍah* movement and a mentor to William Hocking, was designated Syria's first envoy to the UN and was a guest of the institute. These transnational connections have staggering implications for Arab American studies. Therefore, if Arab American studies is to grow as a distinct area of scholarship, it cannot continue a path completely divorced from events in the Arab Middle East; spurious comments either dismissing or overplaying the meaning of 1967 should not circumscribe the conversation on Arab Americans' political activities and their importance overall. There is no substitute for a people writing its own narrative. In this case, the Arab American narrative was not only moved but rather shaped by political calamity as much as by race, ethnicity, gender, and sexuality.

A project of writing a more comprehensive narrative of Arab Americans must also write their experiences into the social history of the United States. Abourezk began his political life by defending the indigenous Americans of the Dakotas and criticizing the U.S. government for training foreign security forces on behalf of repressive regimes. Likewise, activists in the AAUG were clearly influenced by the civil rights movement as much as by international politics. Like Stokely Carmichael and Malcolm X, they were ultimately radicalized by stalled social reforms and experienced a process of drawing upon their national consciousness. Michael Suleiman was among many in the AAUG who were profoundly touched by racial intolerance. He was an engineering student oscillating between careers until he inherited his position as a spokesman for the Palestinian cause, just as Samra, Shatara, Kātibah, and Totah did before him. He explained his transformation by recalling a trip to the southern United States in which he found himself staring down the barrels of a shotgun after a restaurant owner in Georgia took him for a black man. The owner kept shouting, "Get that nigger out of here!" When told that Suleiman was actually an Arab, he continued shouting: "Get that A-rab out of here."[5] Before his passing in March 2010, Suleiman tried to put forty years of defending and explaining the Arab side in perspective to American audiences, emphasizing the "necessary but burdensome and costly task of studying, cataloguing, and archiving the full Arab American experience."[6]

Being viewed as outsiders or radicals may have played a role in the kind of attention the activists received from the B'nai B'rith. One Anti-Defamation League operative described the "professional intellectuals" in the AAUG as "familiar with the U.S. scene" and the AAUG itself as the most effective Arab American organization in the United States.[7] Ironically, William Safire, a vocal Zionist, had spoken of the institute in almost the same terms two decades earlier. Predictably, the AAUG was threatened by the loss of its tax-exempt status by the IRS and targeted by the FBI as part of President Nixon's secretive Operation Boulder. This operation targeted Arabs and Arab Americans after the terrorist attacks on Israeli athletes in 1972.[8] Abdeen Jabara, later the head of the ADC, gained prominence among Arab immigrants and progressives when he sued the government over Operation Boulder and won. The result was that, as I suggested above, the ADC took on the challenges that had faced the institute.

Inquiries into the strides and setbacks experienced by Arab Americans must assess the chilling effect of the tactics used by proponents of Israel in the United States, including the Anti-Defamation League of B'nai B'rith (ADL), against critics of Israel. In many of his appearances at ADC national conventions and other settings, Professor Jack Shaheen has described negative stereotypes as the basis for the political status quo, that is, the basis of sustained support for Israel, while casting Arabs and Muslims as perpetually uncivilized, inarticulate enemies of the West. Shaheen supports his conclusions by analyzing hundreds of made-for-TV programs, newspaper articles, Hollywood movies, comic books, commercials, cartoons, textbooks, magazines, billboards, press releases, and news broadcasts. He finds widespread hostility toward Arabs within various genres: entertainment, scholarly works, and even travel guides. For more than thirty years now, Shaheen's presentations at the ADC annual national conventions have vividly disclosed specific examples of disparaging stereotypes of Arabs and Muslims—especially Palestinians—in dozens of Hollywood movies. He has documented blatant tactics used by mostly Jewish Americans with Israeli citizenship in *The TV Arab*, "Reel Bad Arabs," and a steady stream of articles.[9]

There is no indication that intimidation tactics and cultural violence by proponents of Israel have abated. In 1993 the ADL was involved in a massive spying operation against Arab American activists. At the time that campaign was uncovered, it had been going on for decades and involved providing information to foreign governments on hundreds of groups active in the United States. Among its activities were supplying the Israeli government with information on Arab American activists and probably providing the apartheid government of South Africa information about the African National Congress.[10] Given the ADL's stated goals as early as 1945 in its confidential report of reaching every man, woman, and child through media, schools, and more, the connection between the pervasive unfavorable portrayals of Arabs in the United States and the reach of the ADL's media campaigns deserves to be critically addressed.

Rashid Khalidi, the Edward Said Professor of Modern Arab Studies at Columbia University, finds that Palestinians further defined their identity in opposition to but not solely as a result of Zionist pressures and British colonialism. Ascribing to an Arab American identity by members of the Arab National League was made necessary by structural acculturation and residing in the United States for decades, but the very existence of that organization was directly the result of Zionism and British militarism in Palestine. And it was Syrian national identity—the Syria idea—that sparked experiments with national political organizing in the United States as early as 1915, before the United States entered World War I and well before the outcome of that conflict became evident.

The stages of the development of Arab American identity thus correspond to similar stages of Palestinian national identity in Rashid Khalidi's discourse. Khalidi rejects the dismissal of Palestinian identity and "with it, Palestinian nationalism" as ephemeral and artificial. He has debunked the notion that Palestinian identity "emerged only in the 1960s."[11] In the same vein that Khalidi rejects fables of only recently constructed Palestinian national identity, in this book I debunk the view that it was the war with Israel in 1967 and the resultant scholarship on Arab Americans that led to the emergence of Arab American identity as it is understood today, and I reject as harmful the view that this post-1967 analysis is now largely forgotten or a basis for a narrowly constructed political category.

Understanding the importance of mass political action in the development of Arab American identity is long overdue. Calamity across the waters convinced Arab immigrants to pull together and do what they could to aid those in their homelands. It became clear to them during the early stages of doing so, as Ameen Rihani's book *Letters to Uncle Sam* illustrates, that upholding higher ideals of democracy and self-determination in their homelands overseas was not incompatible with the stated values of their adopted country. When sending aid facilitated a structure and a political role for the organizations in this study, being of and not merely existing in the United States, as Fuad Shatara hoped would happen a century ago, became a goal in itself. Arab immigrants and their descendants did not intend their newfound loyalty to the United States to be a way station on an endless journey of deracination. They began building their economic and intellectual lives from the moment they set foot in the New World, and it mattered little if a sojourner mentality lingered for each wave of immigrants. Ultimately what they did as U.S. citizens in terms of disseminating a better understanding of their homelands satisfied a need to help both their ancestral and adopted lands. The question that deserves more attention than this limited study can offer is: To what extent did Zionism retard building coherence among Arab Americans by putting pressure on them in order to maintain support for Israel? There is little doubt based on the internal documents of the ADL that devastatingly pervasive ugly depictions of Arabs, especially Palestinians and later Muslims, in every form of media every day of the year helped perpetuate favorable impressions of Israel and Zionism and harmed the Arab cause. Also needed is to continue this inquiry for an assessment of the core issues in the lives of Arab Americans in the rapidly shifting political and social landscape across the Middle East. How many members of the Movement of Arab Nationalists, the influential pan-Arabist movement founded by Palestinian students at the AUB, came to the United States in the 1950s and 1960s? How exactly did members of this mostly Palestinian progressive organization, which became the Popular Front for the Liberation of Palestine after 1967, influence Arab American life before 1967 and the emergence of the AAUG?

What Rashid Khalidi has called the "lost years" following the Nakbah in 1948, when Palestinians seem to have "disappeared from the map," created a fog that obscured five decades of political activity on the part of Arab immigrants in the United States. My aim in this study has been to pierce the fog surrounding these lost years and reveal the formerly unseen Arab American nationalists whose work and activities have so far been unfortunately neglected.

NOTES

INTRODUCTION

1. Philip S. Khoury, "Factionalism among Syrian Nationalists during the French Mandate," *International Journal of Middle Eastern Studies* 13.4 (November 1981), 441.

2. Ibid.

3. A useful background on Syria's territorial boundaries can be found in Lamia Rustum Shihadeh, "The Name of Syria in Ancient and Modern Usage," in *The Origins of Syrian Nationhood: Histories, Pioneers, and Identity*, edited by Adel Beshara, 17–29 (London: Routledge, 2011). Emphasis on the territorial boundaries and labeling oscillate from Bilād al-Shām to Syria, Greater Syria, and Geographic Syria, depending on the political context and the authors' dispositions toward the Syria idea even in the above scholarship, itself involving scant discussion on this topic.

4. For writings on gender, ethnicity, and family life, see, for example, Louise Cainkar, "The Social Construction of Difference and the Arab American Experience," *Journal of American Ethnic History* 25.2 (2006): 243–278; Nadine Naber, "Arab American Femininities: Beyond Arab Virgin/American(ized) Whore," *Feminist Studies* 32.1 (2006): 87, 111, 193; Suad Joseph, "Geographies of Lebanese Families: Women as Transnationals, Men as Nationals, and Other Problems with Transnationalism," *Journal of Middle East Women's Studies* 5.3 (2009): 120, 144, 199; Lisa Suhair Majaj, "Into the Wadi," *Journal of Middle East Women's Studies* 2.2 (2006): 137–139.

5. See Alixa Naff, *Becoming American: The Early Arab Immigrant Experience* (Carbondale: Southern Illinois University Press, 1985); Abdo Elkholy, *The Arab Moslems in the United States: Religion and Assimilation* (New Haven, CT: College and University Press, 1966); Michael W. Suleiman, *Arabs in the Mind of America* (Brattleboro, VT: Amana Books, 1988); Earl H. Waugh and Baha Abu Laban, eds., *The Muslim Community in North America* (Edmonton, Canada: University of Alberta Press, 1983).

6. Yvonne Yazbeck Haddad, "Maintaining the Faith of the Fathers: Dilemmas of Religious Identity in the Christian and Muslim Communities," in *The Development of Arab-American Identity*, edited by Ernest McCarus (Ann Arbor: University of Michigan Press, 1994), 61, also n29. Haddad lists these works by pioneering scholars among her references: Elaine C. Hagopian and Ann Paden, eds., *The Arab-*

Americans: Studies in Assimilation (Wilmette, IL: Medina University Press International, 1969); Barbara C. Aswad, ed., *Arabic Speaking Communities in American Cities* (Staten Island, NY: Center for Migration Studies of New York, 1974); Philip M. Kayal and Joseph M. Kayal, *The Syrian-Lebanese in America: A Study in Religion and Assimilation* (Boston: Twayne, 1975); Sameer Abraham and Nabil Abraham, eds., *Arabs in the New World: Studies on Arab American Communities* (Detroit: Wayne State University, 1983); Eric J. Hooglund, *Crossing the Waters: Arabic-Speaking Immigrants to the United States before 1940* (Washington, DC: Smithsonian Institution Press, 1987); Gregory Orfalea, *Before the Flames: A Quest for the History of Arab Americans* (Austin: University of Texas Press, 1988).

7. Janice Terry, "Community and Political Activism Among Arab Americans in Detroit" in *Arabs in America: Building a New Future*, edited by Michael Suleiman (Philadelphia: Temple University Press, 1999), 243.

8. Suleiman, *Arabs in the Mind of America*, 34.

9. Michael W. Suleiman, "Arab-Americans and the Political Process," in *The Development of Arab American Identity*, edited by Ernest McCarus (Ann Arbor: University of Michigan Press, 1994), 37–38.

10. Ibid.

11. Michael Suleiman, "Early Arab Americans: The Search for Identity," in *Crossing the Waters: Arabic-Speaking Immigrants to the United States before 1940*, edited by Eric J. Hooglund (Washington, DC: Smithsonian Institution Press, 1987), 40.

12. Ibid., 41.

13. Ibid.

14. Michael Suleiman, "A History of Arab American Political Participation," in *American Arabs and Political Participation*, edited by Philippa Strum, conference proceedings, Woodrow Wilson International Center for Scholars, Washington, DC, May 5, 2006, 3.

15. Ibid., 10.

16. The ANL files and Ḥabīb Kātibah papers were only recently added to the finding aid of the Alixa Naff Collection, Faris and Yamna Naff Arab American Collection, Smithsonian Institution, Washington, DC (hereafter cited as Naff Collection).

17. Alixa Naff, interview with Farhat Ziadeh on November 8, 1994, in Seattle, WA, subseries A5f, Naff Collection. In this interview Ziadeh wanted to talk about the institute and recalled the Arab National League's last convention in Flint. However, Naff proceeded to ask about other matters. Ziadeh said Rashid Khalidi's parents, Ismail Khalidy and Salwa Juha, met through their volunteer work for the Institute of Arab American Affairs in New York in 1945.

18. Totah's books and papers were transferred to Ziadeh by Totah's wife, Eva, in 1971. The papers were largely neglected, according to Joy Totah Hilden, Khalil and Eva's daughter, until she retrieved them in 1997; e-mail from Joy Totah Hilden to the author, April 5, 2013.

19. Lawrence Davidson, "The Past as Prelude: Zionism and the Betrayal of American Democratic Principles, 1917–48," *Journal of Palestine Studies* 31.3 (Spring 2002): 21–35. In an e-mail message to the author, Davidson confirmed how he located the Arab immigrant activists: "I found mention of the Arab American individuals and groups in the index of the NYT and then went to the articles. The index was my primary guide. Once I identified the individuals and organizations I made a thorough check of all relevant secondary sources. Simultaneously, I was going through the State Department Records (on microfilm) and ran into reports of occasional meetings with some of these individuals. The whole process took me about two years"; e-mail from Davidson to the author, March 1, 2012.

20. Nabeel Abraham and Andrew Shryock, introduction to *Arab Detroit*, ed. Abraham and Shryock (Detroit, MI: Wayne State University Press, 2000), 39.

21. George Khoury, conversations with the author, January 2012.

22. Ibid.

23. Gary C. David, "The Creation of 'Arab American': Political Activism and Ethnic (Dis)Unity," *Critical Sociology* 33.5–6 (September 2007).

24. George Khoury, conversation with the author, January 2012.

25. David, "Creation of 'Arab American,'" 842.

26. Ibid., 843.

27. Orfalea, *Before the Flames*, 140. This number includes a spike after the immigration quotas were repealed in 1965 and an influx of Lebanese Shi'a immigrated after the violent civil war in their country.

28. Ibid., 139.

29. Ibid., 140.

30. Ibid.

31. Ibid., 141.

32. Ibid.

33. Michael W. Suleiman, "'I Come to Bury Caesar, Not to Praise Him': An Assessment of the AAUG as an Example of an Activist Arab-American Organization," *Arab Studies Quarterly* 29.3 (2007): 84.

34. The numbers do reflect accurately return circular migrations. See Ismail Haqqi, *Lubnan: Mabaheth 'Ilmiyah wa 'Ijtima'iyah* (Beirut: N.p., 1913).

35. Alixa Naff, "The Early Arab Immigrant Experience," in *The Development of Arab American Identity*, edited by Ernest McCarus (Ann Arbor: University of Michigan Press, 1994), 30.

36. Naff, *Becoming American*, 128.

37. Ibid.

38. Ibid.; Kayal and Kayal, *Syrian-Lebanese in America*.

39. Motaz Abdullah Alhourani, "The Arab-American Press and the Arab World: News Coverage in *Al-Bayān* and *Al-Dalil*," master's thesis, Kansas State University, 1992; Michael W. Suleiman Collection, Arab American National Museum, Dearborn, MI (henceforth Suleiman Collection).

40. Ibid., 14.

41. Ibid., 18.
42. Ibid., 31.
43. Basil M. Kherbawi, *Tarīkh al Wilāyāt al-Muttaḥidah* [History of the United States] (New York: Al-Dalil, 1913).
44. Rizk Haddad, *Nafahat al-Riyād* (New York: Mirāt al-Gharb Press, 1945).
45. Ibid., 130, 150, 280.
46. Elkholy, *Arab Moslems*.
47. See Reed Ueda, *Postwar Immigrant America: A Social History* (New York: Bedford St. Martin's Press, 1994), 18–26.
48. George Antonius, *The Arab Awakening: The Story of the Arab National Movement*, translated by Ali Haidar Rikabi (New York: G. P. Putnam's Sons, 1946), 36. Originally published as *Yaqzat al-ʿArab tārīkh ḥarakat al-ʿArab al-qawmīyah* (Damascus: Matbaʿat al-Taraqqi, 1938).
49. Al-Bukhari is known for his writings on *ḥadīth*, conversations and interpretations of Islamic teachings by the Prophet Muhammad and his inner circle.
50. I came across many of these books during my research and volunteer work at the Heritage Museum and Library of the Antiochian Village in Pennsylvania. Gifts from Syrian Orthodox Christian homes have contributed to a massive collection on a variety of topics. Nestled in rural Pennsylvania about sixty miles east of Pittsburgh on some 400 acres, the complex is part of the Antiochian Orthodox Christian Church of North America and consists of a conference center, hiking and meditation trails, and a campground for youngsters. It is also home to the Heritage Museum and Library, which contains invaluable Arabic texts from the late nineteenth and early twentieth centuries.
51. Over the past twelve years, I have presented papers on strands of Syrian nationalist thought in *mahjar* literature, the specific organizations discussed here, and the Paris First Arab Conference of 1913. This is a partial list of those presentations: "The Evidentiary Power of Manuscripts," in "A Discursive Approach to the Formation of Arab American Identity: Literature, Politics, and Archival Evidence," a symposium by the Center for Arab American Studies, University of Michigan-Dearborn, March 15, 2010; "Historical Modalities of Arab Immigrant Political Action," at "Arab American Activism: Historical and Contemporary Trends," the Middle East Studies Association Annual Conference, Washington, D.C., November 25, 2008; "Looking beyond September 11: 'New Syria, U.S.A.': Arab American Political Activism from 1915–1950" at "Arabs in America: Communities and Identities after 9/11," Race and Ethnic Studies Institute, Texas A&M University, February 9–12, 2007; "National Consciousness and Arab American Identity. Mapping Arab Diasporas: Gender, Race, and Citizenship," Middle East Studies Association Annual Conference, Washington, DC, 2005; "The Nuaimah-Farah Correspondence (1914–1915)," at "Ethnicity and Change," Middle East Studies Association Annual Conference, Chicago, November 1998; "Arab Nationalism; Caught between Two Continents, 1913 to 1948," American Arab Anti-Discrimination Committee National Convention, Washington, DC, May 1998.

52. Sarah M. A. Gualtieri, *Between Arab and White: Race and Ethnicity in the Early Syrian American Diaspora* (Berkeley: University of California Press: 2009), 109. Gualtieri's scant reference to the New Syria Party is understandable due to the difficulty of locating resources on that organization, although presumably based on letters from NSP chapters to the French government she reached the conclusion that "the New Syria Party had chapters throughout the United States"; 216n133.

53. See, for example, Nuaihed Al-Hut, "Shakib Arslan," *Al-A'rabi*, March 2008. Also important is noting the typical recycled quote from Philip Hitti's 1924 book, *The Syrian in America*, which Gualtieri cites as an example of how love of religion meant a patriotism "devoid of national feelings"; *Between Arab and White*, 82–83. Hitti himself evolved after making that comment in 1923. He was the president of the Institute of Arab American Affairs for a short while and took up the cause of the new Arab states seeking membership in the United Nations in 1945. He defended the Arab cause in congressional hearings alongside Fuad Shatara as representatives of the Palestine National League. See also Lawrence Davidson, *America's Palestine: Popular and Official Perceptions from Balfour to Israeli Statehood* (Gainesville: University Press of Florida, 2001).

54. Anthony D. Smith, *National Identity* (Reno: University of Nevada Press, 1991).

55. Hisham Sharabi, *Arab Intellectuals and the West: the Formative Years 1875–1914* (Baltimore: Johns Hopkins Press, 1970); Ernest Dawn, "The Origins of Arab Nationalism" in *The Origins of Arab Nationalism: A Reassessment*, edited by Rashid Khalidi, Lisa Anderson, Muhammad Muslih, and Riva S. Simon (New York: Columbia University Press, 1991).

56. Antonius, *Arab Awakening*, 15–16.

57. Sachedina Abdulaziz, *The Islamic Roots of Democratic Pluralism* (Oxford, England: Oxford University Press, 2001), 23.

58. Here again, abundant self-serving rhetoric in Mokarzel's Maronite paper, *Al-Hoda*, creates confusion, especially when the historical context is overlooked. Most Orthodox Christians in the Flint and Detroit areas supported the nationalists regardless of sect and religion. *Al-Sa'eh*, too, was a nationalist publication, and for that reason Mokarzel attacked it.

59. Confidential report, June 7, 1943. B-48, INT33AR15, Foreign Nationalities Branch, Office of Strategic Services, National Archives and Records Administration, College Park, MD (henceforth OSS).

CHAPTER 1: ARAB POPULATIONS UNDER OTTOMAN RULE

1. Rashid Khalidi, "Ottomanism and Arabism in Syria Before 1914: A Reassessment," in *The Origins of Arab Nationalism*, ed. Rashid Khalidi, Lisa Anderson, Muhammad Muslih, and Riva S. Simon (New York: Columbia University Press, 1991), 51.

2. Ameen Rihani, *The Book of Khalid* (New York: Dodd, Mead, 1911), 274.

3. Khalidi, "Ottomanism and Arabism," especially page 57.
4. Antonius, *Arab Awakening*, 19.
5. Zeine N. Zeine, *Arab Turkish Relations and the Emergence of Arab Nationalism* (Beirut: Khayat, 1958), 7.
6. Antonius, *Arab Awakening*, 20.
7. Ibid.
8. Ibid., 33.
9. Albert Hourani, *A History of the Arab Peoples* (New York: Warner Books, 1991), 265–295.
10. Roger Owen, *State, Power, and Politics in the Making of the Modern Middle East* (New York: Routledge, 1992).
11. Mohammad Sawaie, "Rifaʿa Rafiʿ Al-Tahtawi and his Contribution to the Lexical Development of Modern Arabic," *International Journal of Middle Eastern Studies* 32 (2000): 395–410.
12. Bassam Tibi, *Arab Nationalism: Between Islam and the Nation-State*, 3rd ed. (London: Macmillan, 1997), 9–15.
13. Antonius, *Arab Awakening*, 28.
14. Ibid., 35–40.
15. Ibid., 40.
16. Muhammad Zuʿaytir, *Al-Mashrūʿ al-Mārūni fi Lubnān: Juḏhūrahu wa taṭawwaruhu* [The Maronite project in Lebanon: Its origins and development] (Lebanon: Al-Wikālah al-ʿĀlamīyah li-al-Tawzīʿ, 1986), 234–251.
17. Ibid.
18. Ibid., 238.
19. Ibid.
20. Zeine N. Zeine, *The Emergence of Arab Nationalism. With a Background Study of Arab-Turkish Relations in the Near East* (Beirut: Khayat, 1966), 68.
21. Philippe de Tarazi, *Tarīkh al-saḥāfah al-ʿarabīyah* [History of the Arab press] (Beirut: Al-Matbaʿah al-Adabīyah, 1913), 82.
22. Antonius, *Yaqzat al-ʿArab*, 46.
23. During my search for manuscripts in the homes of descendants of Syrian immigrants, I came across three copies of Bustāni's volumes: one belonged to Ameen Farah; the second is in Ann Arbor at the home of Amal Dalack and Gregory Dalack, a relative of the historian and Orthodox archpriest Basil Kherbawi; and the third is in the office of Father George Shalhoub, the priest of Saint Mary's Orthodox Basilica in Livonia, Michigan. These are indications that bringing copies of this dictionary with them to the United States was fairly common, at least among the Orthodox immigrants.
24. Antonius, *Yaqzat al-ʿArab*, 61–67.
25. Ibid., 72.
26. Zeine, *Emergence of Arab Nationalism*, 68.
27. Ibid., 69.

28. Roger Owen and Sevket Pamuk, *A History of Middle East Economies in the Twentieth Century* (Cambridge, MA: Harvard University Press, 1999).

29. William Cleveland, *A History of the Modern Middle East* (Boulder, CO: Westview Press, 1994), 48–69.

30. See Wilfrid Scawen Blunt, *Secret History of the English Occupation of Egypt: Being a Personal Narrative of Events* (New York: A. A. Knopf, 1922).

31. See Albert Hourani, Philip S. Khoury, and Mary C. Wilson, eds., *The Modern Middle East* (London: I. B. Tauris, 1993), 171–311.

32. Al-Hadi al-Taymoumi, *Fi usūl al-ḥarakah al-qaumīyah al-ʿarabīyah: 1920–1939* [On the origins of the Arab national movement: 1920-1939] (Tunis: Muhammad Ali Publishing House, 2002).

33. Letter from Jubrān Kuzma to Nicola Qubʿyn, February 9, 1912. Translations by the author unless otherwise indicated. Farah Papers, Hani Bawardi Collection, Arab-American Archive Project, Genesee Historical Collections Center, University of Michigan–Flint Library (hereinafter Bawardi Collection).

34. Taymoumi, *Fi usūl al-ḥarakah*, 84.

35. Kuzma to Qubʿyn, February 9, 1912.

36. Jubrān Kuzma, letter to Nicola Qubʿyn or Ameen Farah, June 30, 1912. Farah Papers, Bawardi Collection.

37. Ibid.

38. James Gelvin, *Divided Loyalties: Nationalism and Mass Politics in Syria at the Close of Empire* (Berkeley: University of California Press, 1998), 8.

CHAPTER 2: THE SYRIAN NATIONALISM
OF THE *MAHJAR* PRESS

1. Zuʿaitir, *Al-mashruʿ al-Maruni fi Lubnān*, 287.

2. De Tarazi, *Tarīkh al-sahāfa al-ʿarabiyah* (1913), 4–68.

3. Rashid Khalidi, *Palestinian Identity: The Construction of Modern National Consciousness* (New York: Columbia University Press), 54–61.

4. Ibid.

5. De Tarazi, *Tarīkh al-sahāfa al-ʿarabiyah*, part 4 (Beirut: Al-Matbaʿa al-Amreekīya, 1933).

6. INT 2AB 16, OSS.

7. INT 2AB 16, 3, OSS.

8. INT 2AB 20, OSS.

9. Ibid.

10. An eloquent response by Kherbawi to Maronite agitation by, among others, Hanania Kassab and Maronite Patriarch Anton Aridah can be found in Basil Kherbawi, *Al-Hijjah al-rahinah fi dafʾ daʾawa batrik al-mawarinah wa rad al-sada ʿala jareedat al-huda*, circa late 1930s. Roughly translated, this title in classical rhymed prose style implies, "A refutation of the Maronite patriarch and a righting

of the errors of *Al-Hoda* newspaper." The publisher may have been *Al-Nisr* newspaper. This eighty-six-page attractively bound reader includes parts of the debates published by *Al-Nisr* and other newspapers. The divisions over ecclesiastical matters may have been the cause of the violence, which attracted the attention of the local press; see "Syrians Riot in Street, and Many Are Hurt," *New York Times*, October 24, 1905.

11. See John Daye, "Syrianist Orientations in the Thought of Mikha'il Nu'aimah," in *The Origins of Syrian Nationhood: Histories, Pioneers, and Identity*, ed. Adel Beshara (London: 2011), 205. Daye claims that Mokarzel was more "French than the French government" when it came to political matters, drawing attention to a 1918–1940 file on the Levant Syrie-Leban, note 74, in the French Foreign Ministry archives.

12. De Tarazi, *Tarīkh al-sahāfa al-ʿarabiyah*, part 4.

13. Ibid., 416.

14. Ibid., 428.

15. Kherbawi, *Tarīkh al-Wilāyāt al-Muttaḥidah*.

16. Henry H. Melki, "Al-Sahāta al-ʿarabiya fi al-mahjar wa ʿilāqatuha bi-al-adab al-mahjari" [The Arab-American press and its relation to diaspora literature], PhD diss., Georgetown University, 1972, University Microfilms, Ann Arbor, MI.

17. Ibid.

18. Ibid.

19. Ibid., 92.

20. *Al-Hoda*, October 10, 1905, 4.

21. *The Word* is still published in English only and distributed to parishioners across the United States from Engelwood, New Jersey.

22. Muhammad Zuʿaitir, *Al-Marūniyah fi Lubnān qadīman wa hadīthan* [The Maronite rite in Lebanon past and present] (Beirut: Al-Wakalah al-sharqyya lil-tawzeeʿ, 1994).

23. Ibid., 363.

24. Ibid., 380.

25. Ibid., 405–407.

26. Melki discloses that in 1929 Marion Mills Miller wrote, "Rihani needs no statute for he resides in the hearts of his people and his life will be immortalized by his books"; "Al-Sahāta al-ʿarabiya," 149, my translation.

27. Ibid., 32.

28. Ibid., 177–191. Rihani's lengthy letter is unpublished save in Melki's dissertation.

29. Ibid., 186–187.

30. Ibid., 188–189.

31. Zuʿaitir, *Al-mashruʿ al-Maruni fi Lubnan*, 355–360. Zuʿaitir's large volume (1,264 pages) is a valuable resource on the intricate events, names, and dates in Lebanon's history. However, it contains many such problematical polemics as claims of a secret Mason-Zionist alliance and dismissal of the idea of an Arab "renaissance"

as a Western invention aimed at "erasing [Islamic] religious values from social life"; 358. His ever-present suspicion of any non-Islamic interpretation as a Christian-colonialist collaboration weakens his work. On page 359, however, Zuʿaitir raises a good point: How can the nationalists call for independence from the Ottomans and remain silent on the occupation of Egypt by Britain and of Algiers by the French? The answer has to do with the pragmatic nature of Arab nationalism in using the Allies against each other and against the Ottomans when they could, as can be gleaned from nationalists' comments in the Arabic press.

32. E-mail from Helen Hatab Samhan, a member of the Mokarzel family, to me on March 8, 2007, provides some insights on Zionist attempts to influence *Al-Hoda*'s editorial policy: "I checked in my family records and found I had made notes of my conversations with my aunt about the Israelis approaching both her father [Salloum Mokarzel] and herself about publishing 'favorable pieces' in *Al-Hoda*. According to my aunt Mary Mokarzel, who published *Al-Hoda* from 1956 to 1971, her father Salloum had been offered $40,000 by the Israelis to include favorable coverage. He refused. After Salloum died and Mary became publisher, an intermediary approached Mary and told her the Israelis wanted to offer her $250,000 to do the same thing, and she also refused. (These conversations took place on July 26, 1997, at my aunt's apartment in NYC, as part of my preparatory work on the centennial celebration of *Al-Hoda*'s founding in 1998.)" With permission.

33. John Daye, *Lakom Jubrānakom wa li Jubrāni* [You have your Gibran and I have mine] (Beirut: Qub Elias Press, 2009), 53.

34. Jean Gibran and Khalil Gibran, *Khalil Gibran: His Life and World* (New York: Interlink Books, 1991), 287.

35. Ibid.

36. In Melki, "Al-Sahāta al-ʿarabiya," 201–204.

37. Daye, *Lakom Jubrānakom*, 181.

38. Gibran and Gibran, *Khalil Gibran*, 289.

39. Ibid., 292.

40. In Melki, "Al-Sahāta al-ʿarabiya," 241–245; my translation from the Arabic.

41. Ibid., 112.

42. Ibid., 130.

43. Mokarzel, in "Al-Aʿālam al-Sūry" (The Syrian world), *Al Saʾeh*, April 4, 1929.

44. Gibran Khalil Gibran, *Syrian World*, July 1926.

45. De Tarazi, *Tarīkh al-sahāfa al-ʿarabiyah*, part 4, 408–409.

46. Afifa Karam, "Thihabi ila al-harb tashabuni ummi" [My departure to the war accompanied by my mother], *Al-aʾalam al-jadid* 3 (December 1912).

47. Anton Zraick, "Khalifat al-Muslimin yadʾu lel-jihad. Fa-ila-l-jihad" [The Muslim caliph calls for war. Then on to war] *Jurāb-ul-Kurdi*, November 12, 1912. The title is intended as political satire by Zraick.

48. Ibid.

49. Anton Zraick, "Hawadeth kharijyya" (Foreign affairs), *Jurāb-ul-Kurdi*, November 19, 1912.

50. Ibid.
51. Ibid.
52. Rafīq al-ʿAẓm, "Al-harakah al-Sūrīya: Asbabaha wa nataʾijaha" [The Syrian movement: Its causes and outcomes], *Jurāb-ul-Kurdi*, May 17, 1913.
53. Ibid.
54. Letters between Jubrān Kuzma in Montpellier and Ameen Farah in Cairo indicate that the practice of mailing newspapers from the United States to the Arab population was practiced widely. The correspondence in question describes hiding newspapers in books and luggage and sending them through the foreign mail service in the Ottoman provinces to serve the purposes of foreign nationals through exchanges usually not subjected to search by the Ottoman police; June 12, 1912, Farah Papers, Bawardi Collection.
55. Rafīq al-ʿAẓm, "Al-harakah al-Sūrīya, III" [The Syrian Movement, 3], *Jurāb-ul-Kurdi*, May 20, 1913.
56. Rafīq al-ʿAẓm, "Al-harakah," *Jurāb-ul-Kurdi*, May 21, 1913.
57. *Mirāt al-Gharb*, "Filastin," April 18, 1913.
58. ʿAẓm, "Al-harakah al-Suryya, III."
59. *Al-Hoda*, "Mahmoud Shawkat Pasha," June 13, 1913.
60. *Mirāt al-Gharb*, "Limatha al-istikhfaf?" (Why belittle?), May 5, 1913.
61. Ibid.
62. *Mirāt al-Gharb*, "Sūrīya wa syasat al-taʾweed" (Syria and the policy of compensation), May 5, 1913.
63. Antonius, *Arab Awakening*, 109.

CHAPTER 3: SOLDIERS FOR SYRIA BEFORE WORLD WAR I

1. *Mirat al-Gharb*, "Daʿwah ilā abnāʾ al-ummah al-ʿarabīyah" [Invitation to the children of the Arab nation], May 5, 1913.
2. Ibid.
3. Al-Hadi al-Taymoumi, *Fi usul al-harakah al-qaumīyah al-ʿarabīyah, 1839–1920* [On the origins of the Arab national movement, 1839–1920] (Tunis: Dār Muhammad ʿAli al-hāmi, 2002), 87.
4. Antonius, *Arab Awakening*, 109, 114.
5. Taymoumi, *Fi usul al-harakah al-qaumīyah al-ʿarabīyah, 1839–1920*, 87.
6. Muhib al-Din al-Khatib, *Al-Muʾtamar al-ʿArabi al-Awwal* [The First Arab Conference] (Cairo: Higher Committee of the Ottoman Decentralization Party in Egypt, Bosphorus Press, 1913).
7. Ibid., 18.
8. Ibid., 20–21.
9. Ibid., 66–67.
10. Ibid., 68.
11. Ibid., 70.
12. Ibid.

13. Ibid., 113–121.

14. Ibid., 120.

15. "Barqīyah min Bārīs ilā Jamʿīyat al-Ittiḥād al-Sūri" [A telegram from Paris to the United Syrian Society], *Mirāt al-Gharb*, June, 23, 1913.

16. Letter to the editor, "Jamʿīyat al-shubān al-Zaḥlīyīn fī wilāyat Ohio" [Zahleh Youth Society in Ohio], *Mirāt al-Gharb*, June 13, 1913.

17. *Mirāt al-Gharb*, "Ṣaḥīfah amrīkīyah wa muʾtamar Bārīs" [An American newspaper and the Paris conference], June 26, 1913.

18. Ibid.

19. Khoury, "Factionalism among Syrian Nationalists," 441.

20. The priest Yaʿqoub Farah, according to his great-grandson Roy, wrote a book titled *The History of Nazareth* that was published circa 1840. It was intended for the Bawardi Collection as part of the gift, but the book went missing. Ameen's father, Saleh, wrote his son extensively from 1913 to 1923. His letters contained lessons on Arab history and analysis recounting generations-old oral traditions of Nazareth and the surrounding area.

21. Elizabeth Farah, interview by the author, 1996, Bawardi Collection. Neman Farah, a Flint-based grocer and Elizabeth's husband, was the son of Raji Farah, the mayor of Nazareth. His compatriots included original members of the Mansour, Khouri, and Jubrān families. Equally as successful as the Farah clan, these families became prosperous retail grocery dynasties and later major developers credited with building large sections of downtown Flint.

22. Ameen Farah, *Rushd wa Suha* (Cairo: Al-Taqaddum, n.d.). I estimate that Ameen began writing the novel while in Nazareth and finished it during his short stay in 1912 in Egypt, where he commissioned its publication by a printing press before leaving for the United States the following year. The printings probably reached Farah in Flint just before World War I commenced. His friend Makhoul Shaheen inscribed a dedication on the inside cover of Farah's copy: "This novel was presented by the loyal friend Ameen Farah in 1915 or 1917, and now Ameen asked for it from yours truly as he no longer owns a copy of his own. If anyone else asked for it, he would not have gotten it. However, the dear Ameen being a longtime friend is hereby presented with this novel from one brother to another. Your friend, Makhoul [Mikhail] Shaheen." An older dedication appears in Farah's impeccable handwriting that he most likely inscribed as a young man: "Presented to the dear friend Mikhail Shaheen." Correspondence between the two friends establishes their intimate acquaintance in the 1920s through the 1940s. I estimate that both men were well into their eighties when this novel found its way back to Ameen's library in the mid-1970s.

23. Farah, *Rushd wa Suha*, 1.

24. Based on my translations of early publications by Syrian intellectuals and community leaders, the United Syrian Society seems to have been the earliest organization to draw wide audiences.

25. Kherbawi, *Tarīkh al Wilāyāt al-Muttaḥidah*, 822.

26. Ibid., 799.

27. Ibid., 816–817.

28. Ibid., 839.

29. In Mikhail Naimy, *Saboun: Ḥikayat Omr, 1889–1959*, 7th ed. (Beirut: Nofal, 1991).

30. Ibid., 53–54.

31. Ibid.

32. Ibid., 55.

33. Mikhail Naimy, letter to Ameen Farah, March 7, 1915, Farah Papers, Bawardi Collection.

34. Naimy, *Saboun*, 55.

35. Ibid., 57.

36. Letter from Mikhail Naimy to Ameen Farah, circa April 1915, Farah Papers, Bawardi Collection.

37. Untitled FSS bylaws, Farah Papers, Bawardi Collection.

38. Although the role of Syrian women nationalists is emphasized in the archival material under study, more work is needed to reveal the extent of their contributions, for example, in churches and ladies auxiliaries collecting aid for the organizations in question. See Ali al-Tarrah, "An Overview of Historical Changes in the Lives of Middle Eastern Women," *Domes* 3.3 (June 30, 1994): 5.

39. Untitled FSS bylaws, Farah Papers, Bawardi Collection.

40. Orfalea, *Before the Flames*, 91–94.

41. Letter from Ameen Rihani to ʿAbdulmassīh Haddād, May 24, 1917, in Melki, "Al-Sahāta al-ʿarabiya," 174.

42. Ameen Farah Diary, August 1919, Farah Papers, Bawardi Collection.

43. Besides writing, all three spoke to a crowd of 500 in opposition to Zionism at the Hotel Bossert; *New York Times*, "Oppose Zionist Plan; Syrians Adopt Resolution of Protest at Brooklyn Meeting," November 9, 1918.

CHAPTER 4: THE SYRIA IDEA AND THE NEW SYRIA PARTY

1. Gabriel E. Ward, *Al-Jundi al-Sūri fi thalath hurub* [The Syrian soldier in three wars] (New York: Al-Maktaba al-Amreekīyah al-Suriya, 1919). This bound volume from the collection of Basil Kherbawi is one of the earliest and most complete and significant publications on military service by Syrians across the United States. The "three wars" in the title are the Spanish-American War, the war in the Philippines, and World War I. The author published rare portraits of several members of the Pen Bond, including Rashid Ayoub, William Catzeflis, Nasib Arida, and others, in addition to glowing accounts of the soldiers' military prowess.

2. *Al-Akhlāq* 6.1 (January 1925); *Al-Akhlāq* 6.6 (June 1925).

3. Suleiman, introduction to *American Arabs and Political Participation*, edited by Michael W. Suleiman (Washington, DC: Woodrow Wilson International Center for Scholars, 2006), 10.

4. Ibid.

5. Charles Malouf Samaha, "A Voice in the Dark: Faris Saleem Malouf (1892–1958)," unpublished biography, 25. The author is a practicing attorney in Saint Petersburg, Florida.

6. Ibid. Noteworthy is that James Ansara gave his interpretation of the events to Michael Suleiman in an interview on November 22, 1981; series 5, subseries 5–6 Oral Histories, Transcripts, Suleiman Collection.

7. See, for example, this news item from a Syrian publication in Indianapolis: "Mid West Federation of Syrian American Clubs Now a Reality. Dr. Waheeb Zarick [sic], First President. Other Officers Unanimously Elected," *Syrian Ark* 1.1 (September 1936). A performance program was attached: "Love or Honor, an Oriental Musical Drama by the Little Syrian Theatre Guild under the Auspices of the Mid-West Federation of Syrian Clubs (The Syrian Ladies Aid Society of Chicago, Illinois: May 1, 1938, Civic Center Theatre, 20 N. Wacker Drive, Chicago, Illinois). Milwaukee Welcomes You to the Third Annual Convention of the Midwestern Federation of Syrian American Clubs, August 5th–7th, 1938," series 9, box 12, folder 6, Naff Collection.

8. The information on the federations is gleaned from my many conversations with Charles M. Samaha, the great-nephew of Faris Malouf, from summer 2010 to February 2012. Samaha said Faris, aided by his cousin Tawfick, established the Eastern Federation in about 1932. It lasted until 1960, before it was replaced by Frank Maria's American Arabic Association (AMARA), founded in 1960 in Boston from remnants of the Eastern Federation's Foreign Relations Committee.

9. Rihani, *Book of Khalid*, 259. For more information on this important intellectual, see the website *Project Khalid: The 100th Anniversary of the First Arab-American Novel*, http://projectkhalid.org/.

10. Gertrude Lowthian Bell, *Syria: The Desert and the Sown* (London: William Heinemann, 1907), 194. Bell, who chronicled her travels to the "exotic East," wrote, "When I returned to my tent I found a visiting card bearing the name and title Hanna Khabbaz of the Protestant Church at Homs. Beneath was written the following message: 'Madam wife and I are ready to do any service you need in Christ and the humanity. We should like to if you kindly accept us I am your obedient servant.'"

11. Hanna Khabbaz, letter to Ameen Farah, December 22, 1919. Farah Papers, Bawardi Collection.

12. Ibid.

13. Khabbaz was no stranger to New York literary circles, as he wrote in *Al-Funūn* alongside Gibran as early as 1916. See, for example, Hanna Khabbaz, "Falsafat al-Ka'ināt, 1: Ana," *Al-Funūn* 2 (November 1916): 503–508; and Hanna Khabbaz, "Falsafat al-Ka'ināt, 2: al-Fida'," *Al-Funūn* 2 (February 1917): 786–793.

14. Ḥabīb Kātibah, "Syria for the Syrians under the Guardianship of the United States," *Bulletin of the Syrian National Society* (Boston) 1.9, February 28, 1919.

15. Ibid., 3.

16. "Habib Ibrahim Katibah," series 9, box 12, file 6, Naff Collection.

17. Peter S. George, "Dr. F. I. Shatara, Biography," *Federal Herald* (Boston) 2.7 (April 8, 1942).
18. Kātibah, "Syria for the Syrians," 10.
19. Ibid., 3.
20. Ibid., 11.
21. Ibid.
22. Taysir Jbara, *Palestinian Leader Hajj Amin al-Husayni, Mufti of Jerusalem* (Princeton, NJ: Kensington Press, 1985), 32-35.
23. Nicola Qubʻyn, letter to Ameen Farah, January 10, 1920. Farah Papers, Bawardi Collection.
24. Ameen Farah Diary, Farah Papers, Bawardi Collection. This is confirmed by a letter from Muhammad Muhaisen, at this point having settled in Detroit, on the letterhead of the Royal (ice cream) Cone Company on the corner of Franklin Street and Dubois in Detroit; letter from Muhammad Muhaisen to Ameen Farah, May 19, 1921, Farah Papers, Bawardi Collection. After visiting Ameen in Flint, Muhaisen asked Ameen to send him 100 copies of *Rushd wa Suha* after selling a dozen copies and suggesting they share the profits on a 50-50 basis.
25. William T. Ellis, "Syrians Seek Liberty: American Influence Has Roused Spirit of National Unity," *Washington Post*, September 7, 1919; Philip Hitti, "The Disposition of Syria," *New York Times*, February 2, 1919; *New York Times*, "Syria and Palestine for Pan-Arabic Rule," November 25, 1923.
26. In Adel Beshara, "A Rebel Syrian; Gibran Khalil Gibran," in *The Origins of Syrian Nationhood: Histories, Pioneers, and Identity*, edited by Adel Beshara (London: Routledge, 2011), 148.
27. Arthur Goldschmidt Jr. and Lawrence Davidson, *A Concise History of the Middle East* (Boulder, CO: Westview Press, 2006), 280.
28. The following are among the headlines that in my view helped the cause of the NSP, including some that indicate active anti-Arab propaganda: *New York Times*, "Proud Druse Race Enraged at French: New Yorker, Back From Syria, Tells How Savage Warfare Started with Insult. Puts Blame on Officers; Villages Bombed with Great Loss of Life, Following Massacre of French Column," November 2, 1925; B. Ybabba, "Americans Blame Sarrail: Those Familiar with Near East Say a Change Is Needed," special cable to *New York Times*, October 30, 1925; *Chicago Daily Tribune*, "Revolt Grows: Syrian Rebels Cut Damascus Road; Win Town," November 7, 1925; Robert Paulaine, "Raid French Posts Near Homs, Syria: Rebels Also Plan Offensives and Form Staff to Prevent Troop Movements. Loot Balbeck Station. French Reinforcements Arrive—More Shelling Is Reported East of Damascus," special cable to *New York Times*, December 15, 1925; Thomas T. Topping, "War Still Rages in Much of Syria: French Military Leaders Say Paris Should Furnish Bigger Army or Quit Mandate," *New York Times*, June 23, 1926; *Chicago Daily Tribune*, "Yank Churches and Schools in Syria Burned," November 8, 1925; *New York Times*, "News of First Trouble Suppressed: Report 200 French Killed in Syria," August 8, 1925; *Los Angeles Times*, "French Quit Syria Area after Loss: Natives Seize Equipment and

Slay Soldiers in Surprise Attack," August 8, 1925; and George Seldes, "Christians of Syria, Led by Priest, Battle Islam Horde," *Chicago Daily Tribune*, November 15, 1925. The racist overtones of the term "Islam Horde" in this last headline obscure the part of the story itself that says the reporter's interpreter, "Najeeb N. Samra . . . a Detroit rug merchant" and one of the "large colony [of] naturalized Americans" visiting their country of birth, was a prolific activist against the French, the British, and Zionism.

29. *Washington Post*, "Sarrail Summoned to Explain French 'Atrocity' in Syria: Paris Gets Its Most Complete News of Damascus from U.S. Envoy. 1,200 Prisoners Killed in Escaping, Is Report. Havas Agency Says Boncour May Be Commissioner, If He Will Accept," October 31, 1925.

30. Ibid.

31. Michele Lotfallah, "Complains of French Acts: Syro-Palestinian Committee Tells of Destruction in Syria," cable to the editor, *New York Times*, October 29, 1925. This cable was sent by Lotfallah himself, relying on French news reports, in an appeal "to the conscience of the civilized world" to put a stop to atrocities such as the bombardment at Sarrail's behest of the Druze enclave Suadah "before evacuating it," resulting in the killing of 200 people. See also *Washington Post*, "Sultan Pasha Atrash Condemned to Death," June 1, 1926.

32. Ameen Farah, letter to Jamal al-Husseini, January 13, 1925. Farah Papers, Bawardi Collection.

33. Nathmi Anabtawi, letter to Suleiman [Baddūr] and Ameen Farah, circa January 1926, Farah Papers, Bawardi Collection.

34. Ameen Farah, letter to Najib Nassar, Flint, April 10, 1926, Farah Papers, Bawardi Collection.

35. Ibid.

36. Michael Provence, *The Great Syrian Revolt and the Rise of Arab Nationalism* (Austin: University of Texas Press, 2005).

37. Ibid., 68.

38. ʿAbbas Abu Shaqra, "Three Month Report," addressed to Ameen Farah, May 3, 1926, Farah Papers, Bawardi Collection.

39. Ibid.

40. Ibid.

41. Ameen Farah, letter to Lutfi al-Saʿdi, May 31, 1926, Farah Papers, Bawardi Collection. Farah kept carbon copies of many of his outgoing correspondences, but these were drafts and did not always indicate the recipients and dates. When possible, I disclose both based on the content.

42. Ameen Farah, letter to Hanna Nasr, May 31, 1926, Farah Papers, Bawardi Collection.

43. L. M. Saʿdi, letter to Ameen Farah, June 6, 1926. Farah Papers, Bawardi Collection.

44. Ameen Farah, letter to Suleiman Baddūr, May 31, 1926, Farah Papers, Bawardi Collection.

45. Ali Muhyiddīn, letter to Ameen Farah, June 26, 1926, Farah Papers, Bawardi Collection.

46. Ameen Farah, letter to Ali Muhyiddīn, June 13, 1926, Farah Papers, Bawardi Collection.

47. Nathmi Anabtawi, letter to Ameen Farah, June 30, 1926, Farah Papers, Bawardi Collection.

48. Ibid.

49. Ibid.

50. ʿAbbas Abu Shaqra to the chapters of the New Syria Party, July 20, 1926, Farah Papers, Bawardi Collection.

51. Badiʿ Thibiyan, letter to Ameen Farah, August 11, 1926, Farah Papers, Bawardi Collection.

52. Muhammad Musa al-Tawīl, Islamic Committee to Aid the Victims (*mankū-bīn*), Damascus Branch of the Beirut Central Committee, letter to the head of the Syrian Arab Committee [Ameen Farah], September 15, 1926, Farah Papers, Bawardi Collection.

53. Ameen Farah, letter to ʿAbbas Abu Shaqra, August 10, 1926, Farah Papers, Bawardi Collection.

54. Ibid.

55. Ameen Farah, notes, Farah Papers, Bawardi Collection.

56. Ibid.

57. ʿAbbas Abu Shaqra, letter to Ameen Farah, October 12, 1926, Farah Papers, Bawardi Collection.

58. Ibid.

59. Hasan Amin al-Buʿaini, *Durūz Sūrīya wa Lubnān* [The Druze of Syria and Lebanon] (Beirut: Arab Center for Research and Documentation, 1993).

60. Ibid., 219.

61. In Provence, *Great Syrian Revolt*, 1.

62. In al-Buʿaini, *Durūz Sūrīya wa Lubnān*, 394. The signature on the letters to Farah and his compatriots matches that of Sultan al-Atrash in Buʿaini's appendix.

63. ʿAbbas Abu Shaqra, letter to chapters of the New Syria Party, December 192[6]. Although the date is listed December 1927, the content spells out preparations for the convention to be held in January 1927, which can only mean that 1927 was written in error and should have read December 1926. Box 6, series III (henceforth 6.3, etc.), Farah Papers, Bawardi Collection.

64. Bayan Nuwaihed al-Hut, "Shakib Arslan," *Al-Arabi*, March 2008.

65. ʿAbbas Abu Shaqra, letter to chapters of the New Syria Party, December 192[6].

66. Ibid.

67. Ibid.

68. Kamel Hamady, Pan-Syrian Society, Flint, letter to New Syria Party, December 31, 1926, Farah Papers, Bawardi Collection.

69. ʿAbbas Abu Shaqra, "Program for the Second Annual Convention of the New Syria Party," sent to chapters of NSP, December 7, 1926, Farah Papers, Bawardi Collection.

70. *Detroit Free Press*, "Syrians Hear Liberty Plea. Emir Chekib Arslan Tells 1000 Delegates Here of Fight Against French," January 17, 1926.

71. Ibid.

72. Ibid.

73. Najīb Diāb, "The Approaching Syria," *Mirāt al-Gharb*, May 4, 1917.

74. Ibid.

75. See, for example, *Al-Hoda*, July 1, 1922, full-page ads under the headline "Demands of the Lebanese" in which the emblem of the Lebanese League of Progress takes center stage.

76. *Al-Hoda*, July 29, 1922.

77. Ibid.

78. *Al-Hoda*, January 4, 1926; *Al-Hoda*, "Akhbar al-Watan" [News of the Homeland], January 5, 1927.

79. *Detroit Free Press*, "400 Syrians Protest Visit of Emir Here," January 18, 1926.

80. Ibid.

81. Ibid.

82. Mokarzel, "Al-Khawāṭer. "Who Will Represent the Lebanese in Paris?" *Al-Hoda*, January 20, 1927.

83. "A Public Meeting of the New Syria Party Convention in the Auditorium of the Wayne Lodge," January 16, 1927. Farah Papers, Bawardi Collection.

84. Ibid.

85. Ibid.

86. ʿAbbas Abu Shaqra, letter to Ameen Farah and Muhammad ʿAjram, undated, Farah Papers, Bawardi Collection.

87. S. Joseph, letter to the Executive Committee of the New Syria Party, March 17, 1927, Farah Papers, Bawardi Collection.

88. Elias Joseph, letter to Ameen Farah, March 18, 1927, Farah Papers, Bawardi Collection.

89. Mahmoud Abu al-Filat, letter to the Executive Committee of the New Syria Party and the Treasurer, March 19, 1927, Farah Papers, Bawardi Collection.

90. Provence, *Great Syrian Revolt*, 139.

91. Ameen Farah, letter to Salman Jaber, April 16, 1927, Farah Papers, Bawardi Collection.

92. Executive Committee of the New Syria Party, letter to the Central Committee, April 22, 1927, Farah Papers, Bawardi Collection.

93. Ali Salman Tab Abi al-Hisn, letter to the New Syria Party, April 27, 1927, Farah Papers, Bawardi Collection.

94. Ibid.

95. George Dibs, letter to the Executive Committee of New Syria Party, April 29, 1927, Farah Papers, Bawardi Collection.
96. ʿAbbas Abu Shaqra, letter and receipts to Ameen Farah, April 28, 1927, Farah Papers, Bawardi Collection.
97. Nasīm Saybaʿa, letter to Ameen Farah, May 5, 1927, Farah Papers, Bawardi Collection.
98. Ibid. Saybaʿa was honored in New York, where Rizk Haddad, M.D., a poet and Lebanese man of letters, gave a speech on the political situation to a large gathering in 1927. Judging from the content of the Arabic-language address extolling the virtues of U.S. independence and giving a brief history of it, the undated address was likely held during the week of the Fourth of July that year. See Haddad, *Nafahat al-Riyād*, 280. Haddad's wife, Shafiqa Gabriel Haddad, published this invaluable volume posthumously in honor of her husband.
99. Ameen Farah, letter to Nasīm Saybaʿa, May 22, 1927, Farah Papers, Bawardi Collection.
100. See Antonius, *Yaqzat al-ʿArab*, 500–508; Cleveland, *History of the Modern Middle East*, 228, 229.
101. Ameen Farah, letter to Nasīm Saybaʿa, May 22, 1927, Farah Papers, Bawardi Collection.
102. Ibid.
103. ʿAbbas Abu Shaqra, letter to NSP chapters, April 22, 1927, Farah Papers, Bawardi Collection.
104. Ameen Farah, letter to ʿAbbas Abu Shaqra, June 12, 1927; ʿAbbas Abu Shaqra, "Official Announcement," New Syria Party, June 16, 1927, Farah Papers, Bawardi Collection.
105. Ameen Farah, letter to ʿAbbas Abu Shaqra, June (no date) 1927, Farah Papers, Bawardi Collection.
106. Nasīm Saybaʿa, letter to Ameen Farah, undated, Farah Papers, Bawardi Collection. For a useful discussion on divisions within the ranks of Syrian nationalists see Khoury, "Factionalism among Syrian Nationalists."
107. Nasīm Saybaʿa, letter to Ameen Farah, undated, Farah Papers, Bawardi Collection; *New York Times*, "Colonizing in Syria Charged to France: Native Commission Lodges Protest with the League, Alleging Misuse of Mandate," September 4, 1927.
108. Nasīm Saybaʿa, letter to Ameen Farah, undated, Farah Papers, Bawardi Collection.
109. Ḥabīb Ibrahīm Kātibah, *Al-Nāṭiqūn bi al-Ḍād fi Amrīkā* [*Arab Speakers in America*], translated by Al-Badawi al-Mulathasm (Jerusalem: Al-Matbaʿa al-tijāriya, 1946).
110. Hitti, *Syrians in America*, 59.
111. Shakib Arslan, letter to Ḥabīb Kātibah, January 6, 1929. Arslan's address is listed as 26 Avenue Les Alpes, Lausanne. Series 9, box 13, folder 2, Naff Collection.
112. Ibid.

CHAPTER 5: THE MANDATE YEARS AND THE DIASPORA

1. Michael Suleiman, *The Arab American Experience in the U.S. and Canada: A Classified Annotated Bibliography* (Ann Arbor, MI: Pierian Press, 2006), 422.

2. Ḥabīb Ibrahīm Kātibah, "The Arab Challenge," unpublished manuscript, 80; series 9, box 15, folder 5, Naff Collection. I estimate that Kātibah wrote his manuscript shortly before his death in February 1951.

3. Ibid., 81.

4. Ibid.

5. Harry Viteles and Khalil Totah, eds., *Palestine, a Decade of Development* (Philadelphia: American Academy of Political and Social Science, 1932).

6. See Rashid Khalidi, *Palestinian Identity: The Construction of Modern National Consciousness* (New York: Columbia University Press, 1998), 146–174. Although Khalidi does not demarcate the period by the Balfour Declaration and San Remo Agreement, he argues that Palestinians began to think of themselves as such even before the mandate was conferred on Britain by the League of Nations. His work does not address immigrant political identity in the United States, but it does provide the transnationalist dimension for this study.

7. See Davidson, *America's Palestine*.

8. See Roger Howard, "Britain, Persia and Petroleum," *History Today* 58.5 (2008): 44–50. However, Iraqis would not be free of British control over the country's resources, foreign policy, and national borders until a bloody coup in 1958.

9. R. Khalidi, *Palestinian Identity*, 147.

10. Ḥabīb I. Kātibah, "Syrian Americans," in *One America: The History, Contributions, and Present Problems of Our Racial and National Minorities*, edited by Francis Brown and Joseph S. Roucek, 3rd edition (Engelwood, CA: Prentice Hall, 1952), 284; originally published 1937.

11. Ibid.

12. Philip Hitti, "Al-Istishraq fi al-Wilayat al-Muttahidah" [Orientalism in the United States], *As-Sameer*, April 1932, 10.

13. Ibid., unnumbered footnote.

14. Elia Madey, "Al-Marhum Naʿūm Muharzal" [The late Naʿūm Mokarzel], *As-Sameer*, April 15, 1932, 108.

15. Ibid.

16. *As-Sameer*, "Jumhuryya bila musawāh" [A republic without equality], April 15, 1932, 111.

17. Nafhat Nasr, "Dual Executive Leadership in Lebanon," *Journal of Arab Affairs* 4.1 (Spring 1985): 89.

18. *As-Sameer*, "Suri wa Lubnani wa . . . " [Syrian and Lebanese and . . .], *As-Sameer*, October 1932, 18–19.

19. Ibid., 20.

20. Aʾ (pseudonym), "Haul Suri Wa Lubnani" [About Syria and Lebanon], *As-Sameer*, November 1932, 26–27.

21. *As-Sameer,* "Ughnya Sauda'" [A black song (translated from English)] *As-Sameer* 4.22 (March 1933): 3.

22. *As-Sameer,* "Maut zaeem filastini kabeer" [The death of a great Palestinian leader] *As-Sameer* 6.22 (March 1935). "Al-Malek al-Arabi" [The Arab king] *As-Sameer* 3.5 (June 1931).

23. Khalidi, *Palestinian Identity,* 165.

24. Ibid.

25. Buʿaini, *Durūz Sūrīya wa Lubnān,* 150–151.

26. In Khalidi, *Palestinian Identity,* 165.

27. Beatrice (Mrs. Stewart) Erskine, *Palestine of the Arabs* (Westport, CT: Hyperion Press, [1935] 1976), 60.

28. Ibid., 81; Ann Mosley Lesch, *Arab Politics in Palestine, 1917–1939: The Frustration of a Nationalist Movement* (Ithaca, NY: Cornell University Press, 1979), 45.

29. Lesch, *Arab Politics,* 45.

30. In Erskine, *Palestine of the Arabs,* 70.

31. Lesch, *Arab Politics,* 160, 161.

32. Ibid., 162–164.

33. Palestine Arab Delegation, "The Holy Land: The Moslem and Christian Case against Zionist Aggression," official statement, 1. The delegation produced the statement in February 1922 from meetings at London's Hotel Cecil during the conference.

34. Ibid., 2.

35. Ibid.

36. Ibid., 3.

37. Ibid., 5.

38. Ibid., 6.

39. Ibid., 4.

40. Lesch, *Arab Politics,* 166n40.

41. Esco Foundation for Palestine, *Palestine, a Study of Jewish, Arab, and British Policies,* vol. 1 (New Haven, CT: Yale University Press for the Esco Foundation, 1945), 281.

42. Ibid., 285.

43. Ibid., 285.

44. Lesch, *Arab Politics,* 156.

45. Ibid., 169.

46. Elia Madey, "Al nar wa-al-dam fi Filastin wa ʿitham Balfor" [Fire and blood in Palestine and the bones of Balfour] *As-Sameer,* May 1936, 2.

47. "Thawrat 1929," [The revolt of 1929] and "La Tasruqu Baitana," [Do not steal our home] *As-Sameer,* May 1936, 6–7.

48. Ibid., 6.

49. Erskine, *Palestine of the Arabs,* 134.

50. Ibid., 132.

51. Among the few surviving records of Fuad Isa Shatara is an aluminum disc

containing the voice of the activist. Judging from the content and the age of the record, the disc dates to the early 1930s. In it Shatara gives information from the Simpson Report. The disc is in the Bawardi Collection courtesy of Barbara Tate Cerato of New York.

52. John Hope Simpson, *Palestine. Report on Immigration, Land Settlement, and Development* (London: His Majesty's Stationery Office, 1930), 64.

53. Ibid., 63. Due to quotas restricting emigration from the region, it is safe to assume that the remittances came from pre–World War I émigrés and immigrants.

54. Ibid., 42.

55. Ibid., 49.

56. Naomi Wiener Cohen, *The Year after the Riots: American Responses to the Palestine Crisis of 1929–30* (Detroit: Wayne State University Press, 1988). Cohen's book is a useful treatment of intra-Jewish debate over support for the Zionists. Cohen reaches predictable conclusions, though, such as viewing attempts at even-handedness by the British as anti-Zionist and giving a critical overview of self-serving U.S. foreign policy.

57. *Chicago Daily Tribune*, "50 Slain in Riots in Jerusalem: Jews Attacked by Moslems at Wailing Wall, British Rush Ships and Troops. Where Riots in Which 50 Were Killed in Jerusalem Started," August 25, 1929; *Chicago Daily Tribune*, "12 Americans Die in Holy Land Riot: Chicago Youth Slain As Arabs Storm College," August 26, 1929; *Washington Post*, "45 Jews Slain As Racial War Nears Hebron: Palestine Death Total Reaches 63; Hundreds Are Wounded. Americans Escape Harm In Jerusalem. British Planes Bombing Arabian Towns near Holy City. U.S. Consul Files Report On Clashes, Representative Celler Asks Instant Dispatch of Cruiser to War Zone," August 26, 1929; *Chicago Daily Tribune*, "Chicago Jews Appeal to U.S. to Protect Kin: Legion Post Offers to Fight in Palestine," August 27, 1929; Vincent Sheehan, "Arabs Kill Americans: Twelve Victims in Holy Land Bloody Riots Continue and British Rush Troops to Halt Bloodshed Hebrew Battle Described; Jaffa Crisis Feared; Fascists Censured," *Los Angeles Times*, August 26, 1929; *New York Times*, "Riots Preventable, Rabbi Wise Asserts: Britain Can 'Redeem Honor' by Prompt Action, Says Jewish Leader in Paris," August 30, 1929; *Washington Post*, "Arab Flames Raze Ancient City of Jews: Safed, in Upper Galilee, Is Fired and Residents Killed or Hurt. Hebrew Chieftains Make Plea for Aid, Extermination Is Threat Hanging over Heads, Appeal Asserts. British Send Planes To Border Of Syria, Jerusalem Is Quiet, Although Sporadic Violence Marks Moslem Sabbath," August 31, 1929. Compare these headlines to others in the *New York Times*: "Americans Safe, Consul Reports: Washington Hears British Have Taken Adequate Precautions in Palestine Riots," August 25, 1929; special to the *New York Times*, "Arabs Ask Stimson to Aid in Palestine: Delegation of Citizens Urge Help to Revoke Balfour Declaration and Cut Immigration. Blame Homeland Project Jewish Movement Means Double Sovereignty, Secretary Is Told—Group Visits British Ambassador," September 7, 1929; special to the *New York Times*, "Arabs Here Appeal To MacDonald for Aid: Urge Revocation of the Balfour Declaration—Voice Regret over His Ref-

erence to "Crime," September 8, 1929; Joseph M. Levy, special cable to the *New York Times*, "Arabs Call Strike On Rules For Jews: They Assail as Far Too Liberal Orders on Wailing Wall—Jews Call Them Harsh. Shops To Close Tomorrow Day of Atonement Passes Quietly, With Synagogues Overflowing With Tearful Worshipers," October 15, 1929; and "Rights in Palestine of Jews Debated: Amin Rihani and M. W. Weisgal Discuss Subject From Opposite Viewpoints. Kaiser And World War, New Evidence on Potsdam Council Is Offered in an Article in November Current History," October 27, 1929.

58. Jewish Telegraphic Agency, "Riot Death Total Now Placed at 119: 83 Jews and 36 Arabs Reported in Official Bulletin—213 Severely Wounded. Many Colonies Deserted, Residents Flee to Cities—Raids Continue in Various Places—More Victims Buried. Colony Fight Lasts Thirty-two Hours. More Victims Buried. Appeals to World for Aid," August 28, 1929.

59. *New York Times*, "Zionists To Raise Relief Fund Here: Committee to Be Formed to Give Information on the Holy Land Outrages. Mass Meeting Is Called. All Jewish Organizations in City Will Be Asked to Participate on Thursday Night," August 27, 1929.

60. This determination is based on my extensive survey of U.S. newspapers; before the *New York Times* was targeted for an effective boycott, it had a different orientation.

61. *New York Times*, "Arabs Here Assail Jewish Riot Views: Call Reports on Palestine Situation Unfair at Meeting—Blame Balfour Declaration. Appeal To World Leaders, Messages Are Sent to League of Nations, Hoover, MacDonald, the Pope and Many Others," August 29, 1929.

62. Ibid.

63. Ibid.

64. Rihani, in "Rights in Palestine of Jews Debated," *New York Times*, October 27, 1929.

65. *New York Times*, "Graduate of Cornell Testifies for Arabs: Nazarene Tells British Inquiry Commission Zionists Turned 945 Families Adrift," November 29, 1929.

66. I am in possession of several hundred land registries in the mayor's handwriting.

67. *Bay City Times*, "Says Occidentals Have False Notions of East. N. H. Samra Explains Traditions of Mohammedans," February 1, 1931.

68. Najīb Samra, "Racial Hatred In Palestine Not Cause of Recent Row: N. H. Samra Lays Trouble To Political Differences of Arab and Jew," *Bay City Times*, March 2, 1930.

69. Ameen Rihani, letter to Ameen Farah, February 18, 1930, Farah Papers, Bawardi Collection. In the letter, Rihani confirmed receiving $12 from Farah for a shipment of his book to Ragheb Mitrage and informed him that books for Khalil Bazi and Wadie Mumari were sent to Detroit and that he informed Dr. Lutfi al-Sa'di about it. Rihani also indicated that he enclosed a shipment of books for Samra with

the Detroit shipment to Dr. Saʿdi at 525 Professional Building, 10 Peterboro, Detroit, Michigan.

70. Najīb Samra, "Arab in Midland Tells Other Side of the Story. Jews Not Rightful Inheritors of Holy Land, Says N. H. Samra," *Midland Republican*, May 1, 1930.

71. Joy Totah, "Biographical Statement," *Passia*, http://passia.org/ (accessed on June 1, 2008). Joy Totah is Khalil Totah's daughter. See the Passia website for extensive biographies of the Syrian contributors.

72. Fuad Shatara, "Arab Jewish Unity," *Palestine, a Decade of Development*, edited by Harry Viteles and Khalil Totah (Philadelphia: American Academy of Political and Social Science, 1932), 178.

73. Ibid, 179.

74. Ibid. Regarding DeHaan's murder in 1924 see David B. Green, "This Day in History: Zionism's First Political Assassination," *Haaretz*, July 30, 2013.

75. Ameen Rihani, "Palestine and the Proposed Arab Federation," in *Palestine, a Decade of Development*, edited by Viteles and Totah, 62.

76. Ibid.

77. Ibid., 63.

78. Ibid., 65. Rihani referred to his book *Around the Coasts of Arabia*, 111.

79. Aouni Abdelhadi, "The Balfour Declaration," in *Palestine, a Decade of Development*, edited by Viteles and Totah, 15–17.

80. Jamal Bey Husseini, "The Proposed Palestine Constitution," in *Palestine, a Decade of Development*, edited by Viteles and Totah, 25–26.

81. Ibid.

82. Bernard Joseph, "Palestine Legislation under the British," in *Palestine, a Decade of Development*, edited by Viteles and Totah, 39.

83. A. P. S. Clark, "Commerce Industry and Banking," in *Palestine, a Decade of Development*, edited by Viteles and Totah, 95.

84. Ibid., 97.

85. J. Elazari-Volcani, "Jewish Colonization in Palestine," in *Palestine, a Decade of Development*, edited by Viteles and Totah, 87.

86. Alfred Bonné, "The Concessions for the Mousul-Haifa Pipe Line," in *Palestine, a Decade of Development*, edited by Viteles and Totah, 116.

87. Ibid., 126.

88. Jamal Muhammad Qaddurah, *Al-qadiyah al-filastiniya wa lijan al-tahqiq* [The Palestinian question and investigative commissions] (Beirut: Dar al-Hamra, 1993), 30–31.

89. Cleveland, *History of the Middle East*.

90. Ibid., 258.

91. Qaddurah, *Al-qadiyah al-filastiniya*, 58, first note marked *.

92. Increased interest in Israel's past has revealed information on the level of competition among these gangs over weapons and influence, although underground weapons factories now serve as museums for visitors. See, for example, Ari Zivotofsky, "In Our History: Remember the Altalena . . . with Shame," *Cleveland*

Jewish News, June 19, 1998; and Herb Geduld, "Haganah Museum: A Monument to a Movement and a Man," *Cleveland Jewish News*, November 22, 1996.

93. Cleveland, *History of the Middle East*, 257–258.

94. Qaddurah, *Al-qadiyah al-filastiniya*, 32.

95. Ibid., 36.

96. Ibid.

97. Ibid., 38.

98. Ibid., 43.

99. *New York Times*, "Jews Here Decree Boycott on Reich: Defense League Asks 2,000,000 in City Area to Stop Buying German Goods and Service. Christians Urged to Join. Untermyer, Cerard, La Guardia Back Move—Say Nazis Menace World Peace," May 15, 1933.

100. *New York Times*, "Weizmann Urges A Refugee Colony. Wants Shelter n Palestine for 250,000 Jews Persecuted in Germany and Other Lands," June 29, 1933.

101. Ibid.

102. *New York Times*, "Assails Assimilation," August 22, 1933, reproduced by the Jewish Telegraphic Agency.

103. *New York Times*, "Calls Jew Victim of Mass Hypnosis: Rabbi B. R. Brickner Tells Hadassah Palestine Must Be Made Homeland for Refugees," November 30, 1935.

104. *New York Times*, "Zionists Reject Boycott of Reich: Revisionists Quit Meeting After Assailing Attitude of Congress Toward Germany. League's Help Is Sought Mildness of Resolution on the Nazis Is Believed Designed to Facilitate Emigration," August 25, 1933.

105. Ibid.

106. Khalidi, *Palestinian Identity*, 147.

107. Ibid., 146.

108. H. I. Kātibah, ed., *The Case against Zionism* (New York: Palestine National League, 1921), 10.

109. Elmer Berger, "Memoirs of an Anti-Zionist Jew," *Journal of Palestine Studies* 5.1/2 (Autumn 1975/Winter 1976): 5–6.

110. Ibid., 4.

111. Ibid., 6.

112. Albert Einstein, *Out of My Later Years* (Westport, CT: Greenwood Press, 1970), 262, in the chapter "Our Debt to Zionism."

113. Ibid.

114. Ibid., 263.

115. Virginia Iris Holmes, "Was Einstein Really a Pacifist? Einstein's Forward-Thinking, Pragmatic, Persistent Pacifism," *Peace and Change* 33.2 (April 2008): 274–307.

116. Letter from Albert Einstein to Fuad Shatara, December 16, 1930, #48–308, Albert Einstein Archives, Hebrew University of Jerusalem.

117. Ibid.

118. Fuad Shatara, "A Proposed Solution for the Arab Jewish Controversy in Palestine," #48-310, Einstein Archives, Hebrew University. Shatara's response reads like a manifesto touting a "correct diagnosis" of the problem of "political Zionism. . . . I mean the creation of a Jewish majority followed by the establishment of a Jewish sovereign state." Shatara's prescribed treatment was an armistice for ten years followed by the establishment of a representative government per the Passfield White Paper, aiding Jewish and Palestinian farmers on equal footing, conserving natural resources to benefit all, and promoting communal development in social, business, and cultural spheres. He included a quote from his letter of December 14, 1930, to Einstein and the response from the latter.

119. Albert Einstein, letter to Fuad Shatara, February 23, 1931, #48-311, Einstein Archives, Hebrew University. Cursory translations from the German were provided by Alexandra Pa'kh, PhD candidate in German literature, Wayne State University.

120. Fuad Shatara, letter to Albert Einstein, April 21, 1938, #54-360, Einstein Archives, Hebrew University.

121. Albert Einstein, letter to Haim Greenberg, April 26, 1938, #54-363, Einstein Archives, Hebrew University.

122. Haim Greenberg, letter to Einstein, April 29, 1938, #54-364. Einstein Archives, Hebrew University.

123. Ibid.

124. Jbara, *Palestinian Leader Hajj Amin al-Husayni*, 157–160.

125. Mahmoud Abu al-Filat, "Ḥadith 'an Filastin" [A Conversation on Palestine] *As-Sameer*, March 1935, 10–13.

126. Ibid.

127. Ibid.

128. Ibid.

129. *As-Sameer*, "Al-A'arab wal Harb al-Muqbilah" [The Arabs and the approaching war], September 1935, 22–30.

130. *As-Sameer*, "Al-Hizb al-sūri al-qaumi fi Sūrīya" [The Syrian National Party in Syria], January 1936, 20.

131. Suleiman, *Arab American Experience*, 422.

132. Fuad Shatara, letter to Ameen Farah, March 26, 1925, Farah Papers, Bawardi Collection.

133. Kātibah, *Al-Nāṭiqūn bi al-Ḍād fī Amrīkā*, 84–85.

134. Davidson, *America's Palestine* and "Past as Prelude."

CHAPTER 6: THE ARAB NATIONAL LEAGUE AND THE EMERGENCE OF ARAB AMERICAN IDENTITY

1. Arab National League (ANL), "Bayān al-Jāmi'ah al-'Arabīyah" [Declaration of the Arab (National) League], New York: Arab National League, circa 1937, 1.

2. Ibid., 2.

3. Ibid., 2.

4. Ibid., 6.
5. Ibid.
6. Fuad Shatara, letter to Philip Hitti, June 23, 1936, IHRC894, box 6, folder 2, Philip Hitti Papers, University of Minnesota.
7. Fuad Shatara, letter to Ḥabīb Kātibah, September 20, 1936, series 9, box 12, folder 6, Naff Collection, Smithsonian.
8. Ibid.
9. The slot for member information reads:

> I have read the Declaration of the Arab League and agree with its principles and its agenda. Accordingly, I want to become a member.
> Name—clearly in English and Arabic
> Street—in English
> City and State
> I am enclosing my membership dues of $6
> Arab National League
> 303 Fifth Avenue, New York, N.Y.

10. Arab National League (ANL), "The Constitution and Bylaws of the Arab National League" (New York: Arab National League, circa 1936), in English and Arabic.
11. Ibid., 10.
12. Arab National League (ANL), *Whither Palestine? A Statement of Facts and of Causes of the Arab-Jewish Conflict in the Holy Land* (New York: Arab National League, circa 1936).
13. Ibid., 9.
14. See, for example, these articles in *Mirāt al-Gharb*: "Al-lughah al-ʿarabīyah fī al-mahjar" [The Arabic language in the diasporas], January 11, 1927; "Limādhā qubiḍa ʿala zaʿīm al-ḥizb al-Sūri al-qaumi?" [Why was the chief of the Syrian Nationalist Party arrested?], January 3, 1937; "Risālah min Bairūt" [A message from Beirut], April 5, 1937 (regarding the return of George Faris carrying a "message of freedom"); "Amām Haikal al-ḥurrīyah: Ḥaul iʿtiqāl al-zaʿīm al-Shaʿbi Anton Saʿādah" [Before the mantel of freedom. On the arrest of the popular leader Anton Saʿadeh], April 2, 1937; "Ṣaut min Baghdād yanʿī lughat al-ḍād fī Lubnān" [A voice from Baghdad eulogizes the Arabic language], April 14, 1937; "Fatḥ Filasṭīn li hijrat al-Yahūd mustaḥīl" [Opening Palestine for Jewish immigration is impossible], April 14, 1937 (decrying persecution of Jews in Poland and Romania and calling on the British to find a place for Jews in Africa or elsewhere with more resources and space); "Al-ḥizb al-Sūri al-qaumi fī al-Maksīk yahtāj . . ." [The Syrian Nationalist Party in Mexico protests to the Lebanese government . . .], April 23, 1937 (about a protest against internal exile of Saʿadeh and members of the Syrian National Bloc including Riad al-Sulh, Khouri, Bakri, and al-Jaberi); Michele Ashqar, "Al-Khaṭar al-istiʿmāri fī Sūrīya" [The colonial danger in Syria], April 28, 1937; "Filasṭīn al-jarīḥah tataʾallam ʿalā al-ṣalīb" [Wounded Palestine is tortured on the cross],

May 10, 1937; "Al-qadīyah al-filasṭīnīyah tuthīr sukhṭ al-ʿArab wa al-Suhyūnīyīn maʿan ʿalā fikrat al-taqsīm" [The Palestine problem angers the Arabs and the Zionists against the idea of partition], July 12, 1937.

15. Curiously, several issues of the newspapers I consulted on microfilm were missing around that date within otherwise complete dates.

16. The website http://ameenrihani.org (accessed August 22, 2012) described the speech as follows:

> This [recording] depicts a gathering at the Town House Club at 123 West 43rd Street in New York on June 5, 1937. Ameen Rihani was the Guest of Honor and was hailed by each of the two opening speakers Faris S. Malouf and Professor [William Ernest] Hocking of Harvard. The Master of Ceremony was Dr. [Fuad] Shatara. The presentations by Malouf and Hocking were about 30 minutes, combined. Rihani's speech was 26 minutes long. During the introduction of Ameen Rihani, Dr. Shatara read two cables praising the Guest of Honor, one from the grand *mufti* of Jerusalem, Ameen Al-Husaini, and the other from Emir Adel Arslan in London. This broadcast was aired by the local radio station WNYC in NY.

17. *New York Times*, "Zionism Decried by Arab Leader," June 6, 1937.

18. Ibid.

19. Jacob Dabronsky, telegram to mayor of New York City, June 7, 1937, MS Am 2375.245, William E. Hocking Papers, Houghton Library, Harvard University (henceforth Hocking Papers).

20. F. J. H. Kracke, letter to Hon. F. H. La Guardia, June 7, 1937, MS Am 2375.245, Hocking Papers.

21. *New York Times*, "Anti-Jewish Bias On WNYC Is Denied," June 16, 1937.

22. Ibid.

23. "We" as opposed to "I" is an expression of humility in written Arabic text. There are no indications that Rihani the *raḥḥālah* (traveling scholar) was accompanied by anyone on his journey.

24. Ameen Rihani, letter to Albert Rihani, February 14, 1937, *Rasāʾil Ameen al-Rihani, 1896–1940* [Letters of Ameen al-Rihani] (Beirut: Dar al-Rihani lil-Nashr, 1959), 514.

25. *Flint Journal*, "Noted Arab Leader Coming Here Monday to Talk about Palestine," July 11, 1937.

26. Rihani, letter to Laila al-Saʿdi, July 31, 1937, *Rasāʾil Ameen al-Rihani*, 518.

27. Rihani, to Husseini, July 31, 1937, *Rasāʾil Ameen al-Rihani*, 519. Rihani mentioned the invitations to Abdelhadi and Ragheb in this letter. The ship, he wrote, would dock in Jaffa on Sunday morning and sail that afternoon to Haifa in the evening before continuing to Beirut at 10 p.m. Rihani informed the *mufti* that access to the ship from the pavement was easier in Haifa, where the port had been built up.

28. Ibid.

29. Davidson, *America's Palestine*, 239.

30. *Mirāt al-Gharb*, "Al-Yahūd musirrūn ʿalā waṭan qaumi" [Jews are insistent on a national home], January 4, 1937.

31. *Mirāt al-Gharb*, "Fī sabīl Filasṭīn" [In the cause of Palestine], July 12, 1937.

32. Ibid.

33. Muhammad Jamil Beyhum, *Filasṭīn: Andalus al-Sharq* (Beirut: Farajallah and Hitti, 1946), 205–207. Beyhum's account is a valuable chronicle of Arab Americans' political lobbying through the Arab National League and the beginnings of the Institute of Arab American Affairs. This area of studies will benefit greatly from a faithful translation of his book. I will have room for scant translations from Beyhum's recollection of his travels and contacts across the United States. Copies of Beyhum's volume from the Farah manuscript collection may be secured on loan from the author.

34. Qaddurah, *Al-qadiyah al-filastiniya*, 37.97.

35. Special cable to the *New York Times*, "Arab Congress Opens: 400 Hear Speech Protesting Plan to Partition Palestine," September 9, 1937.

36. Beyhum, *Filasṭīn*, 61–63.

37. *New York Times*, "Arabs Here Warn of Boycott of U.S.: Two Arrive to Present the Cause of Their People—Will Try to See Roosevelt. They Denounce Zionists. But Deny They Are Anti-Semitic—Say Our Trade Is Threatened All Over Moslem World Says Our Trade Will Suffer Meet Arab Leaders Here," November 12, 1938.

38. Ibid.

39. Beyhum, *Filasṭīn*, 171.

40. Ibid.

41. Ibid., 172.

42. Ibid., 134–136.

43. Ibid., 175. Beyhum indicated that talking to Salloum was the best way to erase traces of "bad influences" from Salloum's mind. Beyhum wrote of a similar exchange with the celebrated Egyptian nationalist and feminist Huda Shaʿrawi in which she admitted that she sympathized with Jews as brethren and victims "before she realized the dire consequences of their actions" in Palestine.

44. Ibid., 202.

45. Ibid., 206.

46. Ibid., 206–207. A copy of the letter from Wallace Murray, Chief, Division of Near Eastern Affairs, to Beyhum dated December 22, 1938, and carrying the reference NE 867N.01/1343 can be viewed in Beyhum's *Filasṭīn* on page 208.

47. Ibid., 180.

48. Ibid., 185.

49. Ibid.

50. Ibid., 211.

51. Beyhum likely was referring to Abdo Salloum Yared, whose name appears in NSP correspondences. I suspect Yared also joined the Free Syria Society.

52. Beyhum, *Filasṭīn*, 193.

53. Ibid., 192.

54. *Detroit News*, "Arab Envoys Visit City Present Other Side of Palestine Revolt," November 23, 1938.

55. Ibid.

56. Beyhum considered "anti-Jewish" each of the "World association of national newspapers," *World Service* in London, *Service Mondial* in Paris, *Verden Jeneste* in Copenhagen, and *Weltdienst* in Germany. These institutions issued, according to Beyhum, "publications against Judaism generally and Zionism especially, in which they pretend to defend the Arabs"; *Filasṭīn*, 198.

57. Ibid., 199. Beyhum chronicled another anecdote in which an aggressive James Miles of the "Association Press of America," claimed to have interviewed Chiang Kai-shek and others and to have done his best to extract a comment from the *mufti*, who declined because he was granted asylum by the French "so long as he avoided politics." While saying goodbye, the American reporter told the *mufti*, "I assure you sir that the hearts of the Americans are with the Arabs." The *mufti* answered with a parable from the ancient Arab Islamic past: "In old times a Bedouin chief declared to Ali bin-abi-Taleb [Prophet Muhammad's cousin and supporter] that his heart and that of his tribe were with Ali, to which Ali, peace be upon him, replied: 'But your swords are with Muawya bin-abi-Sufyan [Islam's archenemy before becoming a Muslim].'" The reporter, Beyhum recalled, came up with a lengthy article based on this encounter and wired it to the United States; 199–200.

58. *Detroit News*, "Arab Envoys Visit."

59. Beyhum, *Filasṭīn*, 218.

60. Ibid. A picture of the lavish banquet can be found with Beyhum's account on page 217.

61. Ibid., 218.

62. Ibid.

63. Khalil Mufarrij, letter to Ameen Farah, November 4, 1938.

64. Fuad Shatara, letter to the Syrian American Club of Pittsfield, undated, MS Am 2375, 245, Hocking Papers.

65. Arab National League (ANL), "Ḥaflah kubrā ʿalā sharaf al-uʾurubah" [Grand reception in honor of the Arab's Delegation], Detroit and Flint, November 21, 1938, Farah Papers, Bawardi Collection.

66. Emil el-Ghouri, letter to Salim Farah and his brothers, November 21, 1938, Farah Papers, Bawardi Collection.

67. Beyhum, *Filasṭīn*, 219.

68. *Al-Bayān*, "The Arab Delegation Is Welcomed in Flint," December 13, 1938.

69. A rudimentary inquiry revealed that the Burton Collections houses copies of each of these Arabic-text periodicals: *Al-Dalīl*, *Al-Ittiḥād*, *Lisān al-ʿAdl*, and *Nahḍ at al-ʿArab*.

70. Beyhum, *Filasṭīn*, 219.

71. Ibid., 220.

72. Ibid., 220–221.

73. Ibid., 224–225. Beyhum lists among his stops these cities without specifying

the states: Michigan City, Ashland, New Virginia, Toledo, and Roanoke, where Ahmad Husain Shams al-Din donated $1,500 during the Depression, no less.

74. Ibid., 227-238.

75. Ibid. 232.

76. Ibid., 179. Beyhum wrote that numerous dignitaries who knew him previously welcomed him and that he would be elected "grand emissary" of Cuban Masons in the Near East in 1932.

77. *Risālat al-Jamīʿah al-ʿarabīyah* [Bulletin of the Arab League], "Mahrajā li-istiqbāl al-wafd al-ʿArabi al-Filasṭīni" [Receptions to honor the Arab Palestinian delegation], November 25, 1938.

78. *Risālat al-Jamīʿah al-ʿarabīyah*, "Muḥāḍarāt al-Duktūr Fuʾād Shaṭārah fī Boston" [The lectures of Dr. Fuad Shatara in Boston], November 25, 1938.

79. *New York Times*, "Church Group Denies Support of Zionism," November 17, 1938; *Risālat al-Jamīʿah al-ʿarabīyah*, "Ittiḥād al-Kanāʾis yujīb ʿalā barqīyat al-baṭrak," [The Council of Churches answers and patriarch's telegram], November 25, 1938.

80. Emil el-Ghouri, letter to Ameen Farah, January 30, 1939, Farah Papers, Bawardi Collection.

81. Emil el-Ghouri, "An Arab View of the Situation in Palestine," *International Affairs* (Royal Institute of International Affairs, 1931-1939) 15.5 (September-October 1936): 684-699.

82. Ḥabīb Kātibah, letter to Ameen Farah, February 8, 1939, Farah Papers, Bawardi Collection.

83. Robert P. Post, "Zionists Adamant in Palestine Row: Continue to Bar Discussion of British Proposals, but Conversations Go On. Rabbi Wise Sails Today. 1916 McMahon Letters Made Public. Arab Claims up for Consideration. Rabbi Wise Returning. 1916 Correspondence Published Excerpts of McMahon Letters. Bodies of Twelve Arabs Found. Plea Sent to MacDonald," *New York Times*, March 4, 1939.

84. Ibid.

85. Ibid.

86. Ibid.

87. Ibid.

88. Ibid.

89. Fuad Shatara, letter to Oswald Villard, March 4, 1939, MS Am 1323, 68, Houghton Library, Harvard University.

90. Oswald Villard to Fuad Shatara, March 8, 1939, MS Am 1323, Houghton Library.

91. Fuad Shatara to Oswald Villard, March 8, 1939, MS Am 1323, Houghton Library.

92. Tom Segev, *One Palestine Complete: Jews and Arabs Under the British Mandate* (New York: Metropolitan Books, 2000), 109.

93. *New York Times*, "White Paper Assailed: Dr. Goldman Tells Sons of Zion Jews Will Stick to Bible," June 12, 1939; Warren Irvin, "M'Donald [sic] Defends Pal-

estine Policy: Tells League Mandates Body Britain Holds It Best Fitted to Attain 'Great Hopes.' Declares Time Is Needed. Insists the Arabs and Jews Be Free to Live Own Lives—Two Slain in Holy Land, Holds Time Is Needed Cites Rising Hostility Fresh Violence in Palestine," *New York Times*, June 16, 1939; *New York Times*, "Asks End of White Paper: Dr. Goldman Calls on British Government to Renounce It," June 24, 1939; *New York Times*, "200 at Jewish Congress," July 31, 1939.

94. *New York Times*, "Geneva Commission Questions M'Donald: Britain's Colonial Secretary Defends Palestine Policy," June 17, 1939.

95. Shatara to Farah, Igram, and Samra, April 17, 1939, Farah Papers, Bawardi Collection.

96. Ameen Farah to Ḥabīb Kātibah, May 14, 1939, Farah Papers, Bawardi Collection.

97. Ameen Farah to Elia Madey, editor of *As-Sameer*, August 18, 1939, Farah Papers, Bawardi Collection.

98. *As-Sameer*, "Risālat al-Jamīʿah al-ʿarabīyah: Muʾtamar Flint wa ḥarakat al-tandḥīm" [The Arab League's message—the Flint conference and movement to mobilize], July (no date). Another snippet of an invitation without the newspaper title (I estimate this to be *Mirāt al-Gharb* based on the font, orientation of ads, and margins) appeared under the title "Daʿwah li ḥuḍūur al-muʾtamar al-ʿarabi al-rābiʿ fī madīnat Flint, Michigan" (An invitation to attend the Fourth Arab Convention in Flint, Michigan), July 15, 1939.

99. *Risalat al-Jāmiʿa al-ʿarabīya* (Bulletin of the Arab National League), August 1939.

100. Farhat Ziadeh, "Winds Blow Where Ships Do Not Wish to Go," in *Paths to the Middle East: Ten Scholars Look Back*, edited by Thomas Naff (New York; University of New York Press, 1993).

101. Ibid.

102. *Arab National League Bulletin*, no. 121 (August 18, 1939).

103. Ibid.

104. Ibid.

105. Kātibah to Farah, August 22, 1939, Farah Papers, Bawardi Collection.

106. Arab National League Bulletin, August 18, 1939.

107. *Flint Journal*, "More than 200 in Arabian Group of U.S. and Canada to Meet Here," August 3, 1939.

108. *Flint Journal*, "Envoy Kennedy's Words Displease. Flint Unit of Arab National League Protest," March 1, 1939.

109. Ibid.

110. *Flint Journal*, "Arab National League Convention Will Be Here Sept. 3 Through 4," August 27, 1939.

111. Ziadeh, "Winds Blow," 301.

112. *Flint Journal*, "Arab National League Convention Will Be Here."

113. *Flint Journal*, "Detroit Artist Will Play Here. Mrs. Adams to Entertain the Arab National League," September 1, 1939.

114. Ralph G. Coulter, "Arabs in Gathering. They Give Their Unqualified Allegiance to the United States," *Flint Journal*, September 5, 1939.

115. Ibid.

116. Ibid.

117. Ibid.

118. Ibid.

119. Ibid.

120. Ibid.

121. Ibid. The Josephs are descendants of Yousef Shihadeh Jalbout, believed to be the first Syrian to settle in Flint, in 1901; Shaker Brackett, interview with the author, August 12, 1998, transcript, Bawardi Collection.

122. Coulter, "Arabs in Gathering."

123. Ibid.

124. Kātibah, letter to Farah, September 23, 1939, Farah Papers, Bawardi Collection.

125. Shatara to Farah, November 1, 1939, Farah Papers, Bawardi Collection.

126. Ibid.

127. Beyhum, *Filasṭīn*, 234.

128. Ibid.

129. Ibid., 235.

130. Davidson, *America's Palestine*, 125.

131. Ibid., 123.

132. Ibid., 124.

133. Only recently have perceptions that Israel is surrounded by enemies who refused to accept its existence been challenged by Western and Israeli scholars. A considerable challenge to this rendition by Arab scholars—beginning with George Antonius—is now supported by a growing number of Israeli historians. One of these is Avi Shlaim, who has documented the use of force in dealing with Arabs from the earliest beginnings of the Zionist movement. See Avi Shlaim, *The Iron Wall: Israel and the Arab World* (New York: W. W. Norton, 2000).

134. In Cleveland, *A History of the Middle East*, 260–261.

135. Ibid., 261.

136. Cheryl A. Rubenberg, *Israel and the National Interest: A Critical Examination* (Urbana: University of Illinois Press, 1986), 29.

137. Ibid., 25–26.

138. Cleveland, *History of the Middle East*, 261; Allon Gal, *David Ben-Gurion and the American Alignment for a Jewish State* (Jerusalem: Magnes Press; Bloomington: Indiana University Press, 1991).

139. Cleveland, *History of the Middle East*, 261.

140. In Nabih Amin Faris, report to Foreign Nationalities of OSS on articles in the Arabic-language press, INT2AB8, May 22, 1942, NE-9-R, OSS records.

141. Ibid.

142. Letter from Ḥabīb Kātibah to Victor Weingarten, circa November 1946, series 9, box 12, file 6, Naff Collection.

143. Ibid.

144. Ibid., 2.

145. Ibid.

146. Ibid., 3.

147. Sworn statement by Ḥabīb Kātibah in October, 1947, New York City Magistrate's Court of the City of New York. This statement was part of a lawsuit by Kātibah against the *Daily Mirror*, the Hearst Corporation, Charles B. McCabe, and Walter Winchell. The transcripts of the court complaint can be found in Kātibah Papers, series 9, box 11, folder 3, Naff Collection.

148. For example, Adolph J. Sabath, remarks on July 24, 1947. Congress, Session 80-1 (1947), CR-1947-0724.

149. Khalidi, *Palestinian Identity*, 147.

CHAPTER 7: THE INSTITUTE OF ARAB AMERICAN AFFAIRS

1. As the title of chapter 2 in Suleiman's book indicates, the scholar conducted "An Evaluation of Middle East News Coverage in Seven American Newsmagazines, July–December, 1956" after the Suez Canal crisis. His findings show that six national U.S. news magazines and the *New York Times* persistently portrayed Arabs as "desert-living nomads"; *Arabs in the Mind of America*, 15–35.

2. Davidson, *America's Palestine*, 102–104.

3. Owen, *State, Power*, 86.

4. Private Office Papers of Sir Anthony Eden, reference FO954/5D, United Kingdom National Archive.

5. Donald Macintyre, "Israel's Forgotten Hero: The Assassination of Count Bernadotte," *The Independent*, September 18, 2008.

6. Ilan Pappé is one of the so-called revisionist Israeli historians who has presented detailed accounts of the expulsion of Palestine's inhabitants; see Pappé, *The Arab Israeli Conflict: The Ethnic Cleansing of Palestine* (Oxford, England: Oneworld, 2006).

7. "Foreign Nationality Groups in the United States. Arab American Political Reflections," memorandum to the head of the Office of Strategic Services, April 9, 1943, no. 118, INT-33AR-10, OSS.

8. The *New York Times* scantily reported on the visit in "Prince Faisal Gives a Reception for 500," November 10, 1943.

9. See no. 157, INT-33R-16, OSS.

10. The report was titled "Arab Americans Lay Plans to Combat Zionism," July 3, 1944, no. B-222, INT-33AR-20, OSS.

11. Ibid.

12. Telegram from Ahmad Bader to Issa Bateh, November 14 and 24, 1944,

Khalil Totah Manuscript Collection, Joy Totah Hilden, Berkeley, California (henceforth Totah Archives). A fourth telegram, from Hassan Haleem, asking Ismail Khalidi to represent the Arab American Committee of Chicago in the institute's meeting was sent February 15, 1945, likely to a subsequent general meeting.

13. Kātibah, *Al-Nāṭiqūn bi al-Ḍād*, 85; Arab American Institute, "Ma'had al-Shu'ūn al-'arabīyah al-amrīkīyah: Nash'atahu-mabādi'uhu wa ma'atih" [The Institute of Arab American Affairs: Its rise, its principles, its accomplishments, its hopes], pamphlet, New York, 1946, Farah Papers, Bawardi Collection.

14. Archbishop Antony Bashir, letter to Senator Tom Connally, December 4, 1944, Totah Archives.

15. In Totah Archives.

16. "Report of Progress I," Institute, March 6, 1945, Totah Archives.

17. Ibid.

18. Kātibah, *Al-Naṭiqūn bi al-Ḍād*, 86.

19. "Progress Report," Institute, "Beginning," June 1, 1945, Totah Archives.

20. "Monthly Report of Progress on Activities," Institute, October 1–31, 1945, Totah Archives.

21. I. R. Khalidi, "Monthly Report of Progress on the Activity of the Institute," October 1–31, 1945, Totah Archives.

22. Kātibah, *Al-Naṭiqūn bi al-Ḍād*, 86.

23. *Arab American Affairs Bulletin* 7 (January 15, 1950): 6, Farah Papers, Bawardi Collection.

24. Institute of Arab American Affairs (Institute), "Ma'had al-shu'ūn al-'arabīyah al-amrīkīyah" [Institute of Arab American Affairs], pamphlet, Farah Papers, Bawardi Collection.

25. Ibid., 87.

26. "Constitution of the Institute of Arab American Affairs," 60 Broadway, New York City, 7, New York, (1945), Farah Papers, Bawardi Collection.

27. "Manifesto of the Institute of Arab American Affairs on Palestine, (Submitted to the honorable delegates of the United Nations Conference on International Organization at San Francisco), New York, April 1945, Archives of the Missionary Research Library, New York.

28. Ibid.

29. Ibid.

30. Ibid.

31. The Yalta Conference facilitated the surrender of Germany and tied up loose ends after World War II, though it gave the Russians influence over Poland. According to some, the conference ushered in the Cold War; Martin H. Folly, "Friends of a Kind: America and Its Allies in the Second World War," *Journal of American Studies* 40.3 (December 2006): 635–644.

32. Ibid.

33. Aside from the many contributions toward explaining Arab culture by

Samra, George, Shatara, and numerous others, Ḥabīb Kātibah authored a book explaining Arab and Middle Eastern mythology and old tales; it is H. I. Kātibah, *Arabian Romances and Folk Tales* (New York and London: Charles Scribner and Sons, 1929). The book relates many popular bedtime stories and features attractive illustrations by W. M. Berger.

34. Teller, telegram to Epstein, June 5, 1945, L35–40, Central Zionist Archives, Jerusalem (henceforth Zionist Archives).

35. Undated report, L35–40, Zionist Archives.

36. Jewish Agency for Palestine, "Memorandum" containing cable from Nahum Goldman to London, September 11, 1945, L35–40, Zionist Archives.

37. See, for example, letters from Khalidi to Epstein, October 9, 1945, and Totah to Epstein, August 16, 1946. A similarly polite letter from Epstein provided "Statistical Data on Palestine, 1945" and thanked Totah "very much for your kindness in arranging for me the receipt of your material," December 5, 1945; L35–40, Zionist Archives.

38. A. S. Yahuda, "A Reply to the 'Manifesto' on Palestine of the Institute of Arab American Affairs," 123/502, Zionist Archives.

39. Ibid., 2.

40. Ibid., 6.

41. The Village Welfare Movement funding is stipulated in Shatara's last correspondence to Ameen Farah about the project. The organization was founded around 1931.

42. Farah Papers, Bawardi Collection, include a letter from Samra, Hasan Tali (Tuleiʾ), Amin Saab, and Kamel Hamady to the St. George's Orthodox Men's Society, January 1, 1945, and a raffle ticket for the Syrian Red Crescent for Palestine Relief on January 18, 1947, at St. George's Hall, Flint. Samra's letter on the stationery of the Arab Committee for Democracy invited the community to a banquet in honor of Dr. Gloria M. Wisner, secretary of the American Missionary Works in All the East (name translated from Arabic) to be held on February 15, 1945.

43. See Virginia Gildersleeve International Fund, http://www.thegildersleeve.org/.

44. Robert Gale Woolbert, "Pan-Arabism Adds to Unrest," *New York Times*, November 20, 1938.

45. Ibid.

46. Ibid.

47. Khalil Totah, "Ārāʾ al-qurrāʾ" [Opinions of the readers], *Al-Hoda*, November 29, 1948. The date on this original issue of the *Al-Hoda* erroneously reads 1941. It is not clear if microfilm collections noted the discrepancy. Totah wrote to *Al-Hoda* again, this letter published on December 13, 1948, to defend his reputation after he suffered a personal attack because of his views.

48. Zuʿaitir, *Al-Marūniyah fi Lubnān*.

49. Institute, "Maʾhad al-shuʾūn al-ʿarabīyah al-amrikīyah."

50. "Khalil Totah, Ph.D.," unpublished autobiography, 1, Totah Archives.

51. *New York Times*, "Truman Favors Parley: Says He Is Following Situation in Levant States Closely," June 2, 1945.

52. Ibid.

53. *New York Times*, "Wants Syria, Lebanon at Parley," March 16, 1945.

54. *Los Angeles Times*, "U.S. Approves Arab League," June 3, 1945; *New York Times*, "American to Back Pan-Arab League: Phillips Predicts Its States Will Aid in Big Tasks Before United Nations," June 3, 1945; *Los Angeles Times*, "U.S. Approves Arab League," June 3, 1945.

55. "Khalil Totah, Ph.D.," 8, Totah Archives. Totah passed away in 1955 before refining his draft and finishing it.

56. Bashir, letter to Connally, December 4, 1944, Totah Archives.

57. Henry L. Feingold, *Zion in America: The Jewish Experience from Colonial Times to the Present* (New York: Twayne, 1974), 273.

58. Ibid.

59. Bashir, letter to Connally, December 4, 1944, Totah Archives.

60. Institute, "Progress Report," March 6, 1945, Totah Archives.

61. Letter from Paul H. Alling, Department of State, to Dr. Philip Hitti, Department of Oriental Languages, Princeton University, April 2, 1945, Totah Archives.

62. *Bulletin of the Institute of Arab American Affairs* 1.1 (July 15, 1945), 2.

63. Ibid., 1.

64. Ibid.

65. Ibid.

66. Bulletin dates are not always clear. Aside from Farah's archives, the largest collection of institute bulletins is housed in the Columbia University Libraries in New York. I found these copies in a distressed state and in need of restoration and preservation.

67. Report of Work for Arab Institute, March 3–18, 1945, Totah Archives.

68. The Totah Archives provide more than can be digested here. However, item-by-item lists in semimonthly reports were replaced with paragraph-length descriptions of the institute's activities by December and issued once a month.

69. Institute, "Monthly Report of Progress on the Activities of the Institute," December 1945, Totah Archives.

70. Institute of Arab American Affairs, "Testimony of Professor Philip K. Hitti before the Committee on Foreign Affairs," in *Papers on Palestine: A Collection of Statements, Articles and Letters Dealing with the Palestine Problem* (New York: Institute of Arab American Affairs, 1945).

71. Chappell J. Hutcheson, "Report of the Anglo-American Committee Of Enquiry Regarding the Problems of European Jewry and Palestine, Lausanne, 20th April 1946" (London: His Majesty's Stationery, 1946).

72. Aron Berman, *Nazism the Jews and American Zionism, 1933–1948* (Detroit: Wayne State University Press, 1990), 139. Berman includes persistent support by Wagner for the Jewish state in all parts of Palestine. To this end, Berman dis-

closes, Wagner even opposed the partition plan of the American Peel Commission, although the context is presented from the Zionist point of view; 55.

73. The full testimony also can be found in Judah Leon Magnes, *Arab-Jewish Unity: Testimony before the Anglo-American Inquiry Commission for the Ihud (Union) Association* (Westport, CT: Hyperion Press 1976). Magnes is attracting some attention lately; see, for example, Lawrence Zuckerman, "A Pacifist Leader Who Was More Prophet than Politician," *Jewish Daily Forward*, January 14, 2011.

74. Institute, "Monthly Report of Progress," December 1945, 2, Totah Archives.

75. A. L. Warnshuis, "Christians and Zionists," Institute, December 1945, Totah Archives.

76. Ibid.

77. "Khalil Totah, Ph.D.," 9, Totah Archives.

78. Ibid.

79. *New York Times*, "The Nation: As Congress Returns. Debate on Palestine," January 13, 1946.

80. Ibid.

81. Ibid.

82. Ibid.

83. Ibid.

84. Ibid.

85. Ibid.

86. Walid Khalidi, "On Albert Hourani, the Arab Office, and the Anglo-American Committee of 1946," *Journal of Palestine Studies* 35.1 (October 2005): 69.

87. Ibid.

88. Institute, "Memorandum of the Institute of Arab American Affairs on the Recommendation of the Anglo-American Committee of Inquiry," 2, August 1946, Totah Archives.

89. Ibid., 7.

90. Ibid., 22–23.

91. Institute, *Papers on Palestine*, 22.

92. Vernon McKay, "The Arab League in World Politics," November 15, 1946, Totah Archives.

93. Totah to Farah, May 14, 1947, and June 10, 1947, Farah Papers, Bawardi Collection. In the interim, material in Farah Papers indicates that a fund-raiser took place, with Tom Mansour giving the lion's share.

94. Quoted in Roy Miller, "More Sinned against than Sinning? The Case of the Arab Office, Washington, 1945–48," *Diplomacy and Statecraft* 15.2 (June 2004): 309.

95. Truman to Atlee, May 8, 1946, as cited in *Diplomacy and Statecraft*, no. 50.

96. Miller, "More Sinned against than Sinning?" 310.

97. Ibid.

98. Ibid., 306.

99. Totah to Farah, June 10, 1947.

100. Feingold, *Zion in America*, 297.

101. *New York Times*, "The Levant Crisis Debated, Action Taken by France Upheld and Opposed by Readers," letters to the editor, June 7, 1945.

102. Ibid., Frederick W. Eisner letter.

103. *New York Times*, "Arabs Oppose Zionists: Institute Here Protests against Immigration to Palestine," August 23, 1945.

104. *New York Times*, "Arabs Decry Zionism: Group Here Tells Truman Jewish Problem Has Another Solution," October 7, 1945.

105. "Hoover Iraq Plan Opposed, Suggested Transfer of Arabs to That Country Is Disapproved," op-ed, *New York Times*, December 24, 1945. Under this headline the *Times* published responses by Vahan H. Kalenderian, James G. Mitchell, Marvin L. Kline, Courtland Grants Bailey, Khalil Totah, and H. E. Bishop.

106. *New York Times*, "Palestine Debate Upset by Heckling," April 14, 1946.

107. Elmer Berger, "Memoirs," 29, Totah Archives.

108. *Chicago Daily Tribune*, "Seek $4,000,000 to Stamp out Anti-Semitism: Plan to Reach All of U.S. with Program," August 30, 1945.

109. Philip Chasin, "Confidential Memorandum," June 15, 1945. Totah Archives.

110. *New York Times*, "Philip Chasin, 87, Professional Fund-Raiser," obituary, February 2, 1997.

111. Ibid., 10.

112. Ibid., 4.

113. Ibid., 5.

114. Ibid., 6–7.

115. It is not clear how this document by Philip Chasin made its way to Totah. I estimate that a Jewish friend with ties to the ADL was responsible for delivering it to him or to the institute directly.

116. "Khalil Totah Ph.D.," 23, Totah Archives.

117. *New York Herald Tribune*, January 14, 1947.

118. *Waterbury Republican*, October 26, 1948.

119. *Herald Tribune*, May 20, 1946.

120. *New York Herald Tribune*, May 15, 1947.

121. *New York Times*, July 10, 1946.

122. *New York Post Home News*, November 19, 1948.

123. A stance against routing Palestinians, previously described as a Palestinian and Arab viewpoint, has been supported by a roster of Israeli scholars. Besides Ilan Pappé's *Arab Israeli Conflict*, his works on the topic include *The Forgotten Palestinians: A History of the Palestinians in Israel* (New Haven, CT: Yale University Press, 2011) and *The Making of the Arab-Israeli Conflict, 1948–1951* (London: St. Antony's College Series, Macmillan; New York: St. Martin's Press, 1988).

124. Cleveland, *History of the Middle East*, 262, 263.

125. Arnold Forester, "The Facts: Reported Monthly by the Civil Rights Division of the Anti-Defamation League of B'nai B'rith," May 1948 and June 1948, edited by Arnold L. Scheuer, Totah Archives.

126. Ibid., May 1948, 1.

127. Ibid.
128. Ibid., 4.
129. Ibid., 5.
130. Ibid., 6.
131. Ibid., June 1948, 1, 9.
132. Richard H. Curtiss, "*New York Times* Editor Abe Rosenthal Had a 'Passionate Attachment' to Israel," *Washington Report on Middle East Affairs*, July 2006, 34–35.
133. Ibid.
134. Cleveland, *History of the Middle East*, 263.
135. Ibid.
136. Johan Franzén, "Communism versus Zionism: The Comintern, Yishuvism, and the Palestine Communist Party," *Journal of Palestine Studies* 36.2 (January 2007): 6–24.
137. Natan Sharansky, "A Tale of Two 'Isms,'" *Jerusalem Report*, November 15, 1990, 14.
138. Peter Grose, *Israel in the Mind of America* (New York: Alfred Knopf, 1983), 145.
139. Michael B. Oren, *Power, Faith, and Fantasy: America in the Middle East, 1776 to the Present* (New York: W. W. Norton, 2007), 488.
140. *Chicago Daily Tribune*, "Truman Balks on Palestine State for Jews," November 30, 1945.
141. *New York Times*, "Taft, Wagner to Talk Here," December 9, 1945.
142. *New York Times*, "Palestine Survey Lists many Groups," May 22, 1946.
143. Oren, *Power, Faith*, 486.
144. Ibid., 488.
145. Ibid., 491.
146. Cleveland, *History of the Middle East*, 266.
147. David Perlman, "Judge Wants Bombs as Proof," *Washington Post*, September 10, 1947.
148. Totah to George C. Marshall, September 10, 1947, Totah Archives.
149. Grose, *Israel in the Mind of America*, 235.
150. Cleveland, *History of the Middle East*, 264.
151. Ibid.
152. Oren, *Power, Faith*, 492.
153. Ibid.
154. Israelis are slowly coming to terms with incidents such as Deir Yaseen, as seen in Elie Podeh, "History and Memory in the Israeli Educational System: The Portrayal of the Arab-Israeli Conflict in History Textbooks (1948–2000)," *History and Memory* 12.1 (June 30, 2000): 65–100. However, several Israeli historians have acknowledged this and other massacres. Among these are Ilan Pappé, *A History of Modern Palestine: One Land, Two Peoples* (Cambridge, England: Cambridge University Press, 2006); Simcha Flapan, *The Birth of Israel: Myths and Realities* (New

York: Pantheon Books, 1987); and Ilan Pappé and Moshe Ma'oz, eds., *Middle Eastern Politics and Ideas: A History from Within* (London: Tauris Academic Studies, 1997).

155. Dana Adams Schmidt, "200 Arabs Killed, Stronghold Taken: Irgun and Stern Groups Unite to Win Deir Yasin," special to the *New York Times*, April 10, 1948.

156. Oren, *Power, Faith*, 493.

157. Ibid., 487.

158. "July 21," *Harry S. Truman 1947 Diary*, Harry S. Truman Library and Museum, http://www.trumanlibrary.org/diary/page21.htm.

159. Oren, *Power, Faith*, 497.

160. Cleveland, *History of the Middle East*, 265, 267.

161. Ahmad H. Sa'di, "Catastrophe, Memory and Identity: Al-Nakbah as a Component of Palestinian Identity," *Israel Studies* 7.2 (July 1, 2002): 175.

162. See, for example, Walid Khalidi, *All that Remains: The Palestinian Villages Occupied and Depopulated by Israel in 1948* (Washington, DC: Institute for Palestine Studies, 1992).

163. *New York Times*, "Witness Admits to Aiding Arab Cause: Freedman, Testifying in Libel Case, Cooperated on Note to State Department," May 7, 1948.

164. Donald Neff, "Middle East History: It Happened in September; Jewish Terrorists Assassinate U.N. Peacekeeper Count Folke Bernadotte," *Washington Report on Middle East Affairs*, September 30, 1995, 83.

165. Ibid.

166. *New York Times*, "Shock Voiced Here at News of Killing," September 18, 1948.

167. Khalil Totah, "The Palestine Problem: Only Permanent Solution Is One Based on Righteousness," letter, *New York Times*, October 1, 1948.

168. Khalil Totah, letter, in "Arab Views on Palestine: Tendency to Underrate Opposition of Arabs Viewed as Folly," *New York Times*, December 23, 1947.

169. *As-Sameer*, "Al-wafd al-Filastini fi Flint," [The Arab delegation in Flint] February 28, 1948.

170. "Statement of Income and Expenses, May 31, 1947, to May 31, 1948," Institute, Farah Papers, Bawardi Collection.

171. The Palestinian Academic Society for the Study of International Affairs (PASSIA) website has maps and quantitative information on Palestinian geography, demographics, and biographies from Palestinians' point of view, at http://www.passia.org/palestine_facts/MAPS/0_pal_facts_MAPS.htm.

172. Minutes, Annual Meeting of the Board of Directors, June 5, 1948, Farah Papers, Bawardi Collection.

173. Minutes, Executive Committee, June 11, 1948, Institute, Farah Papers, Bawardi Collection.

174. Ibid.

175. Bylaws of the American Middle East Relief Organization and poster, Farah Papers, Bawardi Collection.

176. John Hohenberg, "Israel Proclaims Jerusalem Its Capital in Defiance of UN," *New York Post*, December 13, 1949.

177. Institute, "Israel Aligned against the Whole World," *Bulletin of the Institute of Arab American Affairs* 6 (December 15, 1949).

178. Ibid., 2–5.

179. Khalil Totah, letter to William E. Hocking, December 19, 1949, bMS Am 2375 (3019), Hocking Papers.

180. Ibid.

181. Hocking to Totah, January 25, 1950, bMS Am 2375 (3019), Hocking Papers.

182. Institute, *Bulletin of the Institute of Arab American Affairs* 7 (January 15, 1950), Farah Papers, Bawardi Collection.

183. Thomas G. Paterson, "Cold War Revisionism: A Practitioner's Perspective," *Diplomatic History* 31.3 (June 2007): 387–395.

184. The terms "nonaligned" and "nonalignment" denote strident impartiality by many small nations in the Cold War. These policies were incompatible with the Truman Doctrine and the Eisenhower Doctrine of a zero-sum game when it came to communism.

185. David W. Lesch, *Syria and the United States: Eisenhower's Cold War in the Middle East* (Boulder, CO: Westview Press, 1992).

186. Khalil Totah, for example, was so keen on expressing his American patriotism while on a trip to Beirut in the 1950s that his friends were alarmed that he might be mistaken as a spy for the Americans. Conversations with Thomas Ricks in the summer of 2007. See Thomas H. Ricks, *Turbulent Times in Palestine: The Diaries of Khalil Totah, 1886–1955* (Beirut: Institute for Palestine Studies and PASSIA, 2009).

187. Kristin S. Tassin, "'Lift up Your Head, My Brother': Nationalism and the Genesis of the Non-Aligned Movement," *Journal of Third World Studies* 23.1 (April 2006): 147–168; Michael Hudson, "To Play the Hegemon: Fifty Years of US Policy Toward the Middle East," *Middle East Journal* 50.3 (Summer 1996): 329–343; Michael W. Suleiman, *U.S. Policy on Palestine: From Wilson to Clinton* (Association of Arab-American University Graduates, 1995); William Stivers, *America's Confrontation with Revolutionary Change in the Middle East, 1948–83* (New York: St. Martin's Press, 1986).

CONCLUSION

1. See American Arab Anti-Discrimination Committee (ADC), "About ADC," at http://www.adc.org/about-us/.

2. E-mail from Michael Suleiman to the author, February 15, 2009.

3. ADC, "About ADC."

4. *Off Our Backs*, "Issues Concerning Arab Feminists," September 30, 1983, 8.

5. Suleiman, "I Come to Bury Caesar," 76.

6. Ibid., 84.

7. Association of Arab American University Graduates (AAUG), "The First Decade, 1967-1977" (Washington, DC: Tammuz, 1977).

8. Abdeen Jabara, interview, "Targeting Palestinian Activists," video, *Tracked in America*, American Civil Liberties Union (ACLU), at http://www.trackedinamerica.org/timeline/civil_rights/jabara/.

9. Jack G. Shaheen, *The TV Arab* (Bowling Green, OH: Bowling Green State University Popular Press, 1984); Jack G. Shaheen, "Reel Bad Arabs: How Hollywood Vilifies a People," *Annals of the American Academy of Political and Social Science* 588 (July 2003): 171-193; Jack G. Shaheen, "Palestinians on the Silver Screen in the 1980s," *American-Arab Affairs* 31 (Spring 1989): 68.

10. News coverage of the spying operations by the ADL received considerable attention on the West Coast but hardly any attention by the *New York Times*. See, for example, Phil Bronstein, "Suspect in Cop Spy Case Tells his Story," *San Francisco Examiner*, January 22, 1993; Richard Paddock, "San Francisco Probes Private Spy Network," *Los Angeles Times*, February 26, 1993; Robert Friedman, *Village Voice*, May 11, 1993.

11. R. Khalidi, *Palestinian Identity*, 177.

BIBLIOGRAPHY

A' (pseudonym). "Haul Suri Wa Lubnani" [About Syria and Lebanon]. *As-Sameer*, November 1932.

Abdulaziz, Sachedina. *The Islamic Roots of Democratic Pluralism*. Oxford, England: Oxford University Press, 2001.

Abdulhadi, Aouni. "The Balfour Declaration." In *Palestine, a Decade of Development*, edited by Harry Viteles and Khalil Totah, 12–21. Philadelphia: American Academy of Political and Social Science, 1932.

Abraham, Nabeel. "Arabs in America: An Overview." In *The Arab World and Arab-Americans: Understanding a Neglected Minority*, by Sameer Y. Abraham and Nabeel Abraham. Detroit: Wayne State University Press, 1981.

———. "National and Political Politics: A Study of Political Conflict in the Yemeni Immigrant Community of Detroit, Michigan." PhD diss., University of Michigan, 1978.

Abraham, Nabeel, and Andrew Shryock, eds. *Arab Detroit*, edited by Nabeel Abraham and Andrew Shryock. Detroit, MI: Wayne State University Press, 2000.

Abraham, Sameer, and Nabeel Abraham, eds. *Arabs in the New World: Studies on Arab American Communities*. Detroit: Wayne State University, 1983.

Abu-Lughod, Ibrahim. Preface to *The Arab Americans: Studies in Assimilation*, edited by Elaine C. Hagopian and Ann Paden. Wilmette, IL: Medina University Press International, 1969.

Ahmed, Hisham. "Roots of Denial: American Stand on Palestinian Self-Determination from the Balfour Declaration to World War Two." In *U.S. Policy on Palestine: From Wilson to Clinton*, edited by Michael W. Suleiman, 27–58. Normal, IL: Association of Arab American University Graduates, 1995.

Alhourani, Motaz Abdullah. "The Arab-American Press and the Arab World: News Coverage in *Al-Bayan* and *Al-Dalil*." Master's thesis, Kansas State University, 1992. Michael Suleiman Collection, Arab American National Museum, Dearborn, MI.

Anderson, Benedict. *Imagined Communities: Reflections on the Origin and Spread of Nationalism*. London: Verso, 1983.

Antonius, George. *The Arab Awakening: The Story of the Arab National Movement*. Translated by Ali Haidar Rikabi. London: G. P. Putnam's Sons, 1946.

———. *Yaqzat al-ʿArab tārīkh ḥarakat al-ʿArab al-qawmīyah*. Damascus: Matbaʿat al-Taraqqi, 1938.
Arab National League (ANL). "Bayān al-Jāmiʿah al-ʿArabīyah" [Declaration of the Arab (National) League], New York: Arab National League, circa 1937.
———. *Whither Palestine? A Statement of Facts and of Causes of the Arab-Jewish Conflict in the Holy Land*. New York: Arab National League, circa 1936.
Aswad, Barbara C., ed. *Arabic Speaking Communities in American Cities*. Staten Island, NY: Center for Migration Studies of New York, 1974.
———. "Attitudes of Immigrant Women and Men in the Dearborn Area toward Women's Employment and Welfare." In *Muslim Communities in North America*, edited by Yvonne Yazbeck Haddad and Jane I. Smith, 501–520. Albany: State University of New York Press, 1994.
Balibar, Etienne, and Immanuel Wallerstein. *Race, Nation, Class: Ambiguous Identities*. New York: Verso, 1991.
Bell, Gertrude Lowthian. *Syria: The Desert and the Sown*. London: William Heinemann, 1907.
Bentwich, Norman, and Helen Bentwich. *Mandate Memories: 1918–1948*. London: Hogarth Press, 1965.
Berger, Elmer. "Memoirs of an Anti-Zionist Jew." *Journal of Palestine Studies* 5 (Autumn 1975/Winter 1976): 3–55.
Berman, Aron. *Nazism, the Jews and American Zionism, 1933–1948*. Detroit: Wayne State University Press, 1990.
Beshara, Adel. "A Rebel Syrian: Gibran Khalil Gibran." In *The Origins of Syrian Nationhood: Histories, Pioneers, and Identity*, edited by Adel Bishara. London: Routledge, 2011.
Beyhum, Muhammad Jamil. *Filasṭīn: Andalus al-Sharq* [Palestine: The Andalusia of the Orient]. Beirut: Faraj-Allah and Hitti, 1946.
Black, Edwin. *The Transfer Agreement: The Untold Story of the Secret Agreement between the Third Reich and Jewish Palestine*. New York: Macmillan, 1984.
Blunt, Wilfrid Scawen. *Secret History of the English Occupation of Egypt: Being a Personal Narrative of Events*. New York: A. A. Knopf, 1922.
Bonné, Alfred. "The Concessions for the Mosul-Haifa Pipe Line." *Palestine, a Decade of Development*, edited by Harry Viteles and Khalil Totah, 116–126. Philadelphia: American Academy of Political and Social Science, 1932.
Boyle, Susan Silsby. *Betrayal of Palestine: The Story of George Antonius*. Boulder, CO: Westview Press, 2001.
Brecher, F. W. "French Policy toward the Levant 1914–18." *Middle Eastern Studies* 29 (October 1993): 641–663.
Buʿaini, Hasan Amin al-. *Durūz Sūrīya wa Lubnān* [The Druze of Syria and Lebanon]. Beirut: Arab Center for Research and Documentation, 1993.
Bukowczyk, John J. "Forum: Future Directions in American Immigration and Ethnic History—Introduction." *Journal of American Ethnic History* 25 (Summer 2006): 68–73.

Cainkar, Louise. "The Social Construction of Difference and the Arab American Experience." *Journal of American Ethnic History* 25.2 (2006): 243–278.
Chang, Michael. *Racial Politics in an Era of Transnational Citizenship.* New York: Lexington Books, 2004.
Choueiri, Youssef M. *Arab Nationalism: A History. Nation and State in the Arab World.* Oxford, England: Blackwell, 2000.
Clark, A. P. S. "Commerce Industry and Banking." *Palestine, a Decade of Development*, edited by Harry Viteles and Khalil Totah, 95–107. Philadelphia: American Academy of Political and Social Science, 1932.
Cleveland, William. *A History of the Modern Middle East.* Boulder, CO: Westview Press, 1994.
Cohen, Naomi Wiener. *The Year after the Riots: American Responses to the Palestine Crisis of 1929–30.* Detroit: Wayne State University Press, 1988.
Cole, Juan R. I., and Deniz Kandiyoti. "Nationalism and the Colonial Legacy in the Middle East and Central Asia: Introduction." In *Nationalism and the Colonial Legacy in the Middle East and Central Asia*, edited by Juan R. I. Cole, special issue of *International Journal of Middle Eastern Studies* 34 (May 2002): 189–203.
Commins, David Dean. *Islamic Reform: Politics and Social Change in the Late Ottoman Syria.* New York: Oxford University Press, 1990.
Commons, John Rogers. *Races and Immigrants in America.* New York: A. M. Kelly, 1907.
Conklin, Nancy Faires, and Nora Faires. "'Colored' and Catholic: The Lebanese in Birmingham, Alabama." In *Crossing the Waters: Arabic-Speaking Immigrants in the United States before 1940*, edited by Eric J. Hooglund, 69–84. Washington, DC: Smithsonian Institution Press, 1987.
Curtiss, Richard H. "*New York Times* Editor Abe Rosenthal Had A 'Passionate Attachment' to Israel." *Washington Report on Middle East Affairs*, July 2006.
David, Gary C. "The Creation of 'Arab American': Political Activism and Ethnic (Dis)Unity." *Critical Sociology* 33.5–6 (September 2007): 833–862.
Davidson, Lawrence. *America's Palestine: Popular and Official Perceptions from Balfour to Israeli Statehood.* Gainesville: University Press of Florida, 2001.
———. "Debating Palestine: Arab American Challenges to Zionism 1917–1932." In *Arabs in America: Building a New Future*, edited by Michael W. Suleiman, 227–240. Philadelphia: Temple University, 1999.
———. "The Past as Prelude: Zionism and the Betrayal of American Democratic Principles, 1917–48." *Journal of Palestine Studies* 31.3 (Spring 2002): 21–35.
Dawisha, Adeed I. *Arab Nationalism in the Twentieth Century: From Triumph to Despair.* Princeton, NJ: Princeton University Press, 2003.
Dawn, Ernest. "The Origins of Arab Nationalism." In *The Origins of Arab Nationalism: A Reassessment*, edited by Rashid Khalidi, Lisa Anderson, Muhammad Muslih, and Riva S. Simon, 3–30. New York: Columbia University Press, 1991.
Daye, John. *Lakom Jubrānakom wa li Jubrāni* [You have your Gibran and I have mine]. Beirut: Qub Elias Press, 2009.

———. "Syrianist Orientations in the Thought of Mikha'il Nu'aimah." In *The Origins of Syrian Nationhood: Histories, Pioneers, and Identity*, edited by Adel Bishara, 109–209. London: Routledge, 2011.

de Tarazi, Philippe. See Tarazi.

Doumani, Bishara B. "Rediscovering Ottoman Palestine: Writing Palestine into History." *Journal of Palestine Studies* 21 (Winter 1992): 5–28.

Einstein, Albert. *Out of My Later Years*. Westport, CT: Greenwood Press, 1970.

Elazari-Volcani, J. "Jewish Colonization in Palestine." *Palestine, a Decade of Development*, edited by Harry Viteles and Khalil Totah, 84–94. Philadelphia: American Academy of Political and Social Science, 1932.

Elkaisy-Friemuth, Maha. *God and Humans in Islamic Thought: Abd al-Jabbār, Ibn Sīnā and al-Ghazālī*. London: Routledge, 2006.

Elkholy, Abdo. *The Arab Moslems in the United States: Religion and Assimilation*. New Haven, CT: College and University Press, 1966.

Erskine, Beatrice (Mrs. Stewart). *Palestine of the Arabs*. Westport, CT: Hyperion Press, [1935] 1976.

Esco Foundation for Palestine. *Palestine, a Study of Jewish, Arab, and British Policies*. Vol. 1. New Haven, CT: Yale University Press for the Esco Foundation, 1945.

Fakhry, Majid. *Al-Fārābi: Founder of Islamic Neoplatonism: His Life, Works and Influence*. Oxford, England: Oneworld, 2002.

Farah, Ameen. *Rushd wa Suha*. Cairo: Al Ta'qaddum, n.d.

Feingold, Henry L. *Zion in America: The Jewish Experience from Colonial Times to the Present*. New York: Twayne, 1974.

Flapan, Simcha. *The Birth of Israel: Myths and Realities*. New York: Pantheon Books, 1987.

Folly, Martin H. "Friends of a Kind: America and its Allies in the Second World War." *Journal of American Studies* 40.3 (December 2006): 635–644.

Frank, Richard M. *Creation and the Cosmic System: Al-Ghazâlî und Avicenna Vorgelegt Am 27. April 1991*. Heidelberg, Germany: Carl Winter Universitätsverlag, 1992.

Franzén, Johan. "Communism versus Zionism: The Comintern, Yishuvism, and the Palestine Communist Party." *Journal of Palestine Studies* 36 (January 2007): 6–24.

Friedman, Saul S. Review of *The Year after the Riots: American Responses to the Palestine Crisis of 1929–30* by Naomi Wiener Cohen. *American Historical Review* 94 (December 1989): 1503.

Gal, Allon. *David Ben-Gurion and the American Alignment for a Jewish State*. Jerusalem: Magnes Press; Bloomington: Indiana University Press, 1991.

Gellner, Ernest. *Nations and Nationalism*. Ithaca, NY: Cornell University Press, 1983.

Gelvin, James. *Divided Loyalties: Nationalism and Mass Politics in Syria at the Close of Empire*. Berkeley: University of California Press, 1998.

George, Peter S. "Dr. F. I. Shatara, Biography." *Federal Herald* (Boston) 2.7 (April 8, 1942).
Ghouri, Emil el-. "An Arab View of the Situation in Palestine," *International Affairs* (Royal Institute of International Affairs, 1931-1939) 15.5 (September-October 1936): 684-699.
Giannakos, Symeon. "Church and State." *Harvard International Review* 25 (Winter 2004): 52-57.
Gianotti, Timothy J. *Al-Ghazālī's Unspeakable Doctrine of the Soul: Unveiling the Esoteric Psychology and Eschatology of the Ihyā*. Boston: Brill, 2001.
Gibran, Jean, and Khalil Gibran. *Khalil Gibran: His Life and World*. New York: Interlink Books, 1991.
Ginio, Eyal. "Mobilizing the Ottoman Nation during the Balkan Wars (1912-1913): Awakening from the Ottoman Dream." *War in History* 12 (April 2005): 156-177.
Goldschmidt, Arthur Jr., and Lawrence Davidson. *A Concise History of the Middle East*. Boulder, CO: Westview Press, 2006.
Gribetz, Louis J. *The Case for the Jews: An Interpretation of Their Rights under the Balfour Declaration and the Mandate for Palestine*. New York: Bloch, 1930.
Grose, Peter. *Israel in the Mind of America*. New York: Alfred Knopf, 1983.
Gualtieri, Sarah M. A. *Between Arab and White: Race and Ethnicity in the Early Syrian American Diaspora*. Berkeley: University of California Press: 2009.
Haddad, Rizk. *Nafahat al-Riyād*. New York: Mirāt al-Gharb Press, 1945.
Haddad, Yvonne Yazbeck. "Maintaining the Faith of the Fathers: Dilemmas of Religious Identity in the Christian and Muslim Communities." In *The Development of Arab-American Identity*, edited by Ernest McCarus, 61-84. Ann Arbor: University of Michigan Press, 1994.

———. *Not Quite Americans: The Shaping of Arab and Muslim Identity in the United States*. Waco, TX: Baylor University Press, 2004.
Hagopian, Elaine C., and Ann Paden, eds. *The Arab-Americans: Studies in Assimilation*. Wilmette, IL: Medina University Press International, 1969.
Handlin, Oscar. *Race and Nationality in American Life*. Boston: Little Brown, 1957.
Haqqi, Ismail. *Lubnan: mabāheth 'ilmiyah wa 'ijtima'iyah*. Beirut: N.p., 1913.
Herzl, Theodor. *The Complete Diaries*, vol. 1. Translated by Harry Zohn. New York: Hertzl Press and Thomas Yoseloff, 1960.

———. *The Jewish State: A Critical English Translation*. Translated by Henk Overberg. Northville, NJ: Jason Aronson, 1997.
Hitti, Philip K. *The Arabs: A Short History*. Princeton, NJ: Princeton University Press, 1943.

———. "Al-Istishraq fi al-Wilayat al-Muttahidah" [Orientalism in the United States]. *As-Sameer* 4 (April 1932): 10.

———. *The Syrian in America*. New York: George H. Doran, circa 1924.
Hoerder, Dirk. *Cultures in Contact: World Migrations in the Second Millennium*. Durham, NC: Duke University Press, 2002.

Holmes, Virginia Iris. "Was Einstein Really a Pacifist? Einstein's Forward-Thinking, Pragmatic, Persistent Pacifism." *Peace and Change* 33.2 (April 2008): 274–307.
Hooglund, Eric J., ed. *Crossing the Waters: Arabic-Speaking Immigrants to the United States before 1940.* Washington, DC: Smithsonian Institution Press, 1987.
Hourani, Albert. *A History of the Arab Peoples.* New York: Warner Books, 1991.
Hourani, Albert, Philip S. Khoury, and Mary C. Wilson, eds. *The Modern Middle East.* London: I. B. Tauris, 1993.
Howard, Roger. "Britain, Persia, and Petroleum." *History Today* 58.5 (2008): 44–50.
Hudson, Michael. "To Play the Hegemon: Fifty Years of US Policy Toward the Middle East." *Middle East Journal* 50.3 (Summer 1996): 329–343.
Huseby-Darvas, Eva Veronika. "'Coming to America': Dilemmas of Ethnic Groups since the 1880s." In *The Development of Arab American Identity,* edited by Ernest McCarus, 9–22. Ann Arbor: University of Michigan Press, 1994.
Husseini, Jamal Bey al-. "The Proposed Palestine Constitution." In *Palestine, a Decade of Development,* edited by Harry Viteles and Khalil Totah, 22–26. Philadelphia: American Academy of Political and Social Science, 1932.
Hutcheson, Chappell J. "Report of the Anglo-American Committee Of Enquiry Regarding the Problems of European Jewry and Palestine, Lausanne, 20th April 1946." London: His Majesty's Stationery Office, 1946.
Ibrahim Abu-Lughod Institute of International Studies. *Ibrahim Abu-Lughod: Resistance, Exile, and Return: Conversations with Hisham Ahmad-Fararej.* Birzeit, Palestine: Birzeit University, Ibrahim Abu-Lughod Institute of International Studies, 2003.
Ilyas, Juzif. *ʿAflaq wa-al-Baʿth: nisf qarn min al-nidāl.* Beirut: Dār al-Nidāl, 1991.
Institute of Arab American Affairs. "Manifesto of the Institute of Arab American Affairs on Palestine (Submitted to the Honorable Delegates of the United Nations Conference on International Organization at San Francisco), New York, April 1945. Archives of the Missionary Research Library, New York.
———. *Papers on Palestine: A Collection of Statements, Articles and Letters Dealing with the Palestine Problem.* New York: Institute of Arab American Affairs, 1945.
Jabara, Abdeen. Interview, "Targeting Palestinian Activists." Video. At *Tracked in America,* American Civil Liberties Union (ACLU), http://www.trackedinamerica.org/timeline/civil_rights/jabara/.
Jacobson, Mathew Frye. "More 'Trans-,' Less 'National.'" *Journal of American Ethnic History* 25 (Summer 2006): 74–84.
———. *Special Sorrows: The Diasporic Imagination of Irish, Polish, and Jewish Immigrants in the United States.* Cambridge, MA: Harvard University Press, 1995.
Jbara, Taysir. *Palestinian Leader Hajj Amin al-Husayni, Mufti of Jerusalem.* Princeton, NJ: Kensington Press, 1985.
Jewish Encyclopedia. "Ibn Gabirol, Solomon ben Judah (Abu Ayyub Suleiman ibn Yahya Ibn Jabirul)." http://www.jewishencyclopedia.com/view.jsp?artid=17&letter=I.
Joseph, Bernard. "Palestine Legislation under the British." *Palestine, a Decade of*

Development, edited by Harry Viteles and Khalil Totah, 39–46. Philadelphia: American Academy of Political and Social Science, 1932.
Joseph, Suad. "Geographies of Lebanese Families: Women as Transnationals, Men as Nationals, and Other Problems with Transnationalism." *Journal of Middle East Women's Studies* 5.3 (2009): 120–144, 199.
Kallen, Horace M. *Culture and Democracy in the United States: Studies in the Psychology of the American People*. New York: Boni and Liveright, 1924.
Karam, Afifa. "Thihabi ila al-harb tashabuni ummi" [My departure to the war accompanied by my mother]. *Al-a'alam al-jadid* 3 (December 1912).
Kātibah, Ḥabīb Ibrahīm. *Arabian Romances and Folk Tales*. New York: Charles Scribner and Sons, 1929.
———, ed. *The Case against Zionism*. New York: Palestine National League, 1921.
———. *Al-Nāṭiqūn bi al-Ḍād fī Amrīkā [Arab Speakers in America]*. Translated by Al-Badawi al-Mulathasm. Jerusalem: Al-Matba'a al-tijāriya, 1946.
———. "Syria for the Syrians under the Guardianship of the United States." *Bulletin of the Syrian National Society* (Boston) 1.9, February 28, 1919.
———. "Syrian Americans." In *One America: The History, Contributions, and Present Problems of Our Racial and National Minorities*, edited by Francis Brown and Joseph S. Roucek. 3rd edition. Englewood, CA: Prentice Hall, 1952. Originally published 1937.
Kayal, Philip M., and Joseph M. Kayal. *The Syrian-Lebanese in America: A Study in Religion and Assimilation*. Boston: Twayne, 1975.
Khabbaz, Hanna. "Falsafat al-Ka'inat, 1: Ana" (Philosophy of the objects, 1: Ana). *Al-Funūn* 2 (November 1916): 503–508.
———. "Falsafat al-Ka'inat, 2: al-Fida'." *Al-Funūn* 2 (February 1917): 786–793.
Khalidi, Rashid. "Ottomanism and Arabism in Syria Before 1914: A Reassessment." In *The Origins of Arab Nationalism: A Reassessment*, ed. Rashid Khalidi, Lisa Anderson, Muhammad Muslih, and Riva S. Simon, 50–69. New York: Columbia University Press, 1991.
———. *Palestinian Identity: The Construction of Modern National Consciousness*. New York: Columbia University Press, 1998.
Khalidi, Walid. *All That Remains: The Palestinian Villages Occupied and Depopulated by Israel in 1948*. Washington, DC: Institute for Palestine Studies, 1992.
———. "On Albert Hourani, the Arab Office, and the Anglo-American Committee of 1946." *Journal of Palestine Studies* 35.1 (October 2005): 60–79.
Khater, Akram Fuad. *Inventing Home: Emigration, Gender, and the Middle Class in Lebanon, 1870–1920*. Berkeley: University of California Press, 2001.
Khatib, Muhib-al-Din al-. *Al-Mu'tamar al-'Arabi al-Awwal* [The First Arab Conference]. Cairo: Higher Committee of the Ottoman Decentralization Party in Egypt, Bosphorus Press, 1913.
Kherbawi, Basil M. *Tarīkh al Wilāyāt al-Muttaḥidah* [History of the United States]. New York: Al-Dalil, 1913.
Khoury, Philip S. "Factionalism among Syrian Nationalists during the French Man-

date." *International Journal of Middle Eastern Studies* 13.4 (November 1981): 441–469.

Khuri, Wadiʿ Rashid al-. *Zuhur wa tatawwur al-adab al-Arabi fi al-mahjar* [Emergence and development of Arab literature in the diaspora]. Beirut: Dār al-Rihani Lil-nashr, 1969.

Lesch, Ann Mosley. *Arab Politics in Palestine, 1917–1939: The Frustration of a Nationalist Movement.* Ithaca, NY: Cornell University Press, 1979.

Lesch, David W. *Syria and the United States: Eisenhower's Cold War in the Middle East.* Boulder, CO: Westview Press, 1992.

Madey, Elia. "Al-nar wa-al-dam fi Filastin wa ʿitham Balfor" [Fire and blood in Palestine and the bones of Balfour]. *As-Sameer* 7.23 (May 1936): 2.

Magnes, Judah Leon. *Arab-Jewish Unity: Testimony before the Anglo-American Inquiry Commission for the Ihud (Union) Association.* Westport, CT: Hyperion Press, 1976.

Majaj, Lisa Suhair. "Into the Wadi." *Journal of Middle East Women's Studies* 2.2 (2006): 137–139.

Mallah, Abdallah al-. "Mouqif al-jaliya al-Lubnaniya fi al-Argantin min Lubnan al-Kabir: 1918–1920" [The position of the Lebanese immigrant community in Argentine from Greater Lebanon]. In *Dawlat Lubnan al-Kabir (1920–1996), 75 sanah min al-tarikh wa al-munjazat* [Greater Lebanon (1920–1926), 75 years of history and accomplishments]. Beirut: Dairat Manshurat al-Jamiʾa al-Lubnaniya, al-Idara al-Markiziya, al-mathaf [A collection of works by the Department of History, Lebanese University], 1999.

McGoldrick, Monica, Joe Giordano, and John K. Pearce, eds. *Ethnicity and Family Therapy.* 2nd ed. New York: Guilford Press, 1996.

Melki, Henry H. "Al-Sahāta al-ʿarabiya fi al-mahjar wa ʿilāqatuha bi-al-adab al-mahjari" [The Arab-American press and its relation to diaspora literature]. PhD diss., Georgetown University, 1972. University Microfilms, Ann Arbor, MI.

Miller, Roy. "More Sinned against than Sinning? The Case of the Arab Office, Washington, 1945–48." *Diplomacy and Statecraft* 15 (June 2004).

Moubayed, Sami. "Lebanon's Phalange Party: Back from the Grave?" *Washington Report on Middle East Affairs* (American Educational Trust), January 1, 2002.

Naber, Nadine. "Arab American Femininities: Beyond Arab Virgin/American(ized) Whore," *Feminist Studies* 32.1 (2006).

Naff, Alixa. *Becoming American: The Early Arab Immigrant Experience.* Carbondale: Southern Illinois University Press, 1985.

———. "The Early Arab Immigrant Experience." In *The Development of Arab American Identity,* edited by Ernest McCarus, 23–36. Ann Arbor: University of Michigan Press, 1994.

Naimy, Mikhail. *Saboun: Ḥikayat Omr, 1889–1959.* 7th ed. Beirut: Nofal, 1991.

Nasr, Nafhat. "Dual Executive Leadership in Lebanon." *Journal of Arab Affairs* 4.1 (Spring 1985).

Neff, Donald. "Middle East History: It Happened in February; Israeli Leaders Found

Indirectly Responsible for Massacres in Lebanon." *Washington Report on Middle East Affairs* 16.5 (January/February 1998): 90–91.

———. "Middle East History: It Happened in September; Jewish Terrorists Assassinate U.N. Peacekeeper Count Folke Bernadotte." *Washington Report on Middle East Affairs* (September 30, 1995): 83.

Nijim, Basheer K., and Bishara Muammar, eds. *Toward the De-Arabization of Palestine/Israel 1945–1977*. Dubuque, IA: Kendal/Hunt and Jerusalem Fund for Education and Community Development, 1984.

Ochsenwald, William, and Sydney Fisher. *The Middle East: A History*. 6th ed. New York: McGraw-Hill, 2004.

Off Our Backs. "Issues Concerning Arab Feminists," September 30, 1983.

Omar, Saleh. "Philosophical Origins of the Arab Ba'th Party: The Work of Zaki Al-Arsuzi." *Arab Studies Quarterly* 18 (Spring 1996): 23–38.

Oren, Michael B. *Power, Faith, and Fantasy: America in the Middle East, 1776 to the Present*. New York: W. W. Norton, 2007.

Orfalea, Gregory. *Before the Flames: A Quest for the History of Arab Americans*. Austin: University of Texas Press, 1988.

Owen, Roger. *State, Power, and Politics in the Making of the Modern Middle East*. New York: Routledge, 1992.

Owen, Roger, and Sevket Pamuk. *A History of Middle East Economies in the Twentieth Century*. Cambridge, MA: Harvard University Press, 1999.

Oxford Economic Country Briefings. "Saudi Arabia," July 21, 2008, 1–5.

Pappé, Ilan. *The Arab Israeli Conflict: The Ethnic Cleansing of Palestine*. Oxford, England: Oneworld, 2006.

———. *The Forgotten Palestinians: A History of the Palestinians in Israel*. New Haven, CT: Yale University Press, 2011.

———. *A History of Modern Palestine: One Land, Two Peoples*. Cambridge, England: Cambridge University Press, 2006.

———. *The Making of the Arab-Israeli Conflict, 1948–1951*. London: St. Antony's College Series, Macmillan; New York: St. Martin's Press, 1988.

Pappé, Ilan, and Moshe Ma'oz, eds. *Middle Eastern Politics and Ideas: A History from Within*. London: Tauris Academic Studies, 1997.

Paterson, Rubin. "Transnationalism: Diaspora-Homeland Development." *Social Forces* 84 (June 2006): 1891–1907.

Paterson, Thomas G. "Cold War Revisionism: A Practitioner's Perspective." *Diplomatic History* 31.3 (June 2007): 387–395.

Perry, Marvin, and Frederick M. Schweitzer, eds. *Antisemitic Myths: A Historical and Contemporary Anthology*. Bloomington: Indiana University Press, 2008.

Philipp, Thomas. "Identities and Loyalties in Bilad al-Sham at the Beginning of the Early Modern Period." In *From Syrian Land to the States of Syria and Lebanon*, edited by Thomas Philipp and Christoph Schumann, 9–26. Beirut: Orient Institute, 2004.

Podeh, Elie. "History and Memory in the Israeli Educational System: The Portrayal of the Arab-Israeli Conflict in History Textbooks (1948–2000)." *History and Memory* 12.1 (June 30, 2000): 65–100.

Provence, Michael. *The Great Syrian Revolt and the Rise of Arab Nationalism* (Austin: University of Texas Press, 2005.

Qaddurah, Jamal Muhammad. *Al-qadiyah al-filastiniya wa lijan al-tahqiq* [The Palestinian Question and Investigative Commissions]. Beirut: Dar al-Hamra, 1993.

Rhead, Louis. *The Arabian Nights' Entertainments*. New York: Harper Brothers, 1916.

Ricks, Thomas H. *Turbulent Times in Palestine: The Diaries of Khalil Totah, 1886–1955*, Beirut: Institute for Palestine Studies and PASSIA, 2009.

Rigg, Bryan Mark. *Hitler's Jewish Soldiers: The Untold Story of Nazi Racial Laws and Men of Jewish Descent in the German Military*. Modern War Studies Series. Lawrence: University Press of Kansas, 2002.

Rihani, Ameen. *The Book of Khalid*. New York: Dodd, Mead, 1911.

———. *Letters to Uncle Sam*. Washington, DC: Platform International, 2001.

———. *Muluk al-Arab* [Kings of the Arabs]. Beirut: Yousef Sader, Al matba'a al ilmiya, 1929.

———. "Palestine and the Proposed Arab Federation." In *Palestine, a Decade of Development*, edited by Harry Viteles and Khalil Totah, 62–71. Philadelphia: American Academy of Political and Social Science, 1932.

———. *Rasa'il Ameen al-Rihani, 1896–1940* [Letters of Ameen al-Rihani]. Beirut: Dar al-Rihani lil-Nashr, 1959.

———. "Rouh al Thawrah" [The Spirit of the Revolution]. In *Al Qawmiyat Part I*. Beirut: Dar Reehani Lil-Tab', 1956.

Rogers, Lynne D. "Literary Snapshots: Mark Twain's *Innocents Abroad* and William Thackeray's *Notes of a Journey from Cornhill to Grand Cairo*." In *The Landscape of Palestine: Equivocal Poetry*, edited by Ibrahim Abu-Lughod, Roger Heacock, and Khaled Nashef. Birzeit, Palestine: Birzeit University Publications, 1999.

Rubenberg, Cheryl A. *Israel and the American National Interest: A Critical Examination*. Urbana: University of Illinois Press, 1986.

Saʿdi, Ahmad H. "Catastrophe, Memory and Identity: Al-Nakbah as a Component of Palestinian Identity." *Israel Studies* 7.2 (July 1, 2002): 175–200.

Said, Edward W. *The Politics of Dispossession: The Struggle for Palestinian Self Determination, 1969–1994*. New York: Pantheon, 1994.

Sameer, As-. "Al-A'arab wal harb al-muqbilah" [The Arabs and the approaching war]. *As-Sameer* 7 (September 1935): 22–30.

———. "Hadith 'an Filastin" [A conversation on Palestine]. *As-Sameer* 6 (March 1935): 10–13.

———. "Al-Hizb al-Suri al-Qaumi fi Surya" [The Syrian National Party in Syria]. *As-Sameer* 7 (January 1936): 20.

———. "La Tasruqu Baitana" [Do not steal our home]. *As-Sameer* 7 (May 1936): 6, 7.

———. "Al-Malek al-Arabi" [The Arab king]. *As-Sameer* 3 (June 1931).

———. "Maut zaʿem filastini kabeer" [Death of a great Palestinian leader]. *As-Sameer* 6 (March 1935).

———. "Suri wa Lubnani wa..." [Syrian and Lebanese and...]. *As-Sameer* 4 (October 1932): 18, 19.

———. "Thawrat 1929" [The Revolt of 1929]. *As-Sameer* 7 (May 1936): 6–7.

———. "Ughniya Sauda'" [A black song (translated from English)]. *As-Sameer* 4.22 (March 1933): 3.

———. "Al-wafd al-Filastini fi Flint" [The Arab delegation in Flint]. *As-Sameer*, February 28, 1948.

Sampter, Jessie E. *A Course in Zionism*. New York: Federation of American Zionists, 1915.

Sawaie, Mohammad. "Rifaʿa Rafiʿ al-Tahtawi and His Contribution to the Lexical Development of Modern Arabic." *International Journal of Middle Eastern Studies* 32 (2000): 395–410.

Schad, Geoffrey D. "Colonialists, Industrialists, and Politicians: The Political Economy of Industrialization in Syria, 1920–1954." PhD diss., University of Pennsylvania, 2001.

Schumann, Christoph. "Nationalism, Diaspora and 'Civilisational Mission': The Case of Syrian Nationalism in Latin America between World War I and World War II." *Nations and Nationalism* 10 (October 2004): 599–617.

Segev, Tom. *One Palestine Complete: Jews and Arabs Under the British Mandate*. New York: Metropolitan Books, 2000.

Shaheen, Jack G. "Palestinians on the Silver Screen in the 1980s." *American-Arab Affairs* 31 (Spring 1989): 68–80.

———. "Reel Bad Arabs: How Hollywood Vilifies a People." *Annals of the American Academy of Political and Social Science* 588 (July 2003): 171–193.

———. *The TV Arab*. Bowling Green, OH: Bowling Green State University Popular Press, 1984.

Sharabi, Hisham. *Arab Intellectuals and the West: the Formative Years 1875–1914*. Baltimore: Johns Hopkins Press, 1970.

———. *Al-Jamr wa-al-Ramad: Muthakkarat muthaqqaf Aʿarabi* [Chariots and ashes: Memoir of an Arab intellectual]. Beirut: Ibn-Rushd, 1978.

Shatara, Fuad. "Arab Jewish Unity." In *Palestine, A Decade of Development*, edited by Harry Viteles and Khalil Totah, 178–183. Philadelphia: American Academy of Political and Social Science, 1932.

Shihadeh, Lamia Rustum. "The Name of Syria in Ancient and Modern Usage." In *The Origins of Syrian Nationhood: History, Pioneers, and Identity*, edited by Adel Bishara, 17–29. London: Routledge, 2011.

Shlaim, Avi. *The Iron Wall: Israel and the Arab World*. New York: W. W. Norton, 2000.

Simpson, John Hope. *Palestine. Report on Immigration, Land Settlement, and Development*. London: His Majesty's Stationery Office, 1930.

Smith, Anthony D. *National Identity*. Reno: University of Nevada Press, 1991.

Stivers, William. *America's Confrontation with Revolutionary Change in the Middle East, 1948–83.* New York: St. Martin's Press, 1986.

Suleiman, Michael W., ed. *American Arabs and Political Participation.* Washington, DC: Woodrow Wilson International Center for Scholars, 2006.

———. *The Arab American Experience in the U.S. and Canada: A Classified Annotated Bibliography.* Ann Arbor, MI: Pierian Press, 2006.

———. "Arab-Americans and the Political Process." In *The Development of Arab American Identity*, edited by Ernest McCarus, 37–61. Ann Arbor: University of Michigan Press, 1994.

———. *Arabs in the Mind of America.* Brattleboro, VT: Amana Books, 1988.

———. "Early Arab Americans: The Search for Identity." In *Crossing the Waters: Arabic-Speaking Immigrants to the United States before 1940*, edited by Eric J. Hooglund, 37–54. Washington, DC: Smithsonian Institution Press, 1987.

———. "A History of Arab American Political Participation." In *American Arabs and Political Participation*," edited by Philippa Strum, 3–25. Conference proceedings, Woodrow Wilson International Center for Scholars, Washington, DC, May 5, 2006.

———. "'I Come to Bury Caesar, Not to Praise Him': An Assessment of the AAUG as an Example of an Activist Arab-American Organization." *Arab Studies Quarterly* 29 (Summer/Fall 2007): 75–96.

———. Introduction to *American Arabs and Political Participation*, edited by Michael W. Suleiman. Washington, DC: Woodrow Wilson International Center for Scholars, 2006.

———. *Political Parties in Lebanon: The Challenge of Fragmented Political Culture.* Ithaca, NY: Cornell University Press, 1967.

———. *U.S. Policy on Palestine: From Wilson to Clinton.* N.p.: Association of Arab-American University Graduates, 1995.

Tarazi, Philippe de. *Tarīkh al-saḥāfa al-ʿarabīyah* [History of the Arab press]. Beirut: Al-Matbaʿa al-adabiya, 1913.

———. *Tarīkh al-saḥāfah al-ʿarabīyah* [History of the Arab press]. Beirut: Al-Matbaʿa al-Amreekīya, 1933.

Tarrah, Ali al-. "An Overview of Historical Changes in the Lives of Middle Eastern Women." *Domes* 3.3 (June 30, 1994): 5.

Tassin, Kristin S. "'Lift up Your Head, My Brother': Nationalism and the Genesis of the Non-Aligned Movement." *Journal of Third World Studies* 23.1 (April 2006): 147–168.

Taymoumi, Al-Hadi al-. *Fi usūl al-harakah al-qaumīyah al-ʿarabīyah, 1839–1920* [On the origins of the Arab national movement, 1839–1920]. Tunis: Dār Muhammad ʿAli al-hāmi, 2002.

———. *Fi usūl al-harakah al-qaumīyah al-ʿarabīyah: 1920–1939* [On the origins of the Arab national movement, 1920–1939]. Tunis: Dār Muhammad ʿAli al-hāmi, 2002.

Telhami, Shibley, Fiona Hill, Abdullatif A. al-Othman, and Syrus H. Tahmassebi. "Does Saudi Arabia Still Matter?" *Foreign Affairs*, November 2002, 167–178.

Terry, Janice. "Community and Political Activism among Arab Americans in Detroit." In *Arabs in America: Building a New Future*, edited by Michael Suleiman, 241–254. Philadelphia: Temple University Press, 1999.

Tibawi, A. L. "T. E. Lawrence, Faisal and Weizmann: The 1919 Attempt to Secure an Arab Balfour Declaration." *Royal Central Asian Journal* 56 (1969): 156–163.

Tibi, Bassam. *Arab Nationalism: Between Islam and the Nation-State*. 3rd ed. London: Macmillan, 1997.

Ueda, Reed. *Postwar Immigrant America: A Social History*. New York: Bedford St. Martin's Press, 1994.

Vecoli, Rudolph J., and Suzanne Sinke, eds. *A Century of European Migrations, 1830–1930*. Urbana: University of Illinois Press, 1991.

Viteles, Harry, and Khalil Totah, eds. *Palestine, A Decade of Development*. Philadelphia: American Academy of Political and Social Science, 1932.

Ward, Gabriel E. *Al-jundi al-Suri fi thalath hurub* [The Syrian soldier in three wars]. New York: Al-maktba'a al-Amreekiyah al-Suriya, 1919.

Warnshuis, A. L. "Christians and Zionists." Pamphlet. New York: Institute of Arab American Affairs, December 1945.

Watenpaugh, Keith D. "Middle-Class Modernity and the Persistence of the Politics of Notables in Inter-War Syria." *International Journal of Middle East Studies* 35 (May 2003): 257–286.

Waugh, Earl H., and Baha Abu Laban, eds. *The Muslim Community in North America*. Edmonton, Canada: University of Alberta Press, 1983.

Weismann, Itzhak. "Sufi Reformist Diffusion and the Rise of Arabism in Late Ottoman Syria." In *From the Syrian Land to the State of Syria and Lebanon*, edited by Thomas Philipp and Christoph Schumann, 113–126. Beirut: Ergon Verlag Wurzburg In Kommission, 2004.

Wigle, Laurel D., and Samir Abraham. "Arab Nationalism in America: The Dearborn Arab Community." *Journal of University Studies* 10 (1974): 279–302.

Younis, Adele Linda. "The Coming of the Arabic-Speaking People to the United States." PhD diss., Boston University Graduate School, 1961.

Zeine, Zeine N. *Arab Turkish Relations and the Emergence of Arab Nationalism*. Beirut: Khayat, 1958.

———. *The Emergence of Arab Nationalism. With a Background Study of Arab-Turkish Relations in the Near East*. Beirut: Khayat, 1966.

Ziadeh, Farhat. "Winds Blow Where Ships Do Not Wish to Go." In *Paths to the Middle East: Ten Scholars Look Back*, edited by Thomas Naff. New York; University of New York Press, 1993.

Zraick, Anton A. "Hawadeth kharijyya" [Foreign affairs]. *Jurāb-ul-Kurdi*, November 19, 1912.

———. "Khalifat al-Muslimin yadʻu lil-jihād, Fa-ila-l-jihād" [The Muslim caliph calls for war. Then on to war]. *Jurāb-ul-Kurdi*, November 12, 1912.

Zuʻaitir, Muhammad. *Al-Marūniyah fi Lubnān qadīman wa hadīthan* [The Maronite rite in Lebanon past and present]. Beirut: Al-Wikalah al-Sharqiya lil-Tawzeeʻ, 1994.

———. *Al-mashrūʻ al-Marūni fi Lubnān: Judhūrahu wa taṭawurahu* [The Maronite project in Lebanon: Its origins and development]. Lebanon: Al-Wikālah al-ʻĀlamīyah li al-Tawzīʻ, 1986.

Zuckerman, Lawrence. "A Pacifist Leader Who Was More Prophet than Politician." *Jewish Daily Forward*, January 14, 2011.

INDEX

1967 war, 37; Arab American National Museum and, 1, 5; hostility after, 7, 294, 300; identity and, 9, 10, 12, 13; immigration after, 7, 12; political organizations and, 1, 6–7, 10, 12, 36, 37, 298, 301; scholarship and, 6, 10, 12, 13, 241, 298, 299, 302

ʿAbbas, ʿAbd al-Majid, 221
Abbas, Hassan Abu, 150
Abbasi, Muhammad Baradʿi (Baradei), 257, 286
Abdelhadi, Aouni, 175, 176–177, 179, 200
Abduh, Muhammad, 46
Abdulhamid (Sultan), 41, 48, 57, 72, 160; censorship of, 61, 62, 84; removal of, 65, 66, 73, 74; suspension of constitution by, 19, 39
Abdullah (King), 156, 186
Abodeely, Michael, 110
Abourezk, James (Senator), 174, 301, 302
Abramowitz (Rabbi), and debate with Rihani, 199
Abscam, 301
Abulfilāt (Abu-al-Filāt), Mahmoud, 186, 224
Acheson, Dean, 268, 280
Adams, Emily Mutter, 227
Adams, Frank, 175
Adib, Augustus, 139
Afghāni, Jamāl al-Dīn al-, 28, 139
African National Congress, 303

ʿAhd, Al-, (The Promise), 48
Aimen, Alan, 11
ʿAjram, Abi, 150
ʿAjram, Fuad Abu, 121
ʿAjram, Muhammad Abi, 136, 137, 155
Akhbār al-Injīl (News of the Bible), 56
Akhlāq, Al-, 59, 108
ʿĀlam al-Jadid al-Nisāʾi, Al-, (The New World for Women), 74
ʿAlami, Musa al-, 270
Alawane, Ibrahim, 246
Albright, W. F., 175
Alhourani, Motaz Abdullah, 15
Ali, Ibrahim, 41–42
Ali, Muhammad (Egypt's governor), 16, 40–41
Ali, Muhammad Kurd, 48, 50
Ali, Rashid, 268
Alling, Paul H., 262
Amen family, 11
American Academy of Political and Social Science, 161, 175
American Arab Anti-Discrimination Committee (ADC), 174, 291–293, 301
American-Arab Committee for Democracy, 257
American Arabic Association (AMARA), 319n8
American Council for Judaism, 267
American Evangelical Syrian College, 65
American Friends Mission, 220, 227, 230

Americanism, 5, 236
American Jewish Committee, 274
American Jewish Distribution Committee, 267
American League for the Defense of Jewish Rights, 181
American League for a Free Palestine, 278
American Middle East Relief Organization, 288
American Oriental Society, 163–164
American Palestine Campaign, 182
American Syrian Lebanese Clubs (AMSYRLUB), 191
American University of Beirut (AUB), 112, 113, 142, 241, 261, 269
American University in Cairo, 112
American Zionist Emergency Council, 255, 264
Amin, Karen, 11
Amiriyyeh School, al- (Jaffa), 112
Anabtawi, Nathmi, 121–122, 132, 133, 148, 150, 151, 153
Anglo-American Committee of Inquiry, 242, 243, 250, 264, 266–268, 270, 280–281
ANL. *See* Arab National League
Anti-Defamation League, 274–278, 284, 302, 303, 348n10
Anti-Nazi League, 270, 285
Anti-Semitism, 181, 182, 203, 235, 266, 273–274, 276–277, 278
Anton, Farah, 72
Antonius, George, 28–29, 39, 40, 75, 203, 214, 232
Anwar, Al-, 67
ʿArabi al-Fatāt, al- (Arab Youth or Young Arab Society), 48
Arab American Institute (AAI), 293
Arab American National Museum, 1, 5, 11, 299
Arab American studies: 1967 war and, 12; civil rights movement and, 6; dominant themes of, 5, 6; feminism in, 6, 307n4; political organizations in scholarship of, 1–2, 5, 7, 297–304
Arab Bureau of Information, 249
Arab Community Center for Economic and Social Services (ACCESS), 10–11, 293, 300
Arab Council, 175
Arab Detroit, 9–11
Arab Higher Committee, 179, 201–202, 205, 286
Arab hype, 14–15
Arabian American Oil Company (ARAMCO), 290
Arabian Society of Detroit, 246
Arab League. *See* League of Arab States
Arab Literary Club. *See* Muntada al-ʿArabi, al-
Arab Men's Teacher Training College, Jerusalem, 112
Arab National Congress, 203
Arab nationalism, 26, 29–30; American policy on, 34–36, 295; Arabian peninsula and, 45; definition of, 82; local context of, 41; origins of, 53; Ottoman Empire experience and, 39–40; Palestinian advocacy and, 203, 235, 254, 291; socialism and, 201; strategies for, 105–106, 191–192, 235, 254
Arab National League (ANL), 3, 9, 14, 22, 24, 28–29, 109, 235, 300; Muhammad Jamil Beyhum and, 17, 201–212; bylaws of, 195; car accident involving leaders of, 229; chapters of, 208, 215–216, 218; conventions of, 14, 32, 35, 195, 211, 215–229, 235, 238, 297; economic principles of, 197; FBI examination of, 237; functions of, 131, 190–195, 226, 238; geographic distribution of, 216; humanitarian efforts of, 201, 209, 220, 227, 234; al-Husseini's office and, 201;

language usage by, 194–195; media activities of, 227–228, 297; New Syria Party's overlap with, 131–132, 156, 157, 162, 190; origins of, 4, 32, 107, 159, 169, 170, 175, 178, 187–189, 190; Palestinian advocacy of, 187, 234–235, 258; publications of, 194–195, 197; Rihani and, 200; scholarship on, 107; sectarianism and, 191, 209–210, 216, 222; suspension of, 4, 231, 233, 237, 250, 257; Zionist activists versus, 214
Arab Office (London), 232
Arab Office (Washington, DC), 242, 269–270, 277
Arab Party, 179
Arab Revolt of 1916, 167
ʿArbili, Ibrahim, 60, 62
ʿArbili, Najib, 60, 62
ʿArbili, Yousef, 60
ʿĀref, ʿĀref al-, 166
Arida, Nasib, 20, 59, 296, 297; Ameen Farah and, 88, 94; death of, 232; Free Syria Society and, 14, 88, 94, 97, 98–99; Al-Funun and, 70, 97, 121; nationalism of, 56; Orthodox press and, 54, 55; religion of, 23, 59; Syrian Relief Committee and, 118
ʿArīdah, Anton (aka Anton Butros), 60
ʿArīdah, Kāmil, 112
Armenian atrocities, 116
Arslan, Adel, 156, 198, 202
Arslan, Majīd, 140, 232
Arslan, Muhammad, 45
Arslan, Shakib: controversy over visit of, 15, 23, 24, 59, 135–139, 143–144, 145–147, 151; convention of New Syria Party and, 30, 45, 142, 152, 157; First Arab Conference and, 82, 104, 139; Kātibah's correspondence with, 158; at the League of Nations, 122; representation by New Syria Party of, 126, 153

Asʿad, Amin al-, 140
ʿAsali, Shukri al-, 39, 50, 78, 81; social role of, 53
ʿĀṣimah, Al- (The Capitol), 136, 148
Asmar, George N., 146
Association of Arab American University Graduates (AAUG): ACCESS creation and, 11; and analysis of Arab American institutions, 7, 11–12, 239–241, 293, 294, 295, 298, 299; attacks on, 302–303; civil rights movement and, 302; foundation of, 1, 12; Palestinian advocacy of, 240; scholarship and, 6; social services of, 240
Aswad, Barbara, 6
Atlantic Charter, 253
Atlee, Clement, 268, 270
Atrash, Abdel-Ghaffar al-, 140
Atrash, Hasan al-, 138, 140
Atrash, Sayyah Hammoud al-, 140
Atrash, Sultan al-, 30, 119, 137–138, 149, 155
Atrash, Zeid al-, 150
Atwel, Helen, 11
Audi, E. J., 197, 248
Awad, Habib J., 59
Ayoub, Rashid, 20
Ayoubi, Salahaddin al-, 128, 226
Ayyam, Al- (The Days), 73
Azhar, al-, 112
ʿAẓm, Rafīq al-, 15, 48, 57, 76–77, 78, 79, 82, 86, 93, 297
Azzam, Abdelrahman, 270
Azzam, Salman Yousef, 133

Badder, Ahmad, 246
Baddūr, Suleiman, 20, 59, 69, 72, 232
Badr, Ahmad, 216
Badran, Najib, 59
Baihum, Husain, 45
Bailey, J. W., 269
Bakhkhash, Shukri, 73

366 | INDEX

Bakūra al-Durziya, al-, 126
Balfour Declaration, 9, 112, 160, 162, 178, 234, 253, 256, 280; criticisms of, 228; deracination and, 204, 235; McMahon correspondence and, 213; motivations for, 107, 198; Palestinian reaction to, 168; Syrian nationalism and, 102–103; United States' endorsement of, 116; Wilsonianism and, 169
Balkan Wars, 24, 57, 73–74, 77, 79, 88
Bandak, Issa, 156, 202
Bank al-'Arabi, al- (Arab Bank), 140
Baqa' League of Dearborn, 222
Barakat, Fayyad, 248
Barakat, George M., 32, 162, 245
Barbour, Hamad al-, 138
Barghuthi, Omar Saleh al-, 175
Barq, Al-, 51
Barudi, Fauzi al-, 204
Bashīr, Al- (The Good Message), 56
Bashir, Antony, 108, 207, 246–248, 260, 261
Bateh, Isa, 248, 249
Bateh, Joseph, 197
Battle of Maysalūn, 166
Bayān, Al-, 15, 24, 29, 56, 99, 103, 129, 136, 140, 145, 148, 153; Beyhum delegation and, 204; editors of, 59; humanitarian relief and, 68; nationalism of, 69; New Syria Party reports in, 135; Ottoman politics of, 15; Prince Faisal's visit and, 245; Syrian Revolt and, 69, 140
Bazi, (Imam) Khalil, 17, 150, 209, 246, 248
Begin, Menachem, 276, 278
Beirut Reform Society, 64
Bell, Gertrude, 319n10
Ben Gurion, David, 233, 234, 281, 288
Ben-Zvi, Isaac, 175
Berger, Rabbi Elmer, 183–184, 273

Bernadotte, (Count) Folke, 243, 285–286, 288
Berri, Abdallah, 209, 224
Bevin, Ernest, 267, 279
Beyhum, Ahmad, 44
Beyhum, Muhammad Jamil, 16, 17, 45, 201–212, 215, 218, 232, 233, 334n23, 334n43, 335nn56–57, 336n76
Biltmore Program, 233–234, 243, 267, 271, 276
Bliss, Daniel, 241
Bliss, Edward, 192
Bliss, Howard, 241
Blue Star Mothers, 270
Blunt, Wilfred, 48
Bodley, Ronald V. C., 277
Bolshevik Revolution, 134
Bonné, Alfred, 175, 177–178
Book of Khalid, The (1911), 39, 55
Bookstein, Morris, 211
Borah, William, 122, 126, 172, 261
Brandeis, Louis, 103, 184, 185
Brickner, (Rabbi) Barnett, 182
British Mandate, 167, 240; contradictory statements during, 169; protest against, 297; U.S. opinion and, 226; U.S. involvement in, 268
Brown, Philip Marshal, 269
Brown, William B., 205–206
Bu'aini, Hasan Amin al-, 137
Buckley, Charles, 213
Budairi family, 57
Bukhāri, Saḥīḥ al-, 19, 310n49
Bulaq section of Cairo, 41
Bunche, Ralph, 283
Bund, the, 236–237
Burhān, Al- (The Evidence), 60
Bushel, Hayman, 285
Bustān, Al- (The Garden), 73
Bustani, Butrus al-, 19, 44, 45, 56, 57, 312n23
Bustani, Ibrahim al-, 139
Bustani, Suleiman al-, 108

Bustani, Wadiʿ al-, 169
Butros, Anton. See ʿArīdah, Anton

California Alien Land Law, 76
caliphate, 39
Cambou declaration, 64
Carlyle, Thomas, 111
Carson, Robert, 205
Catzeflis, William, 55, 107, 112, 187
Centennial International Exhibition (Philadelphia), 17
Central Relief Committee (Jerusalem), 153
Chamberlain, Neville, 214
Chasin, Philip, 274–276
Chicago World Expo. See World's Columbian Exposition
Churchill, Winston, 167, 169, 215, 254, 267
Civil War (American), 61
Clark, A. P. S., 175, 177
Clifford, Clark, 284
Coffee, John M., 249–250
Cohen, Morris, 185
Cold War, 242–244, 280, 294, 300, 340n31
Collège des Frères (Jerusalem), 112
Comings, Harry, 227
Committee for the Aid of the Syrian Victims, 123, 136
Committee for Palestine's Victims, 155–156, 210
Committee for Peace and Justice in the Holy Land, 276
Committee of Union and Progress (CUP), 48, 50, 51, 66; and Balkan Wars, 74–75; New Provinces Law of, 76
communism, 35, 37, 279, 295
Connally, Tom, 246–248, 249, 260
conspiracy theory, 261
Council of Churches of Christ in America, 211
Council on American Islamic Relations (CAIR), 293
Crane, Charles, 126
CUP. See Committee of Union and Progress

Daʿās, Abdallah, 112
Dabronsky, Jacob, 198
Dajani, Saʿid, 257
Dalīl, Al-, 15
Damous, Nasif, 73
Daouq, Omar, 210
Darwaza, Muhammad ʿIzzat, 203
David, Ameen, 59
David, Gary, 11–12
Davidson, Lawrence, account of political organizations by, 9, 189, 298, 308n19
Dawoud, Suleiman, 210
Dearborn, Michigan, 10, 11, 17
Decentralization Party. See Ottoman Administrative Decentralization Party
DeHaan, Jacob Israel, 176
Deir Yaseen massacre, 283, 284, 345n154
democracy, 160, 229; education and, 142; imperialism and, 236; in Palestine, 177; Syrian immigrant support for, 197, 227–229, 237, 259, 304; Zionism and, 214, 254
deracination, 12, 115, 204
Diāb, Ahmad, 128, 150, 154
Diab, Hajj Yaseen, 210
Diāb, Najīb, 15, 20, 21, 23, 59, 72, 93; First Arab Conference attended by, 67, 79, 81, 82–86; Mirāt al-Gharb founded by; nationalism of, 29, 62, 144, 166; Ottoman politics of, 54; on Palestine, 144; United Syrian Society and, 26
Difāʿ al-ʿArabi, Al- (Arab Defense, 1921), 60, 99

Dīn, Fakhr al-, 40
Dodd, Stuart C., 269
Dodge, Bayard, 277
Drang nach Osten, 46
Druze: alliances of, 67; French treatment of, 119; media attacks on, 15, 23, 145–147, 259; study of Syrian, 137; and Syrian Revolt, 31, 121, 122, 124, 140, 156; and violence with Maronites, 42–43, 65, 95; World War I actions of, 118
Druze immigrants, 14, 139; families of, 112; in media, 24, 57, 59, 60, 62, 68, 69, 129; in Michigan, 17; in New Syria Party; 126, 139; societies of, 124, 126

Eddé, Émile, 164
Egyptian Feminist Union, 99
Einstein, Albert, 35, 184–186, 266, 331n118
Eisner, Frederic, 272
Elazari-Volcani, J., 175, 177
Elkholy, Abdo A., 6
Emerson, Ralph Waldo, 111
Esmail, Jody, 197
ethnie, 26
Exodus (ship), 281

Faisal, Prince (Husain Ibn Ali's son), 46, 144, 166, 173
Farah, Ameen, 1, 25, 51; Arab National League and, 207–209, 215, 216, 217, 224, 229, 230, 231; archives of, ix, x, 21, 26, 37, 49, 189, 242, 250–251; contact with Mikhail Naimy and Nasib Arida by, 54, 94–98; early activity of, 49, 87–90; education support of, 112; Egypt delegation and, 155; fire suffered by, 136; Free Syria Society and, 21, 102–103, 297; and al-Husseini, relationship between, 169; ideology and politics of, 3–4, 72, 163; Institute for Arab American Affairs and, 257, 269; letters of, 49–50, 87; media activities of, 226; and Muhaisen, contact between, 60; and New Syria Party administration, 119–122, 127–129, 132–137, 149–150; and New Syria Party convention program, 140–142; novel by, 88, 90, 93, 116, 317n22, 320n24; report received by, 124; responses to occupations of, 119; revolt reaction by, 122; and Saybaʿa, correspondence between, 151–152, 153; and Abu Shaqra, correspondence between, 154; social role of, 53; World War I service of, 100–102
Farah, Emile, 210
Farah, Farīd ("Fred"), 212, 226
Farah, Nazir, 227, 231
Farah, Neman, 173
Farah, Raji (mayor of Nazareth), 167, 173, 317n21
Farah, Roy, 257
Farah, Saleh (father of Ameen), 317n20
Farah, Salim, 167, 169, 173
Farah, Subhi, 212, 227
Farah, Yaʿqoub (grandfather), 317n20
Faraj, Muhammad, 246
Fares, Nabih, 245
Faris, Philip, 73
Farraj, Yaʿqoub, 203
Fatah (PLO faction), 11
Fatāt, Al- (The Youth), 21, 73, 81, 87, 144, 296; founding of, 175; goals of, 105
Federal Bureau of Investigation (FBI), U.S., 270
Federation of American Syrian Lebanese Clubs, 8, 108, 109
field hollers, 165
Fielding, Michael, 277
Filasṭīn, 57
Finley, John, 192

First Arab Conference (France, 1913), 19, 21, 24, 50, 65, 67, 70, 79, 104, 297; Arslan's view of, 139; motivations for, 81; Syrian views of, 114, 191
Foreign Policy Association, 56, 198–200, 211, 264, 269
France, 60; 1860 conflict and, 43; and Arslan's visit, 146–147; Lebanon, 23; political involvement of, 14, 63; Syrian occupation by, 22, 24, 118, 153, 183, 187, 244
Freedman, Benjamin, 276, 278, 285, 286
Free Syria Society (FSS), 3, 14, 19, 24, 73, 157, 241; agenda of, 21, 99–100, 105, 296–297; bylaws of, 99–100; establishment of, 21, 81, 88; and *Al-Funūn*, 20; goals of, 3–4, 48; membership of, 81, 94–100, 297; nationalism of, 73, 87, 90, 105; Ottoman Administrative Decentralization Party and, 48, 87, 296; uniqueness of, 87
French Mandate, 162, 165; domestic opposition to, 119; end of, 260; history of, 157; treatment of Druze under, 119
Friends of the Arabs Society, 194
Funūn, Al-, 20, 29, 70, 94, 200; Gibran's writings in, 67; financing for, 121
Furlong, Charles Wellington, 277

Gans, Herbert, 227
Garibaldi, Giuseppe, 74
General Arab Orphans Committee in Palestine, 286
Geographic Syria, 10, 244, 307n3; Arab American interest in, 244; definition of, 4; fears for occupation of, 73
George, Jeff, 5
George, Peter, media efforts of, 35, 248, 249, 297
Ghaith, Asʿad, 150
Ghannam, Hamdan, 248

Ghannoum, Abdallah, 150
Gharib (Ghurayeb), Amin al-, 23, 55, 63, 66; nationalism of, 29
Ghouri, (Effendi) Emil el-, 16, 201–212, 215, 218
Gibran, Gibran Khalil (also Khalil Gibran), vi, 20, 54, 55, 66, 71, 88, 296; Islamic influence on, 28; nationalism of, 29, 56, 65–68; Syrian Relief Committee and, 118
Gildersleeve, Virginia, 35, 258, 264, 276, 277, 278, 288
Gossett, Ed, 277–278
Grant, Elihu, 35, 192, 220, 224, 227, 228, 230
Great Depression: Michigan immigrants and, 161; and Palestine, 179; political activities during, 31–32, 159, 169, 174
Greater Syria (Bilād al-Shām), 17, 307n3
Great Syrian Revolt, the, 28, 104–105, 139–140, 162; as challenge to colonialism, 123–124; crushing of, 31, 103, 109, 122, 151, 152, 155, 156; foreign troops in, 139–140; immigrant concern over, 4, 9, 15, 24, 69, 104–105, 107–109, 119, 121, 122, 136, 137, 139, 152, 155, 297; scholarship on, 123–124, 137
Greenberg, Haim, 185
Greensboro Committee for the Abrogation of the White Paper, 269
Grew, Joseph C., 260
groceries, immigrants as vendors of, 13
Gundry, George V., 229

Haddād, ʿAbdulmassīh, 20, 55, 59, 67, 69–70, 100, 296; nationalism of, 29
Haddad, George, 140
Haddad, Gregorios, 203
Haddad, Nadra, 20, 118
Haddad, Ramiz, 248
Haddad, Rizk, 16, 64, 207

Haddad, Yvonne, interpretation of 1967 war by, 7, 12
Haganah, 178, 268, 276, 283, 284
Hagopian, Elaine, 6
Haidar, Najm, 133
haju (diatribe or critique), 16
Halaqāt al-Dhahabīyah, al- (Golden Circles), 66
Haleem, Adel, 248
Hamady, Kamel, 140
Hamady, Mahmoud, 208
Hammer, Gotlieb, 255
Hammoud, Hassan, 150, 207
Hammoud, Saleh, 150
Hamza, Ahmad, 224
Hamzi, Ahmad, 150
Hananiya, Jurji, 57
Harb, Talʿat Pasha, 210
Hariri, Muhammad Uthman al-, 20
Harrison, Earl, 266
Hasan, Fayez, 209, 222–224
Hashemites, 46
Haskell, Mary, 66
Hawawini, Rafael, 63, 66, 108
Hawie, Ashad, 100
Hayes, Patrick Joseph, 173
Hayman, Bushel, 285
Hazam, Hanna (or John), 248, 249, 267
Heider, Kamel, 150
Herzl, Theodore, 280
Highland Park, Michigan, 9, 14
Hilāl, Al-, 28
Hilli, Safi al-Dīn al-, 70
Hisn, Ali Salman Tabi Abi, al-, 150
Hitti, Philip, 163, 261; American Oriental Society and, 163–164; Anglo-American Committee of Inquiry and, 267; Arab National League and, 192; congressional testimony of, 263–264, 268; immigrant press analysis of, 58, 157; Institute of Arab American Affairs, 248, 259, 262, 263–264, 265; media efforts of, 35, 103, 116; nationalism views of, 311n53
Hizb al-Lāmarkizīyah al-Idārīyah al-ʿUthmani. *See* Ottoman Administrative Decentralization Party
Hocking, William Ernest, 35; and the Arab National League, 192, 198, 264, 269, 288, 290, 291
Hoda, Al-, 14, 22, 24, 56, 58, 63, 85, 103, 151, 245; anti-Muslim rhetoric of, 74; attacks in, 64; attacks on Druze by, 259; attacks on *mufti* by, 235; Balkan Wars, views of, in, 78; Beyhum visit and, 204; establishment of, 62; French intervention and, 144; humanitarian relief support of, 68; ideology of, 58; religious provocation of, 60; reprintings in, 77; Rihani and, 65, 70; Syrian nationalism, 69, 311n58; Syrian Revolt and, 69, 145
Holocaust, 35, 233, 266, 267, 285
Homs National College, 112
Hoover, Herbert, 172, 273
Hourani, Albert, 270
Hourani, Cecil, 270
Hourani, Ibrahim al-, 65
Hubaishi, Muhsin, 11
Hull, Cordell, 213, 226, 228
Huroub, Abu Ali, 222
Hurrīyah, Al- (Liberty), 73
Husain (Ibn Ali) (sharif of Mecca, king of the Hijaz), 46, 50, 168
Husseini, Amin al- (brother of Hajj Muhammad Amin), 115
Husseini, Hajj Muhammad Amin al-, 16, 122, 129, 149, 153, 185, 198, 258; aid efforts by, 137, 138, 140, 166, 201, 220; and Ameen Farah, correspondence between, 119–220; Arslan delegation and, 156; Beyhum delegation and, 32, 204, 218; cancellation of

strike by, 180; challenges to authority of, 179; deposal of, 186, 232; exile of, 207, 235–236, 283; fountain pen belonging to, auction of, 222; German flight of, 235–236, 277–278; origin of leadership by, 166–167; Peel Commission testimony of, 180–181; and Rihani, dialogue between, 200–201, 333n27
Husseini, Hilmi, 121
Husseini, Jamal Bey al-, 119, 167, 168, 169, 175, 177, 202, 281
Husseini, Kamal, 121
Husseini, Kazim al-, 156, 166, 167, 169, 175

Ibn Sīna (Avicenna), 45
Ibrahim, Mahdi Ahmad, 210, 216
identity: 1967 war and, 7, 9–10, 304; Arab American, birth of, 5, 7, 23, 26, 33, 183, 190, 217, 229, 234–235, 238, 258–259, 293, 295, 297, 299, 304; Arabic language and, 12; changes in, 23, 229; family and, 8; Islamic, 29; Lebanese, 22, 23, 59, 258, 293; Palestinian, 159–160, 162, 182, 234, 303–304, 325n6; physical environment and, 8; and political advocacy, 2, 12; press and, 15–16; transnationalism and, 11
Igram (changed from ʿAjram), Henry, 215
Igram, Samuel, 226
immigration. *See* Syrian immigrants
Immigration Act of 1924, 5, 17, 239, 299
Independence Party (Palestine), 179
Independence Party of Syria, 118
Inselbuch, Samson, 198
Institute of Arab American Affairs (1944–1950), 3, 28; Arab American identity of, 241; Arab National League and, 244; Association of Arab American University Graduates and, 239–241; chapters of, 249; closing of, 286–288, 290–291, 295; Cold War and, 242–243; financing of, 291; functions of, 131, 252; humanitarian efforts of, 253, 257–258, 285, 286, 294; lobbying by, 248, 249, 258, 260–261, 268, 280; mailings by, 249–250, 261, 262, 263, 265; media efforts of, 242, 244, 264, 273, 275, 278, 285, 288; origins of, 4, 34, 175, 246, 248; Palestine efforts of, 239–241, 243, 246, 250, 253–258, 263–265, 268–269, 293; political strategy of, 34–35, 252, 285, 291; present-day organizations versus, 37, 239, 271, 291–293, 296, 300; publications of, 35–36, 187, 250, 253, 256–257, 268–269, 288, 342n66; records of, 242, 261, 286; structure of, 248–249, 253; support for American interests of, 245, 250, 254–255, 259, 269, 293; United Nations and, 241–242, 260; Zionist groups and, 255–256, 264, 266, 270–271, 273–274, 277, 278, 285, 291
Institute of International Education, 198
International Missionary Council, 265
International Zionist Congress, 168
Irgun, 179, 243, 278, 279
ʿĪsa, ʿĪsa al-, 57
Islāh, Al- (Reform), 73, 204
isolationism, 228, 233, 261
Israel: American support for, 285; founding of, 34, 36, 37, 278, 281, 286, 288; Jerusalem's capture by, 288; recognition of, 284
Issawi, Charles, 270
Istanbul University, 112
Istiqlal Party, 179
ʾIttihād al-ʿUmmāl (Workers Union), 57

Jabara, Abdeen, 174, 298, 303
Jabara, Arif, 248
Jabara, Fayyad, 248
Jabara, Fuad, 249
Jabiri, Hasan, 128
Jabiri, Mannaʿ al-, 11
Jabiri, Ihsan al-, 126, 138, 153
Jabotinsky, Vladimir, 109, 169, 179
Jacobson, Eddy, 284
Jahiẓ, al-, 20
Jamiʿah al-ʿUthmānīyah, Al- (Ottoman college), 72
Jamʿīyat ittiḥād al-ʿummāl al-Sūrīya (Syrian Workers Union Society), 92
Jastrow, Judah, 176
Jawāʾeb, Al-, 57
Jazzār, Aḥmad al-, 40
Jerusalem Aid Committee, 129, 153, 154
Jerusalem Committee for the Refugees, 155
Jewish Agency for Palestine, 178, 180, 182, 255
Jewish National Fund, 114, 167, 172
Jewish Telegraph Agency, 172
Jihād, Al- (The Struggle), 73
Jinān, Al-, 57
Johnson-Reed Act. *See* Immigration Act of 1924
Jordan, creation of, 34; monarchy of, 34, 156, 186, 243, 295; and Palestine, 285; policies of, 233; war defeat of, 37
Joseph, Bernard, 175, 177
Joseph, Elias, 148
Joseph, Joseph, 229, 298
Joseph, S. (Hannibal, Missouri), 143, 148
journalism. *See* press, the
Jurāb-ul-Kurdi, 72, 74–76

Kahn, Julius, 114
Kaibani, Jack, 248
Kalimah, Al- (The Word), 63

Kanʿan, Taufiq, 194
Karam, Afifa, 74, 108
Karmel, Al-, 57, 122, 136
Kātibah, Ḥabīb Ibrahīm, 108, 162, 277; administration of Arab National League by, 208, 215, 216, 222, 229, 231, 235–236; administration of Institute of Arab American Affairs by, 34, 160, 246, 248–250, 265, 285; biography of, 113; creation of Arab National League and, 32, 192–193, 195, 297; humanization of Arabs by, 163; media efforts of, 35, 103, 116, 192, 271–272; Mokarzel, response to, by, 118; Nazi-related attacks on, 236–238, 285, 339n147; papers of, x, 308n16; scholarship on, 8, 9; Syrian nationalism of, 112, 191; Woodhead Report and, 213; writings by, 36, 160, 183, 187, 341n33; and Zionism, 105, 114, 156, 215
Kawākibi, ʿAbdulrahmān, 46, 48
Kawkab Amreeka (Star of America), 60–62
Kawkab al-Sharq, 154
Kawkab al-subḥ al-munīr (Shining Morning Star), 56
Kennedy, Joseph P., 226
Khabbaz, Hanna, 112, 319n10, 319n13
Khairy, Khloussi, 273
Khalaf, Hanna, 17, 209
Khalidi, Hussein al-, 179, 180
Khalidi, Ismail, 248, 249, 250, 255, 264, 297
Khalidi, Rashid, 39, 182, 303–304, 325n98
khalifah. *See* caliphate
Kharoub, Muhammad Husain, 17, 20, 209, 211
Khateeb, Abd M., 172
Kheiralla, George, 197
Kherbawi, Basil (Basilius), 16, 29, 60, 90, 313–313n10

Khouri, Faris al-, 138, 269, 301–302
Khouri, Kareema, 248–249
Khouri, Maroun Khalil al-, 73
Khouri, Naseem, 73
Khouri, Nicola, 128
Khouri, Philip, 3, 187
Khouri, Shukri, 249
Khoury, George, 11, 12
Kigler, I. J., 175
King-Crane Commission, 166, 167, 241
King David Hotel, 243, 279
Kook, Hillel, 271
Korff, (Rabbi) Baruch, 281
Kracke, Frederick J. H., 198–199
Kuroum, Mahmud Abu, 134
Kuzma, Jubrān, 21, 49, 50–51, 81, 87, 88; and Farah, interaction between, 93; and First Arab Conference, 85; and Jewish immigration as matter for concern, 51–53; school established by, 116; social role of, 53

Lacey, Arthur J., 227
La Guardia, Fiorello, 198
Landman, Rabbi, 176
League for Peace with Justice in Palestine, 275, 276
League of Arab States (Arab League), 232, 260, 270, 273, 283
League of Nations, the, 115, 154, 162, 280; Arslan's representation at, 138; British Mandate and, 167, 169, 253; French Mandate and, 166; imperial powers and, 158; and Jewish settlement in Palestine, 182; New Syria Party's representation at, 122, 126, 128, 133, 157; Palestinian grievances sent to, 170, 176–177, 215
Lebanese League of Progress, 64
Lebanese League of Progress of New York, 144
Lebaneseness. *See* identity: Lebanese
Lebanon (al-Lubnān): census in, 165; separatism of, 2, 59, 62, 64, 65, 67, 82, 85, 144, 164, 165; terminology of, 66, 67, 165
Lehi. *See* Stern Zvai Leumi
Lipsky, Louis, 182, 198, 232, 273
Lisān al-hāl, 75
Lisān hāl al-ʿUmmāl fi Filasṭīn (Reporter on the Workers in Palestine), 57
lobbying, 31, 229, 260, 270; Arab American, 4, 31, 32, 80, 205, 222, 263, 334; Arab governments and, 233; Jewish, 35, 37, 167, 200–201, 208, 234, 243, 266, 271, 280–283, 284; language of, 31; rhetoric of, 32
Lotfallah, Michele, 119, 135, 138, 145, 321n31
Lovett, Robert, 284
Lughod, Ibrahim Abu, 6
Luzūmīyāt, Al-, 28, 55

Maʿarri, Abu al-ʿAlāʾ al-, 20, 27
Macaris, Shahin, 65
MacDonald, Malcolm, 213, 214
MacDonald, Ramsay, 173, 178
madeeh (compliments and exaltation), 16
Madey, Elia (also Elia Abu Madey), 20, 55, 59, 88, 163, 296; Arab National League conference and, 217; Balfour Declaration as criticized by, 170; eulogy of Mokarzel by, 164; nationalism of, 29
Magnes, Judah, 35, 176, 264, 265, 281, 343n73
Mahadeen, Ali. *See* Muhyiddīn, Ali
Mahfouz, Husni, 248
Mahmoud, Hassan, 197
Maklani, Ali al-, 11
Malouf, Faris, 162, 198, 245, 261, 319n8; Arab National League and, 32, 297; conference speech of, 227; Institute of Arab American Affairs and, 34,

Malouf, Faris (*continued*)
  248, 249, 263, 268, 286; media efforts of, 35, 116; San Francisco conference attendance of, 253, 259; Syrian borders as seen by, 110, 191
Malouf, Jouseph (Yusef) Nuʿman, 73
Malouf, Nasif, 93
Malti, Michael, 260
Mamluks, 40
Manār, Al-, 57, 77
Mansour, George, 203
Mansour, Shafiq, 286
Mansour, Tawfiq, 208, 217, 227
Mansour, Thomas, 224–226
Maoists, 11
Maria, Frank, 319n8
Maronite Church: and advocacy of First Arab Conference, 85; Arab identity and the, 44; and divisions with Orthodox Church, 59; and Druze, relations between, 43, 259; and France, ties between, 22, 55; and Islam, 272–273; politics of, 22; Syrian nationalism and the, 60; and Zionism, ties between, 64, 259
Maronite Syrian Christian Association, 146
Marshall, George C., 281, 284
Masonic Society (Detroit), 128
Massey, Fred, 142
McAuliffe, Christa, 5
McCormack, John William, 276
McFadden, Louis, 261
Mehmet V (sultan), 74
Meir, Golda, 281
Melki, Henry, 55, 66
Mexico: Beyhum's visit to, 211; Syrian immigrants in, 86, 129, 136, 140, 153, 190, 210, 215, 232, 249, 297
millet (religious minority), 28, 43–44, 75
Mirāt al-Gharb (Mirror of the West), 15, 56, 57, 59, 63, 64, 67, 78, 79, 86, 99, 103, 108–109, 148; Arab National League and, 197–198; Beyhum delegation and, 204; CUP newspaper monitored by, 78; foundation of, 62; humanitarian relief supported by, 68; ideology of, 58; Ottoman Empire politics of, 69; Palestine and, 201; reprintings in, 77
missionaries, 42; aid by, 106; division caused by, 51; literary club support of, 45; presses of, 20, 56, 58, 61–62; schools of, 19, 29, 44, 56, 111, 139, 262
Mitchell, K. S., 268
Mithell, John P., 108–109
Mitrage, Ragheb, 112, 121, 136, 137, 154, 200, 297
Mokarzel, Naʿūm, 59, 64, 67, 151; attacks on Arab National League by, 30; attacks on Al-Gharib, 63; attacks on Muslims by, 118, 145, 209; attacks on New Syria Party by, 30, 139; attacks on Orthodox Church by, 63, 66; attacks on Prince Arslan by, 139, 142, 144, 145, 146; and Beyhum, encounter between, 204; eulogy for, 163–164; First Arab Conference attended by, 82, 85; and France, ties between, 22–24, 60, 63, 119, 314n11; Great Syrian Revolt and, 145–147; *Al-Hoda* established by, 62; Palestine and, 144; politics of, 55, 62, 63
Mokarzel, Salloum, 8, 22, 59; and Beyhum, meeting between, 204; personality of, 71; political activities of, 71, 110; and political differences with brother, 60, 71, 108
Morgenthau, Henry, 5, 116, 176
Morhig, Emile, 118
Morrison-Grady Plan, 281
Moroccan immigration, 207
Mount Lebanon. *See* Lebanon
Movement of Arab Nationalists, 305

Moyne, Lord (Walter Guinness), 243, 279
Mufarrij, Fuad, 208, 211, 221–222, 226–227, 228–229, 230–231, 232, 253, 297
Mufīd, Al-, 57, 75
Mughannam, Mughannam E., 175, 194
Muhaisen, Muhammad, 14, 60, 297; Free Syria Society, 20; and interaction with Ameen Farah, 49, 93; and nationalism, 99; social role of, 53
Muhajir, Al- (The Immigrant), 29, 56, 63, 66
Muhammad, the Prophet, 27
Muhyiddīn, Ali, 129, 133, 134, 197, 248, 249
Muntada al-'Arabi, al- (Arab Literary Club), 48
Muntada al-Sūri al-Amrīki, al- (Syrian-American Literary Club), 91–92
Muqattam, Al-, 77, 154
Muqtabas, Al-, 51, 57, 79, 145
Muqtataf, Al-, 57
Murrah, Ta'an Muhammad, 222
Murray, Wallace, 205
Musa, Muhammad, 209
Musharraf, Hamid, 209
Muslim immigrants, 17
Muslim Student Association of New York, 207
Mutanabbi, Abu al-Tayyib al-, 20
mutaṣarrifīyah, 3

Nader, Ralph, 5
Naff, Alixa, x, 6, 13, 299; scholarship on political organizations by, 8
Nafīr Sūrīya (Trumpet of Syria), 56
Nahar, Al-, 209
nahḍah, 3, 19, 20, 44, 55, 110, 122, 133, 139, 174, 239, 262, 269, 296, 302
Nahhas, Hanna, 112
Nahhasin, Mustapha al-, 203

Nahj al-Balāghah (Method of Eloquence), 19
Naimy (Na'imah), Mikhail, 14, 20, 54, 55, 70, 296, 297; Farah's interaction with, 88, 94–98; Muhaisen's views of, 95; nationalism of, 56, 68; response to Zionism by, 93
Najjar, Qasem al-, 120, 135
Najm, Ahmad Yousef, 206, 217–218
Nakbah, 284, 300, 305
Nakhleh, Isa, 286
Napoleon Bonaparte, 40, 41
Napoleon III, 42
Nashashibi, Anwar, 179, 270
Nashrah al-Usbū'īyah, Al- (Weekly Bulletin), 56
Nasr, George, 128
Nasr, John (Hanna), 128, 136, 142, 246, 248, 264
Nasrallah, Abbas, 248, 249
Nassar, Najib, 57, 122
Nasser, Jamal (Abd-al-Naser), 295
Nathan, Robert, 266–267
National Association of Arab Americans (NAAA), 291, 298–299
National Council of Young Israel, 198
National Defense Party (Palestine), 179
nationalism: academic understanding of, 26–27; identity and, 2; poetry of, 16; Turkish, 20; *ummah* and, 26–30. *see also* Syrian nationalism
Natural Syria, 114, 190–191
Nazism in the Middle East, 273–274
Newman, Louis I., 185
newspapers. *See* press, the
New Syria League of New York, 114
New Syria Party, the, 3, 14, 16, 73, 99; ages of members in, 30; challenges for, 155; chapters of, 124, 134, 138–139, 141, 149, 151; convention program of, 140–142, 147; conventions of, 30, 126, 128, 129, 131, 135, 136, 140–151, 155, 157; decline of, 109,

New Syria Party, the (*continued*)
122, 149, 151, 152; educational differences within, 128–129; Egypt delegation of, 155; executive committee of, 150; financing of, 127–128, 148–150, 151, 156; formation of, 4, 24, 30, 87, 104, 105, 107, 124, 134–135, 138; Great Syrian Revolt boosted by the, 121, 165, 297; humanitarian efforts of, 30, 31, 124, 134, 138, 152, 155, 156; ideology of, 4; information center proposal of, 131–133, 157; language difficulties for, 122, 195; lobbying by, 32, 138, 157; media efforts undertaken by, 150, 320–321n28; memorial service of, 136; nationalism in, 30, 73; New York awareness of, 9; operations of, 138; postwar activity of, 119; research detailing, 108; scholarship on, 24; sectarianism of, 24, 124, 128–129, 139, 146, 147, 158
New York Board of Aldermen, 198
New York Times, boycott of, 35
New York World's Fair, 227
Nietzsche, Friedrich, 72
Niles, David, 284
Nimr, Faris, 57, 65
Nisr, Al-, 59, 60; Beyhum delegation and, 204
Nonsectarian Anti-Nazi League, 275–276, 285
Noor, Queen of Jordan, 5
Nukrashy, Mahmud Fahmi al-, 261

Odeh, Ilias, 249
Office of Strategic Services (OSS), U.S., 38, 58, 59, 244–246, 271
Office of War Information, U.S., 113
Ohrback, Nathan M., 274
oil concessions in Iran, 162
Omar, Abdullah, 140

Operation Boulder, 303
Organization of Arab Students at Wayne State University, 11
Orientalism, 10, 255
Orthodox Archdiocese of North America, 63
Orthodox Benevolent Society, 91
Orthodox Christians: and divisions with Maronites, 20, 23, 44, 59, 60, 63, 67, 70; internal divisions among, 144; libraries of, 20, 29; nationalism of, 24, 139; Ottoman regime's treatment of, 26; press activity of, 14, 15, 24, 62, 63, 70; Russian ties to, 67, 70
Orthodox Fraternity (Detroit), 128
Orthodox Ladies Auxiliary
Oseiran, Hikmet, 229
OSS. *See* Office of Strategic Services
Ottoman Administrative Decentralization Party (Hizb al-Lamarkizīyah al-Idarīyah al-ʿUthmani), 15, 20, 21, 48, 50, 76, 79, 86, 296; conference by, 81, 83; goals of, 105
Ottoman Empire, 3, 4; administration of, 17; European encroachment under, 40–41; Islam as used in, 39; minorities under, 39; "Revolution" of 1908 in, 160; Syrian attitudes about, 15, 24, 46, 83–84, 85

Paasen, Pierre, 198
Palestine: 1920–1921 uprisings in, 162; 1929 uprising in, 22, 31, 109, 160–161, 170–172; 1933 uprising in, 179; 1935 and 1936 uprising in, 178, 179, 192, 212; activism on, 152, 156, 178, 180, 181, 211, 213, 239, 253–258, 297; American knowledge about, 266; Arab Federation and, 176; Arab state advocacy for, 203, 206; boycotts over, 204; British policy in, 161, 267; divisions in, 233; immigrants to U.S.

from, 11, 12; institutional development in, 177; Jewish immigration to, 33, 178, 180, 226, 243, 254, 260, 263–264, 267, 268, 273; nationalism and events in, 109; partition of, 186, 243, 258, 260, 268, 275, 283, 288, 293; refugees from, 286; "Southern Syria" as terminology for, 31, 68; violence triggers in, 119; white papers on, 167, 170, 178, 214, 215 233, 254, 267, 279, 280, 331n118; World War II and, 231, 233

Palestine, a Decade of Development, 161, 175–178

Palestine Arab Action Committee, 119
Palestine Foundation Fund, 171
Palestine Higher Executive, 121
Palestine Liberation Organization (PLO), 10–11
Palestine National League (PNL), 32, 107, 109, 113, 139, 172, 183, 187–189
Palestine Renaissance Society, 187
Palestine Royal Commission, 180. *See also* Peel Commission
Palestinian Congress (1919), 168
Pan-Syrian Congress (1919), 167
Pan-Syrian Party (Flint), 121, 140, 148, 155
Pappé, Ilan, 339n6, 344n123
Paris Peace Conference (1919), 104, 112, 114, 166, 241; effects of, 115; hope for American action at, 169
Pasha, Ahmad Zaki, 138
Pasha, Jamāl, 48, 143
Pasha, Nathem, 75
Passfield White Paper, 178
Patient Aid Project, 25
Patriarchal School (Beirut), 112
peddling among immigrants, 1, 13, 163
Peel Commission, 180–181, 201, 202–203, 212, 233, 258, 279

Pen League (al-Rābitah al-Qalamīyah), 16, 20, 63, 70, 200, 296; scholarship on, 37
Phillips, William, 262
Phoenicians, 62
Picot, George, 60
Pius XI (pope), 173
political organizations: coagulation of, 157; first Arab American, 1, 105, 239, 291–293, 296, 304; motivations for supporting, 107; scholarship on, 7, 8, 10, 90–91, 107, 297–302, 304
Ponsot, Auguste Henri, 154
Pool, David de Sola, 108
Popular Front for the Liberation of Palestine, 10–11, 305
press, the: activist introduction through, 54; and Arab identity, 45; Arabic-language, early American, 60; criticism of, 64; Egypt intellectuals and, 71–72; enabling of, 15–16; foreign coverage in, 73–80; missionary ties of, 56, 58; organizational ties of, 54; in the Ottoman Empire, 56; Palestinian section of, 57; politics of, 2, 60, 63; religious basis of, 14, 44, 58; scholarship on, 54, 55; science and technology in, 79; sectarianism in, 60, 69; strategies regarding the Ottoman Empire in, 54, 57, 72–73, 76–77, 78
Preuss, W., 175
Prophet, The, 28, 66
Proskauer, Joseph, 267

Qaderi, Abdelrazeq al-, 150
Qaderi, Ali al-, 150
Qalam al-Hadidi, Al- (The Iron Pen), 140
Qanawati, Suleiman al-, 232
qaseed (nationalist ode), 16
Qassam, Izz al-Din al-, 179

Qattami, ʿUqlah al-, 150
Qubʿyn, Nicola, 49, 50, 51, 87, 88; and Farah, interaction with, 93; social role of, 53; work with British of, 116
Quds, Al-, 57

Raʾi al-ʿAm, Al- (Public Opinion), 145
Raʾid, Al-, 79
Ramadan, David, 195, 197
Raphael, J. G., 59
Rashidiya school, al- (Jerusalem), 112
Rawi, Al- (The Narrator), 73
Red Scare, 134
Reform Party (Palestine), 179
Rehm, Diane, 5
Renaissance Arab Hashemite Club (Jamʿiyat al-nahḍah al-hashimiyah), 17
Renan, Ernest, 72, 88, 111, 209
Rida, Muhammad Rashīd (1865–1935), 15, 46, 48, 57, 93
Rihani, Albert, 199
Rihani, Ameen al-, 16, 23, 26, 39, 55, 70, 88, 229, 328–329n69; biography of, 55; criticism of the press by, 64; death of, 232; gathering for, 198–199; Islamic influences on, 28; *Letters to Uncle Sam* by, 169, 304; media efforts of, 35; on Morocco, 224; nationalism of, 29, 65, 110–111, 166, 199, 296; Syrian borders as seen by, 191; Syrian Relief Committee and, 118; tours by, 198–200; views on Wahhabism of, 46; World War I and, 100; Zionism and, 173, 175, 176, 199–200
Riḥāniyāt, Al-, 55, 110–111
Rihbany, Abraham, 192
Rihbany, Simon, 248
rithaʾ (lament), 16
Riza, King (Shah), 173
Romley, Edward, 226

Roosevelt, Franklin D., 201, 204, 211, 228, 260, 261
Roosevelt, Kermit, 35, 276, 277, 286
Roosevelt, Theodore, 35, 108
Rosenwald, Lessing, 267
Rothenberg, Morris, 182
Rothschild, Edmond de, 197, 253
Rushd wa Suha. See Farah, Ameen
Rustum, Ali, 208

Saab, Amin, 136
Saʿadeh, Anton, 197
Saba, Fuad, 203
Sabah, Al-, 59
Sabbagh, Elias, 153
Saʿd, Faris, 249
Saʿd, Yousef, 249
Sadaka, Mahmoud, 248
Saʿdi, Laila al-, 200
Saʿdi, Lutfi al-, 128, 200, 209, 227, 261
Sado, Joseph, 248
Saʾeh, Al- (The Traveler), 24, 29, 59, 69, 70, 159, 235, 311n58; communiqué of 1936 published in, 187; Gibran's writing published in, 67; ideology of, 58; and Prince Faisal's visit, 245
Safire, William, 271, 302
Sagath, Adolph J., 270
Sahat Ali (Ali's Field), 73
Said, Edward, 6
Saʿīd, Nuri al-, 262–263, 268
Sakhra, Al-, 63
Salloum, Habib, 54, 59
Sameer, As-, 22, 24, 29, 59, 108–109, 148, 159, 163, 164, 235; Beyhum delegation and, 204; ideology of, 58; Palestinian advocacy in, 169, 186, 224; as praised by Ameen Farah, 217
Samhan, Helen, 301
Samhat, Ali, 224
Samra, Adele, 208
Samra, George, 215
Samra, Najīb, 143–144, 173–175, 183,

200, 208, 257; media activities of, 226
Samuel, Herbert (high commissioner of Palestine), 167, 168, 169
San Remo Agreement, 162, 234, 256, 280
sanjaq, 3
Sarkis, Salim, 73
Sarouf, Jacoub, 65
Sarrail, Maurice, 119
Saud, King Abdulaziz Al, 126, 173, 203, 245
Saudi Arabia, 236; American support for, 34, 245, 255, 271, 279, 295; Arab American assistance to, 36, 245, 301; Arab unity and, 280; position on Palestine of, 37, 245, 290; United Nations and, 263
Sawabini, Iliyas, 248
Saybaʿa, Nasīm, 135, 138, 142, 146, 147–148, 151, 153, 154–155, 324n98
Sayeh, as-. See *Saʾeh, Al-*
Schulman, Samuel, 182
Schwartz, Joseph, 267
secret societies, 48, 73, 81, 99
sectarianism in Arab American identity, 2, 8, 9–10, 44, 65, 296; claims of, 14; in Detroit, 209; in press, 22–26; and violence, 42, 65
Selim I, Sultan, 40
Shahbandar, Abdelrahman (Sunni clergyman), 119, 136, 140
Shaheen, Jack, 303
Shakir, Evelyn, 12
Shalala, Donna, 5
Shaqra, ʿAbbas Abu, 20, 136; convention of New Syria Party and, 136, 137, 148; media efforts of, 172; nationalism of, 29; New Syria Party role of, 124, 133, 134, 135, 138, 140, 148, 150, 151, 153; newspapers of, 60, 69, 99; Syrian Relief Committee service of, 118; writings of, 108

Sharabi, Hisham, 6, 298
Sharanski, Natan, 279
Shaʿrawi, Huda, 99
Shatara, Fuad Isa, 34, 54, 108, 151, 195, 304, 326–327n51; activism of, 113–114, 116, 151, 156, 162; Arab National League organization and, 8, 113, 192–193, 208, 211, 215–216, 227, 229, 230, 234; binational state proposal by, 168, 175–176, 215, 234, 264–265; biography of, 113; Einstein, Albert and, 35, 184–186, 331n118; media efforts undertaken by, 35, 71, 103, 116, 172, 192, 214; nationalism of, 59; Nazi-related attacks on, 236–237; Palestine National League formation and, 32, 107, 109, 139, 188–189, 297; public debate of, 108; reactions to Zionism by, 105; and Saudi representation, 301; scholarship on, 9; suicide of, 237, 244; Syrian borders as seen by, 191; in *Syrian World*, 71; World War I views of, 104; writings of, 175
Shaykh, Fakhri al-, 220–221, 229, 230, 231, 253
Shibli, Jabir, 269
Shidyāq, Ahmad Fāris, 57
Shlaim, Avi, 338n133
Shouman, Abdelhamid, 34, 140, 187
Shryock, Andrew, 9–10, 12
Shuqair, Jaber, 140
Shuqair, Najib, 152–153
Shuqeiri, Ahmad, 269
Sickles, Mrs. John E., 227
Siegel, Seymour, 198
Silver, Abba Hillel (Rabbi), 103, 198, 280, 281, 284
Simmons, Furnifold McLendel, 143
Simpson, Hope, 171, 173, 249, 269
Singleton, John, 266
Smith, Anthony D., 26
Smith, Eli, 42

Smith, Wilbert, 264
Sobe, Emett, 226
social services, 10–11, 12
Society of Friends (Quakers), 111, 258
Soltau, H., 269
Sorbonne, the, 112
Souf, Jenny Abu al-, 222
Soviet Union, 34–35, 262, 295
Spanish-American War, 105
Spanish and Portuguese Synagogue, 108
State Department, U.S., 35; Arab American contacts with, 242, 249, 262, 271; Arabists at, 197; on Palestine, 204, 232, 280, 283
stereotypes: of Arabs, 239, 300–301, 303, 305, 339n1; of Islam, 174
Stern Zvai Leumi, 178, 179, 243, 279, 281, 283, 285
Stettinius, Edward, 261
Stimson, Henry, 109, 172
Suez Canal, 79, 107
Suleiman, Michael, 6, 15; 1967 war and, 12; on political activity by immigrants, 7–8, 13, 108, 109, 298; on racism, 302; on stereotype of Arabs, 7, 302, 339n1
Sulḥ, Riad al-, 153
Sultaniyeh College, 112
Sulzberger, Arthur Hays, 35, 278
Supreme Islamic Council in Jerusalem, 138, 175
Sūrīya al-Jadīdah (New Syria), 73
Sūrīya al-Janūbīyah (Southern Syria), 68
Sykes-Picot Agreement, 4, 60, 106–107, 162
Syria: definition of, 110, 115, 190–191; origins of the name, 3, 112–113; proposed U.S. management of, 115
Syrian American Club of Boston, 114
Syrian American Federation of New England, 109–110
Syrian-American Literary Club. *See* Muntada al-Sūri al-Amrīki, al-
Syrian Arab Committee, 135
Syrian Christians Association, 146
Syrian Educational Society, 111
Syrian immigrants: businesses of, 13; conscription as trigger for, 41; in Detroit, 209; education levels among, 14, 19–20, 28, 29, 56, 60, 111–112, 310n50; influence on Palestinian delegation to London by, 168; Middle Eastern expectations regarding, 222; numbers of, 13; political orientations of, 30, 157, 158, 216–217, 226, 261, 279; religious institutions of, 14; stereotypes of, 174, 235, 258, 300–301; and support for the Great Syrian Revolt, 122–123; visibility of, 163
Syrian Ladies Benevolent Society, 16
Syrian Liberation Committee (Lajnat Tahrīr Sūrīya), 118
Syrian National Bulletin (Boston), 112
Syrian National Congress (1919), 166
Syrian nationalism, 26, 29, 30, 239; and American political organizing, 304; challenge after World War I for, 118–119, 234; Christian support for, 29–30, 203; coherence of, at First Arab Conference, 86; intellectuals involved in, 2, 4; origins of, 3; scholarship of, 3; transition away from, 30, 34; women and, 318n38
Syrian National Society, 112, 114
Syrian Orthodox Archdiocese, 211, 246
Syrian-Palestinian Executive Council, 30
Syrian Palestinian Society, 156
Syrian Protestant College. *See* American University of Beirut
Syrian Red Crescent, 257, 341n33
Syrian Relief Committee, 106, 118
Syrian Revolt. *See* Great Syrian Revolt, the

Syrian Scientific Society (al-Jamʿīyah al-ʿIlmīyah al-Sūrīya), 45
Syrian World, 8, 71, 108
Syrian Wounded Veteran Relief Committee, 134

Taft, Robert, 264, 280
Tahamah, ʿAbdelsalam Bin, 207
Tahtāwī, Rifaʿa Rāfiʿ al-, 28, 41
Tali, Harry, 226
Tamimi, Amin al-, 169
Tannous, ʿIzzat, 201
tanzimāt, 3, 19
Tarazi, Philippe de, 58, 60
Tarīkh al-saḥafah al-ʿarabīyah (History of the Arab Press), 58, 312n21
Tawil, Muhammad Musa al-, 135
Teller, J. L., 255
Terry, Janice, 6, 7, 299
Thabat, Al-, 75
Thani, Muhammad Bin-, 207
Thibiyan, Badiʿ, 120, 134, 136
Third Palestine Congress (1921), 167
Thomas, Helen, 5
Thornburg, Max, 277
Tolstoy, Leo, 72, 88
Totah, Khalil: at U.S. congressional committee, 202, 281; Institute responsibilities of, 249–250, 255, 259, 263–264, 265, 273, 281–283, 288, 290–291, memoirs of, 8–9, 259, 266, 273; papers of, ix, 242, 308n18, 342n68; patriotism of, 347n186; in *Syrian World*, 71; writings of, 175, 255, 285, 341n47
Totah, Selim, 172, 260
Truman, Harry S., 260, 270, 273, 279, 280, 281, 283, 284

Umar, Dhāhir al-, 40
ummah, 26–30
United Nations: 1967 war and, 7; decisions concerning Palestine by, 275, 279, 281, 283, 288; Institute of Arab American Affairs and, 253; lobbying by nations seeking to enter, 33–34, 241–242, 254–255, 259–261, 290, 301, 311n53; San Francisco conference of, 269
United Nations Special Committee on Palestine (UNSCOP), 243, 281, 283
United Syrian Society (USS, 1908), 16, 26, 82, 83, 317n24; press coverage of, 78; politics of, 90
Untermyer, Samuel, 182
ʿUraisi, ʿAbdulghani al-, 26, 57, 81, 82; killing of, 83, 94
ʿUsbah, al- (The Bond), 257

Valentino, Rudolph, 174
Villard, Oswald, 213–214
Viteles, Harry, 175
Voltaire, François, 26–27, 88, 111

Wadsworth, George, 200–201
Wagner, Robert F., 264, 280, 342–343n72
Wahbe, Tawfiq, 205
Wahbeh, Naseeb Amer, 73
Wahhab, Muhammad ibn ʿAbd al-, 46
Wahhabi movement, 46
War Refugee Board, 271
Warnshuis, A. L., 265
Washington Street, 13
Watan, al- (The Homeland) Club, 257
Wayne State University, 11
Weingarten, Victor, 236–237
Weizmann, Chaim, 167, 176, 178, 182, 214
white paper. *See* Palestine: white papers on
wilayet (province), 3
Wilson, Woodrow, 36, 69, 166, 253; as inspiration to Palestinians, 176
Wise, Stephen S., 198–199, 213, 232, 255, 263, 267, 280

WNYC (radio station), 198
Women's Arab League, 222
Woodhead Commission, 181, 212–213
World Islamic Conference, 203
World's Columbian Exposition, 62
World War I: aid during and after, 16, 70, 111, 112, 230; effects on Arab American identity caused by, 8, 69
World War II: as affecting the Arab National League, 32–33, 228, 232, 233, 244; as affecting Syrian nationalism, 21, 30, 93; as affecting U.S. power, 105; and the Arab National League conference, 227; Arab politics and the approach of, 203, 207, 212–213; deaths of Syrians during, 65; and decisions on Palestine by the British, 213; domestic effects of, 217; Syrian immigrants' participation in, 100, 104, 215, 297; political strategies after, 36, 216–217, 233, 238, 242, 244
World Zionist Organization, 114, 167, 172, 255
Wright, Walter L., Jr., 58

Yahuda, A. S., 256
Yahya of Yemen, 173
Yared, Abdo Salloum, 205, 334n51
Yāziji, Ibrahim, 65
Yāziji, Nasīf al-, 44–45
Yāziji, Tawfīq al-, 138, 147, 155
Yemen, immigration from, 5, 11, 207
Young Men's Christian Association, 136
Young Men's Moslem Society of America, 172
Young Turk Revolution, 48, 73
Younis, Don, 11
Younis-Amen, Katherine, 11
Younis family, 11

Zahdi, Khalil, 120, 135
Zahrah, Said, 136
Zahrāwi, ʿAbdulhamīd al-, 39, 50, 82, 83, 86; killing of, 83, 94; political discourse of, 83; social role of, 53
Zain, Ibrahim al-, 205
Zangwill, Israel, 176
Zaydān, Jurji, 28, 44–45
Zeidān, Amin, 107, 187, 195, 197
Zeine, Zeine, 39, 75
Ziadeh, Farhat, 8–9, 36, 220, 227, 245, 248, 249, 308n17
Zionism, 4, 9, 28, 35–36; and advantages for activists, 182, 213, 214, 266, 291; American views on, 265; biblical claims and, 197; binational state and, 279; congressional tactics in lobbying for, 232–233; debates between Jews and Arabs on, 183, 273; and difficulties facing activists, 162–163, 182; expulsion of Palestinians in, 276; German boycotts and, 182; internal Jewish divisions on, 183, 256, 327n56; Jewish debate on, 181; media tactics of activists in United States regarding, 173, 254, 274–278; militant groups within, 243; monitoring of Arab activists by adherents of, 255, 277, 278; New York focus of, 232; statehood efforts of, 281
Zionist Congress, 181, 182
Zionist Organization of America, 172, 182, 232
Zogby, James, 298
Zraick, Anton Anastasias, 69, 72, 74–76; assassination of, 94
Zuʿaytir, Muhammad, 42, 63–64, 259, 315–316n31
Zvai Leumi group. See Stern Zvai Leumi